National Remedies Before the Court of Justice

The Court of Justice has delivered an extensive body of caselaw concerning the obligation of domestic courts to provide effective judicial protection to claimants relying upon Community law rights—including such landmark judgments as *Factortame* and *Francovich*. This book offers a critical analysis of the Court's fast-changing approach to national procedural autonomy, and explores the difficult conceptual framework underpinning the caselaw.

The author demonstrates how Community intervention in the domestic systems of judicial protection cannot remain unaffected by wider debates about the evolving European integration project, in particular, the tension between uniformity and differentiation as competing values influencing the exercise of Community regulatory competence. Because of its emphasis on an ideal of uniformity which has become increasingly untenable within the contemporary Community legal order, much of the existing academic discourse about national remedies and procedural rules now seems ripe for reconsideration. It is argued that the Court's jurisprudence on the decentralised enforcement of Treaty norms needs to be interpreted afresh, having regard to the recent growth of regulatory differentiation within the Community system.

National Remedies Before the Court of Justice provides a challenging account of this crucial field of EU legal studies. It includes detailed discussion of issues such as Member State liability in damages, Community control over national limitation periods, and the principles governing state aid and competition law enforcement. This book will be of value to academics and practitioners alike.

Volume 4 in the series, Modern Studies in European Law

Modern Studies in European Law

Soft Law in European Community Law *Linda Senden*

The Impact of European Rights on National Legal Cultures *Miriam Aziz*

Partnership Rights, Free Movement and EU Law *Helen Toner*

National Remedies Before the Court of Justice *Michael Dougan*

National Remedies Before the Court of Justice

Issues of Harmonisation and Differentiation

MICHAEL DOUGAN
Professor of European Law,
Liverpool University

HART PUBLISHING
OXFORD AND PORTLAND OREGON
2004

Published in North America (US and Canada) by
Hart Publishing
c/o International Specialized Book Services
5804 NE Hassalo Street
Portland, Oregon
97213-3644
USA

Hart Publishing is a specialist legal publisher based in Oxford, England. To order further copies of this book or to request a list of other publications please write to:

Hart Publishing, Salters Boatyard, Folly Bridge, Abingdon Rd, Oxford, OX1 4LB Telephone: +44 (0)1865 245533 Fax: +44 (0)1865 794882
email: mail@hartpub.co.uk
WEBSITE: http//:www.hartpub.co.uk

British Library Cataloguing in Publication Data
Data Available

ISBN 1-84113-395-7 (hardback)

Typeset by Olympus Infotech Pvt Ltd, India (Palatino, 10/12 pts)
Printed and bound in Great Britain by
MPG Limited, Bodmin, Cornwall

Preface

At one level, this book is concerned with the Court of Justice's developing caselaw on the national remedies and procedural rules available for the decentralised enforcement of Community law. But more fundamentally, my objective has been to use the principles of Community intervention in the domestic systems of judicial protection as a prism through which to engage with wider debates about the evolving European integration project, in particular, the tension between uniformity and differentiation as competing conceptual models for Community regulatory activity.

The Court's remedies caselaw, and regulatory differentiation, have both provided the subject-matter for extensive academic research. This book attempts to bring together these hitherto discrete fields of scholarship by asking the following question: what implications does the recent growth of regulatory differentiation within the Treaty system hold for the traditional policy framework which surrounds Community control over the domestic standards of judicial protection? My answer is that, because of its emphasis on an ideal of uniformity which has become increasingly untenable within the contemporary Community legal order, much of the existing academic debate about national remedies and procedural rules is now ripe for reconsideration; and with it much of the critical interpretation usually afforded to the Court's recent jurisprudence on the decentralised enforcement of Treaty norms.

This study is a revised version of my Cambridge doctoral thesis, which was supported by a scholarship from the Arts and Humanities Research Board of the British Academy. I am also very grateful for the generous financial assistance I received as a research student from other organisations, including the Lawlor Foundation and the Sir Isaac Newton Trust. Sincere thanks are offered to Angela Ward, Albertina Albors Llorens and Rosa Greaves for their guidance and support; as well as to Alan Dashwood, John Bell, Catherine Barnard, Catherine Seville, Joanne Scott and Paul Craig for their encouragement and advice. Richard Hart deserves a sainthood, not least for his patience and flexibility. Thanks of a very special class are owed to Eleanor Spaventa, who is not only the best colleague I could ever wish for, but also one of the kindest people on the planet, and a very dear ciccette indeed. This book owes her a lot, and I owe her far more than that. Of course, where would I be without the rest of my closest friends? David Falkner, Alex Forsyth, Christophe Hillion, Anne Myrjord and Damien Kennedy have each brought their own brand of immeasurable happiness into my life, and not only during those dull,

dull days of filling in footnotes and double-checking house-style. And how could I ever express gratitude enough to my family—Eilish and Tommy Dougan, together with Damien, Tara and Karen—for their unfailing love?

This work is dedicated with sadness to the beautiful memory of my two grannies: Brigid Mervyn (died 24 April 1996) and Agnes Dougan (died 18 June 1998).

Contents

Table of Cases

EFTA COURT

EUROPEAN COURT OF HUMAN RIGHTS

EUROPEAN COURT OF JUSTICE AND COURT OF FIRST INSTANCE

(Alphabetical)

(By Case Number)

GERMANY

UNITED KINGDOM

Table of Legislation

COUNCIL OF EUROPE

EUROPEAN UNION

Treaties and Other Primary Acts

Decisions

Directives

Recommendations

Regulations

Other Measures

ITALY

UNITED KINGDOM

Statutory Instruments

1

Effective Judicial Protection Within the Community Legal Order

THIS BOOK IS concerned with the relative competences of the European Community and its Member States to determine the remedies and procedural rules available before the domestic courts for the enforcement of rights and obligations created at the Community level. Two main issues will be investigated: first, the policy rationale for Community intervention in the national systems of judicial protection; and secondly, the contribution of the European Court of Justice as the institution primarily responsible for carrying out such intervention. In particular, we will investigate the supposedly fundamental imperative of uniformity in the formulation and application of Community law: examining its role within both the academic debate and the Court's caselaw on domestic remedies and procedures; and exploring the valuable insights which recent scholarship on regulatory differentiation within the Community legal order might usefully share with existing research into the decentralised enforcement of Treaty norms.

Before addressing these issues, it is necessary to outline the basic legal framework which is essential for understanding the scholarship and the caselaw.

CENTRALISED AND DECENTRALISED ENFORCEMENT OF COMMUNITY LAW

There are two main means by which Community norms can be enforced: centrally (or directly) and decentrally (or indirectly). Centralised enforcement refers to the ability of the Community institutions, Member States and private parties to bring an action before the Community's own courts (the Court of Justice and Court of First Instance).[1] This was the primary method of enforcement envisaged by the Treaty of Rome, but its effectiveness is

[1] Further, eg K Lenaerts and D Arts, *Procedural Law of the European Union* (Sweet & Maxwell, 1999); H Schermers and D Waelbroeck, *Judicial Protection in the European Union* (Kluwer Law International, 2002).

undermined by a number of serious drawbacks. For example, the access of private parties to the Community courts is extremely limited: they can challenge the legality only of Community not national or individual conduct;[2] even then, the rules of *locus standi* are notoriously restrictive.[3] Private parties may bring infringements by the Member States and other individuals to the attention of the Commission, but limited resources demand that the Commission retains a broad discretion to set its own priorities for investigation and prosecution.[4] Even a favourable judgment from the Community courts may prove to be a hollow victory: compliance by the Member States often seems to depend as much upon goodwill as upon compulsion;[5] in any case, the Courts' power to order the cessation of illegal conduct may do little to remedy its consequences for past victims.[6]

Acknowledging the weaknesses of centralised enforcement for both the rule of Community law and the individual relying upon it, the Court of Justice has constructed a supplementary system of decentralised enforcement.[7] Rules of Community law (provided they are sufficiently clear, precise and unconditional) are capable of having direct effect within the national legal order, creating rights and obligations which must be protected and enforced by the domestic courts.[8] By virtue of the principle of supremacy, these directly effective Community provisions take precedence over all conflicting national law—even an act of the English Parliament or rule of the German Constitution.[9] Moreover, those relying on directly effective Community law are entitled to an effective standard of judicial protection as regards the remedies and procedural rules available before the domestic courts. Finally, the Treaty itself established a

[2] Eg Case 46/81 *Bienvenuto* [1981] ECR 809; Case C–181/91 *Parliament v Council and Commission* [1993] ECR I–3685.

[3] Further: ch 6 (below).

[4] Eg Case 247/87 *Star Fruit* [1989] ECR 291; Case T–24/90 *Automec* [1992] ECR II–2223.

[5] Even after the introduction by the Treaty on European Union of Art 228 EC establishing a system of financial sanctions against Member States, eg Case C–387/97 *Commission v Greece* [2000] ECR I–5047; Case C–278/01 *Commission v Spain* (Judgment of 25 November 2003).

[6] Eg the Court has power to award non-contractual damages against the Community institutions under Arts 235 and 288 EC; but cannot *directly* require the Member States to make redress for losses caused to individuals, within the context of either Art 226 or Art 234 proceedings.

[7] Eg E Stein, 'Lawyers, Judges, and the Making of a Transnational Constitution' (1981) 75 AJIL 1; G Mancini, 'The Making of a Constitution for Europe' (1989) 26 CML Rev 595; P Craig, 'Once Upon a Time in the West: Direct Effect and the Federalization of EEC Law' (1992) 12 OJLS 453.

[8] Eg Case 26/62 *van Gend en Loos* [1963] ECR 1, Case 43/75 *Defrenne v Sabena* [1976] ECR 455, Case C–281/98 *Angonese* [2000] ECR I–4131 on Treaty provisions. Eg Case 93/71 *Orsolina Leonesio* [1972] ECR 287, Case 39/72 *Commission v Italy* [1973] ECR 101 on regulations. Eg Case 41/74 *van Duyn* [1974] ECR 1337, Case 148/78 *Ratti* [1979] ECR 1629 on directives.

[9] Eg Case 6/64 *Flaminio Costa v Enel* [1964] ECR 585; Case 11/70 *Internationale Handelsgesellschaft* [1970] ECR 1125; Case 48/71 *Commission v Italy* [1972] ECR 527; Case 106/77 *Simmenthal* [1978] ECR 629; Case C–213/89 *ex p Factortame* [1990] ECR I–2433; Case C–224/97 *Erich Ciola* [1999] ECR I–2517; Cases C–10–22/97 *IN.CO.GE.'90* [1998] ECR I–6307.

framework (the preliminary reference procedure under Article 234 EC) by which the national courts can seek advice from the Court of Justice if they are unsure of the exact requirements imposed by Community law, or their application to any given factual scenario.[10]

By these means, the entire judiciary of Europe from the lowliest tribunal to the most venerable court of appeal has (at least in theory) been harnessed to the service of the Community, all under the guidance of the Court of Justice. This system of decentralised enforcement contributes to the unique character of the European Community as an international organisation: Community economic and social policies can have a direct impact upon the citizen which is unparalleled in its sheer range, volume and detail.

But the current system of decentralised enforcement also suffers from several well-known drawbacks, for example: the rule that un- or incorrectly implemented directives cannot have direct effect between two private individuals;[11] the intermittent and unilateral rejection of the principle of supremacy by certain national judges;[12] and the reluctance of some domestic courts to submit an Article 234 reference even in cases where the Court of Justice's guidance seems necessary and appropriate.[13] Such problems fuel academic speculation about whether the time has come to reconsider the principles of decentralised enforcement at a more fundamental level. For example, Prechal has argued that the doctrine of direct effect has become so broad and diluted, particularly as regards the link between direct effect and the existence or creation of individual rights, that it tends to confuse more than assist; and that the direct effect principles may even undermine the rule of law within the European Community by setting limits to the justiciability of Treaty norms before the domestic courts which do not apply in proceedings before the Court of Justice itself.[14] Similarly, Allott has expressed strong concerns that

[10] Cf C Barnard and E Sharpston, 'The Changing Face of Article 177 References' (1997) 34 CML Rev 1113; D O'Keeffe, 'Is the Spirit of Article 177 Under Attack? Preliminary References and Admissibility' (1998) 23 EL Rev 509; T de la Mare, 'Article 177 in Social and Political Context' in P Craig & G de Búrca (eds), *The Evolution of EU Law* (OUP, 1999); T Tridimas, 'Knocking on Heaven's Door: Fragmentation, Efficiency and Defiance in the Preliminary Reference Procedure' (2003) 40 CML Rev 9.

[11] Eg R Mastroianni, 'On the Distinction Between Vertical and Horizontal Direct Effects of Community Directives: What Role for the Principle of Equality?' (1999) 5 *European Public Law* 417.

[12] Eg N Reich, 'Judge-made "Europe à la carte": Some Remarks on Recent Conflicts between European and German Constitutional Law Provoked by the Banana Litigation' (1996) 7 *European Journal of International Law* 103. Cf C Schmid, 'All Bark and No Bite: Notes on the Federal Constitutional Court's Bananas Decision' (2001) 7 *European Law Journal* 95.

[13] Eg A Robertson, 'Effective Remedies in EEC Law Before the House of Lords?' (1993) 109 LQR 27; P Allott, 'EC Directives and Misfeasance in Public Office' [2001] CLJ 4. Consider, in particular, the situation at issue in Case C–224/01 *Köbler* (Judgment of 30 September 2003).

[14] S Prechal, 'Does Direct Effect Still Matter?' (2000) 37 CML Rev 1047. Also: S Prechal, 'Direct Effect Reconsidered, Redefined and Rejected' in J Prinssen & A Schrauwen (eds), *Direct Effect: Rethinking a Classic of EC Legal Doctrine* (Europa Law Publishing, 2002).

Article 234 references hinder the full and proper integration of Treaty rules into the domestic legal orders by reinforcing the perception that Community law is something foreign and different, rather than an essential element of the citizen's own legal patrimony.[15]

This book is concerned with another of the drawbacks posed by decentralised enforcement: the disputed rationale for, and controversial nature of, Community intervention in domestic remedies and procedural rules, for the sake of ensuring that Treaty-based norms are effectively and uniformly enforced before the national courts.

LEGAL FRAMEWORK OF COMMUNITY INTERVENTION IN NATIONAL REMEDIES AND PROCEDURAL RULES

In the absence of anything approaching comprehensive Treaty legislation, the Court of Justice has developed its own principles to regulate Community intervention in the domestic systems of judicial protection. These principles can be organised around four basic structural concepts: first, the fundamental right of access to judicial process; secondly, the presumption of national competence to determine remedies and procedural rules; thirdly, the limits to that presumption applicable under Community law (consisting primarily of the substantive Treaty provisions, plus the principles of equivalence and effectiveness); and finally, the legal basis for such Community intervention. We shall refer to this caselaw collectively as the 'principles of effective judicial protection'.

Fundamental Right of Access to Judicial Process

Fundamental rights form an integral part of the general principles of Community law whose observance is ensured by the Court. For that purpose, the Court draws inspiration from the constitutional traditions common to the Member States; and from the guidelines supplied by international treaties for the protection of human and fundamental rights on which the Member States have collaborated or to which they are signatories. In that regard, the European Convention for the Protection of Human Rights and Fundamental Freedoms (ECHR) holds particular significance.[16]

Article 6(1) ECHR states that, in the determination of his/her civil rights and obligations or of any criminal charge against him/her,

[15] P Allott, 'Preliminary Rulings: Another Infant Disease' (2000) 25 EL Rev 538.
[16] Eg Case 11/70 *Internationale Handelsgesellschaft* [1970] ECR 1125; Case 4/73 *Nold* [1974] ECR 491.

everyone is entitled to a fair and public hearing within a reasonable time by an independent and impartial tribunal established by law. The Court held in *Johnston v Chief Constable of the RUC* that this fundamental requirement of judicial control is also recognised as a general principle of Community law. Beneficiaries of Community provisions thus enjoy the right to pursue their claim by judicial process, and the Member States must provide access to the national courts for the purposes of obtaining a judicial determination of their Treaty rights.[17] This broad statement of principle has since been affirmed in numerous judgments.[18]

In certain respects, the Court's general principle of access to judicial process is broader in its scope of application than the requirement of judicial control contained in Article 6(1) ECHR. For example, Article 6(1) ECHR applies only to the determination of civil rights and obligations and criminal charges, not to disputes relating exclusively to public law.[19] By contrast, the Community principle of access to judicial control applies to all rights and obligations deriving from the Treaty, and thus extends to decisions taken by national authorities which are purely administrative in nature.[20] This is clearly acknowledged in Article 47 of the Charter of Fundamental Rights of the European Union, which provides simply that everyone whose rights and freedoms under Union law are violated is entitled to a fair and public hearing before an independent and impartial tribunal.[21]

Right to a Fair Hearing Before an Independent and Impartial Tribunal

Community law thus requires Member States to provide claimants with access to an independent and impartial tribunal. For example, Case C–424/99 *Commission v Austria* (2001) concerned the system for challenging decisions by the competent domestic authority to reject applications for inclusion in the list of medicinal products covered by the national

[17] Case 222/84 *Johnston v Chief Constable of the RUC* [1986] ECR 1651.
[18] Eg Case 178/84 *Commission v Germany* [1987] ECR 1227; Cases C–174 & 189/98 P *van der Wal* [2000] ECR I–1; Case C–228/98 *Dounias* [2000] ECR I–577; Case C–54/99 *Église de Scientologie* [2000] ECR I–1335; Case C–7/98 *Krombach* [2000] ECR I–1935. However, the Court sometimes fails to distinguish the right to judicial process from the principle of effectiveness (dealt with below): eg contrast Case C–34/02 *Pasquini* [2003] ECR I–6515; with Case C–63/01 *Evans* (Judgment of 4 December 2003).
[19] Eg *Schouten and Meldrum* [1994] 19 EHRR 432.
[20] Eg AG Ruiz-Jarabo Colomer in Cases C–65 & 111/95 *ex p Shingara* [1997] ECR I–3343; AG Alber in Case C–63/01 *Evans* (Opinion of 24 October 2002; Judgment of 4 December 2003). Further: E G de Enterría, 'The Extension of the Jurisdiction of National Administrative Courts by Community Law: The Judgment of the Court of Justice in *Borelli* and Article 5 of the EC Treaty' (1993) 13 *Yearbook of European Law* 19; C Harlow, 'Access to Justice as a Human Right: The European Convention and the European Union' in P Alston (ed), *The EU and Human Rights* (OUP, 1999).
[21] Charter of Fundamental Rights of the European Union, OJ 2000 C364/1.

health insurance system. Austrian legislation provided that, at the applicant's request, such decisions should be referred to an independent advisory board consisting of technical experts, which could then issue recommendations to the competent domestic authority (if appropriate) urging the latter to reconsider its refusal. The Court held that redress before an administrative body without true decision-making powers was clearly incapable of satisfying the principle of access to judicial process.[22] Similarly, *Johnston v Chief Constable of the RUC* itself concerned UK legislation which permitted derogations from the principle of equal treatment between men and women in relation to acts intended to safeguard national security or protect public safety; and provided that a certificate issued by the national authorities should constitute conclusive evidence that the act in question complied with the terms of such derogations. The Court observed that Article 6 Equal Treatment Directive requires Member States to introduce into their legal systems the measures necessary to enable victims of unlawful discrimination to pursue their claims by judicial process.[23] This provision merely reflects the requirement of access to a court guaranteed as a general principle of Community law. The system of certificate-plus-ouster-clause in question permitted the national authorities to deprive individuals of the opportunity of asserting their right to equal treatment, and was thus contrary to the principle of effective judicial control.[24]

Moreover, Community law also requires Member States to ensure that claimants enjoy a fair hearing before the relevant tribunal. For example, *Steffensen* concerned analyses conducted by the national authorities which indicated that certain foodstuffs failed to comply with domestic rules on labelling, but as regards which the relevant manufacturer had been unable to exercise its right under Community law to obtain a second opinion. The question arose whether such analyses could be admitted as evidence before the competent German court during the manufacturer's appeal against an administrative decision imposing financial penalties. The Court observed that Article 6(1) ECHR does not lay down any rules on evidence as such; but the requirement of a fair hearing, which implies that the parties enjoy an adequate opportunity to participate in proceedings before the competent court, covers also the manner in which evidence was taken. In particular, parties must be afforded a real opportunity to comment effectively upon evidence submitted to the court, especially where that evidence pertains to a technical field beyond the knowledge of the judges.

[22] Case C–424/99 *Commission v Austria* [2001] ECR I–9285.

[23] Dir 76/207 on the implementation of the principle of equal treatment for men and women as regards access to employment, vocational training and promotion, and working conditions, OJ 1976 L39/40. Note the amendments to Art 6 Dir 76/207, introduced by Dir 2002/73, OJ 2002 L269/15.

[24] Case 222/84 *Johnston v Chief Constable of the RUC* [1986] ECR 1651.

If the German court found that, in the circumstances of this case, admitting the analyses would infringe the right to a fair hearing, Community law would then require the evidence to be excluded.[25]

Scope of the Principle of Judicial Control

Several issues concerning the full scope of the Community right of access to judicial process warrant brief consideration: first, how far judicial control must extend to provisional acts; secondly, the degree of judicial review exercised by the national courts in Community cases; and thirdly, the consequences of the Member State's failure to provide access to judicial procedure.

Judicial Control Over Provisional Acts The requirement of judicial control may apply not only in respect of final but also as regards provisional decisions adopted by the national authorities where, in themselves, such acts are capable of affecting the claimant's legal interests. In *Garage Molenheide*, national law provided that, where a taxable person's deductions exceeded the taxes paid to the competent authorities, the refundable sums could nevertheless be retained as a precautionary measure (for example, in cases where there were serious grounds for presuming tax evasion) pending a final administrative decision about the taxable person's status. The Court held that effective judicial review must be available in respect not only of proceedings concerning the substance of the case, but also those concerning the adoption of precautionary measures.[26]

Provisional acts may also fall within the scope of the fundamental Community right to judicial process in situations where decision-making competences are divided between the Member States and the Community institutions. The Court in *Borelli* held that, where the disputed domestic act constitutes a necessary preliminary stage in the overall procedure for adopting a final Community act, as regards which the competent Community institutions enjoy limited or even no discretion, the national courts must assume jurisdiction—even though domestic procedural rules would normally preclude the existence of judicial review in such cases.[27] For example, *Kühne* concerned the Community system for registering geographical indications and designations of origin for foodstuffs. Member States assess whether a given designation satisfies the necessary criteria, then address a request for registration to the Commission. The latter undertakes a formal examination to verify that the necessary criteria

[25] Case C–276/01 *Steffensen* [2003] ECR I–3735. Also, eg Case C–63/01 *Evans* (Judgment of 4 December 2003) on the right to know and answer the opposing case.
[26] Cases C–286, 340 & 401/95 and C–47/96 *Garage Molenheide* [1997] ECR I–7281.
[27] Case C–97/91 *Borelli* [1992] ECR I–6313.

are indeed fulfilled, and if so is obliged to complete the registration process. Were a third party to challenge the Commission's decision to register via Article 230 EC, on the grounds that the underlying domestic act was flawed, the Court would be unable to assist: it has no jurisdiction to rule on the lawfulness of measures adopted by the national authorities. To avoid a vacuum in the system of effective judicial protection, the domestic courts are therefore obliged to entertain challenges to the legality of the Member State's decision to request registration of a designation, on the same terms on which they would review any definitive measure adopted by the relevant domestic authority which is capable of adversely affecting the rights of third parties, even though such 'provisional' national measures would ordinarily be immune from judicial review.[28]

Exercise of Full Jurisdiction The fundamental right to a fair hearing before an independent and impartial tribunal requires that the competent national court must be capable of exercising full jurisdiction over the disputed decision—though what constitutes 'full jurisdiction' for the purposes of Community law depends upon the precise factual and legal context of each case.[29]

For example, Directive 89/665 seeks to coordinate national review procedures for the award of various public contracts, by ensuring that decisions taken by contracting authorities may be reviewed effectively and as rapidly as possible on the grounds that they have infringed Community public procurement rules.[30] In *Hospital Ingenieure*, Austrian law limited judicial review of the legality of the withdrawal by a national authority of its invitation to tender for a public service contract to an examination of whether that decision was arbitrary. The Court held that, having regard to the objective of Directive 89/665 to strengthen review procedures for the award of public contracts, the scope of judicial review could not be interpreted in such a restrictive manner. National courts must be able to verify the compatibility of decisions to withdraw invitations to tender with the relevant substantive rules of Community law.[31] By contrast, *Upjohn v The Licensing Authority Established by the Medicines Act 1968* concerned the question of whether Community law requires the domestic courts, in an action for judicial review of national decisions revoking marketing authorisations for proprietary medicinal products, to substitute their own

[28] Case C–269/99 *Kühne* [2001] ECR I–9517.
[29] Caselaw based upon Art 6(1) ECHR demonstrates that this assessment can often prove controversial: consider, eg the judgment of the House of Lords in *R v Secretary of State for the Environment, Transport and the Regions, ex p Alconbury* [2001] 2 All ER 929.
[30] Dir 89/665 on the coordination of the laws, regulations and administrative provisions relating to the application of review procedures to the award of public supply and public works contracts, OJ 1989 L395/33.
[31] Case C–92/00 *Hospital Ingenieure* [2002] ECR I–5553.

assessment of the facts and scientific evidence for the assessment of the competent national authority. The Court advised that, where national authorities enjoy a wide margin of discretion because they are undertaking complex assessments, judicial review may be limited to verifying that such decisions are not vitiated by a manifest error or misuse of powers, and do not clearly exceed the boundaries of the authority's discretion.[32]

In any case, respect for the fundamental right derived from Article 6(1) ECHR is fulfilled provided that the claimant enjoys *one* fair hearing before an independent and impartial tribunal. The general principles of Community law will not require Member States to create additional courses of redress. For example, the claimant in *Schneider* was able to pursue his claim under national legislation implementing the Equal Treatment Directive, in respect of decisions taken by the Austrian State, before an administrative authority and then before an administrative court.[33] He argued that the latter enjoyed only limited competence to review factual assessments made by the administrative authority, and was thus incapable of satisfying the requirement of access to a fair hearing before an independent and impartial tribunal. However, the claimant was also entitled to bring an action for compensation against the Austrian State before the ordinary civil courts, which were capable of exercising full jurisdiction over both the legal and the factual elements of the dispute. The Court held that this right to redress before the civil courts undeniably met the standards of judicial protection expected under Community law, and made it unnecessary to assess whether that was true also of the system of review before the administrative courts.[34]

Consequences of Failure to Provide Access to the Courts There is some confusion in the caselaw about the exact consequences which flow from the Member State's failure to provide access to a fair hearing before an independent and impartial tribunal. Clearly, where the competent court finds its jurisdiction improperly inhibited by the presence of an ouster clause (in situations like *Johnston*), or the fairness of its hearing distorted by certain evidential rules (in cases like *Steffensen*), such domestic legislation must simply be set aside as incompatible with the binding requirements of Community law.[35] But what if the Member State has failed to designate *any* tribunal competent to adjudicate upon the claimant's rights? Would the ordinary (general, civil or administrative)

[32] Case C–120/97 *Upjohn v The Licensing Authority Established by the Medicines Act 1968* [1999] ECR I–223. Also, eg AG Alber in Case C–63/01 *Evans* (Opinion of 24 October 2002; Judgment of 4 December 2003).
[33] Dir 76/207, OJ 1976 L39/40.
[34] Case C–380/01 *Schneider* (Judgment of 5 February 2004).
[35] Eg Case C–276/01 *Steffensen* [2003] ECR I–3735, para 79.

courts be obliged to assume jurisdiction and deal with the dispute for themselves?

On the one hand, cases such as *Borelli* demonstrated that, if it proved necessary to guarantee the fundamental right of access to judicial process, the domestic courts should be prepared to disregard procedural restrictions which denied them jurisdiction to entertain claims based on the Treaty.[36] If that was true of rules such as ouster clauses, why should it not also apply to a simple vacuum of competence to adjudicate? On the other hand, the basic principle established by the Court in *Bozzetti* is that it is for the legal system of each Member State to determine which court or tribunal has jurisdiction to hear disputes involving individual rights derived from Community law. Although it is the Member State's responsibility to ensure that those rights are effectively protected in each case, it is not for the Court to involve itself in the resolution of questions of jurisdiction to which the classification of certain legal situations based on Community law may give rise in the national judicial system.[37] This principle can also be seen in the Court's earlier judgment in *Simmenthal*: every national court must, *in a case within its jurisdiction*, apply Community law in its entirety and protect rights which the latter confers on individuals; any domestic rule which might impair the effectiveness of Community law, by withholding from the national court *having jurisdiction to apply such law* the power to do everything necessary to set aside national provisions which might prevent Treaty norms from having full force, are incompatible with the very essence of Community law.[38]

More recent judgments suggest that the Court is indeed reticent about obliging national courts to assume jurisdiction in entirely novel situations which lie beyond their prima facie field of competence. In *Dorsch Consult*, Germany had failed to transpose the provisions of Directive 92/50 on the coordination of procedures for the award of public service contracts.[39] The Court observed that, although the Directive requires Member States to ensure effective review mechanisms were available, it does not specify which national bodies were to be competent for that purpose. In such circumstances, the Court was not prepared to insist that the supervisory

[36] Case C–97/91 *Borelli* [1992] ECR I–6313.

[37] Case 179/84 *Bozzetti* [1985] ECR 2301. Similarly, eg Case 13/68 *Salgoil* [1968] ECR 661; Case C–446/93 *SEIM* [1996] ECR I–73; Cases C–10–22/97 *IN.CO.GE.'90* [1998] ECR I–6307; Case C–224/01 *Köbler* (Judgment of 30 September 2003). Cf the parallel principle established as regards the discharge of Treaty obligations by national authorities in Cases 51–54/71 *International Fruit Company* [1971] ECR 1107.

[38] Case 106/77 *Simmenthal* [1978] ECR 629, paras 21–22.

[39] Dir 92/50 relating to the coordination of procedures for the award of public service contracts, OJ 1992 L209/1 (amending Dir 89/665, OJ 1989 L395/33). Note that the relevant provisions of Dir 92/50 have not been repealed by the recent public procurement modernisation package (in particular: Dir 2004/18, OJ 2004 L134/114).

bodies already designated as competent to conduct review procedures in the context of public works and supply contracts should simply assume jurisdiction also as regards public service contracts. If the relevant national legislation could be interpreted to that effect, in accordance with the *Marleasing* caselaw, all well and good.[40] But if not, the claimant's proper recourse was to bring a *Francovich* action against Germany[41] seeking damages for losses caused by its failure to transpose the Directive.[42]

Judgments such as *Dorsch Consult* demonstrate that, where the Member State omits to designate an appropriate court for a given category of dispute, the fundamental Community requirement of judicial control must be equated, in practice, to a right to reparation against the Member State, in accordance with the *Francovich* caselaw, for having breached its obligation to provide access to effective judicial protection.[43] However, *Dorsch Consult* was distinguished by the Court in *Connect Austria*. Directive 90/387 obliged each Member State to ensure that suitable mechanisms exist for parties affected by decisions of the national telecommunications regulatory authority to enjoy a right of appeal to an independent body.[44] Austrian rules recognised that the Administrative Court should have the power to adjudicate over challenges to the lawfulness of decisions taken by the national authorities; but specifically excluded such jurisdiction, inter alia, as regards measures adopted by 'collegiate authorities'—including decisions of the Telekom-Control-Kommission (the competent Austrian authority). Both the Court and Advocate General Geelhoed accepted that the Directive did not specify which tribunal should have the power to hear appeals from decisions of the telecommunications regulatory authority. The Advocate General believed that the reasoning in *Dorsch Consult* should thus apply by analogy: the claimant could not challenge directly the decision of the Telekom-Control-Kommission, only bring a *Francovich* action for reparation against Austria for its failure to guarantee the right of appeal to an independent tribunal. However, the Court held that a national court which satisfies the requirements of Community law, and would be competent to hear appeals against decisions of the telecommunications regulatory authority *if it was not*

[40] Case C–106/89 *Marleasing* [1990] ECR I–4135.

[41] Cases C–6 & 9/90 *Francovich* [1991] ECR I–5357. Further: ch 5 (below).

[42] Case C–54/96 *Dorsch Consult* [1997] ECR I–4961. Also, eg Case C–76/97 *Walter Tögel* [1998] ECR I–5357; Case C–111/97 *EvoBus Austria* [1998] ECR I–5411; Case C–258/97 *Hospital Ingenieure* [1999] ECR I–1405.

[43] Further, eg M Dougan, 'The *Francovich* Right to Reparation: Reshaping the Contours of Community Remedial Competence' (2000) 6 *European Public Law* 103.

[44] Dir 90/387 on the establishment of the internal market for telecommunications services through the implementation of open network provision, OJ 1990 L192/1 (repealed and by Dir 2002/21, OJ 2002 L108/33).

prevented from doing so by a provision of national law specifically excluding its competence, is obliged to disapply that provision.[45]

Connect Austria was clearly not intended simply to overrule *Dorsch Consult*. Instead, the judgment suggests that it is necessary to distinguish between situations where the Member State has failed totally in its obligation to identify an appropriate court, such that Community law can intervene only indirectly through a *Francovich* action for reparation; and cases where national law does make it possible to identify some appropriate tribunal, as regards which Community law need simply neutralise specific limitations imposed upon its competence to dispose of the claim.[46] Express exclusions of jurisdiction can be set aside, but more creative conferrals of jurisdiction are prohibited. Of course, whether a Member State is deemed to have failed to designate a particular court for a certain category of claim, or instead to have specifically excluded that court's jurisdiction over that type of dispute, depends upon the pre-existing framework of the national legal order: for example, the precise wording of the relevant legislative measures; and whether particular tribunals are considered to exercise general or specific competence. As a consequence, the Court's caselaw produces the seemingly odd (and potentially arbitrary) result that the more serious the Member State's infringement of the right of access to an independent and impartial tribunal, the more likely the claimant's redress will assume the form of an action for damages, based upon the existence of a sufficiently serious breach of Community law, for the lost opportunity to enjoy a substantive hearing on the merits of his/her case in compliance with the requirements of Article 6(1) ECHR as protected under the general principles of Community law (as in *Dorsch Consult* itself). This will usually furnish a less meaningful form of relief than insisting that the ordinary courts assume full jurisdiction to conduct just such a hearing for themselves—which would lie closer to the solution the Court pursues for less serious defaults in the scope of effective judicial protection (not only in situations such as *Connect Austria*, but also in cases like *Johnston* and *Steffensen*).[47]

Flanking Protection for the Right of Access to Judicial Process

The principle of access to judicial process is supplemented by certain guarantees of 'flanking protection' against conduct designed to deter the citizen from pursuing his/her Treaty entitlements through the courts.

For example, the Court in *Heylens* decreed that the right of access to judicial procedure in respect of restrictions on the free movement of

[45] Case C–462/99 *Connect Austria* [2003] ECR I–5197.
[46] On this distinction between direct and indirect intervention, see further: ch 5 (below).
[47] Further: M Dougan, 'The *Francovich* Right to Reparation: Reshaping the Contours of Community Remedial Competence' (2000) 6 *European Public Law* 103.

persons implies a duty upon the competent authority to disclose the reasons for its decision, without which the citizen could not decide whether there was any point in bringing legal proceedings in the first place.[48] Other cases support the existence of a link under Community law between the transparency of an administrative procedure and the effectiveness of the right of access to judicial process. Thus, the Court in *Smits and Peerbooms* held that systems of prior authorisation which disrupt the free movement of services must be based upon objective criteria known in advance, so as to ensure that the national authority does not exercise its discretion arbitrarily; and upon a procedural system which is easily accessible and capable of ensuring that requests are dealt with impartially within a reasonable time, and that refusals to grant authorisation can be challenged in judicial or quasi-judicial proceedings.[49]

Another 'flanking protection' can be seen in *Coote v Granada Hospitality*. There, the Court held that the right of access to the courts to protest about a breach of the principle of equal treatment between men and women necessarily implies an ancillary guarantee of protection against retaliatory measures taken by an employer aimed at deterring the victim of discriminatory action from pursuing her grievances by judicial means.[50] Such reasoning also underlies judgments such as *Emmott* and *Levez*, in which the Court held that national limitation periods applicable to actions for equal treatment in social security and employment must be set aside, where the defendant has engaged in misleading conduct which effectively prevented the individual from initiating his/her claim within the proper time-limits.[51]

Although all these judgments involved the exercise of a fundamental Treaty right (to free movement or equal treatment), there seems no reason in principle why the same approach should not apply to broader categories of circumstances (based upon any rights to protection enjoyed as a matter of Community law). One would certainly expect the Court to offer flanking protection in all situations where the beneficiary of Community law suffers from some status of vulnerability which exposes his/her right

[48] Case 222/86 *Heylens* [1987] ECR 4097. Also, eg Case C–340/89 *Vlassopoulou* [1991] ECR I–2357; Case C–104/91 *Borrell* [1992] ECR I–3003; Case C–19/92 *Kraus* [1993] ECR I–1663. This duty applies only to final decisions, not to merely preparatory or intermediate stages in the overall decision-making process: Case C–127/95 *Norbrook Laboratories* [1998] ECR I–1531. Moreover, the duty to provide reasons applies only to administrative decisions adversely affecting individuals, not national measures of general scope: Case C–70/95 *Sodemare* [1997] ECR I–3395.

[49] Case C–157/99 *Smits and Peerbooms* [2001] ECR I–5473. Similarly, eg Case C–205/99 *Analir* [2001] ECR I–1271; Case C–367/98 *Commission v Portugal* [2002] ECR I–4731; Case C–138/02 *Collins* (Judgment of 23 March 2004).

[50] Case C–185/97 *Coote v Granada Hospitality* [1998] ECR I–5199. Also, eg AG Tesauro in Case C–29/95 *Pastoors* [1997] ECR I–285, paras 19–20 Opinion.

[51] Case C–208/90 *Emmott* [1991] ECR I–4269; Case C–326/96 *Levez* [1998] ECR I–7835. Further: ch 5 (below).

to judicial process to particular threat of reprisal, for example, as employee vis-à-vis employer, or as consumer vis-à-vis commercial trader.[52] Indeed, flanking protection of the sort involved in *Coote* or *Emmott* may be appropriate as regards any inherently unequal relationship involving dependence by one party upon another; or in situations where there is some specific assumption of responsibility by one party towards another.[53]

Presumption of National Competence to Determine Remedies and Procedural Rules

Once the requirements imposed by the fundamental right of access to a court have been satisfied, the Court proceeds on the basis of the following principle: in the absence of Community legislation governing the matter, it is for the domestic legal system of each Member State to lay down the detailed remedies, sanctions and procedural rules governing actions for safeguarding rights which individuals derive from Community law.[54] Both limbs of this principle warrant consideration.

Community Legislation on Decentralised Enforcement

The Community legislature often adopts measures dealing with the types of remedy, sanction or procedural rule which Member States must furnish before the national courts as regards the enforcement of particular categories of Treaty norm.

Such legislation has been passed under a variety of Treaty provisions. For example, Article 95 EC provides for the adoption of harmonising measures which have as their object the establishment and functioning of the Internal Market. This has supplied the legal basis for numerous directives which touch upon the remedies and procedures required for the decentralised enforcement of substantive Community rules.[55]

[52] Further: M Dougan, 'The Equal Treatment Directive: Retaliation, Remedies and Direct Effect' (1999) 24 EL Rev 664.
[53] Consider, eg Case C–327/00 *Santex* [2003] ECR I–1877.
[54] Eg Case 28/67 *Molkerei-Zentrale* [1968] ECR 143; Case 34/67 *Lück* [1968] ECR 245; Case 33/76 *Rewe-Zentralfinanz v Landwirtschaftskammer für das Saarland* [1976] ECR 1989; Case 45/76 *Comet* [1976] ECR 2043; Case 74/76 *Iannelli and Volpi* [1977] ECR 557.
[55] Eg Dir 89/665 on the coordination of the laws, regulations and administrative provisions relating to the application of review procedures to the award of public supply and public works contracts, OJ 1989 L395/33 (as amended by Dir 92/50, OJ 1992 L209/1); Dir 92/13 coordinating the laws, regulations and administrative provisions relating to the application of Community rules on the procurement procedures of entities operating in the water, energy, transport and telecommunications sectors, OJ 1992 L76/14; Dir 93/13 on unfair terms in consumer contracts, OJ 1993 L95/29; Dir 99/44 on certain aspects of the sale of consumer goods and associated guarantees, OJ 1999 L171/12. Also: measures based on Art 94 EC, eg Dir 84/450 concerning misleading and comparative advertising, OJ 1984 L250/17 (as amended by Dir 97/55, OJ 1997 L290/18).

Certain sectoral legal bases (relating to policies other than the Internal Market) have also been used for the adoption of legislation impacting upon national remedies and procedures, for example, Article 137 EC on social policy;[56] and Article 175 EC on environmental policy.[57] As has often been observed, action by the Community legislature under these legal bases, so as to intervene in the process of decentralised enforcement, has not followed a coherent or consistent plan. Rather, the political institutions have identified and responded to particular problems very much on an ad hoc basis.[58] This has resulted in a highly diverse body of Community legislation covering a wide variety of matters: some directives prescribe the limitation period applicable to claims based thereunder,[59] whilst other measures address issues of evidence and the burden of proof,[60] and certain directives deal with questions of standing to bring actions before the national courts,[61] whilst other measures are concerned with the range of remedies offered to their beneficiaries.[62]

A more coherent programme for Community action in the field of judicial protection might emerge from the creation of the Area of Freedom, Justice and Security. The Member States have long sought to establish effective cross-border cooperation as regards the mutual recognition of judicial decisions, in particular, through the 1968 Brussels Convention on jurisdiction and the enforcement of judgments in civil and commercial matters.[63] The Treaty of Amsterdam then altered the legal framework governing this field.[64] Article 65 EC empowers the Community to adopt measures in the field of judicial cooperation in civil matters having cross-border implications, insofar as these are necessary for the proper functioning of the Internal Market.[65] Such measures include improving

[56] Eg Dir 97/80 on the burden of proof in sex discrimination cases, OJ 1998 L14/6.

[57] Eg Dir 2003/35 providing for public participation in respect of the drawing up of certain plans and programmes relating to the environment and amending with regard to public participation and access to justice Directives 85/337 and 96/61, OJ 2003 L156/17.

[58] Eg T Heukels and J Tib, 'Towards Homogeneity in the Field of Legal Remedies: Convergence and Divergence' in P Beaumont, C Lyons & N Walker (eds), *Convergence and Divergence in European Public Law* (Hart Publishing, 2002).

[59] Eg Dir 85/374 on the approximation of the laws, regulations and administrative provisions of the Member States concerning liability for defective products, OJ 1985 L210/29; Dir 2004/35 on environmental liability with regard to the prevention and remedying of environmental damage, OJ 2004 L143/56.

[60] Eg Reg 1/2003 on the modernisation of competition law enforcement, OJ 2003 L1/1.

[61] Eg Dir 98/27 on injunctions for the protection of consumers' interests, OJ 1998 L166/51.

[62] Eg Dir 89/665 on public supply, works and service contracts, OJ 1989 L395/33 (as amended by Dir 92/50, OJ 1992 L209/1).

[63] Last consolidated version, OJ 1998 C27/1.

[64] Further, eg J Basedow, 'The Communitarization of the Conflict of Laws Under the Treaty of Amsterdam' (2000) 37 CML Rev 687.

[65] Cf Title VI TEU as originally agreed at Maastricht, which covered judicial cooperation in civil matters, but only through inter-governmental measures. Consider, eg Convention on jurisdiction and the recognition and enforcement of judgments in matrimonial matters, OJ 1998 C 221/1.

and simplifying the system for the cross-border service of documents, cooperation in the taking of evidence, and the recognition and enforcement of decisions in civil and commercial cases. The Community may also adopt measures promoting the compatibility of the rules concerning conflict of laws and of jurisdiction; and eliminating obstacles to the good functioning of civil proceedings (if necessary) by promoting the compatibility of civil procedure rules. On this basis, the Brussels Convention has now been transformed into Regulation 44/2001 on jurisdiction and the recognition and enforcement of judgments in civil and commercial matters;[66] and other regulations have been adopted dealing with insolvency proceedings,[67] and jurisdiction and the recognition and enforcement of judgments in matrimonial matters and matters of parental responsibility.[68] In 1999, the Tampere European Council set out guidelines for Community action to promote judicial cooperation in civil matters based upon facilitating access to justice in cross-border disputes, and further enhancing the mutual recognition of judicial decisions. The European Council admitted that the latter goal in particular would sometimes make it necessary to establish minimum common standards on specific aspects of civil procedure rules, so as to strengthen mutual trust and permit the Member States to dispense with existing limitations on the scope of mutual recognition.[69] Several initiatives have been undertaken within the framework of these Tampere guidelines: for example, Regulation 1206/2001 on judicial cooperation in the taking of evidence in civil or commercial matters;[70] and Directive 2003/8 establishing minimum common rules relating to legal aid for cross-border disputes.[71]

[66] Reg 44/2001 on jurisdiction and the recognition and enforcement of judgments in civil and commercial matters, OJ 2001 L12/1. However, the Brussels Convention (rather than the new Regulation) remains in force for certain purposes, eg in relations between Denmark and the other Member States.

[67] Reg 1346/2000 on insolvency proceedings, OJ 2000 L160/1. This measure does not apply to Denmark.

[68] Reg 2201/2003 concerning jurisdiction and the recognition and enforcement of judgments in matrimonial matters and the matters of parental responsibility, OJ 2003 L338/1 (repealing and replacing Reg 1347/2000, OJ 2000 L160/19). Again, this measure does not apply to Denmark.

[69] Conclusions of the Tampere European Council (15–16 October 1999). Also: Council, *Draft Programme of Measures for Implementation of the Principle of Mutual Recognition of Decisions in Civil and Commercial Matters*, OJ 2001 C12/1.

[70] Reg 1206/2001 on cooperation between the courts of the Member States in the taking of evidence in civil or commercial matters, OJ 2001 L174/1. Again, this measure does not apply to Denmark.

[71] Dir 2003/8 to improve access to justice in cross-border disputes by establishing minimum common rules relating to legal aid for such disputes, OJ 2003 L26/41. Again, this measure does not apply to Denmark. Consider also, eg Commission, *Green Paper on Alternative Dispute Resolution in Civil and Commercial Law*, COM (2002)196 Final; Commission, *Green Paper on a European Order for Payment Procedure and on Measures to Simplify and Speed Up Small Claims Litigation*, COM (2002)746 Final.

The Third Pillar seeks to bolster the Area of Freedom, Security and Justice by making provision (in Article 31 TEU) for judicial cooperation in criminal matters, for example, as regards preventing conflicts of jurisdiction between the Member States, and in establishing minimum rules relating to the definition of criminal acts and penalties in fields such as organised crime and terrorism. Measures adopted under this legal basis might again have a profound impact upon aspects of judicial protection before the national courts. For example, Article 54 of the Convention implementing the Schengen Agreement, now located within the framework of the Third Pillar, sets out the *ne bis in idem* principle, that a person whose trial has been finally disposed of in one Member State may not be prosecuted in another Member State for the same acts; provided that, if a penalty has been imposed, it has been enforced, is actually in the process of being enforced, or can no longer be enforced under the laws of the sentencing State.[72] This principle is intended to ensure that individuals are not prosecuted on the same facts in several Member States, on account of having exercised their right to free movement across the Community. In *Gözütok and Brügge*, the Court held that, where proceedings in one Member State are discontinued after the accused agreed to pay fines under an agreement reached with the public prosecutor, barring further prosecution in that Member State, this was capable of activating the *ne bis in idem* principle as regards the other Member States—even though no court had been involved, and the final decision was not judicial in nature. In particular, the Court stressed that no provision of the Third Pillar makes application of Article 54 of the Convention implementing the Schengen Agreement conditional upon the harmonisation of national criminal laws—which necessarily implies that Member States have mutual trust in their criminal justice systems, and will recognise the criminal law in force in other countries, even if their own national rules would reach a different outcome.[73]

This emphasis on the principle of mutual trust creates a powerful incentive for Member States, some perhaps uneasy at the idea of having extensive obligations of mutual recognition in this field, to agree harmonised (procedural and substantive) standards of criminal justice.[74] In this regard, Article 31 TEU has already led to the adoption of numerous framework decisions concerning, for example: the standing of victims in

[72] Convention implementing the Schengen Agreement, OJ 2000 L239/19.
[73] Cases C–187 & 385/01 *Gözütok and Brügge* [2003] ECR I–1345.
[74] Further, eg D Curtin and I Dekker, 'The Constitutional Structure of the European Union: Some Reflections on Vertical Unity-in-Diversity' in P Beaumont, C Lyons & N Walker (eds), *Convergence and Divergence in European Public Law* (Hart Publishing, 2002). Cf the proposals for greater harmonising powers in this field contained in the Convention on the Future of Europe's Draft Treaty Establishing a Constitution for Europe, OJ 2003 C169/1; and adopted at the 2004 IGC in the final Treaty Establishing a Constitution for Europe, CIG 87/04.

criminal proceedings;[75] confiscation of the proceeds of crime;[76] the European arrest warrant and surrender procedures between Member States;[77] and the execution of orders freezing property or evidence.[78]

National Competence Over Remedies, Sanctions and Procedures

Community legislative measures create binding obligations for the Member States which are (in principle) capable of pre-empting national competence over the standards of judicial protection applicable to actions based on the relevant Community law provisions.[79] However, in the absence of harmonising Community legislation, each Member State is presumed to exercise its own competence over the remedies, sanctions and procedural rules available for the decentralised enforcement of Treaty norms. We have already seen that this presumption of national autonomy extends to limited aspects of the fundamental right of access to judicial process. Thus, it is for the Member State to take the initial step of designating the particular court or tribunal having jurisdiction to entertain a particular category of Community law claim.[80] Similarly, it lies within the discretion of the domestic legislature to decide whether the appropriate remedy for a discriminatory dismissal from employment, in breach of the Equal Treatment Directive, should consist in reinstatement of the victim back to her post, or the award of financial compensation representing losses suffered through the unlawful dismissal.[81]

It seems widely accepted that the presumption of domestic autonomy applies only to determine the modalities under which Treaty rights are exercised before the national courts (such as limitation periods, evidential

[75] Framework Dec 2001/220 on the standing of victims in criminal proceedings, OJ 2001 L82/1.
[76] Framework Dec 2001/500 on money laundering, the identification, tracing, freezing, seizing and confiscation of instrumentalities and the proceeds of crime, OJ 2001 L182/1.
[77] Framework Dec 2002/584 on the European arrest warrant and the surrender procedures between Member States, OJ 2002 L190/1.
[78] Framework Dec 2003/577 on the execution in the European Union of orders freezing property or evidence, OJ 2003 L196/45. Also, eg Commission, *Green Paper on Compensation to Crime Victims*, COM (2001)536 Final; Commission, *Green Paper on Procedural Safeguards for Suspects and Defendants in Criminal Proceedings Throughout the European Union*, COM (2003)75 Final. However, for critical comments, consider S Peers, 'Mutual Recognition and Criminal Law in the European Union: Has the Council Got it Wrong?' (2004) 41 CML Rev 5.
[79] Of course, the situation is more nuanced as regards *Union measures* adopted under the Third Pillar in the sphere of judicial cooperation in criminal measures, thanks to Art 34 TEU.
[80] See above.
[81] Dir 76/207, OJ 1976 L39/40. Eg Case C–271/91 *Marshall II* [1993] ECR I–4367. Also: Case 14/83 *von Colson* [1984] ECR 1891; Case 79/83 *Harz* [1984] ECR 1921; Case 248/83 *Commission v Germany* [1985] ECR 1459.

restrictions, heads of recoverable damages, the payment of interest etc); whereas the conditions governing the very existence and nature of a right under Community law fall to be defined directly by the Court of Justice.[82] However, it is worth noting the argument made by certain commentators that, since the conditions giving rise to liability to make reparation for a breach of the Treaty (for example, whether liability should arise from the infringement per se, or only based upon requirements of fault) are so closely linked to the existence and nature of the substantive Community right itself, competence over those conditions should also vest, as a matter of principle, in Community (not domestic) law.[83]

It is true that the Community legislature can specify whether liability to make reparation for a particular breach of the Treaty is to be incurred on a per se or on a fault basis.[84] It is also true that the Court sometimes sets out for itself the substantive conditions which determine access to a given remedy: for example, as with Member State liability to make reparation under the *Francovich* caselaw;[85] and as regards interim relief before the national courts when challenging the lawfulness of Community acts.[86] But in other cases, the presumption of national autonomy does indeed seem to apply: for example, in respect of interim relief before the national courts when challenging the lawfulness of Member State acts;[87] and as regards the conditions for obtaining compensation from private parties pursuant to an infringement of the Community's competition rules.[88] So, whatever the issue of principle, it nevertheless seems clear that, as matter of practice, the presumption of national autonomy applies unless and until either the Community legislature or the Court have actively assumed responsibility for specifying the conditions under which an infringement of one's Treaty rights will lead to the imposition of liability to make reparation.

In any event, it also seems widely accepted that the presumption of national competence is not justified by some quasi-political sensitivity towards the sovereignty of the Member States to regulate their own national legal orders. The Court's approach is determined rather by the pragmatic realisation that, without systematic harmonisation through secondary legislation, the Community has little choice but to defer

[82] Eg AG Léger in Case C–453/00 *Kühne & Heitz* (Opinion of 17 June 2003; Judgment of 13 January 2004).
[83] Eg W van Gerven, 'Of Rights, Remedies and Procedures' (2000) 37 CML Rev 501.
[84] Eg Dir 85/374 on the approximation of the laws, regulations and administrative provisions of the Member States concerning liability for defective products, OJ 1985 L210/29.
[85] Cases C–6 & 9/90 *Francovich* [1991] ECR I–5357. Further: ch 5 (below).
[86] Eg Cases C–143/88 and C–92/89 *Zuckerfabrik Süderdithmarshen* [1991] ECR I–415. Further: ch 6 (below).
[87] Eg Case C–213/89 *ex p Factortame* [1990] ECR I–2433. Further: ch 6 (below).
[88] Eg Case C–453/99 *Courage v Crehan* [2001] ECR I–6297. Further: ch 6 (below).

in the first instance to the existing domestic judicial systems for the decentralised enforcement of Treaty norms.[89]

Community Limits to the Presumption of National Competence

Nevertheless, the Court's presumption of national competence to determine the remedies and procedural rules applicable to Community law claims is not irrebuttable. Three principles are particularly relevant for present purposes: the substantive rules contained in the Treaty itself; the principle of equivalence; and the principle(s) of effectiveness.

Substantive Treaty Rules

National remedies and procedural rules may be governed directly by the substantive rules contained in directly effective Treaty provisions.

For example, where a domestic measure is held to be incompatible with the free movement of goods under Article 28 EC, or the free movement of persons under Articles 39, 43 and 49 EC, any sanction (criminal or otherwise) intended to enforce that domestic measure is automatically prohibited by the Treaty, without any need to conduct an independent assessment of whether the sanction itself complies with the principle of proportionality.[90] Even where a domestic rule is indeed found to be compatible with the free movement provisions (because it benefits from an express Treaty derogation or pursues an imperative requirement of the public interest), any sanction intended to enforce that domestic rule, imposed upon traders or migrant Community nationals, must not be so disproportionate to the gravity of the infringement that this becomes *in itself* an obstacle to free movement. This is inherent in the general principle of proportionality binding upon the Member States when acting within the scope of application of Community law and, in particular, when derogating from their Treaty obligations.[91] Thus, in *Skanavi*, the Court held that it would be incompatible with Article 43 EC for Germany to

[89] See AG Warner in Case 33/76 *Rewe-Zentralfinanz v Landwirtschaftskammer für das Saarland* [1976] ECR 1989 and Case 45/76 *Comet* [1976] ECR 2043; and AG Mischo in Case C–424/97 *Haim II* [2000] ECR I–5123. Also, eg Case C–394/93 *Alonso-Pérez* [1995] ECR I–4101; Case C–343/96 *Dilexport* [1999] ECR I–579. Further, eg C N Kakouris, 'Do the Member States Possess Judicial Procedural "Autonomy"?' (1997) 34 CML Rev 1389; L M Díez-Picazo, 'Towards a Unified Judicial Protection in Europe(?)' (1997) 9 *European Review of Public Law* 975.

[90] Eg Case 179/78 *Rivoira* [1979] ECR 1147; Case 269/80 *Tymen* [1981] ECR 3079. More recently, eg Cases C–388 & 429/00 *Radiosistemi* [2002] ECR I–5845; Case C–13/01 *Safalero* (Judgment of 11 September 2003); Case C–167/01 *Inspire Art* (Judgment of 30 September 2003); Case C–12/02 *Grilli* (Judgment of 2 October 2003).

[91] Eg Case 203/80 *Casati* [1981] ECR 2595; Case C–387/93 *Banchero* [1995] ECR I–4663. Cf Case 823/79 *Carciati* [1980] ECR 2773.

subject foreign nationals to criminal penalties for failing to comply with the (otherwise perfectly justified) obligation to exchange their driving licence within one year of taking up residence in the host state, having regard to the importance of the right to drive a motor vehicle for exercise of the freedom of establishment.[92]

It is also possible that the domestic standards of judicial protection will raise their own issues of compatibility with substantive Community law prohibiting discrimination on grounds of nationality. The principle of non-discrimination on grounds of nationality is set out in Article 12 EC and given more specific expression in fields such as the free movement of workers, freedom of establishment and free movement of services. It requires 'perfect equality of treatment' as between Community nationals and nationals of the relevant Member State in all situations governed by Community law.[93] The principle of non-discrimination thus prohibits: direct discrimination, ie, the application of criteria which draw a blatant distinction between Community and own-nationals, and can be justified only by reference to the express derogations provided for under the Treaty;[94] and indirect discrimination, ie, the application of prima facie neutral criteria which in practice impose greater burdens on Community than own-nationals, and must be justified by reference to either the Treaty derogations or a broader category of public interest requirements recognised by the Court of Justice.[95] Where there has been an unjustified breach of the principle of non-discrimination, the Community victim is entitled to claim the benefits accorded to his/her domestic comparator, since this is the only point of reference by which to restore true equality of treatment.[96]

The principle of non-discrimination thus plays a fundamental role in attaining the Treaty's objectives of ever closer economic and political union among the peoples of Europe.[97] As such, its reach extends, within the context of the free movement of persons, beyond the substantive to touch also upon the remedial, punitive and procedural provisions of the national legal orders. For example, in Case C–24/97 *Commission v Germany* (1998), the imposition of heavier fines on Community nationals who failed to comply with the obligation to obtain a residence permit

[92] Case C–193/94 *Skanavi* [1996] ECR I–929. Also, eg Case 48/75 *Royer* [1976] ECR 497; Case 118/75 *Watson and Belmann* [1976] ECR 1185; Case 8/77 *Sagulo* [1977] ECR 1495; Case C–265/88 *Messner* [1989] ECR 4209; Case C–348/96 *Calfa* [1999] ECR I–11; Case C–378/97 *Wijsenbeek* [1999] ECR I–6207.

[93] Case C–43/95 *Data Delecta* [1996] ECR I–4661, para 16. Also, eg Case C–274/96 *Bickel and Franz* [1998] ECR I–7637.

[94] Eg on grounds of public policy, security and health, as regards the free movement of persons, under Arts 39(3), 46(1) and 55 EC.

[95] Eg Case 152/73 *Sotgiu* [1974] ECR 153; Case C–237/94 *O'Flynn* [1996] ECR I–2617.

[96] Eg Case C–15/96 *Schöning* [1998] ECR I–47; Case C–18/95 *Terhoeve* [1999] ECR I–345.

[97] AG Jacobs in Cases C–92 & 326/92 *Phil Collins* [1993] ECR I–5145, 5162–3.

than on own-nationals who breached the comparable obligation to possess a valid identity document amounted to direct discrimination contrary to Article 39 EC.[98] Similarly, consider the following rules governing the seizure of assets intended to act as security for civil actions pending before the local courts: in the case of judgments to be enforced within the domestic territory, seizure orders are to be granted only if enforcement would otherwise be rendered impossible or substantially more difficult; whereas in the case of judgments to be enforced in the territory of other Member States, such orders are to be made automatically. The Court held in *Mund and Fester* that these rules constitute indirect discrimination against Community citizens which must be objectively justified by factors unrelated to nationality.[99]

Even where national remedies, sanctions or procedural rules comply with the requirement of non-discrimination on grounds of nationality, they may still breach the substantive Treaty provisions by raising unjustified obstacles to the free movement of goods or persons. The idea of indistinctly applicable barriers is illustrated by the judgment in *Reisebüro Broede*, which concerned national rules whereby judicial debt-collection activities could be carried out in Germany only through the intermediary of a lawyer. The Court held that, although this restriction applied equally to everyone carrying out judicial debt-collection activities in Germany, it nevertheless hindered the ability of undertakings established in other Member States, where they lawfully conducted such activities without the involvement of a lawyer, from offering their services within Germany in accordance with Article 49 EC.[100]

Substantive Treaty provisions other than those regulating free movement may also impact directly upon the national systems of judicial protection. For example, *Promedia* concerned an agreement for the supply of customer data between an independent publisher of telephone directories and a company providing telephone services in Belgium. The company later began to produce its own rival telephone directory, and

[98] Case C–24/97 *Commission v Germany* [1998] ECR I–2133. Cf Case 8/77 *Sagulo* [1977] ECR 1495. Other examples of direct discrimination in remedies, sanctions and procedural rules: Case C–43/95 *Data Delecta* [1996] ECR I–4661; Case C–323/95 *Hayes v Kronenberger* [1997] ECR I–1711; Case C–122/94 *Saldanha* [1997] ECR I–5325. Consider also, eg Case 186/87 *Cowan v Trésor public* [1989] ECR 195; Case C–390/96 *Lease Plan Luxembourg* [1998] ECR I–2553.

[99] Case C–398/92 *Mund and Fester* [1994] ECR I–467. Other examples of indirect discrimination in remedies, sanctions and procedural rules: Case C–29/95 *Pastoors* [1997] ECR I–285; Case C–336/94 *Dafeki* [1997] ECR I–6761; Case C–274/96 *Bickel and Franz* [1998] ECR I–7637.

[100] Case C–3/95 *Reisebüro Broede* [1996] ECR I–6511. Also, eg Case C–255/97 *Pfeiffer Großhandel* [1999] ECR I–2835; Case C–289/02 *AMOK Verlags* (Judgment of 11 December 2003). Consider also judgments dealing with the burden of proof in trade mark disputes, eg Cases C–414–16/99 *Davidoff* [2001] ECR I–8691; Case C–244/00 *Van Doren* [2003] ECR I–3051.

brought an action based upon the agreement seeking to oblige the publisher to surrender its commercial know-how. The publisher complained to the Commission that this legal action was a breach of Article 82 EC. The Commission held that litigation by a dominant undertaking may constitute an abuse contrary to Article 82 EC where two cumulative criteria were fulfilled: the legal action could not reasonably be considered as an attempt to establish the rights of the dominant undertaking, only to harass its rival; and the legal action was conceived within the framework of a plan to eliminate competition on the relevant market. The Court of First Instance (CFI) confined itself to examining whether the Commission had correctly applied these criteria to the facts of the case. However, the CFI did observe that the ability to assert one's rights through the courts constituted a general principle of Community law. Therefore, it was only in wholly exceptional circumstances that the bringing of legal proceedings could constitute an abuse contrary to Article 82 EC. Insofar as the Commission's criteria provided the correct legal test for establishing the existence of such exceptional circumstances, they had to be construed and applied strictly.[101]

In most cases, however, national remedies and procedural rules do not involve any direct breach of the substantive Treaty rules. Indeed, their impact upon the free movement provisions is likely to be considered 'too indirect and uncertain' to warrant scrutiny by the Court. For example, *Italo Fenocchio* concerned an Italian trader who had supplied goods to a customer resident in Germany. The latter failed to pay for the goods, so the trader brought an action before the Italian courts seeking a summary order for payment. National procedural rules provided that such orders could be made only if the defendant was resident within Italy, not where the defendant was resident abroad. The Court held that, although the effect of the Italian rules was to subject traders to different procedural rules depending on whether they supplied goods to the domestic or the Community markets, the possibility that traders would consequently hesitate to sell goods abroad was too remote to consider that the Italian rules hindered trade between Member States contrary to Article 29 EC.[102]

As regards the great majority of national remedial and procedural rules, the Community's interest therefore lies less in securing substantive compliance with specific Treaty provisions on free movement and fair competition, and more in the legal matrix within which *all* Community rules are enforced before the national courts. The principles of equivalence and effectiveness provide the twin means of surveying this legal matrix, to ensure that it does not *in itself* endanger the Community's legitimate interests.

[101] Case T–111/96 *Promedia* [1998] ECR II–2937. Cf Case C–221/99 *Conte* [2001] ECR I–9359.
[102] Case C–412/97 *Italo Fenocchio* [1999] ECR I–3845.

Principle of Equivalence

According to the principle of equivalence, Treaty-based claims brought before the domestic courts may not be furnished with less favourable remedies and procedural rules than those available in respect of similar actions based on purely national law.[103] So, for example, a Member State may not levy interest on the recovery of wrongly paid Community subsidies at a higher rate than that which applies to the recovery of comparable wrongly paid domestic monies.[104]

After years of comparative neglect, the principle of equivalence has recently become the focus of increasing interest by litigants keen to exploit its full potential to improve the levels of protection offered by the national courts in respect of Community law rights. The Court has responded by making clear that the principle of equivalence is not so broad as to oblige the Member States to extend to Community actions any more favourable remedial or procedural rules available in respect of domestic claims falling simply within the same policy field.[105] The test in fact consists of two separate stages.

The first stage concerns when a Community and domestic claim will be considered 'sufficiently similar' to found the basis of an appropriate comparison. This is, in principle, a matter to be determined by the national court. However, the latter's deliberations should be guided by the 'objective' or 'purpose' of the actions in question, determined in the light of their 'essential characteristics.'[106] So, for example, a *Francovich* action for Member State liability in damages seeks to compensate the claimant for losses incurred through a breach of Community law perpetrated by the national authorities; its appropriate comparator is therefore a domestic action for the non-contractual liability of public authorities which have committed an unlawful act in the exercise of their powers.[107] Similarly, an action for the recovery of financial charges levied by a Member State in breach of Community rules should be compared to a claim for the refund of taxes wrongly collected by a public authority under purely domestic rules. Such an action need not be considered 'similar' to a claim for the restitution of monies wrongly demanded by a private individual, in respect of which it is therefore permissible for the Member State to apply different limitation periods than those found in relation

[103] Regardless of the claimant's nationality. The principle of equivalence applies not only to procedural rules before the national courts (such as limitation periods), but also to those applied by the national authorities in reaching administrative decisions, eg Case C–34/02 *Pasquini* [2003] ECR I–6515.
[104] Case 54/81 *Fromme* [1982] ECR 1449.
[105] Case C–326/96 *Levez* [1998] ECR I–7835, para 42.
[106] Eg Case C–326/96 *Levez* [1998] ECR I–7835, paras 39–41 and 43; Case C–78/98 *Preston* [2000] ECR I–3201, paras 49 and 56–57.
[107] Case C–261/95 *Palmisani* [1997] ECR I–4025, paras 32–38.

to public bodies.[108] The principle of equivalence becomes relevant only where conditions for the repayment of charges levied by the State in breach of Community law are less favourable than those applicable to the repayment of other taxes raised by a public body contrary to purely domestic law.[109]

It is possible that no appropriate national comparator can be located in respect of the relevant Community action. In such cases, the principle of equivalence is deemed to have been fulfilled.[110] But if a particular domestic action is considered sufficiently similar to found the basis of comparison, the second question is whether there has been 'less favourable treatment' of the Community claim. For these purposes, the national courts are obliged to conduct a contextual assessment—considering the place of the disputed rule within the relevant domestic procedure, examining that procedure as a whole and taking account of its special features.[111] This means that the principle of equivalence catches rules which discriminate against Community claims either directly or indirectly. Thus, an unfavourable procedural restriction which on its face applies to generic categories of action, but which in practice applies only to claims derived from Community law rather than to those based upon domestic law, would be contrary to the Treaty.[112] It also means that the principle of equivalence catches discrimination against Community claims which arises either from obvious rules such as shorter limitation periods; or from less obvious provisions—such as the degree of formality required by the procedure—which might force a claimant relying upon the Treaty to incur additional costs and delay as compared to a claimant whose action derives from purely domestic law.[113] However, it is also possible that a contextual analysis will reveal apparent differences in the regulation of comparable claims to be in fact objectively justified by factors unrelated to their Community or domestic provenance.[114]

Despite the recent growth in caselaw, the Court's guidance on the full scope and precise application of the principle of equivalence remains far from comprehensive. In particular, a test of comparability based on the 'objectives' of the relevant claims is capable of operating at several different

[108] Eg Case C–231/96 *Edis* [1998] ECR I–4951; Case C–260/96 *Spac* [1998] ECR I–4997; Case C–228/96 *Aprile* [1998] ECR I–7141; Case C–343/96 *Dilexport* [1999] ECR I–579; Case C–88/99 *Roquette Frères* [2000] ECR I–10465.

[109] Consider, eg Cases C–216 & 222/99 *Prisco* [2002] ECR I–6761. Cf Cases C–279–281/96 *Ansaldo Energia* [1998] ECR I–5025.

[110] Case C–261/95 *Palmisani* [1997] ECR I–4025, para 39.

[111] Case C–326/96 *Levez* [1998] ECR I–7835, para 44; Case C–78/98 *Preston* [2000] ECR I–3201, paras 60–62.

[112] Consider, eg AG Jacobs in Case C–147/01 *Weber's Wine World* (Opinion of 20 March 2003, Judgment of 2 October 2003).

[113] Case C–326/96 *Levez* [1998] ECR I–7835; Case C–78/98 *Preston* [2000] ECR I–3201.

[114] Case C–132/95 *Jensen and Korn* [1998] ECR I–2975, paras 50–51.

levels of abstraction; for which purpose the opaque reference to an evaluation based on the 'essential characteristics' of the relevant procedures hardly aids our comprehension. For example, a claim for financial benefits wrongly withheld from an employee in breach of the principle of equal pay between men and women might be said to have the purpose of enforcing the general principle of non-discrimination, and thus to be comparable to domestic claims based on racial or religious prejudice. Alternatively, such a claim might be understood to pursue the objective of recovering remuneration properly due to a worker by his/her employer, and thus properly to be compared with domestic actions for arrears of wages or breach of the employment contract. Moreover, what if the national court identifies several domestic actions, each pursuing the same 'purpose' as the Community claim, but each carrying different remedial and/or procedural rules. Must one select the comparator which most favours the effective as well as the merely equivalent treatment of Community rights? Or is the choice left to the discretion of the Member State?

Conflicting advice on the appropriate level of abstraction to be pursued under the principle of equivalence has been offered by the Advocates General.[115] The Court of Justice often seems reluctant to rule definitively on matters of equivalence, preferring to leave the final decision to the referring judges, particularly in the absence of detailed information about the structure of the national judicial system, and about the procedural rules applicable to various purely domestic legal actions.[116]

Principle(s) of Effectiveness

Principles such as non-discrimination and equivalence implicitly assume that the remedies and procedural rules already provided under the domestic judicial orders are sufficient in scope and character to safeguard the exercise of the citizen's legal rights. Their main concern is to ensure that these existing standards of judicial protection are extended on an equal basis to benefit Community as well as own-nationals, and Treaty-based as much as comparable domestic law claims. By contrast, the principle of effectiveness addresses itself to the possibility that the national systems of judicial protection may sometimes fall short of the

[115] Consider the Opinions in, eg Case 199/82 *San Giorgio* [1983] ECR 3595; Case C–271/91 *Marshall II* [1993] ECR I–4367; Case C–62/93 *BP Supergas* [1995] ECR I–1883; Case C–312/93 *Peterbroeck* [1995] ECR I–4599; Case C–132/95 *Jensen and Korn* [1998] ECR I–2975; Case C–326/96 *Levez* [1998] ECR I–7835; Case C–78/98 *Preston* [2000] ECR I–3201.
[116] Eg Case C–326/96 *Levez* [1998] ECR I–7835; Case C–78/98 *Preston* [2000] ECR I–3201; Case C–472/99 *Clean Car Autoservice* [2001] ECR I–9687. However, the Court does occasionally adopt a more interventionist approach to the principle of equivalence, giving the national courts detailed instructions about issues of comparability and less favourable treatment, eg Case C–34/02 *Pasquini* [2003] ECR I–6515.

standards of enforcement expected under Community law. In correcting these shortcomings, the Court of Justice seeks to ensure that adequate remedies and procedural rules exist within each Member State. Moreover, the incidental effect of such intervention is to promote common Community-wide principles about the sort of legal safeguards which must accompany the enforcement of Treaty norms.

Analysis of the Court's caselaw in fact reveals four chief manifestations of the notion of 'effectiveness,' all of which concern the Community's interest in guaranteeing a satisfactory legal framework for enforcement before the national courts, but each fixing its attention upon different (and sometimes competing) actors or values. Two of these manifestations seek to ensure a smooth transition between the substantive concept or policy pursued by a given provision of Community law, and its practical value after having been filtered through the domestic systems of judicial protection: the effectiveness of subjective rights enjoyed by individuals under the Treaty as they are enforced against Member States or private parties; and the effectiveness of provisions safeguarding the general interest as they are enforced against national authorities and individuals. The remaining two manifestations are concerned with guaranteeing the integrity of certain basic tenets of the Community's judicial architecture at crucial points of intersection with national remedies and procedural rules: the effectiveness of the preliminary reference procedure under Article 234 EC vis-à-vis domestic provisions which would inhibit the possibility of open dialogue between the Court and the national judges; and the effectiveness of the procedural restrictions applicable before the Union courts under the Article 230 EC action for annulment, when faced with the possibility that private parties may instead challenge the legality of Community acts indirectly before the domestic courts.

Effective Protection of Individual Rights The principle of effectiveness *stricto sensu* (ie, referred to by the Court as such) requires that national remedies and procedural rules must not render the exercise of Community rights by their beneficiaries virtually impossible or excessively difficult in practice.[117] This apparently simple formula has proven the most volatile weapon in the Court's armoury, and its development will provide the basis for much of the analysis to follow in subsequent chapters of this book. For present purposes, it is sufficient to identify several core themes in the caselaw.

[117] From innumerable cases, eg Case 199/82 *San Giorgio* [1983] ECR 3595, para 12; Case C–312/93 *Peterbroeck* [1995] ECR I–4599, para 12; Case C–134/99 *IGI* [2000] ECR I–7717, para 34. The principle of effectiveness applies not only to procedural rules before the national courts (such as limitation periods), but also to those applied by the national authorities in reaching administrative decisions, eg Case C–224/02 *Pusa* (Judgment of 29 April 2004).

Individual Rights Enforced Against the Member State Individuals asserting their subjective Community law rights are clearly entitled to invoke the principle of effectiveness in vertical disputes against the Member State.

In this context, sometimes the national systems of judicial protection contain such glaring flaws that the Court can readily find the exercise of Community law rights to have been rendered virtually impossible or excessively difficult. This is particularly true where the Member State has sought to shield itself from the consequences of its own default by blatantly depriving a given Community law right of any practical value. Thus, for example, it is relatively uncontroversial for the Court to insist that, where the Member State has levied taxes contrary to Community law, the national courts must in principle guarantee that such charges are reimbursed to their payor.[118] It is also true where obvious shortcomings in the domestic systems of judicial protection reflect certain historical or constitutional peculiarities which do not find ready sympathy within the Community legal order. Thus, for example, domestic law might feel comfortable with the idea of refusing to provide interim relief against the acts of central government departments—based on the theory that government ministers act on behalf of the sovereign, and the sovereign cannot be injuncted by its own courts—yet that state of affairs is clearly incompatible with a functioning system of judicial protection in cases involving Community law rights.[119]

However, most national remedies and procedural rules do not suffer from such blatant inadequacies. Rather, they are designed to perform some useful function in ensuring the fair and efficient administration of justice. The problem here is to balance the Member State's legitimate interest in respecting its own choices concerning the conduct and resolution of judicial procedures, against the Community's legitimate interest in ensuring the effectiveness of rights conferred by the Treaty upon individuals. Take national limitation periods by way of illustration: on the one hand, the application of such procedural rules clearly engages the Community interest in effective judicial protection because they may result in the complete or partial dismissal of a Treaty-based claim; on the other hand, limitation periods reflect the Member State's perfectly reasonable desire to safeguard legal certainty by protecting public authorities against indefinite liability. Most of the problems arising from the caselaw derive from the Court's apparent uncertainty about how best to strike this difficult balance between potentially conflicting interests.

[118] Case 177/78 *Pigs and Bacon Commission v McCarren* [1979] ECR 2161; Case 199/82 *San Giorgio* [1983] ECR 3595.
[119] Case C–213/89 *Ex p Factortame* [1990] ECR I–2433.

The Court's current approach to resolving this task cannot be analysed without some basic understanding of its historical context. For these purposes, it is possible to identify three main periods in the caselaw.

The early caselaw—dating from the 1970s and early 1980s—can be summarised quite simply: domestic standards were the rule, Community interference an ill-defined exception. This position is best exemplified by judgments such as *Rewe* and *Comet*, where the Court held that domestic limitation periods regulating the initiation of proceedings before the national courts may also apply to Community cases, provided they comply with the principles of equivalence and effectiveness. The latter requires merely that the time-limit in question be reasonable in duration. For this purpose, a 30-day limitation period in respect of actions for the recovery of unlawfully levied charges could not be considered to render the exercise of Treaty rights 'virtually impossible'.[120]

By contrast, the Court's middle-period jurisprudence—dating from the mid-1980s to the early 1990s—was dominated by increasingly dramatic levels of Community intervention. This became immediately apparent in the Court's changing language: national rules must not render Community rights 'virtually impossible *or* excessively difficult'[121]; this negative language was then rephrased into more positive terms, that Community rights must be 'effectively protected.'[122] In outcome, too, the change was marked. For example, the Court held in *Emmott* that, even if a domestic limitation period complies with the conditions of equivalence and effectiveness as set out in *Rewe/Comet*, it must nevertheless be set aside in cases where the Member State has failed correctly to implement a Community directive within the prescribed deadline, and the individual citizen would otherwise be deprived of the opportunity to rely on rights derived from that directive.[123]

However, the most recent period in the caselaw—from around mid-1993 onwards—is characterised by the Court's attempts to strike a more nuanced approach than its two previous extremes.[124] There has been a definite retreat back towards the orthodox presumption of national autonomy in the provision of judicial protection. But the contemporary principle of effectiveness surely remains more intrusive than the caselaw of the 1970s and early 1980s. Indeed, it has been said that the Court now practises a

[120] Case 33/76 *Rewe-Zentralfinanz v Landwirtschaftskammer für das Saarland* [1976] ECR 1989; Case 45/76 *Comet* [1976] ECR 2043. Also, eg Case 35/74 *Mutualités Chrétiennes v Rzepa* [1974] ECR 1241; Case 61/79 *Denkavit Italiana* [1980] ECR 1205.

[121] Eg Case 199/82 *San Giorgio* [1983] ECR 3595 (emphasis added).

[122] Eg Case 179/84 *Bozzetti* [1985] ECR 2301.

[123] Case C–208/90 *Emmott* [1991] ECR I–4269.

[124] Further, eg R Craufurd Smith, 'Remedies for Breaches of EU Law in National Courts: Legal Variation and Selection' in P Craig & G de Búrca (eds), *The Evolution of EU Law* (OUP, 1999); T Tridimas, *The General Principles of EC Law* (OUP, 1999) ch 8; A Ward, *Judicial Review and the Rights of Private Parties in EC Law* (OUP, 2000) chs 2–4.

form of 'selective deference' to national procedural autonomy: sometimes consolidating the achievements of its middle period, and even striking out on bold new initiatives worthy of the hey-day of the effective judicial protection caselaw; but often shying away from fresh invitations to bolster the domestic standards of judicial protection, and sometimes even blunting the impact of its more adventurous middle-period judgments.[125] For example, the Court held in *Fantask* that the ruling in *Emmott* must be understood by reference to its own particular facts: the relevant national authorities had deliberately misled the claimant as to her rights, and thereby prevented her from initiating legal proceedings within the applicable domestic time-limit; but the judgment was not in fact intended to overturn the general rule that reasonable limitation periods are compatible with the principle of effectiveness.[126]

The general approach now used by the Court when applying the principle of effectiveness might be compared to the 'objective justification' model, familiar from areas such as free movement and equal treatment, applied to domestic provisions capable of serving socially valuable aims but prima facie pitted against some fundamental interest of the Community itself. In an idealised form, this model can be summarised as follows. A Community right is being enforced before the national courts, and the application of a domestic remedial or procedural provision is alleged to affect adversely the exercise of that Community right. For the purposes of assessing whether the principle of effectiveness justifies intervention, the Court seems to ask: (i) whether the exercise of the Community right is indeed adversely affected by the operation of the national provision; (ii) if so, whether the national provision pursues a legitimate policy objective; and (iii) if so, whether the national provision pursues that policy objective in a legitimate manner, consistent with the margin of discretion left to the Member State by Community law.

Admittedly, the Court does not explicitly refer to the use of an objective justification model *as such* in its remedies jurisprudence (or clearly articulate each stage in that model during the course of every judgment). Nevertheless, that model is employed implicitly throughout the caselaw. In particular, the Court in *Peterbroeck* and *Van Schijndel* made clear that:

> [E]ach case which raises the question whether a national procedural provision renders application of Community law impossible or excessively difficult must be analysed by reference to the role of that provision in the procedure, its progress and its special features, viewed as a whole, before the various national instances. In the light of that analysis the basic principles of

[125] T Tridimas, 'Liability for Breach of Community Law: Growing Up and Mellowing Down?' (2001) 38 CML Rev 301.
[126] Case C–188/95 *Fantask* [1997] ECR I–6783.

> the domestic judicial system, such as protection of the rights of the defence, the principle of legal certainty and the proper conduct of procedure, must, where appropriate, be taken into consideration.[127]

This dictum, advocating a 'contextual approach' to the principle of effectiveness, was, at the time, identified by Hoskins as a new development in the caselaw. He contended that, during the Court's early and middle-period caselaw, the principle of effectiveness involved an essentially two-dimensional approach to assessing the compatibility of national provisions with Community law: the judges looked simply at the practical effect of the remedial or procedural rule in the circumstances of the case; if its effects transgressed the (less, then more, stringent) limits imposed by Community law, the domestic provision had to be set aside. In *Peterbroeck* and *Van Schijndel*, it was argued, the Court introduced a third dimension to the principle of effectiveness: the judges must look not only at the effect of the procedural rule upon the claimant's Community rights, but also at its role within the domestic judicial system; moreover, they must do so by reference to abstract concepts such as 'legal certainty' and the 'proper conduct of proceedings.'[128] However, one might justifiably query the extent to which *Peterbroeck* and *Van Schijndel* really represented such a radical conceptual departure by the Court, from merely examining the effect of a national procedure upon the exercise of a Treaty right, to evaluating also its policy role within the domestic judicial system. Indeed, balancing the competing Community and Member State interests which are at stake in the debate over effective judicial protection, through an assessment of the rationale and function of a given domestic rule, has always played an integral part in the Court's approach to national remedies and procedural rules. That much was clear even from early cases such as *Rewe/Comet*, where the Court accepted that the obvious restrictive effects of national limitation periods upon the exercise of Community law rights could nevertheless be justified having regard to their role in guaranteeing legal certainty within the domestic systems of judicial protection.[129]

The additional guidance offered by the Court in *Peterbroeck* and *Van Schijndel* seems rather to have been intended to encourage the national judges towards greater critical assessment of the Member State's claim that restrictions on the exercise of Community rights perform an important

[127] Case C–312/93 *Peterbroeck* [1995] ECR I–4599, para 14; Cases C–430–431/93 *Van Schijndel* [1995] ECR I–4705, para 19. Further, eg S Prechal, 'Community Law in National Courts: The Lessons From *Van Schijndel*' (1998) 35 CML Rev 681.

[128] M Hoskins, 'Tilting the Balance: Supremacy and National Procedural Rules' (1996) 21 EL Rev 365.

[129] Case 33/76 *Rewe-Zentralfinanz v Landwirtschaftskammer für das Saarland* [1976] ECR 1989, para 5; Case 45/76 *Comet* [1976] ECR 2043, paras 17–18.

domestic function—advocating a more intrusive level of analysis which in itself helps distinguish the current-period from the early-period caselaw. Indeed, a growing number of judgments insist that restrictive domestic rules cannot be justified by reference to abstract principles such as 'legal certainty' and the 'proper conduct of proceedings' alone, without undertaking more rigorous analysis of how such interests apply in the particular factual circumstances of any given dispute. This means that restrictions on the exercise of Community rights which might well be justified *in principle*, having regard to their particular objectives and their overall procedural environment, may yet infringe the principle of effectiveness *in practice* for reasons specific to the given claimant's situation. For example, the Court held in *Santex* that national rules imposing a 60-day limitation period for challenging public procurement decisions were generally compatible with the principle of effectiveness. However, the Court continued to observe that application of the domestic time-limit, in the particular circumstances of the case, would breach Community law: the national authority had made representations, following publication of the disputed invitation to tender, which persuaded the claimant not to launch legal proceedings; the uncertainty created by that conduct, coupled with the effects of the domestic limitation period, would render excessively difficult the claimant's exercise of its Community law rights.[130] Indeed, the Court stated in *Cofidis* that judgments on national remedies and procedures are merely the result of assessments on a case by case basis, taking account of each case's own factual and legal context as a whole, which cannot be applied mechanically in fields other than those in which they were made.[131]

Certain specialised bodies of caselaw have emerged which elaborate in greater detail upon the requirements of effectiveness in particular fields, for example: interim protection of one's Treaty rights pending their final determination by a competent judicial authority;[132] the recovery of charges levied in breach of Community rules by the Member State;[133] the right to reparation in respect of losses suffered through a breach of Community law for which the Member State can be held responsible;[134]

[130] Case C–327/00 *Santex* [2003] ECR I–1877.
[131] Case C–473/00 *Cofidis* [2002] ECR I–10875.
[132] In particular: Case C–213/89 *Ex p Factortame* [1990] ECR I–2433. Further: ch 6 (below).
[133] In particular: Case 177/78 *Pigs and Bacon Commission v McCarren* [1979] ECR 2161; Case 68/79 *Hans Just* [1980] ECR 501; Case 199/82 *San Giorgio* [1983] ECR 3595; Cases 331, 376 & 378/85 *Bianco* [1988] ECR 1099; Cases C–192–218/95 *Comateb* [1997] ECR I–165; Case C–343/96 *Dilexport* [1999] ECR I–579; Cases C–441–42/98 *Mikhailidis* [2000] ECR I–7145; Cases C–397 & 410/98 *Metallgesellschaft* [2001] ECR I–1727; Case C–147/01 *Weber's Wine World* (Judgment of 2 October 2003); Case C–129/00 *Commission v Italy* (Judgment of 9 December 2003). Further: ch 6 (below).
[134] In particular: Cases C–6 & 9/90 *Francovich* [1991] ECR I–5357; Cases C–46 & 48/93 *Brasserie du Pêcheur* and *Factortame III* [1996] ECR I–1029; Case C–392/93 *Ex p British Telecommunications* [1996] ECR I–1631; Case C–5/94 *Ex p Hedley Lomas* [1996] ECR I–2553;

the measure of compensation due in respect of an infringement of one's Treaty rights;[135] the imposition of time-limits restricting the opportunity for claimants to assert their rights before the domestic courts;[136] and national rules limiting the back-payment of compensation or other financial benefits.[137] In addition, there are a large number of more assorted situations in which claimants have invoked the principle of effectiveness as a means of challenging domestic rules alleged to inhibit the full exercise of their Community rights, for example: by depriving certain documents of any evidential value,[138] or by recognising the admissibility of certain forms of evidence;[139] by undermining the neutrality of expert witnesses;[140] by providing for set-off between sums payable under Community law and outstanding debts owed to the Member State;[141] or by the method for apportioning the costs of bringing legal proceedings.[142]

As well as raising many detailed questions of their own, these clusters of caselaw highlight certain broader problems arising from the underlying principle of effectiveness. In particular, the Court's tacit objective justification model for national remedies emerges primarily as a

Cases C–178–79 & 188–90/94 *Dillenkofer* [1996] ECR I–4845; Cases C–94–95/95 *Bonifaci* [1997] ECR I–3969; Case C–373/95 *Maso* [1997] ECR I–4051; Case C–127/95 *Norbrook* [1998] ECR I–1531; Case C–319/96 *Brinkmann* [1998] ECR I–5255; Case C–302/97 *Konle* [1999] ECR I–3099; Case C–140/97 *Rechberger* [1999] ECR I–3499; Case C–424/97 *Haim II* [2000] ECR I–5123; Case C–150/99 *Stockholm Lindöpark* [2001] ECR I–493; Cases C–397 & 410/98 *Metallgesellschaft* [2001] ECR I–1727; Case C–118/00 *Larsy* [2001] ECR I–5063; Case C–224/01 *Köbler* (Judgment of 30 September 2003). Further: ch 5 (below).

[135] In particular: Case 14/83 *von Colson* [1984] ECR 1891; Case 79/83 *Harz* [1984] ECR 1921; Case C–271/91 *Marshall II* [1993] ECR I–4367; Case C–66/95 *ex p Sutton* [1997] ECR I–2163; Case C–180/95 *Draehmpaehl* [1997] ECR I–2195; Cases C–397 & 410/98 *Metallgesellschaft* [2001] ECR I–1727; Case C–63/01 *Evans* (Judgment of 4 December 2003). Further: ch 5 (below).

[136] In particular: Case 33/76 *Rewe-Zentralfinanz v Landwirtschaftskammer für das Saarland* [1976] ECR 1989; Case 45/76 *Comet* [1976] ECR 2043; Case 309/85 *Barra* [1988] ECR 355; Case 240/87 *Deville* [1988] ECR 3513; Case C–208/90 *Emmott* [1991] ECR I–4269; Case C–188/95 *Fantask* [1997] ECR I–6783; Case C–231/96 *Edis* [1998] ECR I–4951; Case C–260/96 *Spac* [1998] ECR I–4997; Cases C–279–81/96 *Ansaldo Energia* [1998] ECR I–5025; Case C–228/96 *Aprile* [1998] ECR I–7141; Case C–343/96 *Dilexport* [1999] ECR I–579; Case C–78/98 *Preston* [2000] ECR I–3201; Case C–62/00 *Marks & Spencer* [2002] ECR I–6325; Case C–255/00 *Grundig Italiana* [2002] ECR I–8003; Case C–327/00 *Santex* [2003] ECR I–1877. Further: ch 5 (below).

[137] In particular: Case C–338/91 *Steenhorst-Neerings* [1993] ECR I–5475; Case C–410/92 *Johnston II* [1994] ECR I–5483; Case C–394/93 *Alonso-Pérez* [1995] ECR I–4101; Case C–212/94 *FMC* [1996] ECR I–389; Case C–246/96 *Magorrian* [1997] ECR I–7153; Case C–326/96 *Levez* [1998] ECR I–7835. Further: ch 5 (below).

[138] Eg Case C–336/94 *Dafeki* [1997] ECR I–6761.

[139] Eg Case C–276/01 *Steffensen* [2003] ECR I–3735. Consider also caselaw on the burden of proof under Dir 91/533 on an employer's obligation to inform employees of the conditions applicable to the contract or employment relationship, OJ 1991 L288/32, eg Cases C–253–58/96 *Kampelmann* [1997] ECR I–6907; Case C–350/99 *Lange* [2001] ECR I–1061. Further, eg J Malmberg (ed), *Effective Enforcement of EC Labour Law* (Kluwer Law International, 2003) pp 204–13.

[140] Eg Case C–236/92 *Comitato di Coordinamento* [1994] ECR I–483.

[141] Eg Case C–132/95 *Jensen and Korn* [1998] ECR I–2975.

[142] Eg Case C–63/01 *Evans* (Judgment of 4 December 2003).

structural achievement: it provides a clearer and more logical methodology for resolving disputes about the compatibility of domestic procedural rules with the principle of effectiveness, and perhaps prompts the national courts towards a more systematic and articulate analysis of the issues involved. But of itself, the objective justification model cannot provide all the answers (either to explain the nuances of the existing caselaw, or to predict the Court's response to future disputes). For example, which domestic policy interests will be recognised as 'legitimate', such that they might in principle be capable of justifying the adverse effects of national procedural rules upon the exercise of Community law rights? Moreover, what margin of discretion is left to the Member State, such that it may claim to be pursuing those objectives in a 'legitimate' manner, which does not render the exercise of Community rights unduly difficult in practice? Clearly, an objective justification-style approach to national remedies cannot operate in a vacuum, divorced from the framework of substantive values actually required to address such questions—a problem which will be dealt with in greater detail later in this book.[143]

Individual Rights Enforced Against Other Private Parties The principle of effectiveness applies in litigation not only vertically, between an indivdual and the defaulting Member State, but also horizontally, when the claimant's Community law rights have been breached by another private party.[144]

In accordance with the presumption of national autonomy, Member States may legitimately draw distinctions between the levels of judicial protection *available under domestic law* as between vertical and horizontal situations. For example, the Court held in *Edis* that the principle of equivalence does not preclude a Member State from laying down, alongside a limitation period applicable under the ordinary law to actions between private individuals for the recovery of sums paid but not due, less favourable rules governing legal proceedings to challenge charges imposed by public authorities.[145] The more controversial question is whether *Community law itself* draws any comparable distinctions between the levels of judicial protection which must, pursuant to the principle of effectiveness, be made available in vertical and horizontal situations.

Several suggestions to that effect, usually offered as a potential means of explaining puzzling inconsistencies in judicial practice, have not been borne out by the caselaw. For example, we noted how the Court in *Emmott* appeared to decide that national limitation periods must be set aside for so

[143] In particular: chs 5 and 6 (below).
[144] Eg Case C–60/92 *Otto v Postbank* [1993] ECR I–5683; Cases C–430–31/93 *Van Schijndel* [1995] ECR I–4705; Case C–326/96 *Levez* [1998] ECR I–7835; Case C–126/97 *Eco Swiss v Benetton* [1999] ECR I–3055; C–453/99 *Courage v Crehan* [2001] ECR I–6297.
[145] Case C–231/96 *Edis* [1998] ECR I–4951. Also, eg Cases C–279–81/96 *Ansaldo Energia* [1998] ECR I–5025; Cases C–216 & 222/99 *Prisco* [2002] ECR I–6761.

long as the Member State has failed correctly to implement a Community directive within its deadline.[146] Advocate General van Gerven in *Fisscher* therefore argued that this rule should apply only to vertical (not horizontal) situations: it was essentially a means of preventing the Member State benefiting from its own wrongdoing, but private parties cannot be held responsible for failure to implement a directive correctly or on time.[147] However, we also mentioned how the Court later held in *Fantask* that *Emmott* should be distinguished, so as to apply only to situations where the defendant has, by its own conduct, effectively dissuaded the claimant from initiating legal proceedings within the applicable time-limit.[148] That estoppel analysis seems capable of applying to *both* vertical *and* horizontal relationships—so that Advocate General van Gerven's suggestion should no longer be seen as persuasive.[149]

However, there may well be situations in which certain forms of effective judicial protection are—for sound objective reasons—better suited to vertical than to horizontal disputes. Or perhaps it would be more accurate to say that certain aspects of effective judicial protection are better suited to public law situations than to private law situations (regardless of whether the dispute is, from a purely institutional point of view, vertical or horizontal in character).[150]

For example, in the case of *public law*, effective judicial protection may demand that relief be provided for a mere breach of the relevant Treaty right. Consider the reimbursement by Member States of taxes and other charges levied contrary to Community law. The Court in judgments such as *FMC* and *Fantask* made clear that liability to repay is imposed upon the defaulting Member State on the basis of illegality per se, without the need for the claimant to prove fault or unreasonableness on the part of the relevant public authorities.[151] In fact, the only defence available to the Member State is to argue that the quantum due for reimbursement should be reduced to the extent that the claimant would otherwise be unjustly enriched, having already passed on the charge to his/her customers.[152]

[146] Case C–208/90 *Emmott* [1991] ECR I–4269.
[147] Case C–128/93 *Fisscher* [1994] ECR I–4583, para 31 Opinion.
[148] Case C–188/95 *Fantask* [1997] ECR I–6783.
[149] As judgments like Case C–326/96 *Levez* [1998] ECR I–7835 arguably demonstrate.
[150] This distinction between effective judicial protection in public and private law situations has not yet fully emerged from the caselaw, or the academic literature. Further: M Dougan, 'What is the Point of *Francovich*?' in T Tridimas & P Nebbia (eds), *European Union Law for the Twenty-First Century: Rethinking the New Legal Order* (Hart Publishing, 2004).
[151] Case C–212/94 *FMC* [1996] ECR I–389; Case C–188/95 *Fantask* [1997] ECR I–6783.
[152] And even then, subject to strict conditions concerning, inter alia, the burden of proof, eg Case 199/82 *San Giorgio* [1983] ECR 3595; Case 104/86 *Commission v Italy* [1988] ECR 1799; Cases 331, 376 & 378/85 *Bianco* [1988] ECR 1099; Cases C–192–218/95 *Comateb* [1997] ECR I–165; Cases C–441 & 442/98 *Mikhailidis* [2000] ECR I–7145; Case C–343/96 *Dilexport* [1999] ECR I–579; Case C–147/01 *Weber's Wine World* (Judgment of 2 October 2003); Case C–129/00 *Commission v Italy* (Judgment of 9 December 2003).

However, in appropriate circumstances, effective judicial protection may instead permit relief to be made conditional upon the claimant satisfying certain additional considerations, aimed at balancing the individual interest in obtaining redress against the general interest in protecting public authorities in the efficient performance of their functions. This is true, in particular, under the *Francovich* right to reparation—which applies culpability criteria to public law situations such as where the Member State has failed to transpose directives correctly or on time;[153] where the Member State has enacted or maintained legislation incompatible with the Treaty itself;[154] or where public authorities have taken individual administrative decisions which fail to comply with Community law.[155] In such situations, it is legitimate to take into account factors such as the degree of legislative or administrative discretion enjoyed by the Member State in discharging its public functions, and the relative clarity or ambiguity of the relevant Treaty legislation, before transforming a simple infringement of Community law into a breach which is sufficiently serious to warrant imposing liability to make reparation.[156]

In the case of *private law*, effective judicial protection may again require that relief be provided for a mere breach of the claimant's Treaty rights. Sometimes the relevant Community legislation will say so explicitly. For example, the Product Liability Directive provides that producers shall be liable for damage caused by defects in their products; and that such liability shall not, in relation to the injured person, be limited or excluded by any other provisions.[157] In other cases, the Court will construe the relevant Community legislation to achieve the same effect. For example, discrimination against women (or men) as regards their terms and conditions of employment, contrary to the Equal Treatment Directive, of itself gives rise to liability on the part of the defaulting employer.[158] The Court held in *Dekker* and *Draehmpaehl* that national law may not curtail the scope of the consequent duty to make adequate reparation, by imposing additional fault-based requirements, even where these would, in practice, be very easy for the claimant to satisfy.[159] Again, however, in appropriate circumstances, effective judicial protection may instead permit relief to be made conditional upon the claimant satisfying additional criteria pertinent to the particular policy sphere at issue in the relevant dispute.

[153] Eg Case C–140/97 *Rechberger* [1999] ECR I–3499; Case C–371/97 *Gozza* [2000] ECR I–7881.
[154] Eg Case C–242/95 *GT-Link* [1997] ECR I–4449; Case C–302/97 *Konle* [1999] ECR I–3099.
[155] Eg Case C–127/95 *Norbrook* [1998] ECR I–1531; Case C–319/96 *Brinkmann* [1998] ECR I–5255.
[156] In particular: Cases C–46 & 48/93 *Brasserie du Pêcheur* and *Factortame III* [1996] ECR I–1029. Further: ch 5 (below).
[157] Dir 85/374 on the approximation of the laws, regulations and administrative provisions of the Member States concerning liability for defective products, OJ 1985 L210/29.
[158] Dir 76/207, OJ 1976 L39/40.
[159] Case C–177/88 *Dekker* [1990] ECR I–3941; Case C–180/95 *Draehmpaehl* [1997] ECR I–2195.

Consider the judgment in *Courage v Crehan*. Breach of Article 81 EC should, in principle, give rise to an action for compensation in respect of losses incurred through the relevant anti-competitive practice. But this need not necessarily be the case—as, for example, where the claimant was itself party to the unlawful agreement. In such situations, national courts may take into account factors such as the relative bargaining power enjoyed by the claimant and the defendant, and thus their relative degrees of culpability, in determining whether compensation should be recoverable in practice.[160] However, in either type of case, it would seem inappropriate to apply the sorts of culpability criteria developed under the *Francovich* caselaw specifically to deal with public authorities performing their duties in the general interest; there is no pressing reason why Community law should offer a comparable buffer against the imposition of liability as regards purely private law situations.

There may therefore be sound doctrinal reasons for distinguishing between the requirements of effectiveness as they apply in the public law context (usually involving public authorities) when compared to private law disputes (often involving private individuals). Nevertheless, there are certain situations where the existing caselaw points towards certain more artificial distortions in the content of the principles of effective judicial protection as between vertical and horizontal situations. Consider, for example, actions concerning the restitution of unlawfully levied charges, or the payment of wrongly withheld benefits. Where such actions are brought against a defaulting public authority, the Court in *ex parte Sutton* held that the principle of effectiveness does not require interest to be paid automatically and as of right.[161] The claimant's proper course of redress is to bring a *Francovich* action against the Member State, seeking interest *qua* compensatory damages for losses suffered through the effluxion of time.[162]

But where the substantive breach of Community law giving rise to the claimant's right to recover unlawfully levied charges, or to the payment of wrongly withheld sums, is attributable to another individual, this reasoning could hardly apply. On the one hand, the private party which has actually perpetrated the substantive breach of the claimant's Community law rights is not directly susceptible to a *Francovich* action for recovery of the interest. On the other hand, the Member State against which *Francovich* actions can theoretically be initiated has not actually committed any wrong capable of justifying the imposition of liability on its shoulders instead. After all, interest is not an essential aspect of effective judicial protection

[160] Albeit phrased in terms of preventing unjust enrichment and not profiting from one's own wrong: Case C–453/99 *Courage v Crehan* [2001] ECR I–6297.
[161] Cf the position as regards compensatory actions, eg Case C–271/91 *Marshall II* [1993] ECR I–4367; Case C–63/01 *Evans* (Judgment of 4 December 2003). Further: ch 5 (below).
[162] Case C–66/95 *Ex p Sutton* [1997] ECR I–2163.

as regards actions for non-compensatory relief—so the Member State cannot have infringed its own obligations under Community law by failing to empower its national courts to award interest. In the absence of a substantive breach of Community law for which the Member State itself can be held responsible, there is simply nothing onto which *Francovich* can bite. In such situations, the Court would either have to insist that (despite authorities such as *ex parte Sutton*) interest must be recoverable against the defaulting private party as a matter of Community law; or be forced to accept that interest falls squarely within national competence and there is no further possibility of even indirect redress under the *Francovich* caselaw. In either event, the Court seems to have created (probably inadvertently) an artificial cleavage in the standards of effective judicial protection applicable in vertical as compared to horizontal disputes.

Effective Protection of the General Interest The second main type of 'effectiveness' which emerges from the Court's caselaw concerns the enforcement of Community law provisions safeguarding the general interest (without necessarily creating rights, in a subjective sense, for other individuals), such as regulatory standards concerning consumer safety, fair competition and environmental protection.

Enforcement in the General Interest by the Member State Responsibility for the enforcement of Community law in the public interest will often vest directly in the national authorities.[163] The Court's early approach, epitomised in cases such as *Amsterdam Bulb*, was that, in the absence of any provision in a given Community measure providing for specific sanctions to be imposed on individuals for failure to observe the applicable Treaty rules, the Member States are competent to adopt such sanctions as appear appropriate.[164] However, the Court displayed a more prescriptive attitude in Case 68/88 *Commission v Greece* (1989). Where Community legislation does not specifically provide any penalty for an infringement (or refers to domestic rules for that purpose), the Member State is obliged to take all measures necessary to guarantee the application and effectiveness of Community law. For that purpose, the presumption of national competence

[163] For detailed discussion, eg C Harding & B Swart (eds), *Enforcing European Community Rules: Criminal Proceedings, Administrative Procedures and Harmonization* (Dartmouth, 1996); C Harding, 'Member State Enforcement of European Community Measures: The Chimera of "Effective" Enforcement' (1997) 4 *Maastricht Journal of European and Comparative Law* 5; J Vervaele (ed), *Compliance and Enforcement of European Community Law* (Kluwer Law International, 1999). Specifically on the implications of Community effective enforcement requirements for national criminal law, consider, eg H Sevenster, 'Criminal Law and EC Law' (1992) 29 CML Rev 29; C Harding, 'Exploring the Intersection of European Law and National Criminal Law' (2000) 25 EL Rev 374.

[164] Case 50/76 *Amsterdam Bulb* [1977] ECR 137.

applies as much to sanctions imposed in the general interest, as to the remedies made available to individual right-holders. However, the Member State must ensure that infringements of Community law are penalised under conditions (both substantive and procedural) which are analogous to those applicable to infringements of national law of a similar nature and which, in any event, make the penalty effective, proportionate and dissuasive.[165]

Some authors claim that these requirements are simply a mirror image of the principles of judicial protection as they apply to the protection by individuals of their subjective Community law rights.[166] It is true that the first of the limits placed upon the presumption of national competence in the *Commission v Greece* case is clearly identical to the principle of equivalence. Moreover, the idea of 'effective' and 'dissuasive' conditions for the enforcement of Community law by the Member State finds an easy parallel in the caselaw on the effective protection of individual rights.[167] However, it is less clear whether the requirement of 'proportionality' is entirely synonymous with the principle of effectiveness *stricto sensu*.

The Court is clearly prepared to interfere with the sanctions chosen by a Member State, for the purposes of enforcing Community rules, where those sanctions go beyond what is necessary to achieve their objective.[168] But this requirement of proportionality is probably best seen as one of the general principles of Community law applicable to the Member States when acting within the scope of application of the Treaty. Indeed, the requirement that Member States adopt only proportionate sanctions for the purposes of enforcing Community rules (that is, when implementing their Treaty obligations) seems more closely related to the *Skanavi* principle that Member States may adopt only proportionate penalties for the enforcement of national provisions creating justified obstacles to the free movement of goods or persons (that is, when derogating from their Treaty obligations).[169] This is not to deny that there

[165] Case 68/88 *Commission v Greece* [1989] ECR 2965. Also, eg Case C–7/90 *Vandevenne* [1991] ECR I–4371; Case C–186/98 *Nunes and De Matos* [1999] ECR I–4883; Case C–354/99 *Commission v Ireland* [2001] ECR I–7657; Case C–454/99 *Commission v United Kingdom* [2002] ECR I–10323; Case C–140/00 *Commission v United Kingdom* [2002] ECR I–10379; Case C–230/01 *Penycoed Farming Partnership* (Judgment of 15 January 2004).

[166] Eg E Baker, 'Criminal Jurisdiction, the Public Dimension to "Effective Protection" and the Construction of Community–Citizen Relations' (2001) 4 *Cambridge Yearbook of European Legal Studies* 25.

[167] Consider, eg Case 14/83 *von Colson* [1984] ECR 1891; Case C–382/92 *Commission v United Kingdom* [1994] ECR I–2435.

[168] Consider, eg Case C–101/01 *Lindqvist* (Judgment of 6 November 2003).

[169] Case C–193/94 *Skanavi* [1996] ECR I–929 (see above). The fact that proportionality applies in both domestic and Community enforcement cases is important especially in dual enforcement cases, where penalties are imposed partly to enforce obligations derived from Community law, and partly to enforce obligations imposed under national law in derogation from the Treaty, eg Case C–262/99 *Louloudakis* [2001] ECR I–5547.

may be compelling arguments for having a proportionality assessment, within the framework of the principle of effectiveness, in respect of *all* national remedies and procedural rules.[170] After all, the Member State is still acting within the scope of application of the Treaty even when it is furnishing individuals with judicial protection in respect of their subjective rights. However, it seems fair to point out that the Court does not adopt the same (relatively intensive) scrutiny of the Member State's margin of appreciation when it comes to the remedies and procedural rules offered to individuals when enforcing their Community law rights, as it does to the sanctions imposed by national authorities for the enforcement of Treaty norms in the general interest.[171]

In any event, specialised bodies of caselaw again elaborate more fully upon the implications of the principle of effective, proportionate and dissuasive sanctions in particular fields, for example: on the recovery of Community subsidies wrongly paid to their recipients;[172] and the recovery of domestic subsidies paid by the Member State in breach of the Treaty rules on state aids.[173]

Enforcement in the General Interest by Individuals It is also possible that the ability to enforce Treaty norms in the public interest might vest directly in other individuals or organised interests such as consumer and environmental pressure groups. However, such situations tend to engage somewhat different aspects of Community intervention in the national systems of judicial protection on grounds of effective enforcement. Two major issues will serve to illustrate this point.[174]

First, the opportunities for individuals and pressure groups to bring public interest enforcement actions may be curtailed by restrictive national rules on standing. As one might expect,

> while it is, in principle, for national law to determine an individual's standing and legal interest in bringing proceedings, Community law nevertheless requires that … national legislation does not undermine the right to effective

[170] Cf W van Gerven, 'Of Rights, Remedies and Procedures' (2000) 37 CML Rev 501.
[171] Eg Case C–343/96 *Dilexport* [1999] ECR I–579. Further: ch 5 (below).
[172] In particular: Case 265/78 *Ferwerda* [1980] ECR 617; Case 54/81 *Fromme* [1982] ECR 1449; Cases 205–215/82 *Deutsche Milchkontor* [1983] ECR 2633; Case C–366/95 *Steff-Houlberg* [1998] ECR I–2661; Case C–298/96 *Oelmühle Hamburg* [1998] ECR I–4767; Case C–336/00 *Huber* [2002] ECR I–7699. Further: ch 6 (below).
[173] In particular: Case 120/73 *Lorenz* [1973] ECR 1471; Case 94/87 *Commission v Germany* [1989] ECR 175; Case C–5/89 *Commission v Germany* [1990] ECR I–3437; Case C–169/95 *Spain v Commission* [1997] ECR I–135; Case C–24/95 *Alcan Deutschland* [1997] ECR I–1591; Case C–480/98 *Spain v Commission* [2000] ECR I–8717; Cases C–261–262/01 *Van Calster* (Judgment of 21 October 2003). Further: ch 6 (below).
[174] For general analysis, within the particular context of environmental law, see H Somsen, 'The Private Enforcement of Member State Compliance with EC Environmental Law: An Unfulfilled Promise?' (2000) 1 *Yearbook of European Environmental Law* 311.

judicial protection.[175]

For these purposes, the Community legislature will sometimes expressly require the Member States to liberalise their standing rules concerning the protection of diffuse interests, in particular, as regards situations where Community law creates subjective rights for individuals but (for practical reasons) is unlikely to be enforced directly by its beneficiaries. For example, Directive 93/13 obliges Member States to ensure that adequate and effective means exist to prevent the continued use of unfair terms in consumer contracts, including provisions whereby persons or organisations 'having a legitimate interest under domestic law in protecting consumers' may take action before the competent national authorities or courts.[176]

The Court has also contributed to the effective judicial protection of diffuse interests, in particular, as regards situations where Community law seeks to safeguard the general public rather than the rights of any identifiable category of individuals.[177] For example, *Kraaijeveld* concerned an action brought by an economic operator challenging the legality of the decision of a Dutch local authority to approve dyke reinforcement works which would have had a serious and damaging effect on certain local businesses. During the course of the proceedings, it emerged that the local authority had failed to carry out an environmental impact assessment as required under Directive 85/337.[178] The Court observed that it would be incompatible with the binding effect of a directive to exclude in principle the possibility that the obligations it imposes may be invoked by those concerned. In particular, where the Community has imposed on Member States the obligation to pursue a particular course of conduct, the useful effect of the relevant directive would be weakened if individuals were prevented from relying on it before their national courts, and if the latter were prevented from taking it into consideration as an element of Community law in order to rule whether the national legislature had kept within the limits of its discretion.[179]

Some commentators query whether such cases, since they do not entail the vesting of subjective rights in particular individuals, should properly be viewed as examples of the 'direct effect' of Community law at all.[180] They might instead be thought to illustrate a novel kind of 'public interest

[175] Case C–13/01 *Safalero* (Judgment of 11 September 2003), para 50.
[176] Dir 93/13 on unfair terms in consumer contracts, OJ 1993 L95/29.
[177] Cf caselaw on the scope of individuals entitled to enforce subjective rights, eg Cases C–87–89/90 *Verholen* [1991] ECR I–3757; Case C–77/95 *Züchner* [1996] ECR I–5689.
[178] Dir 85/337 on the assessment of the effects of certain public and private projects on the environment, OJ 1985 L175/40.
[179] Case C–72/95 *Kraaijeveld* [1996] ECR I–5403.
[180] Further, eg S Prechal and L Hancher, 'Individual Environmental Rights: Conceptual Pollution in EU Environmental Law?' (2001) 2 *Yearbook of European Environmental Law* 89.

effect', whose focus lies on securing the effective enforcement of Treaty norms, by harnessing the ability of interested parties to bring legal proceedings for the collective benefit.[181] Or one might feel that it is an appropriate conceptual compromise to talk about a directly effective right to standing—recognising that certain citizens have a sufficient interest in the relevant dispute to justify granting them an enforceable right of access to the domestic courts for the purposes of invoking and enforcing Treaty rules which are of benefit primarily to broader societal interests.[182] In any case, although *Kraaijeveld* confirms the idea that Community legislation which is not directly linked to the creation of individual rights can nevertheless produce independent effects within the national legal systems, several important questions remain open. For example, the Court did not clarify precisely which categories of individual might be entitled to initiate legal proceedings before the domestic courts aimed at enforcing those legal effects. *Kraaijeveld* merely referred (very vaguely) to the possibility for 'those concerned' to rely on the relevant directive.[183] But it is difficult to say that the economic operator in *Kraaijeveld* initiated legal proceedings with a view to protecting the general interest in accordance with the aims of the Environmental Impact Assessment Directive (rather than its own financial and business interests, which were likely to be adversely affected by the proposed dyke works). Moreover, *Kraaijeveld* itself had involved judicial review proceedings brought against a defaulting national authority. But how would the Court react if an individual claimed a right of standing, for the purposes of enforcing Community law in the general interest, to bring civil proceedings against another private party—and such proceedings would run alongside any system for enforcement operated directly by the Member State itself?

The Court began to address such issues in its judgment in *Muñoz*. The claimant alleged that a rival undertaking imported grapes into the UK and sold them under incorrect product labels, in breach of the provisions of Regulations 1035/72 and 2200/96 concerning quality standards within the common organisation of the market in fruit and vegetables.[184] Under English law, enforcement of the Regulations was reserved exclusively to a public authority with monopoly power to impose fines for breach of quality standards. The claimant had complained to the public authority several times, but the latter took no action. The claimant

[181] Consider, eg J Scott, *EC Environmental Law* (Longman, 1998) ch 8.

[182] Further, eg P Craig and G de Búrca, *EU Law: Text, Cases and Materials* (OUP, 2003) ch 5.

[183] Case C–72/95 *Kraaijeveld* [1996] ECR I–5403, para 56. Similarly, eg Case C–435/97 *World Wildlife Fund* [1999] ECR I–5613; Case C–287/98 *Linster* [2000] ECR I–6917; Case C–127/02 *Landelijke Vereniging tot Behoud van de Waddenzee* (Judgment of 7 September 2004). Consider also, eg Case C–97/96 *Daihatsu Deutschland* [1997] ECR I–6843.

[184] Reg 1035/72 on the common organization of the market in fruit and vegetables, OJ Special English Edition 1972 (Series II) 437; Reg 2200/96 on the common organization of the market in fruit and vegetables, OJ 1996 L297/1.

therefore initiated its own proceedings before the domestic courts, arguing that the Regulations were directly effective and could be enforced not only by the competent public authorities but also by interested individuals. The Court held that the purpose of the Regulations was to keep unsatisfactory products off the market, for the protection of both consumers and rival undertakings. The full effectiveness of those quality standards implied that it must be possible to enforce obligations contained in the Regulations by means of civil proceedings brought against a trader by one of its competitors. The possibility of bringing such proceedings would supplement enforcement by the Member State itself by discouraging practices which might be difficult to detect.[185]

Muñoz demonstrates conclusively that, just because Community legislation fails to specifically refer to or implicitly envisage the creation of individual rights for any given class of claimant, such legislation is not precluded from producing independent effects within the national legal orders at the behest of a private party. In addition, the judgment indicates that national rules restricting standing for individuals may indeed have to be set aside even in horizontal situations, as regards the conduct of private parties which is already subject to the possibility of administrative measures initiated by the national authorities. The idea that the resources available to individual citizens act as an invaluable supplement to the limited enforcement activities of public authorities is, after all, part of the fundamental rationale underpinning the entire system of direct effect and supremacy for Community law.[186] Furthermore, *Muñoz* sheds light on the sorts of factors the Court might consider relevant in determining exactly which category of individuals should benefit from that possibility. On the one hand, the Court referred specifically to the added value offered by civil actions brought by competitors, which were particularly likely to root out infringements of Community law. Moreover, on the facts of the case, the claimant's commercial interests were directly affected by its rival's conduct in allegedly selling grapes under incorrect labels. This suggests that (at least in certain situations, involving quality standards imposed by agricultural regulations, rather than impact assessment obligations under environmental directives) *not just anyone* will be entitled to challenge national restrictions on standing to bring enforcement actions in the public interest.[187] On the other hand, Advocate General Geelhoed

[185] Case C–253/00 *Muñoz* [2002] ECR I–7289.

[186] Cf Case 26/62 *van Gend en Loos* [1963] ECR 1.

[187] Note that, as regards the Environmental Impact Assessment Directive itself, the Community legislature has now intervened to clarify the categories of people entitled to bring public interest proceedings before the national courts: see Dir 2003/35 providing for public participation in respect of the drawing up of certain plans and programmes relating to the environment and amending with regard to public participation and access to justice Directives 85/337 and 96/61, OJ 2003 L156/17.

had suggested that, for the purposes of determining when the Community's interest in effective enforcement should trump national autonomy over the rules on standing, one should look to the (highly restrictive) caselaw on the standing of natural and legal persons to bring actions for annulment against measures adopted by the Community institutions under Article 230(4) EC. By refusing to follow this advice, the Court sent a clear signal that claimants do not need to be so entangled in the dispute as to be considered 'directly and individually concerned' before they acquire capacity to bring decentralised enforcement actions under Community law.[188]

The peculiar demands made on the principles of effective judicial protection in situations concerning private enforcement of the public interest are also well illustrated by our second major issue: what type of sanction might be imposed upon the national authority or private party in respect of its infringement of Community law? In principle, one would expect the Court to apply by analogy its caselaw on the Member State's obligation to adopt effective, proportionate and dissuasive measures—albeit at the suit of a private party, rather than at the initiative of a public authority. In many situations, the requirement for an *effective* sanction might well be satisfied by the provision of injunctions and restraining orders. However, the demand for a *dissuasive* sanction might well require the courts to go further, for example, by ensuring that financial penalties are also inflicted upon the defaulter. But what form exactly should such financial penalties take?

For example, would it be possible (or even appropriate) for claimants to seek damages under the *Francovich* caselaw against public authorities which have breached the Treaty's environmental standards;[189] or to obtain reparation from private parties for having infringed Community obligations imposed for the general good, relying upon the judgment in *Courage v Crehan*?[190] The answer might well be affirmative in situations such as *Muñoz*, where the claimant's direct commercial interest in the defendant's disputed conduct is deemed relevant to recognising his/her legal capacity to initiate enforcement proceedings before the domestic courts in the first place. After all, it could prove difficult to sustain any persuasive dividing line between recognising a mere right of standing to restrain the marketing of incorrectly labelled goods (without any possibility of also seeking compensation); and creating a more substantive right to protection against unfair competitive practices which might adversely affect the claimant's personal position as a competitor or consumer (including a right to pursue financial redress for any losses incurred).

[188] Further on 'direct and individual concern': ch 6 (below).
[189] Cases C–6 & 9/90 *Francovich* [1991] ECR I–5357. Further: ch 5 (below).
[190] C–453/99 *Courage v Crehan* [2001] ECR I–6297. Further: ch 6 (below).

However, the answer is more likely to be negative in situations such as *Kraaijeveld*, insofar as the relevant Community obligations really are imposed for the public good, rather than the benefit of any identifiable category of individuals. From a legal perspective, it might be difficult in such cases to demonstrate any intention by the Community legislature to confer subjective rights upon the individual, as opposed to the recognition of mere rights to standing. From a policy perspective, it would seem hard to justify enriching an individual whose capacity to bring legal proceedings derives from the effective protection of the public (rather than any strictly private) interest. And *Francovich* damages would surely be difficult to swallow in cases involving general damage to the environment, as regards which the claimant suffers no greater loss than any other citizen.[191] In this type of situation, effectiveness clearly demands a coherent system of penalties (rather than simply of compensation). And the Court-made principles of judicial protection may prove less than adept at meeting this demand than positive intervention by the Community legislature. Consider, in this vein, Directive 2004/35 establishing a framework of environmental liability to help prevent and remedy environmental damage, based upon the recovery from defaulting undertakings of the costs incurred by public authorities in cleaning up certain classes of environmental damage;[192] and the Commission's proposal for a directive on the protection of the environment through criminal law, which would establish common rules on penal offences relating to serious infringements of important Community legislation.[193]

Effectiveness of the Article 234 EC Preliminary Reference Procedure Our two remaining manifestations of effectiveness are concerned with guaranteeing the integrity of certain basic tenets of the Community's judicial architecture at crucial points of intersection with national remedies and procedural rules.

191 However, consider Case C–97/96 *Daihatsu Deutschland* [1997] ECR I–6843, in which the Court contemplated the possibility of *Francovich* damages against a Member State for failing to implement the provisions of a Community directive requiring companies to disclose their annual accounts and permitting 'any interested persons' to apply to the national courts for the imposition of penalties in the event of non-compliance. Consider also: Case C–201/02 *Wells* (Judgment of 7 January 2004), where the Court suggested that the Member State's obligation to remedy the consequences of an unlawful failure to carry out an environmental impact assessment could include compensation for affected individuals, though without specifying the precise legal basis for such an action. Further, eg A Ward, 'Judicial Review of Environmental Misconduct in the European Community: Problems, Prospects and Strategies' (2000) 1 *Yearbook of European Environmental Law* 137.

192 Dir 2004/35 on environmental liability with regard to the prevention and remedying of environmental damage, OJ 2004 L143/56. Cf G Betlem and E Brans, 'The Future Role of Civil Liability for Environmental Damage in the EU' (2001) 2 *Yearbook of European Environmental Law* 183.

193 COM (2001)139 Final; COM (2002)544 Final.

As regards national procedures governing the conduct of preliminary references under Article 234 EC, the ordinary presumption of national competence applies, subject to the principles of equivalence and effectiveness. For example, in *Clean Car Autoservice*, the Court held that national rules which did not permit the successful party in proceedings before a domestic court to recover its proportion of the costs occasioned by an Article 234 EC reference did not render the exercise of Community law rights virtually impossible or excessively difficult.[194] However, the Court's conception of effectiveness becomes more nuanced when considering domestic rules which regulate the ability of either the parties, or the judges themselves, to raise new arguments (including those based on Community law) during the course of litigation or on appeal.

In principle, the supremacy of Community law requires national courts to ensure the full effectiveness of the Treaty by disapplying—if necessary on their own initiative—incompatible provisions of domestic law.[195] Procedural rules restricting the power of the courts even to consider relevant points of Community law may, of course, hinder the potential for Treaty norms to have full and immediate effect within the national legal order—though no more so than ordinary limitation periods or standing requirements, so one might expect the general requirements of effectiveness (as described above) to apply here too. But such procedural rules are also capable of affecting the possibility of open dialogue between the Court and the national judges, in particular, by reducing the possibility of making a reference under Article 234 EC. This latter factor has led the Court to identify fresh considerations of effectiveness, which also count among the limits placed by Community law upon national procedural autonomy.

In *Salonia*, it was established that the fact that the parties to a dispute failed to raise a point of Community law before the national court does not preclude the latter from bringing the matter before the Court of Justice via Article 234 EC.[196] As regards the ability of national courts to raise points of Community law of their own motion in the first place, one would have expected that, by virtue of the principle of equivalence, any duty on or discretion to raise domestic rules on the judge's own initiative would create a similar duty or discretion in respect of comparable Community situations. But in *Van Schijndel*, the Court went further: even if domestic law conferred on the national court a mere *discretion* to raise points of domestic law of its own motion, the principle of cooperation

[194] Case C–472/99 *Clean Car Autoservice* [2001] ECR I–9687.
[195] Case 106/77 *Simmenthal* [1978] ECR 629. More recently, eg Case C–187/00 *Kutz-Bauer* [2003] ECR I–2741; Case C–416/00 *Morellato* (Judgment of 18 September 2003).
[196] Case 126/80 *Salonia* [1981] ECR 1563. Cf Cases C–87–89/90 *Verholen* [1991] ECR I–3757.

enshrined in Article 10 EC nevertheless imposed on the court a *duty* to raise any relevant points of Community law on its own initiative.[197]

What about national procedural rules purporting actively to restrict the ability of the domestic court (or the parties) to raise Community law issues during the course of proceedings? Certain judgments suggested that the Court would adopt a robust interventionist approach in such situations. For example, in *Rheinmühlen-Düsseldorf*, it was held that national rules whereby the decisions of higher courts on points of law were binding upon lower courts could not of themselves have the effect of depriving any tribunal of its power to refer to the Court of Justice under Article 234 EC, in cases which raised questions about the proper interpretation of Community law.[198]

However, the Court eventually adopted a more restrained approach in the leading cases of *Peterbroeck* and *Van Schijndel*. The former concerned a 60-day limitation period on raising new pleas (including Community arguments) before the Belgian Court of Appeal against first instance decisions of the national tax administration.[199] The latter concerned a rule that, in a dispute between private parties, the Dutch appeal court had a duty of passivity and therefore could not consider of its own motion new arguments (including those based on the Treaty) not already advanced by the parties at first instance.[200] Applying the *Rewe/Comet* formula of national autonomy, equivalence and effectiveness, the Court held that the rule in *Van Schijndel* was compatible with Community law. The principle that, in civil suits, it is for the parties to take the initiative reflected conceptions prevailing within most of the Member States concerning relations between state and individual. In addition, it safeguarded the rights of the defence and ensured the proper conduct of proceedings. As regards *Peterbroeck*, whilst the 60-day limitation period was not objectionable per se, the Court highlighted several special features of the procedure which meant it could not be upheld here: the Court of Appeal was the first court able to make a reference under Article 234 EC (since the first instance tribunal was not a court/tribunal within the meaning of Article 234 EC); the Court of Appeal was itself prevented from considering the compatibility of the national tax with Community law because the 60-day limitation period expired before the Court of Appeal even held its hearing; no other national court in subsequent proceedings could of its own motion consider the compatibility question; and finally, this impossibility for national courts to raise points of Community law of their own motion was not

[197] Cases C–430–31/93 *Van Schijndel* [1995] ECR I–4705. Also: Case C–72/95 *Kraaijeveld* [1996] ECR I–5403.
[198] Case 166/73 *Rheinmühlen-Düsseldorf* [1974] ECR 33.
[199] Case C–312/93 *Peterbroeck* [1995] ECR I–4599.
[200] Cases C–430–31/93 *Van Schijndel* [1995] ECR I–4705.

reasonably justified by principles such as legal certainty or the proper conduct of procedure.

Commentators have found it very difficult to distinguish these two cases convincingly.[201] It seems most likely that the Court conceived of *Van Schijndel* as a case in which some national court at some point in the proceedings (presumably at first instance) had the opportunity to consider the claimant's Community law arguments, and, if necessary, make an Article 234 EC reference; whereas in *Peterbroeck*, the domestic procedure was such that, although some national court at some point in the proceedings (again at first instance) had the opportunity to consider the claimant's Community law arguments, that court could not, if necessary, make an Article 234 EC reference. However, is not clear whether the Dutch court of first instance in *Van Schijndel* was bound by the principle of judicial passivity. If not, then national law had indeed provided an opportunity for a competent judicial body to interact with the superior Community courts. But if so, then there was clearly no opportunity for any of the Dutch judges to seek guidance from the Court under Article 234 EC—making it much more difficult to provide a satisfactory means of reconciling *Van Schijndel* with the outcome in *Peterbroeck*.[202]

Nevertheless, this interpretation of the two judgments is supported by the later case of *Eco Swiss v Benetton*, which concerned a Dutch provision requiring judicial passivity (subject to certain exceptions) during the course of an appeal against an arbitration award. The Court held that the circumstances of this dispute differed from those of *Van Schijndel*. In *Eco Swiss*, the private arbitration authority hearing the dispute at first instance was the only body allowed by national law to consider the Community law arguments, but it was not a court/tribunal within the meaning of Article 234 EC and thus could not make a reference to the Court. Moreover, no subsequent court or tribunal was able under national law to consider the Community law arguments and, if necessary, to make a reference under Article 234 EC. As in *Peterbroeck*, this amounted to a total closure of the channel of communication between the domestic and the Community courts. By contrast, the Court had no objection under Community law to domestic procedural rules whereby an arbitration award, in respect of which no application for annulment had been made before the courts within a time-limit of three months, could no longer be called into question by a subsequent arbitration award—even though this would have

[201] Eg T Heukels, Commentary on *Peterbroeck* and *Van Schijndel* (1996) 33 CML Rev 337; F Jacobs, 'Enforcing Community Rights and Obligations in National Courts: Striking the Balance' in J Lonbay & A Biondi (eds), *Remedies for Breach of EC Law* (Wiley, 1997); S Prechal, 'Community Law in National Courts: The Lessons From *Van Schijndel*' (1998) 35 CML Rev 681.

[202] Further: G de Búrca, 'National Procedural Rules and Remedies: The Changing Approach of the Court of Justice' in J Lonbay & A Biondi (eds), *Remedies for Breach of EC Law* (Wiley, 1997).

been necessary in order to examine, in proceedings for annulment of the subsequent award, whether the agreement upheld in the first award was in fact void for breach of Article 81 EC. The limitation period itself was compatible with the principle of effectiveness insofar as it concerned the protection of individual rights derived from Article 81 EC; and the fact that the appeal court did enjoy an opportunity to consider the application of Community law to the first arbitration award meant that the procedure was also compatible with considerations of effectiveness as regards the integrity of Article 234 EC.[203]

It thus seems that this particular line of caselaw is not based on considerations of effective judicial protection for the citizen, who clearly bears the risk of looking after his/her own interests. After all, where the possibility of an Article 234 EC reference is still available, the Court will not intervene, even though the effect of the domestic procedural rule is to deprive the individual of the opportunity to assert his/her Treaty rights. The judicial policy at work in these judgments is instead moulded by the Court's desire to protect Article 234 EC as an effective medium for dialogue between the Community and domestic courts on the interpretation of Treaty law. Domestic procedural rules can restrict that channel of communication (*Van Schijndel*), but cannot exclude it altogether (*Peterbroeck*). And so, the Community's interest in the effectiveness of Article 234 EC succeeds where the individual's interest in effective judicial protection would fail.[204]

However, even if the Court has clarified which policy interests are at stake in cases such as *Peterbroeck* and *Van Schijndel*, important questions remain as to their full potential to interfere in the procedural autonomy of the Member States. For example, *Seymour-Smith* concerned a British rule requiring two years of continuous employment, before a worker was entitled to bring a claim for unfair dismissal based on the Equal Treatment Directive.[205] The Court based its reasoning on whether the UK's requirement of two years' continuous employment in itself amounted to indirect discrimination on grounds of sex. However, Advocate General Cosmas adopted a very different line of analysis, arguing that this rule was incompatible with the principle of effectiveness, because it prevented the national court from ever being able to evaluate the

[203] Case C–126/97 *Eco Swiss v Benetton* [1999] ECR I–3055. Further, eg M Furse and L D'Arcy, Commentary on *Eco Swiss v Benetton* [1999] ECLR 392; A P Komninos, Commentary on *Eco Swiss v Benetton* (2000) 37 CML Rev 459; C Baudenbacher and I Higgins, 'Decentralisation of EC Competition Law Enforcement and Arbitration' [2002] 8 *Columbia Journal of European Law* 1.

[204] However, note certain judgments dealing with the protection of consumers under Dir 93/13 on unfair terms in consumer contracts, OJ 1993 L95/29, eg Cases C–240–244/98 *Oceáno Grupo Editorial* [2000] ECR I–4941; Case C–473/00 *Cofidis* [2002] ECR I–10875. See further below.

[205] Dir 76/207, OJ 1976 L39/40.

claimant's Community law rights and, if necessary, to make a preliminary reference under Article 234 EC.[206] If the latter argument holds true, then the type of effectiveness embodied in *Peterbroeck* and *Van Schijndel* may intrude yet further into the realm of national procedural autonomy.

Effectiveness and Judicial Review Against the Community Institutions The last of our principles of effectiveness is concerned with the need to ensure that claimants do not abuse the possibility of challenging the legality of Community acts indirectly before the domestic courts, so as to overcome certain of the procedural restrictions applicable before the Union courts themselves when questioning the lawfulness of Community measures directly via an Article 230 EC action for annulment.

In particular, the existence of very limited rights of standing directly before Union courts for natural and legal persons (based on the 'direct and individual concern' requirement contained in Article 230(4) EC) has meant that many applicants are encouraged to challenge the legality of Community acts indirectly before the national courts.[207] In such situations, the Court is faced with a legitimate need to preserve the effectiveness of the Treaty's judicial architecture. The existence of a two-track avenue for seeking judicial review against Community measures—where one route operates according to centrally determined procedural rules which are often relatively restrictive in nature, as regards issues such as interim relief and time-limits, but the other route is fragmented into 15 judicial systems which may be much more liberal in character when it comes to such issues—poses particular problems in maintaining the coherent application of Treaty norms.[208] Specialised bodies of caselaw have therefore developed to determine the remedies and procedural rules applicable to decentralised challenges against Community measures, for example: as regards the competence of the national judges finally to dispose of the case;[209] the conditions for granting interim relief against Community acts or their national implementing measures;[210] and the compatibility with Community law of domestic limitation periods.[211]

[206] Case C–167/97 *Seymour-Smith* [1999] ECR I–623.
[207] Eg Case C–209/94 *Buralux* [1996] ECR I–615; Case C–321/95P *Greenpeace* [1998] ECR I–1651; Cases T-172 & 175–77/98 *Salamander* [2000] ECR II–2487.
[208] Cf the situation in English law after the reforms to Order 53 of the Rules of the Supreme Court and the Supreme Court Act 1981, eg *O'Reilly v Mackman* [1982] 3 All ER 1124. Cf the impact of the new Civil Procedure Rules, eg *Clark v University of Lincolnshire* [2000] 3 All ER 752.
[209] In particular: Case 314/85 *Firma Foto-Frost* [1987] ECR 4199.
[210] In particular: Cases C–143/88 and C–92/89 *Zuckerfabrik Süderdithmarshen* [1991] ECR I–415; Case C–465/93 *Atlanta* [1995] ECR I–3761.
[211] In particular: Case C–188/92 *TWD* [1994] ECR I–833; Case C–178/95 *Wiljo* [1997] ECR I–585.

That caselaw will be discussed in greater detail later in this book.[212] Suffice for present purposes to observe that it produces results which may well diverge from the requirements ordinarily imposed by the principle of effectiveness *stricto sensu*. In particular, intervention by the Court of Justice in this category of situation often means that the standards of judicial protection offered to individuals under Community law are lower than those which would otherwise have applied under pre-existing domestic rules alone. For example, interim relief against allegedly invalid Community measures must be granted only under the relatively restrictive conditions set out by the Court, even if this has the effect of reducing the levels of protection offered to individuals by domestic rules on interim relief.[213] Similarly, in all cases where the claimant could clearly have challenged the validity of a Community measure directly before the Union courts, but failed to do so within the two-month limitation period set out in Article 230(5) EC, his/her ability to challenge that Community act indirectly before the national courts must automatically be deemed forfeit (even if the action would have been considered valid having regard to domestic time-limits alone).[214]

Such cases, in which the Court's understanding of 'effectiveness' does not correspond to the interests of the citizen, might lead one to suspect that Community intervention in national remedies and procedural rules has less to do with the protection of individual rights than with the effective execution of Community policies: where the two coincide, the former enjoys the incidental benefits; but where the two conflict, the latter will prevail. And on a broader front, this might provide support for the argument that the Court's commitment to the protection of individual rights under the Treaty is a thinly disguised attempt to legitimise the expansion of Community competence.[215]

However, it would be wrong to overstate this critique. After all, the recovery of Community monies wrongly paid to the individual by the Member State is also a situation in which the interests of the Community in securing repayment of the sums are pitted against the interests of the citizen in retaining them. Yet the Court of Justice has held that national rules restricting the obligation to recover on grounds such as legitimate

[212] Ch 6 (below).

[213] Further, eg P Oliver, 'Interim Measures: Some Recent Developments' (1992) 29 CML Rev 7.

[214] Further, eg D Wyatt, 'The Relationship Between Actions for Annulment and References on Validity After *TWD Deggendorf*' in J Lonbay & A Biondi (eds), *Remedies for Breach of EC Law* (Wiley, 1997).

[215] Cf J Coppel and A O'Neill, 'The European Court of Justice: Taking Rights Seriously?' (1992) 29 CML Rev 669. Cf J Weiler and N Lockhart, '"Taking Rights Seriously" Seriously: The European Court and its Fundamental Rights Jurisprudence' (1995) 32 CML Rev 51 and 579.

expectations and equitable remission are compatible with the principle of effectiveness.[216] Similarly, we have seen that the Member State's duty to impose an effective and dissuasive sanction against those who breach their Treaty obligations is limited by reference to an upper ceiling of proportionality, whereby the sanctions may not go further than is necessary to achieve their desired effect.[217] These examples show that the Court is prepared to impose safeguards for the judicial protection of the citizen, even where this might contradict the interests of the Community. Instead of looking for an inherent bias in favour of the effective enforcement of Treaty policy, as opposed to the effective protection of individual rights, it might be better to recognise that, as regards the particular situation of challenges to the legality of Community acts, the Court's primary concern has been to maintain a coherent parallel between the remedies and procedural rules applicable to the complementary channels of centralised and decentralised enforcement. It is only incidental to this goal that the principle of effectiveness has been reshaped so as to protect the Community rather than the individual interest—and that is ultimately due to the fact that the Court's own standards of judicial protection as provided for in the Treaty itself, concerning issues such as interim relief and time-limits, happen to be relatively ungenerous when compared to the domestic rules of certain Member States.

Legal Basis for and Scope of Community Intervention

The fundamental right of access to a court is clearly binding upon each Member State as a general principle of Community law.[218] The ability of substantive Community norms to impact upon national remedies and procedural rules is clearly binding upon the Member States through the medium of the corresponding directly effective Treaty provisions, for example, Article 12 (and Articles 39, 43 and 49) EC in the case of the principle of non-discrimination on grounds of nationality.[219] The requirement of proportionality, as it applies *both* to national sanctions for the enforcement of domestic rules creating justified obstacles to free movement *and* to national sanctions adopted by the Member State for the enforcement of Community provisions, also finds its legal force through the general principles of Community law.

[216] Eg Cases 205–15/82 *Deutsche Milchkontor* [1983] ECR 2633. Further: ch 6 (below).
[217] See above.
[218] On the binding effect of general principles of Community law for the Member States, eg Case 222/84 *Johnston v Chief Constable of the RUC* [1986] ECR 1651 (implementing Treaty obligations); Case C–260/89 *ERT* [1991] ECR I–2925 (derogating from Treaty obligations).
[219] Eg Case 167/73 *Commission v France* (*French Seamen*) [1974] ECR 359; Case 2/74 *Reyners* [1974] ECR 631; Case 33/74 *Van Binsbergen* [1974] ECR 1299.

What about the principles of equivalence and effectiveness? On the one hand, these requirements are often seen simply as specific manifestations of the Member State's general duty of loyal cooperation towards the Community, which is also binding upon the national courts as regards matters falling within their jurisdiction.[220] As such, equivalence and effectiveness would find their proper legal basis in Article 10 EC—just like, say, the duty of consistent interpretation established by *von Colson* and *Marleasing*.[221] The Court has certainly referred to Article 10 EC to explain many of its decisions on effective judicial protection for the individual's Community law rights. For example, the Court in *Rewe/Comet* held that the national courts are entrusted with ensuring the legal protection which citizens derive from the direct effect of Community law, applying the principle of cooperation laid down in Article 10 EC, as regards the imposition of domestic limitation periods.[222] Similarly, it was stated in *Factortame* that it is for the national courts, in application of the principle of cooperation laid down in Article 10 EC, to ensure the legal protection which persons derive from the direct effect of provisions of Community law.[223] Or again, the Court relied upon Article 10 EC as the legal basis for its caselaw on the need for equivalent and effective sanctions against private parties who breach their obligations under Community law.[224]

On the other hand, the Court sometimes treats equivalence and effectiveness as fully-fledged general principles of Community law, binding upon the Member States as such and without the need for a specific legal basis such as Article 10 EC. For example, the Court in *Pasquini* stated that the principle of equivalence is no more than an expression of the principle of equal treatment, which is itself one of the fundamental principles of Community law;[225] and in *Pflücke* that the requirements of both equivalence and effectiveness were general principles of Community law.[226]

[220] Further: J Temple Lang, 'Community Constitutional Law: Article 5 EEC Treaty' (1990) 27 CML Rev 645; 'The Duties of National Courts under Community Constitutional Law' (1997) 22 EL Rev 3; 'The Duties of National Authorities Under Community Constitutional Law' (1998) 23 EL Rev 109; 'The Duties of Cooperation of National Authorities and Courts Under Article 10 EC: Two More Reflections' (2001) 26 EL Rev 84.

[221] Case 14/83 *Von Colson* [1984] ECR 1891; Case C–106/89 *Marleasing* [1990] ECR I–4135.

[222] Case 33/76 *Rewe-Zentralfinanz v Landwirtschaftskammer für das Saarland* [1976] ECR 1989, para 5; Case 45/76 *Comet* [1976] ECR 2043, para 12.

[223] Eg Case C–213/89 *ex p Factortame* [1990] ECR I–2433, para 19. Also, eg Case C–228/98 *Dounias* [2000] ECR I–577; Case C–1/99 *Kofisa Italia* [2001] ECR I–207; Case C–147/01 *Weber's Wine World* (Judgment of 2 October 2003).

[224] Eg Case 68/88 *Commission v Greece* [1989] ECR 2965. In similar vein, eg S Weatherill, 'Beyond "EC Law Rights, National Remedies"' in A Caiger & D A Floudas (eds), *1996 Onwards: Lowering the Barriers Further* (Wiley, 1996); S Prechal, 'EC Requirements for an Effective Remedy' in J Lonbay & A Biondi (eds), *Remedies for Breach of EC Law* (Wiley, 1997).

[225] Case C–34/02 *Pasquini* [2003] ECR I–6515.

[226] Case C–125/01 *Pflücke* (Judgment of 18 September 2003).

Similarly, the Court in *Francovich* held that the principle of Member State liability to make reparation for harm caused to individuals by breaches of Community law for which the state can be held responsible 'is inherent in the system of the Treaty.' Reference to Article 10 EC followed, but only to provide 'further foundation' for the right to reparation.[227] Moreover, Article 13 ECHR states that everyone whose rights and freedoms as set forth under that Convention are violated shall have an effective remedy before a national authority—making clear that this is in itself a fundamental right, albeit linked to enforcement of the specific human rights contained in the ECHR. Article 47 of the Charter of Fundamental Rights of the European Union carries this principle much further: everyone whose rights and freedoms guaranteed under Union law are violated has the right to an effective remedy—suggesting that this constitutes a general principle of Community law which applies, as such, to the enforcement of any norm derived from the Treaty.[228]

Commentators are divided about which of these two possible legal bases for the principles of equivalence and effectiveness should be preferred.[229] For present purposes, however, it is not necessary to make any firm choice. More important is the fact that both models provide a general legal basis for Community intervention in the process of decentralised enforcement, which is of Treaty status or at least equivalent to Treaty status. And it is from this common feature that all the legally important implications flow: for example, it means that equivalent and effective remedies and procedures must be provided by the Member State, regardless of whether the particular Community legislation at issue lays down any express requirements to this effect.[230] We will therefore accept, as a working proposition, that equivalence and effectiveness are best seen as general principles of Community law, whose implications are in any case binding upon the national courts through the medium of the duty of loyal cooperation enshrined in Article 10 EC.

[227] Cases C–6 & 9/90 *Francovich* [1991] ECR I–5357, paras 31–37.

[228] Charter of Fundamental Rights of the European Union, OJ 2000 C364/1. Art 13 ECHR is also referred to in, eg Case 222/84 *Johnston v Chief Constable of the RUC* [1986] ECR 1651 as the basis for a general principle of Community law. Both Art 47 of the Charter and Art 13 ECHR are referred to by the CFI in, eg Cases T-116 & 118/01 *P&O European Ferries* (Judgment of 5 August 2003).

[229] Consider, eg P Girerd, 'Les principes d'équivalence et d'effectivité: encadrement ou désencadrement de l'autonomie procédurale des Etats membres?' (2002) 38 *Revue trimestrielle de droit européen* 75.

[230] To take one from innumerable possible examples: Cases C–46 & 48/93 *Brasserie du Pêcheur* and *Factortame III* [1996] ECR I–1029 concerned directly effective Treaty provisions on free movement for goods and freedom of establishment which make no express reference to effective remedies. Also, eg Cases 66 & 127–8/79 *Salumi* [1980] ECR 1237; Case 265/78 *Ferwerda* [1980] ECR 617; though cf Case 152/79 *Lee v Minister for Agriculture* [1980] ECR 1495.

Against that background, the requirements of effective judicial protection, taken as a whole, are clearly binding upon the Member States and capable of having direct effect within the domestic legal orders. In turn, where a national court finds that its remedies or procedural rules are not compatible with the requirements of effective judicial protection, it will be obliged to resolve this conflict by simply disapplying the offending domestic provisions pursuant to the principle of supremacy.[231] Thus, prohibitions on the granting of interim relief can be circumvented;[232] and unreasonably short limitations periods can be set aside.[233]

This is not to say that every single aspect of effective judicial protection is apt to have direct effect and prevail over conflicting national rules in this manner. For example, it will be recalled that, where the Member State simply fails to designate any tribunal competent to adjudicate over the claimant's Community law rights, the Court is reluctant to interfere directly so as to insist that another tribunal assumes jurisdiction for itself. We criticised that approach on the grounds that the more serious the Member State's infringement of the fundamental right of access to a court, the less likely the claimant will have access to a satisfactory avenue of redress under Community law.[234] However, the Court's approach still follows an underlying legal rationale. Correcting such a breach of Community law implies a positive act in identifying a particular court or tribunal, rather than merely a negative one in disapplying unacceptable remedial or procedural restrictions. This suggests that the right of access to a court, insofar as it depends upon concrete action on behalf of the Member State, is not capable of having direct effect within the national legal orders, because it is insufficiently clear, precise and unconditional to produce legal effects of its own, without the exercise of a certain degree of national discretion.

We are now in a position to deal with three more problematic questions about the full scope of application of the principles of effective judicial protection: the material range of substantive Community law provisions able to benefit from the requirements of effective judicial protection and, in particular, how far the latter cover not only directly effective but also non-directly effective Treaty norms; the personal range of substantive Community law disputes able to benefit from the requirements of effective judicial protection and, in particular, the horizontal applicability of remedies provisions contained in Community directives; finally, the status of Community secondary legislation dealing with remedies and procedural rules before the national courts which might itself conflict with the Court's caselaw.

[231] Eg Case 106/77 *Simmenthal* [1978] ECR 629; Case C–118/00 *Larsy II* [2001] ECR I–5063.
[232] Eg Case C–213/89 *ex p Factortame* [1990] ECR I–2433.
[233] Eg Case C–125/01 *Pflücke* (Judgment of 18 September 2003).
[234] See above.

Effective Judicial Protection of Non-Directly Effective Rights?

We have just seen how (for the most part) the principles of effective judicial protection are directly effective and capable of prevailing over conflicting national rules. But there is a prior question: what is the material range of substantive Community law provisions which are able to benefit from the requirements of effective judicial protection in the first place? And in particular, are those requirements tied to the existence of directly effective Community law provisions, or can they also cover (at least certain) non-directly effective Treaty rights?

The answer depends partly upon how one defines the concept of direct effect itself. Effective judicial protection clearly applies to substantive provisions of Community law which have direct effect in the narrow sense of creating freestanding individual rights. This category includes a number of situations: for example, where the relevant provisions of Community law have not been properly implemented by the Member State, so that the claimant relies upon directly effective Treaty rights, and a dispute then arises as to the standards of judicial protection available under domestic law;[235] but also where the relevant provisions of Community law have been fully implemented by the Member State, so that the principle of direct effect as regards those substantive provisions is not per se necessary, and the dispute relates only to the level of judicial protection provided by the Member State.[236]

Effective judicial protection clearly applies also in respect of substantive Community law which is directly effective in the broader sense, that is, as regards provisions which are not linked to subjective individual rights, but are still capable of affecting the citizen's legal position because they produce independent effects within the national legal orders. This is certainly the best way of conceptualising the caselaw on the enforcement of Community law in the general interest by the Member States, and by individuals/pressure groups able to invoke Community law before the national courts even though they cannot be described as 'right-holders' as regards anything other than rules of standing.[237]

[235] Eg Case C–208/90 *Emmott* [1991] ECR I–4269; Case C–271/91 *Marshall II* [1993] ECR I–4367.
[236] Eg Case 109/88 *Danfoss* [1989] ECR 3199. This includes situations where the relevant substantive provisions of Community law are deemed to have been fully implemented, thanks to the duty of interpretation under Case C–106/89 *Marleasing* [1990] ECR I–4135 (eg Case C–185/97 *Coote v Granada Hospitality* [1998] ECR I–5199); and also where Community law has been properly transposed into national law, but misapplied by the competent domestic authorities in individual cases, giving rise to disputes about the equivalence or effectiveness of national remedies or procedural rules (eg Case C–62/00 *Marks & Spencer* [2002] ECR I–6325).
[237] See above.

In short, the principles of effective judicial protection clearly apply to situations involving directly effective substantive provisions of Community law, to the extent that 'direct effect' involves the capacity for Community law to produce independent legal effects within the Member States, regardless of whether or not this can be said to involve the creation of individual rights.

Difficulties arise, however, as regards substantive Community norms which do not have direct effect in any sense, because they simply fail to meet the basic threshold criteria for producing independent effects within the national legal orders (in the sense of being sufficiently clear, precise and unconditional; and any relevant deadline for implementation having expired).[238] The status of such Community provisions, vis-à-vis the principles of effective judicial protection, depends partly upon which of the threshold criteria have not been satisfied. For example, if either the nature of a right or the identity of its beneficiary cannot be identified on the basis of Community law alone, then it is difficult to envisage how the principles of effective judicial protection might become engaged.[239] However, if the lack of any direct effect arises from the fact that, although both the right and its beneficiary are clear, the identity of the person or body subject to the corresponding obligation cannot be determined on the basis of Community law alone, the Member State which is responsible for failing to adopt all necessary domestic measures to complete the regulatory system envisaged by the Treaty can be held liable to make reparation under the *Francovich* caselaw.[240] This will, in turn, permit the claimant to challenge any related national remedial and procedural restrictions which raise issues of compatibility with the principles of effective judicial protection (such as rules on the quantum of damages, or on limitation periods).[241]

How do we conceptualise this situation? After the judgment in *Francovich*, some commentators argued that the Court had dramatically expanded the material scope of the domestic courts' duty to furnish citizens with effective standards of judicial protection. In particular, *Francovich* seemed to have exploded the link between effective judicial protection and the direct effect doctrine, so that the principles of equivalence and effectiveness could benefit also certain types of non-directly effective

[238] Cf judgments such as Cases C–6 & 9/90 *Francovich* [1991] ECR I–5357; Case C–336/96 *Gilly* [1998] ECR I–2793; Case C–378/97 *Wijsenbeek* [1999] ECR I–6207.

[239] Further, eg G Anagnostaras, 'State Liability and Alternative Courses of Action: How Independent Can an Autonomous Remedy Be?' (2002) 21 *Yearbook of European Law* 355.

[240] Cases C–6 & 9/90 *Francovich* [1991] ECR I–5357. Further: ch 5 (below).

[241] Note that such situations arise not only as regards substantive Community law provisions, but also in respect of those elements of the principles of effective judicial protection which themselves lack direct effect. Eg it will be recalled that, where the Member State totally disregards its duty to identify a court or tribunal competent to hear certain public procurement actions under Community law, the Court encourages the aggrieved claimant to bring an action under *Francovich* to vindicate this non-directly effective right (see above).

substantive Community law right. It was sufficient for the imposition of liability to make reparation that the relevant Treaty norm was *intended* to confer rights, even if the right itself was insufficiently precise and unconditional to be enforceable on its own terms.[242]

However, one could also interpret the *Francovich* judgment, and subsequent cases which have likewise involved actions for reparation based upon non-directly effective Community provisions,[243] as nevertheless remaining linked to a directly effective Treaty norm, that is, the Member State's obligation to transpose directives into domestic law correctly and on time. According to this argument, *Francovich* merely recognised that Article 249 EC has a limited form of direct effect insofar as it is now capable of producing independent effects within the national legal orders; and used the 'intention to confer rights' criterion as a means to identify the specific class of individuals enjoying standing to bring actions for reparation based upon that directly effective provision.[244]

Or better still, perhaps one should understand *Francovich* as a method for transforming the non-directly effective Community law expectation of a particular substantive benefit (say, to guaranteed payment of outstanding wages when one's employer becomes insolvent), into the directly effective Community law right to reparation against the Member State responsible for failing to deliver a legal framework capable of fulfilling that expectation (because it failed to implement the relevant directive correctly or on time). This transformation is effected through the medium of the liability criteria identified in judgments such as *Brasserie de Pêcheur* and *Dillenkofer* (an intention to confer rights by the Community, a sufficiently serious breach by the Member State, and a direct causal link between breach and damage).[245] The principles of effective judicial protection thus act as the source of a new—substantive and autonomous—right under the Treaty. Since it was created through the medium of the principles of effective judicial protection, this right to reparation is possessed of its own direct effect, thanks to the general principles of Community law/duty of loyal cooperation under Article 10 EC.

[242] Consider, eg J Steiner, 'From Direct Effects to *Francovich:* Shifting Means of Enforcement of Community Law' (1993) 18 EL Rev 3; M Ross, 'Beyond *Francovich*' (1993) 56 MLR 55; C Stefanou and H Xanthaki, 'Are National Remedies the Only Way Forward? Widening the Scope of Article 215(2) of the Treaty of Rome' in J Lonbay & A Biondi (eds), *Remedies for Breach of EC Law* (Wiley, 1997).

[243] Eg Case C–54/96 *Dorsch Consult* [1997] ECR I–4961; Case C–97/96 *Daihatsu Deutschland* [1997] ECR I–6843; Case C–371/97 *Gozza* [2000] ECR I–7881.

[244] Consider, eg W van Gerven, 'Non-contractual Liability of Member States, Community Institutions and Individuals for Breaches of Community Law with a View to a Common Law for Europe' (1994) 1 *Maastricht Journal of European and Comparative Law* 6.

[245] Cases C–46 & 48/93 *Brasserie du Pêcheur and Factortame* III [1996] ECR I–1029; Cases C–178–79 & 188–90/94 *Dillenkofer* [1996] ECR I–4845. Further: ch 5 (below).

According to this argument, the right to reparation is ultimately no different from any other substantive Treaty right (for example, to equal treatment on grounds of nationality or sex). In particular, if we accept that the requirements of effective judicial protection may themselves be constitutive of an autonomous and directly effective right to reparation, then *Francovich* need not imply that the principles of effective judicial protection benefit certain non-directly effective provisions of Community law in anything other than a second-order manner.

Horizontal Applicability of Remedies Provisions in Directives

Our next issue concerns the personal range of substantive Community law disputes which are able to benefit from the requirements of effective judicial protection.

We have seen that effective judicial protection applies whether the dispute in question is properly characterised as vertical or horizontal in nature (though the detailed content of effective judicial protection may well vary between litigation involving individuals and public authorities and litigation involving two private parties).[246] For these purposes, the general principles of Community law, combined with Article 10 EC, provide an appropriate legal basis for intervening in the domestic standards of judicial protection as regards not only vertical but also horizontal situations. Two main arguments are generally invoked to support this proposition. First, it is well established that both the general principles of Community law and the primary Treaty provisions are capable of producing legal effects in litigation between private parties. There is thus no inherent objection to the horizontal application of the requirements of effective judicial protection. Secondly, it is irrelevant for these purposes that Article 10 EC is formally addressed only to the Member States, and might thus seem to rule out the imposition of obligations upon private parties.

This irrelevancy might be explained by the simple observation that the Court has accepted the horizontal application of Treaty provisions such as Articles 39 and 141 EC, rejecting out of hand the argument that Treaty provisions worded in terms of 'the Member States' cannot create obligations also for individuals.[247] One might also point out that in judgments such as *Marleasing*, the Court used Article 10 EC as the legal basis for the duty incumbent upon national judges to construe domestic legislation in conformity with the Member State's Treaty obligations, even in the context of

[246] See above.
[247] Eg Case C–281/98 *Angonese* [2000] ECR I–4131 (on Art 39 EC); Case 43/75 *Defrenne v Sabena* [1976] ECR 455 (on Art 141 EC).

horizontal disputes.[248] Indeed, such judgments might prompt us to adopt a different perspective, arguing that horizontal disputes should actually be understood as triangular in nature. The beneficiary of Community law has a right to effective judicial protection, but that right is binding vertically upon the national court adjudicating upon his/her claim, not upon the other private party involved in the litigation. Discharge by the national court of its obligation to provide effective standards of judicial protection may well have significant consequences for resolution of the horizontal dispute, but that is not the same as saying that Article 10 EC has horizontal direct effect per se.[249]

In any case, the legal basis question acquires particular significance within the context of horizontal disputes which involve rights derived from a Community directive.

It is established law that the substantive provisions of unimplemented directives cannot have direct effect so as to impose novel obligations upon a private party (the '*Dori* principle').[250] Nevertheless, there are a number of judgments in which the Court appears to have sanctioned the direct application of an unimplemented directive, even though the case in question consisted of a horizontal situation involving two private parties. Some of these cases concerned the unimplemented remedial provisions of a Community directive.[251] For example, Article 6 of the Equal Treatment Directive requires the Member State to guarantee effective standards of judicial protection in respect of the substantive right to equal treatment on grounds of sex.[252] On several occasions where the Member State correctly transposed the principle of non-discrimination but failed to comply with the duty to impose an effective sanction in the event of an infringement, the Court of Justice ordered that any domestic rules restricting the availability of satisfactory remedies should be set aside—even though the dispute in question involved two private parties.[253]

[248] Case C–106/89 *Marleasing* [1990] ECR I–4135. Eg Case C–2/97 *Borsana* [1998] ECR I–8597; Case C–343/98 *Collino* [2000] ECR I–6659.
[249] Eg A Komninos, 'New Prospects for Private Enforcement of EC Competition Law: *Courage v Crehan* and the Community Rights to Damages' (2002) 39 CML Rev 447. Cf K Lackhoff and N Nyssens, 'Direct Effect of Directives in Triangular Situations' (1998) 23 EL Rev 397; D Colgan, 'Triangular Situations: The Coup de Grâce for the Denial of Horizontal Direct Effect of Community Directives' (2002) 8 *European Public Law* 545.
[250] In particular: Case 152/84 *Marshall* [1986] ECR 723; Case C–91/92 *Faccini Dori* [1994] ECR I–3325.
[251] Other cases have concerned the unimplemented substantive provisions of Community directives. Consider, eg Case C–201/02 *Wells* (Judgment of 7 January 2004).
[252] Dir 76/207, OJ 1976 L39/40 (as interpreted in Case 14/83 *von Colson* [1984] ECR 1891 and Case 222/84 *Johnston v Chief Constable of the RUC* [1986] ECR 1651). Note the amendments to Art 6 Dir 76/207, introduced by Dir 2002/73, OJ 2002 L269/15.
[253] Eg Case C–177/88 *Dekker* [1990] ECR I–3941; Case C–180/95 *Draehmpaehl* [1997] ECR I–2195.

On its face, this looks like judicial endorsement of the principle of horizontal direct effect for the unimplemented remedial provisions of a Community directive. It has accordingly been argued that such provisions constitute an exception to the general prohibition on horizontal direct effect.[254] However, it is possible to argue that such cases are perfectly compatible with the *Dori* principle. The obligation to provide effective sanctions as set out in measures such as the Equal Treatment Directive merely codifies the general principles of the Court's caselaw on the minimum standards of judicial protection which must be offered in respect of the domestic enforcement of Community rights. These general principles are binding on the national courts by virtue of Article 10 EC, regardless of the vertical or horizontal character of the dispute in question. Since effective remedies must be available to the claimant of Community rights both in the absence of any express legislative provision to that effect and as against another private party, such remedies should still be enforceable even where the relevant directive does direct the Member State to furnish adequate standards of judicial protection, as this cannot amount to the imposition upon the private defendant of obligations not already provided for and enforceable under the Treaty.[255]

To hold otherwise would constitute an extension of the *Dori* principle which is not only unnecessary from a doctrinal perspective, but also undesirable on a policy level: particularly in an era when the Community legislature has developed a certain fondness for crowning growing numbers of directives with a reminder to the Member States of their pre-existing obligation to provide adequate enforcement mechanisms, it would be most unfortunate if the Court were eventually to undermine its own achievements in advancing the cause of effective judicial protection for the sake of an unpersuasive argument based on the lack of horizontal direct effect for directives. [256]

Only where the relevant directive goes beyond a mere duplication of the legal requirements already set out under the Treaty, obliging the Member State to establish remedies which are more effective or at least more specific than those required under the Court's own jurisprudence, could its enforcement against a private party be said to constitute horizontal direct effect contrary to the *Dori* principle. This qualification might well explain the decision in *Océano Grupo Editorial*. In that case, the Court interpreted the Unfair Contract Terms Directive so as to require that a domestic judge must be able to determine of his/her own motion whether the terms of a contract at issue in litigation before the national court

[254] Eg A Ward, 'New Frontiers in Private Enforcement of EC Directives' (1998) 23 EL Rev 65.
[255] Cf the relationship between Art 141 EC and Dir 75/117 on equal pay between men and women, OJ 1975 L45/19 (eg Case C–381/99 *Brunnhofer* [2001] ECR I–4961).
[256] Further: M Dougan, 'The "Disguised" Vertical Direct Effect of Directives?' [2000] CLJ 586.

should be regarded as 'unfair' within the meaning of the Directive.[257] However, in situations where the Directive has not been properly transposed, the Court did no more than remind the national judges of their duty to interpret domestic rules so far as possible to achieve the objectives set by Community law—implicitly ruling out any direct effect for the relevant provisions of the Directive within the context of a horizontal dispute.[258] This obligation for national courts to consider of their own motion the unfairness of contractual terms was justified by considerations of consumer protection specific to the applicable Directive,[259] and goes further than the duty for domestic judges to raise points of Community law on their own initiative as it results from the general principles of effective judicial protection elaborated in the caselaw.[260] As such, the fact that the Court in *Océano Grupo Editorial* did not endorse the horizontal direct effect of a particular Community law restriction upon national procedural autonomy remains perfectly consistent with the idea that the fundamental requirements of effective judicial protection developed in the caselaw are binding upon the national courts within the context of disputes between private parties—even where these overlap with the unimplemented remedies provisions of Community directives.[261]

Effective Judicial Protection and Community Secondary Legislation

Our final question concerns the status of Community secondary legislation dealing with remedies and procedural rules before the national courts which might itself conflict with the Court's caselaw on effective judicial protection.

Since they enjoy the status of general principles of Community law, binding through the medium of Article 10 EC, the requirements of effective judicial protection apply as much to Community secondary legislation dealing with remedies and procedures before the national courts as to the standards of judicial protection adopted by the Member State pursuant to their presumptive domestic competence. For example, the Court in *Kofisa Italia* and *Siples* considered provisions of Regulation 2913/92 which purported to confer the power to suspend implementation of contested

[257] Dir 93/13 on unfair terms in consumer contracts, OJ 1993 L95/29.
[258] Cases C–240–4/98 *Océano Grupo Editorial* [2000] ECR I–4941.
[259] See also Case C–473/00 *Cofidis* [2002] ECR I–10875.
[260] In particular: Case C–312/93 *Peterbroeck* [1995] ECR I–4599; Cases C–430–31/93 *Van Schijndel* [1995] ECR I–4705; Case C–126/97 *Eco Swiss v Benetton* [1999] ECR I–3055. See above.
[261] Note also the problems posed by Case C–185/97 *Coote v Granada Hospitality* [1998] ECR I–5199. Further: M Dougan, 'The Equal Treatment Directive: Retaliation, Remedies and Direct Effect' (1999) 24 EL Rev 664.

customs decisions exclusively upon the national customs authorities.[262] It was held that the Regulation could not restrict the fundamental right to effective judicial protection, and therefore could not deprive the domestic courts of their general jurisdiction to grant interim relief.[263]

However, certain cases are more equivocal about how far the principles of effective judicial protection will prevail over any apparently conflicting measures adopted by the Community institutions.[264] Consider the remedies provisions of Directive 64/221.[265] Article 8 states that Community nationals exercising their right to free movement shall enjoy the same legal remedies in respect of any decision concerning entry, the refusal of a residence permit, or expulsion from the national territory as are available to nationals of the Member State in respect of acts of the administration. However, as regards a decision by the host state to refuse renewal of a residence permit or to expel from the national territory, Article 9(1) provides that, where domestic remedies as envisaged under Article 8 grant no right to appeal to a court of law, or where such appeal can only challenge the legal validity of the decision rather than re-assess the facts, or where the appeal cannot have suspensory effect, the relevant decision cannot be taken (save in cases of urgency) until an opinion has been obtained from an independent authority before which the Community national enjoys rights of defence and representation. Similarly, as regards a decision by the host state to refuse issue of a first residence permit or to expel from the national territory before the first residence permit has been issued, Article 9(2) provides that, where domestic remedies grant no right of appeal to a court of law, or where such appeal can only challenge the legal validity of the decision rather than re-assess the facts, or where the appeal cannot have suspensory effect, the decision may, at the Community national's request, be referred to an independent authority for consideration.

It is clear that the Community framework of effective judicial protection applies *in principle* to Member State decisions refusing entry into or

[262] Reg 2913/92 establishing the Community customs code, OJ 1992 L302/1.

[263] Case C–1/99 *Kofisa Italia* [2001] ECR I–207; Case C–226/99 *Siples* [2001] ECR I–277. Consider also the judgments in Case C–62/00 *Marks & Spencer* [2002] ECR I–6325 and Case C–17/01 *Sudholz* (Judgment of 29 April 2004) on Member State and Community measures (respectively) retroactively authorising improper national taxes.

[264] Though, of course, the Court can hardly be criticised for rejecting *unfounded* claims that Community secondary legislation somehow breaches the principles of effective judicial protection, eg Case C–52/00 *Commission v France* [2002] ECR I–3827; Case C–154/00 *Commission v Greece* [2002] ECR I–3879.

[265] Dir 64/221 on the coordination of special measures concerning the movement and residence of foreign nationals which are justified on grounds of public policy, public security or public health, OJ English Special Edition (Series I) 1963–64, p 117. However, see now Dir 2004/38 on the right of citizens of the Union and their family members to move and reside freely within the territory of the Member States, OJ 2004 L158/77.

expulsion from the national territory.[266] However, Advocate General Ruiz-Jarabo Colomer in *ex parte Shingara* queried whether the Member State's failure to provide a right to appeal to a court of law, or to ensure that such appeal could have suspensory effect, as specifically envisaged by Article 9 Directive 64/221 itself, would be compatible with the Court's caselaw on effective judicial protection—in particular, with cases like *Johnston v Chief Constable of the RUC* on the fundamental right to legal redress before a court of law,[267] and with judgments such as *Factortame* on the jurisdiction to grant interim relief as required by the principle of effectiveness.[268] In effect, the Advocate General argued that Directive 64/221 had become outdated in the light of subsequent developments in the Court's caselaw, and that Article 9 cannot exempt the Member States from their more fundamental obligation, under the general principles of Community law and Article 10 EC, to ensure effective standards of judicial protection in respect of Community law rights.[269]

The Court itself had an opportunity to clarify this problem in the *MRAX* case, which raised issues about the procedural protection against refusals of entry and expulsion available under Community law to the third-country national family members of migrant Union citizens. The Court recalled that the existence of judicial control over every decision of a national authority constitutes a general principle of Community law. However, it also pointed out that the provisions of Article 9 Directive 64/221 are complementary to those relating to the system of appeals to a court of law (referred to in Article 8) and are intended to mitigate the effect of certain deficiencies in those remedies. The Court then continued to interpret the provisions of Article 9, without questioning whether they were actually compatible with the fundamental requirements of judicial control.[270]

It is possible that, in such situations, the Court feels its legitimate room for manoeuvre constrained by the fact that the Community legislature has intervened to establish a particular regulatory scheme for national remedies and procedural rules. However, this defies the logic of the hierarchy of norms established by the Treaty: if access to a court and interim relief are rights derived from the general principles of Community law and/or primary provisions of the Treaty itself, they should prevail over incompatible secondary measures adopted by the Community institutions just as much as incompatible provisions adopted by the Member States themselves. Moreover, the Court need not feel moved to invalidate the relevant

[266] Eg Cases 482 & 493/01 *Orfanopoulos* (Judgment of 29 April 2004).
[267] Case 222/84 *Johnston v Chief Constable of the RUC* [1986] ECR 1651.
[268] Case C–213/89 *ex p Factortame* [1990] ECR I–2433.
[269] Cases C–65 & 111/95 *ex p Shingara* [1997] ECR I–3343.
[270] Case C–459/99 *MRAX* [2002] ECR I–6591.

Community legislation altogether: it could just as easily create a cleavage between the provisions of the relevant directive and the standards expected under the Treaty, and require the Member States to fill the resulting gap between what Community legislation says and what Community law actually means.[271] In any case, the odd result of the Court's approach is that measures such as Directive 64/221, which were clearly intended to advance the cause of effective judicial protection across the Community, may in some cases actually undermine it, by inducing the Court to respect a national autonomy extrapolated from the legislative text which it would not otherwise tolerate under the general principles of the Treaty legal order. *MRAX* thus reinforces perceptions that the Court has failed to consider with necessary rigour the relationship between its general remedies caselaw, and the more explicit enforcement provisions now contained in several secondary measures.[272]

NATURE AND STRUCTURE OF ANALYSIS TO FOLLOW

This quartet of concepts—fundamental right of access to judicial process, rebuttable presumption of national autonomy, overriding Community requirements as embodied in substantive Treaty rules and the principles of equivalence and effectiveness, direct effect within the domestic legal orders as general principles of Community law and/or through primary Treaty provisions—provides the basic legal framework through which the Court of Justice has elaborated its understanding of the underlying policy concerns at stake in the decentralised enforcement of Community rules.

In fact, the Court of Justice's intervention in the domestic systems of judicial protection may be rationalised and assessed along two complementary axes. The first is the imperative of effectiveness, demanding an adequate standard of enforcement for Treaty norms within each Member State. It is readily apparent that inadequate national remedies and procedural rules can frustrate the effective application of Community law within each Member State. For example, a substantive policy that Member States should not impose import duties, or that employers should not sack women for being pregnant, risks being undermined at the purely remedial level if national law does not provide for the reimbursement of unlawfully levied taxes, or for substantial damages to deter discriminatory dismissals. In this regard, the Court of Justice continues its struggle to define the

[271] A phenomenon which is already familiar in the law on free movement of persons: see M Dougan and E Spaventa, 'Educating Rudy and the (Non-)English Patient: A Double Bill on Residency Rights Under Article 18 EC' (2003) 28 EL Rev 699.
[272] Further, eg M Dougan, 'The *Francovich* Right to Reparation: Reshaping the Contours of Community Remedial Competence' (2000) 6 *European Public Law* 103.

Member State's margin of discretion to regulate or restrict the exercise of Community rights through the national courts. This struggle has provided inexhaustible fuel for an effervescence of academic discourse: assessing the unstable and often inconsistent meaning of effective judicial protection; querying its relationship with competing Member State interests in (say) legal certainty and the fair administration of justice; or pondering its implications for wider debates about (for example) the constitutional limits of judicial activism.[273]

The second axis, which has by comparison provoked a less vigorous and less varied response, is the imperative of uniformity, demanding equality of treatment between the Member States (without necessarily implying any particular level of treatment, so long as it is the same across the entire Community). Again, it is apparent that differences between national standards of judicial protection may result in the unequal enforcement of Treaty policy across the Community territory. This may have the effect of distorting competition between undertakings within the Single Market: manufacturers of dangerous consumer goods who can be fined up to €100,000 are put at a competitive disadvantage as compared to those who risk paying only €1,000 for the same breach of their Community obligations. Moreover, a lack of uniform remedies and procedures might also run counter to the principle of equal treatment between citizens of the European Union: individuals intended to benefit from the same substantive right across the Community will in fact receive very different treatment according to where they happen to live and work.

This book seeks to contribute to academic debate over the true nature and proper resolution of the 'enforcement deficit' thus generated by the Community's reliance upon domestic remedies and procedural rules, by investigating the appropriate role to be performed by the imperative of uniformity. In particular, we will explore two competing conceptual models of the need for uniformity in the formulation and application of Community law, and their respective implications for ongoing controversy about the decentralised enforcement of Treaty norms.

The first is the traditional 'integration through law' approach: the success of the European integration project depends on the progressive establishment of uniform legal norms throughout the Community; against this background, national remedies and procedural rules present a serious threat to the coherency of the Treaty order which must be countered by creating a unified system of judicial protection in Europe (Chapter 2).

[273] Eg C Himsworth, 'Things Fall Apart: The Harmonisation of Community Judicial Procedural Protection Revisited' (1997) 22 EL Rev 291; A Biondi, 'The European Court of Justice and Certain National Procedural Limitations: Not Such a Tough Relationship' (1999) 36 CML Rev 1271; A Ward, *Judicial Review and the Rights of Private Parties in EC Law* (OUP, 2000) chs 2–4. Further: ch 2 (below).

However, it will be argued that this model has failed to keep pace with significant politico-legal changes within the Treaty system as a whole. In particular, the relationship between Community and national institutions in the formulation of substantive Treaty policy has become increasingly complex. A survey of the current position (Chapter 3) supports the claim that regulatory differentiation is fast becoming one of the dominant operational and indeed constitutional characteristics of the modern European Union. Moreover, the dynamic forces inherent in both the concept and practice of regulatory differentiation make it not only a symptom but also a potentially potent cause of constitutional change, demanding the re-evaluation of several long-held assumptions which surround the Community legal order but unduly emphasise its integrative character. Those assumptions include the supposed need for absolute or generalised uniformity in the application of Community law such as inspires an 'integration through law' approach to the enforcement deficit. We will therefore propose a second (and alternative) 'sectoral' model: Community remedial competence should, so far as possible, be selectively matched to the actual degree of Community substantive competence exercised over any given policy matter (Chapter 4). Thus, some sectors (such as competition law and state aids) remain characterised by high levels of substantive harmonisation such as to warrant corresponding levels of approximation for the existing standards of domestic judicial protection; whereas other sectors (including environmental, consumer and social policies) are marked by a degree of differentiation that makes it difficult to identify any genuinely uniform Community policy which is being undermined by the present lack of common remedies and procedural rules for its enforcement before the national courts.

These two models will then act as critical perspectives through which to assess the developing caselaw of the Court of Justice and, in particular, to investigate changing judicial understandings of the Community's interest in harmonising national remedies and procedural rules. This investigation (highlighted by case-studies of the *Francovich* right to reparation, and limitation periods for the commencement of proceedings) demonstrates that the Court's general approach is now to prescribe incomplete and, in particular, merely minimum standards of effective judicial protection—leaving each Member State free to pursue independent remedial policies over and above the basic Community requirements. It will be argued that this represents a fair reflection of the Community's legitimate interest in attaining uniformity of enforcement within an increasingly differentiated Europe, at least as regards sectors such as environmental, consumer and employee protection (Chapter 5). However, further analysis (focusing upon decentralised challenges to acts of the Community institutions, then the caselaw on domestic enforcement of both the state aids rules and Community competition policy) reveals that the Court struggles to pursue a coherent agenda of more tight-knit remedial harmonisation as regards those sectors whose centralised substantive legal framework should still warrant it. This leads to the conclusion that the Court of Justice seems to lack any consistent conception of the Community's interest in interfering with the domestic systems of judicial protection for the sake of the imperative of uniformity: on the one hand, the Court indeed appears sensitive to the limits of an outmoded 'integration through law' analysis; on the other hand, a fully-fledged 'sectoral' interpretation of the current position ultimately proves unconvincing (Chapter 6). It will be suggested (Chapter 7) that this apparent conceptual muddle might well be attributable to the difficult institutional position of the Court vis-à-vis the other Community institutions, the Member States and the domestic judiciaries.

It is time now to examine the 'integration through law' model of the imperative of uniformity, and explore its implications for the academic debate on the appropriate parameters of judicial review by the Court over domestic remedies and procedural rules.

2

'Integration Through Law' and the Enforcement Deficit Debate

THE PREVIOUS CHAPTER offered a brief explanation of why the remedies and procedural rules applied by domestic courts in cases involving Community law are usually perceived as posing a problem for the Treaty order. The familiar argument, dominating almost the entire academic discourse, is that national remedies and procedures threaten the fundamental imperatives of uniformity and effectiveness in the application of Community law. This chapter begins by exploring in greater detail what these imperatives actually mean, then examines the manner in which they have structured our understanding of and responses to the Community's enforcement deficit.

'INTEGRATION THROUGH LAW': UNIFORMITY AND EFFECTIVENESS

At least as they are employed in the context of the enforcement deficit debate, accepted ideas of uniformity and effectiveness are closely tied to a particular conceptual approach to the study of Community law, characterised by its own interpretation of the nature of European union, and consequently by its own understanding of the proper role to be performed by the Treaty legal order. For convenience, this approach shall be referred to as 'integration through law.'[1] Distilled to its simplest level of expression, 'integration through law' refers to an interpretation of the Treaty project which asserts: first, that the basic function of the Community is to promote an 'ever closer union among the peoples of Europe'; and secondly, that the concomitant function of the Community legal order is to advance and consolidate this process of convergence through the creation of a uniform body of binding norms guaranteed to be applied effectively throughout the Member States.

[1] This terminology is *not* intended to refer directly to the major research project by M Cappelletti, M Seccombe & J Weiler (eds), *Integration Through Law: Europe and the American Federal Experience* (Walter de Gruyter, 1985).

This interpretation is often articulated as little more than a rhetorical flourish or self-evident truth. In 1983, for example, Dagtoglou asserted that '[t]he European Community's new legal order simultaneously presupposes and creates unity.'[2] Similarly, Borchardt wrote in 1994 that '[u]nity is the Community's leitmotiv': present-day problems can be mastered only if European countries move forward along the path that leads them to unity; the realisation of such unity is the task of the Treaty legal system.[3] Enunciated at such a high level of abstraction, these definitions beg more questions than they can possibly answer. After all, to say that 'integration through law' advocates an ongoing process of European integration belies the complexity of opinions that such a viewpoint could potentially embrace: integration for what purpose, and to what degree? One could simply desire the creation of a Common Market aimed at improving economic efficiency and increasing prosperity. Or one could go further, calling for the strengthening of a shared social and cultural heritage through the promotion of a common framework of citizens' rights and obligations. One might even look forward to the building of a federal political entity designed to replace the flawed ideology of the nation-state which has brought such ignominy upon European civilisation.

Nevertheless, it is possible to identify with tolerable clarity some more principled motivation for an 'integration through law' approach to EC legal studies. To help illuminate some of the main facets of and tensions within the idea of 'integration through law,' it is accordingly proposed briefly to explore its interpretation of the twin notions of uniformity and effectiveness, and to do so against the background of the historical development and changing emphases of the Community system as a whole.

Uniformity and Effectiveness as Economic Imperatives

Uniformity and effectiveness have traditionally been understood from a primarily economic perspective. The immediate objective of the original Treaty of Rome, and the primary goal of the evolving Community system, was to stimulate economic integration among the Member States. This was to be achieved, in particular, through the creation of a Common Market in which goods, persons and services (later also capital) could move freely across the entire territory of the Community. Thus, for example, Article 25 EC prohibits the Member States from imposing customs duties and other charges having an equivalent effect on imported goods.

[2] P Dagtoglou, 'The Legal Nature of the European Community' in European Commission (ed), *Thirty Years of Community Law* (Office for Official Publications of the European Communities, 1983) pp 40–41.
[3] K-D Borchardt, *The ABC of Community Law* (Office for Official Publications of the European Communities, 1994) pp 12 and 32f.

Similarly, Article 39 EC outlaws discrimination against Community nationals as regards their access to and conditions of employment within the domestic labour markets.[4]

In addition, it was widely believed that the Community should facilitate the gradual realisation of a level playing-field whereby enterprises established in every Member State could operate under equal conditions of competition. On one level, this objective implied the need to control private bodies whose market conduct damages healthy competition within the Community. For example, Article 82 EC forbids undertakings occupying a dominant economic position from perpetrating abusive behaviour, such as arbitrary discrimination between customers or consumers as regards the supply of goods and services.[5] But the creation of any genuine level playing-field was also threatened in a less obvious manner: the simple co-existence of different collections of national rules (say, on product specifications or marketing techniques) means that economic undertakings bear unequal regulatory burdens, depending on no other factor than the Member State within which they happen to be established. So at another level, building a Common Market also implies the need to replace the existing patchwork of domestic rules with a single norm applicable across every country. Equalisation of compliance costs is not the only economic benefit to be gained from realising the uniform legal regulation of the Common Market. There is also a widespread belief that existing differences in national legislation generate higher transaction costs as undertakings have to adjust to diverse legal environments; impede economies of scale which could otherwise have been achieved through the adoption of pan-European business plans; and deter both undertakings and consumers from engaging in cross-border trade through a climate of aggravated business uncertainty and a lack of legal transparency.[6]

Opinions differ, of course, about how best to deliver these objectives. Many commentators believe that the task of attaining regulatory uniformity

[4] Also, eg Art 90 EC on discriminatory internal taxation; Art 28 EC on free movement for goods; Arts 43 and 49 EC on freedom of establishment and free movement of services; Art 133 EC on the Common Commercial Policy. Cf the definition in Art 14 EC (introduced by the Single European Act).

[5] Also, eg Art 81 EC on anti-competitive agreements and practices; Art 34(2) EC on the Common Agricultural Policy; Arts 87 and 88 EC on state aids.

[6] Consider, by way of illustration, the debate over whether it is desirable to construct a more unified European contract law, eg European Parliament, *Resolution on Action to Bring Into Line the Private Law of the Member States*, OJ 1989 C158/400; European Parliament, *Resolution on the Harmonisation of Certain Sectors of the Private Law of the Member States*, OJ 1994 C205/05–22; Commission, *Communication on European Contract Law*, COM (2001)398 Final; Commission, *Action Plan on a More Coherent European Contract Law*, COM (2003)68 Final. Further, eg G Wagner, 'The Economics of Harmonization: The Case of Contract Law' (2002) 39 CML Rev 995; C Bar, 'From Principles to Codification: Prospects for European Private Law' (2002) 8 *Columbia Journal of European Law* 379; M Kenny, 'The 2003 Action Plan on European Contract Law: Is the Commission Running Wild?' (2003) 28 EL Rev 538.

across the Member States should be entrusted to the Community legislature. In this regard, for example, Article 95 EC empowers the Community to adopt measures for the approximation of national rules which have as their object the establishment and functioning of the Internal Market.[7] Such Treaty-level approximation of national law is often stereotyped in terms of a model of 'total harmonisation': the Community exhaustively regulates a given field, thereby pre-empting national competence to take independent action therein.[8] Even if a novel and potentially undesirable development in scientific technology or market behaviour threatens (for example) the interests of consumers or the environment in a manner unforeseen by the Community legislature, regulatory adaptation is in principle to be achieved by the Treaty authorities—not the Member States.[9]

The adoption of pre-emptive harmonising legislation by the central authorities has several perceived advantages: in removing the residual obstacles to genuine free movement across national frontiers which persist under primary Community law via the express derogations provided for by the Treaty and the mandatory/imperative requirements doctrine developed under the Court of Justice's caselaw; and in eliminating the distortions of competitive conditions between economic undertakings operating on the Common Market which result from divergent domestic regulatory standards and consequent differences in compliance costs. For example, Advocate General Tesauro observed in 1991 that

> the 'area without internal frontiers' referred to in Article [14 EC] is to be seen as a truly integrated area where the prevailing conditions are as close as possible to those of a single internal market: an area, therefore, in which there is harmonisation not only of the rules concerning products but also of those which more generally affect the conditions of competition between undertakings. Indeed, [one cannot] see how it is possible to achieve a genuinely single, integrated market without eliminating divergences between national legislation which, by having a differing impact on production costs, prevents the development of competition based on the basis of real equality within the Community.[10]

[7] Subject to the limits laid down, eg in Case C–376/98 *Germany v Parliament and Council* [2000] ECR I–8419. Also, eg Art 37 EC on the Common Agricultural Policy; Art 40 EC on free movement for workers; Arts 44 and 47 EC on freedom of establishment; Arts 52 and 55 EC on free movement for services; Art 93 EC on taxation; Art 94 EC on the Common Market.

[8] The true position is, of course, more complex, eg D Vignes, 'The Harmonisation of National Legislation and the EEC' (1990) 15 EL Rev 358; P J Slot, 'Harmonisation' (1996) 21 EL Rev 378. Further: ch 3 (below).

[9] Eg Case 60/86 *Commission v United Kingdom* [1988] ECR 3921; Cases C–129–130/97 *Chiciak and Fol* [1998] ECR I–3315.

[10] Case C–300/89 *Commission v Council (Titanium Dioxide)* [1991] ECR I–2867, para 10 Opinion.

However, other commentators believe that, rather than embark upon a quest of systematic legislative harmonisation, the Treaty system should instead seek to facilitate regulatory competition between the Member States. The primary Treaty provisions on free movement guarantee the principle of open market access as between the Member States, but otherwise respect the competence of each country to enact its own (potentially divergent) standards of market regulation. In theory, this results in a competition between legal orders: differences in regulatory standards across the EU encourage mobile economic factors to locate in the jurisdiction most favourable to their needs; Member States then compete to attract the maximum share of Community goods, persons, services and capital by adapting existing domestic legislation to meet the expressed/perceived needs of these market actors.[11]

Neo-liberal economic analysis would argue that this model of competition between legal orders is beneficial for the Community, in particular, because it will lead to the regulation of the Single Market with maximum efficiency. Laws are seen as products, supplied by states, in response to the demands of end-users (businesses, workers, consumers). Before, protected by external trade barriers, states were permitted to operate (in effect) as regulatory monopolies, manufacturing inefficient legal products which failed to correspond to the true needs of their end-users. Now, within the Single Market, the principles of free movement guarantee that the regulatory choices made by each Member State remain mutually exposed to the discipline of market forces. Businesses, workers and consumers are free to reject poorly designed legislation by exercising their Treaty rights to move from the inefficient Member State, and to settle instead within a jurisdiction whose regulatory products better correspond to their needs. The threat of mobile factors leaving the national territory, and the converse promise of economic actors relocating within the domestic territory, creates a powerful incentive for all Member States to manufacture more efficient legal products.[12]

Ultimately, such competition between legal orders will encourage the Member States to converge around a legislative regime which regulates the Common Market in optimal fashion. This should happen without the need for Community-level positive harmonisation—which not only artificially distorts the conditions of competition, but also acts as a straightjacket on regulatory innovation and adaptation.[13] Instead, the proper

[11] Eg N Reich, 'Competition Between Legal Orders: A New Paradigm of EC Law?' (1992) 29 CML Rev 861.

[12] Similarly with mobile service provision: providers penetrating the territory to offer/consumers looking beyond the territory to receive cheaper services puts pressure on the Member State to reduce compliance costs for domestic undertakings.

[13] Further, eg J Smits, 'A European Private Law as a Mixed Legal System: Towards a Ius Commune through the Free Movement of Legal Rules' (1998) 5 *Maastricht Journal of European*

role of the Community authorities should be limited to enforcing the basic principles of free movement upon which the operation of regulatory competition depends: for example, by prosecuting Member State practices which discriminate against foreign businesses; and insisting upon the fully mutual recognition of regulatory standards as the gateway to unhindered cross-border market access.[14]

Despite these differences in opinion about how to strike a proper balance between the free operation of economic forces and the exercise of legislative competence, the end-goal remains the same: realising a (formally or at least functionally) common regulatory framework for the Common Market. In any case, it was recognised from an early stage that for economic integration to succeed, the relevant Treaty rules and Community legislation had to be formulated and applied both effectively within each Member State (so as to prevent the principles of free movement from being reduced in practice to mere paper guarantees), and uniformly as between the various Member States (so as to minimise the persistence of unfair competitive advantages in the European marketplace). It is upon such considerations, for example, that the Court of Justice has consistently justified the doctrines of the direct effect and supremacy of Community law: without the possibility of decentralised enforcement, Member States and private parties could undermine the Single Market project by unilaterally maintaining or introducing rules or practices contrary to the Treaty.[15]

Conversely, it is also upon such considerations that many commentators continue to criticise certain aspects of the Court's own jurisprudence. Consider the rule that if a Member State fails correctly to implement a Community directive into national law within the prescribed time-limit, that directive is in principle capable of imposing obligations upon public authorities or other emanations of the state but not upon purely private parties.[16] The practical effect of this rule is to undermine both the effective attainment within the defaulting Member State of the Treaty

and Comparative Law 328. Cf the classical analysis of Charles Tiebout, 'A Pure Theory of Local Expenditures' (1956) 64 *Journal of Political Economy* 416.

[14] Note the variant analysis known as 'competitive federalism,' which acknowledges the need for positive Community intervention to correct market failures (such as negative externalities) and replicate the end-solution that would have been reached by the undistorted interplay of economic forces. Further, eg R Van den Bergh, 'The Subsidiarity Principle in European Community Law: Some Insights From Law and Economics' (1994) 1 *Maastricht Journal of European and Comparative Law* 337; and 'Subsidiarity as an Economic Demarcation Principle and the Emergence of European Private Law' (1998) 5 *Maastricht Journal of European and Comparative Law* 129. Also: D Esty & D Geradin (eds), *Regulatory Competition and Economic Integration: Comparative Perspectives* (OUP, 2001).

[15] Further, eg R Kovar, 'The Relationship Between Community Law and National Law' in European Commission (ed), *Thirty Years of Community Law* (Office for Official Publications of the European Communities, 1983).

[16] Eg Case 41/74 *van Duyn* [1974] ECR 1337; Case 148/78 *Ratti* [1979] ECR 1629; Case 8/81 *Becker* [1982] ECR 53; Case 152/84 *Marshall* [1986] ECR 723; Case C–91/92 *Faccini Dori* [1994] ECR I–3325.

objectives embodied in the relevant directive, and the uniform application of the Community rules in question as between the Member States so as to preserve equal competitive conditions for economic undertakings.[17] Similarly, there is controversy over the nature and limits of the doctrine of supremacy: while the Court of Justice insists that this is an unconditional obligation, the domestic courts of several Member States purport to exercise a continuing supervisory jurisdiction over the legality and thus the binding nature of Community rules as within the national legal orders, judged against what are essentially domestic constitutional principles.[18] Again, it is feared that the Treaty's free trade objectives will be undermined within, and conditions of competition distorted as between, the Member States, if secondary Community legislation is applied by some national courts but rejected at the unilateral discretion of others.[19]

Horizontal Expansion of Community Power, and the Introduction of Union Citizenship

However, the imperatives of uniformity and effectiveness in the formulation and application of Community law need no longer be justified by reference to economic considerations alone. The latter have been supplemented and in some respects surpassed by what might be termed a 'rights-based' or rather a 'social welfare' perspective.

The inauguration by the Court of Justice of the doctrines of direct effect and supremacy marked an important shift in the emphasis of European integration. The Community legal system was no longer concerned solely with the obligations of Member States entered into under public international law pursuant to the conclusion of a traditional treaty-contract and

[17] Eg AG Jacobs in Case C–316/93 *Vaneetveld* [1994] ECR I–763; AG Lenz in Case C–91/92 *Faccini Dori* [1994] ECR I–3325. Further, eg G de Búrca, 'Giving Effect to European Community Directives' (1992) 55 MLR 215; T Tridimas, 'Horizontal Effect of Directives: A Missed Opportunity?' (1994) 19 EL Rev 621; J Coppel, 'Rights, Duties and the End of *Marshall*' (1994) 57 MLR 859. Cf I Sebba, 'The Doctrine of Direct Effect: A Malignant Disease of Community Law' [1995] *Legal Issues of Economic Integration* 35; H Schermers, 'No Direct Effect for Directives' (1997) 3 *European Public Law* 527.

[18] In Germany, eg Judgment of the Federal Constitutional Court in *Brunner* [1994] 1 CMLR 57. More recently: the 'Bananas Regulation' cases discussed by U Everling, 'Will Europe Slip on Bananas? The Bananas Judgment of the Court of Justice and National Courts' (1996) 33 CML Rev 401; C Schmid, 'All Bark and No Bite: Notes on the Federal Constitutional Court's Bananas Decision' (2001) 7 *European Law Journal* 95. In the United Kingdom, eg *Ex p Factortame* [1990] 3 WLR 818; *Ex p Equal Opportunities Commission* [1995] 1 AC 1; Lord Denning in *Macarthys Ltd v Smith* [1979] 3 All ER 325. More recently: *Thoburn v Sunderland City Council* [2002] 4 All ER 156; *Gouriet v Secretary of State for Foreign and Commonwealth Affairs* (Court of Appeal Judgment of 5 March 2003).

[19] Eg M Herdegen, 'Maastricht and the German Constitutional Court: Constitutional Restraints for an "Ever Closer Union"' (1994) 31 CML Rev 235; N Reich, 'Judge-Made "Europe à la carte": Some Remarks on Recent Conflicts between European and German Constitutional Law Provoked by the Banana Litigation' (1996) 7 *European Journal of International Law* 103.

enforceable before the Court of Justice. Rather, the Community was capable of bestowing rights directly upon individual citizens and undertakings, enforceable through the domestic courts against the Community institutions, the domestic authorities and each other.[20] By this means, the vast potential resources of the general European population were enlisted to supplement the Commission in its efforts to secure the uniform and effective application of Community law. But the inevitable by-product of this innovation was the growth of an ethos of 'individual rights' within the Treaty order: empowering the citizen to act implied a reciprocal obligation to safeguard and promote the rights thereby created.

This commitment added weight to the imperative of securing the uniformity and effectiveness of Community law within the domestic legal orders, and did so independently of the purely economic objectives of the Common Market. Now, failure to secure the full application of Community rules on unhindered cross-border trade in goods or on non-discrimination against foreign citizens seeking employment could be described not only as a threat to economic integration, but also as an infringement of the individual's concrete legal entitlements within the defaulting Member State, and an affront to the principle of equality before the law as regards every intended beneficiary of Treaty norms across the entire Community territory.[21]

As the Treaty system developed, this rights-based emphasis on the uniformity and effectiveness of Community law has strengthened. The impetus behind this development derives from two major characteristics of the modern Treaty order: first, the horizontal expansion of the Community's competences so as to embrace not only economic issues which impinge directly upon the operation of the Single Market, but also important aspects of social welfare policy; and secondly, the current legal reality and future political potential of citizenship of the European Union.

Horizontal Expansion of Community Competences

Within the scheme of the original Treaty of Rome, dominated by the demands of the Common Market, social actors were seen as the ultimate but indirect beneficiaries of the Community's primarily economic achievements. A free market and increased competition would stimulate prosperity, in turn raising the standard of products and services offered to the public, the levels of wages paid to workers etc.[22] But such blind faith

[20] Cf Opinion 1/91 *(Draft Agreement Relating to the Creation of the European Economic Area)* [1991] ECR I–6079, para 21.

[21] For criticism of the Court's rights-based discourse, eg G de Búrca, 'The Language of Rights and European Integration' in J Shaw & G More (eds), *New Legal Dynamics of European Union* (Clarendon Press, 1995).

[22] There were limited Treaty references to more welfare-orientated concerns, eg Art 141 EC on equal pay for men and women.

in the philanthropic benefits of the liberal capitalist model soon passed as the Community looked beyond the narrow objective of securing market integration to embrace new policy competences in fields such as environmental protection, consumer rights, social policy, education and vocational training, culture and public health. It would seem appropriate briefly to recall some of the factors behind this change.[23]

First, the development of new Community policies was, in part, a necessary incident of the ongoing process of economic integration itself. On the one hand, overturning national laws and practices which pursued purely protectionist goals was relatively uncontroversial: customs duties and import quotas are inherently antagonistic to the functioning of the Common Market. But on the other hand, the wholesale demolition of domestic regimes which promoted certain essential social values (such as environmental or consumer protection) was unacceptable and undesirable, even though their continuing diversity impaired the attainment of true free movement or competitive equality. Thus, in interpreting directly effective Treaty provisions on goods, persons and services, the Court of Justice could not assess the validity of such domestic rules without forming some idea of what sort of interests they could legitimately advance, and of the appropriate balance to be struck with the objective of free trade.[24] Similarly, when adopting harmonisation measures intended to replace divergent national rules on product specifications and marketing practices, the Community legislature was required to decide not merely to approximate but to do so at a particular pitch, taking account of the competing societal concerns which had prompted the original domestic action now being pre-empted.[25] Thus, although the primary purpose of both strategies was economic, the judicial and legislative quest to build a Common Market additionally and inevitably implied the articulation of a Community-wide approach to welfare regulation in the areas affected.

Secondly, the willing elaboration of welfare-inspired 'flanking policies' reflected growing concerns that the Community was indeed too economic in its orientation and appeal. The creation of 'Europe with a Human Face' became a genuine political ambition in the early 1970s, encouraged

[23] There are many sectoral accounts of the development of the Community's social competences. On environmental policy, eg A Ziegler, *Trade and Environmental Law in the European Community* (Clarendon Press, 1996); L Krämer, *EC Environmental Law* (Sweet & Maxwell, 2000); J Jans, *European Environmental Law* (Europa Law Publishing, 2000). On consumer policy, eg S Weatherill, *EC Consumer Law and Policy* (Longman, 1997); G Howells and T Wilhelmsson, *EC Consumer Law* (Dartmouth, 1997). On social policy, eg R Nielsen and E Szyszczak, *The Social Dimension of the European Union* (Handelshøjskolens Forlag, 1997); C Barnard, *EC Employment Law* (OUP, 2000).

[24] Eg in the context of free movement for goods: under the express Treaty derogations provided for under Art 30 EC; or the mandatory requirements developed under Case 120/78 '*Cassis de Dijon*' [1979] ECR 649.

[25] Eg adopted under Art 94 EC or (after the Single European Act) Art 95 EC.

by the belief that a broader conception of the Community's social mandate would provide an essential legitimising force for the evolving but still relatively aloof Treaty system. For example, the Heads of Government of the Member States meeting in Paris in 1972 declared that

> [e]conomic expansion, which is not an end in itself, must as a priority help to attenuate the disparities in living conditions … It must emerge in an improved quality as well as an improved standard of life. In the European spirit special attention will be paid to non-material values and wealth and to protection of the environment so that progress shall serve mankind.[26]

This concern bore fruit in a series of action programmes designed to structure the Community's first forays into fairly unchartered waters such as environmental, consumer and employee protection.[27] In similar spirit, the 1985 report on the promotion of 'A People's Europe,' commissioned and approved by the European Council, stressed the need for action which would be 'of direct relevance to Community citizens and which will visibly offer them tangible benefits in their everyday lives'; such action was recognised as being 'of great importance in making the Community more credible in the eyes of its citizens.'[28]

Thirdly, it should be recalled that the underlying rationale of the entire Treaty project (sometimes known as the 'Monnet method') was indeed to use economic integration as the springboard for closer European cooperation across a broader range of policy concerns. Learning from the failure of the ambitious but premature plan to create a European Defence and Political Community in 1954, the founding fathers believed that the dream of unifying Europe would more realistically be attained through manageable gradations and concrete practical results, rather than by any immediate and definitive political settlement. The manifestation of Community action beyond the realm of the Common Market, so as to touch upon an array of welfare issues not obviously contemplated by the original Treaty of Rome, thus presented a catalyst not only for greater public legitimacy, but also for increased supranational integration.

Initially, both the 'flanking policies' and the potential for social change/closer integration which they presented were constrained by the lack of any independent legal bases within the Treaty. Welfare action was possible only through provisions such as Articles 94 and (after the

[26] Declaration by the Heads of Government of the Member States meeting at Paris on 19–20 October 1972 (The First Summit Conference of the Enlarged Community) EC Bull 10–1972.
[27] Declaration of the Council of the European Communities and of the Representatives of the Governments of the Member States, *Programme of Action of the European Communities on the Environment*, OJ 1973 C112/1; Council, *Resolution Concerning a Social Action Programme*, OJ 1974 C13/1; Council, *Resolution on a Preliminary Programme of the European Economic Community for a Consumer Protection and Information* Policy, OJ 1975 C92/1.
[28] Reports from the ad hoc Committee on 'A People's Europe' EC Bull Supp 7/85.

Single European Act) 95 EC; its form was therefore closely related to the requirements of economic integration which justified the exercise of legislative power under these Treaty competences. Nevertheless, subsequent changes heralded the Community's ability to pursue a variety of social imperatives independently of their Single Market surrogate. In particular, successive Treaty revisions provided explicit bases for Community policies: for example, on the environment (Single European Act),[29] consumer rights (Treaty on European Union),[30] and employee protection (Treaties on European Union and of Amsterdam).[31] Henceforth, such initiatives could be pursued not only through the old Internal Market harmonisation articles, but also through their own legal bases and according to their own framework of principles and institutional procedures. Moreover, the Community institutions are now expressly instructed to integrate environmental, consumer and human health concerns into the pursuit of every Treaty policy;[32] and to base approximation of law proposals under Article 95 EC on high levels of health and safety, environmental and consumer protection.[33]

These developments were encouraged and consolidated by the Court of Justice. First, it offered judicial support for the initiatives being pursued by the political and legislative institutions even before any formal Treaty amendments were effected. For example, in its judgment in *ADBHU*, the Court held that environmental protection was one of the Community's 'essential objectives,' and therefore legitimate subject-matter for secondary legislation. This validation of expanding Community activities pre-dated by several years the formal introduction into the Treaty of an environmental policy title.[34] Secondly, the Court's caselaw on the correct legal basis of Community legislation has contributed to a more evenhanded relationship between the Treaty's Internal Market and broader social policy competences. In particular, the *Waste Directive* judgment held that, where the primary purpose of a Community measure is to advance

[29] Arts 174–76 EC.
[30] Art 153 EC.
[31] Arts 136–45 EC.
[32] Arts 6, 153(2) and 152(1) EC (respectively). These provisions are more hortatory than legally binding, eg Case C–192/94 *El Corte Inglés* [1996] ECR I–1281; Case C–233/94 *Germany v Parliament and Council (Deposit-Guarantee Schemes Directive)* [1997] ECR I–2405; Case C–284/95 *Safety Hi-Tech* [1998] ECR I–4301; Case C–341/95 *Bettati* [1998] ECR I–4355. However, they may still provide the legal basis for significant changes in Community policy, eg Case C–379/98 *PreussenElektra* [2001] ECR I–2099.
[33] Art 95(3) EC.
[34] Case 240/83 *ADBHU* [1985] ECR 531. See also the caselaw on mandatory requirements under Art 28 EC, whereby the ECJ recognises a range of social interests as being compatible with the Treaty and therefore permitted in principle to restrict free movement, eg consumer protection in judgments such as Case 178/84 *Commission v Germany* [1987] ECR 1227; environmental protection in judgments such as Case 302/86 *Commission v Denmark* [1988] ECR 4607.

environmental protection, the fact that it also has an incidental or ancillary effect on the establishment or functioning of the Internal Market does not prevent it from being passed under Article 175 rather than Article 95 EC.[35] The same approach has been extended to action undertaken via the consumer and social policy titles.[36] Its effect is to confirm that the formal Treaty amendments mentioned above do not merely consolidate but actually expand the Community's sphere of interest, entailing a definite shift in our appreciation of fields such as environmental protection from the relative immaturity of 'flanking policies' to the stature of autonomous heads of action.[37]

As a result, it is clear that the Community no longer dances to the tune of the Internal Market alone. Instead, and as even a cursory glance through Articles 2 and 3 EC will confirm, the Treaty sanctions the simultaneous pursuit of a range of policies, the demands of which may well conflict with the traditional economic motif of open markets and equal competition.[38] Indeed, the trend discerned by many commentators has been towards the gradual adoption by the Community of a range of responsibilities for the provision of social welfare more usually associated with the Member (nation-)States.[39] By expanding the Community's activities to cover diverse aspects of daily life, the architects of European integration have certainly encouraged changing perceptions of the Treaty project. Far from being a shallow front for unfettered free-market capitalism, the

[35] Case C–155/91 *Commission v Council (Waste Directive)* [1993] ECR I–939; affirmed in Case C–187/93 *Parliament v Council (Waste Regulation)* [1994] ECR I–2857. Cf the additional guidance in Case C–268/94 *Portugal v Council (Cooperation Agreement between the European Community and the Republic of India)* [1996] ECR I–6177. Contrast with the previous position under Case C–300/89 *Commission v Council (Titanium Dioxide)* [1991] ECR I–2867.

[36] Case C–233/94 *Germany v Parliament and Council (Deposit-Guarantee Schemes Directive)* [1997] ECR I–2405; Case C–84/94 *UK v Council (Working Time Directive)* [1996] ECR I–5755.

[37] Further: D Chalmers, 'The Single Market: From Prima Donna to Journeyman' in J Shaw & G More (eds), *New Legal Dynamics of European Union* (Clarendon Press, 1995); A Dashwood, 'The Working Time Judgment in a Wider Perspective' in *The ECJ's Working Time Judgment: The Social Market Vindicated*, Centre for European Legal Studies Occasional Paper No 2 (CUP, 1997).

[38] The mutual co-existence of objectives which now characterises the Community's activities was stressed by the ECJ in Case C–233/94 *Germany v Parliament and Council (Deposit-Guarantee Schemes Directive)* [1997] ECR I–2405, para 48. Cf discussion of the relationship between competition policy and employee protection in judgments such as Case C–67/96 *Albany International* [1999] ECR I–5751; Cases C–115–17/97 *Brentjens' Handelsonderneming* [1999] ECR I–6025. Cf also the ECJ's willingness to accommodate environmental protection concerns into the legal framework of free movement for goods, eg Case C–2/90 *Commission v Belgium (Wallonian Waste)* [1992] ECR I–4431; Case C–379/98 *PreussenElektra* [2001] ECR I–2099.

[39] Eg W Wessels, 'An Ever Closer Fusion? A Dynamic Macropolitical View on Integration Processes' (1997) 35 JCMS 267; and 'The Growth and Differentiation of Multi-Level Networks: A Corporatist Mega-Bureaucracy or an Open City?' in H Wallace & A Young (eds), *Participation and Policy-Making in the European Union* (Clarendon Press, 1997). Further: J Caporaso, 'The European Union and Forms of State: Westphalian, Regulatory or Post-Modern?' (1996) 34 JCMS 29; R Dehousse, 'European Institutional Architecture After Amsterdam: Parliamentary System or Regulatory Structure?' (1998) 35 CML Rev 595; M Pollack, 'The End of Creeping Competence? EU Policy-Making Since Maastricht' (2000) 38 JCMS 519.

Community has become the focus of an increasing sense of expectation of social and political change in Europe.[40]

Creation of Union Citizenship

This trend took a new step forward with the creation of 'citizenship of the Union' at Maastricht.[41] On the one hand, the legal content of Union citizenship is relatively clear and, in certain respects, unambitious. Construed narrowly, it consists of the modest catalogue of rights set out in Part Two EC: for example, to vote and stand in European and local elections; to diplomatic protection from any Member State when in third countries; to petition the Parliament, apply to the Ombudsman and write to the Community institutions.[42] Of greater potential significance is the right set out in Article 18 EC to move and reside within the Member States, which has created a free-standing principle of free movement for citizens, without the need to prove any viable economic status *qua* worker or self-employed person.[43] Construed more broadly, the concept of citizenship is shaped by provisions well beyond the confines of Part Two EC. It embraces the Treaty's welfare-orientated competences in fields such as environmental, consumer, health and social policy (as outlined above); a clearly stated commitment to respect fundamental human rights, including the ability of citizens to challenge Community and certain domestic actions on this basis;[44] the power under Article 13 EC to enact measures designed to combat a range of debilitating social prejudices;[45] and the 'transparency' provisions which seek to expose Community decision-making processes to broader public scrutiny.[46]

[40] Cf the results of a Community-wide survey of public opinion conducted before the 1999 European Parliament elections: 'L'autre Europe que veulent les Européens' *Le Monde* (Paris, France 1 June 1999).

[41] Arts 17–22 EC. Further, eg C Closa, 'The Concept of Citizenship in the Treaty on European Union' (1992) 29 CML Rev 1137; S O'Leary, *The Evolving Concept of Community Citizenship: From the Free Movement of Persons to Union Citizenship* (Kluwer, 1996).

[42] Arts 19–21 EC.

[43] In particular: Case C–413/99 *Baumbast* [2002] ECR I–7091. Further: M Dougan and E Spaventa, 'Educating Rudy and the (Non-)English Patient: A Double Bill on Residency Rights Under Article 18 EC' (2003) 28 EL Rev 699. See now: Dir 2004/38 on the right of citizens of the Union and their family members to move and reside freely within the territory of the Member States, OJ 2004 L158/77.

[44] Arts 6, 7 and 46 TEU. Also, eg Case 11/70 *Internationale Handelsgesellschaft* [1970] ECR 1125; Case 4/73 *Nold* [1974] ECR 491; Case 222/84 *Johnston v Chief Constable of the RUC* [1986] ECR 1651; Case C–260/89 *ERT* [1991] ECR I–2925. And now: Charter of Fundamental Rights of the European Union, OJ 2000 C364/01.

[45] Eg Dir 2000/78 establishing a general framework for equal treatment in employment and occupation, OJ 2000 L303/16.

[46] Art 255 EC (introduced by the Treaty of Amsterdam). See, eg Reg 1049/2001 regarding public access to European Parliament, Council and Commission Documents, OJ 2001 L145/43. Cf the contribution of the Community courts, eg in Case T–14/98 *Hautala* [1999] ECR II-2489; Case C–353/99P *Hautala* [2001] ECR I–9565.

On the other hand, the present (though admittedly expanding) legal reality of citizenship remains vastly overshadowed by its nascent political potential. Cynics portray the very idea of Union citizenship as a largely cosmetic device, designed to increase the Community's appearance of democratic respectability, but lacking in any real substance. More adventurous minds recognise in Union citizenship an opportunity to revitalise the important yet long-neglected issue of accountability.[47] At its grandest, citizenship could act as the fulcrum for an evolving supranational demos, capable of legitimating the Community's exercise of massive public power, and of doing so independently of the parochial constituencies currently supplied by the nation-states.[48] At the very least, citizenship forms an additional bond between governors and governed in the complex European system of multi-level administration, fostering a greater awareness of the Treaty institutions and their activities, a greater appreciation of the value of European integration, and thereby an improved level of democratic participation in the process of Union governance.[49]

The promulgation at the Nice summit in December 2000 of the Charter of Fundamental Rights of the European Union supplies a comprehensive statement of the social rights and aspirations respected and pursued by the Community institutions, providing a convenient panorama from which to survey several decades of incremental achievement in the adoption of secondary legislation and Treaty revision (not to say judicial innovation) which offer something to a constituency other than big business.[50] Coupled with the direct channel between individual and Community embodied in the creation of Union citizenship, this could pick up where the 'Monnet method' of integration left off—opening up new possibilities for convergence and consolidating the Community's long-term role as guardian of important aspects of social well-being and basic welfare for ordinary Europeans.[51]

[47] Further, eg M Everson, 'The Legacy of the Market Citizen' in J Shaw & G More (eds), *New Legal Dynamics of European Union* (Clarendon Press, 1995); A Wiener and V Della Sala, 'Constitution-Making and Citizenship Practice: Bridging the Democracy Gap in the EU?' (1997) 35 JCMS 595; J Shaw, 'The Many Pasts and Futures of Citizenship in the European Union' (1997) 22 EL Rev 554; and 'The Interpretation of European Union Citizenship' (1998) 61 MLR 293.

[48] Though note the Amsterdam amendment to Art 17 EC: Union citizenship exists alongside and will not replace national citizenship.

[49] Further, eg J Weiler, 'Does Europe Need a Constitution? Reflections on Demos, Telos and the German Maastricht Decision' (1995) 1 *European Law Journal* 219; G Mancini, 'Europe: The Case for Statehood' (1998) 4 *European Law Journal* 29; J Weiler, 'Europe: The Case Against the Case for Statehood' (1998) 4 *European Law Journal* 43; I Ward, 'Amsterdam and the Continuing Search for Community' in D O'Keeffe & P Twomey (eds), *Legal Issues of the Amsterdam Treaty* (Hart Publishing, 1999); H Lindahl, 'European Integration: Popular Sovereignty and a Politics of Boundaries' (2000) 6 *European Law Journal* 239; N Prentoulis, 'On the Technology of Collective Identity: Normative Reconstructions of the Concept of EU Citizenship' (2001) 7 *European Law Journal* 196.

[50] Charter of Fundamental Rights of the European Union, OJ 2000 C364/1.

[51] Cf AG Jacobs in Case C–274/96 *Bickel and Franz* [1998] ECR I–7637: the introduction of citizenship 'was largely inspired by the concern to bring the Union closer to its citizens and to give expression to its character as more than a purely economic union' (para 23 Opinion).

Uniformity and Effectiveness as Social Imperatives

The Community's process of horizontal expansion, crowned by the inauguration of Union citizenship, has important implications for the basis and nature of the imperatives of uniformity and effectiveness in the formulation and application of Treaty norms.

On the one hand, the further the Community pursues social policies such as environmental and consumer protection which are increasingly removed from the traditional dynamics of the Internal Market, the more difficult it becomes to argue the case for a uniform and effective supranational legal order solely by reference to the essentially economic logic of free movement and undistorted competition. On the other hand, the growth of such welfare-orientated policy sectors, combined with the consolidation of a firmly rights-based approach to Community law, ultimately provides an alternative or at least additional justification, whereby uniformity and effectiveness in the application of Treaty rules are understood as essential components as much of a 'citizen's Europe' as of a 'free trade Europe.' It is perhaps worth exploring these tensions in greater detail.

Towards an Autonomous Social Policy Agenda

Consider first the imperative of effectiveness. In the past, securing the effective application of Community law was seen as a necessary precondition for the economic success of the Common Market. Now, the Community's metamorphosis from guarantor of free movement and fair competition to promoter of individual rights and collective social well-being means that the effectiveness of Community law can also be justified as an essential component in realising the broadening welfare objectives set out under the Treaty, and inherent in the consolidation of a politically credible form of Union citizenship. This is true in respect of measures adopted under legal bases such as Articles 94 and 95 EC, where the Treaty's primary objective is the completion of the Single Market, but Community action must incorporate high standards of protection for vulnerable social interests. It is true even more of legislation based on Articles 137, 153 or 175 EC, which sanction the Community's pursuit of autonomous policies on the welfare of workers, consumers and the environment. Conversely, the failure of the Treaty system to secure adequate mechanisms for the effective observance of its own norms may now be measured in terms of its impact on the protection of individual rights. Thus, for example, the lack of horizontal direct effect for non- or incorrectly implemented directives might be seen not only to undermine the full force of market integration as provided for under the original Treaty of Rome, but also unfairly to deprive Union citizens of an effective legal framework for the enjoyment of the social benefits specifically envisaged for them by the Community legislature.[52]

Consider next and in greater detail the imperative of uniformity. It was observed above that, for many commentators, the regulatory ideal of the Common Market consists in the creation of a level playing-field on which all economic actors can operate under equal competitive conditions, and do so freely across the entire Community territory. It was also remarked that this goal implies the approximation of divergent national regimes so as to conform as closely as possible to a single uniform standard. For some, this is a job best left to the operation of market forces themselves, whereby the process of free movement identifies the most efficient regulatory regime for the Common Market and encourages all the Member States to emulate it. For others, responsibility for guaranteeing uniform market regulation lies with the Community institutions, acting also to pre-empt the Member States from maintaining or introducing new domestic provisions that might thenceforth distort the Treaty paradigm. In short: a model of 'total harmonisation'; justified by the impulse towards economic integration.

However, the steady horizontal expansion of Community powers, so as to cover not only a wider range of economic matters but also a panoply of social welfare responsibilities, means that the process of harmonisation now performs very different functions than it did traditionally. This is true to a certain extent of both the judicial (negative) harmonisation achieved through the Court of Justice's interpretation of directly effective Treaty provisions such as Article 28 EC on free movement for goods and Article 49 EC on free movement for services, and the legislative (positive) harmonisation pursued by the Community under Internal Market legal bases such as Articles 94 and 95 EC. In each case, the responsible Treaty institutions must seek, not merely to reduce those regulatory/competitive disparities which persist between the legal orders of the Member States, but also to elaborate a Community conception of what consumer or environmental protection means, and how far it should restrain the full manufacturing and marketing capabilities of the entrepreneurial class. The point is doubly true in respect of measures adopted under the new welfare-orientated Treaty legal bases such as Articles 153, 175 and 137 EC. In these situations, harmonisation more clearly promotes common values about the quality of life Europeans are entitled to enjoy—values which merely interface with rather than serve the economic demands of the Single Market.[53]

[52] Further, eg A Ward, *Judicial Review and the Rights of Private Parties in EC Law* (OUP, 2000) ch 5.

[53] Cf the related issues analysed by R Dehousse, *Integration v Regulation? Social Regulation in the European Community*, European University Institute Working Paper LAW No 92/23 (EUI, 1992).

'Integration through law' in fact offers three possible reactions to this phenomenon. First, one might continue to postulate a primarily economic justification for the objective of uniformity in the formulation and application of Community law. After all, it is perfectly arguable that once the Community has legislated in defence of the relevant social interests now falling under its protection (whether through Internal Market provisions such as Articles 94 or 95, or pursuant to the autonomous welfare policy legal bases), diverse domestic rules should still be dismantled, residual national competence pre-empted, and a level playing-field installed. This level playing-field may not necessarily be pitched at a standard conducive to optimal economic efficiency. And the increased scope of Community harmonising activities would surely add insult to injury against the values of certain regulatory competition theorists. But there is no reason, in principle, why a 'social Community' cannot be a 'uniform Community' and thus designed to accommodate important welfare interests within a regulatory framework which supports a continuing commitment to free movement and equal competitive conditions. In short: a model of 'total harmonisation'; still justified by the impulse towards economic integration; but sensitive to the Community's need to incorporate into the substance of this uniform regulatory framework an adequate standard of protection for vulnerable societal interests.

Secondly, one might offer an economic justification for the ideal of uniformity in Community law which embraces rather than merely suffers the Union's growing responsibilities in the welfare sphere. Social rights (particularly those concerned with labour protection) can be seen as a positive input into the economic process: for example, by giving real substance to the otherwise often formal freedom to engage in gainful employment (as in the case of anti-discrimination rules); or by linking increased levels of efficiency and productivity to the quality of the working environment enjoyed by the individual (as in the case of health and safety requirements, or the right to fair treatment by employers).[54] Echoes of this theory can be found in the European Council's 'Lisbon strategy' advocating an active and dynamic programme of social protection which encourages and rewards participation in the employment market, and thus forms an integral means of promoting the competitiveness of the European economy.[55] On the one hand, this viewpoint might imply

[54] Eg Brian Bercusson *et al*, 'A Manifesto for Social Europe' (1997) 3 *European Law Journal* 189. Also: S Deakin and J Browne, 'Social Rights and Market Order: Adapting the Capability Approach' in T Hervey & J Kenner (eds), *Economic and Social Rights Under the EU Charter of Fundamental Rights* (Hart Publishing, 2003).

[55] Eg Presidency Conclusions of the Lisbon European Council (23–24 March 2000); and of the Nice European Council (7–9 December 2000). Also: Commission, *A Concerted Strategy for Modernising Social Protection*, COM (1999)347 Final; Commission, *Social Policy Agenda*, COM (2000)379 Final.

the creation, through Community legislative intervention, of a level playing-field which guarantees high standards of social rights but is perfectly conducive to enhancing economic efficiency. On the other hand, regulatory competition theorists might argue that, if social rights are such a positive input into the market process, the free play of economic forces should encourage Member States to converge around high standards of employment protection anyway—making legislative intervention by the central authorities unnecessary.[56] But in any case, our emergent 'social Community' can indeed be reconciled to the functioning of our traditional 'economic Community'—offering a double justification for the construction of a 'uniform Community.'

Thirdly, one might argue that it is time to bypass these economic arguments, which stubbornly refuse to conceive of uniformity in any terms other than as a mere precondition to the success of the Common Market. An alternative approach would be to construct an independent conceptual justification for uniformity which stresses its vital role in advancing the social and political integration of the European Union. In particular (and this is true as regards not only labour rights; but also policies such as environmental, consumer and public health protection), one may advocate high standards of welfare provision, not merely as contributory factors favouring economic efficiency, but also as autonomous values which must be safeguarded and promoted within the process of European integration.[57]

Equality as a General Principle of Community Law

Such a perspective draws support, in particular, from the principle of equality between citizens and other social actors within the Community legal order. The notion of equal treatment is enshrined in several different guises in the Treaty, and its character has indeed been transformed by the Community's gradual process of horizontal expansion, away from a purely economic conception of non-discrimination based on the desire to eliminate distortions of competition within the Common Market, and towards a greater appreciation of the independent role performed by the principle of equal treatment in the sphere of social welfare.

In particular, the principle of non-discrimination on grounds of nationality played an important role in the establishment and functioning of the Common Market, for example, in the field of free movement for goods.[58]

[56] Cf B Ryan, 'Pay, Trade Union Rights and European Community Law' (1997) 13 *International Journal of Comparative Labour Law and Industrial Relations* 305.

[57] Particularly having regard to the influence of the Charter of Fundamental Rights: see above. On the treatment of social rights by the Court of Justice, consider eg K Lenaerts and P Foubert, 'Social Rights in the Caselaw of the European Court of Justice' (2001) 28 *Legal Issues of Economic Intergration* 267.

[58] Eg Arts 25, 30 and 90 EC.

However, the double life of the principle of equal treatment—as both instrumental agent for achieving economic integration, and important element of fundamental individual rights—soon became evident within the provisions on free movement of persons. Thus, Article 39 EC creates the right not only to enter and work in another Member State, but to do so free from any discrimination on grounds of nationality as regards access to or conditions of employment.[59] Secondary legislation has extended the principle of equal treatment also to cover certain social and tax benefits.[60] These provisions were intended to remove barriers to economic integration by creating incentives for workers to move freely across the labour markets of the various Member States. But they also tend inherently to promote the welfare of the individual by enhancing his or her quality of life, as employee and as citizen, within the host Member State.[61] Moreover, the expansive interpretation of the principle of non-discrimination adopted by the Court of Justice now permits the migrant worker to enjoy equality of treatment in matters (ranging from discount train passes to discretionary childbirth loans and grants covering funeral expenses) which are more closely related to the social thrust of European integration than to the needs of free movement within the Common Market.[62]

Similarly, Article 141 EC sets out the principle of equal treatment between men and women in matters of pay.[63] Secondary legislation has made parallel provision as regards access to and conditions of employment, and for those who are self-employed.[64] Such measures seek to create a level playing-field between Community undertakings as regards the regulatory burdens imposed by anti-discrimination legislation. However, in *Defrenne v Sabena*, the Court of Justice observed that the principle of equality was also intended to promote improved working conditions for,

[59] Similar principles apply as regards freedom of establishment and free movement for services: Arts 43 and 50 EC (respectively).

[60] Art 7(2) Reg 1612/68 on freedom of movement for workers within the Community, OJ 1968 L257/2. In the context of establishment and services, the ECJ has held that an equivalent right to equal treatment in social and tax advantages derives directly from the Treaty itself, particularly when read together with Art 12 EC.

[61] Eg AG Jacobs in Cases C–92 & 326/92 *Phil Collins* [1993] ECR I–5145, 5162–3.

[62] Eg Case 32/75 *Fiorini* [1975] ECR 1085; Case 65/81 *Reina* [1982] ECR I–33; Case C–237/94 *O'Flynn* [1996] ECR I–2617. Similarly as regards freedom of establishment (eg Case 197/84 *Steinhauser* [1985] ECR 1819; Case C–168/91 *Konstantinidis* [1993] ECR I–1191; Case C–337/97 *Meeusen* [1999] ECR I–3289); and free movement of services (eg Case 63/86 *Commission v Italy* [1988] ECR 29; Case 186/87 *Cowan v Trésor public* [1989] ECR 195; Case C–45/93 *Commission v Spain* [1994] ECR I–911; Case C–274/96 *Bickel and Franz* [1998] ECR I–7637).

[63] Also: Dir 75/117 on the approximation of the laws of the Member States relating to the application of the principle of equal pay for men and women, OJ 1975 L45/19.

[64] Dir 76/207 on the implementation of the principle of equal treatment for men and women as regards access to employment, vocational training and promotion, and working conditions, OJ 1976 L39/40; Dir 86/613 on the application of the principle of equal treatment between men and women engaged in an activity including agriculture, in a self-employed capacity, and on the protection of self-employed women during pregnancy and motherhood, OJ 1986 L359/56 (respectively).

and safeguard the dignity of, Community workers.[65] More recently, the Court in *Sievers* stressed that Article 141 EC

> forms part of the social objectives of the Community, which is not merely an economic union but is at the same time intended, by common action, to ensure social progress and seek constant improvement of the living and working conditions of the peoples of Europe.

Indeed,

> the economic aim pursued by Article [141] of the Treaty, namely the elimination of distortions of competition between undertakings established in different Member States, is secondary to the social aim pursued by the same provision, which constitutes the expression of a fundamental human right.[66]

Many commentators argue that provisions such as Articles 39 and 141 EC should be seen merely as specific manifestations of a more general principle of equality—which constitutes one of the basic values protected within and promoted by the Community legal order, and has attained this status not only as a matter of Common Market economic philosophy but also as a matter of moral and political necessity.[67] This view finds support in the caselaw. For example, the Court has consistently held that the right to equal treatment guaranteed to economically active market agents under the Treaty rules on free movement merely reflects the prohibition on discrimination on grounds of nationality set out in Article 12 EC and which applies across the entire scope of application of the Treaty.[68] Similarly, the Court has proclaimed that Directive 76/207 on equal treatment for men and women as regards access to and conditions of employment

> is simply the expression, in the relevant field, of the principle of equality, which is one of the fundamental principles of Community law.[69]

In his Opinion in *Grant v South West Trains*, Advocate General Elmer stated that

> [e]quality before the law is a fundamental principle in every community governed by the rule of law and accordingly in the Community as well.[70]

[65] Case 43/75 *Defrenne v Sabena* [1976] ECR 455, paras 8–12.

[66] Cases C–270–271/97 *Deutsche Post v Sievers* [2000] ECR I–929, paras 53–57. Also: Case C–50/96 *Deutsche Telekom v Schröder* [2000] ECR I–743, paras 53–57.

[67] For discussion, eg G de Búrca, 'The Role of Equality in European Community Law' in A Dashwood & S O'Leary (eds), *The Principle of Equal Treatment in EC Law* (Sweet & Maxwell, 1997); G More, 'The Principle of Equal Treatment: From Market Unifier to Fundamental Right?' in P Craig & G de Búrca (eds), *The Evolution of EU Law* (OUP, 1999); T Tridimas, *The General Principles of EC Law* (OUP, 1999) ch 2.

[68] Eg Case 186/87 *Cowan v Trésor public* [1989] ECR 195; Case C–20/92 *Hubbard v Hamburger* [1993] ECR I–3777; Cases C–92 & 326/92 *Phil Collins* [1993] ECR I–5145; Case C–43/95 *Data Delecta* [1996] ECR I–4661.

[69] Case C–13/94 *P v S and Cornwall County Council* [1996] ECR I–2143, para 18; Dir 76/207, OJ 1976 L39/40. Cf Case C–25/02 *Rinke* (Judgment of 9 September 2003).

[70] Case C–249/96 *Grant v South West Trains* [1998] ECR I–621, para 42 Opinion.

The Court of Justice itself in *SFI v Belgium* observed that 'equality is one of the fundamental principles of Community law' which requires that similar situations should not be treated differently unless objectively justified.[71] The idea of equality as a general principle of Community law received a further boost with the introduction of Article 13 EC by the Treaty of Amsterdam, supplementing the Union's existing commitment to fight sex and nationality discrimination with additional powers to promote equality between individuals in spheres such as race, religion, disability and sexual orientation.[72]

Equality Between Union Citizens

However, the cynosure around which hopes for the emergence of any more general principle of equality now coalesce is the concept of Union citizenship. It has been argued that uniformity of treatment between individuals across the Community is an essential value implicit in the emerging concept of citizenship. For example, Advocate General La Pergola in *Stöber and Pereira* maintained that the ultimate purpose of Part Two of the EC Treaty is 'to bring about increasing equality between citizens of the Union, irrespective of their nationality.'[73] Moreover, Advocate General Léger in *Boukhalfa* observed that

> [i]f all the conclusions inherent in [the concept of citizenship] are drawn, every citizen of the Union must, whatever his nationality, enjoy exactly the same rights and be subject to the same obligations. Taken to its ultimate conclusion, the concept should lead to citizens of the Union being treated absolutely equally, irrespective of their nationality.[74]

Similarly, Advocate General Jacobs in *Bickel and Franz* argued that

> [t]he notion of citizenship of the Union implies a commonality of rights and obligations uniting Union citizens by a common bond transcending Member State nationality.[75]

The Court itself in judgments such as *Grzelczyk* stated that Union citizenship is 'destined to be the fundamental status of nationals of the Member States,' enabling those who find themselves in the same situation to enjoy the same treatment in law irrespective of their nationality.[76]

[71] Case C–85/97 *SFI v Belgium* [1998] ECR I–7447, paras 29–30. Or that different situations should not be treated in the same manner (unless objectively justified), eg Case C–148/02 *Garcia Avello* (Judgment of 2 October 2003).
[72] Also: Dir 2000/78 establishing a general framework for equal treatment in employment and occupation, OJ 2000 L 303/16.
[73] Cases C–4–5/95 *Stöber and Pereira* [1997] ECR I–511, para 51 Opinion.
[74] Case C–214/94 *Boukhalfa* [1996] ECR I–2253, para 63 Opinion.
[75] Case C–274/96 *Bickel and Franz* [1998] ECR I–7637, para 23 Opinion.
[76] Case C–184/99 *Grzelczyk* [2001] ECR I–6193, para 31.

Of course, one might lobby for such equality of treatment between Union citizens at very different levels of abstraction. First, one might simply insist, through the medium of Article 12 EC, that Member States must treat migrant Union citizens in the same manner as own nationals as regards all situations falling within the scope of the Treaty (subject to such exceptions as are expressly provided for)—thus guaranteeing the assimilation of Community nationals (both economically active and economically inactive) into their host societies, but without questioning the continued existence of regulatory differences between Member States.[77] Indeed, the Court has made clear in cases such as *Milk Marque* that Article 12 EC is not concerned with any disparities in treatment which may result from divergences between the laws of the various Member States (so long as such national laws affect all persons subject to their jurisdiction without regard to their nationality).[78] Secondly, however, the ideals which many commentators see embodied in the concept of Union citizenship might extend much further—requiring real equality of treatment not just within any given Member State (and benefiting primarily those who exercise rights to free movement), but across the entire Community (embracing situations which would otherwise be considered wholly internal), as regards all situations falling within the material field of application of the Treaty. Here, the aim would be precisely to replace the disparities in treatment for Union citizens which result from divergences between the laws of the various Member States.

In this regard, a 'strong' interpretation of Union citizenship might insist on the need for absolute legal equality as regards all significant aspects of economic and welfare provision falling within the scope of Community law. From this perspective, the existing Treaty system may fairly be said to suffer from numerous shortcomings. For example, while the Community has been endowed with competence to develop supranational policies in fields such as education and public health, it is expressly deprived of the power to achieve these objectives through the harmonisation of domestic laws, and thus of the opportunity to develop a body of truly shared social rights for its citizens.[79] Similarly, even though Article 13 EC is a major improvement in the Community's commitment to the individual's protection against discrimination, it represents only a shadow of what might have been. The Amsterdam drafters consciously sought to limit the scope of Article 13 EC by making it difficult for this provision

[77] Eg Case C–85/96 *María Martínez Sala* [1998] ECR I–2691; Case C–184/99 *Grzelczyk* [2001] ECR I–6193; Case C–224/98 *D'Hoop* [2002] ECR I–6191; Case C–138/02 *Collins* (Judgment of 23 March 2004).

[78] Case C–137/00 *Milk Marque* (Judgment of 9 September 2003). Also, eg Case C–92/02 *Kristiansen* (Judgment of 4 December 2003).

[79] Arts 149–50 and 152 EC. Also: Art 151 EC on Community cultural policy. Further: ch 3 (below).

of itself to have direct effect within the domestic legal orders (instead furnishing a legal basis for the adoption of secondary legislation by the Community's political institutions).[80] Moreover, the Court of Justice has affirmed that, despite the creation of Union citizenship, the phenomenon of reverse discrimination (whereby Member States may impose harsher restrictions upon their own nationals than on foreigners in wholly internal situations) remains perfectly compatible with the current state of the Treaty's development.[81]

By contrast, a 'weak' interpretation of Union citizenship might insist simply on securing equality of treatment in respect of legal rights and obligations created pursuant to such competences as do currently exist under Community law, so that rules enacted at the Treaty level are applied uniformly to all citizens within the relevant sphere. However, even this less ambitious approach has in some cases been frustrated by unsatisfactory examples of discrimination in the enjoyment of Treaty norms as between individuals in fact intended to enjoy the same rights. For example, the Court's denial of horizontal direct effect for non- or incorrectly implemented directives has been lambasted not only for perpetuating distortions of competitive conditions within the Common Market which the Community legislature had taken positive steps to eradicate, but also for generating imbalances in the levels of legal protection provided for different groups of citizens depending on no other factor than the Member State in which they happen to find themselves—an inequality of treatment which should be viewed as politically unacceptable in the modern Union.[82]

These difficulties notwithstanding, it is still possible for those inclined towards an 'integration through law' perspective to postulate a new conceptual understanding of the imperative of regulatory uniformity within the Treaty legal order—an understanding which offers great prescriptive value, even if it does not possess full descriptive force. The Community's horizontal expansion, the pervasive influence of the principle of equality and the institution of Union citizenship after Maastricht all combine to provide a strong basis for arguing that the contemporary European integration

[80] Further, eg L Waddington, 'Article 13 EC: Mere Rhetoric or a Harbinger of Change?' (1998) 1 *Cambridge Yearbook of European Legal Studies* 175; M Bell, 'The New Article 13 EC Treaty: A Sound Basis For European Anti-Discrimination Law?' (1999) 6 *Maastricht Journal of European and Comparative Law* 5; L Flynn, 'The Implications of Article 13 EC: After Amsterdam, Will Some Forms of Discrimination be More Equal Than Others?' (1999) 36 CML Rev 1127.

[81] Eg Cases C–64–65/96 *Uecker and Jacquet* [1997] ECR I–3171; Case C–148/02 *Garcia Avello* (Judgment of 2 October 2003).

[82] Eg AG Lenz in Case C–91/92 *Faccini Dori* [1994] ECR I–3325. Further: E Szyszczak, 'Building a European Constitutional Order: Prospects for a General Non-Discrimination Standard' in A Dashwood & S O'Leary (eds), *The Principle of Equal Treatment in EC Law* (Sweet & Maxwell, 1997). A comparable threat to equality of treatment between Union citizens is posed by those national courts which (as seen above) unilaterally reject the unconditional supremacy of Community law within their domestic legal orders.

project should rightly be seen to consist in the creation of a common body of social as well as economic rights, enjoyed by all the citizens of the Union. In short: yet another model of 'total harmonisation'; but this time, one which refuses either to take as its justification the impulse towards economic integration alone, or to be treated as a necessary but unwelcome dilution of the full free-trade ambitions pursued by the overbearing Common Market; and is instead prepared to defend the pursuit of uniformity in the formulation and application of Treaty law as the natural continuation of recent trends towards Community-level convergence in the socio-political spheres.

Combating a 'Race to the Bottom'

Indeed, some commentators point out that pre-emptive harmonisation by the Community is not merely a desirable step towards realising uniform levels of generous social rights for Union citizens, but an essential counterweight to the inherent bias against the protection of vulnerable welfare interests which afflicts the operation of the Single Market.

Rights to free movement have traditionally favoured the economically active. Even within this category, barriers of an economic, cultural and linguistic character mean that individual workers and consumers are unable simply to leave those Member States which offer unsatisfactory legal products, and relocate in other jurisdictions whose regulatory regimes better protect their welfare interests.[83] The economic pressure generated by competition between legal orders to attract mobile individuals is therefore minimal, and produces little incentive for the Member States to pursue higher standards of welfare protection. Moreover, these limitations on 'exit' power may be exacerbated by restrictions on 'voice' opportunities, whereby inadequate channels of representation and unequal access to decision-making procedures hamper the ability of non-mobile citizens nevertheless to express their regulatory preferences to the domestic authorities.[84]

By contrast, medium and large undertakings are much better placed in terms of economic resources and transnational mobility to exercise their rights to free movement, and thus to relocate in Member States with favourable regulatory regimes—generally meaning countries with minimal welfare legislation, and thus with reduced compliance costs for businesses.[85] Such 'social dumping' in turn raises the spectre of a 'race to the bottom.' Member States feel obliged to lower their own welfare

[83] Eg Commission, *Action Plan for Skills and Mobility*, COM (2002)72. Further, eg S O'Leary, 'The Free Movement of Persons and Services' in P Craig & G de Búrca (eds), *The Evolution of EU Law* (OUP, 1999).
[84] Eg M P Maduro, 'Striking the Elusive Balance Between Economic Freedom and Social Rights in the EU' in P Alston (ed), *The EU and Human Rights* (OUP, 1999).
[85] Though not necessarily: higher labour and social standards can be reflected in higher levels of productivity, and attract mobile factors of production to the relevant territory on that basis.

standards and compliance costs, in the hope of both attracting inward investment from mobile economic factors, and minimising competitive disadvantages for their own undertakings as they battle with new foreign rivals on the domestic market, or act as cross-border service providers on the wider European stage. While some hail this as a rational choice by society to trade off some of the luxuries of welfare provision against increased economic growth, others see in the flawed process of competition between legal orders the kindler for a vicious deregulatory cycle which threatens to undermine basic standards of social protection throughout the entire Community.[86]

From a perspective which stresses the autonomous value of social rights within the Community legal order, the problem of social dumping and threat of a race to the bottom clearly represent unacceptable consequences of the process of regulatory competition. In direct opposition to the advocates of regulatory competition, many commentators have identified the solution to this problem precisely in the systematic pursuit of 'market correcting' positive harmonisation at the European level, whereby the Community authorities adopt binding legislative norms common to every Member State, which guarantee in themselves the high standards of social protection and welfare regulation necessary to ensure the political credibility of the European Union. And in principle, such norms should be fully pre-emptive in nature—so as to fatally undermine the legal infrastructure which supports competition between legal orders within the Single Market, by eliminating those regulatory differences which nurture the inequitable pursuit of rights to free movement by mobile economic actors, and depriving the Member States of their capacity to engage in any short-sighted and destructive exercise of legislative autonomy.[87]

Thus, harmonisation in the field of welfare rights is not simply an idle indulgence, aimed at carrying the integration process forward towards an

[86] Eg S Deakin & F Wilkinson, 'Rights vs Efficiency? The Economic Case for Transnational Labour Standards' (1994) 23 ILJ 289; S Deakin, 'Labour Law as Market Regulation: the Economic Foundations of European Social Policy' in P Davies, A Lyon-Caen, S Sciarra & S Simitis (eds), *European Community Labour Law: Principles and Perspectives* (OUP, 1996); L Delsen, N van Gestel and J van Vugt, 'European Integration: Current Problems and Future Scenarios' in J van Vugt & J Peet (eds), *Social Security and Solidarity in the European Union* (Physica-Verlag, 2000); A Lo Faro, *Regulating Social Europe: Reality and Myth of Collective Bargaining in the EC Legal Order* (Hart Publishing, 2000) ch 2. There is disagreement about the extent of social dumping within the Internal Market, eg D Goodhart, 'Social Dumping Within the EU' in D Hine & H Kassim (eds), *Beyond the Market: the EU and National Social Policy* (Routledge, 1998); C Barnard, 'Social Dumping and the Race to the Bottom: Some Lessons For the European Union From Delaware?' (2000) 25 EL Rev 57. However, even the threat or perception of social dumping may emasculate the bargaining power of trade unions and governments, eg W Streeck, 'Neo-Voluntarism: A New European Social Policy Regime?' (1995) 1 *European Law Journal* 31.

[87] Further, eg K Van Wezel Stone, 'Labour in the Global Economy: Four Approaches to Transnational Labour Regulation' in W Bratton, J McCahery, S Picciotto & C Scott (eds), *International Regulatory Competition and Coordination: Perspectives on Economic Regulation in Europe and the United States* (OUP, 1996).

ideal of equality between Union citizens; but a necessary corollary of the imperfect functioning of the Internal Market itself, since the mobilisation of economic forces, left to its own devices, might threaten the very social values upon which the Union claims to be constructed.

Assessment

Even after attempting to shed some light on its underlying nature, the idea of 'integration through law' remains in certain respects an unashamedly ambiguous term which masks as much controversy as it suggests common ground. The impulse towards European convergence is capable of manifesting itself in myriad guises, ranging from the purely economic ideal of a Single Market at one extreme, to the political ambition of a full-blown federal state at the other. In any case, the Community's actual experience of horizontal expansion has rendered more complex the central concept of a uniform and effective Treaty legal order: traditional arguments based on the legitimate needs of the Common Market have been supplemented by a more contemporary rationale which stresses the importance of the Treaty's commitment to a mature agenda of social welfare. Notwithstanding this complexity and potential contradiction, it is possible to extract with tolerable clarity some common idea: the success of the Community depends upon the promotion of a regulatory code which is enforced effectively within each Member State and applied uniformly across the Community territory as a whole. 'Integration through law' thus represents a convenient shorthand for these widely held views about the essentially integrative nature of the Treaty project, and the sort of legal system which is required to sustain it.

'INTEGRATION THROUGH LAW': THE TRADITIONAL PARAMETERS OF THE ENFORCEMENT DEFICIT DEBATE

It is now possible to examine more fully the traditional parameters within which the opposing sides in the enforcement deficit debate have constructed their varying interpretations of why the national remedies and procedures employed during the decentralised enforcement of Community law present a particular problem and require a particular solution.

The Need For a 'Unified System of Judicial Protection'

The basic conceptual framework has been provided by an 'integration through law' analysis, which both diagnosed the initial malady and prescribed the appropriate cure.

The Problem With National Remedies and Procedural Rules

Direct effect and supremacy are the central pillars of the legal order developed by the Court of Justice with a view to securing the uniform and effective application of Community law across the Member States, and thus of realising the Treaty's multifarious objectives in the economic, social and political spheres. These principles may not be unproblematic even in themselves—we have already noted criticisms relating to the Court's approach to horizontal direct effect for directives, and the intermittent resistance on the part of some national judges to the full logic of supremacy—but their contribution to the jurisprudential character and operational efficiency of the Treaty legal order are beyond question. However, even assuming that a provision of Community law has direct effect and the domestic courts are prepared to enforce it in preference to contradictory national rules, this may not in itself be sufficient to satisfy the underlying demands of either uniformity or effectiveness. In particular, it is possible that the sanctions and procedures available for the decentralised enforcement of Community norms may be inadequate within any given Member State, or simply different from those available in other jurisdictions.

By way of illustration, imagine that a woman has been dismissed from her post contrary to the Community regime outlawing sexual discrimination in the workplace.[88] The relevant directive has been correctly implemented by all the Member States. The victim therefore seeks redress before the national courts, and one might expect the principles of direct effect and supremacy to guarantee that such redress is of an adequate and equivalent standard regardless of the Member State in which the offending dismissal took place. However, this expectation may well prove to be misguided. In Member State A, applicants challenging sexual discrimination have one year in which to commence legal proceedings and will be awarded (at most) a declaration that the employer has acted illegally. In Member State B, the relevant limitation period is five years and the remedy is in damages, but subject to a statutory ceiling of € 5,000. In Member State C, the time-limit is just one month, but successful applicants are entitled to be reinstated back in their original posts. The right to equal treatment on grounds of sex, which should in theory benefit all citizens in the same manner throughout the Community, actually means very little in practice to citizens of Member State A, and in any case means something very different to citizens who happen to work in Member States B or C. Likewise, the varying economic consequences of failing to comply with the principle of equal treatment, which result from the varying remedies

[88] Dir 76/207 on the implementation of the principle of equal treatment for men and women as regards access to employment, vocational training and promotion, and working conditions, OJ 1976 L39/40 (overlooking Art 6, and the Court's caselaw, for the purposes of this example).

and procedural rules applied across the Community, mean that defaulting undertakings established in one Member State might enjoy appreciable competitive advantages over their rivals operating on the Common Market but which happen to be established in other Member States.

From the standpoint of the Internal Market, the Community's reliance upon domestic remedies and procedures disrupts the operation of fundamental policies such as free movement for goods and persons, and distorts competitive conditions between Community undertakings.[89] This is particularly true as regards those sectors of Treaty activity which remain dominated by the objectives of economic integration (for example: Articles 81 and 82 EC on competition policy, and Articles 87 and 88 EC on state aids).[90] Viewed from a rights or welfare-based perspective, the same situation undermines the standards of protection individuals are supposed to enjoy under Community law, and contradicts the principle of equal treatment between citizens of the Union. This is particularly true as regards those sectors of Treaty activity which pursue increasingly autonomous social objectives (for example: environmental, employee and consumer protection).[91]

Proceeding from those basic assumptions about the nature of European integration and the concomitant role of the Treaty legal order which characterise an 'integration through law' perspective, it is possible to demonstrate that the Community suffers from an 'enforcement deficit,' brought on by its reliance upon the fragmented systems of judicial protection presently offered by the Member States.

This analysis reverberates across the scholarship. For example, writing in 1984, Bridge observed that:

> [T]here are possible serious disadvantages from the point of view of the Community of reliance on the laws and authorities of the Member States to

[89] Lack of effective domestic enforcement mechanisms also risks undermining the essential framework of mutual trust and recognition between Member States, upon which depends the successful operation of the new approach to harmonisation. Cp S Woolcock, 'Competition Among Rules in the Single European Market' in W Bratton, J McCahery, S Picciotto & C Scott (eds), *International Regulatory Competition and Coordination: Perspectives on Economic Regulation in Europe and the United States* (OUP, 1996).

[90] Eg T Hartley, 'The Effects in National Law of Judgments of the European Court' (1980) 5 EL Rev 366; M Bronckers, 'Private Enforcement of 1992: Do Trade and Industry Stand a Chance Against the Member States?' (1989) 26 CML Rev 513; B Ryan, 'Private Enforcement of European Union Labour Laws' in C Kilpatrick, T Novitz & P Skidmore (eds), *The Future of Remedies in Europe* (Hart Publishing, 2000). Cf Council, *Resolution on the Effective Uniform Application of Community Law and on the Penalties Applicable for Breaches of Community law in the Internal Market*, OJ 1995 C188/1.

[91] Eg A P Tash , 'Remedies for European Community Law Claims in Member State Courts: Toward a European Standard' (1993) 31 *Columbia Journal of Transnational Law* 377; E Szyszczak, 'Making Europe More Relevant To Its Citizens: Effective Judicial Process' (1996) 21 EL Rev 351 and 'Building a European Constitutional Order: Prospects for a General Non-Discrimination Standard' in A Dashwood & S O'Leary (eds), *The Principle of Equal Treatment in EC Law* (Sweet & Maxwell, 1997); C Himsworth, 'Things Fall Apart: The Harmonisation of Community Judicial Procedural Protection Revisited' (1997) 22 EL Rev 291.

> determine the procedures for the enforcement of Community law. The availability and effectiveness of remedies to enforce the law are dependent on the applicable rules of procedure. The national rules of procedure of the various Member States are unlikely to be uniform. Therefore… the nature of the remedies for the enforcement of Community law is likely to vary from Member State to Member State. This, in turn, is likely to result in inequality and unfairness in the protection of individual rights conferred by Community law. In such circumstances the attainment of the principal and crucial objective of Community law that it be applied and enforced uniformly and equally throughout the Community will be obstructed.[92]

Commentators have continued to deliver such unfavourable diagnoses. For example, writing in 1997, Chiti remarked that,

> [t]he uniformity of substantive European law is in fact often jeopardised by the peculiarities of national procedural laws. … not only the Community policies, but also the rights conferred by Community law, can acquire different characters depending on the various national systems of protection, and this is incompatible with the principle of direct and uniform application of Community law.[93]

The 'integration through law' analysis is perhaps best embodied in the 1994 Storme Report on the approximation of judiciary law in the European Union.[94] This collaborative project recalls the diversity which currently exists between national procedural rules on crucial issues relating to the costs and duration of litigation, and the potential remedies or sanctions which might result from legal action. It stresses that such inequalities in the national systems of judicial protection are clearly incompatible with the functioning of the Internal Market: they distort the conditions of competition between economic undertakings, and might deter potential cross-border trade through their lack of transparency.

[92] J Bridge, 'Procedural Aspects of the Enforcement of European Community Law through the Legal Systems of the Member States' (1984) 9 EL Rev 28, 31–32.

[93] M P Chiti, 'Towards a Unified Judicial Protection in Europe(?)' (1997) 9 *European Review of Public Law* 553, 555. Similarly, eg D Curtin, 'Directives: The Effectiveness of Judicial Protection of Individual Rights' (1990) 27 CML Rev 709; K Lenaerts, 'Some Thoughts About the Interaction Between Judges and Politicians in the European Community' (1992) 12 *Yearbook of European Law* 1; W van Gerven, 'Bridging the Gap Between Community and National Laws: Towards a Principle of Homogeneity in the Field of Legal Remedies' (1995) 32 CML Rev 679; L Flynn, 'Taking Remedies Too Seriously? National Procedural Autonomy in the European Court of Justice' (1996) XXXI *The Irish Jurist* 110; M Jarvis, *The Application of EC Law by National Courts: The Free Movement of Goods* (Clarendon Press, 1998) pp 367–68; J Steiner, 'The Limits of State Liability for Breach of European Community Law' (1998) 4 *European Public Law* 69. Note the more nuanced (though still essentially integrationist) analysis offered by W van Gerven, 'Of Rights, Remedies and Procedures' (2000) 37 CML Rev 501; and 'Harmonization of Private Law: Do We Need It?' (2004) 41 CML Rev 505.

[94] M Storme (ed), *Approximation of Judiciary Law in the European Union* (Martinus Nijhoff, 1994).

Storme himself also highlights the political relevance of the enforcement deficit:

> Citizens in Europe cherish the hope that Community policy will not be confined to economic purposes but will also recognise the necessity of a properly functioning 'fabric of justice'.

Indeed, he asserts that

> [c]itizens must accordingly have the feeling that those in authority will constantly be bending their minds to the pursuit of a harmonising policy in the field of procedural law.[95]

Creating More Uniform and Effective Standards of Judicial Protection

The necessary cure is prescribed with admirable logic: if national remedies and procedural rules undermine the uniformity and effectiveness of Community law, Community law must render national remedies and procedural rules more uniform and effective. A substantial body of academic opinion therefore argues that the only way genuinely to overcome the difficulties posed by the enforcement deficit is to construct a 'unified system of judicial protection' in Europe.

What this solution actually means in practice is rarely articulated with any satisfactory degree of clarity. On the one hand, few appear to support the logistically impractical and politically unacceptable idea that we should legislate into existence a single European legal system—root-and-branch reform of the entire infrastructure for the administration of justice across the Union.[96] Even the Storme Report, despite its highly integrationist philosophy, shied away from proposals relating to the organisation of the national judiciaries—considering this to be a structural expression of national sovereignty pertaining to the fundamental character of the state.[97] On the other hand, a more modest proposal would be to achieve a progressive harmonisation of the present panoply of national remedial and procedural provisions so as to conform to a common Community-wide standard, which could then be administered through the existing

[95] M Storme, 'General Introductory Report' available at <www.storme.be/euroius.html>. Cf M Shapiro, 'The European Court of Justice' in P Craig & G de Búrca (eds), *The Evolution of EU Law* (OUP, 1999), who suggests that harmonisation of domestic remedies and procedural rules is a useful tool in enhancing the democratic accountability of the Community decision and lawmaking systems.

[96] Further, eg M Brenner, 'Administrative Judicial Protection in Europe: General Principles' (1997) 9 *European Review of Public Law* 595; M P Chiti, 'Towards a Unified Judicial Protection in Europe(?)' (1997) 9 *European Review Public Law* 553; W van Gerven, 'European Standards for Civil Liability of the State' in J Vervaele (ed), *Compliance and Enforcement of European Community Law* (Kluwer Law International, 1999).

[97] M Storme (ed), *Approximation of Judiciary Law in the European Union* (Martinus Nijhoff, 1994).

domestic legal systems without necessarily attempting otherwise to reconcile their major structural differences and doctrinal peculiarities.[98] Thus, the Storme Report itself contained a draft directive proposing the harmonisation of limited aspects of procedural rules as they would be applied before the various domestic courts (for example: the use of mediation and conciliation procedures; the commencement of civil proceedings; rules of discovery, witness examinations and evidence; the apportionment of the costs of proceedings; and provisional remedies and orders for payment)—falling far short of any sort of comprehensive 'European Judicial Code.'[99]

Whatever its shortcomings as a concrete blueprint for future reform, the ideal of a unified system of judicial protection has nevertheless provided those who reason from an 'integration through law' perspective with a workable conceptual yardstick against which to assess the Community's existing efforts to address the enforcement deficit. Those efforts can be categorised into three different types—the process of regulatory competition, legislative intervention by the political institutions and judicial harmonisation by the Court of Justice—but in each case, more often than not, they are found to be sadly lacking.

Consider first the theory of regulatory competition. Many commentators have argued that the existence of diverse national remedies and procedural rules permits undertakings to engage in forum-shopping within the Internal Market—choosing to do business (or even to establish themselves) in Member States which offer the most favourable conditions for litigation as regards issues such as compensation for unlawful acts.[100] Some authors have gone further, suggesting that such forum-shopping might stimulate a competition between national legal orders, whereby Member States are forced to reform their domestic standards of judicial

[98] Further, eg J Bridge, 'Procedural Aspects of the Enforcement of European Community Law through the Legal Systems of the Member States' (1984) 9 EL Rev 28; G de Búrca, 'Giving Effect to European Community Directives' (1992) 55 MLR 215; J Steiner, *Enforcing EC Law* (Blackstone Press, 1995) Ch 5; C Himsworth, 'Things Fall Apart: The Harmonisation of Community Judicial Procedural Protection Revisited' (1997) 22 EL Rev 291; L Neville Brown, 'National Protection of Community Rights: Reconciling Autonomy and Effectiveness' in J Lonbay & A Biondi (eds), *Remedies for Breach of EC Law* (Wiley, 1997); E Deards, 'Curiouser and Curiouser? The Development of Member State Liability in the Court of Justice' (1997) 3 *European Public Law* 117.

[99] M Storme (ed), *Approximation of Judiciary Law in the European Union* (Martinus Nijhoff, 1994). For critical comments, eg C Himsworth, 'Things Fall Apart: The Harmonisation of Community Judicial Procedural Protection Revisited' (1997) 22 EL Rev 291; E Werlauff, *Common European Procedural Law: European Law Requirements Imposed on National Administration of Justice* (DJØF Publishing, 1999).

[100] Eg R Whish, 'The Enforcement of EC Competition Law in the Domestic Courts of Member States' [1994] ECLR 60; L Hiljemark, 'Enforcement of EC Competition Law in National Courts: The Perspective of Judicial Protection' (1997) 17 *Yearbook of European Law* 83; S Kon and A Maxwell, 'Enforcement in National Courts of the EC and New UK Competition Rules: Obstacles to Effective Enforcement' [1998] ECLR 443.

protection so as to satisfy the actual/perceived needs of mobile market actors.[101] And as with substantive law, therefore, the simple operation of economic forces might ultimately result in the desired level of uniform remedies and procedural rules, without the need for any specific intervention by the Community institutions. Indeed, the sort of uniformity produced by the market can be more successful than that attempted through positive intervention by the central authorities: economic actors are better placed to identify functional equivalences between apparently diverse national legal systems, such that regulatory competition need not interfere with the structural or doctrinal specificities of each Member State where these have no genuine impact upon competitive conditions.[102]

However, many comparative lawyers argue that rules of judicial protection are so embedded in their own national legal environments as to prove peculiarly immune to the possibility of cross-border transplantation—thus blunting the pressure for convergence exerted by the market alone.[103] Indeed, certain scholars have pointed out that, for any system of regulatory competition to function according to theoretical expectations, there must exist an effective process for translating the economic preferences expressed by mobile actors into corresponding policy choices on the part of the Member States. But the reality of this interaction is much more complex and unpredictable: it may be difficult for businesses (or individuals) to gather the information required to make an 'economically wise' decision about the relative benefits of different types of governmental regulation across different Member States; similarly, government policy-making is influenced not only by the simple economic logic of regulatory competition, but also by a host of other considerations and the intervention of other institutional actors. Such factors distort the conceptual model of competition between legal orders, and make it difficult to assert that it leads inexorably to optimally efficient regulation.[104] One might have particular cause to wonder (if only intuitively) how far the duration of limitation periods or the rules on discovery of documents might really sway the decision to transact or invest in a given Member State;[105] or how

[101] Eg S Weatherill, 'Compulsory Notification of Draft Technical Regulations: the Contribution of Directive 83/189 to the Management of the Internal Market' (1996) 16 *Yearbook of European Law* 129, who argues that Member States might be induced to pursue a race to the bottom in national remedies so as to protect domestic industries against competitive disadvantages within the Single Market.

[102] Cf A Ogus, 'Competition Between National Legal Systems: A Contribution of Economic Analysis to Comparative Law' (1999) 48 ICLQ 405.

[103] Eg O Kahn-Freund, 'On Uses and Misuses of Comparative Law' (1974) 37 MLR 1.

[104] Further, eg J-M Sun and J Pelkmans, 'Regulatory Competition in the Single Market' (1995) 33 JCMS 67; S Woolcock, 'Competition Among Rules in the Single European Market' in W Bratton, J McCahery, S Picciotto & C Scott (eds), *International Regulatory Competition and Coordination: Perspectives on Economic Regulation in Europe and the United States* (OUP, 1996).

[105] The ECJ at least seems sceptical, eg Case C–412/97 *Italo Fenocchio* [1999] ECR I–3845.

far the national systems of judicial protection are genuinely receptive to reforms inspired by regulatory competition with other Member States.[106]

Consider secondly the legislative contribution. It typically remains the case that secondary legislation passed under the Treaty will fail to make any Community-level provision for the remedies and procedures to be applied during its enforcement before the national courts. True, it has become increasingly common for Community measures to impose upon the Member States an obligation to provide appropriate means of judicial protection for beneficiaries of the substantive provisions in question.[107] However, it seems clear that such clauses merely codify the general principles developed in the caselaw of the Court of Justice, without expanding in any significant manner the standards of enforcement already expected from the Member States.[108] Even measures which purport to establish a Community-level remedies regime in respect of a particular policy field tend to be relatively unambitious. For example, Directive 97/80 enacts rules governing allocation of the burden of proof in sex discrimination cases which largely duplicate the position already followed by the Court of Justice in cases such as *Bilka-Kaufhaus*.[109]

The Public Procurement Remedies Directive 89/665 is often viewed as the pinnacle of the Community legislature's creative endeavours in the sphere of remedies.[110] Article 1(1) states that the Member States shall take the measures necessary to ensure that public procurement decisions taken by contracting authorities may be reviewed effectively and, in particular,

[106] Eg A Ogus, 'Competition Between National Legal Systems: A Contribution of Economic Analysis to Comparative Law' (1999) 48 ICLQ 405.

[107] Eg Dir 75/117 on the approximation of the laws of the Member States relating to the application of the principle of equal pay for men and women, OJ 1975 L45/19; Dir 76/207 on the implementation of the principle of equal treatment for men and women as regards access to employment, vocational training and promotion, and working conditions, OJ 1976 L39/40; Dir 91/533 on an employer's obligation to inform employees of the conditions applicable to the contract or employment relationship, OJ 1991 L288/32; Dir 92/85 on the introduction of measures to encourage improvements in the safety and health at work of pregnant workers and workers who have recently given birth or are breastfeeding, OJ 1992 L348/1; Dir 94/33 on the protection of young people at work, OJ 1994 L216/12; Dir 98/59 on the approximation of the laws of the Member States relating to collective redundancies, OJ 1998 L225/16; Dir 2001/23 on the approximation of the laws of the Member States relating to the safeguarding of employees' rights in the event of transfers of undertakings, businesses or parts of undertakings or businesses, OJ 2001 L82/16.

[108] Eg Case 14/83 *von Colson* [1984] ECR 1891; Case C–271/91 *Marshall II* [1993] ECR I–4367; Case C–185/97 *Coote v Granada Hospitality* [1998] ECR I–5199.

[109] Dir 97/80 on the burden of proof in cases of discrimination based on sex, OJ 1998 L14/6; Case 170/84 *Bilka-Kaufhaus* [1986] ECR 1607. Similarly, eg Case 109/88 *Danfoss* [1989] ECR 3199; Case C–381/99 *Brunnhofer* [2001] ECR I–4961.

[110] Dir 89/665 on public supply, works and service contracts, OJ 1989 L395/33 (as amended by Dir 92/50, OJ 1992 L209/1). Cf Dir 92/13, OJ 1992 L76/14 setting out similar (but not identical rules) on public utilities contracts. Further, eg C Bovis, *The Liberalisation of Public Procurement and its Effects on the Common Market* (Ashgate, 1998). Note that the Commission recently launched a consultation on reform of the various public procurement remedies directives: see Press Release IP/03/1455.

as rapidly as possible in accordance with the conditions contained in the Directive. For these purposes, the Directive contains relatively detailed provisions on issues such as *locus standi* to challenge public procurement decisions,[111] and the composition of independent review bodies.[112] However, the Directive's system of redress as regards (for example) the availability of interim relief and compensatory damages may have anticipated but hardly exceeds the Court's own achievements in judgments such as *Factortame* and *Francovich*.[113] Moreover, the coverage of the Directive remains limited. When it comes to issues such as the limitation periods applicable to challenges against public procurement decisions,[114] the intensity of judicial review over such decisions,[115] and the ability of national judges to raise of their own motion issues of incompatibility with Community law,[116] it is necessary to have regard to the general principles of the Court's caselaw on effective judicial protection. In any case, the Directive has also been criticised for failing to tackle more deep-seated structural problems buried within the domestic legal systems—such as inadequate resources and inordinate delays in the administration of justice.[117]

The Community's competence under Article 65 EC in the field of judicial cooperation as regards civil matters having cross-border implications has not yet produced any more comprehensive legislative programme. In principle, the Area of Freedom, Security and Justice could offer fertile justification for Community intervention to promote common standards of judicial protection.[118] After all, the full mutual recognition of judicial decisions across the Member States presupposes a climate of mutual trust between the domestic legal orders, which in turn presupposes the existence of certain common procedural safeguards relating (for example) to the admissibility of evidence and the effective exercise of rights to defence. More broadly, the Tampere European Council's guidelines on

[111] Art 1(3). Cf Case C–57/01 *Makedoniko Metro* [2003] ECR I–1091; Case C–249/01 *Hackermüller* [2003] ECR I–6319; Case C–410/01 *Fritsch, Chiari & Partner* [2003] ECR I–6413; Case C–230/02 *Grossmann Air Service* (Judgment of 12 February 2004).

[112] Art 2(8). Cf Case C–103/97 *Köllensperger* [1999] ECR I–551; Case C–258/97 *Hospital Ingenieure* [1999] ECR I–1405. Cf also Case C–54/96 *Dorsch Consult* [1997] ECR I–4961; Case C–76/97 *Walter Tögel* [1998] ECR I–5357.

[113] Case C–213/89 *ex p Factortame* [1990] ECR I–2433; Cases C–6 & 9/90 *Francovich* [1991] ECR I–5357. See the various provisions contained in Art 2. On interim relief, cf Case C–236/95 *Commission v Greece* [1996] ECR I–4459; Case C–214/00 *Commission v Spain* [2003] ECR I–4667.

[114] Eg Case C–470/99 *Universale-Bau* [2002] ECR I–11617; Case C–327/00 *Santex* [2003] ECR I–1877.

[115] Eg Case C–92/00 *Hospital Ingenieure* [2002] ECR I–5553.

[116] Eg Case C–315/01 *Gesellschaft für Abfallentsorgungs-Technik* [2003] ECR I–6351.

[117] Eg J M Fernández Martín, *The EC Public Procurement Rules: A Critical Analysis* (Clarendon Press, 1996).

[118] Note also the Third Pillar provisions on judicial cooperation in criminal matters: see ch 1 (above).

Community action in the sphere of judicial cooperation, covering not only the mutual recognition of judicial decisions but also issues such as effective access to justice in cross-border disputes, are inspired by the desire to realise the economic and political benefits of the Internal Market as an area truly without internal frontiers.[119]

By these means, national procedural rules become more fully absorbed into the Treaty's substantive policy ambitions. Indeed, we have so far considered the domestic standards of judicial protection as a field in which the Community's interest is merely derivative, that is, justified by the second order impact which national remedies might have upon the enforcement of other more substantive Treaty norms. But the development of an Area of Freedom, Justice and Security now sees the domestic standards of judicial protection beginning to constitute a primary object of the 'integration through law' concern for the imperatives of uniformity and effectiveness. The simple co-existence of different procedural regimes in different Member States might constitute *in itself* an obstacle to the free movement of judicial decisions, warranting the harmonisation of essential legal safeguards as a precondition for complete mutual recognition (just as the simple co-existence of different regulatory regimes on product specifications or professional conduct in different Member States might *in itself* constitute an obstacle to the free movement of goods and persons, warranting the harmonisation of essential public interest requirements as a precondition for complete mutual recognition).

But in practice, the Community legislature seems so far not to have construed Article 65 EC as a legal basis for the widespread harmonisation of national civil procedure rules. The Council's 2001 draft programme of measures for implementing the principle of mutual recognition of judicial decisions in civil and commercial matters foresees the harmonisation only of specific civil procedure rules: for example, on the recovery of uncontested claims and litigation on small claims.[120] Even in those particular fields, difficult questions arise about whether harmonisation should apply only in cross-border disputes or also to claims arising in wholly internal situations. In this regard, the Commission has hinted its support for a classic 'integration through law' analysis: it would be contrary to the principle of equality between citizens, and between business partners, if litigants within the Union did not have access to equally rapid and efficient instruments for the recovery of uncontested claims, or for litigation on small claims. In particular, the Commission suggested that such discrepancies between the domestic standards of judicial protection—within as well as between Member States—could have a direct bearing on the functioning of the Internal Market by offering competitive advantages

[119] Conclusions of the Tampere European Council (15–16 October 1999).

[120] Council, *Draft Programme of Measures for Implementation of the Principle of Mutual Recognition of Decisions in Civil and Commercial Matters*, OJ 2001 C12/1.

to undertakings established in Member States which offer fast and effective enforcement mechanisms.[121] However, the Council seems less receptive to this strain of analysis. Consider Directive 2003/8, one of the legislative measures already adopted pursuant to Article 65 EC, which establishes minimum common rules on legal aid for the purposes of facilitating access to justice.[122] The Commission had originally proposed that the Directive should apply to all civil disputes, including those wholly internal to one Member State.[123] But in its final version, the Directive states that it applies only to cross-border disputes, in accordance with the specific objectives for judicial cooperation established by Article 65 EC.[124]

For the time being at least, the prospects for harmonising the domestic systems of judicial protection by exercising the competences conferred under Article 65 EC therefore remain weak. More generally, as Heukels and Tib have observed,

> it appears difficult to distinguish a coherent overall policy underlying the Community's [legislative] activities. Rather, the impression is one of fragmentation and of an ad hoc approach.[125]

Indeed, in the search for a 'unified system of judicial protection,' at whatever level of abstraction such a goal is postulated, the Community legislature appears to have been conspicuously unforthcoming.[126]

Consider thirdly the judicial contribution (though for the time being only briefly, since this will form the subject of more detailed treatment later in this book).[127] In the early stages of the caselaw, the Court of Justice's extensive deference to national procedural autonomy (as demonstrated in judgments such as *Rewe/Comet*, *Russo* and the *Butter Buying Cruises* litigation)[128] was criticised for permitting the Member States to maintain inadequate and disparate sanctions and procedural rules, and thus

[121] Commission, *Green Paper on a European Order for Payment Procedure and on Measures to Simplify and Speed Up Small Claims Litigation*, COM (2002)746 Final.
[122] Dir 2003/8 to improve access to justice in cross-border disputes by establishing minimum common rules relating to legal aid for such disputes, OJ 2003 L26/41.
[123] Commission, *Proposal for a Directive to Improve Access to Justice in Cross-Border Disputes by Establishing Minimum Common Rules Relating to Legal Aid and Other Financial Aspects of Civil Proceedings*, COM (2002) 13 Final.
[124] Arts 1 and 2 Dir 2003/8.
[125] T Heukels and J Tib, 'Towards Homogeneity in the Field of Legal Remedies: Convergence and Divergence' in P Beaumont, C Lyons & N Walker (eds), *Convergence and Divergence in European Public Law* (Hart Publishing, 2002).
[126] Further, eg J Steiner, *Enforcing EC Law* (Blackstone Press, 1995) ch 5. Cf judicial discussion of the Community's competence to impose sanctions in Case C–240/90 *Germany v Commission* [1992] ECR I–5383.
[127] See chs 5 and 6 (below).
[128] Case 33/76 *Rewe-Zentralfinanz v Landwirtschaftskammer für das Saarland* [1976] ECR 1989 and Case 45/76 *Comet* [1976] ECR 2043; Case 60/75 *Russo* [1976] ECR 45; Case 158/80 *Rewe-Handelsgesellschaft Nord v Hauptzollamt Kiel* [1981] ECR 1805 (respectively).

indirectly to frustrate the efficacy of the Common Market.[129] As the Court's commitment to 'effective judicial protection' gathered pace in its middle-period caselaw (as demonstrated by judgments such as *Emmott*, *Francovich* and *Factortame*),[130] many commentators excitedly prophesied the birth of a Community remedial system which would overcome the dilemmas—in terms of effectiveness and uniformity—posed by the administration of Treaty rules through the domestic systems of justice.[131] Then, when the Court lurched back towards a more conservative approach, it was lampooned for having sacrificed the interests of the Treaty order in constructing a more coherent system of legal protection suited to the needs of supranational integration, in the face of political pressure from disgruntled Member States intent on holding the Community's natural development hostage to their own parochial and—given the budgetary costs of effective judicial protection, usually financial—interests.[132]

The overall assessment of the current legal position suggested by an 'integration through law' perspective is perhaps summed up in the tone of van Gerven's recent observations: the objective of uniform enforcement for Treaty rules throughout every Member State is a fundamental requirement of the Community legal order; yet as a matter of political necessity and legal reality, and surely to its own misfortune, the Community is forced to rely on the divergent remedies and procedural rules provided by the national legal orders.[133]

Objections to a 'Unified System of Judicial Protection'

The underlying essentials of this 'integration through law' analysis have been accepted as orthodox not only by its adherents, but also by its detractors.

[129] Eg D Curtin, 'Directives: The Effectiveness of Judicial Protection of Individual Rights' (1990) 27 CML Rev 709.

[130] Case C–208/90 *Emmott* [1991] ECR I–4269; Cases C–6 & 9/90 *Francovich* [1991] ECR I–5357; Case C–213/89 *ex p Factortame* [1990] ECR I–2433.

[131] Eg AP Tash, 'Remedies for European Community Law Claims in Member State Courts: Toward a European Standard' (1993) 31 *Columbia Journal of Transnational Law* 377; D Curtin and K Mortelmans, 'Application and Enforcement of Community Law by the Member States: Actors in Search of a Third Generation Script' in D Curtin & T Heukels (eds), *Institutional Dynamics of European Integration* (Martinus Nijhoff, 1994); R Caranta, 'Judicial Protection Against Member States: A New *Jus Commune* Takes Shape' (1995) 32 CML Rev 703; S Weatherill, 'Beyond "EC Law Rights, National Remedies"' in A Caiger & D A Floudas (eds), *1996 Onwards: Lowering the Barriers Further* (Wiley, 1996).

[132] Consider contemporary analyses offered, eg by B Fitzpatrick and E Szyszczak, 'Remedies and Effective Judicial Protection in Community Law' (1994) 57 MLR 434; J A Sohrab, Annotation of *Steenhorst-Neerings* (1994) 31 CML Rev 875; I Higgins, 'Equal Treatment and National Procedural Rules: One Step Forward, Two Steps Back' (1995) 4 *Irish Journal of European Law* 18; A Ward, 'Effective Sanctions in EC Law: A Moving Boundary in the Division of Competence' (1995) 1 *European Law Journal* 205.

[133] W van Gerven, 'Of Rights, Remedies and Procedures' (2000) 37 CML Rev 501, 521–22.

Interaction With Legitimate National Interests

First, certain commentators have questioned the manner in which the (admittedly valid) Community goal of effectiveness interacts with competing interests operating at the level of each Member State—such as the need to protect legal certainty in administrative or contractual relationships, or to maintain fairness and efficiency in the provision of justice. For example, imagine that the Community were to impose a general rule whereby all actions for the recovery of charges levied by the Member State contrary to the prohibition on customs duties contained in Article 25 EC may be brought before the national courts without restriction as to time. Such a procedural rule might well advance the cause of effective enforcement for an important Community norm, but it is also likely to interfere with budgetary certainty in a Member State whose administrative framework is not adapted to cope with the financial and evidential burdens such a rule would undoubtedly impose. Similarly, consider the *Francovich* principle that Member States must make reparation for breaches of their Treaty obligations which cause loss to citizens.[134] Should the substantive conditions under which the Member State incurs liability be framed permissively, so as to maximise the effective protection of individual Community rights; or should the Community be satisfied with more restrictive requirements, thereby accommodating concerns about the dangers of exposing public authorities to excessive levels of liability such as would hamper the efficient performance of their duties in the general interest? Alternatively, imagine a principle of Community law whereby arguments based on Treaty rights may be raised by claimants at any point during litigation before the domestic courts: such intervention might also increase the likelihood that Treaty norms are enforced effectively within each Member State; but conversely, might not such a requirement prejudice the fair administration of justice, by granting to parties who rely on Community measures a significant procedural advantage over those who claim rights derive solely from domestic provisions?

The basic thrust of this criticism is that 'integration through law' should not simply identify a problem and postulate a solution reasoned solely on the basis of abstract Treaty-centred concerns: Community law operates not in a vacuum, but in the daily context of its administration by the national authorities and enforcement through the domestic judiciaries. The imperative of effectiveness may therefore have to be compromised to the extent of those limitations which result inevitably from the Community's reliance upon the legal orders of the various Member States.[135] At the very

[134] Cases C–6 & 9/90 *Francovich* [1991] ECR I–5357. Further: ch 5 (below).
[135] Further, eg M Hoskins, 'Tilting the Balance: Supremacy and National Procedural Rules' (1996) 21 EL Rev 365; C Himsworth, 'Things Fall Apart: The Harmonisation of Community Judicial Procedural Protection Revisited' (1997) 22 EL Rev 291; A Biondi, 'The European

least this requires that, when the Court is applying the principles of effective judicial protection in particular cases, it must negotiate a careful balance between Community and legitimate domestic interests; and when the Community legislature is adopting secondary measures dealing with national remedies and procedural rules, it must strike that balance anew.

Interference With Local Cultural Choices

Secondly, consider the criticism that Community-wide principles for the grant of legal remedies interfere unduly with the cultural fabric of each Member State. Harlow has suggested that most Community rights remain essentially economic in nature, or in any case are of greatest benefit to those multinational corporations which are best placed in terms of financial resources and cross-border mobility to exploit their full potential. When transplanted into the context of each individual Member State, such Treaty rules will often clash with domestic provisions promoting (for example) citizens' welfare and environmental protection. For the Court of Justice to insist that these extraneous Community rights enjoy increased levels of judicial protection, the balance struck within each national order about how to value economic rights vis-à-vis other more fundamental social interests is disrupted even further.[136] Harlow cites the example of *Hedley Lomas*, where the United Kingdom was required to pay compensation to exporters whose commercial interests were adversely affected by a government ban on the shipment of live sheep to Spain, imposed on the grounds that the recipient Spanish slaughterhouses were guilty of perpetrating acts of cruelty against the animals.[137] The Community's economic interest in free movement for goods within the Single Market prevailed over the United Kingdom's cultural preference for defending high standards of animal welfare; and the Court's robust approach to the judicial protection of the Community right to free trade, through means of a *Francovich* action in damages, reinforced this intrusive interference still more.[138]

This argument in fact fits into Harlow's wider critique of Community intervention in the national legal systems (particularly as regards public

Court of Justice and Certain National Procedural Limitations: Not Such a Tough Relationship' (1999) 36 CML Rev 1271.

[136] C Harlow, '*Francovich* and the Problem of the Disobedient State' (1996) 2 *European Law Journal* 199.

[137] Case C–5/94 *ex p Hedley Lomas* [1996] ECR I–2553.

[138] Also: T Hartley, *Constitutional Problems of the European Union* (Hart Publishing, 1999) pp 59–65. Cf J Bridge, 'Procedural Aspects of the Enforcement of European Community Law through the Legal Systems of the Member States' (1984) 9 EL Rev 28, 42:

> [i]t is difficult to believe that there are any issues of high policy here or that very important interests of the Member States are at stake.

and administrative law). The latter should not be debased by an analysis which treats them merely as 'regulatory compliance costs' and 'distortions of competition'. National legal systems reflect a delicate balance between competing economic, political and social interests within any given country. Community intervention not only disrupts that balance, but also has a negative impact upon the democratic processes which underpin it. In this regard, Harlow asserts that popular identity and political participation within the European Union remain primarily focused upon the domestic level. By contrast, the Community system fosters undemocratic channels of public power—particularly though the disproportionate influence of the Court of Justice over the evolution of EU law. Thus, principles created at the supranational level by relatively less democratic institutions are capable of upsetting the compromises struck at the national level by relatively more democratic institutions. Against that background, one is entitled to query whether the arguments in favour of a 'unified system of judicial protection' in Europe are really so persuasive as to outweigh the potential threat to local cultural preferences.[139]

Uniformity On Paper and In Practice

Thirdly, other commentators have queried how far the creation of a unified system of judicial protection would actually serve the (admittedly valid) objective of increasing the uniform application of Community law. After all, the daily administration of any harmonised system of judicial protection would still lie in the hands of national authorities, and the latter would retain broad discretion as regards matters such as prosecution policy and the assessment of damages.[140] Moreover, socio-legal research suggests that there are marked national and regional variations as regards important aspects of rule-enforcement, such as the willingness of individuals and undertakings to have recourse to litigation as a means of dispute settlement.[141] In short: it is one thing to devise idealised remedies and

[139] In particular: C Harlow, 'A Common European Law of Remedies?' in C Kilpatrick, T Novitz & P Skidmore (eds), *The Future of Remedies in Europe* (Hart Publishing, 2000); and 'Voices of Difference in a Pluralist Community' in P Beaumont, C Lyons & N Walker (eds), *Convergence and Divergence in European Public Law* (Hart Publishing, 2002). Of course, these views have not gone uncontested, eg C Lyons, 'Perspectives on Convergence Within the Theatre of European Integration' in the same collection edited by P Beaumont, C Lyons & N Walker.

[140] Eg C Harding, 'Member State Enforcement of European Community Measures: The Chimera of "Effective" Enforcement' (1997) 4 *Maastricht Journal of European and Comparative Law* 5; A Biondi, 'The European Court of Justice and Certain National Procedural Limitations: Not Such a Tough Relationship' (1999) 36 CML Rev 1271. Cf the observations of both AG van Gerven and the ECJ in Case C–326/88 *Hansen* [1990] ECR I–2911.

[141] Eg S Deakin and F Wilkinson, 'Contract Law and the Economics of Inter-Organisational Trust' in C Lane & R Bachmann (eds), *Trust Within and Between Organisations* (OUP, 1998). Also: F Snyder, 'The Effectiveness of European Community Law: Institutions, Processes, Tools and Techniques' (1993) 56 MLR 19.

procedures to be transposed into the domestic legal orders; but it is a much more difficult and unpredictable task to maintain the supranational coherency of such remedies and procedures in the face of their practical application to meet the subtly different problems and demands of what remain, in certain important respects, compartmentalised nation-states.

This argument can also find support in broader theoretical critiques of European integration. Teubner's analysis of law as an autopoietic system stresses the closed character of the national legal orders, each constructing and perpetuating its own elements and processes in a self-referential manner. Such a state of operational closure renders the domestic legal systems highly resistant to any intervention by the Community authorities which seeks to prescribe supranational legislative norms understood and applied identically in every Member State. Of course, individual autopoietic orders remain cognitively open to their external environment, such that the latter can exert an indirect influence on the formers' evolution. In particular, Teubner identifies a process of 'interference': phenomena from the Community order are brought into immediate contact with each national order via a series of institutional and conceptual 'linkages' (for example: the transposition of directives into domestic legislation; or the Article 234 EC preliminary reference procedure). This in turn stimulates a process of 'perturbation': each domestic system reconstructs and incorporates the new information according to its own internal reality such that it becomes absorbed into, but also stimulates the ongoing evolution of, the self-referential unit. By such means, it is possible to envisage the mutual—but complex and often unpredictable—development of what nevertheless remain autonomous legal systems.[142] Such an analysis suggests that there are inherent limitations to the possibility of genuine legal convergence in Europe—and might thus reinforce doubts about whether centralised intervention in the domestic systems of judicial protection can ever really achieve its stated goal of uniform of treatment between individuals *qua* economic actors or *qua* Union citizens.

Discrimination Against Purely Domestic Situations

Finally, another objection points out that whenever the Community legislature or the Court of Justice takes steps towards the 'Europeanisation' of national remedies and procedures in cases involving the application of Treaty-based norms, the inevitable by-product of such ventures is to discriminate against cases involving the application of purely domestic norms. The Court is adamant that, by virtue of the principle of equivalence,

[142] G Teubner, *Law as an Autopoietic System* (Blackwell, 1993). On the application of this theoretical framework within the EC context, eg I Maher, 'Community Law in the National Legal Order: A Systems Analysis' (1998) 36 JCMS 237; G Teubner, 'Legal Irritants: Good Faith in British Law or How Unifying Law Ends Up in New Divergences' (1998) 61 MLR 11.

Community rights may not suffer a lesser level of protection than that enjoyed by comparable national rights.[143] However, it is prepared to tolerate reverse discrimination, whereby citizens relying on national rights are treated less favourably than those relying on Treaty provisions.[144] Consider by way of illustration the judgments in *Factortame* and *Marshall II*. The Court of Justice held that rules of English law proscribing the grant of interim relief against the Crown, and limiting the damages recoverable against employers guilty of having carried out a discriminatory dismissal, were inapplicable in Community cases because they offered claimants inadequate levels of judicial protection.[145] But there was nothing to prevent such rules from continuing to apply in analogous domestic cases involving litigation against the Crown or allegations of racial discrimination, and therefore from continuing to deprive claimants in those situations of satisfactory standards of legal redress.[146] The creation of such dual systems of judicial protection has been criticised as running counter both to equalised conditions of competition between economic undertakings operating within the Common Market, and to the principle of equality between all citizens of the Union—exactly the same imperatives upon which an 'integration through law' analysis claims to justify Community intervention in domestic remedies and procedures in the first place.[147]

Assessment

The purpose of the above exposition was twofold: first, to offer a representative summary of contemporary academic discussion about what to

[143] Eg Case C–261/95 *Palmisani* [1997] ECR I–4025; Case C–326/96 *Levez* [1998] ECR I–7835; Case C–78/98 *Preston* [2000] ECR I–3201.

[144] Reverse discrimination is, in fact, the result of the ECJ's own limited jurisdiction to interfere with remedies and procedural rules falling outside the scope of application of Community law. Cf Case 355/85 *Driancourt v Michel Cognet* [1986] ECR 3231; Case 98/86 *Arthur Mathot* [1987] ECR 809; Cases C–64–65/96 *Uecker and Jacquet* [1997] ECR I–3171; Case C–148/02 *Garcia Avello* (Judgment of 2 October 2003).

[145] Case C–213/89 *ex p Factortame* [1990] ECR I–2433; Case C–271/91 *Marshall II* [1993] ECR I–4367.

[146] Though in fact the Member States are sometimes prepared to remove such anomalies for themselves. Eg the English House of Lords in *M v Home Office* [1994] 1 AC 377 adapted domestic law on interim relief (at least in part) in the light of Case C–213/89 *Ex p Factortame* [1990] ECR I–2433. Similarly, eg the House of Lords in *Woolwich Building Society v IRC* [1993] AC 70 also adapted domestic rules on the recovery of unlawful taxes (at least in part) in the light of Case 199/82 *San Giorgio* [1983] ECR 3595.

[147] Eg M P Chiti, 'Towards a Unified Judicial Protection in Europe(?)' (1997) 9 *European Review of Public Law* 553. Further: R Caranta, 'Judicial Protection Against Member States: A New *Jus Commune* Takes Shape' (1995) 32 CML Rev 703; and 'Learning from our Neighbours: Public Law Remedies, Homogenisation from Bottom Up' (1997) 4 *Maastricht Journal of European and Comparative Law* 220. Also, eg M L F Esteban, 'National Judges and Community Law: The Paradox of the Two Paradigms of Law' (1997) 4 *Maastricht Journal of European and Comparative Law* 143; W van Gerven, 'Mutual Permeation of Public and Private Law at the National and Supranational Level' (1998) 5 *Maastricht Journal of European and Comparative Law* 7.

do with the remedies and procedural rules available for the purposes of enforcing Treaty law before the domestic courts of the Member States; and secondly, to demonstrate that this entire debate has been dominated by a particular approach to European integration, and hence a particular understanding of the proper role to be performed by the Community legal order. 'Integration through law' dictates that national remedies and procedures present a threat to the Treaty's fundamental economic and/or socio-political objectives, and that the solution to this problem is to strive towards the creation of a 'unified system of judicial protection.' Critics of this analysis tend merely to point out the alleged shortcomings of Community intervention, in terms of achieving its own Treaty-orientated goals of uniformity and effectiveness, or of striking an appropriate balance with competing Member State concerns (for example) as regards legal certainty and the fair administration of justice.

The remainder of this book will seek to construct a more far-reaching critique, by challenging the internal assumptions which support the initial 'integration through law' analysis, and thus structure the subsequent enforcement deficit debate.

The problem with the argument that uniformity and effectiveness provide a sufficient rationale for Community intervention in the national systems of judicial protection lies in its unwavering faith in the belief that the vocation of the Treaty project is to promote a continuous process of supranational convergence. The Community is meant to achieve an 'ever closer union among the peoples of Europe.' Community law is one of the central tools available to bring this ideal of unity to fruition. Therefore, chinks in the Community armour—such as the lack of horizontal direct effect for directives, the ambivalent attitude of certain domestic courts to the supremacy of Treaty rules, and the provision of inadequate and disuniform national procedures—each in their own way present obstacles to the proper realisation of the Treaty's ultimate raison d'être. At least as regards the problem posed by domestic remedies, the solution is obvious if possibly difficult to attain: increasing the degree of Community review over, or ultimately the approximation of, the legal infrastructure for the domestic administration of justice.

However, it will be argued that this interpretation has failed to keep pace with wider trends in the Treaty's political and legal evolution. In particular, the imperative of uniformity is under direct challenge from within the Community order itself, through the increasingly common phenomenon of regulatory differentiation. Chapter 3 offers an overview of the contemporary nature and scope of regulatory differentiation. Chapter 4 then addresses in greater detail the implications of this process of differentiation both for the Community system in general, and for the enforcement deficit debate in particular. It will be argued that the modern Treaty project is concerned as much with managing our respective differences as with removing them, and that the modern Community legal order has an equally valid role in forwarding both these objectives. Once the underlying assumptions of 'integration through law' are challenged, so too our traditional diagnosis of the problem posed by national remedies and procedures, and our traditional prescription of the cure required to address it, will need to be updated and refined.

3

Regulatory Differentiation Within the Community Legal Order

THIS CHAPTER ANALYSES the relative competences of the Community institutions and national authorities in the extrapolation of legal rules to govern matters falling within the Treaty's sphere of interest, and thus seeks to provide an outline of the phenomenon of regulatory differentiation within the Community legal order. In particular, it is proposed to examine some of the ways in which the Treaty system permits the Member States to participate in the formulation of substantive rules falling within the scope of Community policies. The intention is to demonstrate that, just because the Community is involved in a given sphere of activity, this does not mean that the regulatory regime it establishes to achieve its objectives will provide uniform norms across the Member States, or indeed that such uniformity is its ultimate goal.

For the purposes of exposition, we will distinguish between two principal categories of differentiation. 'Vertical differentiation' refers to the ability of Member States to contribute to substantive regulatory policy within the context of any given sector of Community activity or legislative measure. 'Horizontal differentiation' refers to the ability of Member States to decide whether or not to participate in any given sector of Community activity or legislative measure at all. To help illustrate this distinction, consider the Social Protocol as annexed to the EC Treaty by the Treaty on European Union: the ability of the United Kingdom to opt out of this sphere of Community activity altogether was a clear instance of horizontal differentiation; for those Member States which did participate in the Social Protocol, the fact that the Community set only minimum standards, and that even these were punctuated by numerous derogations, provided an example of vertical differentiation.[1]

[1] This particular instance of horizontal differentiation has now been terminated by the agreement of the UK, under the Treaty of Amsterdam, to be bound by the provisions of the Social Protocol as integrated into the main body of the Treaty (Arts 136–45 EC).

VERTICAL DIFFERENTIATION

Principle of Attributed Powers

The starting point for any analysis of Community competences is the principle of attributed powers set out in Article 5(1) EC: the Community shall act within the limits of the powers conferred upon it by the Treaty and of the objectives assigned to it therein. In other words, the Community has no primary or inherent competence; its powers are secondary and derive solely from the provisions of the Treaty.[2] This principle is undoubtedly one of the fundamental concepts defining the nature of the Community order.[3] However, there are significant limits to its utility for the purposes of apportioning regulatory competence between the Community and the Member States.

First, the Treaty text does not necessarily offer an accurate description of the 'scope' or 'breadth' of the powers actually enjoyed by the Community. For example, Articles 94 and 95 EC appear on their face to sanction the adoption of legislation for the completion of the Internal Market. However, these provisions were sufficiently broad in both wording and concept to allow for the development of additional Community interests in environmental and consumer policy which, at the time, had no apparent textual basis.[4] Moreover, the Court of Justice has traditionally tended to interpret the Community's powers expansively. In the 1971 *ERTA* judgment, for instance, the Court recognised a doctrine of implied external competence, whereby the adoption by the Community institutions of a common policy for the Member States could in principle generate a corresponding power to negotiate and enter into international agreements with third countries and organisations in respect of the subject matter of that common policy, even where the Treaty made no explicit provision in this regard.[5] Similarly, in the 1987 *Migration Policy* judgment, the Court began to develop a limited principle of implied internal competence, whereby the Community institutions must be understood to enjoy those powers which are indispensable in order to carry out

[2] Opinion 2/94 (*Accession by the Communities to the Convention for the Protection of Human Rights and Fundamental Freedoms)* [1996] ECR I–1759, para 23.
[3] A Dashwood, 'The Limits of European Community Powers' (1996) 21 EL Rev 113.
[4] See ch 2 (above). Consider also Art 308 EC as discussed by, eg R Schütze, 'Organised Change Towards an "Ever Closer Union": Article 308 EC and the Limits to the Community's Legislative Competence' (2003) 22 *Yearbook of European Law* 79. On the other hand, there are signs that the Court is adopting an increasingly circumspect approach to the construction of Community competence, more compatible with the idea of attributed powers, eg Opinion 2/94 (*Accession by the Communities to the Convention for the Protection of Human Rights and Fundamental Freedoms)* [1996] ECR I–1759; Case C–249/96 *Grant v South-West Trains* [1998] ECR I–621; Case C–376/98 *Germany v Parliament and Council* [2000] ECR I–8419.
[5] Case 22/70 *Commission v Council (ERTA)* [1971] ECR 263.

the specific tasks conferred on them by the Treaty, even if the measures in question are not clearly authorised by the Treaty.[6]

Secondly, the Treaty text does not necessarily define the 'strength' or 'depth' of the powers actually enjoyed by the Community, vis-à-vis the existence of domestic competence. To be sure, there are situations in which the boundary between Community and Member State regulatory power is spelt out with relative clarity. In particular, the Treaty confers upon the Community certain 'complementary competences': policy fields in which both the Community and the Member States are legally capable of carrying out independent action; but legally binding acts adopted by the Community are incapable of harmonising national laws or of having pre-emptive effects vis-à-vis national competence. Regulatory power therefore rests primarily with the Member States, and Community action merely supports, coordinates or complements domestic policies. For example, Article 149 EC states that the Community shall contribute to the development of quality education by encouraging cooperation between Member States and, if necessary, by supporting and supplementing their action, whilst fully respecting the responsibility of the Member States for the content of teaching and the organisation of education systems. To this end, the Council is empowered to adopt incentive measures, excluding any harmonisation of the laws and regulations of the Member States.[7] Such complementary competence also exists as regards cultural policy and most aspects of public health policy.[8] In addition, complementary competence can be considered to apply to employment policy (where the Community merely facilitates the coordination of national activities) and industrial policy (where the Community is empowered to adopt specific measures in support of action taken by the Member States).[9] However, even in fields of complementary competence, the Member States remain bound by the obligations imposed by directly effective Treaty provisions (for example) on free movement of goods or non-discrimination on grounds of nationality.[10] Moreover, the Community can pass approximation measures which have an educational, cultural or public health dimension on the basis of Articles 94 and 95 EC, where this can be justified by reference to the operation of the Single Market.[11]

The designation of a given policy sector as one of complementary competence clearly has a drastic impact upon the potential for regulatory

[6] Cases 281, 283–85 & 287/85 *Germany v Commission (Migration Policy)* [1987] ECR 3203.

[7] Also: Art 150 EC (vocational training).

[8] Arts 151 and 152 EC (subject to the limited power to harmonise domestic laws contained in Art 152(4)(a) EC).

[9] Arts 125–30 EC and Art 157 EC (respectively).

[10] Consider, in the sphere of education, eg Case 293/83 *Gravier v City of Liège* [1985] ECR 593; Case 39/86 *Lair* [1988] ECR 3161; Case C–184/99 *Grzelczyk* [2001] ECR I–6193.

[11] Consider, in the sphere of cultural policy, eg Dir 93/7 on the return of cultural objects unlawfully removed from the territory of a Member State, OJ 1993 L74/74.

uniformity across the Community: without any direct power to harmonise domestic provisions, individual rights and obligations will clearly continue to differ from Member State to Member State. But clauses such as Article 149 EC are the exception rather than the rule. Neither Article 5(1) EC, nor the great majority of more specific Treaty provisions, seek to elaborate on the consequences of the existence of any given Community power, in particular, as regards its relationship with national competence over the same or similar subject-matter.

Exclusive and Shared Competences

In the absence of any comprehensive guidance from the Treaty text itself, scholars have therefore sought to devise some useful analytical framework for describing the balance between Community and national regulatory power.[12] We shall adopt the threefold categorisation proposed by the Convention on the Future of Europe in its 2003 draft Treaty establishing a Constitution for Europe, and accepted by the Member States at the 2004 IGC.[13] Complementary competence, as discussed above, is one of those categories.[14] The remaining two are exclusive and shared competences.

In fact, the distinction between exclusive and shared competences has long occupied a central place in the conceptual framework by which commentators have sought to explain the nature of Community powers.[15] And indeed, we shall see how these two categories do *in themselves* tell us something useful about the relationship between uniformity and differentiation in regulatory standards across the European Union. But their utility in this regard is often limited. The fact that a particular power is exclusive to the Community need not mean that substantive policy is uniform across the Member States. Conversely, the fact that a particular power is shared by the Community need not imply that substantive policy differs as between the Member States within the territory occupied by the Treaty.

Exclusive Competence

Exclusive competence refers to the idea that only the Community institutions are legally capable of carrying out independent action within

[12] Consider, eg A Von Bogandy and J Bast, 'The European Union's Vertical Order of Competences: The Current Law and Proposals For Its Reform' (2002) 39 CML Rev 227.
[13] Draft Treaty Establishing a Constitution for Europe, OJ 2003 C169/1; final text of the 2004 Treaty, CIG 87/04. Not that the Convention's proposals are perfect in this regard: consider, eg M Dougan, 'The Convention's Draft Constitutional Treaty: Bringing Europe Closer To Its Lawyers?' (2003) 28 EL Rev 763; J Kokott and A Rüth, 'The European Convention and its Draft Treaty Establishing a Constitution for Europe: Appropriate Answers to the Laeken Questions?' (2003) 40 CML Rev 1315.
[14] Arts 11 and 16 of the Draft Treaty Establishing a Constitution for Europe, OJ 2003 C169/1. See now Arts I-12 and I-17 of the 2004 Treaty, CIG 87/04.
[15] The distinction is also crucial when attempting to define the potential scope of / limits to the principles of subsidiarity and enhanced cooperation: Arts 5(2) EC and 43(d) TEU (respectively).

the relevant policy field; any such action by the Member States is strictly precluded.

Competence of this nature is in fact relatively rare. The first situation in which exclusivity was identified concerned the Common Commercial Policy based on Article 133 EC. In Opinion 1/75, the Court stressed that the success of the Common Commercial Policy depends on common and uniform rules throughout the Community, an objective which would be seriously jeopardised were the individual Member States to retain freedom of action in their relations with third countries with regard to matters falling within the scope of Article 133 EC.[16] Accordingly, the Member States may not, for example, impose by means of national legislation alone charges having equivalent effect to customs duties in trade with third countries.[17] However, the Treaty of Nice amended Article 133 EC so as to qualify the principle of exclusivity as regards the 'new' aspects of the expanded Common Commercial Policy. First, Article 133(5) EC states that, as regards the negotiation and conclusion of agreements in the fields of trade in services and the commercial aspects of intellectual property which were not already covered by the pre-Nice Common Commercial Policy, the Treaty shall not affect the right of the Member States to maintain or conclude agreements with third countries or international organisations.[18] Here, the Community has competence, but it is not exclusive, though it may be exercised autonomously. Secondly, Article 133(6) EC now provides that, by way of derogation, agreements relating to trade in cultural and audiovisual services, educational services, and social and human health services, shall fall within the shared competence of the Community and its Member States—and must be concluded jointly by the Community and the Member States. Here, the Community has competence, and again it is not exclusive, but this time it may only be exercised jointly with the Member States.[19]

The Court has also held that exclusive competence vests in the Community as regards the preservation of marine biological resources within the context of the Common Fisheries Policy.[20] Moreover, it is widely assumed that the Community enjoys exclusive competence over monetary policy for those Member States which have adopted the euro.[21] But

[16] Opinion 1/75 (*Understanding on a Local Cost Standard)* [1975] ECR 1355, pp 1363–5. Also, eg Case 41/76 *Donckerwolcke* [1976] ECR 1921.

[17] Case C–125/94 *Aprile* [1995] ECR I–2919, paras 32–37. Also, eg Case C–83/94 *Peter Leifer* [1995] ECR I–3231.

[18] In so far as such agreements comply with Community law and other relevant international agreements.

[19] These provisions are extremely complex and their full legal effects are controversial. Further, eg M Cremona, 'A Policy of Bits and Pieces? The Common Commercial Policy After Nice' (2001) 4 *Cambridge Yearbook of European Legal Studies* 61.

[20] Eg Cases 3–4 & 6/76 *Kramer* [1976] ECR 1279; Case 804/79 *Commission v UK* [1981] ECR 1045; Case C–25/94 *Commission v Council* [1996] ECR I–1469.

[21] Eg N Bernard, 'The Future of European Economic Law in the Light of the Principle of Subsidiarity' (1996) 33 CML Rev 633.

whether exclusive competence should be taken to exist in other fields has been a matter of considerable controversy.[22] The Court certainly seems reluctant to adopt too expansive a conception of the policy fields governed by exclusivity. For example, several Advocates General had argued that Community competence under Article 95 EC, to adopt measures which have as their object the establishment of the Internal Market, should be considered exclusive in nature.[23] Yet the Court in its *Tobacco Labelling Directive* judgment held that Article 95 EC merely confers upon the Union 'a certain competence' for improving the functioning of the Internal Market—expressly rejecting the claim that Article 95 EC was characterised by exclusivity.[24] The European Convention's draft Treaty Establishing a Constitution for Europe likewise adopts a relatively narrow approach to the scope of exclusivity.[25]

On the one hand, the designation of a given policy sector as one of exclusive Community competence has an immediate and drastic impact upon the existence of Member State regulatory power. Moreover, there is obviously a strong affinity between the recognition of exclusive Community competence and the imperative of uniformity in the application of Treaty norms. In particular, the principle of exclusivity can be seen as an effective legal contribution (albeit within limited spheres) to achieving the Treaty's substantive policy objectives as regards economic integration based on free trade and equal competition. On the other hand, the link between exclusive Community competence and the imperative of uniformity is far from absolute. Just because a particular regulatory sector is one of exclusive Treaty competence does not necessarily mean that potentially divergent national action ceases altogether. Although, with regard to the subject matter of an exclusive competence, *independent* action by the Member States is prohibited, the national authorities may still pursue differentiated policy goals *as permitted* (and within the limits set) by Community law.[26]

[22] Eg contrast the views of A G Toth, 'A Legal Analysis of Subsidiarity', with those of J Steiner, 'Subsidiarity under the Maastricht Treaty', both in D O'Keeffe & P Twomey (eds), *Legal Issues of the Maastricht Treaty* (Wiley, 1994). Note also the views of A Arnull, A Dashwood, M Ross & D Wyatt, *Wyatt and Dashwood's European Union Law* (Sweet & Maxwell, 2000), pp 157–59. In any case, it is important to define the sectoral boundaries of the Community's exclusive competences, eg Opinion 1/78 *(International Agreement on Natural Rubber)* [1979] ECR 2871; Opinion 1/94 *(Competence of the Community to conclude international agreements concerning services and the protection of intellectual property)* [1994] ECR I–5267; Opinion 2/92 *(Competence of the Community to participate in the Third Revised Decision of the OECD on national treatment)* [1995] ECR I–521.
[23] Eg in Case C–233/94 *Germany v Parliament and Council (Deposit Guarantee Schemes Directive)* [1997] ECR I–2405; Case C–376/98 *Germany v Parliament and Council (Tobacco Advertising Directive)* [2000] ECR I–8419; Case C–377/98 *Netherlands v Parliament and Council (Biotech Directive)* [2001] ECR I–7079.
[24] Case C–491/01 *ex p British American Tobacco* [2002] ECR I–11453.
[25] See Arts 11 and 12 of the Draft Treaty Establishing a Constitution for Europe, OJ 2003 C169/1. See now Arts I-12 and I-13 of the 2004 Treaty, CIG 87/04.
[26] Further, eg T Tridimas and P Eeckhout, 'The External Competence of the Community and the Caselaw of the Court of Justice: Principle versus Pragmatism' (1994) 14 *Yearbook of*

Such authorisation will usually be explicit. For example, within the context of the Common Commercial Policy, Regulation 2603/69 provides that exports from the Community to third countries shall not be subject to any quantitative restrictions or measures having equivalent effect; but grants the Member States the right to adopt obstacles to external trade on grounds identical to those contained in Article 30 EC.[27] But in addition, there exists a limited doctrine of implied authority for Member State action. Exclusive competence creates the potential danger of 'regulatory gaps,' whereby the Community is solely competent to adopt legislative measures, but has failed to exercise its powers. In order to protect the vital interests of the Community from the dangers posed by such a legal vacuum, the Court of Justice has recognised that the Member States may act as 'trustees of the common interest.' For example, in the *Sea Fisheries Conservation* case, the Community had failed to exercise its exclusive competence to adopt the measures necessary to achieve the preservation of marine biological resources. The Member States were therefore impliedly authorised to adapt existing conservation measures to new biological and technological developments—provided that such measures were of a limited scope and did not involve a new national conservation policy, and that the Member States obtained prior Commission approval for their actions and collaborated with the Commission throughout.[28]

Shared Competence

Shared competence refers to the idea that both the Community and the Member States are legally capable of carrying out independent action within the relevant policy field. By contrast with areas of exclusive Union competence, Member States do retain the power to adopt independent legislative strategies in respect of the relevant policy sector. However, the exercise of Community regulatory power takes precedence over the exercise of national regulatory power, in the sense that rules enacted by the Community institutions may create binding obligations for the Member States which the latter must respect.

Such shared competence applies to many sectors of Community activity: for example, the Internal Market; the Area of Freedom, Justice and Security; social policy; environmental policy; consumer policy; certain

European Law 143; H W Micklitz and S Weatherill, *European Economic Law* (Ashgate, 1997) ch 9; P Koutrakos, 'The Elusive Quest for Uniformity in EC External Relations' (2001) 4 *Cambridge Yearbook of European Legal Studies* 243.

[27] Reg 2603/69 establishing common rules for exports, OJ 1969 L324/25. See: Case C–83/94 *Peter Leifer* [1995] ECR I–3231. Also: Case 41/76 *Donckerwolcke* [1976] ECR 1921; Case C–394/97 *Sami Heinonen* [1999] ECR I–3599. Further: M Cremona, 'The External Dimension of the Single Market: Building (on) the Foundations' in C Barnard & J Scott (eds), *The Law of the Single European Market: Unpacking the Premises* (Hart Publishing, 2002).

[28] Case 804/79 *Commission v UK* [1981] ECR 1045.

aspects of public health policy; transport policy; and agricultural policy.[29] In each case, the relevant legal bases contained in the Treaty elaborate in greater detail the precise impact of Community competence upon national regulatory power: for example, whether harmonisation is to establish merely minimum standards; or whether certain specific aspects of the policy field are not amenable to harmonisation at all. Nevertheless, it is possible to discuss certain general principles, based on a distinction between two main categories of situations: those arising *before* and those arising *after* the adoption of Community harmonising legislation.

Before the Adoption of Harmonising Measures Where the Community has not yet exercised its power to adopt harmonising legislation on a given matter, the Member States are free to legislate—but must respect the obligations imposed under primary Treaty provisions. However, this does not in itself have a decisive impact upon the relationship between regulatory uniformity and differentiation within the relevant sector. Much depends on the nature of the relevant Treaty provisions. In certain fields, the Treaty itself acts like a regulatory code—the completeness of which means that the Member States make little contribution to substantive policy. In such cases, the relevant sector may be characterised by shared competence; but this does not prevent regulatory standards from being relatively uniform across the entire Community.

Complete Regulatory Code: The Example of Competition Law By way of illustration, consider the cross-border competition policy sector. Articles 81 and 82 EC control abusive market practices which are capable of having an appreciable effect on intra-Community trade, and thereby justify intervention to protect the operation of the Common Market.[30] These Community competition rules are characterised by a genuine measure of uniformity within their own particular scope of application. Indeed, the Treaty eschews any formal degree of influence by the Member States over the substantive policy objectives pursued under Articles 81 and 82 EC, and thereby excludes almost entirely the phenomenon of regulatory differentiation from the sphere of interest occupied by Community law. In particular, the threshold requirements which activate Community supervision over various types of market conduct, the existence of an infringement of Community competition rules, and the justifications which might exempt abusive agreements and practices from punitive sanction, are all defined exhaustively by the Treaty itself.[31]

[29] Cf Arts 11 and 13 of the Draft Treaty Establishing a Constitution for Europe, OJ 2003 C169/1; now Arts I-12 and I-14 of the 2004 Treaty, CIG 87/04.
[30] Eg Case 56/65 *STM v MUG* [1966] ECR 235; Cases 56 & 58/64 *Consten and Grundig* [1966] ECR 299; Case 5/69 *Volk v Vervaecke* [1969] ECR 295; Case 22/78 *Hugin* [1979] ECR 1869.
[31] As interpreted by the CFI / ECJ and supplemented by secondary measures adopted by the Community institutions, eg Reg 2790/1999 on the application of Article 81(3) of the

Member States retain the power to regulate anti-competitive conduct the effects of which are confined entirely to the national territory. But, as the Court confirmed in the *Walt Wilhelm* case, the cross-border competition sector is one of shared competence: the Member States may (in principle) apply their domestic competition regimes also to agreements and practices falling within the scope of Articles 81 and 82 EC.[32] Article 83(2) EC expressly empowers the Council to adopt regulations to determine the relationship between Community competition law and national competition law. It did so for the first time with Regulation 1/2003, which entered into force on 1 May 2004.[33]

Before that date, the Court had developed certain rules to control the possible parallel application of Community and domestic competition rules to conduct affecting inter-State trade. The fundamental principle was that national law should not prejudice the uniform application of Community law, or the full effect of implementing measures adopted under the Treaty. In particular, domestic action could not result in a situation where the binding effect of Community competition law differed from one Member State to another. Thus, it was clear from the principle of supremacy that national law could not prejudice the full operation of Article 81 EC by purporting to validate an agreement or practice which the Commission had already judged to be void. It also seemed fairly certain (though not beyond doubt) that Member States could not purport to invalidate an agreement or practice which had been granted block or individual exemption under Article 81(3) EC—since that would undermine choices made by the Community institutions about how best to foster economic development within Europe.[34] However, the legal framework of other situations was less clear: for example, whether national competition rules could apply to agreements or practices which were judged to fall outside Article 81(1) EC altogether (say) thanks to a reasoned assessment of their pro- and anti-competitive effects.[35]

Altogether, the Court's caselaw suggested a situation of almost de facto exclusivity in the cross-border competition law sector: Member States were able to apply domestic rules to intra-Community situations, but their margin of discretion was strictly limited by the need to preserve the uniformity of the Treaty provisions. Nevertheless, academic commentators

Treaty to categories of vertical agreements and concerted practices, OJ 1999 L336/21. Such secondary legislation is better seen as implementing the relevant Treaty provisions (rather than harmonising national rules in the field). Further, eg R Whish, *Competition Law* (Butterworths, 2003); D Goyder, *EC Competition Law* (OUP, 2003).

[32] Case 14/68 *Walt Wilhelm* [1969] ECR 1. More recently, eg Case C–137/00 *Milk Marque* (Judgment of 9 September 2003).

[33] Reg 1/2003 on the implementation of the rules on competition laid down in Articles 81 and 82 of the Treaty, OJ 2003 L1/1.

[34] Case 14/68 *Walt Wilhelm* [1969] ECR 1.

[35] Further: R Whish, *Competition Law* (Butterworths, 2003) pp 322–29.

were harsh on the principle of shared competence,[36] and the Commission's 2001 proposal for a new regulation on the implementation of Articles 81 and 82 EC proposed the mutually exclusive application of Community and domestic competition rules according to whether situations have or lack cross-border effects.[37]

However, the Council ultimately rejected this particular option. Since 1 May 2004, Regulation 1/2003 has introduced a new regime governing the relationship between Community and national competition law which is intended 'to create a level playing field for agreements, decisions by associations of undertakings and concerted practices within the internal market.'[38] Article 3(1) Regulation 1/2003 provides that, where Member States apply national competition law to conduct which may affect intra-Community trade, they shall also apply Articles 81 and 82 EC (as appropriate). It remains clear from the principle of supremacy that national law cannot purport to validate an agreement or practice which the Commission has judged to be void under Article 81 EC. In addition, Article 3(2) Regulation 1/2003 finally makes clear that the application of national competition law may not lead to the prohibition of agreements and concerted practices which may affect trade between Member States but which do not restrict competition under Article 81(1) EC, or which are entitled to individual or block exemption under Article 81(3) EC. However, as regards Article 82 EC, Article 3(2) Regulation 1/2003 provides that Member States shall not be precluded from adopting and applying on their territory stricter national laws which prohibit or sanction unilateral conduct engaged in by undertakings.[39] Thus, it remains the case that Member States cannot excuse conduct which is deemed abusive under Community law; but it is now clear that they can penalise conduct which has survived censure under Article 82 EC.[40] In any case, Article 3(3) Regulation 1/2003 provides that (without prejudice to general principles and other provisions of Community law) Articles 3(1) and (2)

[36] Cf R Walz, 'Rethinking *Walt Wilhelm*, Or the Supremacy of Community Competition Law Over National Law' (1996) 21 EL Rev 449; R Wesseling, 'Subsidiarity in Community Antitrust Law: Setting the Right Agenda' (1997) 22 EL Rev 35.

[37] COM (2000)582 Final.

[38] Reg 1/2003, OJ 2003 L1/1, 8th recital to the preamble.

[39] This seems to cover *both* unilateral conduct engaged in by a single dominant undertaking *and* non-collusive abuses by members of a collectively dominant group of undertakings. But it implies that Member States cannot adopt more stringent rules as regards collusive abuses by a collectively dominant group of undertakings. If the latter interpretation is correct, the situation would remain covered by the principle in Case 14/68 *Walt Wilhelm* [1969] ECR 1, ie that Member States cannot reach results under national competition rules which would deviate from Art 82 EC.

[40] But some commentators believe that the restrictions in Case 14/68 *Walt Wilhelm* [1969] ECR 1 will still apply: if an abuse is justified under Community law, it cannot be precluded under national competition rules. Eg H Gilliams, 'Modernisation: From Policy to Practice' (2003) 28 EL Rev 451.

shall not apply when Member States enforce national merger control laws, and do not preclude the application of domestic rules which predominantly pursue an objective different from that pursued by Articles 81 and 82 EC (for example, by prohibiting unfair trading practices).[41]

In some respects, Regulation 1/2003 therefore reinforces regulatory uniformity within the cross-border competition sector: even more so than the Court's pre-existing caselaw, it stresses the de facto exclusivity of Article 81 EC, so as to leave little room for national deviation.[42] That de facto exclusivity is augmented by the fact that, as a matter of the Member States' own regulatory choice, national competition regimes are now based closely upon the substantive model supplied by Article 81 EC.[43] But in other respects, the new Regulation establishes the potential for a certain degree of regulatory differentiation across the Member States: the parallel application of Community and domestic competition rules as regards abusive conduct under Article 82 EC might lead to a limited degree of unequal treatment for cross-border situations.[44]

Complete Regulatory Code: The Example of State Aids Another field where the Treaty acts as a complete code, and regulatory standards are relatively uniform across the entire Community, is state aids under Articles 87 and 88 EC. These provisions define, again exclusively by reference to Community law, the threshold concepts which determine the scope of application of the state aids rules, the conditions for establishing the existence of an infringement by the Member State, and the conditions for recognising both mandatory and discretionary exemptions from the prohibition on granting state aids.[45]

Moreover, to an even greater degree than Community competition law, the state aids regime is characterised by a strict division of competence between the Commission and the national authorities (including the domestic courts). As the Court observed in *Iannelli & Volpi*, the rules

[41] Further: R Whish, *Competition Law* (Butterworths, 2003) pp 76–77.
[42] Indeed, in a manner akin to pre-emptive harmonisation (see below).
[43] Eg as with the UK's Competition Act 1998. Further: H Gilliams, 'Modernisation: From Policy to Practice' (2003) 28 EL Rev 451.
[44] Indeed, in a manner akin to minimum harmonisation (see below). However, consider the potential impact of the Draft Treaty Establishing a Constitution for Europe, OJ 2003 C169/1: Art 12 envisages that the Union should have exclusive competence over the competition rules necessary for the functioning of the Internal Market. See now Art I-13 of the 2004 Treaty, CIG 87/04.
[45] Again as interpreted by the CFI / ECJ and supplemented by secondary measures adopted by the Community institutions, eg block exemptions passed under Reg 994/98 on the application of Articles 87 and 88 of the Treaty establishing the European Community to certain categories of horizontal State aid, OJ 1998 L142/1. Again such secondary legislation is best seen as implementing the Treaty provisions (rather than harmonising national rules). Further, eg A Arnull, A Dashwood, M Ross and D Wyatt, *Wyatt and Dashwood's European Union Law* (Sweet & Maxwell, 2000) ch 24; P Craig and G de Búrca, *EU Law: Text, Cases, & Materials* (OUP, 2002) ch 27; A Biondi, P Eeckhout & J Flynn (eds), *The Law of State Aid in the European Union* (OUP, 2004).

governing the substantive compatibility of state aids with the Common Market are neither absolute nor unconditional; and the Treaty gives the Commission a wide discretion to sanction the grant of state aid, in derogation from the general prohibition, under Article 87 EC. The Treaty thereby intended that any finding that aid might be incompatible with the Common Market should (subject to judicial review by the Community courts) be the outcome of the procedures envisaged by Article 88 EC under the responsibility of the Commission. For that reason, individuals are not entitled to rely upon Article 87 EC to challenge the substantive compatibility of state aids with Community law before the national courts.[46] The latter police the purely procedural requirements of notification and standstill contained in the last sentence of Article 88(3) EC—though this might admittedly require the domestic judges to determine whether the disputed measure in fact constitutes state aid within the meaning of Article 87(1) EC at all.[47] Moreover, when the grant of state aid is found to be incompatible with Community law, the role of the national authorities is merely to give effect to the Commission's decision. Member States lack any discretion as regards revocation of a decision granting aid, and are not entitled to reach any finding other than the Commission's order for recovery.[48] Whether or not this state aids regime is seen as an example of exclusive rather than shared competence, it is surely a sector in which regulatory standards across the Community remain remarkably undifferentiated.[49]

Incomplete Regulatory Codes However, there are other sectors where, in the absence of Community harmonising legislation, the Treaty cannot be construed as a complete regulatory code and the Member States remain free to contribute to substantive policy formulation—such that it is difficult to see the rights enjoyed and obligations borne by businesses and individuals across the Community as being particularly uniform.

Consider, for example, the primary Treaty provisions on free movement of goods, persons, services and capital. It is true that these Treaty provisions also establish threshold concepts, prohibitions and exemptions defined entirely according to Community law itself. But that does not result in any sort of uniform regulation for the Internal Market. National competence to pursue independent regulatory strategies remains intact, even if it is partially curtailed by the existence of directly effective obligations not to create

[46] Case 74/76 *Iannelli & Volpi* [1977] ECR 557.
[47] Eg Case C–53/00 *Ferring* [2001] ECR I–9067; Case C–280/00 *Altmark Trans* [2003] ECR I–7747.
[48] Eg Case C–24/95 *Alcan Deutschland* [1997] ECR I–1591. Further: ch 6 (below).
[49] The argument in favour of exclusivity is that the Member States cannot adopt state aids rules unilaterally, only through the authorising procedure established by the Treaty. The argument against exclusivity is that the Treaty rules merely provide a regulatory code which governs (albeit in a relatively intrusive manner) the exercise of national competence.

unjustified obstacles to free movement. For example, insofar as there has been no harmonisation of a particular product specification, the Member States remain free to establish their own (potentially divergent) regulatory standards, provided that, as regards imported and exported products, they do not transgress the ceiling set by Articles 28–30 EC on the free movement of goods.[50] Thus, the Internal Market is a substantive policy field still characterised by different levels of regulation drawn along distinct national lines—tolerating barriers to free movement which can be justified by some derogation contained in the Treaty or recognised by the Court as an imperative requirement of the public interest; and leaving in place potentially significant differences in regulatory compliance costs which distort the conditions of competition between undertakings operating on the Community market, and potentially far-reaching variations in the rights and obligations of individuals which are hardly consonant with the goal of equality between Union citizens.[51]

What is true of the Internal Market is even more so for sectors like environmental, consumer and social policy. In such fields, the Member States remain free, in accordance with the shared competence doctrine, to adopt independent regulatory strategies—this time without any directly effective, autonomous Treaty obligations to mould the exercise of domestic legislative power towards any particular model, scope or level of environmental, consumer or employment protection.[52] Indeed, the primary Treaty provisions specifically governing those fields are largely of a programmatic character—setting out fundamental principles for action, and empowering the Community to adopt the necessary secondary measures.[53] For large swathes of substantive policy activities falling with the Treaty's scope of application, shifting the balance from regulatory differentiation to regulatory uniformity therefore depends upon the Community exercising its competence to harmonise.

In this respect, it is worth recalling that the Community's lack of harmonising power is not limited to marginal activities, such as education and culture, categorised *in toto* as fields of complementary competence. As regards specific aspects of fields otherwise considered to be shared competence, the Community may have no power to adopt harmonisation measures at all—placing inherent limits to the pursuit of regulatory

[50] Eg Case 120/78 *'Cassis de Dijon'* [1979] ECR 649.
[51] Though regulatory competition theorists might argue that the market itself will eventually generate the desired level of uniformity: see ch 2 (above).
[52] Though, of course, the primary rules on free movement of goods/services etc may still apply.
[53] Even then, these programmatic Treaty provisions have only limited legal effects. Consider, eg Case C–192/94 *El Corte Inglés* [1996] ECR I–1281 and Case C–233/94 *Germany v Parliament and Council (Deposit-Guarantee Schemes Directive)* [1997] ECR I–2405 (on consumer policy); Case C–284/95 *Safety Hi-Tech* [1998] ECR I–4301 and Case C–341/95 *Bettati* [1998] ECR I–4355 (on environmental policy).

uniformity through centralised legislative intervention. And this is true, in particular, of certain crucial compliance costs directly related to the conditions of competition within the Internal Market.[54] For example, the Community lacks competence to establish a minimum wage, whether applicable across the entire Single Market, or tailored to each Member State on the basis of functional equivalency. Article 137 EC specifically excludes pay from the scope of the Community's power to adopt minimum standards of social protection. The competence to adopt approximation measures under Article 95 EC for the purposes of completing the Internal Market cannot provide an alternative legal basis for intervention, since it does not apply to provisions relating to the rights and interests of employed persons.[55] The Community has therefore been forced to accept the ring-fenced existence of wage differences between the Member States.[56] Similarly, the Community enjoys only limited competence to harmonise social security contributions and benefits. In particular, Article 137 EC provides a legal basis for the Community to adopt (by unanimity in Council) directives in the field of social security and other forms of social protection for workers. However, the Treaty of Nice amended Article 137 EC so as to exclude the adoption of harmonising measures as regards combating social exclusion and modernising social protection for individuals other than workers; and also Article 18 EC so as to provide that secondary legislation adopted by the Community to facilitate exercise by Union citizens of their right to free movement shall not apply to the domestic systems of social security or social protection. Even as regards workers, exercise of the existing Treaty competence to harmonise welfare benefits is undermined in practice by the daunting political and logistical obstacles erected by widely divergent national attitudes towards the role and nature of social protection.[57] This fact is reinforced by the Nice Treaty amendments, which require that Community action under Article 137 EC should not affect the right of Member States to define the

[54] Though again, regulatory competition theorists might argue that the market itself will eventually generate the desired level of uniformity: see ch 2 (above).

[55] Note also the Nice amendments to Art 157 EC, excluding 'provisions relating to the rights and interests of employed persons' from the 'specific measures' the Community may adopt in the sphere of industrial policy. Further (including possible reliance upon Art 94 EC): B Ryan, 'Pay, Trade Union Rights and European Community Law' (1997) 13 *International Journal of Comparative Labour Law and Industrial Relations* 305.

[56] Though note that Community law has a more indirect influence on the development of national minimum wages, eg as regards the legal position of posted workers, where both the caselaw under Art 49 EC and Dir 96/71 concerning the posting of workers in the framework of the provision of services, OJ 1997 L18/01 seek to minimise the potential for social dumping in favour of low-wage countries. Further, eg P Davies, 'Posted Workers: Single Market or Protection of National Labour Law Systems?' (1997) 34 CML Rev 571; R Giesen, 'Posting: Social Protection of Workers vs. Fundamental Freedoms?' (2003) 40 CML Rev 143.

[57] Further, eg M Rhodes, 'Defending the Social Contract: The EU Between Global Constraints and Domestic Imperatives' in D Hine & H Kassim (eds), *Beyond the Market: the EU and National Social Policy* (Routledge, 1998).

fundamental principles and maintain the basic financial equilibrium of their own social security systems. So again, Community policy must accept the ring-fenced existence of significant differences in welfare provision (and their consequent economic costs) between the Member States.[58]

After the Adoption of Harmonising Measures Where the Community has *and* has actually exercised its power to adopt secondary legislation on any given matter, the Member States in principle remain free to legislate—but must respect both the obligations imposed under primary Treaty provisions, *and also* the obligations imposed by the relevant Community secondary legislation. This includes the possibility for Community secondary legislation to have pre-emptive effects, occupying the relevant regulatory field, and preventing Member States from exercising their competence therein.

Pre-Emption and Exclusivity Pre-emptive Community harmonisation is often treated as a form of exclusivity. Certainly, the practical effect of pre-emptive Community secondary legislation upon national regulatory power within the occupied field may often appear to differ little from that experienced in the Common Commercial Policy or as regards the preservation of marine biological resources. That might seem particularly true of sectors such as the Common Agricultural Policy, where the sheer volume and density of Community legislative activity leaves very little scope for the exercise in practice of residual Member State regulatory power.[59] But it is perhaps better to keep the two phenomena conceptually separate. Pre-emptive Community secondary legislation does not affect the existence of Member State competence—somehow converting a field of shared competence into one of exclusive Community competence, and thus stripping the Member States of their inherent power to regulate. Pre-emptive Community harmonisation merely affects the exercise of national competence—imposing obligations of such a nature and extent that the Member State is thenceforth unable to exercise its regulatory powers, as concerns the occupied field, without infringing the obligations imposed upon it through the Treaty. The issue can thus be framed in terms of the incompatilibity of domestic rules with Community law, rather than any more fundamental abrogation of the Member State's competence to enact those rules in the first place.

[58] Further, eg S Leibfried and P Pierson, 'Social Policy: Left to Courts and Markets?' in H Wallace & W Wallace (eds), *Policy-Making in the European Union* (OUP, 2000). Again, note that Community law can have a more indirect influence on the development of national social security rules, eg as regards the legal position of migrant workers and other Union citizens. Further, eg M Dougan & E Spaventa (eds), *Social Welfare and EU Law* (Hart Publishing, forthcoming).

[59] Eg A Von Bogandy and J Bast, 'The European Union's Vertical Order of Competences: The Current Law and Proposals For Its Reform' (2002) 39 CML Rev 227.

Our suggested approach has the benefit of explaining why the revision or repeal of a pre-emptive Community measure allows the Member State to resume the exercise of its competence.[60] After all, if pre-emption had the effect of converting shared into exclusive competence, one might expect revision or repeal of the relevant Community act to leave in its wake a regulatory vacuum—akin to those which sometimes arise in the Common Commercial Policy or as regards the preservation of marine biological resources—with the Member States unable independently to adopt alternative legislation for themselves.[61] Our suggested approach also explains why the Community must respect the principle of subsidiarity even when exercising its competence to amend or replace existing pre-emptive secondary measures with further pre-emptive secondary measures.[62] After all, subsidiarity applies only as regards fields covered by shared competence. If the doctrine of pre-emption really generated exclusivity within the regulated field, subsidiarity would no longer be relevant to the exercise of Community regulatory power therein. The fact that the Court continues to apply the principle of subsidiarity even to areas already subject to pre-emptive harmonisation suggests that shared Community-Member State competence has not been usurped by exclusive Community competence.

Degree and Scope of Pre-emptive Action In any case, harmonisation (whether pursuant to an Internal Market legal basis such as Article 95 EC; or under sectoral legal bases such as Article 175 EC on environmental policy or Article 137 EC on social policy) can assume various forms: covering very different material scopes of application; and carrying very different degrees of pre-emption. And so, just because the Community adopts secondary legislation on a given subject-matter does not mean that it thereby creates uniform regulation of the marketplace, or of Union citizens' rights and obligations.

To be sure, Community secondary legislation is sometimes fully pre-emptive in character: the Member States are totally prevented from exercising regulatory competence in the relevant field. Many harmonisation measures adopted under Articles 94 and 95 EC for the completion of the Internal Market follow this model.[63] For example, Directive 73/173 set out rules on the classification, packaging and labelling of dangerous preparations.[64] The Court has held that this measure was intended to eliminate

[60] Cf Case C–3/99 *Cidrerie Ruwet* [2000] ECR I–8749.
[61] See above.
[62] Cf Case C–491/01 *Ex p British American Tobacco* [2002] ECR I–11453.
[63] Again, however, it is vital to define the sectoral boundaries of the measure in question, eg Case C–2/90 *Commission v Belgium* [1992] ECR I–4431; Case C–323/93 *Société Civile Agricole du Centre d'Insémination de la Crespelle v Coopérative d'Élevage et d'Insémination artificielle du Départment de la Mayenne* [1994] ECR I–5097; Case C–400/96 *Harpegnies* [1998] ECR I–5121.
[64] Dir 73/173 on the approximation of Member States' laws, regulations and administrative provisions relating to the classification, packaging and labelling of dangerous preparations,

barriers to intra-Community trade, by introducing an exhaustive regulatory regime which pre-empted Member State competence to introduce additional or even simply different provisions in respect of either domestic or imported production.[65] In fields characterised by fully pre-emptive harmonisation, regulatory adaptation is in principle to be achieved by the Treaty, not the national authorities—even where a novel and potentially undesirable development in scientific technology or market behaviour threatens the interests (for example) of the consumer or the environment in a manner unforeseen by the Community legislature.[66]

This model of total harmonisation is closely linked to the realisation of regulatory uniformity across the Member States. However, it should be borne in mind that many Community measures deal with only limited aspects of an overall policy sector. One prominent example is the New Approach to Technical Harmonisation adopted in the later 1980s. This legislative technique was a crucial element in the drive to complete the Single Market: directives adopted under Article 95 EC set out common standards to be implemented in each Member State as regards only the essential health and safety requirements to be expected of any given product offered for sale on the Community market; in respect of all other aspects of product specification (and often as regards the precise technical standards necessary to comply with harmonised public interest requirements), the Member States were permitted to maintain their own particular rules. Each Member State was required to ensure that goods manufactured within its territory complied with the essential health and safety requirements laid down under Community law (the home state control principle); but was also obliged to respect free movement for goods manufactured in other Member States, and certainly could not block importation on the grounds that other non-essential specifications might differ from domestic rules (the mutual recognition principle).[67]

OJ 1973 L189/7 (repealed by Dir 88/379, OJ 1988 L187/14; itself repealed and replaced by Dir 1999/45, OJ 1999 L200/1).

[65] Eg Case 148/78 *Ratti* [1979] ECR 1629; Case 278/85 *Commission v Denmark* [1987] ECR 4069.
[66] Eg Case 60/86 *Commission v United Kingdom* [1988] ECR 3921; Cases C–129–30/97 *Chiciak and Fol* [1998] ECR I–3315. Pre-emptive secondary legislation is capable of having such legal effects not only internally, but also externally. The latter arises either by express provision in the relevant secondary legislation, or implicitly under the *ERTA* doctrine, eg Case 22/70 *Commission v Council* [1971] ECR 263; Cases 3–4 & 6/76 *Kramer* [1976] ECR 1279; Opinion 1/76 *(Draft Agreement establishing a European laying-up fund for inland waterway vessels)* [1977] ECR 741; Opinion 2/91 *(Convention No 170 of the International Labour Organisation concerning safety in the use of chemicals at work)* [1993] ECR I–1061; Opinion 1/94 *(Competence of the Community to conclude international agreements concerning services and the protection of intellectual property)* [1994] ECR I–5267; Opinion 2/92 *(Competence of the Community to participate in the Third Revised Decision of the OECD on national treatment)* [1995] ECR I–521.
[67] Consider, in particular, Commission, *White Paper on Completing the Internal Market*, COM (1985)310 Final (and note also the important role played by European standardisation). Further, eg J Pelkmans, 'The New Approach to Technical Harmonisation and Standardization' (1987) 25 JCMS 249; N Burrows, 'Harmonisation of Technical Standards: Reculer Pour Mieux

Such Community secondary legislation certainly contained elements of total harmonisation, and hence promoted a certain degree of regulatory uniformity—but this was combined with the continued exercise of national competence, and hence the persistence of regulatory diversity, within the relevant policy sector.[68]

Another example might be the Community's efforts to safeguard and promote consumers' economic interests, where centralised legislative intervention has focused largely on improving standards of information (say) by imposing labelling requirements for goods placed on the Community market, or requiring service providers to communicate certain written terms to actual or potential service recipients.[69] Indeed, Community consumer policy has made few significant incursions into the substance of contractual relations between consumers and suppliers, which is left largely to domestic law (subject to the ad hoc impact of directly effective Treaty obligations), and may therefore continue to vary significantly from Member State to Member State.[70] The Community's record on employee protection might also be seen as relatively piecemeal.[71] For example, the Collective Redundancies Directive merely insists on the information and consultation of employees in the event of economic dismissals, without affecting the employer's freedom to carry out such dismissals as provided for under national law.[72] Similarly, the Acquired Rights Directive is intended only to guarantee the transfer of employees' rights between employers, without harmonising either the definition or content of the employment relationship itself.[73] In 1993, the Court

Sauter?' (1990) 53 MLR 597; A McGee and S Weatherill, 'The Evolution of the Single Market: Harmonisation or Liberalisation' (1990) 53 MLR 578.

[68] Though insofar as the result of the New Approach was to facilitate competition between legal orders as regards non-harmonised specifications, certain economists might argue that the obligation of mutual recognition still facilitated regulatory uniformity through the operation of market forces.

[69] Eg Dir 84/450 concerning misleading and comparative advertising, OJ 1984 L250/17; Dir 94/47 on the protection of purchasers in respect of certain aspects of contracts relating to the purchase of the right to use immovable properties on a timeshare basis, OJ 1994 L280/83. Even many of these measures are minimum harmonisation only: see below.

[70] Notables exceptions are the Dir 93/13 on unfair terms in consumer contracts, OJ 1993 L95/29; Dir 99/44 on certain aspects of the sale of consumer goods and associated guarantees, OJ 1999 L171/12. Further, eg S Weatherill, *EC Consumer Law and Policy* (Longman, 1997) chs 3 and 4; G Howells and T Wilhelmsson, *EC Consumer Law* (Dartmouth, 1997) ch 9.

[71] And again, most of these measures have been minimum harmonisation only: see below.

[72] Dir 98/59 on the approximation of the laws of the Member States relating to collective redundancies, OJ 1998 L225/16. Eg Case 284/83 *Nielsen* [1985] ECR 553; Case C–383/92 *Commission v UK* [1994] ECR I–2479; Case C–449/93 *Rockfon* [1995] ECR I–4291.

[73] Dir 2001/23 on the approximation of the laws of the Member States relating to the safeguarding of employees' rights in the event of transfers of undertakings, businesses or parts of undertakings or businesses, OJ 2001 L82/16. Eg Case 105/84 *Danmols Inventar* [1985] ECR 2639; Case 324/86 *Daddy's Dance Hall* [1988] ECR 739; Case C–382/92 *Commission v UK* [1994] ECR I–2435. Consider also Dir 91/533 on an employer's obligation to inform employees of the conditions applicable to the contract or employment relationship, OJ 1991 L288/32.

of Justice felt able to state that social policy was a matter which fell predominantly within the competence of the Member States.[74] More recent developments suggest that this remains true today. Commission action programmes, setting out strategies for achieving the Treaty's objectives of increased living standards and greater worker emancipation, indicate a fundamental change of emphasis: legislation creating legal rights for the individual should be consolidated rather than expanded; attention should instead concentrate on tackling macro-economic issues such as mass unemployment and social exclusion through the monitoring and coordination of domestic economic policies.[75] This trend was reinforced by the introduction at Amsterdam of a new Title VIII, Part Three EC on employment, providing for cooperation between the Commission and the Member States on labour market issues.[76]

Moreover, even within its own (often limited) scope of application, Community secondary legislation need not have fully pre-emptive effects. Harmonising measures may still offer opportunities for Member States to enact higher regulatory standards than, or equally to derogate from, the centralised Community norm—and thus to shape the final contours of substantive policy even within the field now (partially) occupied by Community law. For example, Directive 91/629 on the protection of calves has been held to regulate exhaustively the powers of the Member States in this area, but it still permits the maintenance of stricter welfare standards within each national territory, and also grants temporary derogations from the common Community rules.[77]

Indeed, it is possible to identify several important legislative techniques by which the Community legal order facilitates a process of vertical differentiation, placing itself even further at odds with the ideal of regulatory uniformity advocated by an 'integration through law'-style analysis: the use of minimum harmonisation clauses; the grant of derogations; reliance upon variable norms and conceptual renvois to the domestic legal orders; and even the choice of legal instrument itself. These devices will now be examined in turn.[78]

[74] Opinion 2/91 *(Convention No 170 of the International Labour Organisation concerning safety in the use of chemicals at work)* [1993] ECR I–1061, para 30.
[75] Eg Commission, *Medium-Term Social Action Programme 1995–1997*, COM (1995)134; Commission, *Social Action Programme 1998–2000*, COM (1998)259.
[76] Further, eg D Chalmers and E Szyszczak, *European Union Law Volume II: Towards a European Polity?* (Ashgate, 1998) ch 10; C Barnard, *EC Employment Law* (OUP, 2000) ch 1. Though, of course, this has not entirely stopped the pressure for individual rights measures, eg Commission, *Amended Proposal for a Directive on Working Conditions for Temporary Workers*, COM (2002)701 Final.
[77] Dir 91/629 laying down minimum standards for the protection of calves, OJ 1991 L340/28. See, eg Case C–1/96 *ex p Compassion in World Farming* [1998] ECR I–1251.
[78] Many of the examples employed to illustrate the following discussion have been drawn from case-studies on the Community's environmental, consumer and employee protection policies.

Minimum Harmonisation

We have just seen how, under a model of total harmonisation, the regulatory standards established by a Community measure act as both a floor (below which the Member States must not fall) and a ceiling (beyond which national law may not impose additional requirements). Indeed, the Community exhaustively regulates the relevant field, depriving the Member States of their capacity to carry out not only independent but indeed any divergent action therein: the uniform Community norms can be neither supplemented, nor derogated from, by domestic rules.[79]

But total harmonisation is not the only model employed by Community secondary legislation. For example, certain directives effect merely optional harmonisation: Member States are bound by the mutual recognition principle as regards imported goods which satisfy the essential product specifications set out under Community law; but Member States need not require all goods manufactured within their territory to comply with the particular rules contained in the directive. To that extent, domestic competence to establish potentially divergent regulatory standards is not pre-empted. Indeed, undertakings are free to choose between the Community's technical standards (which guarantee access to foreign markets); or their home state's own technical rules (which might better suit the undertaking's manufacturing and marketing preferences).[80] Optional harmonisation enjoyed a brief period of popularity in the 1970s,[81] but since then it has not proved a very common legislative technique.[82]

Of much greater practical significance is the contrast between total and minimum harmonisation. In the latter case, Member States are permitted to maintain and/or to introduce more stringent regulatory standards than those prescribed by Community legislation, for the purposes of advancing a particular social or welfare interest, and provided that such additional requirements are compatible with the Treaty. National competence within the occupied territory is not completely ousted: the applicable Community legislation sets a floor, the Treaty itself sets a ceiling, and the Member States are free to pursue an independent domestic policy between these two parameters.[83]

[79] Also, eg Case C–369/89 *Peeters I* [1991] ECR I–2971; C–85/94 *Peeters II* [1995] ECR I–2955. Cf Case C–385/96 *Goerres* [1998] ECR I–4431; Case C–33/97 *Colim v Biggs* [1999] ECR I–3175.
[80] Eg Dir 71/316 on measuring instruments, OJ 1971 L202/1. Though again, the result of optional harmonisation is to facilitate competition between legal orders, and might thus ultimately encourage regulatory uniformity through the operation of market forces: see ch 2 (above).
[81] P J Slot, 'Harmonisation' (1996) 21 EL Rev 378.
[82] C Barnard, *The Substantive Law of the EU* (OUP, 2004) ch 18.
[83] Further, eg S Weatherill, 'Beyond Preemption? Shared Competence and Constitutional Change in the European Community' in D O'Keeffe & P Twomey (eds), *Legal Issues of the*

Minimum harmonisation has become an increasingly common characteristic of Community regulation. Indeed, since the Single European Act it has been 'institutionalised' through express incorporation into the Treaty text itself. General minimum harmonisation clauses are now found in respect of the Community's competences to pursue policies on the environment,[84] consumer protection[85] and social policy,[86] as well as the more restricted legislative powers available in respect of public health.[87] Even Article 95 EC contains a (much more limited) minimum harmonisation facility in respect of measures adopted under that legal basis for the completion of the Internal Market, and which themselves fail to make provision for more stringent domestic standards.[88]

But well before these Treaty amendments were enacted, minimum harmonisation clauses were common in Community secondary legislation. That tradition continues despite the general provisions now enshrined in primary Community law, and particularly where socially valuable Community action is being pursued through legal bases such as Articles 94 and 95 EC, rather than under the more specifically welfare-orientated policy chapters. Minimum harmonisation clauses are therefore common in environmental directives,[89] and standard in measures dealing with consumer policy,[90] and employee protection.[91]

Maastricht Treaty (Wiley, 1994); M Dougan, 'Minimum Harmonisation and the Internal Market' (2000) 37 CML Rev 853. This includes the competence to make only partial use of a derogation provided under the relevant harmonisation measure, eg Case 228/87 *Pretura unificata di Torino v X* [1988] ECR 5099.

[84] Art 176 EC, in respect of measures adopted under Art 175 EC.
[85] Art 153(5) EC, in respect of measures adopted under Art 153(3)(b) and (4) EC.
[86] Art 137(5) EC, in respect of measures adopted under Art 137(2) and (3) EC.
[87] Art 152(4)(a) EC.
[88] Art 95(4)–(9) EC. Consider, eg Case C–512/99 *Germany v Commission* [2003] ECR I–845; Case C–3/00 *Denmark v Commission* [2003] ECR I–2643. Further, eg N de Sadeleer, 'Procedures for Derogations From the Principle of Approximation of Laws Under Article 95 EC' (2003) 40 CML Rev 889.
[89] Eg Art 7(2) Dir 76/160 concerning the quality of bathing water, OJ 1976 L31/1; Art 9 Dir 79/923 on the quality required of shellfish waters, OJ 1979 L281/47; Art 16 Dir 80/778 relating to the quality of water intended for human consumption, OJ 1980 L229/11; Art 4(3) Dir 88/609 on the limitation of emissions of certain pollutants into the air from large combustion plants, OJ 1988 L336/1.
[90] Eg Art 8 Dir 85/577 to protect the consumer in respect of contracts negotiated away from business premises, OJ 1985 L372/31; Art 15 Dir 87/102 for the approximation of the laws, regulations and administrative provisions of the Member States concerning consumer credit, OJ 1987 L42/48; Art 8 Dir 90/314 on package travel, package holidays and package tours, OJ 1990 L158/59; Art 8 Dir 93/13 on unfair terms in consumer contracts, OJ 1993 L95/29; Art 11 Dir 94/47 on the protection of purchasers in respect of certain aspects of contracts relating to the purchase of the right to use immovable properties on a timeshare basis, OJ 1994 L280/83; Art 14 Dir 97/7 on the protection of consumers in respect of distance contracts, OJ 1997 L144/19; Art 7 Dir 98/27 on injunctions for the protection of consumers' interests, OJ 1998 L166/51; Art 8 Dir 99/44 on certain aspects of the sale of consumer goods and associated guarantees, OJ 1999 L171/12.
[91] Eg Art 5 Dir 98/59 on the approximation of the laws of the Member States relating to collective redundancies, OJ 1998 L225/16; Art 8 Dir 2001/23 on the approximation of the laws

Finally, minimum harmonisation need not be provided for explicitly. The Court of Justice has on several occasions held Community measures to constitute non-exhaustive regulatory standards by process of implication. This is illustrated by the judgment in *ex p Gallaher*.[92] Directive 89/622 on the labelling of tobacco products required that cigarette packets must carry warnings about the health risks associated with smoking, covering 'at least' four per cent of the relevant surface area of the packet.[93] The United Kingdom enacted rules stipulating that the relevant coverage should be six per cent. The Court held that this was compatible with the Directive, which had sought to establish only minimum standards.[94]

By laying down a compulsory floor of rights across the Community, measures adopted under a minimum harmonisation facility offer a concrete guarantee against the uniformity of legal rules which might otherwise follow from the unrestrained operation of market forces. But their lack of fully pre-emptive effect also provides a safeguard against the uniformity of legal rules which might otherwise result from centralised intervention by the Community authorities. This creates a safe regulatory space within which the Member States remain free to experiment with individual legislative initiatives.[95]

The potential for minimum harmonisation to produce more diverse welfare policies within each relevant sector of Community activity is illustrated by reference to the Commission's report on the operation of the Consumer Credit Directive.[96] Although adopted under Article 94 EC with a view to reducing those discrepancies between the relevant national regimes which impeded the proper functioning of the Common Market, Article 15 of the Directive provides that the measure

of the Member States relating to the safeguarding of employees' rights in the event of transfers of undertakings, businesses or parts of undertakings or businesses, OJ 2001 L82/16; Art 9 Dir 80/987 on the approximation of the laws of the Member States relating to the protection of employees in the event of the insolvency of their employer, OJ 1980 L283/23; Art 1 Dir 89/391 on the introduction of measures to encourage improvements in the safety and health of workers at work, OJ 1989 L183/1; Art 7 Dir 91/533 on an employer's obligation to inform employees of the conditions applicable to the contract or employment relationship, OJ 1991 L288/32; Cl 4(1) Framework Agreement annexed to Dir 96/34 on the framework agreement on parental leave concluded by UNICE, CEEP and the ETUC, OJ 1996 L145/4; Cl 6(1) Framework Agreement annexed to Dir 97/81 concerning the framework agreement on part-time work concluded by UNICE, CEEP and the ETUC, OJ 1998 L14/9.

[92] Case C–11/92 *ex p Gallaher* [1993] ECR I–3545.
[93] Dir 89/622 on the labelling of tobacco products, OJ 1989 L 359/1 (now repealed and replaced by Dir 2001/37, OJ 2001 L194/26).
[94] Also, eg Case C–222/91 *Philip Morris Belgium* [1993] ECR I–3469; Case C–128/94 *Hans Hönig* [1995] ECR I–3389; Case C–389/96 *Aher-Waggon* [1998] ECR I–4473; Case C–376/90 *Commission v Belgium* [1992] ECR I–6153.
[95] Eg N Reich, 'Competition Between Legal Orders: A New Paradigm of EC Law?' (1992) 29 CML Rev 861.
[96] Dir 87/102 for the approximation of the laws, regulations and administrative provisions of the Member States concerning consumer credit, OJ 1987 L42/48.

shall not preclude Member States from retaining or adopting more stringent provisions to protect consumers consistent with their obligations under the Treaty.

Observing the considerable extent to and variety by which the Member States had taken advantage of this facility to improve on the level and scope of substantive protection guaranteed by the Directive, the Commission remarked that, as a result, the measure had only a modest impact on the original objective of harmonisation.[97]

This scope for diversity has, moreover, been reinforced by the general approach adopted by the Court of Justice. For example, the Court has held that 'minimum' harmonisation does not mean merely 'minimal,' such as would reserve to the national authorities the preponderance of regulatory competence as regards (say) employment protection regulation.[98] But nor does the Community's commitment to pursuing 'high standards' of environmental protection mean 'the highest possible,' such as would leave little room for independent domestic initiatives.[99] In reaching this conclusion, the Court referred expressly to the Article 176 EC minimum harmonisation clause: high Community standards cannot mean the highest possible precisely because the Treaty envisages that the Member States may set more stringent safeguards at the national level.[100] The effect of these decisions is to affirm the legitimate right of Member States to put clear blue water between the Community and the domestic legal orders, even within a sphere of interest currently occupied by the Treaty.

However, the full capacity of minimum harmonisation to act as a vehicle for higher and thus differentiated standards of social welfare protection remains unclear. Many subsidiary issues about the scope of minimum harmonisation within the Community legal order remain controversial, for example: whether minimum harmonisation clauses contained in the Treaty itself may be ousted by secondary legislation which purports to be fully pre-emptive in nature;[101] and conversely, whether a minimum harmonisation clause contained in one legal basis (such as Article 153 EC) can apply automatically across the rest of the Treaty as well (including secondary measures adopted under Article 94 or 95 EC).[102]

The same is true of the precise relationship between minimum harmonisation and the principles of free movement and undistorted

[97] COM (1995)117 Final.

[98] Case C–84/94 *UK v Council* [1996] ECR I–5755, paras 17 and 56.

[99] Case C–284/95 *Safety Hi-Tech* [1998] ECR I–4301, para 49; Case C–341/95 *Bettati* [1998] ECR I–4355, para 47.

[100] Also: Case C–233/94 *Germany v Parliament and Council* [1997] ECR I–2405, para 48.

[101] Consider, eg Case C–203/96 *Dusseldorp* [1998] ECR I–4075; Case C–324/99 *DaimlerChrysler* [2001] ECR I–9897; Case C–6/00 *Abfall Service* [2002] ECR I–1961.

[102] Consider, eg Case C–52/00 *Commission v France* [2002] ECR I–3827; Case C–154/00 *Commission v Greece* [2002] ECR I–3879; Case C–183/00 *González Sánchez* [2002] ECR I–3901.

competition within the Internal Market. On the one hand, it is clear that minimum harmonisation necessarily distorts at least to some extent the ideal of equal competitive conditions between economic actors within the European marketplace, and the notion of equal social rights between Union citizens. In particular, producers and service providers established in a Member State which has enacted more stringent protective standards may be burdened by more onerous costs than their rivals established in Member States which prescribe the Community norm alone.[103] Similarly, Union citizens living in a Member State which has enacted higher social standards than the Treaty requires may enjoy greater levels of welfare provision than their fellow Union citizens living elsewhere in the Community.[104] On the other hand, there is considerable controversy about how far minimum harmonisation may also result in the maintenance of post-harmonisation barriers to intra-Community trade: for example, whether Member States may apply their own more stringent domestic regulatory standards to foreign goods and services which complied with the basic Community norm in their state of origin; or instead, whether Member States which make use of minimum harmonisation clauses choose (in effect) to create a situation of reverse discrimination, whereby additional regulatory provisions may only be enforced against domestic undertakings.[105]

Nevertheless, the phenomenon of minimum harmonisation makes clear that, for significant sectors of Community activity, regulatory uniformity across the Member States does not reflect the reality (or even the objective) of the European integration process.

Derogations

Just as minimum harmonisation distorts the notion of uniformity in the application of Treaty norms by permitting the Member States to maintain more stringent regulatory standards than those set out in Community legislation, so too any idealised model of total harmonisation is contradicted

[103] Eg Case C–11/92 *ex p Gallaher* [1993] ECR I–3545, para 22; Case C–128/94 *Hans Hönig* [1995] ECR I–3389, para 17; AG Cosmas in Case C–389/96 *Aher-Waggon* [1998] ECR I–4473, para 15 Opinion; AG Jacobs in Case C–6/98 *ARD v PRO Sieben Media* [1999] ECR I–7599, para 84 Opinion.

[104] Eg M Poiares Maduro, 'The Scope of European Remedies: The Case of Purely Internal Situations and Reverse Discrimination' in C Kilpatrick, T Novitz & P Skidmore (eds), *The Future of Remedies in Europe* (Hart Publishing, 2000).

[105] On all these issues, see further: M Dougan, 'Vive La Différence? Exploring the Legal Framework for Reflexive Harmonisation within the Single European Market' in R Miller & P Zumbansen (eds), *Annual of German and European Law (Volume 1: 2003)* (Berghahn Books, 2004), and the extensive references contained therein.

by the practice of granting derogations exempting the Member States from certain of the obligations otherwise imposed under the Treaty.

Derogations are very common in secondary legislation.[106] In many cases, they concern specific and limited matters. For example, the Product Liability Directive (as originally enacted) contained three possible derogations,[107] by which the Member States could choose to exclude primary agricultural produce from the definition of 'product' used in determining the scope of application of the Directive (though this particular derogation was deleted by an amendment in 1999);[108] to limit the principle of strict liability for defective goods by reference to a 'development risk defence'; and to impose a ceiling on the amount of damages recoverable in respect of certain categories of injury. Virtually every possible combination of these three derogations could be seen in the implementing legislation of the various Member States.[109]

In other cases, the number and character of derogations may be such that the Community standard itself appears to be the exception rather than the rule. For example, the original Working Time Directive was very generous as regards the number and extent of derogations which Member States were able to adopt when implementing the legislation;[110] and the new Working Time Directive continues to offer Member States extensive opportunities to derogate from its basic health and safety rules.[111] Indeed, certain Community measures offer Member States an opt-out from entire sections of the purportedly harmonised subject-matter. Thus, the amended Acquired Rights Directive 'gives Member States a quite remarkable range of choices to make at the transposition stage.'[112] In particular, the Member States may exclude insolvent undertakings from the scope of the Directive altogether. Alternatively, even if such enterprises are included, it remains open for national rules to provide that the transferee shall not be obliged to meet the employees' claims against the insolvent transferor,

[106] Consider the analysis of G de Búrca, 'Differentiation Within the Core: The Case of the Common Market' in G de Búrca & J Scott, *Constitutional Change in the EU: From Uniformity to Flexibility?* (Hart Publishing, 2000).
[107] Dir 85/374 on the approximation of the laws, regulations and administrative provisions of the Member States concerning liability for defective products, OJ 1985 L210/29.
[108] Dir 1999/34, OJ 1999 L141/20.
[109] Further: W Hoffman and S Hill-Arning, *Guide to Product Liability in Europe* (Kluwer Law and Taxation Publishers, 1994); P Kelly & R Attree (eds), *European Product Liabilities* (Butterworths, 1997).
[110] Dir 93/104 concerning certain aspects of the organization of working time, OJ 1993 L307/18, esp Arts 17 and 18(1)(b). Further: C Barnard, 'The Judgment of the ECJ in *United Kingdom v Council*: The Working Time Directive' in *The ECJ's Working Time Judgment: The Social Market Vindicated*, CELS Occasional Paper No 2 (CUP, 1997).
[111] Dir 2003/88 concerning certain aspects of the organization of working time, OJ 2003 L299/9, esp Arts 17–22.
[112] P Davies, 'Amendments to the Acquired Rights Directive' (1998) 27 ILJ 365.

in derogation from the full standards of employee protection established by the Directive.[113]

Moreover, there may exist a limited *implied* right to derogate from certain Community measures. In principle, the Court of Justice has held that Member States must comply with their Community obligations under regulations and directives, except insofar as there is express provision to the contrary.[114] However, there are two possible qualifications to this proposition.

First, the Court has held that the 'absolute impossibility' of complying with Community law may justify a Member State's failure to fulfil its obligations, despite the fact that there are no (or at least no applicable) express derogations in the relevant legislation.[115] However, it is unclear whether this would affect relations between private parties and the Member State within the national legal orders, as opposed to relations between the Commission and the Member State during Article 226 EC enforcement proceedings before the Court of Justice.

Secondly, there is authority to suggest that, where Community legislation fails to make provision for the adaptation of existing regulatory standards to changing circumstances, there may nevertheless be implied authority to derogate where this seems necessary for the effective achievement of the Treaty's underlying objectives. The main case is Case C–57/89 *Commission v Germany* (1991), which concerned Directive 79/409 on the conservation of wild birds.[116] This measure required Member States positively to identify territories suitable for classification as special protection areas (SPAs), and conferred upon Member States a degree of discretion in doing so, but made no express provision for Member States to reduce the physical extent of SPAs once the latter had been properly designated. Germany granted permission for certain dyke-building operations to be carried out, despite the fact that this would damage a designated SPA. The Court held that a power to reduce the physical extent of SPAs could be implied on 'exceptional grounds' which corresponded to 'a general interest which is superior to the general interest represented by the ecological objective of the directive.'[117] In this case, the danger of flooding and protection

[113] Art 5 Dir 2001/23 on the approximation of the laws of the Member States relating to the safeguarding of employees' rights in the event of transfers of undertakings, businesses or parts of undertakings or businesses, OJ 2001 L82/16.

[114] Eg Case 101/78 *Granaria* [1979] ECR 623; Case C–42/89 *Commission v Belgium* [1990] ECR I–2821; Case C–337/89 *Commission v UK* [1992] ECR I–6103.

[115] Case C–56/90 *Commission v UK (Bathing Water Directive)* [1993] ECR I–4109, paras 45–46. Also, eg Case C–198/97 *Commission v Germany* [1999] ECR I–3257; Case C–307/98 *Commission v Belgium* [2000] ECR I–3933. Consider, in particular, state aids cases such as Case C–280/95 *Commission v Italy* [1998] ECR I–259; Case C–6/97 *Italy v Commission* [1999] ECR I–2981.

[116] Dir 79/409 on the conservation of wild birds, OJ 1979 L103/1.

[117] Case C–57/89 *Commission v Germany (Wild Birds Directive)* [1991] ECR I–883, paras 21–22.

of the coast were sufficient justification for the dyke works, provided the latter's effect on the SPA was kept to the minimum necessary.[118]

The judgment in *Commission v Germany* supports the existence of an implied right to derogate where this is absolutely necessary for the protection of national interests which outweigh the Community objectives in question; or at least where the national measures would in fact further rather than undermine the general Community objectives at stake.[119] But subsequent cases suggest that the conditions for relying upon an implied right to derogate may sometimes be less rigorous. For example, in Case C–92/96 *Commission v Spain* (1998), the Court rejected an argument that several freshwater bathing areas within Spain were no longer used for that purpose due to a change in social habits, and therefore no longer needed to comply with the provisions of Directive 76/160 concerning the quality of bathing water.[120] This reasoning did not fall within any of the express derogations provided for under the Directive, and could not therefore be used to justify the Member State's failure to comply with its Treaty commitments.[121] On the one hand, this might have suggested that a mere change of material circumstances is not enough to justify the avoidance of Community obligations, without also demonstrating that such avoidance would serve some valuable welfare function compatible with the Treaty. On the other hand, Advocate General Lenz suggested that Spain's argument could have succeeded, had it supplied clear proof that there was no causal link between the fact that people no longer went bathing in the relevant waters, and the existence of pollution caused by the Member State's failure to comply with the Directive in the first place.[122]

The latter (more generous) approach was ultimately vindicated by the Court itself in Case C–307/98 *Commission v Belgium* (2000): a Member State that wishes no longer to treat certain areas as bathing areas under the Directive must prove that bathing is no longer habitually practised there, and that that situation is not the result of the Member State's own failure to comply with the quality standards fixed by Community law.[123] However, the Court's approach was clearly inspired by the reasoning of Advocate General Ruiz-Jarabo Colomer. He pointed out that the legal framework of the Bathing Water Directive differed fundamentally from that governing the Wild Birds Directive: whereas the latter applied only to

[118] Although the site of the new dyke was partly influenced by a desire to ensure access for local fishing boats to the harbour, this economic interest did not invalidate a decision which would otherwise have considerable ecological benefits. Cf AG Fennelly in Case C–96/98 *Commission v France* [1999] ECR I–8531, para 38 Opinion.

[119] J H Jans, *European Environmental Law* (Europa Law Publishing, 2000) pp 129–32. Also: Case C–374/98 *Commission v France* [2000] ECR I–10799.

[120] Dir 76/160 concerning the quality of bathing water, OJ 1976 L31/1.

[121] Case C–92/96 *Commission v Spain* [1998] ECR I–505, paras 26–29. Cf Case C–198/97 *Commission v Germany* [1999] ECR I–3257.

[122] Case C–92/96 *Commission v Spain* [1998] ECR I–505, paras 37–40 Opinion.

[123] Case C–307/98 *Commission v Belgium* [2000] ECR I–3933.

areas positively identified by the Member States, the former applied to all areas which met objective threshold criteria set out by the Directive itself. So, even though the Bathing Water Directive did not contain any express derogation covering changes of social habits, protected areas which were no longer habitually used for bathing purposes no longer fulfilled the objective threshold criteria for application of the Directive in the first place.[124] If this analysis is correct, neither *Commission v Spain* nor *Commission v Belgium* necessarily illustrate the existence of any implied right to derogate at all, and thus cannot be said to have liberalised the conditions first established by the Court in Case C–57/89 *Commission v Germany* (1991).

Indeed, it seems clear that the Court is very reluctant to recognise the existence of any implied right to derogate (beyond the strict confines suggested by *Commission v Germany* itself). For example, the Court in *Kreil* held that it was not possible to infer from the express derogations provided for in respect of the free movement of goods and persons that there was, inherent in the Treaty, a general exception from binding Community obligations for measures taken on grounds of public security. To recognise any such implied exception (for example) in the sphere of social policy might impair the uniform application of Community law.[125] In any case, even as regards situations such as *Commission v Germany*, it is again unclear how far any implied right to derogate would produce legal effects beyond Article 226 EC proceedings before the Court of Justice, so as also to impact upon relations between the Member State and private individuals within the domestic legal system.

The potential for regulatory differentiation produced by the existence of (at least express) derogations is clear. Different groups or interests enjoy different levels of protection in different Member States, not only above but also below the supposed Community norm—in blatant contradiction of an 'integration through law' model which anticipates equality of regulatory burdens on the Common Market, and/or equality of welfare rights between Union citizens. However, it is important to recall that, according to the Court's well-established caselaw, derogations are to be interpreted strictly and in accordance with the objectives of the measure in question.[126] For example, the categories of employee excluded from the scope of protection offered by the Insolvency Directive cannot be extended beyond those explicitly listed in the Annex, even if the workers in question are in an analogous position to those already excluded.[127] Similarly, the categories

[124] Case C–307/98 *Commission v Belgium* [2000] ECR I–3933, paras 25–30 Opinion.

[125] Case C–285/98 *Kreil* [2000] ECR I–69, paras 15–19. Cf Cases C–19–20/90 *Karella* [1991] ECR I–2691.

[126] From innumerable cases, eg Case C–321/96 *Mecklenburg* [1998] ECR I–3809.

[127] Dir 80/987 on the approximation of the laws of the Member States relating to the protection of employees in the event of the insolvency of their employer, OJ 1980 L283/23. Eg Case 22/87 *Commission v Italy* [1989] ECR 143; Case C–334/92 *Wagner Miret* [1993] ECR I–6911. Also: Case C–53/88 *Commission v Greece* [1990] ECR I–3917 on the alternative treatment of excluded employees as required by the Directive.

of transport (such as refuse collection and public services) which are excluded from the obligations imposed by Regulation 3820/85 on the harmonisation of certain social legislation relating to road transport must be interpreted restrictively and in accordance with the measure's twin aims of equalising conditions of economic competition and improving working conditions and road safety.[128] Another example is the Court's determination to limit strictly the exceptions to the fundamental principle of equal treatment between men and women as regards access to employment and working conditions contained in Directive 76/207.[129]

Variable Norms and Conceptual Renvois

It has been observed how minimum harmonisation accommodates national action above the Community norm, while derogations permit such action below the Community standard. But some measures go further—giving the Member States a range of options, any one of which might equally be said to constitute 'the Community norm'. For example, the Insolvency Directive allows the Member States to choose from a number of possible dates from which the guarantee institution becomes responsible for meeting workers' unpaid wage claims against their insolvent employer; together with options to impose corresponding limits to the extent of the guarantee institution's liability, and to place an overall ceiling on pay-outs.[130]

More recent social policy measures even allow the Member States to replace the obligations defined by Community law with equivalent rules formulated either by the national authorities or the social partners. In such cases, national participation in the regulatory elaboration of substantive Community policy might appear to reach its apex. For example, Article 17 Working Time Directive permits the Member States to replace whole swathes of its protective provisions with alternative arrangements agreed at a national, regional or even local level between the social partners, subject to certain guarantees to ensure that the basic aim of the

[128] Reg 3820/85 on the harmonisation of certain social legislation relating to road transport, OJ 1985 L370/1. Case C–335/94 *Mrozek and Jäger* [1996] ECR I–1573; Case C–39/95 *Pierre Goupil* [1996] ECR I–1601; Case C–387/96 *Anders Sjöberg* [1998] ECR I–1225.

[129] Dir 76/207 on the implementation of the principle of equal treatment for men and women as regards access to employment, vocational training and promotion, and working conditions, OJ 1976 L39/40. Eg Case 222/84 *Johnston v Chief Constable of the RUC* [1986] ECR 1651; Case C–285/98 *Kreil* [2000] ECR I–69. However, consider the changing caselaw on the scope for 'affirmative action' in favour of women to help redress pernicious discrimination: Case C–450/93 *Kalanke* [1995] ECR I–3051; Case C–409/95 *Marschall* [1997] ECR I–6363; Case C–158/97 *Badeck* [2000] ECR I–1875; Case C–407/98 *Abrahamsson* [2000] ECR I–5539; Case C–476/99 *Lommers* [2002] ECR I–2891. Note also: Art 141(4) EC (introduced at Amsterdam).

[130] Dir 80/987, OJ 1980 L283/23. However, cf judgments such as Cases C–19, 50 & 84/01 *Barsotti* (Judgment of 4 March 2004).

Directive as regards the health and safety of workers is not undermined.[131] Similarly, Article 5(2)(b) Acquired Rights Directive provides that, even where insolvent undertakings are included within its scope and therefore subject to the general principle that employees' contracts are to be transferred intact from old to new employer, national law may still permit the social partners to agree alterations to the workers' terms and conditions of employment.[132] If Member States and even private bodies are permitted to exchange their own standards for those of a given Community measure, the idea of 'uniformity' in the formulation and application of Treaty policy for that field begins to look increasingly tenuous.

This trend towards the decentralised formulation of protective standards in respect of matters falling within the Community's sphere of regulatory competence is closely related to the increased emphasis placed by the Treaty on European Union on fully involving both sides of industry in the Community's social policy decision-making processes.[133] However, the trend is not limited to the sphere of social policy. Community environmental legislation shows an increasing preference for establishing 'target standards' rather than the more traditional technique of 'command and control.' In the latter case, Community legislation sets down legally binding requirements which seek directly to regulate the conduct of national economic operators. In the former case, the Community merely sets out objectives forming part of a long-term strategy of (say) pollution control; compliance with these targets is a goal rather than a legally binding obligation, with increased emphasis on the participation of both the national authorities and industry itself.[134] For example, Directive 96/61 concerning integrated pollution prevention and control seeks to prevent or minimise air, water and soil pollution caused by industrial emissions through an environmental licensing system. While the Council and the Member States may fix common emission standards for industrial sectors, such standards are in principle to be determined at the local level and taking account of local factors.[135] Indeed, the

[131] Dir 2003/88, OJ 2003 L299/9 (repealing and replacing Dir 93/104, OJ 1993 L307/18).

[132] Dir 2001/23, OJ 2001 L82/16.

[133] In particular: Arts 137(4), 138 and 139 EC (previously Arts 2(4), 3 and 4 of the Agreement on Social Policy contained in the Protocol on Social Policy annexed to the EC Treaty by the Treaty on European Union). Cf B Bercusson, 'Regulatory Competition in the EU System: Labour' in D Esty & D Geradin (eds), *Regulatory Competition and Economic Integration: Comparative Perspectives* (OUP, 2001).

[134] Further: J Scott, *EC Environmental Law* (Longman, 1998) ch 2.

[135] Dir 96/61 concerning integrated pollution prevention and control, OJ 1996 L257/26. For detailed discussion of this measure: J Scott, 'Flexibility in the Implementation of EC Environmental Law' (2000) 1 *Yearbook of European Environmental Law* 37. For additional examples and discussion, see: L Krämer, 'Recent Developments in EC Environmental Law' in J Holder (ed), *The Impact of EC Environmental Law in the United Kingdom* (Wiley, 1997). Cf also Commission, *White Paper on European Governance*, COM (2001)428 Final: environmental policy is a potential candidate for a new scheme of 'tripartite contracts' between the Community,

Commission's 2002 *Action Plan for Simplifying and Improving the Regulatory Environment* suggested that such forms of co-regulation—whereby the Community legislature sets out only the essential aspects of a given policy initiative, and active stakeholders then define and implement those basic principles according to their knowledge and experience—might warrant more widespread use within the Community legal order.[136] Again, identifying a genuine 'Community norm' within such measures is a very difficult task.

The variable character of Treaty rules as between the Member States is also facilitated by conceptual renvois to the domestic legal orders—permitting the Member States to define for themselves key threshold terms which determine the scope and content of Community legislative initiatives.

In some situations, competence to define a particular matter is expressly reserved to the Member States by the relevant Community legislation. This is the case, for example, with the definition of 'employee' for the purposes of the Insolvency Directive,[137] the Employment Conditions Directive,[138] and the Parental Leave Directive;[139] of 'worker' for the purposes of the Part-Time Work Directive;[140] and of 'workers' representatives' for the purposes of the Collective Redundancies Directive.[141] The same result is often achieved in practice when secondary Community legislation explains key terms in only a cursory manner. Without an accurate Community-wide definition, the same word or phrase can carry widely different meanings and implications when transposed into the various legal and social traditions of the Member States. For example, Article 3(1) of the Unfair Contract Terms Directive sets out the test for unfairness as follows:

> [a] contractual term which has not been individually negotiated shall be regarded as unfair if, contrary to the requirement of good faith, it causes a significant imbalance in the parties' rights and obligations arising under the contract, to the detriment of the consumer.[142]

Member State and regional authorities aimed at offering greater flexibility in attaining Treaty objectives, particularly those which have a strong territorial / local impact (p13).

[136] COM (2002)278 Final.
[137] Art 2(2) Dir 80/987 on the approximation of the laws of the Member States relating to the protection of employees in the event of the insolvency of their employer, OJ 1980 L283/23.
[138] Art 1(1) Dir 91/533 on an employer's obligation to inform employees of the conditions applicable to the contract or employment relationship, OJ 1991 L288/32.
[139] Cl 1(2) Framework Agreement annexed to Dir 96/34 on the framework agreement on parental leave concluded by UNICE, CEEP and the ETUC, OJ 1996 L145/4.
[140] Cl 2(1) Framework Agreement annexed to Dir 97/81 concerning the framework agreement on part-time work concluded by UNICE, CEEP and the ETUC, OJ 1998 L14/9.
[141] Art 1(1)(b) Dir 98/59 on the approximation of the laws of the Member States relating to collective redundancies, OJ 1998 L225/16. Also: Art 2(e) Dir 2002/14 establishing a general framework for informing and consulting employees, OJ 2002 L80/29.
[142] Dir 93/13 on unfair terms in consumer contracts, OJ 1993 L95/29.

Yet 'good faith' means one thing to a German lawyer (whose corpus of contract law is familiar with such a concept), and another to an English lawyer (for whom such a criterion is almost entirely unknown in the context of contractual relations).[143]

On the one hand, it is possible for the Court of Justice to offer Community-level interpretations, and thereby develop a common understanding, of many key concepts. The consequence of such a process is to stem the potential for differentiation and encourage greater uniformity in the application of Community measures.[144] Indeed, the Court has stated that

> [t]he need for uniform application of Community law and the principle of equality require that the terms of a provision of Community law which makes no express reference to the law of the Member States for the purpose of determining its meaning and scope must normally be given an autonomous and uniform interpretation throughout the Community.[145]

Thus, for example, in *Hoeskstra,* the Court stated that the definition of 'worker' for the purposes of delimiting the scope of the right to free movement contained in Article 39 EC must, in the interests of uniformity, be determined according to Community rather than national criteria.[146] Similarly, the application of the Collective Redundancies Directive depends on identifying an 'establishment' which is proposing to carry out the relevant dismissals. Article 1(1)(a) does not elaborate on this term, but in *Rockfon,* the Court held that a single Community definition, not a series of divergent national ones, was appropriate, and interpreted the measure accordingly.[147] Even where Community legislation does specifically refer to national concepts and definitions, the Member States may find their margin of discretion curtailed by the fundamental principles of Community law. For example, the Court held in *Caballero* that, although the concept of 'pay' for the purposes of the Insolvency Directive was to be determined by domestic rules, the Member States were still obliged to respect the requirement of equal treatment when implementing Community law. Spain was thus prohibited from subjecting various categories workers, who actually found themselves in the

[143] Further: S Weatherill, *EC Consumer Law and Policy* (Longman, 1997) ch 4; G Teubner, 'Legal Irritants: Good Faith in British Law or How Unifying Law Ends Up in New Divergences' (1998) 61 MLR 11.

[144] Further: S Weatherill, 'Prospects for the Development of European Private Law Through "Europeanisation" in the European Court: The Case of the Directive on Unfair Terms in Consumer Contracts' (1995) 3 *European Review of Private Law* 307.

[145] Case C–287/98 *Luxembourg v Linster* [2000] ECR I–6917, para 43.

[146] Case 75/63 *Hoekstra* [1964] ECR 177. Also, eg Case 53/81 *Levin* [1982] ECR 1035; Case 139/85 *Kempf* [1986] ECR 1741; Case 66/85 *Lawrie-Blum* [1986] ECR 2121; Case 196/87 *Steymann* [1988] ECR 6159; Case 344/87 *Bettray* [1989] ECR 1621.

[147] Case C–449/93 *Rockfon* [1995] ECR I–4291.

same situation as regards their remuneration, to arbitrary differences in the categories of payments which would be assumed by the competent guarantee institution.[148]

On the other hand, this process of 'Europeanisation' by the Court of Justice has its limits. In particular, the Court has sometimes declined to give certain concepts a Community definition, inferring from the context of the measure in question that the Community legislature's failure to provide a common definition was intentional. For example, the Court has explicitly left to the competence of domestic law the detailed definition of 'insolvency' for the purposes of determining the basic scope of the Insolvency Directive: even though this has the inevitable effect of jeopardising a uniform level of protection for workers throughout the Community, it is nevertheless consistent with the limited ambition of the measure in question, which seeks to attain no more than partial harmonisation in a complex regulatory field.[149] The same is true of the term 'employee' in the context of the Acquired Rights Directive: this measure seeks only to ensure that the existing rights of employees under national law are not diminished by the process of transferring their undertaking from one management to another; it does not seek to establish common levels of protection throughout the Community by harmonising the categories of worker entitled to rely upon the Directive.[150]

Choice of Legal Instrument

Regulatory diversity between the Member States within the sphere of interest occupied by the Treaty can also result from the Community's choice of legislative instrument for intervening within the domestic legal orders.

In this regard, the principal choice is between regulations and directives. Sometimes there is no choice at all: under the Treaty's social policy chapter, Community action is instructed to take the form of directives.[151] However, in sectors such as consumer and environmental policy, the Community legislature is permitted to adopt both regulations and directives.[152] The same is true of Article 95 EC as regards approximation measures adopted for the

[148] Case C–442/00 *Caballero* [2002] ECR I–11915.
[149] Case C–479/93 *Francovich II* [1995] ECR I–3843. Cf Case C–117/96 *Carina Mosbæk* [1997] ECR I–5017.
[150] Case 105/84 *Danmols Inventar* [1985] ECR 2639. More recently, eg Case C–343/98 *Collino* [2000] ECR I–6659. This judicial approach has now been codified by legislative amendment: Arts 2(1)(d) and 2(2) Dir 2001/23 on the approximation of the laws of the Member States relating to the safeguarding of employees' rights in the event of transfers of undertakings, businesses or parts of undertakings or businesses, OJ 2001 L82/16.
[151] Art 137(2) EC.
[152] Arts 153 and 175 EC (respectively).

completion of the Internal Market. Nevertheless, Clause 6 of the Protocol on the application of the principles of subsidiarity and proportionality annexed to the EC Treaty provides that, other things being equal, directives should be preferred to regulations. In practice, the Community has usually followed this preference.[153]

The basic characteristics of regulations and directives, as set out in Article 249 EC, might lead one to suppose that the former necessarily encourage uniformity and the latter diversity—and thus that Community policy on social, consumer and environmental matters allows for an added dimension of differentiation merely through the choice of legislative instrument by which Community policy is enacted. On the one hand, regulations have general application and are binding in their entirety and directly applicable in all Member States. Indeed, the Court of Justice has held that Member States may not in principle 'translate' regulations into national legislation, lest this obscure the Treaty provenance or alter the nature of their provisions.[154] On the other hand, directives are binding as to the result to be achieved, but leave to the national authorities the choice of form and methods.[155] The Treaty therefore seemed to conceive of directives as an 'incomplete' form of Community legislative act: they become fully effective only when transposed into the domestic legal order through the medium of the Member State itself; this process of adaptation seems to imply the existence of national discretion and some leeway for diversity.[156] And indeed, the Commission still tends to prefer proposing the use of regulations in policy areas which require a high level of regulatory uniformity; whereas directives are considered more appropriate for initiatives which will survive a certain degree of differentiation across the Member States.[157]

However, while the scheme of Article 249 EC may still hold true as a general principle, a combination of institutional practice and judicial creativity means that the picture has become more complex in practice.

First, the substantive obligations laid down in directives may be very detailed, leaving little room for variation when transposed into national law.[158] This is particularly true of product specification measures passed

[153] Eg R Macrory and R Purdy, 'The Enforcement of EC Environmental Law Against Member States' in J Holder (ed), *The Impact of EC Environmental Law in the United Kingdom* (Wiley, 1997) observe that the vast majority of legal instruments adopted in the environmental field have been directives; regulations are normally used when the Community wants to establish a uniform regime for dealings with third countries.

[154] Eg Case 34/73 *Variola* [1973] ECR 981; Case 50/76 *Amsterdam Bulb* [1977] ECR 137.

[155] Also: Cl 6 Protocol on the application of the principles of subsidiarity and proportionality (annexed to the EC Treaty).

[156] Cf Commission, *White Paper on European Governance*, COM (2001)428 Final: regulations are appropriate where uniformity across the Union is desired; but otherwise framework directives should be used more often to offer greater flexibility (p 20).

[157] Eg Commission, *Proposal for a Regulation Concerning Sales Promotions in the Internal Market*, COM (2001)546 Final.

[158] As sanctioned by the ECJ itself, eg in Case 38/77 *Enka* [1977] ECR 2203.

before the New Approach to Technical Harmonisation, but many commentators believe that the tendency for over-enthusiastic Community regulation soon crept back into institutional practice.[159] In any case, the distinction drawn in Article 249 EC, between the binding nature of a directive's objective and the Member State's discretion as to the method by which it is attained, does not necessarily imply any choice with regard to substantive policy-making:

> the [Member State's] choice is limited to the *kind* of measures to be taken; their *content* is entirely determined by the directive at issue. Thus the discretion as far as the form and methods is concerned does not mean that Member States necessarily have a margin in terms of policy making.[160]

Conversely, regulations can lay down broad principles which require or imply some degree of independent creativity at the Member State level before they can take meaningful practical effect.[161] Moreover, regulations as well as directives can make provision for minimum harmonisation, and for derogations.[162] In short, there is no *necessary* difference between directives and regulations in terms of the degree of regulatory uniformity they seek to achieve, or the extent of national autonomy they are prepared to tolerate.[163]

Secondly, this analysis suggests that the only inherent difference between regulations and directives lies in their respective preclusion of/need for national transposition measures, before being capable of producing independent effects within the domestic legal orders. Again, however, this distinction has been eroded considerably. On the one side, the Court has held that, although regulations can generally produce immediate effects within the national legal orders, where certain provisions of a regulation do necessitate the adoption of implementing measures by the domestic authorities, individuals may not derive rights from

[159] Eg C Timmermans, 'Community Directives Revisited' (1997) 17 *Yearbook of European Law* 1. Cf Cl 6 Protocol on the application of the principles of subsidiarity and proportionality (annexed to the EC Treaty): framework directives should be preferred to more detailed measures.

[160] S Prechal, *Directives in European Community Law: A Study of Directives and Their Enforcement in National Courts* (Clarendon Press, 1995) p 86.

[161] Eg Reg 2988/95 on the protection of the European Communities' financial interests, OJ 1995 L312/1 sets out general notions about the effective enforcement of Community law by the national authorities which require further reference to / implementation by domestic rules.

[162] This is the case, eg with regulations adopted under Art 175 EC, and automatically subject to the minimum harmonisation clause contained in Art 176 EC (see Case C–203/96 *Dusseldorp* [1998] ECR I–4075).

[163] Though note Commission, *Action Plan for Simplifying and Improving the Regulatory Environment*, COM (2002)278 Final, which acknowledges the tendency for Community legislation to be too detailed; and plans to revert to the original definition of a directive, ie as a measure which sets out only the essential aspects of the relevant policy initiative.

the relevant Community legislation in the absence of such national implementing measures.[164] On the other side, the Court has established that directives as well as regulations may have direct effect, provided the deadline for transposition has passed (and of course that the relevant provisions are sufficiently clear, precise and unconditional).[165] This caselaw still has the potential to produce significant—if unintended—patterns of differentiation in the application of Community substantive policy. Directives can have direct effect only vertically against the Member States, not horizontally against private individuals.[166] Furthermore, their vertical direct effect rests on a definition of the 'state' which, though wide, can nevertheless vary from country to country depending on the precise degree of centralisation or privatisation which characterises the infrastructure of public service provision within any given Member State.[167] Moreover, the possibility of un- or incorrectly implemented directives having so-called 'indirect effect' against private individuals (through the interpretation of existing national legislation so as to conform as closely as possible to Community requirements) again depends upon the precise legislative context prevailing within each Member State.[168]

This survey suggests that the choice between employing regulations or directives is not per se a crucial, only a potential, factor in terms of the existence of regulatory differentiation within the Community legal order. However, there is another choice to be made as regards the legal instruments available under the Treaty: between binding legislative measures such as regulations and directives, and the increasingly widespread reliance upon 'soft law' as an alternative means of promoting substantive Community policy objectives.

[164] Eg Case C–403/98 *Monte Arcosu* [2001] ECR I–103.

[165] Eg Case 41/74 *van Duyn* [1974] ECR 1337; Case 148/78 *Ratti* [1979] ECR 1629; Case 8/81 *Becker* [1982] ECR 53; Case C–62/93 *BP Supergas* [1995] ECR I–1883; Case C–118/94 *World Wildlife Fund v Regione Veneto* [1996] ECR I–1223; Cases C–74 & 129/95 *Criminal Proceedings Against X* [1996] ECR I–6609. Cf Cases C–6 & 9/90 *Francovich* [1991] ECR I–5357; Case C–54/96 *Dorsch Consult* [1997] ECR I–4961; Case C–131/97 *Carbonari* [1999] ECR I–1103; Case C–365/98 *Brinkmann Tabakfabriken* [2000] ECR I–4619.

[166] Eg Case 152/84 *Marshall* [1986] ECR 723; Case C–91/92 *Faccini Dori* [1994] ECR I–3325; Case C–472/93 *Spano v Fiat* [1995] ECR I–4321; Case C–192/94 *El Corte Inglés* [1996] ECR I–1281; Case C–97/96 *Daihatsu Deutschland* [1997] ECR I–6843; Cases C–253–58/96 *Kampelmann* [1997] ECR I–6907; Case C–185/97 *Coote v Granada Hospitality* [1998] ECR I–5199; Case C–2/97 *Borsana* [1998] ECR I–8597; Case C–456/98 *Centrosteel v Adipol* [2000] ECR I–6007; Case C–343/98 *Collino* [2000] ECR I–6659.

[167] Eg Case 222/84 *Johnston v Chief Constable of the RUC* [1986] ECR 1651; Case 152/84 *Marshall* [1986] ECR 723; Case 103/88 *Fratelli Costanzo* [1989] ECR 1839; Case C–188/89 *Foster v British Gas* [1990] ECR I–3313.

[168] Eg Case 14/83 *von Colson* [1984] ECR 1891; Case 80/86 *Kolpinghuis Nijmegen* [1987] ECR 3969; Case C–106/89 *Marleasing* [1990] ECR I–4135; Case C–334/92 *Wagner Miret* [1993] ECR I–6911; Case C–168/95 *Luciano Arcaro* [1996] ECR I–4705.

'Soft law' refers to non-binding Community measures, which (for present purposes) can be categorised under several headings.[169] First, exhortatory statements of principle, intended to guide future Community conduct or legislative activity. For example, the Solemn Declaration by the Member States (excluding the UK) on a Community Charter of the Fundamental Social Rights of Workers was intended to re-launch the Community's commitment to increased levels of employee protection, at the same time as construction of the Internal Market was nearing completion.[170] This category would also include the 'action programmes' which have become a familiar feature of Community policies on the environment, consumer protection and employment.[171]

Secondly, measures intended to supplement existing binding legislation. Such measures are often intended to act as an interpretative guide to the current state of Community law, for example, by clarifying the Commission's understanding of the obligations imposed under a given regulation or directive. This was true of the Commission's code of practice on sexual harassment, which was intended to complement the provisions of the Equal Treatment Directive.[172] This category also covers measures intended to provide guidance to third parties about how the Community institutions intend to exercise decision-making powers vested in them under the Treaty. For example, the Commission has published several guidelines informing the Member States and economic actors of the substantive policy framework by which it will exercise its discretion to authorise state aids under Article 87 EC.[173]

Thirdly, measures which act as substitutes for binding legislation. This includes acts adopted in areas where Treaty competence to adopt legally binding instruments is limited or non-existent, but the Community institutions still wish to influence the exercise of Member State regulatory choices. For example, in the absence of any formal power to harmonise employees' pay, the Community has adopted several (relatively modest)

[169] Further, eg F Snyder, 'The Effectiveness of European Community Law: Institutions, Processes, Tools and Techniques' (1993) 56 MLR 19; J Kenner, 'EC Labour Law: The Softly, Softly Approach' (1995) 11 *International Journal of Comparative Labour Law and Industrial Relations* 307.

[170] Also: Commission, *Social Action Programme to Implement the Solemn Declaration by the Member States, excluding the UK, on a Community Charter of the Fundamental Social Rights of Workers*, COM (1989)568.

[171] Eg Council, *Declaration on the Programme of Action of the European Communities on the Environment*, OJ 1973 C112/1; Council, *Resolution Concerning a Social Action Programme*, OJ 1974 C13/1; Council, *Resolution on a Preliminary Programme of the European Economic Community for a Consumer Protection and Information Policy*, OJ 1975 C92/1.

[172] Commission Recommendation 92/131 on the protection of the dignity of women and men at work (including an annexed code of practice on measures to combat sexual harassment), OJ 1992 L49/1. Also, eg Commission, *Communication on a Code of Practice on the Implementation of Equal Pay for Work of Equal Value for Women and Men*, COM (1996)336.

[173] Eg Commission, *Community Guidelines on State Aid for Environmental Protection*, OJ 2001 C37/3.

soft law measures intended to encourage the Member States to maintain wage levels within the Single Market. The 1989 Charter of the Fundamental Social Rights of Workers enunciated the principle that all employment should be fairly remunerated;[174] and the 1993 Commission Opinion on an Equitable Wage observes that very low wage levels raise problems of equity and social cohesion which might harm long-term economic effectiveness.[175] However, this category also covers measures adopted in cases where the Community does have regulatory competence, but nevertheless chooses to steer national policy choices rather than adopt binding legislation.[176] Indeed, recent years have witnessed a discernible shift away from reliance on hard law regulation in favour of soft law instruments, even in areas of Community activity where a genuine choice exists. Thus, in the environmental sphere, Krämer has observed that, in the period since 1991, a significant decrease in Community legislative activity has been matched by increased numbers of non-binding communications and declarations.[177] For example, the Community preferred to establish voluntary rather than compulsory schemes for both 'eco-labelling' and 'eco-auditing.'[178]

Where soft law is being employed either to structure the exercise of discretionary powers under existing Community legislation, or in the complete absence of Community regulatory competence, it may actually encourage greater uniformity in economic compliance costs, or the treatment of individual citizens, than would otherwise have existed.[179] For example, faced with only limited competence to intervene in the domestic welfare systems, the Community has instead pursued a (relatively far-reaching) programme of measures intended to encourage convergence by the Member States around basic common values, to facilitate the exchange of information about best practice in other jurisdictions, and to stress the benefits of modernisation to ensure the long term viability of the European social model. Beginning with instruments such as Recommendation 92/441 on common criteria concerning sufficient resources and social assistance,[180] and Recommendation 92/442 on the convergence of

[174] Solemn Declaration by the Member States, excluding the UK, on a Community Charter of the Fundamental Social Rights of Workers. Also: Commission, *Social Action Programme to Implement the Solemn Declaration by the Member States, excluding the UK, on a Community Charter of the Fundamental Social Rights of Workers*, COM (1989)568.
[175] COM (1993)388 Final.
[176] Cf Case C–57/95 *France v Commission* [1997] ECR I–1627.
[177] L Krämer, 'Recent Developments in EC Environmental Law' in J Holder (ed), *The Impact of EC Environmental Law in the United Kingdom* (Wiley, 1997).
[178] Reg 880/92 on a Community eco-label award scheme, OJ 1992 L99/1; Reg 1836/93 allowing voluntary participation by companies in the industrial sector in a Community eco-management and audit scheme, OJ 1993 L168/1.
[179] Further: L Senden and S Prechal, 'Differentiation In and Through Community Soft Law' in B de Witte, D Hanf & E Vos (eds), *The Many Faces of Differentiation in EU Law* (Intersentia, 2001).
[180] Recommendation 92/441, OJ 1992 L245/46.

objectives and policies in the area of social protection,[181] the process has gained momentum and intensity since the Commission's publication in 1999 of *A Concerted Strategy for Modernising Social Protection*, and the promotion in this sector of the open method of coordination following the Lisbon European Council of March 2000.[182] The open method of coordination can be seen as the mobilisation of soft law on a grand scale, aimed at achieving a high degree of regulatory consensus among the Member States, despite the absence of hard Community competence.[183] It is already used not only as regards the modernisation of social protection, but also for the coordination of national employment policies, and increasingly in fields such as combating social exclusion, education policy, and research and development.[184] But even if the use of soft law in such situations does indeed encourage greater uniformity than might otherwise have been the case, the Community nevertheless remains characterised by high levels of regulatory differentiation between the Member States.

This assessment is true also of fields where the Community employs soft law in preference to hard law (even though the institutions do in fact possess legislative power). But in such cases, it is worth pointing out that soft law can sometimes have more concrete legal consequences. First, soft can be transformed into hard law indirectly by judicial decision. The Court of Justice has imposed on national courts a duty to take into account Community soft law when interpreting any relevant domestic provisions, particularly where the non-binding measure was specifically intended to supplement a binding instrument.[185] Secondly, soft can also be transformed into hard law directly by legislative action. Non-binding measures often provide a first stage in the development of more intensive Community involvement within any given field. In particular, codes of practice or recommendations which do not satisfactorily achieve their objectives may well later be replaced with binding measures. For example,

[181] Recommendation 92/442, OJ 1992 L245/49.

[182] Commission, *A Concerted Strategy for Modernising Social Protection*, COM (1999)347 Final; Presidency Conclusions of the Lisbon European Council (23–24 March 2000); and of the Nice European Council (7–9 December 2000).

[183] Further, eg E Szyszczak, 'The New Paradigm For Social Policy: A Virtuous Circle?' (2001) 38 CML Rev 1125; S Regent, 'The Open Method of Coordination: A New Supranational Form of Governance?' (2003) 9 *European Public Law* 190.

[184] Further, eg G de Búrca, 'The Constitutional Challenge of New Governance in the European Union' (2003) 28 EL Rev 814.

[185] Case C–322/88 *Grimaldi* [1989] ECR 4407; Case C–207/01 *Altair Chimica* (Judgment of 11 September 2003) (interpretative value of Community recommendations). Also, eg Case C–188/91 *Deutsche Shell* [1993] ECR I–363 (interpretative value of recommendations adopted under an international agreement concluded by the Community); Case C–3/96 *Commission v Netherlands* [1998] ECR I–3031 (interpretative value of Commission expert scientific evidence). Further: A Arnull, 'The Legal Status of Recommendations' (1990) 15 EL Rev 318; J Klabbers, 'Informal Instruments Before the European Court of Justice' (1994) 31 CML Rev 997.

a Commission recommendation on deposit guarantee schemes eventually gave way to a fully-fledged directive, imposing the sorts of standards which Member States and industry players had proven reluctant to undertake voluntarily.[186]

Assessment

The overall impression generated by the above survey is of a sliding scale of Community and national competence to construct regulatory frameworks capable of furthering substantive Treaty policy objectives. At one extreme, it is still perfectly plausible to describe the rules on cross-border competition policy and the grant of state aids as 'uniform' in the sense that the scope of Community action within the relevant sectors is relatively extensive and, within the sphere of interest occupied by the Treaty, the relevant legal framework is determined almost entirely at the centre and with little input from each individual Member State. At another extreme, it seems difficult to describe Europe's regulatory framework for dealing with the environment, consumers or social matters (let alone issues such as education or culture) as being particularly 'uniform' when the scope of Community action within the relevant sectors is often extremely limited and, even as regards the territory occupied by the Treaty, vertically differentiated regulatory techniques permit the Member States to enjoy significant influence over the content of substantive policy.[187]

HORIZONTAL DIFFERENTIATION

This complex web of mixed responsibility and regulatory diversity has been carried to a new degree along what shall be termed the horizontal plane. Whereas vertical differentiation refers to the ability of the Member States to contribute to the regulatory expression of substantive policy within

[186] Commission Recommendation 87/63 concerning the introduction of deposit-guarantee schemes in the Community, OJ 1987 L33/16; Dir 94/19 on deposit-guarantee schemes, OJ 1994 L135/5. Also, eg Commission Recommendation 90/109 on the transparency of banking conditions relating to cross-border financial transactions, OJ 1990 L67/39; Dir 97/5 on cross-border credit transfers, OJ 1997 L43/25. It has also been argued that 'soft law' may be converted into 'hard law' by administrative decision: F Snyder, 'Soft Law and Institutional Practice in the European Community' in S Martin (ed), *The Construction of Europe: Essays in Honour of Emile Noël* (Kluwer, 1994).

[187] Cf L Woods and C Villiers, 'The Legislative Process and the Institutions of the European Union: A Case-Study of the Development of European Company Law' in P Craig & C Harlow (eds), *Law-Making in the European Union* (Kluwer, 1998): recent Community initiatives to harmonise domestic company law have been characterised by increasing regulatory diversity, eg through the use of minimum harmonisation clauses and framework directives.

any particular sector of Community activity, horizontal differentiation refers to the ability of Member States to decide whether or not to participate in that sector at all.

Before outlining how far such horizontal differentiation is currently permitted under Community law, it might first be useful to explain some of the basic concepts involved. Unfortunately, there is no academic consensus as to the appropriate terminology to be employed here.[188] Nevertheless, three main models can be identified and employed as the background for discussion. First, multi-speed integration. This refers to a situation wherein all the Member States agree to a set of common objectives but, for pragmatic political or economic reasons, do not adhere to a common timetable for their realisation. Secondly, variable geometry. Here, the Member States abandon their commitment to pursue a truly common body of objectives. Instead, certain countries are authorised to pursue deeper or broader degrees of integration with regard to a particular sector or sectors of activity. Thirdly, Europe *à la carte*. This also implies diverse rather than common objectives, with Member States able to pick-and-choose the areas of integration in which they wish to participate.

It can sometimes be difficult to draw any meaningful distinction between variable geometry and Europe *à la carte*. It seems that variable geometry implies the maintenance of a minimum core of common Community activities, over and above which certain Member States agree to carry the integrative momentum forward together. By contrast, Europe *à la carte* implies that there is no such common core, participation in every or at least most sectors of Community activity being voluntary and optional. Accordingly, the differentiation which results from Europe *à la carte* is not aimed at carrying the integration process forward, but at accommodating the diverse expectations of each individual Member State.

Some authors express the contrast in terms of 'opting into' or 'opting out of' integrative initiatives.[189] However, such a distinction can be difficult to apply as a matter of watertight theory, particularly since determining whether a given question belongs to the 'core' or to the 'periphery' of Community activity is a controversial task.[190] For example, the United Kingdom's exclusion from the Social Protocol of the post-Maastricht EC Treaty has been interpreted both as an example of Europe *à la carte* (whereby the United Kingdom 'opted out of' the Community core),[191] and as an extreme form of variable geometry (whereby all the other

[188] Eg A Stubb, 'A Categorization of Differentiated Integration' (1996) 34 JCMS 283.
[189] Just as some distinguish between 'minimum harmonisation' (going further) and 'the right to derogate' (falling behind) in the field of vertical differentiation.
[190] Cf S Weatherill, 'Safeguarding the *Acquis Communautaire*' in T Heukels, N Blokker & M Brus (eds), *The European Union After Amsterdam: A Legal Analysis* (Kluwer Law International, 1998); C Delcourt, 'The *Acquis Communautaire*: Has the Concept Had Its Day?' (2001) 38 CML Rev 829.
[191] Eg A Duff, *Reforming the European Union* (The Federal Trust, 1997) ch 8.

Member States were authorised to 'opt into' a form of closer integration which lay outside the Community's Internal Market heartland).[192] The question therefore appears to be rather subjective: variable geometry is seen as less destructive of Community solidarity and more favourable to the process of integration than Europe *à la carte*; but how any particular example of horizontal differentiation is classified depends on one's perspective and (in particular) upon whether one favours the image of a vanguard of countries carrying forward, or the perception of a recalcitrant minority holding back, the Community's natural development.

Bearing in mind the limitations of the theoretical models offered by the academic literature, these three categories nevertheless help one to observe and interpret the phenomenon of horizontal differentiation actually at work within the European Union. The history of horizontal differentiation within the Community legal order can be divided into two main periods: pre-Treaty of Amsterdam (from the founding Treaties to the Treaty on European Union, including the various Accession Treaties); and post-Treaty of Amsterdam (including the reforms agreed under the Treaty of Nice, and those proposed in 2003 by the Convention on the Future of Europe, which were largely accepted by the Member States at the 2004 IGC).

Position Pre-Treaty of Amsterdam

The period before the Maastricht Treaty can be dealt with briefly. It serves merely to illustrate the point that multi-speed integration has long been a feature of the European political and legal landscape. It has also been relatively uncontroversial: there is no undue threat to the unity or solidarity of the *acquis communautaire* in allowing new Member States transitional periods within which to adapt their administrative or economic infrastructures to the demands of Community membership,[193] or in granting to established Member States temporary derogations from Internal Market measures which are unsuited to their current state of economic development.[194]

In certain respects, the Treaty on European Union merely continued this pattern. For example, the amended EC Treaty sets out the convergence criteria which Member States must satisfy before they are permitted to proceed to the third stage of Economic and Monetary Union.[195] The Member States involved thus committed themselves to the attainment of

[192] Eg J Usher, *EC Institutions and Legislation* (Longman, 1998) ch 9. This interpretation is suggested by the language of the Protocol itself. Further: D Curtin, 'The Constitutional Structure of the Union: A Europe of Bits and Pieces' (1993) 30 CML Rev 17, 52–61.

[193] As commonly provided for in the Acts of Accession, eg C Preston, *Enlargement and Integration in the European Union* (Routledge, 1997). The most recent Accession Treaty is no exception, eg C Hillion, 'Commentary on the Accession Treaty 2003' (2004) 29 EL Rev (forthcoming).

[194] Eg Art 15 EC (introduced by the Single European Act).

[195] In particular: Arts 121 and 122 EC; Protocol on the convergence criteria referred to in Article 121 of the Treaty establishing the European Community.

a common objective, but not necessarily to reaching that goal all at the same time. In the event, only Greece was excluded from the first wave of potential entrants;[196] once its economy was verified as meeting the requisite conditions, it became obliged to proceed to the full realisation of monetary union.[197]

However, the Treaty on European Union also introduced several instances of horizontal differentiation which (at the time) were without precedent in the Community legal order. For example, two Member States were allowed to exclude themselves entirely from proceeding to the third stage of Economic and Monetary Union, irrespective of their ability to satisfy the applicable economic criteria.[198] Similarly, the achievements of the Protocol and Agreement on Social Policy in broadening and deepening the Community's previously tenuous competences in the field of employee protection were overshadowed by the splendid isolation of the United Kingdom, which refused to participate in what it saw as anti-competitive over-regulation of the workplace.[199] As a result, the Community's social policy became fractured into health and safety measures binding on all the Member States; and other employee protection initiatives which did not extend to the UK.[200]

The Treaty of Amsterdam erased this particular example of horizontal differentiation by ending the United Kingdom's opt-out and incorporating the Social Protocol into the main text of the Treaty.[201] Nevertheless, its wider significance was profound. The idea of common Community high-policy objectives (albeit sometimes and by necessity achieved at different times by different Member States) had clearly been breached. Instead, the stage was set for Member States to voice and provide for apparently

[196] Council Dec 98/317 in accordance with Article 109j(4) of the Treaty, OJ 1998 L139/30. Sweden was also excluded from proceeding to the third stage of EMU, but it had patently failed to fulfil the convergence criteria.

[197] Council Dec 2000/427 in accordance with Article 122(2) of the Treaty on the adoption by Greece of the single currency on 1 January 2001, OJ 2000 L167/19. On the new Member States and the euro, see C Million, 'Commentary on the Accession Treaty 2003' (2004) 29 EL Rev (forthcoming).

[198] Protocols on certain provisions relating to the UK and to Denmark.

[199] Protocol on Social Policy containing the Agreement on Social Policy concluded between the Member States of the European Community with the exception of the United Kingdom.

[200] The following Social Protocol measures were not binding on the UK: Dir 94/45 on the establishment of a European Works Council or a procedure in Community-scale undertakings and Community-scale groups of undertakings for the purposes of informing and consulting employees, OJ 1994 L254/64; Dir 96/34 on the framework agreement on parental leave concluded by UNICE, CEEP and the ETUC, OJ 1996 L145/4; Dir 97/80 on the burden of proof in cases of discrimination based on sex, OJ 1998 L14/6; Dir 97/81 concerning the framework agreement on part-time work concluded by UNICE, CEEP and the ETUC, OJ 1998 L14/9. Contrast with Dir 93/104 concerning certain aspects of the organization of working time, OJ 1993 L307/18; cf Case C–84/94 *United Kingdom v Council* [1996] ECR I–5755.

[201] Now Arts 136–145 EC. The secondary legislation noted above was also extended to cover the UK: Dir 97/74, OJ 1997 L10/22, Dir 97/75, OJ 1998 L10/24, Dir 98/52, OJ 1998 L205/66, and Dir 98/23, OJ 1998 L131/10 (respectively).

irreconcilable differences of opinion about the proper scope and nature of Community activity. So, the Treaty on European Union also saw the adoption of a number of other protocols, similar in spirit to that on social policy: for example, Ireland's stance on abortion, and Denmark's special treatment as regards the ownership of second homes.[202] For many, such provisions put flesh on the bones of an integration model based not only on the principle of variable geometry, but also on the possibility of Europe *à la carte*.

Position Post-Treaty of Amsterdam

Again, certain provisions of the Treaty of Amsterdam merely continued the same pattern as its predecessor. The most significant is perhaps the legal regime established in the new Title IV EC, based on a transfer to the Community Pillar of provisions previously contained in the Justice and Home Affairs Pillar of the European Union. In itself, the new Title constitutes a significant expansion of the Community's powers to facilitate the free movement of persons, in particular, through the abolition of internal border controls and the adoption of Community-level measures on matters relating to third country nationals (such as visas, asylum and immigration policy). Moreover, provision is made for the incorporation into European Union law of the Schengen regime created by certain Member States outside the institutional framework of the European Union as a matter of ordinary international law.[203] However, these new competences remain subject to special provisions regarding the United Kingdom and Ireland, and regarding Denmark.[204] The basic scheme is that the former two states are excluded from the ambit of Title IV, but both may seek to participate in certain individual measures, and Ireland may in addition chose to opt into the general Community regime at any time. Denmark's position is different again: it is also exempted from the new Title and the incorporation of the Schengen *acquis* into Community law; whilst it may implement additional measures into domestic law, in doing so Denmark will create obligations vis-à-vis the other Member States only under international (not under Community) law. In short: Community policy on the free movement of persons now consists of four

[202] Protocol annexed to the Treaty on European Union and to the Treaties establishing the European Communities; Protocol on the Acquisition of Property in Denmark (respectively).
[203] Protocol integrating the Schengen *acquis* into the framework of the European Union (annexed to the Treaty on European Union and to the EC Treaty).
[204] Art 69 EC; Protocol on the position of the United Kingdom and Ireland; Protocol on the position of Denmark; Protocol on the application of certain aspects of Article 14 of the Treaty establishing the European Community to the United Kingdom and Ireland.

separate but overlapping identities, depending on the Member State under consideration.[205]

Closer Cooperation Under the Treaty of Amsterdam

However, the Treaty of Amsterdam's real innovation lies in the institutionalisation of horizontal differentiation, not simply in specific and pre-determined situations, but generally and for the future.

Accommodating diversity was one of the main themes of the negotiations which led to the signing of the Treaty of Amsterdam. The Union had to find a way to reconcile the clear differences of opinion which had emerged between the United Kingdom (which appeared to promote the idea of a Europe *à la carte*) and France and Germany (who wanted to free the integrative urges of the majority of Member States from the constrictive tendencies of a minority of lukewarm sceptics through some form of variable geometry)—as well as addressing the concerns of other national and Community institutions (who sought to protect the Community from harmful fragmentation).[206] This general debate necessarily involved more specific questions about the nature and form differentiation might take. For example, should those Member States wishing to engage in closer forms of integration do so outside or within the institutional and legal framework of the Community? Extra-Union cooperation was the established model, as evidenced by the Schengen Agreement on free movement and border controls, and by the Western European Union on collective defence. But such intergovernmental regimes were thought to exacerbate the already difficult problems of democratic legitimacy and accountability of decision-making within Europe. At least if brought within the Union framework, such initiatives could be more clearly monitored and controlled. Furthermore, if differentiation was to be accommodated within rather than outside the Treaties, should it be on a purely ad hoc

[205] For illustrations of how this situation is being played out in practice, consider, eg Dir 2003/86 on the right to family reunification, OJ 2003 L251/12; Dir 2003/109 concerning the status of third country nationals who are long-term residents, OJ 2004 L16/44. Further, eg J Monar, 'Justice and Home Affairs in the Treaty of Amsterdam: Reform at the Price of Fragmentation' (1998) 23 EL Rev 320; J W de Zwaan, 'Opting In and Opting Out of Rules Concerning the Free Movement of Persons: Problems and Practical Arrangements' (1998) 1 *Cambridge Yearbook of European Law Studies* 107.

[206] Consider academic discussion of the pre-Amsterdam flexibility debate, eg R Harmsen, 'A European Union of Variable Geometry: Problems and Perspectives' (1994) 45 *Northern Ireland Law Quarterly* 109; A Dashwood (ed), *Reviewing Maastricht: Issues for the 1996 IGC* (Sweet & Maxwell Law Books in Europe, 1996); C-D Ehlermann, 'Increased Differentiation or Stronger Uniformity?' in J Winter, D Curtin, A Kellermann & B de Witte (eds), *Reforming the Treaty on European Union: The Legal Debate* (Kluwer Law International, 1996); R Dehousse, *Europe: The Impossible Status Quo* (McMillan Press, 1997); A Stubb, 'Negotiating Flexible Integration in the Amsterdam Treaty' in K Neunreither & A Wiener, *European Integration After Amsterdam: Institutional Dynamics and Prospects For Democracy* (OUP, 2000).

basis, or by means of some more general provision? Again, precedent favoured the former option. But experience highlighted the shortcomings of this strategy: ad hoc provisions could only be introduced or altered by the cumbersome procedure of a formal Treaty amendment; given the growing pressure for differentiation, such a framework might prove hopelessly inflexible. On the other hand, there were fears that inviting a broad principle of horizontal regulatory diversity into the Community's constitution might endanger the *acquis communautaire*, unless subjected to clear and adequate control mechanisms, aimed at preserving the existing achievements of the integration process.

Amsterdam Provisions on Closer Cooperation The provisions on closer cooperation introduced by the Treaty of Amsterdam reflected all of these concerns. Title VII TEU set out the basic terms of the closer cooperation regime in respect of both the First and Third Pillars; Article 11 EC then laid down additional rules on closer cooperation within the First Pillar in particular.[207] Given the substantial body of academic literature on this subject, and the scope of our present investigation, only the basic scheme applicable to closer cooperation under the First Pillar need be summarised here.[208]

The general idea was that a majority of the Member States could choose, in the future and in respect of a range of Community activities, to pursue closer integration between themselves using the institutional and legislative framework provided under the Treaties. To this end, the Treaties imposed a range of substantive conditions. The basic parameters of closer cooperation were established: on the one hand, it had to respect the principle of attributed powers and could not expand the Community's competences beyond those enumerated by the Treaty; on the other hand, it could not concern areas which fell within the exclusive competence of the Community, nor citizenship of the Union. Within those confines, closer cooperation had to further the objectives and protect the interests of the Union, and to respect the principles and the single institutional framework

[207] The Treaty of Amsterdam made no provision for closer cooperation as regards the Second Pillar.

[208] Eg G Edwards and E Philippart, *Flexibility and the Treaty of Amsterdam: Europe's New Byzantium?*, Centre for European Legal Studies Occasional Paper No 3 (CUP, 1997); V Constantinesco, 'Les clauses de "coopération renforcée"' (1997) 33 *Revue trimestrielle de droit européen* 751; J Shaw, 'The Treaty of Amsterdam: Challenges of Flexibility and Legitimacy' (1998) 4 *European Public Law* 63; H Kortenberg, 'Closer Cooperation in the Treaty of Amsterdam' (1998) 35 CML Rev 833; G Gaja, 'How Flexible is Flexibility Under the Amsterdam Treaty?' (1998) 35 CML Rev 855; C-D Ehlermann, 'Differentiation, Flexibility, Closer Cooperation: The New Provisions of the Amsterdam Treaty' (1998) 4 *European Public Law* 246; W Wessels, 'Flexibility, Differentiation and Closer Cooperation: the Amsterdam Provisions in the Light of the Tindemans Report' in M Westlake (ed), *The European Union Beyond Amsterdam: New Concepts of European Integration* (Routledge, 1998); F Tuytschaever, *Differentiation in European Union Law* (Hart Publishing, 1999).

of the Union. More specifically, closer cooperation could only be used as a last resort where the objectives of the Treaty could not be attained by ordinary procedures. In any case, closer cooperation could not affect the *acquis communautaire*, nor Community policies, actions or programmes adopted under the Treaty. Finally, closer cooperation could neither discriminate between nationals of Member States, nor constitute a discrimination or restriction of intra-Community trade, nor distort conditions of competition between the Member States.

On the procedural front, any proposed closer cooperation had to concern at least a majority of the Member States. Those Member States had then to submit a request to the Commission, which could decide whether to refer a proposal to the Council. If not, the Commission needed only to explain its reasons for this decision. If a proposal was made, the Council could authorise closer cooperation acting by qualified majority and after having consulted the European Parliament. However, the Treaty gave every Member States a right of veto over the initial authorisation by Council of closer cooperation: it was possible for any country to oppose closer cooperation 'for important and stated reasons of national policy'. In that event, the Council could, acting by a qualified majority, refer the matter for a unanimous decision by the Council meeting in the composition of the Heads of State or Government. Once a closer cooperation had been established, measures were to be adopted according to the relevant procedures set out in the Treaties. However, whilst all members of the Council could take part in its deliberations, decisions would be taken according to a restricted formation, compromising only the representatives of the participating Member States.[209]

Finally, the Amsterdam Treaty sought to regulate the relationship between participating and non-participating Member States. Where a closer cooperation was authorised, it could not affect the competences, rights, obligations and interests of non-participants. Conversely, non-participants could not impede the implementation of closer cooperation measures by participating Member States. In any case, closer cooperation had in principle to be open to all countries and allow them to become parties at any time (provided they complied with the basic authorising decision and any measures adopted under the closer cooperation). Member States wishing to participate in a closer cooperation had to notify their intention to the Council and Commission. The latter would give its opinion, on the basis of which the former would then reach a decision on admitting the newcomer, and on any specific arrangements for its participation. For these purposes, the Council was again to act in its restricted formation.

[209] Further: A Dashwood, 'Community Decision-Making After Amsterdam' (1998) 1 *Cambridge Yearbook of European Law Studies* 25.

Regulatory Differentiation Under the Amsterdam Provisions Closer cooperation as introduced at Amsterdam was certainly no Europe *à la carte*: Member States could only add to the existing body of Community law, not subtract from it. Nevertheless, the variable geometry inherent in the notion of closer cooperation reinvigorated the potential for horizontal differentiation within the Community legal order.

In theory, Member States could now coalesce into shifting regulatory groupings, each of which legislated for wider and/or deeper integration on any given subject, but only for themselves. Thus, the Community was faced with the prospect of social, consumer or environmental policies which no longer consisted of a body of common provisions applicable throughout all the Member States, albeit shaped by sometimes higher, sometimes lower, national standards. Instead, it was possible that entire Community measures and even initiatives would apply only in certain countries, whilst others could retain their own domestic policies. One could therefore envisage the emergence of ever more complex regulatory patterns: instruments applying throughout the whole Community laid down certain common but not identical standards, while additional layers of obligation were added by new measures, each embracing different combinations of Member States, and each in turn laying down certain common but not identical standards. Such a model would have serious implications for many established assumptions within the Treaty order as regards (for example) the efficient functioning and democratic legitimacy of the Community legislative process.[210] And in particular, to search for genuinely 'uniform' Community rules (for the purposes either of consolidating economic integration within a Single Market based on free movement and equal competitive conditions, or of enhancing socio-political integration within a more mature European Union by creating a common body of citizens' welfare rights) would seem an ever more elusive task.

However, many commentators rightly wondered whether the substantive and procedural conditions outlined above were such as to make it unlikely that the closer cooperation provisions as agreed at Amsterdam could ever have been used in practice.[211] First, the total exclusion of areas falling within the Community's exclusive competence, coupled with the fundamental obligation to respect the *acquis communautaire*, placed

[210] Eg G Edwards and E Philippart, *Flexibility and the Treaty of Amsterdam: Europe's New Byzantium?*, CELS Occasional Paper No 3 (CUP, 1997); J Shaw, 'The Treaty of Amsterdam: Challenges of Flexibility and Legitimacy' (1998) 4 *European Law Journal* 63; N Walker, 'Sovereignty and Differentiated Integration in the European Union' (1998) 4 *European Law Journal* 355.

[211] Cf S Weatherill, 'Flexibility or Fragmentation: Trends in European Integration' in J Usher (ed), *The State of the European Union: Structure, Enlargement and Economic Union* (Longman, 2000).

immediate limits upon the potential for horizontal differentiation. Secondly, taken in a literal sense, it was hard to imagine a situation in which competitive conditions would not have been distorted by the existence of distinct legal regimes as between different Member States —particularly since exactly such inequalities of regulatory burden have provided the justification for much of the Community's harmonising activities under legal bases such as Articles 94 and 95 EC. However, one might perhaps have drawn a distinction in this regard between situations where the Community had already adopted fully pre-emptive harmonising measures (and closer cooperation measures would surely have re-distorted competitive conditions which had been equalised and become part of the *acquis communautaire*); and situations where the Community had not yet intervened with fully pre-emptive secondary legislation (as regards which closer cooperation measures could not be said to make competitive conditions any worse than before).

Thirdly, it might also have seemed inevitable that any form of horizontal differentiation would result in some level of discrimination between the nationals of participating and non-participating Member States—with some individuals enjoying greater levels of environmental, social or consumer protection than others, depending on their Member State of residence or employment. But again, one might perhaps have drawn a distinction in this regard between the variations in legislative standards across Member States which were inherent in any system of regulatory differentiation; and closer cooperation measures which themselves imposed specific conditions amounting to direct or indirect discrimination against nationals from non-participating Member States. The latter would surely have been incompatible with Article 11 EC, and in any event also with the prohibition of discrimination on grounds of nationality under Article 12 EC.[212] The former might well have been incompatible with a single-mindedly integrationist analysis of the Community legal order—but given that such differences in individual rights and obligations were true as much of existing vertical as of new horizontal forms of regulatory differentiation, including minimum harmonisation and express derogations, they were unlikely to fall foul per se of the Amsterdam closer cooperation provisions.[213] Fourthly, the fact that closer cooperation could not restrict intra-Community trade meant that, even where further integrative measures were adopted, they could not disrupt the free movement of goods or services coming from Member States which complied only with general Community standards—thus

[212] Cf Case 41/84 *Pinna* [1986] ECR 1.

[213] Cf Case C–137/00 *Milk Marque* (Judgment of 9 September 2003). Similarly, eg S van Raepenbusch and D Hanf, 'Flexibility in Social Policy' in B de Witte, D Hanf & E Vos (eds), *The Many Faces of Differentiation in EU Law* (Intersentia, 2001).

incorporating into the closer cooperation provisions an economic incentive for participating Member States not to stray too far from the common Treaty norms, for fear of placing domestic undertakings at a competitive disadvantage or of deterring direct foreign investment into the national territory, as a result of the process of regulatory competition with non-participating Member States.[214]

Finally, and perhaps most importantly, a majority of Member States had to participate in the closer cooperation and a qualified majority had to support it. Even then, first the Commission and then each Member State enjoyed a right of veto over the ultimate use of closer cooperation. While the latter seemed intended only to be able to exercise that possibility in fairly extreme circumstances, the former appeared to enjoy a wide discretion to block closer cooperation based upon its own appreciation of the substantive criteria set out in Article 11 EC. Moreover, the fact that closer cooperation could only be used as a last resort, where the objectives of the Treaty could not be attained by ordinary procedures, seemed to suggest that the Member States could only submit a proposal for embarking upon a horizontally differentiated policy initiative where previous attempts to pass the relevant legislation through the ordinary Council had already been attempted and failed.

With so many hurdles in its path, small wonder some commentators speculated that closer cooperation would struggle to rear its head beyond spheres such as culture, education or public health—precisely those areas where common Community competence already stood at its weakest, and legal regulation was already highly diverse.[215] Even in such fields, the fact that closer cooperation measures had to remain within the limits of the Community's ordinary competences (in accordance with the principle of attributed powers contained in Article 5(1) EC) meant that Member States willing to pursue additional integration could still adopt nothing more than complementary Treaty action, excluding any harmonisation of relevant domestic laws. Indeed, it seemed generally assumed that closer cooperation's direct or formal impact upon the Community legal order would be marginal, and that its greatest significance would instead be indirect or informal, concerning how the Community institutions and the Member

[214] Further, eg M Dougan, 'Vive la différence? Exploring the Legal Framework for Reflexive Harmonisation within the Single European Market' in R Miller & P Zumbansen (eds), *Annual of German and European Law (Volume 1: 2003)* (Berghahn Books, 2004).

[215] Eg S Langrish, 'The Treaty of Amsterdam: Selected Highlights' (1998) 23 EL Rev 3; H Kortenberg, 'Closer Cooperation in the Treaty of Amsterdam' (1998) 35 CML Rev 833. Further: S Weatherill, 'If I'd Wanted You to Understand I Would Have Explained it Better: What is the Purpose of the Provisions on Closer Cooperation Introduced by the Treaty of Amsterdam?' in D O'Keeffe & P Twomey (eds), *Legal Issues of the Amsterdam Treaty* (Hart Publishing, 1999); and 'Finding Space for Closer Cooperation in the Field of Culture' in G de Búrca & J Scott (eds), *Constitutional Change in the EU: From Uniformity to Flexibility?* (Hart Publishing, 2000).

States managed the Treaty's more traditional decision-making processes. On the one hand, it was possible that the existence of the closer cooperation mechanism provided the impetus for compromise between conflicting national viewpoints, and therefore (paradoxically) the maintenance of a single Community-wide legislative programme: for example, Member States prepared to enter into closer cooperation might have felt unable to placate those opposed to and capable of preventing it; whilst Member States unsure of the wisdom of a given initiative may have been persuaded to join nevertheless, rather than suffer the inconvenience of having to opt in later on.[216] On the other hand, it was also possible that, where compromise was not possible, the inflexibility of the closer cooperation procedure might simply have encouraged integrationist Member States to resort once again to extra-Treaty associations and institutions in pursuance of their joint interests.[217]

However, to have thus marginalised the potential impact of the closer cooperation provisions was perhaps to risk adopting an overly legalistic analysis of the situation. It seems generally agreed that Article 11 EC lent itself to only a limited interpretative or interventionist role on the part of the Court of Justice.[218] For example, it was hard to imagine that the Court would have overturned a Council decision that any given Community objective could no longer be attained by ordinary Treaty procedures, such that closer cooperation might properly have been considered a last resort; or that the Court would have rejected an individual Member State's decision to veto closer cooperation on the grounds that it would affect 'important and stated reasons of national policy.' Such issues fell primarily within the political not the judicial field, and that was where their true meaning was likely to be clarified. In turn, the potential for regulatory differentiation contained within the closer cooperation provisions might well have been shaped less by the strict letter of the Treaty than by the attitude of the Member States and, in particular, by the delicate balance negotiated between those governments keen to reinforce the momentum for European integration and those reluctant to be left behind in the process.

[216] Eg G Edwards and E Philippart, *Flexibility and the Treaty of Amsterdam: Europe's New Byzantium?*, CELS Occasional Paper No 3 (CUP, 1997); W Wessels, 'Flexibility, Differentiation and Closer Cooperation: the Amsterdam Provisions in the Light of the Tindemans Report' in M Westlake (ed), *The European Union Beyond Amsterdam: New Concepts of European Integration* (Routledge, 1998).

[217] Eg G Gaja, 'How Flexible is Flexibility Under the Amsterdam Treaty?' (1998) 35 CML Rev 855; C-D Ehlermann, 'Differentiation, Flexibility, Closer Cooperation: The New Provisions of the Amsterdam Treaty' (1998) 4 *European Public Law* 246.

[218] Eg A Duff, *The Treaty of Amsterdam: Text and Commentary* (The Federal Trust, 1997) ch 5; J Shaw, 'The Treaty of Amsterdam: Challenges of Flexibility and Legitimacy' (1998) 4 *European Law Journal* 63.

Enhanced Cooperation After the Treaty of Nice

In any case, the Treaty of Nice has now reformed the closer (renamed enhanced) cooperation system: the complex and fragmented Amsterdam provisions have been simplified and reorganised; the possibility of entering into an enhanced cooperation has been extended, albeit under limited circumstances, to the Second Pillar; and certain of the substantive and procedural hurdles applicable to enhanced cooperation under the First and Third Pillars have been relaxed. The principal provisions are now contained in Title VII TEU, and Articles 11 and 11a EC. Again, we are concerned only with the general scheme of enhanced cooperation under the First Pillar.[219]

Nice Provisions on Enhanced Cooperation Some of the Nice changes are largely hortatory: for example, enhanced cooperation must be aimed at reinforcing the process of European integration; the Council and Commission must ensure that activities undertaken on the basis of enhanced cooperation are consistent with each other and with the activities of the Union; the Commission and participating Member States must ensure that as many Member States as possible are encouraged to take part in the enhanced cooperation. More significantly, it is now provided that enhanced cooperation must respect the *acquis communautaire* (watering down the Amsterdam requirement that closer cooperation must not affect the *acquis communautaire*).[220] In similar vein, enhanced cooperation must not undermine the Internal Market or economic and social cohesion (replacing the Amsterdam provision whereby closer cooperation could not affect Community policies, actions or programmes in general). In particular, there is no longer any express prohibition against enhanced cooperation concerning Union citizenship; and the specific direction that enhanced cooperation should not discriminate between nationals of the Member States has likewise been suppressed.

Crucially for the Union's development post-enlargement into Central and Eastern Europe, enhanced cooperation need now involve a minimum of only eight Member States (and thus a potential minority in the expanded Union, whereas under Amsterdam closer cooperation had to concern at least a majority of Member States). Furthermore, enhanced cooperation will remain a last resort—but this is to be established within the Council, according to the criterion that the objectives of the proposed enhanced cooperation cannot be attained within a reasonable period by applying

[219] For general comments, eg K St Bradley, 'Institutional Design in the Treaty of Nice' (2001) 38 CML Rev 1095; T Stein, 'The Treaty of Nice and Enlargement of the EU with Special Regard to Enhanced Cooperation' (2001) 25 *Polish Yearbook of International Law* 277.

[220] Similarly, enhanced cooperation must respect (rather than must not affect) the competences, rights and obligations of non-participating countries.

the relevant Treaty provisions. Another vital amendment applies to the procedure for authorising an enhanced cooperation under the First Pillar: the existing national veto held by every Member State has been removed. Instead, any Member State objecting to a proposed enhanced cooperation might request that the matter be referred to the European Council—after which the Council can still reach its decision by qualified majority vote.[221] However, where a proposed enhanced cooperation under the First Pillar relates to an area subject to co-decision between Parliament and Council under Article 251 EC, the Council must obtain the assent of Parliament before authorising the enhanced cooperation to proceed (whereas under the original Amsterdam provisions, Parliament was merely consulted on all closer cooperation proposals). Finally, authorisation for a non-participating Member State to join an existing enhanced cooperation is to be granted by the Commission (whereas the original Amsterdam provisions reserved such decisions to Council).

Regulatory Differentiation Under the Nice Provisions Academic opinion again seems unsure exactly what to make of enhanced cooperation after Nice. On the one hand, the chances that horizontal differentiation will become a more common phenomenon have been increased by lowering the threshold of participating Member States to eight within a Union of 25, and removing the national veto over the initial authorisation decision.[222] Indeed, it has been suggested that the post-Nice flexibility provisions have greatly increased the potential for the emergence of a two-tier European Union, split into a core of Member States pursuing deeper political integration through enhanced cooperation across a broader range of economic and social policies, and a periphery of countries who see the Treaties essentially as a forum for promoting free trade.[223] But some commentators have pointed out that requiring parliamentary assent in areas of co-decision has erected fresh procedural hurdles to launching an enhanced cooperation,[224] and others feel that the reformed enhanced cooperation provisions remain sufficiently complex and ambiguous that the Member States will still hesitate about putting them into practice.[225] And indeed, despite Nice's liberalisation of their substantive and

[221] Note that the national veto remains, even after Nice, in respect of the new enhanced cooperation provisions applicable to the Second Pillar. Further, eg A Dashwood, 'The Constitution of the European Union After Nice: Law-Making Procedures' (2001) 26 EL Rev 215.

[222] Eg R Barents, 'Some Observations on the Treaty of Nice' (2001) 8 *Maastricht Journal of European and Comparative Law* 121.

[223] Further, eg J M de Areilza, 'The Reform of Enhanced Cooperation Rules: Towards Less Flexibility?' in B de Witte, D Hanf & E Vos (eds), *The Many Faces of Differentiation in EU Law* (Intersentia, 2001).

[224] Eg D Hanf, 'Flexibility Clauses in the Founding Treaties, From Rome to Nice' in B de Witte, D Hanf & E Vos (eds), *The Many Faces of Differentiation in EU Law* (Intersentia, 2001).

[225] Eg P Pescatore, 'Nice: Aftermath' (2001) 38 CML Rev 265.

procedural conditions, the provisions on enhanced cooperation have still not been used.

However, even before the Treaty of Nice entered into force, the parameters of the flexibility debate began to shift once again. Fears that the Union's impending enlargement would lead to a lot of widening, but very little deepening, sparked serious political debate about carrying the idea of flexibility even further. Some indication of that debate can be gleaned from a speech delivered by President Chirac at the Bundestag in June 2000, in which he set out his vision of:

> l'approfondissement des politiques, à l'initiative de ces pays ... qui souhaitent aller plus loin ou plus vite. Rassemblés avec l'Allemagne et la France, ils pourraient se constituer en un <<groupe pionnier>>. Ce groupe ouvrirait la voie en s'appuyant sur la nouvelle procédure de coopération renforcée définie pendant la [conférence intergouvernementale de l'année 2000] et en nouant, si nécessaire, des coopérations hors traité, mais sans jamais remettre en cause la cohérence et l'acquis de l'Union. ... Je souhaite ainsi que, dès l'an prochain, le <<groupe pionnier>> puisse s'atteler, notamment, à une meilleure coordination des politiques économiques, à un renforcement de la politique de défense et de sécurité et à une plus grande efficacité dans la lutte contre la criminalité. Faut-il que ces Etats concluent entre eux un nouveau traité et se dotent d'institutions sophistiquées? Je ne le crois pas. ... Il fraudrait plutôt envisager un mécanisme de coordination souple, un secrétariat chargé de veiller à la cohérence des positions et des politiques des membres de ce groupe, qui devrait rester ouvert à tous ceux qui souhaitent le rejoindre.[226]

President Chirac's proposal for a 'pioneer group' of states—pursuing closer forms of integration either through the enhanced cooperation provisions or (if necessary) through extra-Union agreements—did not meet with universal approval, particularly in Britain.[227] But it echoed calls for debate on the possibility of pursuing greater flexibility made by the German Foreign Minister in a speech at Humboldt University in May 2000. Joschka Fischer recalled that the European Economic Community had itself been built by a small group of states, whose success then paved the way for others to join the integration project. He queried whether that tried-and-tested model might not represent the way forward once again, particularly after the Eastern enlargement—permitting certain countries to form a 'centre of gravity' pushing forward with economic and political union, including enhanced cooperation on policies such as environmental protection, the fight against crime, immigration and asylum, and foreign and security policy. That centre of gravity could conclude a new treaty providing the nucleus for a federal constitution—including its own institutions, a single government speaking on as many issues as

[226] Full text reproduced in *Le Monde* (Paris France 28 June 2000) pp 16–17.
[227] Eg *The Independent* (28 June 2000) p 1; *The Guardian* (26 July 2000) p 8.

possible, a strong parliament and a directly elected president—with mechanisms to ensure that this avant-garde cooperated smoothly with those countries which remained part of the broader European Union.[228]

Enhanced Cooperation Proposals from the European Convention

Against this background, it is perhaps understandable that the Convention on the Future of Europe, charged by the Laeken European Council with drawing up proposals for major constitutional reform of the EU, should have devoted considerable attention to revising the existing legal framework of enhanced cooperation.

In this regard, the Convention sought to simplify further the still complex provisions on enhanced cooperation found in the current Treaties (and to adapt those provisions to the general principle of depillarisation, particularly as regards police and judicial cooperation in criminal matters currently falling under the Third Pillar; coupled with continued differentiation, especially as regards the common foreign and security policy (CFSP) presently dealt with under the Second Pillar). But more fundamentally, the Convention's proposals are based upon the understanding that enhanced cooperation should evolve into a workable mechanism for responding to the increasingly heterogeneous nature of the enlarged Union. In particular, the Convention sought to facilitate the use of enhanced cooperation, not merely to overcome deadlock within the Council over a particular legislative act, but to engage more systematically in differentiated integration as regards a given policy sphere. Indeed, the Convention envisaged that initiatives undertaken through the enhanced cooperation provisions could eventually emulate the scope and character of the current Schengen and Euro arrangements.[229] The principal provisions are contained in Articles I–43 and III–322–29 of the Convention's draft Treaty establishing a Constitution for Europe.[230]

As regards the substantive conditions for launching enhanced cooperation, the draft Constitution contains three significant changes. First, according to Article I–43(2), the number of Member States required to engage in a new enhanced cooperation would change from a fixed number of eight to a floating number of one-third. In the enlarged Union, this could actually make enhanced cooperation more difficult to initiate, by raising the threshold to at least nine countries in a Union of 25. Secondly, although enhanced cooperation would remain a last resort, Article I–43(2)

[228] Full text available at <http://www.auswaertiges-amt.de/www/en/eu_politik/aktuelles/index_html>.

[229] Further, in particular: CONV 723/03; CONV 724/03; CONV 783/03; CONV 847/03; CONV 853/03.

[230] OJ 2003 C169/1. See now Arts I-44 and III-416–23 of the 2004 Treaty, CIG 87/04, which largely adopt the Convention's proposals. The main changes concern voting requirements within the Council. Readers should cross-refer from the Convention draft discussed in the text of this chapter to the final Treaty as agreed by the Member States.

reformulates the Nice text so as to make clear that there would be no need for any particular proposal, designed for the Union as a whole, to have already been put to the vote within Council; or indeed for Council to have already considered any specific measures, only the general objectives of the proposed programme of enhanced cooperation. Thirdly, the Convention agreed to a major extension of the potential scope of enhanced cooperation as regards the CFSP, including certain specialised forms of enhanced cooperation within the context of the common security and defence policy (which will not be dealt with further in this discussion).[231]

As regards the procedural conditions for authorising the initiation of enhanced cooperation outside the sphere of the CFSP, the Constitution contains three main reforms. First, the Commission would retain its discretion to refuse to submit an initial proposal to Council. But that de facto veto would be extended so as also to cover police and judicial cooperation in criminal matters (whereas the Nice provisions currently allow the Member States to bypass the Commission's refusal to submit a proposal, as regards enhanced cooperation under Title VI TEU, by seeking authorisation directly from the Council). Secondly, the Convention proposed abolishing the lingering possibility that a Member State which objects to the initiation of enhanced cooperation by QMV within Council may still refer the matter to the European Council for further discussion. Thirdly, Article III–325(1) would ensure that Parliament's consent is required for any enhanced cooperation to proceed (thus going further than the existing First Pillar rules, whereby Parliament's assent is required only when the relevant proposal relates to a legal basis governed by co-decision; and also further than Article 40a(2) TEU, which provides for no more than consultation with Parliament across the scope of police and judicial cooperation in criminal matters).

Article I–43(1) states that enhanced cooperation shall be open to every Member State when it is being established and at any time. However, Article III–324(1) recognises that, when enhanced cooperation is being established, the Council's authorising decision may impose conditions of participation. Thus, Member States must be not only willing, but also (where appropriate) able to take part in the enhanced cooperation. The criteria for participation in the third stage of EMU provide a model for the sorts of objective conditions which the Convention had in mind here. Moreover, when Member States wish to join an existing enhanced cooperation, they must comply not only with the acts already adopted within the framework of that enhanced cooperation, but also with the conditions of participation contained in the Council's initial authorisation.

For these purposes, Article III–326(1) provides that, as regards enhanced cooperation outside the scope of the CFSP, the Commission must verify

[231] Arts III-211 and 213–14 of the Convention draft. The 2004 Treaty adopts a more restrictive approach here: see now Arts III-310, III-312 and III-419(2).

whether the Member State fulfils the conditions for participation; and may also adopt any necessary transitional measures. If the Commission twice refuses to approve a Member State's request for subsequent participation in an enhanced cooperation, on the grounds that it does not fulfil the requisite conditions, Article III–326(1) offers that Member State (in effect) a right of appeal to the Council. The Council would decide upon the request to participate, meeting in its restricted formation.[232]

Article III–328 contains one final innovation. Where enhanced cooperation relates to a legal basis under which Council either acts by unanimity, or adopts legislative measures according to a legislative procedure other than co-decision, Council may decide either to act instead by qualified majority vote, or to apply the co-decision procedure (respectively).[233] This mirrors the European Council's general power, under Article I-24(4), to extend qualified majority voting, and/or the co-decision procedure, to any legal basis within Part III of the draft Constitution which would otherwise be governed by unanimity,[234] or where Council would otherwise adopt legislative acts according to a different legislative procedure.[235] However, such organic revision clauses take on an added importance within the context of enhanced cooperation. There was widespread dissatisfaction with the Convention's refusal to extend qualified majority voting still further than the Constitution proposes (for example, to cover areas such as tax harmonisation, and sensitive aspects of the Area of Freedom, Security and Justice);[236] and a high probability that certain Member States would exercise their veto within those fields still subject to unanimity, as regards both the specific legal bases contained in Part III, and the general revision clause under Article I–24(4). The revamped provisions on enhanced cooperation could help bypass the awkward squad for the purposes not just of adopting a specific act, but also of authorising the principle of horizontally differentiated integration, and then transforming the relevant policy field into a system of qualified majority voting for the participating countries. But it remains open to question whether the substantive conditions now contained in Article III–322, relating to barriers to trade and distortions of competition, which have been carried over almost unaltered from the existing Treaties into the draft Constitution, would restrict the use of

[232] As defined in Art I-43(3) of the Convention draft. Again, the distinct provisions currently applicable to police and judicial cooperation in criminal matters under Art 40b TEU would be suppressed.

[233] Acting unanimously, in its restricted formation under Art I-43(3) of the Convention draft, and on its own initiative. In the latter case, Council would also have to consult Parliament.

[234] Now to be found in Art IV-444 of the 2004 Treaty, CIG 87/04.

[235] In a handful of situations, this could also be achieved by unanimous decision of the Council itself: Arts III-104(3), 130(2) and 170(3) of the Convention draft.

[236] Eg Commission Press Release IP/03/836 (13 June 2003). Also, eg CONV 783/03; CONV 849/03.

enhanced cooperation in areas (such as taxation) still governed by unanimity in Council.

Assessment

The Convention's proposals seek to ensure that the evident political pressure in favour of greater flexibility finds legal expression in the more widespread use of the enhanced cooperation procedures within a Union still characterised by a single institutional framework, rather than by encouraging a 'pioneer group' of Member States to form some new 'centre of gravity' within what would effectively become a two-tier Union. The stakes were made dramatically clear when, within hours of the Member States' failure to reach agreement on the draft Constitutional Treaty at the IGC in Rome in December 2003, the debate on how to accommodate increased political diversity shifted again to the feasibility of an 'avant-garde' of countries pursuing closer integration over and above the general Union framework.[237] But in any case, this issue provides a good illustration of the discussions currently unfolding about the future nature and direction of European integration, in which the tension between regulatory uniformity and greater differentiation now plays a central role. That debate, and its implications for both the Community legal order in general and the enforcement deficit in particular, provides the backdrop for discussion in our next chapter.

[237] Eg The Federal Trust, *EU Constitution Project Newsletter* (January 2004). Further: T Konstadinides, 'Now and Then: Fischer's Core Europe in the Aftermath of the Collapse of the December 2003 Constitutional Talks' (2004) 13 *Irish Journal of European Law* 113.

4

Regulatory Differentiation and the Enforcement Deficit Debate

CHAPTER THREE SOUGHT to demonstrate that regulatory differentiation within the Community legal order is a fact, and sought to give some indication of its nature and extent. The next question is: what significance should we attach to this fact? In particular: how far does an increasing degree of differentiation within the Community legal order affect our understanding of, and condition our responses to, the enforcement deficit debate?

'INTEGRATION THROUGH LAW': DIFFERENTIATION AND THE ENFORCEMENT DEFICIT DEBATE

One possible reaction to differentiation within the Community legal order is inspired by an 'integration through law' analysis: to approach increasing levels of regulatory diversity with suspicion, even hostility. The concept and practice of differentiation implicitly threaten the coherence of the Community legal order, and therefore the underlying economic and / or socio-political objectives of the European integration process. How can one speak of a genuine level playing-field for commercial undertakings, or of equal treatment between Union citizens, when the Treaty permits and even encourages different regulatory regimes to apply in different Member States, and some people to enjoy higher levels of social welfare protection than others?

The logic of this viewpoint is to see diversity within the Community legal order as another aspect of an all-too-familiar problem. Facilitating myriad deviations from a supposedly centralised norm differs little in substance from denying the horizontal direct effect of directives, suffering the fair-weather commitment to supremacy shown by certain domestic courts, or indeed relying on an unchecked network of national remedies and procedural rules for the decentralised enforcement of Community provisions. Each of these factors serves, in its own way, to detract from the uniform and effective application of the Treaty system, and therefore to undermine the integrity of the European integration project. More fundamentally, certain commentators have expressed fears that the patterns of differentiation currently emerging under the Treaty have begun to deconstruct the Community's underlying sense of purpose—without suggesting any clear or comprehensible alternative.[1]

The answer to this problem seems simple enough and, on its own terms, is wholly understandable: the Community legal order should be deployed to limit, so far as possible, the supposedly detrimental effects of differentiation, and thereby reinstate integration as the central point of reference by which the identity of the entire Community project defines and sustains itself. In certain respects, this task could be achieved through conventional legal techniques: for example, by construing derogations granted to the Member States in respect of certain Treaty obligations as strictly as possible.[2] But in other cases, a more controversial approach might be called for: nothing less than invoking the principle of uniformity as a fully fledged fundamental constitutional imperative, against which certain manifestations of diversity within the Community legal order could be assessed and (if necessary) declared invalid. For example, some commentators had suggested that the Court might strike down as unconstitutional the United Kingdom's solitary exclusion from the Social Protocol and Agreement, negotiated as part of the Treaty on European Union.[3] This example of regulatory diversity posed a grave threat to the functioning of the Single Market, by affording British enterprises an unfair competitive advantage over their counterparts on the mainland.[4] Moreover, the Union's purported commitment to equal treatment between Community nationals held something of a hollow ring for British workers, deprived of certain of the rights to fair employment conditions enjoyed by all other European citizens.[5] The fact that the United Kingdom's opt-out had been ratified by all the Member States, and that the EC Treaty had been amended accordingly, was not thought to pose an insurmountable obstacle to such judicial review.[6]

[1] The best known academic exposition of this view was offered by D Curtin, 'The Constitutional Structure of the Union: A Europe of Bits and Pieces' (1993) 30 CML Rev 17.
[2] See ch 3 (above).
[3] Eg D Curtin, 'The Constitutional Structure of the Union: A Europe of Bits and Pieces' (1993) 30 CML Rev 17. Cf B Fitzpatrick, 'Community Social Law After Maastricht' (1992) 21 ILJ 199.
[4] Cf C Barnard, 'A Social Policy for Europe: Politicians 1:0 Lawyers' (1992) 8 *International Journal of Comparative Labour Law and Industrial Relations* 15; Editorial Comments, 'Are European Values Being Hoovered Away?' (1993) 30 CML Rev 445.
[5] Cf G de Búrca, 'The Role of Equality in European Community Law' in A Dashwood & S O'Leary (eds), *The Principle of Equal Treatment in EC Law* (Sweet & Maxwell, 1997).
[6] Even though Art 230 EC gives the ECJ jurisdiction to rule on the legality of only the secondary acts of the Community institutions, not the primary Treaty texts or acts of the Member States. Consider, eg Case T–584/93 *Roujansky* [1994] ECR II–585. Further: J Wouters, 'Constitutional Limits of Differentiation: The Principe of Equality' in B de Witte, D Hanf & E Vos (eds), *The Many Faces of Differentiation in EU Law* (Intersentia, 2001).

'Integration through law' may therefore be stereotyped as a conceptual model which assumes that the Community and its legal order are organised around a rationale of convergence—preserving uniformity as a regulatory ideal and dismissing diversity as an undesirable anomaly. Thus marginalised, there is no reason why differentiation should prompt any fundamental change in our understanding of the enforcement deficit. For example, in a recent contribution to academic thinking on effective judicial protection in the administrative law sphere, Himsworth argued that law is the vehicle for the achievement of the Common Market, and other Community policy objectives; and that such law must be capable of being enforced across the whole Union territory. It is true that the imperative of uniformity must now be read subject to the possibilities of differential treatment which are created under Community law itself—but this should not be taken to mean that Community rules no longer demand a very high degree of uniformity as regards their implementation and enforcement. Indeed, the variations produced by legal pluralism as regards national remedies and procedural rules are simply too haphazard and unpredictable to be accommodated comfortably within the Community legal system.[7]

If anything, it has been suggested that differentiation should actually strengthen the Community's determination to approximate national remedies and procedural rules. Just like the strict construction of derogations from harmonised norms, a centrally planned remedial regime for the decentralised enforcement of Community law would form a legitimate part of an integrationist strategy designed to counter, or at least limit, the detrimental effects of increasing levels of substantive policy disuniformity within the Treaty system.[8] For example, consider the right of employees not to suffer collective redundancies without prior consultation by their employer, as set out in Directive 98/59.[9] Through a complex combination of minimum harmonisation, derogations, variable norms and conceptual renvois, this right may differ between Member States as regards the relevant categories of protected worker, the number of proposed redundancies required to trigger the employer's obligations, or even the nature of the consultation itself. But a uniform guarantee that any breach of the Directive would entitle employees to claim, within a defined limitation period, reinstatement pending full compliance by their employer with its obligations might restore some equality of treatment

[7] C Himsworth, 'Convergence and Divergence in Administrative Law' in P Beaumont, C Lyons & N Walker (eds), *Convergence and Divergence in European Public Law* (Hart Publishing 2002). Consider also: G Wagner, 'The Economics of Harmonization: The Case of Contract Law' (2002) 39 CML Rev 995.

[8] Eg M P Chiti, 'Towards a Unified Judicial Protection in Europe(?)' (1997) 9 *European Review of Public Law* 553.

[9] Dir 98/59 on the approximation of the laws of the Member States relating to collective redundancies, OJ 1998 L225/16.

across the Community. At the very least, it would be preferable to reinforcing existing inequalities of treatment by permitting national rules in one Member State to order reinstatement, while national rules in another Member State grant only a limited award of damages, each governed by limitation periods of widely varying duration.

However, it will be argued that, in its assumptions about the nature of European union—and consequently about the nature of both regulatory differentiation and the problems posed by national remedies and procedural rules—'integration through law' is a viewpoint which is at best controversial and at worst seriously flawed. The following sections will identify some of the political, social and economic dynamics which have produced a momentum for diversity to rival the traditional notion that the Community project is one centred on the goal of ever increasing integration between the Member States. As such, regulatory differentiation must be understood both as a symptom of fundamental restructuring within the European Union, and also as a cause of constitutional revision within the Community legal order itself. It will be argued that this process of doctrinal reconsideration and adaptation should extend to the supposedly fundamental concerns—particularly that for uniformity—which continue to structure debate about the nature of the enforcement deficit, and to inspire solutions for its resolution.

DIFFERENTIATION AS A SYMPTOM OF CONSTITUTIONAL CHANGE

'Integration through law' offers an approach to the study of Community law which is prescriptive rather than descriptive in nature—basing itself around an economic/political ideal (of ever closer European unity) and a concomitant legal manifesto (for the construction of a centralised system of uniform and effective regulation) which do not necessarily represent an accurate analysis of the forces which are actually shaping the Community's evolution. In particular, 'integration through law' focuses almost entirely on the expansionist limb, but neglects the equally important contractionist element, of the Treaty system.

Systemic Tensions and Regulatory Differentiation

In many ways, it is true that the history of the Community is that of its expanding spheres of interest. This expansion can be rationalised along four main inter-related axes. First, the horizontal—the expansion of the Community's power to regulate different sectors of activity. This process was outlined in Chapter 2: beginning with the Common Market (based on free movement and fair competition), the Community has acquired competence to regulate important aspects of social policy (environment, consumer rights, public health, employee protection); and is also increasing its involvement in fields such as education, culture, citizenship and fundamental rights. Secondly, the vertical—the expansion of the Community's competence relative to that of the Member States within any given sector of activity. Again, the basic elements of this process have already been outlined: the recognition by the Court of Justice that the Community might possess exclusive competence over certain fields; the possibility that Community secondary legislation might pre-empt the exercise of national regulatory power in other sectors; and in any case, the direct effect of Community rules within the domestic legal orders, together with their supremacy over competing provisions of national law. Thirdly, the institutional—the expansion of the Community's competence to adopt legislation through supranational rather than intergovernmental styles of decision-making procedure. In this regard, the most important developments concern the introduction of co-decision between Council and the European Parliament; and the steady spread of qualified majority rather than unanimous voting within Council itself. Finally, the geographical—from the original six Member States, the number has now risen to 25, with the future possibility that the Union might embrace 30 or more countries.

However, such expansion represents only one of two essential tenets in the Community's evolution.

It has been convincingly argued that the Member States accepted not only the benefits but also the burdens of the original Treaty of Rome because they were in a position to control the day-to-day running of the Community system: for example, through unanimity in a Council which dominated the legislative process. The Member States remain prepared to accept the economic and political advantages yielded by their Treaty membership, even despite the process of aggrandisement identified above, but only on condition that the system retains safeguards to accommodate their own national interests where these do not coincide with the common Community goal. Thus, the recent history of the Community has been characterised not only by a continuing process of Treaty expansion, but also—*and largely as a result*—by a counter-process which attempts to define more clearly the limits to the Community's powers in their relationship with pre-existing national competences, and to accommodate those Member States which wish to retain a greater degree of control over their own policy-making prerogatives.[10]

[10] Further: J Weiler, 'The Community System: The Dual Character of Supranationalism' (1981) 1 *Yearbook of European Law* 267; J Weiler and U Haltern, 'Constitutional or International? The Foundations of the Community Legal Order and the Question of Judicial Kompetenz-Kompetenz' in A-M Slaughter, A Stone Sweet & J Weiler (eds), *The European Court and National Courts: Doctrine and Jurisprudence* (Hart Publishing, 1998).

Examples of this counter-process at work can be seen across the full spectrum of Community law. For example, the Member States remain reluctant to accept the full and equal participation of the European Parliament in the legislative process: consultation rather than co-decision is retained for financially important sectors such as Article 37 EC on agriculture, and for more recent but equally sensitive competences such as Article 13 EC on protection against discrimination.[11] Similarly, there is continued resistance to the general use of majority voting in Council: although the Treaty of Nice expanded qualified majority voting to many new areas,[12] unanimity is retained for controversial fields such as tax harmonisation, and significant elements of environmental and social policy.[13] The desire to create safeguards for the expression of national sovereignty has been identified not only at the political but also the judicial level, precisely through the rejection by certain domestic courts of the unconditional supremacy of Treaty rules where they feel important national interests to be at stake, and do not entirely trust the Community institutions with their protection.[14]

This analysis draws heavily on what political scientists might label a 'neo-realist' model for explaining the dynamics of Community development. By stressing the predominant role played within the Treaty system by the Member States, and presuming that the latter act in pursuit of their individual national preferences, as much as for the sake of some collective vision of a shared political destiny, European union is therefore interpreted as a system of 'state bargains,' albeit of a relatively complex and stable nature.[15]

The convenience of such an analysis lies in the fact that it offers a linear explanation of why and how one finds regulatory differentiation within the Community legal order: certain Member States no longer feel their national

[11] Further: A Dashwood, 'Community Legislative Procedures in the Era of the Treaty on European Union' (1994) 19 EL Rev 343; and 'Community Decision-Making After Amsterdam' (1998) 1 *Cambridge Yearbook of European Legal Studies* 25.

[12] Further: A Dashwood, 'The Constitution of the European Union After Nice: Law-Making Procedures' (2001) 26 EL Rev 215.

[13] Cf the proposals contained in the Draft Treaty Establishing a Constitution for Europe, OJ 2003 C169/1. Further: M Dougan, 'The Convention's Draft Constitutional Treaty: Bringing Europe Closer to Its Lawyers?' (2003) 28 EL Rev 763. See now the 2004 Treaty, CIG 87/04.

[14] Consider, in particular, the German Constitutional Court in *Brunner* [1994] 1 CMLR 57. Further: J Weiler and U Haltern, 'Constitutional or International? The Foundations of the Community Legal Order and the Question of Judicial Kompetenz-Kompetenz' in A-M Slaughter, A Stone Sweet & J Weiler (eds), *The European Court and National Courts: Doctrine and Jurisprudence* (Hart Publishing, 1998).

[15] Further, eg M Jachtenfuchs, 'Theoretical Perspectives on European Governance' (1995) 1 *European Law Journal* 115; D Wincott, 'Political Theory, Law and European Union' in J Shaw & G More (eds), *New Legal Dynamics of European Union* (Clarendon Press, 1995); I Ward, 'The European Constitution and the Nation State' (1996) 16 OJLS 161. On the complexity of national reactions to European integration, consider, eg T Börzel, 'Pace-Setting, Foot-Dragging and Fence-Sitting: Member State Responses to Europeanisation' (2002) 40 JCMS 193.

interests to be compatible with a strategy of continuous integration; they therefore use their position at the centre of the Treaty system to resist undesirable levels of uniformity, and instead to promote forms of diversity more accommodating of their own needs. Regulatory differentiation is thus interpreted as a pragmatic attempt to resolve the tensions generated by the Community's simultaneous pressure for continuing expansion and counter-pressure for delimitation or contraction.[16]

Consider the Community's involvement in welfare-orientated sectors such as environmental, consumer and employee protection. Horizontal and vertical expansion, increasing the Treaty's potential to impinge upon national competence in not only a broader but also a deeper manner, obviously poses problems for those Member States which already possess well-developed regulatory regimes in the relevant policy areas, and are wary of replacing them with a harmonised Community norm; and equally for those Member States likely to resist Community approximation which entails a commitment to higher levels of social welfare than they felt able or willing to attain. For example: Member State A might enjoy a tradition of strong employee protection legislation; whereas Member State B believes that the imposition of similar standards upon its employers would fatally undermine their economic competitiveness through excessive labour costs. Finding a harmonised Community norm to suit both preferences could be a difficult task, particularly if the combined principles of pre-emption, direct effect and supremacy mean that the end-result would supplant the possibilities for adopting supplementary or derogating domestic rules.

Moreover, the impact of institutional changes favouring supranational rather than intergovernmental decision-making within the Treaty legislative processes mean that Member State A might find itself alone in Council in defending the virtues of strong labour protection, then obliged by the demands of total harmonisation to lower its own existing standards of regulation for the sake of complying with the majority's preference for a minimalist Community norm. Conversely, if Member State B were to be outvoted in Council, its concerns over the competitiveness of domestic industry could be sacrificed to meet the demands of traditional Community-wide regulatory techniques. Finally, such tensions are exacerbated by the Community's success in extending membership to other European countries, undermining the solidarity of six relatively homogenous Member States in favour of the increasing diversity of 12, 15 or 25. The presence of countries with very different and often conflicting cultural and political visions both of the appropriate intensity of

[16] Further: S Weatherill, 'On the Depth and Breadth of European Integration' (1997) 17 OJLS 537; M Dougan, 'Minimum Harmonisation and the Internal Market' (2000) 37 CML Rev 853.

social regulation on any given matter, and of the acceptable degree of Community involvement in its realisation, reduces drastically the chances of attaining such regulatory consensus as would be necessary to facilitate the uniform realisation of the Treaty's emergent social policies.[17]

These factors throw some light on the rising tide of what we referred to in Chapter 3 as vertical differentiation, particularly within the more welfare-orientated sectors of the Community legal order. Traditional regulatory techniques such as total harmonisation have not single-mindedly been maintained, precisely because it became necessary to balance the Community's original objective of maintaining a genuinely level playing-field for the purposes of the Common Market against its more recent mandate to develop a social policy agenda, and in doing so to accommodate the desires of the various Member States for differing levels of welfare provision where legislative compromise was difficult to achieve and majority voting to outflank the detractors was either unavailable or simply politically impossible to sustain.[18] Instead, regulatory differentiation permits both the Community and its various Member States to participate in the realisation of common goals, but not necessarily by common means. The widespread occurrence of derogations from the substantive obligations enacted by Community regulations and directives can be interpreted as a safety-valve intended to placate those Member States reluctant to accept the more ambitious standards of social regulation agreed upon by the rest of the Community.[19] Similarly, the widespread preference for minimum harmonisation which has emerged in both secondary and primary Treaty rules can be seen as a device for satisfying those Member States determined to maintain their own high standards of environmental, consumer or employee protection in the face of less ambitious Community harmonisation proposals. Moreover, it seems no coincidence that such regulatory differentiation is most acute not so much in the Community's core and relatively uncontested competences to administer the Internal Market (such as competition policy and state aids), but rather as regards the Community's more recent and much more controversial powers to regulate the environment or the workplace.[20]

Consider also the sorts of pressures which have stimulated the trend towards horizontal differentiation as described in Chapter 3. Regulatory

[17] Eg E Vos, 'Differentiation, Harmonisation and Governance' in B de Witte, D Hanf & E Vos (eds), *The Many Faces of Differentiation in EU Law* (Intersentia, 2001).
[18] Cf the ECJ's sympathy towards institutional constraints which often frustrate the possibility of the Community pursuing more intensive harmonisation, eg Case C–63/89 *Les Assurances du crédit v Council and Commission* [1991] ECR I–1799.
[19] A similar explanation applies to the UK's 'horizontal' opt-out from the Social Policy Protocol and Agreement, annexed to the EC Treaty by the TEU.
[20] Further: G de Búrca, 'Legal Principles as an Instrument of Differentiation?' in B de Witte, D Hanf & E Vos (eds), *The Many Faces of Differentiation in EU Law* (Intersentia, 2001).

diversity on the scale suggested by the enhanced cooperation provisions is again the result of deep-seated and intractable political differences between the various Member States and the Community institutions as regards the purpose and ultimate destiny of the entire European integration project. It will be recalled that the earlier expansion of Community powers was fuelled by a combination of logical necessity in the creation of a Common Market, and faith in the 'Monnet method' of uniting the continent by stealth.[21] However, the combined momentum of economic rationality and post-war political idealism could only carry the Community's growth so far. As the Internal Market neared completion, it would become increasingly difficult to continue justifying novel fields of Community intervention on this ground alone. With the passage of time, the original integrative impetus born of the experience of war and disillusionment with the old 'Europe of nation states' was losing its power to inspire those domestic elites which had, until then, built the Community on the back of only tacit mass support.

Indeed, the integration process had reached a point which was bound to attract the attention and concern of not only the politicians but also the usually complacent public and press. Again, expansion and contraction/delimitation have gone hand-in-hand. For example, as the Community's powers grew horizontally, it inevitably began to touch upon areas of concern (such as social welfare, culture, security, the administration of justice) which aroused public and media opinion, and stimulated debate about the full implications of Community membership (or at least did so to a degree which issues such as freedom of establishment and state aids could never really achieve). This process was reinforced by patterns of vertical growth within each sector of policy activity: when Community law did exist, it had a much more potent effect on the rights and obligations of citizens, administrators and legislators alike. It is significant, for example, that although the principles of direct effect and supremacy were already well established in the Court's caselaw, it was only with the *Factortame* litigation in the early 1990s that the public, press and even parts of the political establishment began fully to appreciate the impact of Community membership upon the constitutional order of the United Kingdom.[22] Mounting concern at the national level was reinforced by changes in the Community's decision-making processes. The thrust of institutional reform has, at least within the First Pillar, clearly favoured the extension of supranational at the expense of domestic control over the developing integration project. The greater legislative and supervisory powers of the directly elected European Parliament, coupled with the trend to replace unanimity with majority voting in the Council, have

[21] Further: ch 2 (above).

[22] Cf Lord Bridge in *R v Secretary of State for Transport, ex parte Factortame II* [1991] 1 AC 603, 658.

attenuated the ability of individual Member States to resist the will of the Community, even when they feel important questions of national policy to be at stake. And inevitably, the geographical growth of the Community has made the problem even more acute: uniformity of goals and methods became less plausible in a Community of 15 increasingly heterogeneous countries, each with their own individual interpretation of the purpose, benefits and limits of the integration process. Enlargement into central and eastern Europe can only have increased this pressure to accommodate the fundamental idiosyncrasies of particular domestic traditions.[23]

A climate therefore evolved in which many central assumptions about the Community entity were thrown open to reflection, challenge and change. Post-war political consensus and public apathy about the administration of the Common Market has given way to broad and heated debate about the Community's potential ambitions, and thus the full implications of Treaty membership. From this debate—which has reached its zenith in the process of constitutional reform initiated in earnest by the Laeken Declaration of the European Council, carried forward by the Convention on the Future of Europe, and played out in the 2003–04 intergovernmental negotiations to finalise a new constitutional treaty—it should be sufficient for present purposes to consider a small but representative sample of viewpoints. At one extreme, there are those who see the European Union as the launch-pad for some more developed form of political union or federation, exercising a range of powers equivalent to those of a traditional nation-state (for example: in welfare, taxation and foreign policy), and therefore implying the continuing integration of the national legal infrastructures.[24] At another extreme, there are those who are concerned to maintain an acceptable balance between the benefits of Union membership and the continuing integrity of national identity—and, in politico-legal terms, national sovereignty. This implies the careful surveillance of the boundaries between domestic and Community power so as to counteract the latter's centralising tendencies and, in particular, the danger of important national interests bending under the will of the

[23] Indeed, it has been argued—in the present author's view, rather unfairly—that recently acceding Member States see Community membership primarily as an economic expediency, rather than as a deeply felt expression of solidarity between shared cultures and values, and will therefore feel even less inclined to support initiatives which elevate supranational over parochial interests: N Petersen, 'National Strategies in the Integration Dilemma: An Adaptation Approach' (1998) 36 JCMS 33.

[24] Even among supporters of this viewpoint, there are those who express reservations about the wisdom of expanding/deepening the powers of the Community to affect the daily lives of European citizens, before more adequate structures of democratic legitimacy and accountability have been developed, eg W van Gerven, 'Towards a Coherent Constitutional System Within the European Union' (1996) 2 *European Public Law* 81; G Mancini, 'Europe: The Case for Statehood' (1998) 4 *European Law Journal* 29.

majority.[25] Yet another school interprets the Union as a postmodern experiment: the Treaty system performs largely ad hoc functions, not according to any clear or pre-conceived scheme or plan, but rather by identifying those issues which it finds itself better placed to regulate than the Member States acting individually, such as (for example) cross-border environmental pollution or abuses of consumer trust. According to this view, the scope and nature of Community competences relative to those of the national authorities should not be determined by ideological preconceptions, but by the requirements of the efficient administration of public power in a changing international economic and political environment—offering integration where it is needed, but also diversity where that is appropriate.[26]

Given such differences of outlook, it is unsurprising that maintaining a genuine consensus on how best to carry forward the process of supranational cooperation began to look increasingly idealistic. The task was no longer naively to pursue an agenda based upon integration that failed to tally with practical political possibilities, but to find a realistic way of reconciling the range of national and Community interests each now clamouring to be heard. On one side of the negotiating table sat Member States with grave reservations about the further strengthening of Community policies; on the other side, Member States more inclined towards increased solidarity. The only solution which would preserve uniformity in the Treaty system was to follow the lowest common denominator. But those Member States who styled themselves the vanguard of European unification had already grown impatient with what they saw as stragglers holding the integration process to ransom. The alternative solution—embodied in the closer/enhanced cooperation provisions agreed at Treaty of Amsterdam, developed by the Treaty of Nice, and under reflection once more during the current process of constitutional reform—was to introduce some form of variable geometry which would reassure the sensitivities of both camps, but necessarily detract from the ideal of uniformity.[27]

[25] Cf A Dashwood, 'The Limits of European Community Powers' (1996) 21 EL Rev 113; and 'States in the European Union' (1998) 23 EL Rev 201. Also: I Ward, 'Amsterdam and the Continuing Search for Community' in D O'Keeffe & P Twomey (eds), *Legal Issues of the Amsterdam Treaty* (Hart Publishing, 1999).

[26] Further: I Ward, 'Identity and Difference: The European Union and Postmodernism' in J Shaw & G More (eds), *New Legal Dynamics of European Union* (Clarendon Press, 1995); J Caporaso, 'The European Union and Forms of State: Westphalian, Regulatory or Postmodern?' (1996) 34 JCMS 29.

[27] Further: F Tuytschaever, *Differentiation in European Union Law* (Hart Publishing, 1999) ch 7. Cf E Philippart and M Sie Dhian Ho, 'From Uniformity to Flexibility: The Management of Diversity and Its Impact on the EU System of Governance' in G de Búrca & J Scott, *Constitutional Change in the EU: From Uniformity to Flexibility?* (Hart Publishing, 2000).

It is not only horizontal differentiation of the sort embodied in the enhanced cooperation provisions which results from differences in macro-political vision between the Member States. Many of the limitations imposed upon the existence of Community competence in accordance with the principle of attributed powers seem to stem from the same basic tensions: for example, as regards the harmonisation of education and cultural policies, or of workers' remuneration and social protection for the economically inactive.[28] And indeed, we might do well to point out that the politically pragmatic acceptance of different regulatory standards across the Community is hardly an entirely recent phenomenon. For example, Community social security policy as envisaged under the original Treaty of Rome seeks to overcome the obstacles to the free movement of persons which arise from the existence of diverse social security systems across the Member States. However, the Community's approach has never been based on any attempt at the full-scale harmonisation of national social security rules. As the Court explained in *Pinna*, the Treaty leaves in place differences between the Member States' social security systems and, consequently, in the rights of persons working in different Member States. It follows that substantive and procedural differences between the social security systems of individual Member States, and therefore in the rights of persons working in the Community, are unaffected by the Treaty.[29] The Community's approach is instead based on a policy of coordination: to ensure that Member States do not organise their social security systems in a manner contrary to Community law; and in particular, contrary to the principle that migrant workers should not lose social security benefits guaranteed under national law as a result of exercising their right to free movement.[30] This limited regulatory ambition—based upon an evident inequality both of compliance costs (social security contributions) for economic undertakings, and of welfare rights (social security benefits) for individual citizens—has been heavily criticised from an integrationist perspective.[31] But others believe that the evolution of the European welfare protection systems is linked to the process of social conflict and political resolution which characterised the history of the various nation states in the 19th and earlier 20th centuries. As a result of experiences peculiar to each individual country, welfare provision across Europe now differs remarkably in terms of its organisation and funding, the groups of people who benefit, and the types of social

[28] Arts 149, 151 and 137 EC (respectively).
[29] Case 41/84 *Pinna* [1986] ECR 1.
[30] Eg Case 24/75 *Petroni* [1975] ECR 1149.
[31] Eg C Laske, 'The Impact of the Single European Market on Social Protection for Migrant Workers' (1993) 30 CML Rev 515; M P Maduro, 'Europe's Social Self: The Sickness Unto Death' in J Shaw (ed), *Social Law and Policy in an Evolving European Union* (Hart Publishing, 2000).

problems which are addressed. When read together with the extreme sensitivity of transferring vast redistributive competences from the Member States to the Union institutions, these factors make the idea of a federal welfare state seem remote indeed.[32]

In any case, it is useful to bear in mind that regulatory differentiation generates a momentum of its own. Once the principle of solidarity in the process of ever-increasing integration has been breached for the sake of accommodating one Member State's self-interest, the incentive for other Member States to advance their own claims grows, and the ability of the Community system to resist the pressure for fragmentation diminishes. Reference to the ideal of uniformity no longer persuades because that uniformity has long since been compromised. Many commentators see the United Kingdom's opt-out from the Social Policy provisions of the post-Maastricht Community Treaty as a watershed in this regard—acting as a template for similar Protocols accompanying both the Treaty on European Union and the Treaty of Amsterdam, and ultimately for the enhanced cooperation provisions themselves.[33]

Multi-level Governance and Regulatory Differentiation

The trouble with models such as neo-realism is that none can *by itself* claim to offer a completely convincing explanation of the changing dynamics of European integration. It cannot be entirely true to say that the Member States are the sole masters of the Treaties, or of the constitutional order which those Treaties sustain. External forces—such as unexpected geopolitical convulsions which lie beyond the control of the Member States to do anything other than respond—can also play an important role.[34] For example, the end of the Cold War and collapse of the Eastern Bloc created a power vacuum in the European continent which redefined the Union's role—fuelling an expansion in its breadth of ambition over issues such as

[32] Further, eg G Majone, 'The European Community Between Social Policy and Social Regulation' (1993) 31 JCMS 153; M Rhodes, 'Defending the Social Contract: The EU Between Global Constraints and Domestic Imperatives' in D Hine & H Kassim (eds), *Beyond the Market: the EU and National Social Policy* (Routledge, 1998); S Leibfried and P Pierson, 'Social Policy: Left to Courts and Markets?' in H Wallace & W Wallace (eds), *Policy-Making in the European Union* (OUP, 2000); T Faist, 'Social Citizenship in the European Union: Nested Membership' (2001) 39 JCMS 37.

[33] Eg A Duff, *The Treaty of Amsterdam: Text and Commentary* (The Federal Trust, 1997) ch 5; Editorial, 'The Treaty of Amsterdam: Neither a Bang Nor a Whimper' (1997) 34 CML Rev 767; J Usher, *EC Institutions and Legislation* (Longman, 1998) ch 9.

[34] Eg R Harmsen, 'A European Union of Variable Geometry: Problems and Perspectives' (1994) 45 *Northern Ireland Law Quarterly* 109; N Blokker and T Heukels, 'The European Union: Historical Origins and Institutional Challenges' in T Heukels, N Blokker & M Brus (eds), *The European Union After Amsterdam: A Legal Analysis* (Kluwer Law International, 1998).

security and defence.[35] Moreover, the tense international atmosphere which followed the events of 11 September 2001 in New York and Washington pushed the Member States into cooperating more closely in the Area of Freedom, Security and Justice, so as to combat the perceived threat of international terrorism—again illustrating how external pressures can drive important but highly sensitive developments in Union policy.[36]

Similarly, many political scientists regard the neo-realist analysis as seriously flawed by the manner in which it dismisses the possibility that supranational institutions such as the Commission, the European Parliament and the Court of Justice might exercise any substantial, autonomous influence over the Community's development.[37] There is a genuine diffusion of power within the Union system, which offers institutions other than those representing purely national interests the opportunity to participate in decision-making processes, and thus to shape both the Union's constitutional affairs and its substantive policies.[38] Indeed, it is now almost universal practice to see the Union as a *sui generis* legal order—much more than an ordinary international organisation, though not quite a traditional federal state—carefully balancing the intergovernmental and supranational constituencies of interest which act as primary stakeholders in the process of European integration. One attempt to capture this unique quality uses the term 'a constitutional order of sovereign states'.[39] Others describe the Union as a system of multilevel governance in which political power is exercised by actors operating at several different levels (such as the supranational, the national and the local), with each actor making an independent (sometimes lesser, sometimes greater) contribution to the formulation and implementation of substantive Union policies.[40] As Bernard puts it: power is dispersed into a multiplicity of

[35] Eg H Wallace, 'Flexibility: A Tool of Integration or a Restraint on Disintegration?' in K Neunreither & A Wiener, *European Integration After Amsterdam: Institutional Dynamics and Prospects For Democracy* (OUP, 2000).
[36] Consider, in particular, Framework Dec 2002/584 on the European arrest warrant and the surrender procedures between Member States, OJ 2002 L190/1.
[37] Eg J Vandamme, 'European Federalism: Opportunity or Utopia?' in M Westlake (ed), *The European Union Beyond Amsterdam: New Concepts of European Integration* (Routledge, 1998).
[38] Consider, eg R Dehousse and G Majone, 'The Institutional Dynamics of European Integration: From the Single Act to the Maastricht Treaty' in S Martin (ed), *The Construction of Europe: Essays in Honour of Emile Noël* (Kluwer, 1994); U Sedelmeier and H Wallace, 'Eastern Enlargement: Strategy or Second Thoughts' in H Wallace & W Wallace (eds), *Policy-Making in the European Union* (OUP, 2000).
[39] In particular: A Dashwood, 'States in the European Union' (1998) 23 EL Rev 201.
[40] Further: M Jachtenfuchs, 'Theoretical Perspectives on European Governance' (1995) 1 *European Law Journal* 115; G Marks, L Hooghe and K Blank, 'European Integration from the 1980s: State-Centric v Multi-level Governance' (1996) 34 JCMS 341; M Jachtenfuchs, 'The Governance Approach to European Integration' (2001) 39 JCMS 245; W Wessels, 'An Ever Closer Fusion? A Dynamic Macropolitical View on Integration Processes' (1997) 35 JCMS 267; K Armstrong, 'Legal Integration: Theorising the Legal Dimension of European Integration'

sites, which constitute nodes in a heterarchical network rather than layers in a hierarchical pyramid, and the relationship between these nodes is one of mutual influence rather than simply one of control.[41] This analysis offers some fresh insights into the causes of regulatory differentiation within the Community legal order.

In the first place, a multilevel governance perspective shifts our attention away from the purely institutional considerations which have previously dominated discussion, and towards the sorts of substantive policy issues confronting and shaping the modern European polity as a whole—such as economic globalisation, widespread social exclusion and environmental pollution. This allows us to identify certain sector-specific needs, militating against uniformity and legitimising some degree of differentiation, to which the relevant actors within the Union's governance network have responded.

For example, many specialists in fields such as environmental, consumer and social policy have commented on a noticeable trend towards deregulation within the Community. The primary aim here is to increase the economic efficiency and competitive position of European industry in the globalised economy by cutting the burden of often unnecessary or over-detailed regulation, and therefore the costs incurred by industry in achieving compliance. Indeed, Title XI EC tempers the Community commitment to improved social provisions by referring to 'the need to maintain the competitiveness of the Community economy' and to 'avoid imposing administrative, financial and legal constraints in a way which would hold back the creation and development of small and medium-sized undertakings'.[42] The inevitable by-product of such a strategy is to increase the potential for diversity within the purview of Community competences. If centralised Community norms are enacted at all, they may well take the form of directives rather than regulations, and indeed of framework directives rather than specific and detailed provisions. There is also a greater incentive to pepper legislation with devices such as the derogation, a point clearly illustrated by the experience of the Working Time Directive: this measure is characterised as much by derogation as by any centralised norm, reflecting widespread anxieties among the Member States that the Community's concern to promote health and safety in the workplace had to be balanced against the need for flexibility in the European labour market.[43] Similarly, the Commission's retreat from

(1998) 36 JCMS 155; P Craig, 'The Nature of the Community: Integration, Democracy, and Legitimacy' in P Craig & G de Búrca (eds), *The Evolution of EU Law* (OUP, 1999).

[41] N Bernard, *Multilevel Governance in the European Union* (Kluwer Law International, 2002) p 9.
[42] Arts 136 and 137(2) EC (respectively).
[43] Dir 2003/88 concerning certain aspects of the organisation of working time, OJ 2003 L299/9 (repealing and replacing Dir 93/104, OJ 1993 L307/18).

the centralised creation of individual employment rights in favour of both the increased involvement of the social partners in the formulation of legislative measures (as embodied in the Social Chapter), and the new commitment to tackling macro-economic issues affecting the labour market (as embodied in the Employment Policy Chapter) represents a new initiative which it is hoped will prove more effective in the fight against the twin demons of unemployment and social exclusion.[44]

Consider along similar lines the fall from grace of traditional 'command and control' style environmental regulation, which has been attributed to the fact that this particular legislative technique failed to make any substantial impact in combating unacceptable levels of pollution. Consequently, the Commission has searched for alternative strategies which rely more on trust and cooperation with local actors, emphasise targets rather than obligations, and focus on results rather than mere formal compliance. In particular, Community law now emphasises the role of procedural (as well as, or even instead of, substantive) duties—requiring national agencies to incorporate environmental concerns into their decision-making processes, but without necessarily demanding any particular outcome, in an attempt to instil a culture of environmental awareness among relevant actors within the governance network.[45] The benefits of such strategies in terms of increased environmental protection are believed to outweigh the costs in terms of departing from the paradigm of a uniform regulatory regime.[46]

In the second place, a multilevel governance model draws attention to certain institutional structures and processes that might facilitate greater regulatory differentiation by engaging a broader range of actors in Union decision-making. After all, it is not simply a question of identifying the existence of diverse local and national interests, or certain sector-specific needs favouring greater decentralisation. It is also necessary to construct channels of communication which permit such interests / needs to be expressed, and forms of interaction that accommodate their influence over policy outputs—and which do so not just at the grand moments of Treaty revision, but also in the quotidian functioning of the Community institutions.[47] But the existence of a constitutional order fundamentally characterised by a system of diffused power might *of itself* foster the growth of a political culture in which the task of satisfying local preferences is seen as a positive value, rather than some necessary yet unwelcome

[44] Further, eg C Barnard, *EC Employment Law* (OUP, 2000) ch 1.

[45] Eg R MacCrory and S Turner, 'Participatory Rights, Transboundary Environmental Governance and EC Law' (2002) 39 CML Rev 489.

[46] Eg J Scott, *EC Environmental Law* (Longman, 1998) ch 2.

[47] Consider, by way of illustration, the role played by the comitology system, eg C Joerges & E Vos (eds), *EU Committees: Social Regulation, Law and Politics* (Hart Publishing, 1999); M Andenas & A Türk (eds), *Delegated Legislation and the Role of Committees in the EC* (Kluwer, 2000).

compromise. Particularly in an era when the Union's efforts to address its democratic deficit (greater legislative powers for the European Parliament, a more politically accountable Commission, increased transparency in the working of the institutions) do not appear to have made substantial inroads into improving its popular acceptance, paying greater attention to local needs and making greater efforts to accommodate national differences might be understood as an important contribution towards legitimising the Union's exercise of massive public power. For example, the Commission's 2001 *White Paper on European Governance*, having registered a widening gulf between the European Union and its citizens, argued that solutions should be based (*inter alia*) on ensuring a more inclusive interaction within the Union's multilevel partnership, so as national, regional and local actors were able to participate effectively in decision-making processes. Moreover, the Commission recognised that the diversity and complexity of the enlarging Union made it difficult to establish a single set of rules for the entire territory, or to achieve basic policy objectives through the traditional medium of centralised legislation.[48]

Reflexive Harmonisation and Regulatory Differentiation

Even if the primary causes of regulatory differentiation are institutional (whether better explained more by a neo-realist analysis here, more by a multilevel governance perspective there), the Community's departure from a programme of ever increasing uniformity in the management of the Internal Market can also find solid support among economic theorists. Indeed, the evolution of legal techniques capable of accommodating the differentiated application of Community rules across the Member States, and the preservation of domestic regulatory competence alongside the existence of centrally adopted norms, has had important implications for the theory and practice of competition between legal orders, in particular, by inspiring the evolution of an alternative model of regulatory competition known as 'reflexive harmonisation.'

Reflexive harmonisation stresses the value of preserving and promoting legal diversity and experimentation across the European Union. On the one hand, it thus differs from classical regulatory competition: it does not envisage that market forces should eventually generate some single regulatory model for the economically optimal management of the Single Market; and indeed, it calls upon the Community authorities to devise interventionist strategies which will avoid this very result. On the other hand, reflexive harmonisation also differs from traditional regulatory

48 COM (2001)428 Final.

centralisation: it does not espouse a template for intervention by the central authorities which creates some uniform legislative code, suppressing altogether the possibility for individual domestic regulatory choices within the harmonised fields. The proper goals of reflexive harmonisation are rather: first, to permit the general thrust of common legal solutions to be tailored more precisely and appropriately to local needs and preferences within each Member State; and secondly, to enable the Community to maintain a healthy stock of legal ideas from which Member States may draw inspiration to meet the challenges posed by changes in scientific technology or market behaviour that create new regulatory dilemmas and require fresh policy solutions. For these purposes, reflexive harmonisation seeks to harness the *process* of regulatory competition, in particular, by exploiting the opportunities for cross-fertilisation of information between Member States and the pressure for reform exerted upon existing national legal orders by the free movement of economic factors; but without being trapped into accepting the sort of static regulatory *outcomes* which the debate over competition between legal orders so often offers by way of final resolution.[49]

What role, more precisely, does this invite from the Community? According to reflexive harmonisation theorists, the Community authorities should seek to establish certain basic parameters for Member State action, but otherwise respect the autonomy and diversity of the national legal orders, thus steering the process of domestic evolution in the light of the general principles of EU law.[50] For example, the growing preference expressed by the Community institutions for the adoption of framework directives, rather than detailed regulations, helps to strike a better balance between the development of a common European legal culture, and the desire to maximise the scope of individual Member State creativity.[51] Similarly, reflexive harmonisation theorists welcome the increasing role offered to soft law initiatives (rather than hard law intervention) as a means of achieving the Union's objectives. In particular, the open method of coordination adopted in fields such as employment policy and the modernisation of social protection seeks to identify and exchange information about best practice across the Community, and to encourage voluntary

[49] S Deakin, 'Two Types of Regulatory Competition: Competitive Federalism Versus Reflexive Harmonisation. A Law and Economics Perspective on *Centros*' (1999) 2 *Cambridge Yearbook of European Legal Studies* 231.

[50] S Deakin, 'Regulatory Competition Versus Harmonisation in European Company Law' in D Esty & D Geradin (eds), *Regulatory Competition and Economic Integration: Comparative Perspectives* (OUP, 2001).

[51] Eg Protocol on the application of the principles of subsidiarity and proportionality annexed to the EC Treaty by the Treaty of Amsterdam; Commission, *European Governance: A White Paper*, COM (2001)428 Final; Commission, *Action Plan for Simplifying and Improving the Regulatory Environment*, COM (2002)278 Final.

convergence by the Member States around certain agreed principles and objectives, with an emphasis on benchmarking, monitoring and peer review.[52] However, in principle at least, the most attractive legal vehicle for facilitating the model of reflexive harmonisation is the adoption of Community measures which envisage only minimum harmonisation. That legal framework might seem to combine the best of both worlds: free movement across a complex legislative landscape, to encourage the identification and dissemination throughout the entire Community of varying regulatory practices, which economic actors and Member States alike can draw upon to help inform their decision and policy-making processes; coupled with centralised harmonisation to establish a common floor of welfare provisions which all the Member States must respect, to preserve the conditions under which each country feels able to pursue new and potentially divergent approaches to the protection of vulnerable social interests, without undue risk of social dumping.[53]

DIFFERENTIATION AS A CAUSE OF CONSTITUTIONAL CHANGE

It thus emerges that regulatory differentiation within the Community legal order has a marked sectoral dimension: it is possible to distinguish between core Internal Market activities (such as competition law and state aids) which remain relatively uniform; shared welfare competences (such as environmental and employment protection) which are relatively more diverse; and complementary welfare competences (such as education and culture) which remain primarily in the hands of the Member States. It also seems clear that regulatory differentiation within the Community legal order has a significant temporal dimension: whereas attaining uniformity of compliance costs seemed a genuine policy aspiration during the 1960s–70s, vertical differentiation gained increased prominence and legitimacy during the 1980s–90s, paving the way for the more recent emergence of new methods of governance such as the open method of coordination, and for the introduction of horizontal flexibility as embodied in the closer/enhanced cooperation provisions.[54] We have also seen that the commentators suggest myriad factors to account for these dual

[52] Further, eg E Szyszczak, 'The New Paradigm for Social Policy: A Virtuous Circle?' (2001) 38 CML Rev 1125; G de Búrca, 'The Constitutional Challenge of New Governance in the European Union' (2003) 28 EL Rev 814.

[53] Further, eg N Reich, 'Competition Between Legal Orders: A New Paradigm of EC Law?' (1992) 29 CML Rev 861; M Dougan, 'Vive La Différence? Exploring the Legal Framework for Reflexive Harmonisation within the Single European Market' in R Miller & P Zumbansen (eds), *Annual of German and European Law (Volume 1: 2003)* (Berghahn Books, 2004).

[54] Even if we have seen that this temporal dimension is not complete, eg as with the Community's approach to social security. Consider also recent developments in Community consumer policy (discussed below).

dimensions: from a fundamental tension between the expansion of Community competence and the desire to subject that competence to more clearly defined limits, through the identification of sector-specific pressures for regulatory differentiation inspired by analysis of the Union as a system of multi-level governance, to the potential economic benefits of treating the Internal Market as a managed system of regulatory competition which encourages experimentation and diversity within a common framework of reference.

Against that background, we are now in a position to draw together the various strands of argument and observation which have so far been presented, and to develop them into a more coherent analysis of the key relationships between integration and differentiation, differentiation and enforcement deficit. So, we shall now return to the questions posed at the start of this chapter: what significance should we attach to the fact that differentiation exists within the Community legal order? In particular, how far does an increasing degree of regulatory differentiation affect our understanding of, and condition our responses to, the enforcement deficit?

Doctrinal Revision Resulting From Regulatory Differentiation

The underlying weakness of 'integration through law' lies in its skewed vision of the Community's historical development. Its analysis is inspired and informed almost entirely by the expansion of the Treaty system along horizontal, vertical, institutional and geographical axes. Such expansion both demonstrates and reinforces the 'integration through law' conviction that the Community's vocation is to create an ever closer degree of economic and/or political union. From this ever closer union springs the desire to build a level playing-field on which all economic actors can operate under equal competitive conditions, and/or all beneficiaries of Community norms can enjoy the same levels of social and welfare rights. This in turn fuels the argument for harmonising divergent national regulatory regimes so as to conform as closely as possible to a single uniform standard set by the Community institutions, and justifies a critical interpretation of everything from the lack of horizontal direct effect for directives, to tolerance of the fair-weather commitment to supremacy shown by certain domestic judges, to reliance on fragmented systems of national remedies and procedural rules.

However, it has been argued that the process of expansion must now be seen in its wider context alongside the counter-process of contraction. As the Community has evolved, so it has been forced to rethink the degree of its commitment to a genuine economic or socio-political level playing-field. Horizontal, vertical and geographical growth in the Community's powers, coupled with periodic waves of institutional reform, have themselves unleashed a dynamic, the inevitable by-product of which was to challenge the ideal of uniformity in the elaboration of substantive Treaty policies. Differentiation emerged as the alternative: an important—indeed necessary—aspect of governance in a Community which celebrates an ever more accentuated state of diversity. As phenomena such as minimum harmonisation, derogations, policy opt-outs and enhanced cooperation all demonstrate, this fundamental momentum favouring diversity as well as integration, and which it is in the interests of the Member States and Community institutions to forward or at least accommodate, has been translated into the contemporary legal reality of differentiated regulation. As a result, the idea of a level playing-field in either an economic or a socio-political sense is difficult to defend as a general characteristic of the contemporary Treaty legal order. The mere fact of Community involvement in a given sphere of activity does not mean that the regulatory regime established to achieve its objectives will consist of uniform norms, or indeed that uniformity is its ultimate goal.

Against this background, 'integration through law' presents a preconceived constitutional model of the Treaty and its legal system which has become increasingly untenable. A more appropriate approach would be to accept the reality of a political and legal shift in the outlook of the Community: European union is as much about managing our respective differences as it is about promoting uniformity; and Community law has an equally valid role in forwarding both these aims. Indeed, one might justly argue that differentiation is fast attaining the status of a central organisational principle within the Treaty system.[55]

This interpretation generates further implications of its own. In particular, it suggests the need to undertake a process of doctrinal reconsideration and adaptation, the goal of which should be to up-date and rationalise our conceptual understanding of the Community legal order, in particular, through the re-evaluation of certain long-held assumptions which unduly emphasise the Treaty's integrative mission and consequent need for regulatory uniformity, and have therefore fallen out of step with the Community's recent patterns of development.[56]

To some extent this process has already begun. Consider, for example, the traditional doctrine of pre-emption: when the Community legislates for the totality of a given matter, national competence to enact additional or even different regulations is effectively usurped; the risk that the newly

[55] See the wide-ranging contributions in G de Búrca & J Scott (eds), *Constitutional Change in the EU: From Uniformity to Flexibility?* (Hart Publishing, 2000); and in B de Witte, D Hanf & E Vos (eds), *The Many Faces of Differentiation in EU Law* (Intersentia, 2001).

[56] In particular: J Shaw, 'European Union Legal Studies in Crisis? Towards a New Dynamic' (1996) 16 OJLS 231.

established Community regime will be undermined or fragmented by independent domestic initiatives is therefore neutralised.[57] Thus stated, pre-emption serves greatly to reinforce the centralising tendencies of the harmonisation process, and has long been seen as making a vital contribution to the Treaty's integrationist endeavours. However, the spread of minimum rather than total harmonisation has necessitated a change in both judicial and intellectual interpretations of the doctrine of pre-emption. As was shown in Chapter 3, it is now recognised that where the Community legislates for only minimum standards in respect of a given issue, domestic competence is not entirely suppressed: the national authorities retain some discretion to enact more protective provisions in respect of the same subject-matter.[58] This change obviously detracts from the uniformity of many Community norms, but that is a price the Treaty legislature and judiciary are prepared to pay for the sake of advancing high standards of social welfare in the absence of a sustainable supranational consensus.

Consider also the *ERTA* principle that exclusive Community competence to conduct external relations can arise not only from primary Treaty provisions, but also and implicitly from the internal competence to enact secondary legislation.[59] Again, the aim of this doctrine is to prevent the uniformity of Community rules from being undermined by independent domestic action (this time by entering into obligations under international law with third countries). However, in its *Opinion on the ILO Convention*, the Court of Justice adopted a more nuanced approach: where internal competence in the sector in question is shared between the Community and the Member States, implied external competence must also be joint rather than exclusive. The Court then applied this approach to help determine the nature of the Community's competence to negotiate and conclude agreements with third countries in the social policy sphere. It held that both ex-Article 118a EC (now subsumed into Article 137 EC), conferring on the Community power to legislate on the health and safety of workers, and the majority of related secondary measures adopted under the Common Market harmonisation powers set out in ex-Article 100 EC (now Article 94

[57] Eg Case 60/86 *Commission v United Kingdom* [1988] ECR 3921; Cases C–129–130/97 *Chiciak and Fol* [1998] ECR I–3315.
[58] Eg Case C–11/92 *ex p Gallaher* [1993] ECR I–3545; Case C–389/96 *Aher-Waggon* [1998] ECR I–4473. Also: R Bieber, 'On the Mutual Completion of Overlapping Legal Systems: The Case of the European Communities and the National Legal Orders' (1988) 13 EL Rev 147; ED Cross, 'Pre-emption of Member State Law in the European Economic Community: A Framework for Analysis' (1992) 29 CML Rev 447; S Weatherill, 'Beyond Pre-emption? Shared Competence and Constitutional Change in the European Community' in D O'Keeffe & P Twomey (eds) *Legal Issues of the Maastricht Treaty* (Wiley, 1994); AG Soares, 'Pre-emption, Conflicts of Powers and Subsidiarity' (1998) 23 EL Rev 132.
[59] Case 22/70 *Commission v Council (ERTA)* [1971] ECR 263.

EC) stated explicitly that internal Community action in this sector was to take the form of minimum standards only. Conclusion of the relevant International Labour Organisation Convention was therefore a matter for the joint competence of the Community and the Member States.[60] Again, the existence of regulatory differentiation logically stimulated the reformulation of an already established principle within the Community legal order.

Moreover, academic interest is now thoroughly engaged with the potential of increased legal diversity within the Treaty system to inform wider debates about the nature of the European project as a whole. For example, Jachtenfuchs has suggested that a state of variable degrees of 'Europeanisation' in the regulatory intensity of Community activity across different policy sectors has implications for the Union's alleged 'democratic deficit'. Why insist on rigorous application of the principle of democratic legitimacy in those areas where Community action merely plays at the margins of national competences, and the latter remain subject to domestic channels of accountability? If the Community is now characterised by a more complex relationship between the centre and the periphery in terms of responsibility for the exercise of public power, then Community commentators must be prepared to adopt a more sophisticated analysis of the concomitant structures of democratic accountability.[61] Similarly, Walker has argued that horizontal differentiation of the sort introduced by the Treaties of Maastricht, Amsterdam and Nice might eventually redraw the boundaries of long-running controversy over the location of ultimate legal sovereignty within the Community. The current two-dimensional competition between the supranationalist claims of the Court of Justice (to the unconditional supremacy of EC norms) and the nationalist reactions of several domestic courts (asserting the residual competence of Member State laws to prevail even over Treaty dictates) could be augmented by a third axis. If enhanced cooperation sees the *de facto* emergence of relatively stable groupings of Member States committed to different degrees of integration, the hard-core might concede that a greater portion of their sovereignty has seeped away to the Community, or indeed claim to constitute a new 'demos' distinct from the remainder of the Union. If so, the possibility of locating any unitary source of sovereignty within the European integration project would indeed seem an implausible prospect.[62]

[60] Opinion 2/91 *(Convention No 170 of the International Labour Organisation concerning safety in the use of chemicals at work)* [1993] ECR I–1061. For detailed analysis of the impact of internal differentiation upon external Community competences, see E De Smijter, 'The External Relations of a Differentiated European Community' in B de Witte, D Hanf & E Vos (eds), *The Many Faces of Differentiation in EU Law* (Intersentia, 2001).

[61] M Jachtenfuchs, 'Democracy and Governance in the European Union' in A Føllesdal & P Koslowski (eds), *Democracy and the European Union* (Springer, 1997).

[62] N Walker, 'Sovereignty and Differentiated Integration in the European Union' (1998) 4 *European Law Journal* 355.

The preceding paragraphs lend a shoulder of intellectual solidarity to the argument that regulatory differentiation implies the need to reconsider certain aspects of the more established corpus of Community jurisprudence. But that argument can also draw on the more solid doctrinal foundations by reference, in particular, to the principles of subsidiarity and proportionality.

Of course, it is true that Article 5(2) EC does not provide a firm basis for the detailed judicial review of Community acts alleged to infringe the principle of subsidiarity;[63] and that even Article 5(3) EC permits only limited judicial review where the Community institutions are called upon to exercise wide discretionary powers.[64] But whatever the practical limits of constitutional adjudication within the Treaty system,[65] subsidiarity and proportionality still have something of substance to say about the nature of the Community and its legal order—providing the basis for an institutional and intellectual obligation to think more carefully about the ambit of Community activities, and of the legal rules which serve to support them.[66] The objective of Article 5 EC is to submit the exercise of Community power to more clearly defined boundaries, by questioning the need for and nature of collective action, particularly as regards its impact on the pre-existing competences of the Member State.[67] In this regard, Article 5 EC reflects and contributes to the shift in the Community's continuing politico-legal evolution identified above: the emergence of a counter-process of 'disintegration' and 'differentiation' which challenges the more traditional assumption that continuous 'integration' and greater 'uniformity' are the necessary or ultimate goals of the Treaty project.

In particular, the principle of subsidiarity recognises explicitly the purely relative value of integration-centralisation as a model for Community development, and contemplates the equally valid existence of alternative national or regional levels of substantive policy formulation, and therefore the tolerance of diverse regulatory frameworks within the Treaty

[63] Consider, eg Case C–84/94 *United Kingdom v Council (Working Time Directive)* [1996] ECR I–5755; Case C–377/98 *Netherlands v Parliament and Council (Biotech Directive)* [2001] ECR I–7079; Case C–491/01 *ex p British American Tobacco* [2002] ECR I–11453.

[64] Consider, eg Case C–331/88 *ex p Fedesa* [1990] ECR I–4023; Case C–233/94 *Germany v Parliament and Council (Deposit Guarantee Schemes)* [1997] ECR I–2405; Case C–491/01 *ex p British American Tobacco* [2002] ECR I–11453.

[65] This distinction between the abstract requirements and the enforceable justiciability of the principle of proportionality is drawn by the ECJ itself, eg Case C–189/01 *Jippes* [2001] ECR I–5689.

[66] Consider academic work on the institutional culture of subsidiarity, eg N Reich, 'The "November Revolution" of the European Court of Justice: *Keck*, *Meng* and *Audi* Revisited' (1994) 31 CML Rev 459; G de Búrca, 'The Principle of Subsidiarity and the Court of Justice as an Institutional Actor' (1998) 36 JCMS 217.

[67] Cf A Dashwood, 'The Limits of European Community Powers' (1996) 21 EL Rev 113.

system. Indeed, even though subsidiarity does not act as an intrusive ground of judicial review, the Court still employs the principle as an interpretative tool—construing Community legislation, in cases of ambiguity, so as to favour the continued exercise of national regulatory competence.[68] A critique of integration for integration's sake is also inherent in the principle of proportionality: the Community may well have a valid interest in acting to further a particular aim; but does it need to do so, for example, by setting out an exhaustive regime which excludes the possibility of more protective national standards, or of derogations to deal with certain domestic peculiarities? That Article 5 EC both contemplates and actively promotes a process of differentiation within the Community legal order is supported by the Protocol introduced at Amsterdam, which directs that '[t]he Community shall legislate only to the extent necessary' and, in particular, that Community action should be 'restricted or discontinued where it is no longer justified'.[69]

Managing the Implications of Regulatory Differentiation

Regulatory differentiation therefore has the potential to act as a motor for constitutional change within the Community legal order. But one should not lose sight of the fact that integration remains a central—albeit modified—characteristic of the Community system. Taken beyond its appropriate boundaries, differentiation could seriously endanger certain fundamental values, embodied in the Treaty and protected by Community law, which should be considered sacrosanct in any programme of doctrinal revision. What is proposed therefore is not a revolution in the Community legal order, but rather a realignment: identifying more clearly the truly common core, while thinking more flexibly about other aspects of the European integration project. Again, there is already clear evidence of such a process at work: as regulatory differentiation has become more familiar, so too has open-minded speculation about how it can be 'managed', that is, accommodated into the framework of the Community legal order without disrupting unduly the latter's underlying integrity.[70]

[68] Eg Case C–114/01 *AvestaPolarit Chrome Oy* (Judgment of 11 September 2003).
[69] Paras 6 and 3 Protocol on the application of the principles of subsidiarity and proportionality.
[70] Though the goal of 'managing differentiation' is complicated by the fact that identifying the core values of the Community project has necessarily proven a difficult and controversial task. Consider, eg S Weatherill, 'Safeguarding the *Acquis Communautaire*' in T Heukels, N Blokker & M Brus (eds), *The European Union After Amsterdam: A Legal Analysis* (Kluwer Law International, 1998); C Delcourt, 'The *Acquis Communautaire*: Has the Concept Had Its Day?' (2001) 38 CML Rev 829.

In a positive sense, the duty of sincere cooperation enshrined in Article 10 EC has become the focus of growing expectation that a balance can be struck between differentiation and solidarity within the Community legal order, based around the idea that Member States should be obliged to use their discretion in a manner which facilitates rather than undermines the Treaty's economic and social objectives. This can be seen in the Court of Justice's jurisprudence concerning joint national-Community competence to conduct external relations: the Court has often stressed the importance of ensuring that there is a close association between the institutions of the Community and the Member States both in the process of negotiation and conclusion and in the fulfilment of the obligations entered into.[71] The same approach is embodied in the Protocol on the application of the principles of subsidiarity and proportionality introduced at Amsterdam: if the Community refrains from collective action in pursuit of a particular policy goal on the basis that it would be inappropriate under Article 5 EC, the Member States are nevertheless reminded of their obligation under Article 10 EC to take all appropriate steps to fulfil their Treaty obligations, and to refrain from any action that might jeopardise the attainment of Community objectives.[72]

In a more negative sense, some forms of regulatory diversity are susceptible to criticism even in the light of the process of doctrinal adaptation outlined above, on the grounds that they are incompatible with the existence of an adequately uniform and integrated Community legal order. This is true, in particular, of differentiation which results not from the deliberate will of the appointed Community legislature (as is the case, say, with minimum harmonisation clauses and the grant of derogations from secondary measures); but from the unilateral assertion of national competence in the face of binding Treaty obligations (for example, through the rejection of the principle of unconditional supremacy by certain national courts).[73] This critique could be carried further: the inequalities of rights and obligations which flow from the lack of horizontal direct effect for non- or incorrectly implemented directives create a pattern of differentiation which might at first sight be attributed to the deliberate will of the Court of Justice, but result more fundamentally from the unilateral

[71] Eg Opinion 2/91 *(Convention No 170 of the International Labour Organisation concerning safety in the use of chemicals at work)* [1993] ECR I–1061, paras 36–37; Opinion 1/94 *(Competence of the Community to conclude international agreements concerning services and the protection of intellectual property)* [1994] ECR I–5267, paras 106–8.

[72] Para 8 Protocol on the application of the principles of subsidiarity and proportionality.

[73] Eg M Herdegen, 'Maastricht and the German Constitutional Court: Constitutional Restraints for an "Ever Closer Union"' (1994) 31 CML Rev 235; N Reich, 'Judge-Made "Europe à la carte": Some Remarks on Recent Conflicts between European and German Constitutional Law Provoked by the Banana Litigation' (1996) 7 *European Journal of International Law* 103.

default of the relevant Member States, in defiance of the clear intention of the Community legislature to enact some minimum body of common legal provisions to govern particular categories of situation.[74]

Indeed, it is even possible to criticise certain forms of differentiation which result from the constitutive power of the Member States when amending the Treaties—though from a perspective which relies less on the idea of ever closer European integration than on more enduring values such as the right to fair and effective judicial redress, and the need for transparency in the exercise of democratic power. Thus, several commentators have attacked the provisions introduced by the Treaty of Amsterdam relating to the jurisdiction of the Court of Justice to receive Article 234 EC references from the domestic judges under the new Title IV, Part Three EC on visas, asylum and immigration. In particular, Article 68(1) EC affirms the obligation of national courts and tribunals against whose decision there is no remedy to make a reference, but precludes any other courts or tribunals from doing so. This represents a significant break from the principle of open communication between the domestic and Treaty judicial authorities, and in practice will mean that particularly vulnerable people (such as asylum-seekers) will have to exhaust all local remedies before being able to refer a simple point of Community law to the Court of Justice.[75]

Similarly, it has been suggested that differentiation in general, and enhanced cooperation in particular, have the potential gravely to exacerbate the problems facing the Community in its earnest quest to achieve greater popular legitimacy and democratic accountability. The complicated prospect of overlapping regulatory regimes offering different levels of legal protection as between different Member States can do little to improve public understanding of the Treaty system. One might well argue that the Union could never hope to replicate the democratic credentials of an ordinary nation or federal state. Indeed, Europe's system of

[74] Cf AG Saggio in Cases C–240–4/98 *Océano Grupo Editorial* [2000] ECR I–4941.

[75] Consider the judgment in Case C–555/03 *Warbecq* (10 June 2004). Note also the Third Pillar provisions contained in Art 35(3) TEU. Further: A Albors Llorens, 'Changes in the Jurisdiction of the European Court of Justice Under the Treaty of Amsterdam' (1998) 35 CML Rev 1273; N Fennelly, 'Preserving the Legal Coherence Within the New Treaty' (1998) 5 *Maastricht Journal of European and Comparative Law* 185; A Arnull, 'Taming the Beast? The Treaty of Amsterdam and the Court of Justice' in D O'Keeffe & P Twomey (eds), *Legal Issues of the Amsterdam Treaty* (Hart Publishing, 1999); A Ward, 'The Limits of the Uniform Application of Community Law and Effective Judicial Review: A Look Post-Amsterdam' in C Kilpatrick, T Novitz & P Skidmore (eds), *The Future of Remedies in Europe* (Hart Publishing, 2000). Cf the proposals contained in the Draft Treaty Establishing a Constitution for Europe, OJ 2003 C169/1; and adopted into the 2004 Treaty, CIG 87/04; M Dougan, 'The Convention's Draft Constitutional Treaty: Bringing Europe Closer To Its Lawyers?' (2003) 28 EL Rev 763. Consider also issues about access to judicial protection before the Community courts in the light of the enhanced cooperation provisions, eg J Usher, 'Flexibility: The Experience So Far' (2000) 3 *Cambridge Yearbook of European Legal Studies* 477.

multilevel governance—where it is difficult enough to identify any 'institution' responsible for exercising decision-making authority, and even harder to imagine that individual citizens feel able to exert effective control thereover—might seem inevitably to strain the bond between governors and governed. But even then, there is perhaps a case to be made for balancing the Community's internal pressure to fragment against the desire to create a political structure compatible with Western expectations about the manner in which public power is structured and exercised.[76]

Finally, it is worth pointing out that the balance between uniformity and differentiation can be highly contested. The dice are not always weighted against greater integration, since the Community institutions can sometimes display ambivalence towards regulatory differentiation bordering on outright hostility. Consider, by way of illustration, the Commission's 2001 *Green Paper on European Union Consumer Protection*, and its *Consumer Policy Strategy 2002–2006*.[77]

In these documents, the Commission refers to the objectives of Community consumer policy as laid out in Article 153 EC, but firmly locates the legal basis for legislative action under Article 95 EC and thus closely tied to the operation of the Single Market. In this regard, the Commission shows an unconcealed antipathy towards the existence of significant differences between national rules, both in the absence of Community secondary measures, and even post-harmonisation due to the inclusion of minimum harmonisation clauses. Drawing upon a classic 'integration through law' analysis, the Commission believes that this situation hinders the creation of a genuine Internal Market for European consumers: inequalities in the burden of regulatory compliance costs distort conditions of competition for economic undertakings established in different Member States; while the lack of clarity as regards their legal rights in other countries (with consequent increases in transaction costs required to ascertain the correct legal position) deters both businesses and consumers from engaging in cross-border trade, and therefore suppresses the greater choice and more intense competition which market integration should bring about. The answer, it is claimed, lies in greater harmonisation so as to achieve a high uniform level of protection for all the Union's citizens.[78]

[76] Further: J Shaw, 'The Treaty of Amsterdam: Challenges of Flexibility and Legitimacy' (1998) 4 *European Law Journal* 63; N Walker, 'Sovereignty and Differentiated Integration in the European Union' (1998) 4 *European Law Journal* 355.

[77] Commission, *Green Paper on European Union Consumer Protection*, COM (2001)531 Final; Commission, *Consumer Policy Strategy 2002–2006*, COM (2002)208 Final. The former has been followed up by the Commission, in the light of responses to its initial consultation (COM (2002)289 Final); while the latter has been approved by the Council (*Resolution on Community Consumer Policy Strategy 2002–2006*, OJ 2003 C11/1).

[78] The *Green Paper* suggested that greater harmonisation could be achieved through the adoption of additional sector-specific directives. But the Commission's *Follow-Up to the Green Paper*, COM (2002)289 Final, indicated a preference for a general framework law on fairness

In particular, the Commission proposes that both existing and new Community legislation should move away from the current practice of minimum harmonisation. For example, the *Consumer Policy Strategy 2002–2006* states that, in proposing amendments to the Timeshare and Package Travel Directives,[79] one of the Commission's reform priorities will be the achievement of total harmonisation.[80] In its 2001 proposal for a regulation concerning sales promotions in the Internal Market, the Commission argues for uniform consumer protection rules across the Member States, with no possibility of adopting more stringent domestic standards. Indeed, the Commission specifically identifies those existing national practices it believed were unduly protective of consumers, and as regards which the proposed regulation would require Member States to harmonise downwards.[81] Similarly, in its 2003 proposal for a framework directive on unfair business-to-consumer commercial practices, the Commission argues for a model based on fully pre-emptive harmonisation as regards essential consumer protection standards, coupled with full mutual recognition as regards extraneous regulatory provisions.[82] Thus, it might appear that the Community's long tradition of minimum harmonisation as regards the protection of consumers' economic interests is under serious threat.

Clearly, the Commission's view of the consequences of minimum harmonisation seems highly orthodox. Any difference in national law capable of erecting barriers to free movement or distorting the conditions of competition is viewed in a dim light. Uniformity of regulation across the Single Market (in particular, through the pre-emptive harmonisation of essential public interest requirements, coupled with full mutual recognition of all remaining national rules) is presented as the end-goal of Community policy. Although the Commission pays lip-service to the idea that consumer protection is a 'shared responsibility' and a 'collective endeavour,' it clearly believes that in many cases regulatory diversity

in consumer transactions, combined (where necessary) with more detailed sectoral measures. That is now reflected in Commission, *Proposal for a Directive Concerning Unfair Business-to-Consumer Commercial Practices in the Internal Market*, COM (2003)356 Final.

[79] Dir 94/47 on the protection of purchasers in respect of certain aspects of contracts relating to the purchase of the right to use immovable properties on a timeshare basis, OJ 1994 L280/83; Dir 90/314 on package travel, package holidays and package tours, OJ 1990 L158/59 (respectively).

[80] Commission, *Consumer Policy Strategy 2002–2006*, COM (2002)208 Final, para 3.1.2.2. This antipathy towards minimum harmonisation as regards consumer protection directives is also evident in the Commission's *Follow-Up to the Green Paper*, COM (2002)289 Final.

[81] Commission, *Proposal for a Regulation Concerning Sales Promotions in the Internal Market*, COM (2001)546 Final.

[82] Commission, *Proposal for a Directive Concerning Unfair Business-To-Consumer Commercial Practices in the Internal Market*, COM (2003)356 Final.

(including minimum harmonisation) is suffered only until the Member States can be brought back to their *communautaire* senses.[83] At the very least, the Commission seems optimistic about the prospects of doing so, particularly post-enlargement into Central and Eastern Europe, when the institutional challenges of negotiating any uniform regulatory standards might seem even more daunting. More fundamentally, the Commission appears deaf to those voices which highlight the positive virtues of differentiation in the legal management of the Single Market. One might have expected that the goals of adapting common principles to local preferences, and maintaining a healthy stock of legal ideas through which to encourage mutual learning, to win greater favour with the authors of the 2001 *White Paper on European Governance*.[84]

Regulatory differentiation within the context of Community consumer policy is particularly vulnerable to adverse institutional responses because its primary legal basis remains Article 95 EC—and Community regulatory activity thus lacks the constitutional guarantee of minimum harmonisation which is enjoyed by sectors such as environmental protection under Article 176 EC, or social policy under Article 137 EC.[85] But even within the Internal Market core, the trend can swing both ways. For example, we saw in Chapter 3 how Regulation 1/2003 will have an important impact upon the relationship between Community and national competition rules in cross-border cases: as regards Article 81 EC, the Regulation reinforces uniformity by reducing still further the potential for domestic law to reach different outcomes from Community law; but as regards Article 82 EC, the Regulation explicitly provides that Member States can apply more stringent rules prohibiting unilateral abuse of a dominant position—thereby increasing the potential for (albeit still limited) differentiation in this field.[86]

THE ENFORCEMENT DEFICIT DEBATE: AN ALTERNATIVE SECTORAL MODEL

There may well be constitutional and political limits to how deeply regulatory flexibility can penetrate the Community legal order. The balance

[83] Commission, *Consumer Policy Strategy 2002–2006*, COM (2002)208 Final, para 2.1.

[84] COM (2001)428 Final. In any case, a move to total harmonisation rather than minimum harmonisation in consumer protection measures raises other difficult issues, in particular, about the substantive nature of Community policy in this field, once the Community sets itself up as the sole regulator. Further, eg G Howells and T Wilhelmsson, 'EC Consumer Law: Has it Come of Age?' (2003) 28 EL Rev 370.

[85] Further, eg P Rott, 'Minimum Harmonisation for the Completion of the Internal Market: The Example of Consumer Sales Law' (2003) 40 CML Rev 1107.

[86] Reg 1/2003 on the implementation of the rules on competition laid down in Articles 81 and 82 of the Treaty, OJ 2003 L1/1.

between uniformity and disintegration may well prove unstable, and institutional attitudes can certainly seem unpredictable. Nevertheless, it has become difficult to speak of regulatory differentiation as some regrettable anomaly. This is true not only in terms of political reality or intellectual pragmatism, but also as a matter of legal doctrine and in the light of the parameters established by primary provisions of the Treaty itself (such as Article 5 EC).

Instead, differentiation must be understood both as a symptom of fundamental restructuring within the European Union, and also as a cause of constitutional revision within the Community legal order itself. Accordingly, both the responsible institutional actors and interested academic commentators should reconsider those aspects of the relationship between Community and domestic law which no longer reflect the underlying character of the Treaty system, by reason of their undue emphasis on the imperative of uniformity, and thereby of their demands for an unnecessarily intrusive quantity and quality of Community regulatory action—albeit balanced against the need to ensure that regulatory differentiation does not threaten certain irreducible interests embedded within the Community legal order. This section proposes how such a process of doctrinal reconsideration and adaptation might extend to the supposedly fundamental Community concerns which continue to structure debate about the nature of the enforcement deficit.

A 'Sectoral Approach' To Community Intervention in Domestic Remedies and Procedural Rules

The most obvious implication of differentiation for the development of an updated conceptual framework when approaching the Community's enforcement deficit concerns the imperative of uniformity. From the survey conducted in Chapter 3, it is clear that phenomena such as minimum rather than total harmonisation, the tolerance of frequent and far-reaching derogations, a preference for loose-knit regulation through the employment of framework directives etc, all combine to produce a situation in which any general principle of uniformity in the Community legal order is rendered somewhat illusory. As observed above, this situation has prompted a response from the 'integration through law' school: diversity in the substantive content of Treaty rules should strengthen, not weaken, the Community's determination to regulate national procedural rules, since a harmonised remedial regime for the decentralised enforcement of Community law would help to counter or at least limit the detrimental effects for the uniform application of Treaty norms which result from increasing degrees of substantive fragmentation.

However, one can now appreciate that this 'integration through law' interpretation of the relationship between differentiation and the enforcement deficit suffers from serious weaknesses. In particular, it is out of step with the modern development of both the Community and its legal order. Continual integration no longer represents the consensus viewpoint on Europe's future, such as could justify portraying differentiation as an unfortunate deviation from the path towards uniformity of regulatory burdens for economic actors within the Common Market and/or equality of rights for individual citizens, and thus as an extraneous attack on the only viable constitutional values the Treaty system possesses. It is instead clear that uniformity is neither a general principle nor even a primary goal of the Community legal order, and can no longer be portrayed as a blanket justification for pursuing the maximum possible degree of harmonisation. Thus, it seems difficult to find any sound conceptual rationale for some grand scheme to create a unified system of judicial protection in Europe by harmonising the remedies and procedural rules applicable to the decentralised enforcement of Community law.

But, keeping in mind the goal of 'managing' the implications of regulatory differentiation, this is resolutely not to say that the imperative of uniformity has become redundant. The point is rather that the Community has evolved into a more complex entity than 'integration through law' permits, characterised by varying degrees of integration and differentiation across different policy fields. As such, uniformity is now possessed of only relative merit, and the policy framework surrounding the debate about national remedies and procedures should display greater sensitivity towards this fact. It is therefore suggested that uniformity should be interpreted at a sectoral level—selectively matching the required level of remedial and procedural harmonisation to the actual degree of substantive approximation achieved within any given policy area, and therefore to the variegated nature of the Community's current programmes for supranational integration.

Sectors Characterised By Substantive Uniformity

Thus, in some such sectors—generally those closely connected to the functioning of the Internal Market—the Community does continue to insist upon the creation and maintenance of a high degree of substantive uniformity. We saw in Chapter 3 how this was true of the competition regime under Articles 81 and 82 EC, which is essential to the goal of market integration and the creation of a genuine level playing-field among economic operators.[87] In this situation, one concedes that the goal of

[87] Further: ch 3 (above).

uniformity lying at the heart of Community regulation is threatened by significant variations in the relevant legal frameworks subsisting at the national level, and that this is true as much of remedial as of substantive rules. Indeed, competition lawyers have for some time complained about discrepancies in domestic procedural rules giving rise to distortions in the conditions for enforcement of Articles 81 and 82 EC, and the concomitant risk of forum-shopping by undertakings across the Member States.[88] In principle, Community legislation harmonising the procedures available for decentralised enforcement might therefore seem entirely appropriate. This is particularly true in the light of the modernisation of competition enforcement initiated by the Commission's 1999 White Paper,[89] and culminating in Regulation 1/2003.[90]

Under Regulation 17/62, the system for enforcing Community competition policy was semi-centralised.[91] Articles 81(1) and (2) EC, the block exemptions for certain categories of agreements and practices, and Article 82 EC in its entirety had direct effect and could be enforced by the national competition authorities and before the domestic courts (as well as by the Commission undertaking its own investigations).[92] However, only the Commission had competence to grant individual exemptions under Article 81(3); and only agreements/practices which were notified to the Commission (or were specifically exempted from the requirement of notification) could be considered for such exemption. According to the 1999 White Paper, this system played a necessary role in the development of European competition policy. At a time when both competition law and Single Market integration were in their infancy, semi-centralised enforcement enabled the Commission to develop a uniform body of principles on the application of Article 81 EC which could be applied across the

[88] Eg R Whish, 'The Enforcement of EC Competition Law in the Domestic Courts of Member States' [1994] ECLR 60; L Hiljemark, 'Enforcement of EC Competition Law in National Courts: The Perspective of Judicial Protection' (1997) 17 *Yearbook of European Law* 83; S Kon and A Maxwell, 'Enforcement in National Courts of the EC and New UK Competition Rules: Obstacles to Effective Enforcement' [1998] ECLR 443.

[89] Commission, *White Paper on Modernisation of the Rules Implementing Articles 81 and 82 of the EC Treaty*, OJ 1999 C132/1. For critical assessment, eg A Klimisch and B Krueger, 'Decentralised Application of EC Competition Law: Current Practice and Future Prospects' (1999) 24 EL Rev 463; J Nazerali and D Cowan, 'Modernising the Enforcement of EU Competition Rules: Can the Commission Claim to be Preaching to the Converted?' [1999] ECLR 442; B Rodger, 'The Commission White Paper on Modernisation of the Rules Implementing Articles 81 and 82 of the EC Treaty' (1999) 24 EL Rev 653; R Wesseling, 'The Commission White Paper on Modernisation of EC Antitrust Law: Unspoken Consequences and Incomplete Treatment of Alternative Options' [1999] ECLR 420.

[90] Reg 1/2003 on the implementation of the rules on competition laid down in Articles 81 and 82 of the Treaty, OJ 2003 L1/1. For a general overview, eg R Whish, *Competition Law* (Butterworths, 2003) chs 7 and 8.

[91] Reg 17/62 implementing Articles 81 and 82 of the Treaty, OJ Special English Edition 1959–62 (Series I) 87.

[92] In particular: Case 127/73 *BRT v SABAM* [1974] ECR 51.

entire territory of the Community; to raise the profile of this relatively new body of law among Europe's business and legal communities, creating a culture of compliance or at least awareness which fostered the development of an effective competition system; to become acquainted with the existing structure of production and distribution networks across Europe and therefore to identify those agreements or practices which constituted real barriers to effective competition and economic integration; and to keep up-to-date with changing patterns in such production and distribution networks, by shadowing the Member State and Community markets as they evolved over the past several decades.

However, the 1999 White Paper argued that the semi-centralised enforcement system—and especially the process of notification and exemption—was no longer appropriate to the modern Community's needs. This was so for two sets of reasons. First, it was no longer clear that the system established by Regulation 17/62 worked well in practice. The Commission's monopoly over individual exemptions under Article 81(3) EC had led to excessively large numbers of agreements being notified to the Commission—far more than could be settled by formal decision, leading to an explosion in the issue of informal 'comfort letters'. Moreover, this workload was not just a serious drain on Commission resources; it was also largely unproductive in terms of identifying priorities for the development of Community competition policy. Most of the agreements notified to the Commission posed no genuine threat to healthy competition or market integration; serious restraints on trade tended in practice not to be notified to the Commission at all, but to be revealed through complaints and investigations. In any case, the Commission's monopoly had encouraged abuse by large companies seeking to block the progress of decentralised actions before the national courts by arguing that exemption was possible, and proceedings should therefore be stayed until the Commission had adopted a final decision under Article 81(3) EC.

Secondly, the Commission argued that its own role had to change to meet the requirements of a more mature Community. On the one hand, progressive enlargement of the Community and the growing complexity of commercial agreements in an increasingly integrated European market meant that more and more agreements fell within the scope of Article 81 EC and required exemption under Article 81(3) EC—exasperating the problems posed by Regulation 17/62 itself. On the other hand, the basic principles of Community competition policy were well established, and their profile among Europe's industrial and legal communities was now beyond doubt. In such circumstances, the burden of enforcement could indeed be shared with the national administrative and judicial authorities without risking any adverse impact upon the overall coherency and uniform application of the Treaty rules. This would leave the Commission free to devote its resources to issues of particular legal and economic importance for the Community (such as cross-border cartels).

The White Paper argued that it was no longer possible to maintain a semi-centralised enforcement system, requiring a decision from the Commission before Article 81(3) EC exemptions could be granted, and therefore proposed radical reform: abolition of the entire notification system, and abolition of the Commission's monopoly over individual exemptions, thus permitting the fully decentralised enforcement of Articles 81 and 82 EC by the domestic administrative and judicial authorities. These proposals were intended to free up the Commission's resources to deal with the most serious infringements of Community competition policy, and exploit the full potential of the Member States as vehicles for the effective enforcement of the Treaty rules. The White Paper led to a formal Commission proposal for a new competition enforcement regulation.[93] This proposal was adopted by the Council (with certain modifications) as Regulation 1/2003, which entered into force on 1 May 2004 (replacing Regulation 17/62 in its entirety). Articles 1, 5 and 6 of the Regulation indeed provide for the full direct effect of Articles 81 and 82 EC—permitting the national competition authorities and courts to apply the conditions for exemption under Article 81(3) EC. And notification to the Commission, as a precondition for individual exemption, has been abolished in its entirety.

But the White Paper also recognised that reform might exasperate certain problems posed by decentralised enforcement, in particular, in ensuring the uniform application of Community competition rules across the Member States. Regulation 1/2003 therefore contains mechanisms to ensure greater coherence within the enforcement network. For example, Article 11 requires domestic competition authorities to cooperate closely with the Commission (by informing the latter of any investigation under Article 81 or 82 EC, and by consulting the Commission before adopting certain decisions); and further provides that the initiation of proceedings by the Commission shall extinguish the competence of the domestic competition authorities over the same matter.[94] Similarly, Article 15 provides for cooperation between the domestic courts and the Commission (by notifying the latter of judgments applying Article 81 or 82 EC, and by

[93] Commission, *Proposal for a Council Regulation on the Implementation of the Rules on Competition Laid Down in Articles 81 and 82 of the Treaty*, COM (2000)582 Final. For critical assessment, eg W Möschel, 'Change of Policy in European Competition Law?' (2000) 37 CML Rev 495; C-D Ehlermann, 'The Modernisation of EC Anti-Trust Policy: A Legal and Cultural Revolution' (2000) 37 CML Rev 537; R Wesseling, 'The Draft Regulation Modernising the Competition Rules: The Commission is Married to One Idea' (2001) 26 EL Rev 357; J Bourgeois and C Humpe, 'The Commission's "New Regulation 17"' [2002] ECLR 43.

[94] Consider the guidance set out by the Commission, *Notice on Cooperation Within the Network of Competition Authorities*, OJ 2004 C101/43.

permitting the Commission to submit written and, with the permission of the competent tribunal, oral observations during the course of domestic court proceedings). Furthermore, Article 16 reminds the national authorities and competent courts of their general obligation to refrain from taking any measure which would conflict with decisions already adopted by the Commission; and the domestic courts of their particular obligation to avoid delivering judgments which would conflict with any decision being contemplated by the Commission (if necessary by considering whether it is necessary to stay proceedings).[95]

However, the new Regulation has been criticised for not going far enough to ensure the uniform and coherent application of Community competition rules. Problems have been identified on three levels. The first concerns the substantive content of Community competition law itself. Some commentators see it as inevitable that any decentralised enforcement system will increase the input of the national competition authorities and domestic courts into the development of Community policy, and thereby lead to certain variations in the substantive legal rules applicable within each Member State.[96] Others believe this need not necessarily be a bad thing: the scope for greater experimentation in finding appropriate solutions to regulatory needs, and the potential for mutual learning between actors within the network, indeed justify some loss of uniformity.[97] That may well be true, but it would nevertheless represent a shift away from the current model. And given the Commission's insistence that decentralisation should not lead to the fragmentation of Community competition policy, such a shift would also appear to be unintended.[98]

The second level concerns problems associated with case allocation—focusing on the complicated relationship between the overlapping jurisdictions of the Commission and the national authorities/courts, and especially the overlapping jurisdictions of the competent Member State institutions *inter se*. For example, if an agreement is made between undertakings established in several Member States, which domestic competition authorities will have jurisdiction? And what if different national competition authorities in different Member States reach

[95] Cf Case C–234/89 *Delimitis* [1991] ECR I–935; Case C–344/98 *Masterfoods* [2000] ECR I–11369. Also: Commission, *Notice on Cooperation Between National Courts and the Commission In Applying Articles 81 and 82 EC*, OJ 1993 C39/6; Commission, *Notice on the Cooperation Between the Commission and the Courts of the EU Member States in the Application of Articles 81 and 82 EC*, OJ 2004 C101/54.

[96] Eg H Gilliams, 'Modernisation: From Policy to Practice' (2003) 28 EL Rev 451.

[97] Eg J Venit, 'Brave New World: The Modernisation and Decentralisation of Enforcement Under Articles 81 and 82 of the EC Treaty' (2003) 40 CML Rev 545. Further: D Geradin, 'Competition Between Rules and Rules of Competition: A Legal and Economic Analysis of the Proposed Modernisation of the Enforcement of EC Competition Law' (2002) 9 *Columbia Journal of European Law* 1.

[98] In particular: Commission, *White Paper on Modernisation of the Rules Implementing Articles 81 and 82 of the EC Treaty*, OJ 1999 C132/1.

conflicting decisions on the application of the Treaty rules to the same agreement or practice? Articles 11 and 12 Regulation 1/2003 seek to address such problems by encouraging cooperation and shared information between the domestic competition authorities. Moreover, Article 13 provides that, where two or more domestic competition authorities are dealing with the same agreement or practice, the fact that one body is dealing (or has already dealt) with the case shall be sufficient grounds for the other/s to suspend proceedings or reject the complaint. The Commission may also reject a complaint on the ground that the domestic competition authority is dealing (or has dealt) with the case.[99] But declining jurisdiction in this manner is voluntary, not mandatory, and many commentators believe that the system therefore does genuinely risk different authorities reaching different decisions as regards the compatibility with the Treaty of one and the same agreement.[100] Only as a last resort can the problem be solved through binding intervention by the Commission itself under Article 11, so as to extinguish altogether the concurrent competence of the domestic enforcement agencies. The position as regards national courts is no less difficult: although the jurisdictional rules contained in Regulation 44/2001 will help allocate disputes between national courts in certain situations,[101] the possibility of multiple actions based upon the same agreement or practice being heard across different Member States is mitigated primarily by the voluntary cooperation of the domestic judges *inter se*. The option of binding intervention from the centre is also available—but this time, the Commission cannot automatically divest national courts of their jurisdiction from the outset of its own investigation; Article 16 Regulation 1/2003 merely debars the domestic judges from adopting a different conclusion from that already reached or now being contemplated by the Commission.[102]

The third layer of problems brings us back to more familiar territory. The tension between encouraging increased decentralisation of enforcement while still maintaining uniformity of substantive policy focuses attention on the case for some sectoral harmonisation of domestic remedies and procedures. This issue was not addressed in the 1999 White Paper itself, but the prospect of procedural harmonisation was raised during the consultation process which followed.[103] Any general

[99] Again, consider the guidance set out by the Commission, *Notice on Cooperation Within the Network of Competition Authorities*, OJ 2004 C101/43.

[100] Eg J Nazerali and D Cowan, 'Modernising the Enforcement of EU Competition Rules: Can the Commission Claim to be Preaching to the Converted?' [1999] ECLR 442; B Rodger, 'The Commission White Paper on Modernisation of the Rules Implementing Articles 81 and 82 of the EC Treaty' (1999) 24 EL Rev 653.

[101] Reg 44/2001 on jurisdiction and the recognition and enforcement of judgments in civil and commercial matters, OJ 2001 L12/1, esp Arts 27–31.

[102] H Gilliams, 'Modernisation: From Policy to Practice' (2003) 28 EL Rev 451.

[103] Part 8.2 of the Commission's *Summary of Observations on the White Paper* (29 February 2000).

programme of procedural harmonisation, to be achieved during the modernisation process, was rejected by the Commission in its 2000 proposal for a new enforcement regulation (perhaps because it believed that would seriously delay and unduly complicate the reform process).[104] Regulation 1/2003 does contain limited provisions concerning remedies and procedural rules. For example, Article 2 states that, in any proceedings (Community or domestic) for the application of Articles 81 and 82 EC, the burden of proving an infringement of Article 81(1) or 82 EC shall rest on the party or authority alleging the infringement; whereas the undertaking or association claiming the benefit of Article 81(3) EC shall bear the burden of proving that the conditions for exemption are fulfilled. Nevertheless, many commentators still feel that greater Community intervention in the national systems of judicial protection is an essential precondition to striking a successful balance between greater decentralisation and continuing uniformity in Community competition policy: for example, as regards the availability of remedies such as interim relief, compensatory damages, punitive damages and restitutionary actions; and in respect of procedural rules such as limitation periods, the discovery of documents and the admissibility of evidence.[105] As we shall see later, the question remains: might this apparent 'enforcement deficit' be fixed, even in the absence of harmonising legislation, through the caselaw of the Court of Justice?[106]

A similar picture emerges from the state aids sector. We saw in Chapter 3 how the substantive rules created under Articles 87-88 EC are also defined by a high degree of regulatory uniformity, which is again essential to the creation of a genuine level playing-field among undertakings operating within the Single Market. We also saw how, to an even greater degree than Community competition law, the application of the state aids regime has traditionally been characterised by a strict division of competence between the Commission and the national authorities (including the domestic courts). Against that background, one concedes that the goal of uniformity lying at the heart of Community state aids regulation is

[104] Part 3 of the Explanatory Memorandum: COM (2000)582 Final.

[105] Further, eg M Todino, 'Modernisation From the Perspective of National Competition Authorities: Impact of the Reform on Decentralised Application of EC Competition Law' [2000] ECLR 348; S Kingston, 'A "New Division of Responsibilities" in the Proposed Regulation to Modernise the Rules Implementing Articles 81 and 82 EC? A Warning Call' [2001] ECLR 340; F Louis, 'Les conséquences pratiques de la réforme envisagée par le Livre Blanc de la Commission' [2001] *Cahiers de droit européen* 218; J Venit, 'Brave New World: The Modernisation and Decentralisation of Enforcement Under Articles 81 and 82 of the EC Treaty' (2003) 40 CML Rev 545. Consider, in particular, W van Gerven, 'Substantive Remedies for the Private Enforcement of EC Antitrust Rules Before National Courts' in C-D Ehlermann & I Atanasiu (eds), *European Competition Law Annual 2001* (Hart Publishing, 2003).

[106] Further: ch 6 (below).

threatened by significant variations in the remedies and procedural rules applicable at the national level. In principle, harmonisation therefore seems entirely appropriate.

As with competition law, the Commission's desire to reduce its own crippling workload, and concentrate on only the most serious infringements of the state aids rules, has encouraged a process of greater decentralised enforcement. In particular, Regulation 994/98 empowered the Commission to adopt group exemption regulations declaring that certain categories of aid are compatible with the Common Market within the meaning of Article 87 EC, and should not be subject to the notification and standstill requirements contained in Article 88(3) EC.[107] The Commission has since adopted block exemptions on matters such as training aid,[108] aid to small and medium-sized enterprises,[109] and employment aid.[110] These block exemptions dilute the Commission's ability to ensure the compatibility of proposed aid measures with Community law based upon the traditional system of *ex ante* monitoring and assessment. Conversely, the exemption regulations increase the responsibilities of the national judges, in the *ex post* enforcement of the state aids regime, during legal challenges brought by disgruntled competitors. It remains the case that a domestic court cannot make its own autonomous assessment of whether state aid is compatible with the Common Market in accordance with Article 87 EC. But the national judge is now required to analyse whether the disputed measure complies with the detailed substantive provisions of the relevant exemption regulation, before being able to assess whether that measure constitutes irregular state aid adopted in breach of the notification and standstill requirements under Article 88(3).[111]

Reform of the state aids regime gives rise to the same dilemma as modernisation of the competition rules. While greater decentralisation might be necessary to relieve the Commission of its unfeasible administrative burdens, it increases the risk that the application and enforcement of

[107] Reg 994/98 on the application of Articles 87 and 88 of the Treaty to certain categories of horizontal state aid, OJ 1998 L142/1.

[108] Reg 68/2001 on the application of Articles 87 and 88 of the EC Treaty to training aid, OJ 2001 L10/20.

[109] Reg 70/2001 on the application of Articles 87 and 88 of the EC Treaty to State aid to small and medium-sized enterprises, OJ 2001 L10/33.

[110] Reg 2204/2002 on the application of Articles 87 and 88 of the EC Treaty to State aid for employment, OJ 2002 L337/3.

[111] Further: M Ross, 'State Aids and National Courts: Definitions and Other Problems—A Case of Premature Emancipation?' (2000) 37 CML Rev 401; A Sinnaeve, 'Block Exemptions for State Aid: More Scope for State Aid Control by Member States and Competitors' (2001) 38 CML Rev 1479. Reg 994/98 also empowered the Commission to adopt a regulation defining certain state aids which are deemed not to meet all the criteria of Article 87(1) EC, and are thus exempted from the procedural controls contained in Article 88(3) EC; see Reg 69/2001 on *de minimis* aids, OJ 2001 L10/30.

Articles 87 and 88 EC will be fragmented across the Member States. Indeed, as decentralised enforcement of the state aids rules becomes more common, the case for a sectoral harmonisation of national remedies and procedural rules grows stronger: for example, to establish uniform conditions for the recovery of irregular and unlawful state aids from their beneficiaries; and common rules on supplementary remedies, such as injunctions and damages actions, against the Member State and / or the beneficiary.

In this regard, it is true that Regulation 659/1999 sets out certain principles regarding the procedural framework for dealing with state aids.[112] For example, Article 11(2) provides that the Commission may, under specified conditions, adopt decisions requiring the Member State provisionally to recover state aid granted in breach of the notification or standstill obligations contained in Article 88(3) EC, pending a final decision on its compatibility with the Common Market. However, this power is without prejudice to the obligation of the national courts, in cases of non-compliance with the procedural requirements of Article 88(3) EC, to take all measures necessary under domestic law to protect the rights of interested parties.[113] The Regulation does not contain any detailed provisions governing discharge of that autonomous obligation relating, in particular, to the remedies and procedural rules expected under Community law.

Moreover, Article 14(1) states that, where the Commission adopts a negative decision finding state aid to be incompatible with the Common Market, it shall order the Member State to take all necessary measures to recover the aid from its beneficiary.[114] But the implementation of recovery decisions under Article 14(1) (and indeed of recovery injunctions under Article 11(2)) shall be effected in accordance with the relevant national legal system, provided that the latter allows for the immediate and effective execution of the Commission's decision.[115] Again, the Regulation falls silent when it comes to the detailed conditions imposed by Community law for enforcing Commission decisions before the domestic courts. As with competition law, the Community legislature therefore seems to have snubbed demand for greater Community intervention in the national systems of judicial protection, so as to preserve the substantive uniformity of

[112] Reg 659/1999 laying down detailed rules for the application of Article 88 of the EC Treaty, OJ 1999 L83/1. Further, eg A Sinnaeve and PJ Slot, 'The New Regulation on State Aid Procedures' (1999) 36 CML Rev 1153.
[113] Cf Case C–354/90 *FNCE ('French Salmon')* [1991] ECR I–5505; Case C–39/94 *SFEI* [1996] ECR I–3547. Further: ch 6 (below).
[114] Unless this would be contrary to a general principle of Community law.
[115] Arts 11(2) and 14(3).

the Treaty's state aids rules.[116] All eyes turn once again to the Court, if a genuine 'enforcement deficit' is to be avoided.

Sectors Characterised By Regulatory Differentiation

By contrast, in other sectors of Community activity, it seems more difficult to argue that regulatory uniformity constitutes an absolute or even significant objective of the Treaty's policy activities. As regards welfare-orientated fields such as environmental, consumer and employee protection, the interaction between Community and national authorities in determining substantive policy (through the use of minimum harmonisation, the grant of derogations etc) means that the latter will differ from Member State to Member State—both tolerating and legitimising cross-border variations in the compliance costs actually suffered by different groups of economic undertaking, and in the levels of protection actually enjoyed by different categories of Union citizen. In turn, this makes it much more difficult to identify a single Community substantive regime the uniformity of which is necessarily undermined by the lack of a harmonised Community remedial regime applicable to decentralised enforcement before the national courts. And if the Treaty has no real or immediate ambition to establish a completely uniform substantive regime in fields such as environmental, consumer or employee policy, why should the Community nevertheless harbour any real or immediate ambition to establish a completely uniform set of remedial and procedural provisions?

This challenge to the legitimacy of an 'integration through law' approach to national remedies and procedural rules in an era of Community-sanctioned regulatory differentiation is reinforced by the demands of subsidiarity and proportionality. If the Community's programme of environmental, consumer or employee protection is based around a general policy, for example, of minimum harmonisation admitting of more stringent national welfare standards, the Community has clearly admitted that its goal here is only the partial unification of the relevant substantive regimes, and that there is scope for variation between the Member States as regards the compliance costs actually suffered by different groups of economic undertaking, and the levels of protection actually enjoyed by different categories of citizen. For the Community nevertheless to insist that these partially harmonised rights be accompanied by fully harmonised remedies and procedural rules would surely represent Treaty action going further than is necessary to achieve its own objectives.

[116] Further: M Karpenschif, 'La récupération des aides nationales versées en violation du droit communautaire à l'aune du règlement no. 659/1999: du mythe à la réalité?' (2001) 37 *Revue trimestrielle de droit européen* 551.

Thus, the putative 'integration through law' agenda of redoubling the Community's efforts at greater remedial harmonisation in the face of spreading patterns of regulatory differentiation would appear in contravention of the principles set out in Article 5 EC.

Difficulties Posed by a Sectoral Understanding of the Imperative of Uniformity

However, this idea of a sectoral approach to the Community's enforcement deficit poses certain problems. These difficulties can be organised under three main headings: first, a practicability critique based on the difficulties of actually defining the requisite sectors of Treaty activity with any satisfactory degree of certainty; secondly, a policy critique inspired by Weatherill's identification of an implementation imbalance in EC law; and thirdly, the questions which arise as regards the residual role to be performed within any sectoral model by the imperative of effectiveness.

Practicability Critique: Defining the Requisite Sectors

On the one hand, adopting a sectoral analysis might seem to resolve, or at least to mitigate, certain of the doubts which have been raised in the past about the practicability of Community interference in the domestic judicial systems. For example, a frequent objection to the sort of all-embracing programme for judicial or remedial harmonisation advocated by an 'integration through law' analysis is that such a task would prove incapable of realistic achievement. A sectoral understanding of the enforcement deficit takes the sting from the tail of this objection without having to enter into discussion of the sort of complicated imponderables required to address it on its own terms: as has been observed, there is simply no need for general harmonisation of the European legal or remedial systems, because in most cases the Community itself has no real interest in pursuing any unified system of judicial protection.

On the other hand, the notion of a sectoral approach generates logistical reservations of its own. In particular, how does one actually define a 'sector' for the purposes of examining the extent of the Treaty's interest in substantive uniformity, and therefore of the appropriate need for remedial harmonisation? The preceding paragraphs have referred to 'sectors' as if they were self-evident units of Treaty policymaking and legislative activity, and there is an undoubted convenience in dividing the Community's activities into manageable conceptual compartments such as 'competition policy,' 'state aids,' 'environmental protection,' 'consumer protection' or 'social policy.' However, the reality is much more complicated than such a scheme admits: the idea of a discrete sector of

Community policy which can be marked off from all others by clearly ascertainable boundaries is in many respects unsustainable; postulating the appropriate level of abstraction at which any sort of sectoral analysis should take place is therefore an inherently troublesome task.

This problem is acutely illustrated by the case of the 'Single Market'. Application of the primary Treaty provisions on free movement requires the Court to balance the demands of greater market integration (by dismantling divergent national rules which hinder cross-border trade) against the need for continuing market regulation (by respecting domestic legislation which performs a socially useful function), and thus to articulate both the welfare goals recognised as worthwhile under the Treaty, and their value relative to the efficient operation of the Internal Market—including (for example) environmental, consumer and employee protection.[117] This complex intertwining of apparently sectoral Treaty objectives is further illustrated by recent developments on free movement for persons. The Court has accepted that Article 18 EC creates a right to move and reside freely across the Member States for Union citizens, irrespective of their economic status and therefore of their contribution to the process of market integration.[118] Together with the introduction of Title IV EC on Visas, Asylum and Immigration, and the commitment to creating an Area of Freedom, Justice and Security, this confirms that the *acquis communautaire* on free movement for persons must now be located within a broader policy framework than the Internal Market alone. Even competition policy—a Treaty competence with Common Market credentials *par excellence*—finds itself increasingly expected to renegotiate its own turf with competing social policy concerns, as (for example) in caselaw excluding the application of Article 81 EC to collective agreements between management and labour which seek to create high levels of employment protection, and thus to advance the welfare objectives set out in Article 2 EC.[119]

[117] Eg Case 120/78 *'Cassis de Dijon'* [1979] ECR 649; Case 178/84 *Commission v Germany* [1987] ECR 1227; Case 302/86 *Commission v Denmark* [1988] ECR 4607; Cases C–369 & 376/96 *Arblade and Leloup* [1999] ECR I–8453. In particular: Case C–2/90 *Commission v Belgium (Wallonian Waste)* [1992] ECR I–4431; Case C–379/98 *PreussenElektra* [2001] ECR I–2099. Further: ch 2 (above).

[118] Though still subject to certain requirements of financial independence. In particular: Case C–413/99 *Baumbast* [2002] ECR I–7091; Case C–456/02 *Trojani* (Judgment of 7 September 2004). Further: M Dougan and E Spaventa, 'Educating Rudy and the (Non-)English Patient: A Double Bill on Residency Rights Under Article 18 EC' (2003) 28 EL Rev 699. See now: Dir 2004/38 on the right of citizens of the Union and their family members to move and reside freely within the territory of the Member States, OJ 2004 L158/77.

[119] Eg Case C–67/96 *Albany International* [1999] ECR I–5751; Cases C–115–17/97 *Brentjens' Handelsonderneming* [1999] ECR I–6025; Case C–219/97 *Maatschappij Drijvende Bokken* [1999] ECR I–6121; Cases C–180–84/98 *Pavel Pavlov* [2000] ECR I–6451; Case C–222/98 *van der Woude* [2000] ECR I–7111. Further, eg R Van den Bergh and P Camesasca, 'Irreconcilable Principles? The Court of Justice Exempts Collective Labour Agreements From the Wrath of Anti-Trust' (2000) 25 EL Rev 492. Consider also the judgment in Case C–309/99 *Wouters*

Moreover, as regards secondary legislation, it will be recalled that many of the Community's welfare-orientated competences originally developed as off-shoots from the Common Market. This was so in terms of both their rationale (as the logical extension of a process of economic integration which sought to minimise discrepancies of regulatory burden) and their legal basis (as harmonisation measures adopted under Articles 94 and 95 EC). A significant number of Community acts which we have grown accustomed to think of as 'environmental', 'consumer' or 'social' legislation were therefore introduced to pursue economic as well as welfare objectives, and cannot easily be assigned to one policy sphere or another.[120] It is true that the old 'flanking policies' have now been granted autonomous legal bases of their own within the Treaty.[121] However, this apparent separation of policy sectors is often more a matter of form than of substance. Many Community initiatives still pursue not only a welfare but also an economic objective, such as potentially to straddle more than one legal basis. Moreover, the guidelines developed by the Court of Justice to ascertain the correct legal basis for any given measure mean that the dividing line between formal Treaty sectors may well be difficult to draw.[122] The problem is exacerbated by the fact that the Community is expressly required to pursue high standards of protection for interests such as the environment, consumers and public health not only through their own autonomous legal bases, but also by integrating these objectives into all other initiatives pursued under authority of the Treaty.[123] This legal framework perhaps explains how, for example, Community consumer policy continues to rely chiefly on the Internal Market legislative competences provided under Articles 94 and 95 EC, despite the opportunities for regulatory action provided under the designated Treaty title on Consumer Policy.[124] Thus, legal basis alone is not a reliable test for defining with a satisfactory degree of clarity the scope of any given sector of Community activity, or for determining whether any particular legislative measure falls within or outside that sector's purported boundaries.

[2002] ECR I–1577; as discussed by, eg G Monti, 'Article 81 EC and Public Policy' (2002) 39 CML Rev 1057.

[120] Further: ch 2 (above).
[121] Eg Title XIX EC on environmental policy; Title XIV EC on consumer policy; Title XI EC on social policy.
[122] In particular: Case C–155/91 *Commission v Council (Waste Directive)* [1993] ECR I–939. More recently, eg Case C–376/98 *Germany v Parliament and Council (Tobacco Advertising Directive)* [2000] ECR I–8419. Contrast with the previous approach in Case C–300/89 *Commission v Council (Titanium Dioxide)* [1991] ECR I–2867.
[123] Arts 6, 153(2) and 152(1) EC (respectively). Also: Art 95(3) EC.
[124] Further: J Stuyck, 'European Consumer Law After the Treaty of Amsterdam: Consumer Policy In or Beyond the Internal Market?' (2000) 37 CML Rev 367. One notable exception is Dir 98/6 on consumer protection in the indication of the prices of products offered to consumers, OJ 1998 L80/27, which was indeed adopted under Art 153 EC.

Even having defined a particular sector and ascertained those measures which it should properly be understood to comprise, it does not necessarily follow that analysis of the relevant Treaty provisions and secondary measures will yield a homogenous or consistent degree of approximation/ differentiation. For example, when defining the scope of the Community's employee protection competence (whether viewed through the prism of the Internal Market, or as an autonomous policy basis in its own right), one might include a range of measures: from the directives on collective redundancies, transfers of undertakings and employer insolvency;[125] to equal pay and equal treatment between men and women in matters relating to employment;[126] and the more recent directives on working time, European works councils and the protection of young employees.[127] Most of these measures rely in common upon the use of minimum harmonisation. However, equal pay and equal treatment stand out as a subsector characterised by a high degree of uniformity across the entire Community.[128] Similarly, although the protection of consumers' economic interests is a sector dominated by minimum harmonisation, certain aspects of Community activity here involve measures which are fully pre-emptive in effect: for example, the rules on comparative advertising contained in Directive 84/450;[129] and Directive 76/768 on the packaging

[125] Dir 98/59 on the approximation of the laws of the Member States relating to collective redundancies, OJ 1998 L225/16; Dir 2001/23 on the approximation of the laws of the Member States relating to the safeguarding of employees' rights in the event of transfers of undertakings, businesses or parts of undertakings or businesses, OJ 2001 L82/16; Dir 80/987 on the approximation of the laws of the Member States relating to the protection of employees in the event of the insolvency of their employer, OJ 1980 L283/23 (respectively).

[126] Arts 3(2) and 141 EC; Dir 75/117 on the approximation of the laws of the Member States relating to the application of the principle of equal pay for men and women, OJ 1975 L45/19; Dir 76/207 on the implementation of the principle of equal treatment for men and women as regards access to employment, vocational training and promotion, and working conditions, OJ 1976 L39/40; Dir 86/613 on the application of the principle of equal treatment between men and women engaged in an activity including agriculture, in a self-employed capacity, and on the protection of self-employed women during pregnancy and motherhood, OJ 1986 L359/56; Dir 97/80 on the burden of proof in cases of discrimination based on sex, OJ 1998 L14/6.

[127] Dir 2003/88 concerning certain aspects of the organisation of working time, OJ 2003 L299/9 (repealing and replacing Dir 93/104, OJ 1993 L307/18); Dir 94/45 on the establishment of a European Works Council or a procedure in Community-scale undertakings and Community-scale groups of undertakings for the purposes of informing and consulting employees, OJ 1994 L254/64; Dir 94/33 on the protection of young people at work, OJ 1994 L216/12 (respectively).

[128] However, note Art 8 Dir 2000/78 establishing a general framework for equal treatment in employment and occupation, OJ 2000 L303/16: Member States may introduce or maintain provisions which are more favourable to the protection of the principle of equal treatment than those laid down in the Directive. Similarly, note Art 8e Dir 76/207 on the implementation of the principle of equal treatment for men and women as regards access to employment, vocational training and promotion, and working conditions, OJ 1976 L39/40 (as introduced by Dir 2002/73, OJ L269/15).

[129] Dir 84/450 concerning misleading and comparative advertising, OJ 1984 L250/17 (as amended by Dir 97/55, OJ 1997 L290/18). Eg Case C–44/01 *Pippig Augenoptik* [2003] ECR I–3095.

and labelling of cosmetic products.[130] This presents problems for developing a coherent remedial strategy for the 'employment sector' or the 'consumer protection sector': to follow the dominant substantive regulatory theme, and support only a loose coordination of the domestic standards of judicial protection, would ignore the strong case for uniform remedies and procedural rules as regards important elements within the relevant policy sphere.

If and when enhanced cooperation becomes a more familiar feature of the Community legal order, this issue would grow correspondingly more complicated. Certain Member States would adopt more detailed Community rights and obligations to govern certain matters, while other Member States continue to participate only in the basic stratum of Treaty regulatory activity. The idea that the relationship between substantive and remedial harmonisation within any particular policy sector can be abstracted into a single identifiable point along the two-dimensional scale between substantive uniformity and differentiation would become even more difficult to sustain. Moreover, the combination of Member States participating in enhanced cooperation might change according to each individual measure and indeed over time. By way of analogy, consider the impact on the negotiations which led to the Treaty of Amsterdam brought about by a change in government in the United Kingdom: whereas the Conservative administration were adamant that the British opt-out from the Social Protocol would stay, the newly elected Labour government soon agreed to the full incorporation of the Social Policy Agreement into the Treaty.

In short: the idea of a 'sectoral approach' to the enforcement deficit debate implies that it is possible to identify with an adequate degree of clarity and stability both a particular sector of Community activity, and a particular relationship between regulatory uniformity and differentiation therein. However, these assumptions do not necessarily reflect the reality of the Community's complex and dynamic regulatory agenda. As a result, it seems hard to imagine how a coherent policy of matching remedial to substantive harmonisation on a sectoral basis could be maintained in practice. While (at one extreme) the quest for uniformity in fields such as environmental, consumer and social protection seems more illusory than real, and (at the other extreme) the weight of the enforcement deficit falls on soundly market-orientated policy concerns such as competition law and state aids, the intractable problems raised by any attempt to map out the fluid boundaries of the wider Internal Market mean that it is difficult

[130] Dir 76/768 on the approximation of the laws of the Member States relating to cosmetic products, OJ 1976 L262/169. Eg Case C–315/92 *Clinique Laboratories and Estée Lauder* [1994] ECR I–317.

to ascertain what level of substantive uniformity this tentative 'sector' pursues, and therefore what degree of remedial harmonisation it deserves. At the very least, it seems clear that such uniformity is not so absolute as stereotyped assumptions about free movement and equalised competitive conditions would appear to suggest, given the intimate interweaving of social welfare concerns (and consequent pressure for differentiated regulatory techniques) into the economic fabric of the market integration process.[131]

Policy Critique: An Implementation Imbalance?

The second main criticism that might be levelled against our proposed sectoral model is that it would reinforce perceptions of a neo-liberal economic bias within the Community legal order.

Writing in 2000, Weatherill identified an 'implementation imbalance' in EC law, whereby Treaty norms aimed at market deregulation (and whose constituency is primarily made up of large business interests) are more likely to be effectively enforced before both the Community and the national courts than other Treaty norms aimed at market re-regulation (and whose constituency tends to consist primarily in disparate social welfare interests). This imbalance was attributed to several factors, including (for example): a sense that the Commission is more likely to identify and pursue obstacles to (economic) free movement than imperfections in the implementation of (welfare-inspired) harmonising directives; and the fact that Community regulatory strategies are themselves becoming less uniform and more differentiated, thus making it more

[131] For further discussion of differentiated regulatory techniques within the Internal Market (against the background of innately blurred sectoral boundaries outlined above): G de Búrca, 'Differentiation Within the Core: The Case of the Common Market' in G de Búrca & J Scott (eds), *Constitutional Change in the EU: From Uniformity to Flexibility?* (Hart Publishing, 2000). Cf F Snyder, *New Directions in European Community Law* (Weidenfeld and Nicolson, 1990):

> much contemporary European Community legislation … does not aim to unify the European economy by means of uniform law. Instead, it serves primarily as a supranational umbrella, beneath which the European Community increasingly recognises the validity of diverse national policies. Common Market law, in a fragmented Europe, is thus mainly a co-ordinating device (p 18).

Cf also Council, *Resolution on the Effective Uniform Application of Community Law and on the Penalties Applicable for Breaches of Community Law in the Internal Market*, OJ 1995 C188/1:

> if there prove to be serious difficulties for the smooth operation of the internal market due to disparities in national penalty arrangements, solutions will have to be sought … so that penalties are such as to ensure that legislation is applied equally effectively throughout the Union, with due regard for the respective jurisdictions of the Community and the Member States and the principles of Member States' national law, and in the light of the subsidiarity and proportionality principles.

difficult to monitor compliance by the Member States with their obligations under the relevant secondary legislation.[132]

This thesis is highly suggestive of a potential critique that might well be raised in response to our proposed sectoral model for resolving the Community's interest in harmonising domestic remedies and procedural rules within the context of the enforcement deficit debate. Consider those policy sectors where the Community's quest for high standards of substantive uniformity continues to hold sway: this category focuses on the familiar territory of the Internal Market, and especially fields such as competition law and state aids. Then consider those areas where differentiation has established a firm foothold in the regulatory strategies adopted under the Treaty in pursuit of its underlying policy goals: this category gravitates towards the Community's social welfare competences, and would comprise fields such as environmental, consumer and social policy (not to mention public health, education and culture). Adopting a sectoral approach to the enforcement deficit would therefore suggest that both the desire for uniformity and the Community's concomitant interest in harmonising the domestic systems of judicial protection are concentrated around the Treaty's economic rather than its social policy objectives. Might this sectoral approach to the Community's enforcement deficit merely reinforce Weatherill's 'implementation imbalance', and thus heighten the critical perception that European integration is more concerned to advance the economic interests of capitalist enterprise than it is to protect those individual or collective welfare interests which are most vulnerable to the forces unleashed by a free market economy?

It is one thing to adopt a (subjective) policy perspective which sees in the Treaty a rich opportunity for effecting social change towards a more just and equal society, and criticises the Community for remaining too heavily influenced by neo-liberal economic theory. However, there is no necessary connection between our sectoral approach to the enforcement deficit, and the sorts of distorted privileges identified by Weatherill at work within the existing framework for implementing Community law.

First, it is true that remedial policy is inextricably linked to the substantive policy it seeks to supplement. Fragmented remedies may undermine a uniform substantive regime—as will usually be the case in the 'economic' sectors—and thereby distort the Community's commitment to equality of treatment between undertakings operating on the Single Market. Conversely, uniform remedies could bolster a fragmented substantive regime—as will usually be the case in the 'welfare' sectors—and thereby

[132] S Weatherill, 'Addressing Problems of Imbalanced Implementation in EC Law: Remedies in an Institutional Perspective' in C Kilpatrick, T Novitz & P Skidmore (eds), *The Future of Remedies in Europe* (Hart Publishing, 2000).

contribute to a greater degree of Community involvement in creating common standards of legal rights for citizens of the Union. But however much one might advocate the pursuit of remedial uniformity by reference to some principle of equality in the enjoyment of social and welfare rights by citizens of the Union, that position is simply not reflected in substantive Community law. A policy of smuggling through the back door what it remains difficult to march through the front hardly seems an adequate substitute for lobbying directly for change in the Community's overall political agenda. This is especially true given that the principles of subsidiarity and proportionality articulate a particular view of the relationship between the relative uniformity of Community rules and the relative harmonisation of national remedies which (as we have seen) makes it difficult to justify such a policy in terms of legal doctrine.

Secondly, it should in any case be recalled that the imperative of uniformity is concerned only with achieving (substantive and remedial) *equality* of treatment across the Community—without necessarily prescribing any particular (substantive or remedial) *level* of treatment. So, just because the Community might have a legitimate interest in harmonising national remedies and procedures as regards (for example) the decentralised enforcement of competition policy or state aids does not mean that the Community will necessarily create a framework of legal protection favourable to the interests of big business. Indeed, we shall see that, in several cases where the Court has relied upon the imperative of uniformity to develop exhaustive Community rules on the remedies and procedures to be applied before the domestic courts, the result has been to lower the standards of effective judicial protection previously available under national law.[133] For example, in *Zuckerfabrik* and *Atlanta*, the Court harmonised the conditions for granting interim relief against allegedly invalid Community measures before the domestic courts at a level less generous than the pre-existing regime (say) in Germany.[134] Similarly, in *Alcan II*, the Court insisted that, for the sake of preserving the uniform application of the Articles 87 and 88 EC, undertakings could not invoke more favourable domestic limitations periods so as to bar proceedings brought by the national authorities for the recovery of unlawful state aids.[135] Conversely, just because the Community might lack any legitimate interest in harmonising the remedies and procedural rules applicable to the decentralised enforcement of more welfare-orientated sectors (such as environmental, consumer and employee protection) does not

[133] Further: ch 6 (below).
[134] Cases C–143/88 and C–92/89 *Zuckerfabrik Süderdithmarshen* [1991] ECR I–415; Case C–465/93 *Atlanta* [1995] ECR I–3761. Further, eg P Oliver, 'Interim Measures: Some Recent Developments' (1992) 29 CML Rev 7; R Voss, 'The National Perception of the Court of First Instance and the European Court of Justice' (1993) 30 CML Rev 1119.
[135] In particular: Case C–24/95 *Alcan Deutschland* [1997] ECR I–1591.

necessarily mean that the Community cannot still insist on Member States respecting minimum guarantees of effectiveness—which may well enshrine particularly robust standards of judicial protection.

In short: the matter depends not so much on the imperative of uniformity as on the imperative of effectiveness, which determines the quality of Community supervision over the domestic systems of judicial protection rather than their simple approximation. A policy-based critique which wrongly equates the Community's competence to harmonise for the purposes of uniformity with its competence to prescribe for the purposes of effectiveness, and consequently assumes that, because the former power would generally affect big business more than the individual citizen, so too the Community as a whole must favour its economic over its social constituency, loses much of its initial force. In fact, there is nothing inherently incompatible between a perspective which supports the Community's continuing process of horizontal expansion so as to embrace important issues of social welfare for the citizen body as well as economic integration for the purposes of creating a Single Market, and a perspective which supports the Community's legitimate desire to pursue common standards of judicial protection only as regards those predominantly economic policy spheres which are characterised by a strong commitment to regulatory uniformity.

Differentiation and the Imperative of Effectiveness

Those comments lead directly to the main third problem posed by our sectoral model. The fact that in certain sectors a lack of uniformity as regards substantive Community regulation may imply some readjustment in our conceptual understanding of the extent of the Treaty's legitimate interest in harmonising the rules for decentralised enforcement, clearly does not detract from the continuing need for effectiveness in the enforcement of all Community rules, and thus for a minimum level of Treaty supervision over national remedies and procedures. It remains axiomatic that every Community measure pursues some identifiable objective (whether in protecting free movement and fair competition within the Single Market, or in advancing the collective and individual welfare rights of Union citizens), the attainment of which may be imperilled by, and must therefore be protected against, inadequate or even obstructionist implementation mechanisms provided by the Member States. This is true regardless of the degree of discretion left to the domestic authorities to assist in the substantive elaboration of the policy objectives in question.

In keeping with the need to 'manage' the impact of regulatory differentiation in the light of certain irreducible characteristics of the Community legal order, it is thus apparent that, even in any sectoral approach to the enforcement deficit, the axis of effectiveness provides a floor below which the Community's interest in the satisfactory character of national remedies and procedures cannot afford to fall. But the relationship between uniformity and effectiveness will not always be so clear-cut. What is an effective means of protecting one right may not be at all sufficient to protect another, and it is thus possible to envisage that the minimum standards of remedial protection expected under Community law will in certain cases be pitched at a relatively high level.

Consider, for example, consumer policy. On the one hand, this is a sector characterised (in particular) by minimum harmonisation, as regards which one would expect less need for Community intervention in national remedies and procedural rules on grounds of uniformity. On the other hand, the problems of effectively enforcing consumer protection legislation are aggravated by a serious of sector-specific factors: many consumers are simply unaware of the rights which they enjoy under Community law; many individuals have little incentive to pursue their rights *qua* consumers because claims tend to involve small amounts of money; consumers often find themselves in a position of weakness when attempting to argue their case against large business undertakings with greater resources and better legal advice; cross-border situations, where consumers are required to pursue claims against undertakings established in another Member State, involve additional legal and practical obstacles (for example, unfamiliarity with foreign legal rules or avenues of redress, barriers imposed by simple considerations of distance and language etc).[136] Such factors might well demand a high level of Community intervention in the domestic systems of judicial protection, so as to address some of those structural imbalances between individual consumers and economic undertakings.

For example, the effective enforcement of consumer protection rules has required the Community legislature to recognise the valuable role played by organised consumer welfare groups—whether national authorities, or private organisations—prepared to identify and pursue in the collective interest instances of market malpractice, which individual consumers would probably be unable or unwilling to pursue for themselves. Thus, the Misleading Advertising and Unfair Contract Terms Directives require Member States to recognise the standing of persons of organisations having a legitimate interest (recognised as such under national law) in protecting consumers, to pursue actions for breach of the relevant Community rules before the competent national judicial or admnistrative authorities.[137] Similarly, the Consumer Injunctions

[136] Further, eg S Weatherill, *EC Consumer Law and Policy* (Longman, 1997); G Howells and T Wilhelmsson, *EC Consumer Law* (Dartmouth, 1997).

[137] Dir 84/450 concerning misleading and comparative advertising, OJ 1984 L250/17; Dir 93/13 on unfair terms in consumer contracts, OJ 1993 L95/29.

Directive requires each Member State to ensure that the national consumer authority or other organisations whose purpose is to protect collective consumer interests may commence legal proceedings seeking the cessation or prohibition of conduct which infringes various Community consumer protection directives. Each country must also ensure that the equivalent organisations from other Member States also have standing, in cases where infringements of the relevant Community directives produce cross-border effects.[138] Moreover, the Commission has proposed a regulation aimed at enhancing mutual administrative cooperation between the national authorities in each Member State responsible for enforcing consumer protection rules, based around the confidential exchange of information and an obligation to bring about the speedy cessation of any infringement identified within the national territory.[139]

Community legislation (as construed by the Court of Justice) has also made more specific provision for the effective judicial protection of individual consumers than of other categories of claimant intended to benefit from Community law. For example, the Court held in *Oceáno Grupo Editorial* that national courts must set aside procedural rules limiting their ability to raise of their own motion the existence of unfair terms in consumer contracts. This conclusion was reached through a teleological interpretation of Directive 93/13.[140] The sums at issue in consumer disputes are often smaller than the cost of lawyers' fees. Given consumers' ignorance of their legal rights, this might deter individuals from contesting the application of an unfair contract term against them. Effective judicial protection in accordance with the purpose of the Directive therefore required national judges to evaluate the possible existence of an unfair contract term of their own motion. Moreover, such a power would contribute to the Directive's specific aim of deterring sellers and suppliers from using unfair terms in consumer contracts in the first place.[141] The Court went even further in *Cofidis*: the same considerations precluded the application of a two-year time-limit within which national judges could examine (either of own motion or at the request of the consumer) whether contract terms were unfair within the meaning of Directive 93/13, at least where the litigation had been initiated by the seller or supplier, and possibility also where the litigation had been commenced by the consumer him/herself.[142] This clearly goes beyond the

[138] Dir 98/27 on injunctions for the protection of consumers' interests, OJ 1998 L166/51. Cf COM (2003)241 Final.

[139] Commission, *Proposal for a Regulation on Cooperation Between National Authorities Responsible for the Enforcement of Consumer Protection Laws*, COM (2003)443 Final.

[140] Dir 93/13 on unfair terms in consumer contracts, OJ 1993 L95/29.

[141] Cases C–240–44/98 *Oceáno Grupo Editorial* [2000] ECR I–4941.

[142] Case C–473/00 *Cofidis* [2002] ECR I–10875.

general principles of effective judicial protection concerning restrictions on the raising of arguments based on Community law, as laid down in cases like *Peterbroeck, Van Schijndel* and *Eco Swiss v Benetton*[143]: provided any time-limits for raising arguments are reasonable in duration, Member States may restrict their judges to performing a passive role in litigation, leaving the parties to look after their own interests; subject only to the requirement that the relevant procedural restrictions should not preclude altogether the possibility of any national court making an Article 234 EC reference to the Court of Justice.[144]

Community consumer protection legislation provides other illustrations of the same phenomenon. For example, the Consumer Sales Directive 99/44 requires Member States to guarantee a time-limit of not less than two years, from the time of delivery of the relevant goods, within which consumers can bring legal actions based on their Community law rights.[145] That is considerably longer than the sorts of limitation period the Court has accepted as being reasonable in duration for the purposes of the general principles of effective judicial protection.[146] Moreover, Directive 90/314 specifically provides for the payment of compensation to consumers in respect of damage resulting from failure to perform, or the improper performance of, package travel obligations.[147] The Court held in *Leitner* that this included the payment of damages for non-material losses: first, that would contribute to the Directive's aim of reducing disparities between national rules which distorted conditions of competition between undertakings within the Internal Market; secondly, it would also contribute to the Directive's aim of offering protection to consumers, as regards which non-material damage resulting from the loss of enjoyment of a holiday is of particular importance.[148] Again, Community consumer protection law in that regard offers a more developed remedial regime than the general principles of effective judicial protection, where the idea of a right to damages between private parties has so far focused on infringement of the competition rules, especially in situations where the parties do not bargain from positions of equal strength.[149]

It is thus clear that effective judicial protection in the consumer policy sector is driven less by the imperative of uniformity than by that of

[143] Case C–312/93 *Peterbroeck* [1995] ECR I–4599; Cases C–430–31/93 *Van Schijndel* [1995] ECR I–4705; Case C–126/97 *Eco Swiss v Benetton* [1999] ECR I–3055.
[144] Further: ch 1 (above).
[145] Dir 99/44 on certain aspects of the sale of consumer goods and associated guarantees, OJ 1999 L171/12.
[146] Under Case 33/76 *Rewe-Zentralfinanz v Landwirtschaftskammer für das Saarland* [1976] ECR 1989; Case 45/76 *Comet* [1976] ECR 2043. Further: ch 5 (below).
[147] Dir 90/314 on package travel, package holidays and package tours, OJ 1990 L158/59.
[148] Case C–168/00 *Leitner* [2002] ECR I–2631.
[149] Under Case C–453/99 *Courage v Crehan* [2001] ECR I–6297. Further: ch 6 (below).

effectiveness. But it is equally apparent that this in itself can result in greater interference by the Community with the presumption of national competence over remedies and procedural rules.

Moreover, it follows from the continuing relevance of the imperative of effectiveness that our sectoral analysis cannot purport to offer a panacea for the complex problems thrown up by the decentralised enforcement of Community norms—such as the perennially controversial task of striking an appropriate balance between the Treaty interest in guaranteeing minimum standards of judicial protection, and competing domestic concerns over the prejudicial impact of Community intervention on (for example) the need for legal certainty or the fair and efficient administration of justice. One might observe, however, that the sort of doctrinal reconsideration of the imperative of uniformity prompted by increasing levels of regulatory diversity within the Community legal order offers some fresh insights into the prima facie separate task of mediating between conflicting Treaty and domestic interests in the effectiveness of decentralised enforcement.

It was argued above that the recent history of the Community has been characterised by both a continuing process of expansion in the horizontal, vertical, geographical and institutional scope of supranational governance pursued under the Treaty, and a counter-process which attempts to define more clearly the limits to the Community's powers as regards their relationship with pre-existing national competences. The gathering process of regulatory differentiation was identified as one symptom of this fundamental tension operating at the heart of the ongoing process of European integration, whereby the need to accommodate those Member States which wish to retain a greater degree of control over their own policy-making prerogatives implies some pragmatic compromise of the objective of achieving absolute uniformity in the application of Community norms, as otherwise required for the purposes of fair competition within the Internal Market and/or equality of treatment between citizens of the Union.

The specific phenomenon of regulatory differentiation may well be less relevant to the imperative of effectiveness. However, the underlying tension between the expansion and the contraction / delimitation of Treaty power remains the same, and inspires a parallel process of doctrinal reflection. An 'integration through law' interpretation of the imperative of effectiveness which focuses purely upon the Community's interest in the adequacy of the legal framework supporting decentralised enforcement would seem to place an unduly one-sided emphasis on the process of expansion. If the enforcement deficit debate is to be located and resolved within the wider context of the Community's politico-legal evolution, any analysis of the imperative of effectiveness should take into account not only the process of expansion, but also the counter-process of contraction/delimitation, and therefore recognise a similarly pragmatic need to arrive at some more balanced reconciliation between Community-orientated demands for intervention in the standards of judicial protection available through the national legal orders, and legitimate concerns voiced by individual Member States about the feasibility or appropriateness of such intervention within the often logistically fraught or politically sensitive context of litigation before the domestic courts.[150]

Assessment

The established 'integration through law' approach to the enforcement deficit debate is based upon a viewpoint which sees the Community as a singularly integrative project, requiring a degree of regulatory uniformity which renders national remedies and procedural rules problematic, and implies that harmonisation is the most appropriate solution. The alternative 'sectoral model' instead sees the Community as a more complex entity characterised by varying degrees of integration and differentiation across different policy fields. This means that the diversity of national remedies and procedures available in the process of decentralised enforcement should not be seen as an automatic impediment to securing the uniform application of Community law, and therefore that wholesale harmonisation would exceed legitimate Treaty interests in this regard. It is instead proposed that the requirements of uniformity should be viewed in a purely relative light, and thus assessed at a sectoral level to determine the true nature of the Community's need for substantive, and thus remedial, approximation—subject to the minimum standards of Treaty control over the framework of decentralised enforcement demanded by the independent imperative of effectiveness.

However, the previous discussion sought to highlight not only the advantages, but also the very real limits of any sectoral approach to analysing and resolving the Community's enforcement deficit. In fact, the utility of the sectoral model depends largely on the purpose to which it is put and, in particular, on the institutional actor to whose activities it is applied. Clearly, a sectoral understanding of the problems posed by national remedies and procedures does not easily translate into a manifesto for detailed policy development, such as could be taken up by a legislature and used as a blueprint for concrete change. But this should not detract from the relevance of the sectoral approach viewed primarily as a

[150] Cf authors such as M Hoskins, 'Tilting the Balance: Supremacy and National Procedural Rules' (1996) 21 EL Rev 365; C Himsworth, 'Things Fall Apart: The Harmonisation of Community Judicial Procedural Protection Revisited' (1997) 22 EL Rev 291; A Biondi, 'The European Court of Justice and Certain National Procedural Limitations: Not Such a Tough Relationship' (1999) 36 CML Rev 1271. Further: ch 2 (above)

conceptual model—offering an interpretation of the Community's interest in national remedies and procedures which is more rigorous in its articulation of the internal Treaty imperatives at stake, and is thus apt to replace the outdated 'integration through law' analysis as the grand perspective through which the Community's enforcement deficit is visualised and its continuing progress monitored.

Against this background, Chapters 5 and 6 will seek to apply our sectoral model in the manner of a critical conceptual tool by which to analyse the Court of Justice's approach to Community control over national remedies and procedural rules. What does the Court have to say about the importance of uniformity? How far does the caselaw reflect, exceed or frustrate the Community's legitimate interests in harmonising the remedial aspects of the decentralised enforcement of its own norms, as understood from a sectoral viewpoint?

5

The Court of Justice's Caselaw on National Remedies and Procedural Rules I

THE COURT OF Justice rarely articulates its approach to the imperative of uniformity explicitly. Ascertaining the nature of changing judicial attitudes towards the enforcement deficit therefore becomes an exercise in conceptual tectonics: by mapping the shifting contours of the legal landscape, one begins to understand something of the underlying policy forces which have shaped it. From this perspective, we already know that it is possible to identify three main historical periods in the caselaw: an early period of extensive deference to national autonomy; a middle-period of increasing Community remedial competence; and the most recent period, in which the Court attempts to strike some acceptable balance between its previous extremes.[1]

EARLY PERIOD: EXTENSIVE DEFERENCE TO NATIONAL AUTONOMY

The early period of the Court of Justice's caselaw can be summarised quite simply: domestic standards were the rule, Community interference an ill-defined exception. For example, the Court held in *Rewe/Comet* that domestic limitation periods regulating the initiation of proceedings before the national courts may also apply to Community cases, provided they comply with the principles of equivalence and effectiveness. The latter requires merely that the time-limit in question be reasonable in duration. For this purpose, a 30-day limitation period in respect of actions for the recovery of unlawfully levied charges could not be considered to render the exercise of Treaty rights 'virtually impossible'.[2] Moreover, in the *Butter Buying Cruises* case, it was bluntly stated that the Treaty was not intended to create any new forms of relief not already available under national

[1] Cf ch 1 (above).

[2] Case 33/76 *Rewe-Zentralfinanz v Landwirtschaftskammer für das Saarland* [1976] ECR 1989; Case 45/76 *Comet* [1976] ECR 2043. Also: Case 35/74 *Mutualités Chrétiennes v Rzepa* [1974] ECR 1241; Case 61/79 *Denkavit Italiana* [1980] ECR 1205.

law.[3] In particular, the Court held in *Russo* that the availability of compensatory damages in respect of losses suffered through a breach of Community law for which the Member State could be held responsible was a matter to be determined by domestic rules.[4] Similarly, *Roquette Frères* established the principle that the Member States were entitled to apply their own rules regarding the payment of interest, its rate and the date from which it should be calculated.[5]

Such cases might be thought to embody a loose-knit strategy of negative harmonisation. The Court paid more than mere lip-service to the presumption of domestic autonomy in the provision of remedies and procedural rules to govern the exercise of Treaty rights. Indeed, the Court seems to have assumed that, since national rules were adequate to protect national rights, it would in most cases be sufficient to require that comparable Community rights were assimilated into this system, via the requirement of equivalence. The principle of effectiveness justified only limited patterns of Community intervention in the pre-existing systems of judicial protection, where the Member State transgressed the relatively generous boundaries of domestic discretion appointed by the Court: for example, where national law failed to provide in principle for the reimbursement of domestic taxes levied contrary to Community law.[6]

On the one hand, this approach might seem to suggest that the Court of Justice devoted little conceptual importance to the quest for uniformity of enforcement as between the Member States. Indeed, on several occasions the Court asserted that divergent systems of remedies and procedural rules, provided they complied with the basic requirements of equivalence and effectiveness, could not be said to distort competition within the Common Market.[7] On the other hand, dicta in several judgments also suggest that Court was sensitive to the problems posed by inequality of treatment under the fragmented domestic systems of judicial protection, but was equally mindful of its own institutional limitations, and preferred to leave the necessary task of harmonisation to the Community legislature.[8] The Court's observations in *Rewe/Comet* offer an apt summary of the position: where necessary, Articles 94 and 308 EC would enable appropriate measures to be adopted by the political institutions to remedy differences between the remedial and procedural provisions laid down by domestic law, if these were likely to distort or harm the functioning of the Common Market.[9]

[3] Case 158/80 *Rewe-Handelsgesellschaft Nord v Hauptzollamt Kiel* [1981] ECR 1805.
[4] Case 60/75 *Russo* [1976] ECR 45. Also: Case 101/78 *Granaria* [1979] ECR 623.
[5] Case 26/74 *Roquette Frères* [1976] ECR 677. Also: Case 6/60 *Humblet* [1960] ECR 559.
[6] Eg Case 177/78 *Pigs and Bacon Commission v McCarren* [1979] ECR 2161.
[7] Eg Case 811/79 *Ariete* [1980] ECR 2545; Case 826/79 *MIRECO* [1980] ECR 2559.
[8] Eg Case 265/78 *Ferwerda* [1980] ECR 617; Cases 66 & 127–8/79 *Salumi* [1980] ECR 1237; Case 130/79 *Express Dairy Foods* [1980] ECR 1887; Case 54/81 *Fromme* [1982] ECR 1449; Cases 205–15/82 *Deutsche Milchkontor* [1983] ECR 2633.
[9] Case 33/76 *Rewe-Zentralfinanz v Landwirtschaftskammer für das Saarland* [1976] ECR 1989, para 5; Case 45/76 *Comet* [1976] ECR 2043, para 14.

In either case, the preponderance of academic opinion asserts that the Court's response was inadequate. Throughout the 1970s and early 1980s, the Treaty order was still dominated by the quest to create a Common Market based upon free movement for economic factors such as goods and services, and upon equalised conditions of competition as between undertakings operating within the Community market. Moreover, the forms of regulatory differentiation recognised under Treaty law were of a relatively limited nature: minimum harmonisation was common in secondary legislation, but had not yet been 'institutionalised' within the Treaty text itself; derogations were also widespread, but the sort of wholesale opt-outs from entire policy sectors found at Maastricht, and the more generalised principle of closer/enhanced cooperation found under Amsterdam and Nice, belonged to the entirely transformed political landscape of the future. Uniformity might thus appear to have constituted a genuine aspiration of Community policy, and in turn to have provided a legitimate template for Community intervention in the domestic systems of legal protection. The Court could hardly have been faulted for pursuing on the remedial plane the sort of approximation still sought after at a substantive level. The fact that it failed to do so seemed a valid criticism of this particular era in the caselaw.

MIDDLE PERIOD: THE ASSERTION OF INCREASING COMMUNITY REMEDIAL COMPETENCE

By contrast, the Court's middle-period jurisprudence was dominated by increasing levels of Community remedial competence. For example, the Court held in *Emmott* that, even if a domestic limitation period complies with the conditions of equivalence and effectiveness as set out in *Rewe/Comet*, it must nevertheless be set aside in cases where the Member State has failed correctly to implement a Community directive within the prescribed deadline, and the individual citizen would otherwise be deprived of the opportunity to rely on rights derived from that directive.[10] Moreover, despite the dictum in *Butter Buying Cruises* that the Treaty was not intended to create new forms of relief, the judgment in *Factortame* established that national courts must be able to offer interim protection to claimants seeking to assert their Community rights by judicial process, even if such relief is not ordinarily available under domestic rules.[11] Similarly, despite the finding in *Russo* that the availability of damages was a matter falling squarely within the presumption of domestic competence, the Court in *Francovich* held that it is inherent in the system of the Treaty that individuals must in principle be able to obtain compensation in

[10] Case C–208/90 *Emmott* [1991] ECR I–4269. See further below.
[11] Case C–213/89 *ex p Factortame* [1990] ECR I–2433. Noted by, eg J Hanna (1990) 106 LQR 2; M Ross (1990) 15 EL Rev 476; AG Toth (1990) 27 CML Rev 573.

respect of losses suffered through a breach of their Community rights for which the Member State could be held responsible.[12] Another good illustration is *Marshall II*, where it was established that the victim of a discriminatory dismissal contrary to the provisions of the Equal Treatment Directive must be able to obtain full compensation for her losses.[13] Notwithstanding the judgment in *Roquette Frères*, such reparation must include the payment of interest to represent losses suffered through the effluxion of time.[14] It was true that the Member States remained free to choose whether such claimants should have a remedy either in reinstatement or in compensation. But those two options could still be seen as functional equivalents—so that uniformity of treatment across the Community was achieved in substantive (even if not in formal) terms.

This change in judicial policy has been attributed to a number of factors.[15] First, it was clear that the Court was wrong to have so much faith in the adequacy of national rules: in fact, as the dispute in *Factortame* demonstrated, they often offered less than adequate levels of protection. Secondly, more and more Community claims were coming before the domestic courts, making the problem more visible. Thirdly, the character of such claims was changing significantly. As well as the economic interests of big business, the Court was being confronted with ordinary citizens asserting their right to the social benefits of Community membership. Bearing in mind the drive for a 'Europe with a human face,' coupled with the natural tendency of a system of decentralised enforcement to emphasise the role of the individual, this change may well have increased the Court's inclination to increase the levels of protection guaranteed by Community law. Finally, the Court's repeated requests for legislative intervention to address the 'problem' of national remedies had gone largely unheeded. So, if anything was to be done to help the increasing numbers of citizens invoking the Community's aid, the initiative lay with the judiciary.

It is thus clear that the primary conceptual engine for the Court's newfound willingness to intervene in the domestic systems of judicial protection was the imperative of effectiveness. Throughout much of this middle-period, the imperative of uniformity often appeared less as an equal partner in laying the intellectual foundations of the Court's change of policy, than as the passive beneficiary of a momentum to which it had

[12] Cases C–6 & 9/90 *Francovich* [1991] ECR I–5357. See further below.

[13] Dir 76/207 on the implementation of the principle of equal treatment for men and women as regards access to employment, vocational training and promotion, and working conditions, OJ 1976 L39/40.

[14] Case C–271/91 *Marshall II* [1993] ECR I–4367. Noted by, eg N Grief (1993) 22 ILJ 314; S Moore, (1993) 18 EL Rev 533.

[15] Further, eg A Ward, 'Effective Sanctions in EC Law: A Moving Boundary in the Division of Competence' (1995) 1 *European Law Journal* 205.

contributed little decisive influence of its own.[16] Nevertheless, whether by conscious design or happy coincidence, the caselaw did witness a significant degree of remedial centralisation. Indeed, the early 1990s saw the birth of widespread academic expectations that the Court had embarked upon a strategy of positive harmonisation—promoting a single Community-level code of procedural rules for the decentralised enforcement of Treaty norms, which would replace the various pre-existing domestic systems.[17]

Viewed from an 'integration through law' perspective, this prospect seemed no more than a faithful reflection of the growing maturity of the Treaty legal order itself. After all, the later 1980s and early 1990s witnessed a period of significant expansion in the scope and intensity of Community power. Consider: first, the consolidation by the Court of its own system of decentralised enforcement (based upon a generalised acceptance by the Member States and the domestic judiciaries of the doctrines of direct effect and supremacy); secondly, the drive to realise the full economic ambitions of the Single Market (initiated by the judgment in *Cassis de Dijon*,[18] and continued both in the new approach to harmonisation, and by the institutional amendments introduced by the Single European Act to facilitate the process of economic integration); and thirdly, the gathering pace of Community competence to regulate ever wider fields of social welfare for the ordinary citizen (consumer protection, social policy, environmental protection, public health, education and culture). Taken together, these developments all seemed naturally to justify the Court's apparent policy of increasing Community control over domestic remedies and procedures, so as finally to achieve the sort of uniform application for Treaty norms which the Community's established economic and growing social ambitions demanded, but which the fledgling mechanisms of decentralised enforcement had thus far proved unable to deliver.

However, when viewed from the alternative perspective developed in Chapter 4, the roots of this middle-period caselaw were in fact feeding from shallow soil. Indeed, with the benefit of hindsight, one can discern how this new and robust jurisprudence was incapable of sustaining its

[16] Advocates General tended to be more forthcoming than the Court in their reliance upon considerations of uniformity, to justify the Community's increasingly interventionist approach to national remedial autonomy. Consider, eg AG Mischo in Cases C–6 & 9/90 *Francovich* [1991] ECR I–5357, paras 61 and 70 Opinion; AG van Gerven in Case C–271/91 *Marshall II* [1993] ECR I–4367, para 28 Opinion.
[17] Eg D Curtin and K Mortelmans, 'Application and Enforcement of Community Law by the Member States: Actors in Search of a Third Generation Script' in D Curtin & T Heukels (eds), *Institutional Dynamics of European Integration* (Martinus Nijhoff, 1994); MP Chiti, 'Towards a Unified Judicial Protection in Europe(?)' (1997) 9 *European Review of Public Law* 553.
[18] Case 120/78 *'Cassis de Dijon'* [1979] ECR 649.

own conceptual momentum. It will be recalled that the recent history of the Community consists essentially of two inter-related strands: not only expansion (along horizontal, vertical, institutional and geographical axes); but also, and in large part in consequence, contraction (or at least the urge to define more clearly the limits of Treaty power, and its relationship to the competing claims of divergent national policies). The consistent and continuing growth of Community power may well have injected fresh impetus into the Court's assertion of remedial competence relative to that of the Member States; but it also unleashed that array of socio-political tensions whose practical resolution lay in the steady spread of differentiated regulatory techniques within the Treaty legal order; such regulatory diversity has in turn undermined the very imperative of uniformity upon which any notion of a unified system of judicial protection depends.

Thus, by concentrating almost exclusively on the strand of expansion and neglecting the strand of contraction, an 'integration through law' perspective seeks to portray the Court's middle-period caselaw as a desirable, even necessary, step on the path towards full-scale remedial harmonisation. But this task appears increasingly misguided, the more its intellectual foundations are undermined by the tide of regulatory differentiation seeping through much of the Community legal order, and by the elevation of 'flexibility' to the status of a central constitutional principle within the Treaty itself. Indeed, current trends towards regulatory diversity have attained such extent and depth that the sort of general drive towards the positive harmonisation of national remedies and procedural rules suggested by the Court's middle-period caselaw and championed by many of the commentators appears increasingly to embody an over-inflated definition of the Community's interest in the imperative of uniformity, and thus an unduly intrusive conception of the Court's mandate to pursue the approximation of the domestic systems of judicial protection.

CURRENT CASELAW: A GENERAL TREND TOWARDS NEGATIVE HARMONISATION

However, the Court of Justice has since moved on to forge a new legal framework. The main characteristic of the most recent caselaw consists in a definite retreat away from the idea of positive harmonisation (the promotion of a single Community-level system of remedies and procedures for the decentralised enforcement of its own norms, which replaces the various pre-existing domestic systems), and back towards the more orthodox pattern of negative approximation (whereby the Court applies a presumption of national autonomy in the provision of judicial protection, and the principle of effectiveness justifies more limited patterns of Community intervention).[19]

On the one hand, it would be wrong to overstate the Court's shift in policy here. The general tide of effective judicial protection may have reached its high-water mark in 1993, failing to lead the Treaty's remedial competence ever-upwards towards the dizzy heights many commentators had so eagerly anticipated. But it still left an indelible imprint on the relationship between Community and Member State competence in the enforcement of Treaty rights before the domestic courts: the jurisdiction to grant interim relief against national measures allegedly contrary to Community law; a right to reparation for losses suffered through unlawful acts perpetrated by the Member State, including even the national legislature; a claim for the inclusion of interest on at least certain awards of compensatory damages. This general trend away from the positive towards a mere negative harmonisation of national remedies and procedures should not therefore be mistaken for an outright judicial rout which has led Community competence back to the extensive deference towards national autonomy practised in the 1970s and early 1980s.

On the other hand, the Court's reaffirmation of its basic preference for negative harmonisation does mean that Community law usually acts as an incomplete rather than exhaustive template for the approximation of the Member States' pre-existing systems of judicial protection. In particular, the Court tends to prescribe only the minimum guarantees expected under the Treaty, leaving significant scope for national autonomy to elaborate more favourable standards of remedial and procedural rules for the enforcement by individual citizens of their Community rights. This general trend will be illustrated by reference to two key strands in the Court's remedies caselaw: the right to reparation for damage caused by a Member State's breach of its Treaty obligations; and the imposition of limitation periods for the commencement of proceedings.

The Right to Reparation

The facts of *Francovich* are too well known to justify more than a brief summary. The Insolvency Directive requires Member States to establish a guarantee institution, to cover the unpaid wage claims of workers whose employer has gone bankrupt.[20] Italy failed to implement the Directive

[19] Further, eg R Craufurd Smith, 'Remedies for Breaches of EU Law in National Courts: Legal Variation and Selection' in P Craig & G de Búrca (eds), *The Evolution of EU Law* (OUP, 1999); T Tridimas, *The General Principles of EC Law* (OUP, 1999) ch 8; A Ward, *Judicial Review and the Rights of Private Parties in EC Law* (OUP, 2000) chs 2–4; P Craig & G de Búrca, *EU Law: Text, Cases, & Materials* (OUP, 2002) ch 6.

[20] Dir 80/987 on the approximation of the laws of the Member States relating to the protection of employees in the event of the insolvency of their employer, OJ 1980 L283/23.

within its prescribed deadline. A group of workers attempted to rely on the provisions of the Directive directly, but were unable to do so because the latter were insufficiently precise and unconditional to have direct effect within the national legal order: although the identify of the beneficiaries and the nature of the wage guarantee were clear, the identify of the guarantee institution itself was dependent upon further domestic implementing measures. In the alternative, the claimants sought damages from Italy for the losses they had suffered through the Member State's failure to transpose the Directive into national law.

In this regard, the Court observed that the full effectiveness of Community rules would be impaired and the protection of the rights which they grant would be weakened if individuals were unable to obtain redress when their rights are infringed by a breach of Community law for which a Member State can be held responsible. Furthermore, it had been consistently held that the national courts, whose task it is to apply the provisions of Community law in areas within their jurisdiction, must ensure that those rules take full effect, and must protect the rights which they confer on individuals. From these considerations, the Court held that it is a principle of Community law that the Member States are obliged to make good loss and damage caused to individuals by breaches of Community law for which they can be held responsible.[21]

The Court continued to observe that, although Member State liability is required by Community law, the substantive conditions under which that liability gives rise to a right to reparation depend on the nature of the breach giving rise to the claimant's loss. Where, as in *Francovich* itself, a Member State has failed to fulfil its obligation under Article 249(3) EC to take all the measures necessary to achieve the result prescribed by a directive, the full effectiveness of Community law requires that there should be a right to reparation when three conditions are fulfilled: first, the result prescribed by the directive should entail the grant of rights to individuals; secondly, it should be possible to identify the content of those rights on the basis of the provisions of the directive; thirdly, there should exist a causal link between the Member State's breach of its Treaty obligation and the damage suffered by the claimant. The Court concluded that those three conditions were sufficient to give rise to a right to obtain reparation founded directly on Community law.[22]

In the immediate wake of the decision, there was extensive speculation about the potential scope and content of the rule it had enunciated.[23] For

[21] Cases C–6 & 9/90 *Francovich* [1991] ECR I–5357, paras 31–37.
[22] Cases C–6 & 9/90 *Francovich* [1991] ECR I–5357, paras 38–41.
[23] Eg A Barav, 'Damages Against the State for Failure to Implement EC Directives' (1991) 141 NLJ 1584; G Bebr, Annotation of *Francovich* (1992) 29 CML Rev 557; D Curtin, 'State Liability Under Community Law: A New Remedy for Private Parties' (1992) 21 ILJ 74; P Duffy, 'Damages Against the State: A New Remedy for Failure to Implement Community Obligations' (1992) 17 EL Rev 133; C Greenwood, 'Effect of EC Directives in National Law'

example, how far would the right to reparation extend beyond the *Francovich* situation of a failure by the Member State to implement a directive within its prescribed deadline? And in what ways might the substantive conditions regulating the availability of relief differ depending on the type of Community obligation which had been breached? In particular, although *Francovich* itself had not expressly referred to any criterion of fault (negligence, bad faith etc) before the Member State should incur liability for an outright failure to implement a directive within its deadline, would the Court really impose strict liability to make reparation in respect of every other potential breach of Community law?

Nevertheless, most commentators seemed to agree at least on the remedial implications of the judgment: *Francovich* represented the logical next-step in the evolution of the Court's caselaw on effective judicial protection. Indeed, there is a still-popular belief that the right to reparation is the dynamic expression of an expanding Community jurisdiction to prescribe the remedies available under the domestic legal orders in respect of the enforcement of Treaty-based rights: the Court has created a 'Community remedy in damages,' a general action for compensation prescribed by the Treaty, which carries its own substantive conditions for the availability of relief. However, through over a decade of judicial refinement, much of the promise which many saw contained in the original *Francovich* judgment has slowly dissipated. Despite its dramatic start, subsequent treatment of the right to reparation must be understood in terms of the Court's broader tendency to retreat from an aggressive approach to effective judicial protection, in favour of greater deference to national competence when redressing breaches of Community law.[24] This phenomenon can be observed in relation to four crucial aspects of the right to reparation: the substantive conditions under which liability may be imposed; the definition of 'the state' for the purposes of *Francovich* liability; the character and extent of reparation which must be provided to successful claimants; and the procedural conditions for exercising the right to reparation.

[1992] CLJ 3; K Parker, 'State Liability in Damages for Breach of Community Law' (1992) 108 LQR 181; E Szyszczak, 'European Community Law: New Remedies, New Directions?' (1992) 55 MLR 690; R Caranta, 'Governmental Liability After *Francovich*' [1993] CLJ 272; P Craig, '*Francovich*, Remedies and the Scope of Damages Liability' (1993) 109 LQR 595; C Lewis and S Moore, 'Duties, Directives and Damages in European Community Law' [1993] PL 151; M Ross, 'Beyond *Francovich*' (1993) 56 MLR 55; J Steiner, 'From Direct Effects to *Francovich*: Shifting Means of Enforcement of Community Law' (1993) 18 EL Rev 3; C Plaza Martin, 'Furthering the Effectiveness of EC Directives and the Judicial Protection of Individual Rights Thereunder' (1994) 43 ICLQ 26; W van Gerven, 'Non-contractual Liability of Member States, Community Institutions and Individuals for Breaches of Community Law with a View to a Common Law for Europe' (1994) 1 *Maastricht Journal of European and Comparative Law* 6.

[24] Further: M Dougan, 'The *Francovich* Right to Reparation: Reshaping the Contours of Community Remedial Competence' (2000) 6 *European Public Law* 103. Cf the alternative 'integration through law' perspective suggested by, eg J Steiner, 'The Limits of State Liability for Breach of European Community Law' (1998) 4 *European Public Law* 69.

Substantive Conditions under which Liability may be Imposed

The primary objective of the *Francovich* decision and most of its subsequent jurisprudence has been to develop a minimum Community standard of accountability for those exercises of public power which affect the existence of Treaty rights and obligations.[25] The national laws of the various Member States have traditionally offered to public authorities in general, and to the exercise of legislative functions in particular, a partial or total immunity from liability.[26] At least according to the jurisprudence on direct effect and supremacy developed by the Court of Justice, such a situation was unacceptable. The Court's established caselaw on effective judicial protection demanded that, where any breach of Community law caused harm to the victim, then the perpetrator must provide some adequate form of redress. What distinguished *Francovich* from most of the cases that went before is that the Court not only required the availability of a remedy where none already existed under national law,[27] but also set out explicitly the substantive conditions under which relief was to be made available within the domestic legal systems.[28] According to Advocate General Mischo in *Francovich* itself, this could be justified by the fundamental need to guarantee the uniform enforcement of Community law rights across the Member States.[29]

However, accurately identifying the substantive conditions for exercising the right to reparation has proven a slow and speculative task. The first important judgments after *Francovich* itself were *Brasserie du Pêcheur* and *Factortame III*.[30] Again, the facts are well known: in the former case, the claimants sought damages from Germany in respect of losses suffered through national legislation related to the marketing of beer which breached Article 28 EC; in the latter case, the claimants sought compensation from the United Kingdom in respect of damage suffered through

[25] Though other considerations were no doubt involved, eg the benefits of *Francovich* in persuading Member States correctly to implement the large body of directives on which the successful completion of the Internal Market depended; eg the value of *Francovich* in reducing the injustices caused by the much aligned doctrine that directives can have vertical but not horizontal direct effect.

[26] For the relatively restrictive position under English law, eg P Craig, *Administrative Law* (Sweet & Maxwell, 2003) ch 26; W Wade and C Forsyth, *Administrative Law* (OUP, 2000) ch 21. Even in a jurisdiction like France, which possesses a more developed system of compensation in respect of official action, liability for legislative measures is very limited, eg L Neville Brown and J Bell, *French Administrative Law* (Clarendon Press, 1998).

[27] As already in Case 177/78 *Pigs and Bacon Commission v McCarren* [1979] ECR 2161 (recovery of unlawfully levied charges); Case C–213/89 *Ex p Factortame* [1990] ECR I–2433 (interim relief against national measures allegedly in breach of Community law).

[28] As before only in Cases C–143/88 and C–92/89 *Zuckerfabrik* [1991] ECR I–415 (interim relief against national measures implementing allegedly invalid secondary Community legislation).

[29] Cases C–6 & 9/90 *Francovich* [1991] ECR I–5357, paras 70–71 Opinion. Also: AG Tesauro in Cases C–46 & 48/93 *Brasserie du Pêcheur* and *Factortame III* [1996] ECR I–1029, paras 48–50 Opinion.

[30] Cases C–46 & 48/93 *Brasserie du Pêcheur* and *Factortame III* [1996] ECR I–1029.

national legislation relating to the registration of fishing vessels which infringed Article 43 EC.

The Court recalled that the conditions under which Community law confers a right to reparation depend upon the nature of the breach giving rise to the claimant's damage. In order to determine those conditions for the purposes of the disputes at hand, the Court considered it pertinent to refer to its own caselaw on the non-contractual liability of the Community institutions under Articles 235 and 288(2) EC. This was true for two reasons: first, Article 288(2) EC refers to the general principles common to the laws of the Member Sstates, from which the Court also draws inspiration in other areas of Community law; and secondly, the conditions under which the Member State may incur liability for damage caused to individuals by a breach of Community law cannot (in the absence of particular justification) differ from those governing the liability of the Community in like circumstances, since the protection of the rights which individuals derive from Community law cannot vary depending on whether a national authority or a Community authority is responsible for the damage.[31]

The Court observed that it had adopted a strict approach towards the liability of the Community in the exercise of its legislative activities under Article 288(2) EC. This was due to two considerations. First, exercise of the legislative function must not be hindered by the prospect of actions for damages whenever the general interest of the Community requires legislative measures to be adopted which may adversely affect individual interests. Secondly, in a legislative context characterised by the exercise of a wide discretion, which is essential for implementing a Community policy, the Community cannot incur liability unless the institution concerned has manifestly and gravely disregarded the limits on the exercise of its powers. The Court continued to observe that, where a Member State acts in a field where it has a wide discretion, comparable to that of the Community institutions in implementing Community policies, the conditions under which it may incur liability must in principle be the same as those under which the Community institutions incur liability in a comparable situation. In such circumstances, Community law conferred a right to reparation where three conditions are met: first, the rule of law infringed must be intended to confer rights on individuals; secondly, the breach must be sufficiently serious; and finally, there must be a direct

[31] Note, however, that recent caselaw shows the influence to run in both directions: developments in Member States liability under *Francovich* can shape the legal framework of Community liability under Art 288(2) EC. Consider, in particular, Case C–352/98P *Bergaderm* [2000] ECR I–5291; Case C–312/00 P *Camar* [2002] ECR I–11355; Case C–472/00 P *Fresh Marine* [2003] ECR I–7541. Further, eg T Tridimas, 'Liability for Breach of Community Law: Growing Up and Mellowing Down?' (2001) 38 CML Rev 301.

causal link between the breach of the obligation resting on the Member State and the damage sustained by the claimant.[32]

Brasserie made clear that the *Francovich* caselaw was not limited to a simple failure by the Member State to implement a directive within its prescribed deadline, and that the right to reparation would not always be available on a strict liability basis. After all, culpability criteria (the 'sufficiently serious breach' test) had been incorporated into the substantive conditions applicable to disputes involving legislation adopted by the Member State in breach of directly effective Treaty provisions. The Court subsequently applied its *Brasserie* conditions to other categories of dispute: for example, those concerning decisions of the national administration taken in breach of the Treaty itself;[33] and cases involving the incorrect implementation of directives by the Member State.[34] But this raised the question: why did the Member State's simple failure to implement a directive seem to be governed by different substantive conditions than every other type of Treaty infringement?

The situation became clearer in the light of *Dillenkofer*. Like *Francovich*, it involved a claim for damages against a Member State for having failed to take any measures to transpose a directive into the national legal system within the prescribed deadline. The Court observed once again that the conditions under which Community law confers a right to reparation depend on the nature of the breach giving rise to the claimant's losses. As regards the substantive conditions for liability, the Court recalled the principles set out in *Francovich*, and those set out in *Brasserie*. It held that, in substance, the two sets of substantive conditions were the same, since the requirement of a sufficiently serious breach, although not expressly mentioned in *Francovich*, was nevertheless evident from the circumstances of that case. Indeed, when the Court held that the conditions under which Community law gives rise to a right to reparation depended on the nature of the breach causing the damage, it simply meant that those conditions are to be applied according to each type of situation.[35]

Dillenkofer therefore generalised the three substantive conditions required in *Brasserie* for imposing liability under the *Francovich* caselaw. Each of these conditions is worth exploring in greater detail.

Intention to Confer Rights on Individuals The rule of Community law breached by the Member State must have been intended to confer rights on the individual claimant. This means that directly effective provisions (in the narrow sense of conferring subjective rights on individuals) will be covered. Article 28 EC on free movement of goods and Article 43 EC on

[32] Cases C–46 & 48/93 *Brasserie du Pêcheur* and *Factortame III* [1996] ECR I–1029, paras 38–51.
[33] Case C–5/94 *ex p Hedley Lomas* [1996] ECR I–2553.
[34] Case C–392/93 *ex p British Telecommunications* [1996] ECR I–1631.
[35] Cases C–178–79 & 188–90/94 *Dillenkofer* [1996] ECR I–4845.

freedom of establishment, at issue in *Brasserie* and *Factortame III*, provide useful examples. Indeed, the Court in *Brasserie* expressly rejected an argument that, insofar as individuals can assert their rights under directly effective provisions of Community law, it is unnecessary also to grant individuals a right to reparation under the *Francovich* caselaw. The right of individuals to rely on directly effective Treaty provisions before national courts is only a minimum guarantee, and is not sufficient in itself to ensure the full and complete implementation of Community law. The purpose of that right is to ensure that provisions of Community law prevail over national provisions, but it cannot in every case secure for individuals the benefits conferred on them by Community law and, in particular, avoid their sustaining damage as a result of a breach of Community law attributable to the Member State. *Francovich* had established that the full effectiveness of Community law would be impaired if individuals were unable to obtain redress when their rights were infringed by a breach of the Treaty. The Court concluded that that is true in the event of infringement of a directly effective right, where reparation is indeed the necessary corollary of the direct effect of the Community provision whose breach caused the damage sustained.[36]

Certain non-directly effective provisions may also be covered, where they are nevertheless intended to confer identifiable rights on an identifiable category of individuals of which the claimant is a member. This is true where the lack of direct effect derives only from the fact that the relevant provisions of Community law are insufficiently clear, precise and unconditional to identify the party intended to bear the corresponding obligation. The Member State's failure to adopt all necessary measures to transpose the directive into national law, and thus complete the conditions required for the free-standing justiciability of the claimant's right, becomes the actionable breach for the purposes of the right to reparation. This was the case, for example, with the Insolvency Directive at issue in *Francovich* itself.[37] The same analysis also holds true where the lack of direct effect derives merely from the fact that, although the relevant provisions of a directive may be sufficiently clear, precise and unconditional to have direct effect against a public authority, they are incapable of having direct effect against another private party due to the rule confirmed by the Court in *Faccini Dori*.[38] Again, the Member State's failure to adopt all necessary measures to transpose the directive into national law becomes the actionable breach for the purposes of the right to reparation.[39]

[36] Cases C–46 & 48/93 *Brasserie du Pêcheur* and *Factortame III* [1996] ECR I–1029, paras 18–22.
[37] Also, eg Case C–131/97 *Carbonari* [1999] ECR I–1103. Cf Case C–54/96 *Dorsch Consult* [1997] ECR I–4961.
[38] Case C–91/92 *Faccini Dori* [1994] ECR I–3325.
[39] Eg Case C–192/94 *El Corte Inglés* [1996] ECR I–1281; Case C–97/96 *Daihatsu Deutschland* [1997] ECR I–6843.

However, there are limits to how far *Francovich* can apply. First, provisions which are not directly effective, and require further implementation before the proper nature of the benefits intended or the full identify of their beneficiaries can be ascertained, will be incapable of giving rise to *Francovich* liability. This would be true, for example, of Article 293 EC on the obligation of the Member States to enter into negotiations with each other with a view to securing for the benefit of their nationals (inter alia) the abolition of double taxation within the Community.[40] Secondly, provisions which are not directly effective, and are clearly not intended to confer any rights on individuals, will also be unable to found the basis of a claim for reparation. This would be true, for example, of the Member State's obligation under Directive 75/442 to notify the Commission of any measures intended to encourage the prevention or reduction of waste production, and the recovery of waste by means of recycling—provisions which are purely inter-institutional in nature, and are not meant to affect the legal situation of third parties.[41] Thirdly, it seems unlikely that *Francovich* will apply to provisions which may well be directly effective (in the broad sense of actually creating independent effects within the national legal systems), but are still not intended to confer rights on individuals. This would be true, for example, of the Member State's obligation to undertake environmental impact assessments in accordance with Directive 85/337—a provision which can be enforced directly before the national courts at the suit of private parties, but is intended to protect the collective interest in environmental protection rather than to create subjective rights for individuals.[42] It would also, on its face, seem true of the Member State's obligation to notify draft technical regulations to the Commission under Directive 83/189—a measure whose breach renders the procedurally defective national provisions inapplicable against private parties, but is still not strictly intended to create rights or obligations for individuals.[43]

[40] See: Case 137/84 *Mutsch* [1985] ECR 2681; Case C–336/96 *Gilly* [1998] ECR I–2793.

[41] Dir 75/442 on waste, OJ 1975 L194/39 (as amended by Dir 91/156, OJ 1991 L78/32). See: Case 380/87 *Enichem Base* [1989] ECR 2491; Case C–159/00 *Sapod Audic* [2002] ECR I–5031. Cf AG Stix-Hackl in Case C–222/02 *Peter Paul* (Opinion of 25 November 2003; Judgment pending).

[42] Dir 85/337 on the assessment of the effects of certain public and private projects on the environment, OJ 1985 L175/40. See: Case C–72/95 *Kraaijeveld* [1996] ECR I–5403; Case C–435/97 *World Wildlife Fund* [1999] ECR I–5613; Case C–287/98 *Linster* [2000] ECR I–6917; Dir 2003/35 providing for public participation in respect of the drawing up of certain plans and programmes relating to the environment and amending with regard to public participation and access to justice Directives 85/337 and 96/61, OJ 2003 L156/17. Further: ch 1 (above).

[43] Dir 83/189 laying down a procedure for the provision of information in the field of technical standards and regulations, OJ 1983 L109/8 (now repealed and replaced by Dir 98/34, OJ 1998 L204/37). See: Case C–194/94 *CIA Security* [1996] ECR I–2201; Case C–443/98 *Unilever*

One major issue which remains unresolved is how far *Francovich* applies to breaches by a Member State not only of its *public law* obligations, but also of its purely *private law* duties (for example, in the field of contract or employment). It is true that *Francovich* cases have so far always involved what we would probably think of as 'public law obligations': failing to transpose directives correctly or on time;[44] enacting or maintaining legislation incompatible with the Treaty itself;[45] or taking individual administrative decisions within a general regulatory framework which fail to comply with Community law.[46] Moreover, the Court in *Brasserie* alluded to the existence of a distinction between the general duty to make reparation for one's legal defaults, and the particular situation of imposing liability upon public authorities performing public functions.[47] However, the basic principles remain framed so broadly as to be capable of catching public authorities, not only when acting as legislators or regulators, but also as employers or contractors. The Court consistently states that *any* breach of a Community norm which is intended to confer rights on the individual is capable of activating the *Francovich* right to reparation against the wrongdoing Member State.[48]

The academic debate is similarly unclear. Pre-*Brasserie*, some observers saw *Francovich* as conferring a general right to reparation based on unlawful conduct by the Member State, without further reference to any requirement of culpability, and thus applicable to the realms of both public and private law;[49] whereas other commentators speculated that the Court would soon introduce fault-based criteria more appropriate to an administrative law context, and thus implied that *Francovich* was best considered a form of public law action.[50] Post-*Brasserie*, many writers recognised the administrative law provenance of the substantive liability conditions borrowed by the Court from its caselaw under Article 288(2)

Italia [2000] ECR I–7535. However, consider the Court's reference to the protection of individual rights under Dir 83/189 in Case C–159/00 *Sapod Audic* [2002] ECR I–5031.

[44] Eg Case C–140/97 *Rechberger* [1999] ECR I–3499; Case C–81/98 *Alcatel Austria* [1999] ECR I–7671; Case C–371/97 *Gozza* [2000] ECR I–7881.

[45] Eg Cases C–46 & 48/93 *Brasserie du Pêcheur* and *Factortame III* [1996] ECR I–1029; Case C–242/95 *GT-Link* [1997] ECR I–4449; Case C–302/97 *Konle* [1999] ECR I–3099.

[46] Eg Case C–127/95 *Norbrook* [1998] ECR I–1531; Case C–319/96 *Brinkmann* [1998] ECR I–5255; Case C–118/00 *Larsy* [2001] ECR I–5063.

[47] Eg Cases C–46 & 48/93 *Brasserie du Pêcheur* and *Factortame III* [1996] ECR I–1029: contrast paras 20–23 with paras 43–45. Also: AG Tesauro in Cases C–46 & 48/93 *Brasserie du Pêcheur* and *Factortame III* [1996] ECR I–1029, paras 12 and 67–68 Opinion.

[48] Eg Cases C–46 & 48/93 *Brasserie du Pêcheur* and *Factortame III* [1996] ECR I–1029, para 51.

[49] Consider, eg C Lewis and S Moore, 'Duties, Directives and Damages in European Community Law' [1993] PL 151.

[50] Eg P Craig, '*Francovich*, Remedies and the Scope of Damages Liability' (1993) 109 LQR 595. Cf J Steiner, 'From Direct Effects to *Francovich*: Shifting Means of Enforcement of Community Law' (1993) 18 EL Rev 3.

EC;[51] but some commentators still interpreted *Francovich* as providing a general right to reparation against the defaulting Member State, without drawing any further distinction between the different public and private law contexts in which public authorities might operate.[52] Indeed, Advocate General Léger in *Hedley Lomas* seemed happy to use the benefit of hindsight to recategorise *Foster v British Gas* as a *Francovich*-style case. Yet *Foster* clearly involved a purely operational breach of Community law by an emanation of the state,[53] which had arisen within a private law context, and as regards which the claimant already had access to effective private law remedies.[54] For the most part, however, the issue of whether *Francovich* applies to vertical-yet-private-law disputes appears simply to have gone unnoticed, or at least unaddressed.[55]

Against this background, it is arguable that the Court should not permit *Francovich* to be available in private law situations at all, because this would be conceptually inappropriate. *Francovich* contributes to the system of principles governing the administrative law responsibilities of public authorities under the Treaty, in particular, by establishing a threshold of culpability designed to balance the private interest in obtaining reparation against the public interest in limiting liability. Yet in the private law sphere, the substantive liability conditions established in *Brasserie* serve no useful purpose, because the public authority is not acting in the general interest, and we have no expectation that a 'sufficiently serious breach' of Community law should furnish a gateway to reparation under the Treaty. This suggests that the Court should not treat *Francovich* as running parallel with every Community norm intended to confer rights on the individual. *Francovich* should only be available (if at all) where the dispute concerns the public law liabilities of national authorities, not where it concerns their private law liabilities. The latter should be determined either on the basis of liability per se; or as liability judged according to fault criteria suited to the particular private law sphere at issue.[56]

[51] Eg P Craig, 'Once More Unto the Breach: The Community, the State and Damages Liability' (1997) 113 LQR 67. More recently, eg W van Gerven, 'Harmonization of Private Law: Do We Need It?' (2004) 41 CML Rev 505.

[52] Eg N Emiliou, 'State Liability Under Community Law: Shedding More Light on the *Francovich* Principle?' (1996) 21 EL Rev 399; though note the query raised by E Deards, 'Curiouser and Curiouser? The Development of Member State Liability in the Court of Justice' (1997) 3 *European Public Law* 117.

[53] Actionable as such through the vertical direct effect of Dir 76/207, OJ 1976 L39/40; and triggered, of course, by the transpositional breach committed by the Member State itself.

[54] Case C–5/94 *ex p Hedley Lomas* [1996] ECR I–2553; Case C–188/89 *Foster v British Gas* [1990] ECR I–3313. Also: W van Gerven, 'Non-contractual Liability of Member States, Community Institutions and Individuals for Breaches of Community Law with a View to a Common Law for Europe' (1994) 1 *Maastricht Journal of European and Comparative Law* 6.

[55] All three of the main English language textbooks are basically silent on this issue: S Weatherill and P Beaumont, *EU Law* (Penguin Books, 1999); A Arnull, A Dashwood, M Ross, and D Wyatt, *Wyatt and Dashwood's European Union Law* (Sweet & Maxwell, 2000); P Craig and G de Búrca, *EU Law: Text, Cases, & Materials* (OUP, 2003).

[56] Further: ch 1 (above).

In itself, this is hardly a very radical idea: after all, the Member States learned exactly the same sorts of lesson decades ago. For example, under French law, the early post-revolutionary notion that public law applied to all legal relations involving the state, whilst private law applied only to legal relations between individuals, gave way in the later 19th century to a more complex approach, based on the concept of 'the performance of a public service,' by which the activities of public authorities may be subject to private law before the ordinary courts (say) when carrying out activities of a commercial or industrial character, and as regards other types of conduct which can be classified as essentially private in nature.[57] Conversely, the Diceyan ideal of the English constitution, whereby the rule of law requires public authorities to be subject to the same legal obligations as any private individual, has given way to the development of administrative legal principles imposing special duties upon bodies engaged in the performance of public functions; and also to extensive adaptations of ordinary tort law principles which make it more difficult to impose liability (say) in negligence, when a public authority is performing duties in the general interest.[58] In neither legal system can public authorities shelter behind simply their capacity *qua* public authorities, so as to evade the responsibilities which they would otherwise engage as a matter of private law.[59]

Sufficiently Serious Breach of Community Law The Member State's breach of the relevant Community provision must be sufficiently serious to warrant imposing liability to make reparation. In this regard, it is necessary to demonstrate that the Member State has committed a manifest and grave disregard of the limits of its powers.[60] However, for these purposes, it is possible to identify two main approaches in the caselaw.

Older judgments (such as *Hedley Lomas* and *Dillenkofer*) suggested that a sufficiently serious breach/manifest and grave disregard could be established in one of two ways.[61] First, where the Member State had an appreciable degree of discretion in discharging its Treaty obligations, whether that discretion was legislative or administrative in nature, the national court should take into account the various factors identified in

[57] See, eg L Neville Brown and J and Bell, *French Administrative Law* (Clarendon Press, 1998) ch 6.
[58] Eg *X v Bedfordshire CC* [1995] 2 AC 633; *Stovin v Wise* [1996] AC 923. Note the impact of the ECHR here, in particular: *Osman v United Kingdom* (Judgment of ECtHR, 28 October 1998); *Barrett v Enfield LBC* [1999] 3 All ER 193; *Phelps v Hillingdon LBC* [2001] 2 AC 619; *Z v United Kingdom* (Judgment of ECtHR, 10 May 2001).
[59] For further discussion of these issues, see: M Dougan, 'What is the Point of *Francovich*?' in T Tridimas & P Nebbia (eds), *European Union Law for the Twenty-First Century: Rethinking the New Legal Order* (Hart Publishing, 2004). See also: ch 1 (above).
[60] Cases C–178–79 & 188–90/94 *Dillenkofer* [1996] ECR I–4845.
[61] Case C–5/94 *ex p Hedley Lomas* [1996] ECR I–2553; Cases C–178–79 & 188–90/94 *Dillenkofer* [1996] ECR I–4845. Also, eg AG Tesauro in Cases C–46 & 48/93 *Brasserie du Pêcheur* and *Factortame III* [1996] ECR I–1029; AG Cosmas in Cases C–94–5/95 *Bonifaci* [1997] ECR I–3969.

Brasserie: the clarity and precision of the rule breached; the measure of discretion left by that rule to the national authorities; whether the infringement was intentional or involuntary; whether any error of law was excusable or inexcusable; whether the position taken by the Community institutions may have contributed towards the breach. On any view, a breach of Community law would be sufficiently serious if it persisted despite a judgment from the Court of Justice finding the infringement to be established, or settled case-law from which it was clear that the Member State's conduct constituted an infringement.[62] Secondly, where the Member State had no appreciable degree of discretion in discharging its Treaty obligations, the mere breach of Community law will be considered sufficiently serious to incur liability to make reparation—without the need to take into account any other factors.[63] For example, in *Dillenkofer*, the Court held that the obligation to implement directives by a particular deadline was clear and left no discretion to the Member States; so where that deadline passed and the Member State had failed to take any measures to implement the directive, that in itself would amount to a sufficiently serious breach of the Treaty.[64]

Thus, in this line of caselaw, discretion is the overriding factor which determines the imposition of *Francovich* liability.[65] Viewed from the perspective of our 'sectoral model,' the right to reparation thus incorporated a degree of sensitivity towards the relationship between regulatory differentiation and effective judicial protection. True, the criteria for determining the existence of a sufficiently serious breach were harmonised at the Community level. But those harmonised criteria still recognised that the greater the discretion enjoyed by the Member States under Community law, assessed at least in part by reference to whether the relevant Treaty norms were relatively more or less centralised in character, the less likely it would prove necessary to recognise the individual's right to obtain reparation in respect of losses incurred through a breach of the Treaty attributable to the national authorities.

However, there was always some element of circularity in the Court's reasoning in this line of caselaw. After all, some of the factors listed in *Brasserie de Pêcheur* for the purposes of assessing the existence of a

[62] Cases C–46 & 48/93 *Brasserie du Pêcheur* and *Factortame III* [1996] ECR I–1029, paras 55–57. Further: Case C–392/93 *ex p British Telecommunications* [1996] ECR I–1631; Cases C–283 & 291–292/94 *Denkavit* [1996] ECR I–5063; Case C–127/95 *Norbrook* [1998] ECR I–1531; Case C–140/97 *Rechberger* [1999] ECR I–3499; Case C–150/99 *Stockholm Lindöpark* [2001] ECR I–493.

[63] Cases C–178–179 & 188–190/94 *Dillenkofer* [1996] ECR I–4845, para 27. Also, eg AG Jacobs in Case C–112/00 *Schmidberger* [2003] ECR I–5659.

[64] Cases C–178–79 & 188–90/94 *Dillenkofer* [1996] ECR I–4845.

[65] Consider also recent caselaw on Art 288(2) EC, eg Case C–352/98 P *Bergaderm* [2000] ECR I–5291; Case C–312/00 P *Camar* [2002] ECR I–11355; Case C–472/00 P *Fresh Marine* [2003] ECR I–7541.

sufficiently serious breach in situations where the national judge had found that the Member State enjoyed an appreciable margin of discretion in complying with its Treaty obligation could *also* be considered relevant in deciding whether the Member State enjoyed any such margin of discretion in the first place.[66] Perhaps for that very reason, more recent judgments (such as *Haim* and *Larsy*) suggest an important change in the Court's approach.[67] Again, a sufficiently serious breach may be established in one of two ways. First and as before, where the Member State had an appreciable degree of discretion, the claimant must demonstrate a manifest and grave disregard, taking into account the various factors listed in *Brasserie*. Secondly, where the Member State had no appreciable degree of discretion, the mere breach of Community law *may* be considered sufficiently serious—but not necessarily so. It is still necessary to take into account the various factors listed in *Brasserie*. In other words, this caselaw recognises that discretion is not the only factor involved in limiting the liabilities of public authorities performing functions in the public interest. There might well be an insufficiently serious breach, even though the Member State had no real discretion in discharging its Treaty obligations, for example, because the relevant Community provisions were ambiguous and the Member State acted reasonably and in good faith.[68]

This caselaw suggests that the Court is prepared to dispense altogether with its previous bipartite approach to establishing the existence of a sufficiently serious breach/manifest and grave disregard, based around the existence or absence of an appreciable degree of Member State discretion under Community law, and instead adopt a genuinely unified approach to liability based in each case upon a global assessment of the *Brasserie* factors (discretion being only one among them).[69] Indeed, Advocate General Léger in *Köbler* argued that, given the manner in which the caselaw has recently developed, the decisive factor for establishing *Francovich* liability seems to be whether the error of law at issue can be considered excusable or inexcusable—an approach which would at least

[66] Similarly, eg C Hilson, 'The Role of Discretion in EC Law on Non-contractual Liability' (forthcoming).

[67] Case C–424/97 *Haim* [2000] ECR I–5123; Case C–118/00 *Larsy* [2001] ECR I–5063. Also, eg Case C–319/96 *Brinkmann* [1998] ECR I–5255; Case C–224/01 *Köbler* (Judgment of 30 September 2003); Case C–63/01 *Evans* (Judgment of 4 December 2003). Further, eg AG Léger in Case C–5/94 *Hedley Lomas* [1996] ECR I–2553; AG Saggio in Case C–140/97 *Rechberger* [1999] ECR I–3499.

[68] Also, eg J Steiner, 'The Limits of State Liability for Breach of European Community Law' (1998) 4 *European Public Law* 69. Cf R Van den Bergh and H-B Schäfer, 'State Liability for Infringement of the EC Treaty: Economic Arguments in Support of a Rule of "Obvious Negligence"' (1998) 23 EL Rev 552.

[69] Consider, in this regard, eg AG Jacobs in Case C–319/96 *Brinkmann* [1998] ECR I–5255; AG La Pergola in Case C–302/97 *Konle* [1999] ECR I–3099.

have the merit of simplicity.[70] In any case, judged according to our 'sectoral model,' *Francovich*'s in-built sensitivity towards the balance between regulatory uniformity and differentiation may have been reduced, but the degree of the Member State's autonomous policy competence remains relevant to legal framework of the right to reparation.

Of course, in all cases, the existence and extent of the Member State's discretion must be determined by reference to Community law, not national rules.[71]

Direct Causal Link Between Breach and Damage The third substantive condition which claimants must fulfil before acquiring a right to reparation under the *Francovich* caselaw concerns the existence of a direct causal link between the Member State's breach and the damage suffered.

The Court in *Brasserie* seemed to envisage that the Member States would retain a significant degree of influence over this particular substantive condition. It was simply stated that:

> it is for the national courts to determine whether there is a direct causal link between the breach of the obligation borne by the State and the damage sustained by the injured parties.[72]

By contrast with its extensive discussion of the 'intention to confer rights' and 'sufficiently serious breach' conditions, the Court did not elaborate any further on the criteria applicable to the requirement of a direct causal link. This was widely interpreted to mean that causation should (at least in principle) be determined on the basis of national (rather than Community) law. That position was heavily criticised: first, because of fears that domestic discretion over the test of causation might be exploited so as to limit the practical impact of the *Francovich* caselaw, by providing a loophole through which Member States with relatively restrictive principles of causation could escape liability;[73] and secondly, because of concerns that variations in national causation rules would in any event lead to the disuniform application of the right to reparation across the Member States, thus undermining the ideal of *Francovich* as a genuinely harmonised Community law remedy.[74]

[70] Case C–224/01 *Köbler* (Judgment of 30 September 2003), para 139 Opinion of 8 April 2003. Cf the approach of the EFTA Court in Case E-9/97 *Sveinbjörnsdóttir* (Judgment of 10 December 1998); and the approach of the House of Lords in *ex p Factortame (No 5)* [2000] 1 AC 524.

[71] Case C–424/97 *Haim* [2000] ECR I–5123, paras 38–40.

[72] Cases C–46 & 48/93 *Brasserie du Pêcheur* and *Factortame III* [1996] ECR I–1029, para 65.

[73] Consider, eg the judgment of the German Federal Supreme Court in *Brasserie du Pêcheur* [1997] 1 CMLR 971. Further: E Deards, '*Brasserie du Pêcheur*: Snatching Defeat from the Jaws of Victory?' (1997) 22 EL Rev 620.

[74] Further, eg F Smith and L Woods, 'Causation in *Francovich*: The Neglected Problem' (1997) 46 ICLQ 925.

The Court seems to have responded to such fears by tightening its grip over the direct causal link requirement—continuing to acknowledge that it is, in principle, for the national courts to determine whether causation exists, but sometimes deciding that the Court itself has sufficient information to judge whether a causal link should, in fact, be found in a particular dispute. For example, *Brinkmann* concerned Denmark's failure to implement Directive 79/32 concerning tobacco taxes into national law within the prescribed deadline.[75] However, the Danish administration still sought to comply with the relevant provisions of the Directive in practice. The Court held that this broke the chain of causation between the legislature's total failure to implement the Directive and the claimant's losses, thus precluding liability on the basis of a breach which would otherwise have been treated as sufficiently serious per se. Instead, liability could only be incurred on the basis of a manifest and grave disregard by the Danish administration of the limits of the Member State's discretion, assessed according to the *Brasserie* criteria, so as to take into account the relative clarity or complexity of the relevant provisions of the Directive.[76] Similarly, in *Rechberger*, Austria failed to implement the Package Holidays Directive within its time-limit.[77] The claimant consumers suffered losses when their private tour operator went bankrupt, and they were unable to rely upon the guarantee of reimbursement contained in the Directive. The Court specifically pointed out that the claimants' action for *Francovich* damages against Austria could not be dismissed on the grounds that the chain of causation (which had already been found by the national court prima facie to exist in accordance with domestic law) had been broken by the imprudent conduct of the private tour operators, since that was precisely the risk the Directive was intended to protect consumers against.[78]

Although this caselaw demonstrates the Court's increasing intervention in matters of causation within the context of the *Francovich* right to reparation, it would not seem entirely accurate to claim that the causal link requirement has now been subjected to full judicial harmonisation—effectively pre-empting existing domestic rules in favour of a centralised Community standard.[79] It seems more appropriate to say that causation rules remain within the presumptive competence of the national legal

[75] Dir 79/32 on taxes other than turnover taxes which affect the consumption of manufactured tobacco, OJ 1979 L10/8 (now repealed and replaced by Dir 95/59, OJ 1995 L 291/40).
[76] Case C–319/96 *Brinkmann* [1998] ECR I–5255.
[77] Dir 90/314 on package travel, package holidays and package tours, OJ 1990 L158/59.
[78] Case C–140/97 *Rechberger* [1999] ECR I–3499.
[79] Consider the views of T Tridimas, 'Liability for Breach of Community Law: Growing Up and Mellowing Down?' (2001) 38 CML Rev 301, who argues that causation is now governed by substantive Community rules; only its application to the facts of any given dispute falls within the competence of the national courts.

order, subject to negative harmonisation through the residual application of the principles of equivalence and effectiveness.[80]

Sufficient Conditions, But Minimum Standards The Court in *Brasserie* clearly stated that the three substantive conditions set out above are sufficient to found a right in individuals to obtain redress.[81] National rules may not impose more rigorous requirements for the exercise of the right to reparation. Thus, the requirement under English law that public authorities must have been guilty of malice before incurring liability under the tort of misfeasance in a public office is relevant to *Francovich* liability only insofar as bad faith has already been incorporated into the test for a manifest and grave disregard by the Member State of the limits of its powers.[82] Similarly, the Court observed that the *Brasserie* test does take into account certain objective and subjective factors connected with the concept of fault under the national legal systems; but ruled that the Member State's obligation to make reparation cannot depend upon any concept of fault (whether intentional or negligent) going beyond that of a sufficiently serious breach of Community law, since the imposition of any such supplementary condition would be tantamount to calling in question the right to reparation founded upon the Community legal order.[83]

However, the substantive conditions established in *Brasserie* are merely minimum standards of judicial protection for the individual. Member States remain free to grant relief under more generous conditions than those laid down by Community law itself.[84] Indeed, by virtue of the principle of equivalence, any less stringent standards of liability, applicable to comparable domestic law claims against public authorities for having exceeded the limits of their powers, must be extended also to the *Francovich* right to reparation.[85]

Definition of 'the State' for the Purposes of Francovich Liability

Having discussed the substantive conditions required for *Francovich* liability to be imposed, our next issue concerns the range of bodies whose acts might lead to the attribution of *Francovich* liability upon the Member State. The basic principle was established by the Court in *Brasserie*: the

[80] Similarly, eg C Kremer, 'Liability for Breach of European Community Law: An Analysis of the New Remedy in the Light of English and German Law' (2003) 22 *Yearbook of European Law* 203.

[81] Cases C–46 & 48/93 *Brasserie du Pêcheur* and *Factortame III* [1996] ECR I–1029, para 66.

[82] Consider Cases C–46 & 48/93 *Brasserie du Pêcheur* and *Factortame III* [1996] ECR I–1029, paras 66–73.

[83] Consider Cases C–46 & 48/93 *Brasserie du Pêcheur* and *Factortame III* [1996] ECR I–1029, paras 75–80.

[84] Cases C–46 & 48/93 *Brasserie du Pêcheur* and *Factortame III* [1996] ECR I–1029, para 66.

[85] Further: ch 1 (above).

right to reparation applies to any case in which a Member State breaches Community law, whichever is the authority of the Member State whose act or omission was responsible for the breach. The Court justified this principle by the fact that, under international law, a state which incurs liability for breach of an international commitment is viewed as a single entity, irrespective of whether the breach is attributable to the legislature, the judiciary or the executive. According to the Court, that principle must apply *a fortiori* in the Community legal order since all national authorities are bound in performing their tasks to comply with the rules laid down by Community law which directly govern the situation of individuals. In addition, the Court observed that, having regard to the fundamental requirement that Community law be uniformly applied, the obligation to make good damage caused to individuals by breaches of the Treaty could not depend upon domestic rules as to the division of powers between constitutional authorities.[86]

Against that background, it is possible to identify a range of public bodies whose acts will lead to the attribution of *Francovich* liability upon the Member State. First, acts of the national legislature which breach Community law may found the basis of the right to reparation. The Court in *Brasserie* made clear that, even where a breach of the Treaty is attributable to the national legislature, this cannot affect the requirements inherent in the protection of the rights of individuals who rely on Community law to obtain redress for damage caused by that breach.[87] Secondly, acts of the national executive (such as administrative decisions taken by central government departments) may also engage Member State liability under *Francovich*. For example, in *ex parte Hedley Lomas*, a policy by the Ministry of Agriculture systematically to refuse the issue of licences for the export of live animals to Spain, in clear breach of Article 29 EC, was sufficient to justify the United Kingdom's liability to make reparation.[88]

Thirdly, the Court in *Köbler* established that decisions of a national supreme court may, in certain circumstances, also give rise to a right to reparation against the Member State. *Köbler* concerned a finding by the Austrian Supreme Administrative Court that loyalty bonuses paid to professors only upon completion of a certain period of service within the national university system did not constitute an infringement of Article 39 EC and Article 7(1) Regulation 1612/68.[89] That finding was in fact based upon an erroneous assessment of Community law. Moreover, the Supreme Administrative Court made that assessment after withdrawing a reference to the Court of Justice under Article 234 EC, having wrongly taken

[86] Cases C–46 & 48/93 *Brasserie du Pêcheur* and *Factortame III* [1996] ECR I–1029, paras 31f.
[87] Cases C–46 & 48/93 *Brasserie du Pêcheur* and *Factortame III* [1996] ECR I–1029, paras 34–36.
[88] Case C–5/94 *Ex p Hedley Lomas* [1996] ECR I–2553.
[89] Reg 1612/68 on freedom of movement for workers within the Community, OJ 1968 L257/2.

the view that resolution of the issue fell within the scope of the *acte clair* doctrine in the light of the judgment in *Schöning*.[90] On an action for damages against Austria, brought by the claimant on the basis of the judgment delivered by the Supreme Administrative Court, the Court of Justice found that the full effectiveness of the Treaty would be called into question, and the protection of rights derived from Community law would be weakened, if individuals were unable to obtain reparation in respect of infringements resulting from judicial decisions delivered at last instance in respect of which there could be no further possibility of correction.[91] However, when applying the substantive conditions for reparation, liability in respect of an infringement of the Treaty resulting from a judicial decision delivered at last instance should be incurred only in exceptional cases where the national court has manifestly breached Community law—taking into account the usual *Brasserie* factors, but also whether the domestic court had abrogated its obligation to make a preliminary reference under Article 234 EC. Perhaps surprisingly, the Court of Justice found that no such manifest breach had been established on the facts: the compatibility of loyalty bonuses with the Treaty rules on free movement for workers had not been addressed clearly in the caselaw extant at the date of the Supreme Administrative Court's judgment, and the Article 234 EC reference had been withdrawn on the basis of an incorrect interpretation of the ruling in *Schöning*.[92]

Köbler is undoubtedly an important judgment—not least because of the indirect implications of *Francovich* liability for related debates about judicial dialogue between the national and Community judiciaries. For example, *Köbler* clearly increases the incentive for national judges not to abuse their discretion under the *CILFIT* caselaw, by refraining from making Article 234 EC references in respect of issues which are not genuinely covered by the *acte clair* doctrine.[93] Similarly, *Köbler* has the potential to shift the goalposts of the supremacy debate: national judges might be more reluctant to shirk their obligation to disapply any provision of domestic law which conflicts with the Treaty, in flagrant defiance of the Court's well-established caselaw, if that would almost certainly constitute

[90] Case C–15/96 *Schöning* [1998] ECR I–47.

[91] In reaching that conclusion, the Court dismissed arguments that *Francovich* liability might undermine the principle of *res judicata*, or the independence of the judiciary. The Court also noted that the principle of liability for judicial decisions was accepted by the legal orders of most Member States; and had been established under the caselaw of the European Court of Human Rights. Further on these issues: G Anagnostaras, 'The Principle of State Liability for Judicial Breaches: The Impact of EC Law' (2001) 7 *European Public Law* 281.

[92] Case C–224/01 *Köbler* (Judgment of 30 September 2003). Indeed, the judgment seems to suggest that *Francovich* liability for judicial decisions will be incurred only in extreme and really very unlikely circumstances, eg where the claimant can demonstrate that the judges of the national supreme court were motivated by improper purposes.

[93] Case 283/81 *CILFIT* [1982] ECR 3415.

a manifest breach of Community law justifying the imposition of *Francovich* liability upon the Member State. However, the Court in *Köbler* repeatedly stressed that its ruling applied only to national judges acting at last instance, which carry a particular responsibility both for ensuring the effective enjoyment by individuals of their Treaty rights, and for making preliminary references to the Court under Article 234 EC. For the time-being, therefore, it seems that infringements of the Treaty perpetrated via decisions delivered by lower courts and tribunals will not furnish the basis for Member State liability under *Francovich*.[94] In any case, the implications of *Köbler* also pose some tricky problems for the Member States (though such problems are not necessarily unique to the Community law sphere). For example, legal systems based upon a unitary court structure may encounter problems in offering access to justice which complies with the standards expected under Article 6 ECHR and the general principles of Community law, given that any judgment of the lower courts concerning *Francovich* liability would remain subject to appeal before the very supreme court whose past failure to comply with the Treaty now constitutes the subject-matter of the claimant's action for reparation.[95]

Fourthly, it is clear that the right to reparation can become engaged not only by acts of the central government institutions, but also by the conduct of local and regional authorities. *Konle* raised the question whether, in federal states, reparation must necessarily be provided by the central authorities, even though the relevant breach of Community law was committed by a regional authority. The Court held that it was for each Member State to ensure that individuals obtain redress for infringements of their Community rights, irrespective of which specific public authority was responsible either for the actual breach or (under domestic rules) for making reparation. However, although a Member State could not plead the distribution of powers and responsibilities between the bodies which exist in its national legal order in order to evade liability, Community law does not require Member States to make any change in the distribution of powers and responsibilities between the public bodies which exist on their territory.[96] In other words, although the federal government was ultimately responsible for the acts of regional authorities under Community law, the federal government could still insist that those regional authorities should make the required reparation.

[94] Especially bearing in mind the duty to exhaust available remedies (such as rights of appeal): see further below. Cf Case C–129/00 *Commission v Italy* (Judgment of 9 December 2003).

[95] The Court did not seem to consider this problem insurmountable: Case C–224/01 *Köbler* (Judgment of 30 September 2003), paras 44–47.

[96] Case C–302/97 *Konle* [1999] ECR I–3099.

Fifthly, the Member State may incur liability also in respect of the acts of autonomous public authorities and regulatory agencies. For example, *Haim* concerned a decision by the Association of Dental Practitioners for Social Security Schemes in Nordrhein refusing to examine whether professional experience acquired in another Member State was equivalent to the standards expected under German rules, thus hindering exercise of the claimant's freedom of establishment under Article 43 EC. The Court repeated its findings in *Konle* that it is for each Member State to ensure that individuals obtain reparation, whichever public authority is responsible for the breach and (under domestic law) for making reparation; but that this did not necessarily imply that reparation must be provided by the Member State itself in order for its obligations under Community law to be fulfilled. This principle applied not only to federal states, but also as regards Member States in which certain legislative or administrative tasks have been devolved to bodies with a certain degree of autonomy, or to public law bodies legally distinct from the state. In such cases, reparation might validly be made by the entity responsible for the relevant infringement.[97]

This caselaw suggests that the relationship between the Member State and other public authorities, as regards the establishment and discharge of liability under *Francovich*, is relatively fluid. On the one hand, *Francovich* liability can be attributed to the Member State whatever the organ responsible for the relevant breach of Community law—including local authorities and autonomous public law bodies.[98] On the other hand, the final discharge of *Francovich* liability as incurred by the Member State can be passed back onto the local authority or autonomous public law body which was directly responsible for breaching Community law. In this regard, the Court in *Konle* and *Haim* held merely that Community law *does not preclude* a local authority/public law body, in addition to the Member State itself, from being liable to make reparation. By implication, nor does Community law *permit* the citizen to bring an action for reparation directly against the wrongdoing local authority/public law body *as of right*. The possibility of direct liability would appear to depend upon the internal organisation of the Member State itself. Moreover, although the Court seemed to envisage that, in cases where the Member State decided to permit direct actions against recalcitrant public bodes, liability to make reparation would be shared jointly between the two entities, *Brasserie* established that domestic procedural rules may impose a requirement to exhaust alternative remedies before bringing a *Francovich*

[97] Case C–424/97 *Haim* [2000] ECR I–5123.

[98] Also: Case C–118/00 *Larsy II* [2001] ECR I–5063. Cf AG Ruiz-Jarabo Colomer in Case C–77/95 *Züchner* [1996] ECR I–5689, paras 65f.

claim.[99] It is thus possible, not only that the Member State may (at its own discretion) permit direct actions for reparation based on the liability of a public authority, but also that the Member State may (again at its own discretion) insist that such direct actions are the citizen's primary means of redress, which must be pursued before any default claim can be brought against the central government.[100]

This fluidity applies not only where the Member State incurs vicarious liability for the acts of a public authority, then devolves responsibility for making reparation back onto that entity; but also where the Member State incurs liability on the basis of its own unlawful acts, then delegates responsibility for making reparation onto some entity in no way directly responsible for the relevant breach of Community law. This possibility arises, in particular, where the Member State chooses to make reparation for its own wrongdoing through the retroactive application of the relevant provisions of Community law. For example, *Carbonari* concerned the Italian legislature's failure to transpose a Community directive concerning the mutual recognition of medical qualifications within its deadline, causing the claimants to be denied appropriate remuneration in respect of certain periods of specialist training as envisaged by the directive. The Court accepted that Italy could make reparation for its infringement by permitting the claimants to seek remuneration retroactively, in accordance with the national legislation subsequently adopted to implement the directive. In practice, that might well mean that the financial consequences of Italy's breach of the Community law are borne by the universities offering specialist medical training, rather than by the Member State which failed to implement the directive on time.[101]

These cases raise difficult questions, for example, about the possibility of seeking indemnification (on the basis of national or even Community law) within the diffuse network of public authorities now governed by the *Francovich* principles.[102] For present purposes, however, judgments such as *Konle* and *Haim* are important because they suggest that the Court has decentralised competence to determine the nature of the remedy due pursuant to a finding of *Francovich* liability, by envisaging a distinction (drawn by the Member State itself) between the author whose conduct attracts substantive liability, and the identity of the body from which subsequent reparation may be obtained.

Finally, the question arises: might the Member State incur *Francovich* liability in respect of acts committed by 'emanations of the state' in the

[99] Cases C–46 & 48/93 *Brasserie du Pêcheur* and *Factortame III* [1996] ECR I–1029, paras 84–85.
[100] See further below.
[101] Case C–131/97 *Carbonari* [1999] ECR I–1103. Consider also, eg Case C–373/95 *Maso* [1997] ECR I–4051; Cases C–94–5/95 *Bonifaci* [1997] ECR I–3969. See further below.
[102] Further, eg G Anagnostaras, 'The Allocation of Responsibility in State Liability Actions for Breach of Community Law: A Modern Gordian Knot?' (2001) 26 EL Rev 139.

sense of *Foster v British Gas*?[103] Although there is authority for the proposition that public undertakings may be caught by the *Francovich* caselaw,[104] the Court has not yet addressed the *Foster v British Gas* issue directly in its caselaw.[105]

On the one hand, there might seem to be a convenient parallel in using the same body of caselaw to determine both the scope of direct effect in situations involving the non-transposition of directives, and the range of entities in respect of whose conduct the Member State may incur liability under *Francovich*. From an 'integration through law' perspective, this parallel might seem especially attractive when compared to the difficulties, as regards maintaining a uniform application of the *Francovich* right to reparation across the Member States, of simply leaving the definition of 'public authorities' to national law.[106] On the other hand, it is clear that the definition of the state for the purposes of Community law does indeed vary across different fields, depending on the purpose and context of the relevant Treaty provisions.[107] The definition of the state adopted by the Court as regards the direct effect of directives is intended to prevent the Member State deriving any advantage whatsoever from the failure to comply with its Treaty obligation to implement directives correctly and on time. This is a more narrow purpose than that of the *Francovich* action, which contributes to the effective judicial protection of *all* Community rights, not just those arising from the non-implementation of directives by the Member States. So, there is no necessary connection between the two lines of caselaw which would require using in each situation an identical definition of the state.

Indeed, there are good reasons for not treating *Foster* as a relevant authority in the context of *Francovich*. To hold the Member State responsible for breaches committed by an 'emanation of the state' would in fact amount to an unfair reallocation of financial responsibility in respect of

[103] Case C–188/89 *Foster v British Gas* [1990] ECR I–3313.

[104] In particular: Case C–242/95 *GT-Link* [1997] ECR I–4449, where the Court suggested that infringements committed by a public undertaking which is responsible to a national ministry and whose budget is governed by a national budget law could give rise to *Francovich* liability on the part of the Member State.

[105] Indeed, there has been only limited academic discussion of this issue, eg P Craig, 'Once More Unto the Breach: The Community, the State and Damages Liability' (1997) 113 LQR 67; D Waelbroeck, 'Treaty Violations and Liability of Member States: The Effect of the *Francovich* Case Law' in T Heukels & A McDonnell (eds), *The Action for Damages in Community Law* (Kluwer Law International, 1997).

[106] As indeed seems to have been the Court's approach in Case C–424/97 *Haim* [2000] ECR I–5123.

[107] By way of illustration: contrast the definition of employment in the public service under Art 39(4) EC (eg Case 149/79 *Commission v Belgium* [1980] ECR 3881; Case C–473/93 *Commission v Luxembourg* [1996] ECR I–3207); with the definition of the Member State for the purposes of Art 28 EC (eg Case 222/82 *Apple and Pear Development Council* [1983] ECR 4083; Case C–292/92 *Hünermund* [1993] ECR I–6787). Further: AG van Gerven in Case C–188/89 *Foster v British Gas* [1990] ECR I–3313 itself.

breaches of Community law. In situations of vertical direct effect following the non-transposition of directives, responsibility for respecting the relevant provisions of Community law falls directly upon the emanation of the state itself: for example, in situations such as *Foster*, the regulatory compliance costs imposed upon employers by the Equal Treatment Directive are incurred and discharged by the emanation of the state.[108] Community lawyers accept that this is a fiction in terms of the Court's underlying rationale for having vertical but not horizontal direct effect, since it is difficult to maintain either that the Member State is being punished by enforcing the directive against an autonomous organisation, or that such autonomous organisations are in any way responsible for the Member State's underlying failure to implement. But this fiction is convenient in that it reduces unnecessary hardship for individuals, and does not fundamentally alter the allocation of legal responsibility and concomitant financial incumbrances as envisaged by the Community legislature. By contrast, in situations involving the imposition of *Francovich* liability, responsibility for making reparation falls ultimately onto the Member State itself. Yet why should a Member State be held in all cases vicariously liable for unlawful acts perpetrated by an 'emanation of the state' as defined under *Foster v British Gas*? The Member State itself has done nothing wrong, and it hardly seems plausible that the connection between Member State and autonomous organisation is so close as to warrant any such vicarious liability. It is true that, under *Konle* and *Haim*, Member States could devolve their liability back onto the state emanation, and require aggrieved individuals to pursue claims against that state emanation in the first instance. But this will not help, for example, if the autonomous organisation has become insolvent.

There are therefore grounds for arguing that the *Francovich* principle should not draw upon the *Foster* caselaw. For now, this implies that the full definition of the 'state' for the purposes attributing liability is left to each national legal order, particularly as regards the outer limits of the concept of a 'public authority,' though the Court may yet develop autonomous Community law criteria for delimiting the personal scope of the *Francovich* right to reparation.

Character and Extent of Reparation

The Court clearly sought to develop a Community system of liability in respect of the abuse of power by national authorities—even if the substantive conditions for imposing such liability can still differ across the Member States, and the full scope of the bodies whose acts can be attributed to the Member State remains unclear. But did the Court also intend

[108] Dir 76/207, OJ 1976 L39/40.

in *Francovich* to create some specifically 'Community remedy in damages'? Perhaps a good starting point in this regard is the Court's statement that, once Member State liability has been established *in principle*, it is on the basis of the rules of national law on liability that the Member State must make reparation for the loss and damage caused *in practice*—provided only that the conditions for reparation laid down by national law must not be less favourable than those relating to similar domestic claims (the principle of equivalence), and must not make it impossible or excessively difficult to obtain reparation (the principle of effectiveness).[109]

Character of Reparation Against this background, the judgments in *Maso* and *Bonifaci* suggest that compensatory damages are not the only form of relief which might constitute valid 'reparation' under the *Francovich* caselaw.[110]

Based upon the same breach of Community law which had given rise to the *Francovich* case itself, *Maso* and *Bonifaci* concerned Italy's total failure to implement the Insolvency Directive within its prescribed deadline.[111] The Court held that the retroactive application of national implementing legislation which complied with the Directive to claimants who had suffered loss through its belated transposition was sufficient to remedy the harmful consequences of that breach of Community law, since the claimants were granted the rights from which they would have benefited had the Directive been implemented on time. However, the national courts had to ensure that reparation of the claimants' loss was adequate. If the latter could establish the existence of consequential or complementary loss, sustained on account of the fact that they were unable to benefit at the appropriate time from the rights provided by the Directive, such loss had also to be made good.[112] The Court applied those principles in the analogous context of an incorrectly transposed directive in its judgments in *Carbonari* and *Gozza*.[113] There seems no reason in principle why the same approach should not extend to any other breach of Community law, for example, involving a Treaty provision, regulation or decision.

One of the central assumptions of the 'Community remedy' view of the right to reparation is that the *Francovich* caselaw creates an action before the national courts for damages representing the losses caused to the claimant as a result of the Member State's breach of Community rules.[114] However, *Maso* and *Bonifaci* suggest that the right to reparation may not be so easy to classify in remedial terms: the Court seems to have significantly

[109] Cases C–6 & 9/90 *Francovich* [1991] ECR I–5357, paras 42–43; Cases C–46 and 48/93 *Brasserie du Pêcheur & Factortame III* [1996] ECR I–1029, para 67.
[110] Case C–373/95 *Maso* [1997] ECR I–4051; Cases C–94–5/95 *Bonifaci* [1997] ECR I–3969.
[111] Dir 80/987, OJ 1980 L283/23.
[112] Also: Case C–261/95 *Palmisani* [1997] ECR I–4025.
[113] Case C–131/97 *Carbonari* [1999] ECR I–1103; Case C–371/97 *Gozza* [2000] ECR I–7881.
[114] Consider, eg M Ross, 'Beyond *Francovich*' (1993) 56 MLR 55.

expanded the Member State's discretion to choose the precise form of reparation it will make.

In particular, it is arguable that *Francovich* does not create a right specifically to damages against the Member State for its breach of Community law, but has instead introduced a general right to reparation in whatever form the Member State finds it most convenient to provide. In *Maso* and *Bonifaci*, reparation was validly made through the retroactive application of belated national implementing measures to those who had suffered loss through the Member State's original breach of Community law, coupled if necessary with an action before the national courts for any additional damage which this failed to rectify. However, the claimants' original rights under the Insolvency Directive were financial in character (to payment of a fixed sum representing wages still owed by their bankrupt employer), and to that extent similar in nature to a right to compensatory damages.[115] But what if the Community right in question is not of an essentially financial nature: can the Member State choose retrospective application of the relevant Community provisions as the sole possible means of reparation (subject to an action for damages in respect of any complementary losses); or does the *Francovich* caselaw always entitle the claimant to a remedy that is monetary in nature? After all, in many cases the retrospective application of a non-stipendiary Community right may well remedy the major consequences of its breach. For example, consider the position of a pregnant woman who is dismissed from employment in breach of the Equal Treatment Directive, and seeks reparation from the Member State which has incorrectly transposed this measure into national law.[116] The Member State chooses to implement the Directive by requiring all employers to reinstate wronged employees,[117] and to make reparation for its past failures by applying this provision retrospectively to the claimant.[118] Would reinstatement (plus a supplementary claim for damages representing wages lost in the interim) comply with the requirements of the *Francovich* caselaw? Or must the claimant always be entitled to seek damages to cover her entire losses resulting from the dismissal?

In short: the question is whether the *Francovich* action is intended always to provide a financial remedy; or whether it can lead also to a remedy which is primarily non-stipendiary in character. At the very least, the judgments in *Maso* and *Bonifaci* suggest a certain confusion over the Court's conception of the remedial character of the right to reparation. However, a broad reading of the cases would imply a more basic

[115] This was also true of Case C–131/97 *Carbonari* [1999] ECR I–1103, and Case C–371/97 *Gozza* [2000] ECR I–7881.

[116] Dir 76/207, OJ 1976 L39/40.

[117] Cf Case C–271/91 *Marshall II* [1993] ECR I–4367.

[118] At least as regards public authorities. Whether it could also do so as regards private employers is open to dispute, especially in the light of the fundamental principle of legal certainty.

reappraisal of the remedial nature of the *Francovich* caselaw and, in particular, of the traditional assumption that it has created some 'Community remedy in damages'. Indeed, *Maso* and *Bonifaci* suggest the basis for an alternative conceptual model. *Francovich* is primarily a reflection of the general principle that every breach of a Community right must carry with it an effective level of redress. However, the precise form of such relief remains initially within the autonomy of the domestic legal system—subject to a supplementary Community remedy in damages before the national courts in respect of excess losses. Thus, despite the importance of the right to reparation in developing the imperative of effective judicial protection (through a general guarantee of redress against the abuse of public power), *Maso* and *Bonifaci* suggest that it does not represent such an original contribution to the Community's evolving remedial system. *Francovich* would become a cause of action but would not necessarily offer any particular form of relief.[119]

Extent of Reparation The next issue is not the character but the extent of reparation due pursuant to a finding of *Francovich* liability: precisely when will the relief offered to a claimant (in whatever form) be deemed sufficient under Community law? Against the general background of presumptive domestic competence over the remedial aspects of the right to reparation, the Court has sent out confusing signals about what the principle of effectiveness requires as regards the level of compensation which must be guaranteed under national law.

On the one hand, the general rule established in the caselaw is that reparation for losses caused to individuals as a result of breaches of Community law must be 'commensurate' with the damage sustained so as to ensure effective protection for the claimant's rights.[120] Reparation commensurate with the damage sustained would appear, on its face, to mean that compensation must reflect fully the claimant's losses. On the other hand, there is a dictum in *Maso* and *Bonifaci* that it is for the national court to ensure that reparation of the loss or damage sustained by the beneficiaries is 'adequate'.[121] Adequate compensation is not necessarily

[119] However, consider the problems raised in this regard by the judgment in Case C–261/95 *Palmisani* [1997] ECR I–4025; discussed by M Dougan, 'The *Francovich* Right to Reparation: Reshaping the Contours of Community Remedial Competence' (2000) 6 *European Public Law* 103.

[120] Eg Cases C–46 & 48/93 *Brasserie du Pêcheur* and *Factortame III* [1996] ECR I–1029, para 82; Case C–261/95 *Palmisani* [1997] ECR I–4025, para 26; Cases C–94–95/95 *Bonifaci* [1997] ECR I–3969, para 48; Case C–373/95 *Maso* [1997] ECR I–4051, para 36.

[121] Case C–373/95 *Maso* [1997] ECR I–4051, para 41; Cases C–94–95/95 *Bonifaci* [1997] ECR I–3969, para 53. Cf Case C–261/95 *Palmisani* [1997] ECR I–4025: the right to reparation seeks to make good 'to a sufficient extent' the loss or damage sustained through the Member State's breach of Community law (para 34).

full compensation, but rather implies a degree of leeway for domestic law to restrict the damages available to the claimant (subject only to a guaranteed Community minimum measure of recovery). Indeed, the Court in *Brasserie* asserted that, in the absence of relevant Community provisions, it is for the domestic legal system of each Member State to set the criteria for determining the extent of reparation, provided that national rules for the valuation of damages comply with the familiar principles of equivalence and effectiveness.[122] In particular, the Court explicitly stated that it is for domestic law to determine the types of damage in respect of which claimants are entitled to seek reparation.[123]

For example, consider a claim for pure economic losses resulting from a breach of Community law. In *Brasserie*, the Court held that national rules could not totally exclude lost profits as a head of recoverable damage: especially in the context of economic or commercial litigation, based on an infringement of the fundamental principle of free movement for goods, such a total exclusion of lost profits would be such as to make reparation virtually impossible in practice.[124] However, it seems that the various Member States deal with the recovery of economic damage in different ways, some being comfortable with the concept, others fearing the imposition of a liability indefinite in scope and extent.[125] There is no indication in the caselaw that the Court has sought to establish some uniform requirement that all (or any particular level of) economic losses must always (or in any particular circumstances) be compensated for.[126] Similarly, as regards the award of punitive damages based on a finding that public authorities have acted oppressively or arbitrarily, the Court was prepared to go no further than insist that Member States must comply with the principle of equivalence: if punitive damages are available in respect of comparable domestic legal claims, they must also be awarded within the context of actions based upon Community law. Again, the principle of effectiveness did not require Member States to recognise a uniform requirement to offer (or refrain from offering) punitive damages for the purposes of the *Francovich* right to reparation.[127]

There are those commentators who would advocate the building of a *ius commune* of administrative liability throughout Europe, and who seem

[122] Cases C–46 & 48/93 *Brasserie du Pêcheur* and *Factortame III* [1996] ECR I–1029, para 83.
[123] Cases C–46 & 48/93 *Brasserie du Pêcheur* and *Factortame III* [1996] ECR I–1029, para 88.
[124] Cases C–46 & 48/93 *Brasserie du Pêcheur* and *Factortame III* [1996] ECR I–1029, paras 86–87.
[125] Further: C Harlow, '*Francovich* and the Problem of the Disobedient State' (1996) 2 *European Law Journal* 199. Cf the Court's own approach to economic loss under Art 288(2) EC, eg Cases 83 & 94/76 *Bayerische* [1978] ECR 1209.
[126] For further discussion of the legal framework surrounding the recovery of lost profits under *Francovich*, consider AG Jacobs in Case C–112/00 *Schmidberger* (Judgment of 12 June 2003).
[127] Cases C–46 & 48/93 *Brasserie du Pêcheur* and *Factortame III* [1996] ECR I–1029, paras 88–89.

to see the *Francovich* jurisprudence as a major step in this direction.[128] But clearly the national legal orders lack any real consensus as to what sort of interests to protect and how they are to be valued. As the Court itself seems to have acknowledged, this makes either a principle of 'full reparation' or some otherwise uniform 'Community remedy' difficult to realise in practice.[129]

Relevance of the Equal Treatment Directive Caselaw One issue which warrants particular attention is the fact that many commentators have looked to the Court's (essentially private law) jurisprudence on the requirement of effective judicial protection under the Equal Treatment Directive as an appropriate model for the measure of compensation due pursuant to the (essentially public law) *Francovich* action.[130] After all, the caselaw concerning Article 6 Equal Treatment Directive on the remedies available against discrimination on grounds of sex is generally accepted to reflect and inform wider notions of effective judicial protection under the general principles of Community law—which could include the level of damages recoverable in *Francovich* cases.[131]

The Court decided in *von Colson* that, as regards a discriminatory refusal of employment, where national law chooses to offer a remedy by way of financial compensation (rather than requiring the employer to re-advertise the position), any damages offered by national law must be 'adequate' in relation to the losses sustained. Nominal compensation (such as the reimbursement of travel costs incurred in attending for interview) manifestly fails to fulfil that criterion.[132] But the Court later held in *Marshall II* that, for the purposes of a discriminatory dismissal from employment, where national law chooses to offer a remedy by way of

[128] Eg W van Gerven, 'Non-contractual Liability of Member States, Community Institutions and Individuals for Breaches of Community Law with a View to a Common Law for Europe' (1994) 1 *Maastricht Journal of European and Comparative Law* 6; and 'Bridging the Unbridgeable: Community and National Tort Laws after *Francovich* and *Brasserie*' (1996) 45 ICLQ 507. Also, eg R Caranta, 'Judicial Protection Against Member States: A New *Jus Commune* Takes Shape' (1995) 32 CML Rev 703; and 'Learning from our Neighbours: Public Law Remedies, Homogenisation from Bottom Up' (1997) 4 *Maastricht Journal of European and Comparative Law* 220.

[129] Cf AG Mischo in Cases C–6 & 9/90 *Francovich* [1991] ECR I–5357, para 80 Opinion; AG Tesauro in Cases C–46 & 48/93 *Brasserie du Pêcheur* and *Factortame III* [1996] ECR I–1029, para 111 Opinion; AG Cosmas in Cases C–94–5/95 *Bonifaci* [1997] ECR I–3969, paras 63 and 103–106 Opinion.

[130] Dir 76/207, OJ 1976 L39/40. Eg AG van Gerven in Case C–128/92 *Banks v BCC* [1994] ECR I–1209, para 54 Opinion; AG Léger in Case C–5/94 *Hedley Lomas* [1996] ECR I–2553, paras 184–186 Opinion; AG Jacobs in Case C–150/99 *Sweden v Stockholm Lindöpark* [2001] ECR I–493, para 81 Opinion.

[131] See: AG Rozès in Case 14/83 *von Colson* [1984] ECR 1891; AG van Gerven in Case C–271/91 *Marshall II* [1993] ECR I–4367. Also: S Prechal, 'Remedies after *Marshall*' (1990) 27 CML Rev 451; D Curtin, Commentary on *Marshall II* (1994) 31 CML Rev 631; E Steindorff, Commentary on *Draehmpaehl* (1997) 34 CML Rev 1259; A Ward, 'New Frontiers in Private Enforcement of EC Directives' (1998) 23 EL Rev 65.

[132] Case 14/83 *von Colson* [1984] ECR 1891. Cf Case 79/83 *Harz* [1984] ECR 1921.

financial compensation (rather than reinstatement into post), the claimant's recoverable damages must enable her losses to be made good 'in full.' For these purposes, the national courts should set aside any statutory ceiling automatically limiting the value of compensation; and must be able to award interest representing losses suffered by the claimant through the effluxion of time.[133]

Marshall II clearly went far beyond the Court's early period laissez-faire caselaw: something less than full compensation can hardly be said to render the exercise of Community rights excessively difficult, let alone virtually impossible. But the Court's insistence on full rather than merely adequate compensation seemed to overshadow even the previous middle-period judgment in *von Colson*. Thus, questions arose as to how far *Marshall II* would extend beyond the situation of a discriminatory dismissal from employment, so as also to cover the valuation of compensation required in respect of the enforcement of other Community rights.[134]

As regards statutory ceilings, partial clarification was offered in *Draehmpaehl*, where the Court found that a maximum limit on the damages recoverable for a discriminatory refusal of employment was also unacceptable under Article 6 Equal Treatment Directive, except where the claimant would not have been appointed anyway on the basis of his/her inferior qualifications.[135] This reinforces perceptions that the Court has a strong distaste for any form of absolute statutory ceiling on the availability of compensation under the Equal Treatment Directive, preferring national courts to assess appropriate levels of compensation free from the strictures of any prior upper limit set by legislation, save where the statutory ceiling does offer a reasonable assessment of the claimant's likely losses. Although these particular judgments have now been incorporated into the legislative text of the Equal Treatment Directive itself,[136] the general policy of preserving judicial discretion in the assessment of a claimant's true losses could still apply to Community actions in other fields—including the *Francovich* right to reparation. Support for this interpretation comes from the Commission's enforcement proceedings against the United Kingdom in respect of the latter's implementation of the Acquired Rights Directive.[137] Domestic rules provided that, in the event of

133 Case C–271/91 *Marshall II* [1993] ECR I–4367.

134 Contrast, eg N Grief, Commentary on *Marshall II* (1993) 22 ILJ 314; and A Barav, 'Omnipotent Courts' in D Curtin & T Heukels (eds), *Institutional Dynamics of European Integration* (Nijhoff, 1994); with B Fitzpatrick and E Szyszczak, 'Remedies and Effective Judicial Protection in Community Law' (1994) 57 MLR 434; and S Prechal, 'EC Requirements for an Effective Remedy' in J Lonbay & A Biondi (eds), *Remedies for Breach of EC Law* (Wiley, 1997).

135 Case C–180/95 *Draehmpaehl* [1997] ECR I–2195.

136 Art 6(2) Dir 76/207, OJ 1976 L39/40 (as amended by Dir 2002/73, OJ 2002 L269/15).

137 Dir 77/187 on the approximation of the laws of the Member States relating to the safeguarding of employees' rights in the event of transfers of undertakings, businesses or parts of undertakings or businesses, OJ 1977 L61/26 (now repealed and replaced by Dir 2001/23, OJ 2001 L82/16).

an employer failing to comply with its obligation of collective information and consultation concerning a prospective transfer of the undertaking, the employees should receive compensation limited to a maximum of the equivalent of two weeks' pay.[138] Having already concluded that the UK's sanctions fell short of Community requirements by imposing overly restrictive set-off provisions, Advocate General van Gerven refrained from expressing any opinion on the statutory ceilings.[139] But the Court went further, observing that the imposition of a ceiling on the amount of compensation payable by the employer and particularly at the level of two weeks' pay aggravated the failure to provide a sanction that was effective and dissuasive.[140] Admittedly, the Court made no reference to *Marshall II*, and did not condemn the statutory ceilings as an unacceptable restriction on the employees' Community law rights as such.[141] But in the light of *Draehmpaehl*, one can see the same policy at work: the Court is hostile to statutory limits on the valuation of Community rights which impose an inherent restriction on the ability of domestic law to award an effective remedy.

As regards the recovery of interest, another partial answer was offered in *ex parte Sutton*. In that case, the United Kingdom had refused to award certain social security benefits to women, in breach of Directive 79/7.[142] The Court imposed a duty upon the Member State to pay the withheld benefits, but did not require the payment of interest. In particular, the Court drew a distinction between cases of compensation (such as *Marshall II*, where effective judicial protection requires interest to be made available), and the payment of wrongly withheld monies (such as *ex parte Sutton*, where effective judicial protection does not require interest to be paid).[143] This distinction seems unconvincing: insofar as interest is intended to reflect the inevitable losses suffered by a claimant who is unable to enjoy his/her rights at the intended time, such losses can clearly arise as much with wrongly withheld social security benefits

[138] During the course of the proceedings, this maximum was raised to four weeks' wages.
[139] Case C–382/92 *Commission v UK* [1994] ECR I–2435, para 32 Opinion.
[140] Case C–382/92 *Commission v UK* [1994] ECR I–2435, para 57 Judgment. Further: P Davies, 'A Challenge to Single Channel' (1994) 23 ILJ 272.
[141] Note that, in the parallel proceedings in Case C–383/92 *Commission v UK* [1994] ECR I–2479, the ECJ made no reference to the identical statutory ceilings applied by the UK to the assessment of damages for the employer's breach of its obligation to inform and consult the workforce of forthcoming collective redundancies under Dir 75/129 on the approximation of the laws of the Member States relating to collective redundancies, OJ 1975 L48/29 (now repealed and replaced by Dir 98/59, OJ 1998 L225/16). But in that case, it seems that neither the Commission nor the Advocate General raised this issue before the ECJ, so it is not altogether surprising that the Court failed to address it either.
[142] Dir 79/7 on the progressive implementation of the principle of equal treatment for men and women in matters of social security, OJ 1979 L6/24.
[143] Case C–66/95 *ex p Sutton* [1997] ECR I–2163.

as with compensatory damages for dismissal from employment.[144] Nevertheless, the reasoning in *ex parte Sutton* seemed to suggest that the payment of interest as a recoverable head of damage should apply to compensatory actions based on the *Francovich* caselaw—thus permitting the requirement of effective judicial protection embodied in *Marshall II* to qualify the general presumption of national competence established under *Brasserie*.

However, the Court's response in the *Metallgesellschaft* case was more complex. In that case, the United Kingdom had breached the Treaty provisions on freedom of establishment, by giving the subsidiaries of domestic companies a longer time within which to pay a particular tax than the period offered to the subsidiaries of foreign companies. The Court held that, in such circumstances, national judges entertaining a claim for reparation under the *Francovich* caselaw must be able to award interest because losses suffered through the effluxion of time represent the essential value of the claimant's Treaty rights. Additional dicta suggest that the Court favours the more generous authority of *Marshall II*, over the more restrictive approach adopted in *ex parte Sutton*.[145] Yet the Court did not go so far as to insist that the presumption of national autonomy in determining the heads of recoverable damage must always give way to the availability of interest as a general requirement of effective judicial protection for the purposes of a *Francovich* claim.[146]

In any case, striking down unduly restrictive statutory ceilings, and awarding interest on recoverable damages, is not the same as imposing a general principle of 'full compensation.' It remains true that the only situation in which full compensation is required as a matter of Community law concerns a discriminatory dismissal from employment (as in *Marshall II* itself). Beyond this, the Court has gone no further than to require that compensation is adequate depending on the type of breach at issue. This is true as regards other types of discrimination caught by the Equal Treatment Directive;[147] and we have seen that it is also true as regards the *Francovich* right to reparation itself.[148]

[144] Eg M Dougan, 'Cutting Your Losses in the Enforcement Deficit: A Community Right to the Recovery of Unlawfully Levied Charges?' (1998) 1 *Cambridge Yearbook of European Legal Studies* 233.

[145] Cases C–397 & 410/98 *Metallgesellschaft* [2001] ECR I–1727.

[146] Though the likelihood of the Court reaching that conclusion has increased since Case C–63/01 *Evans* (Judgment of 4 December 2003), in which the Court relied on *Marshall II* to guarantee that compensation for victims of car accidents, relying on Dir 84/5 on insurance against civil liability in respect of the use of motor vehicles, OJ 1984 L8/17, covered losses suffered through the effluxion of time. Also: AG Jacobs in Case C–150/99 *Sweden v Stockholm Lindöpark* [2001] ECR I–493, para 81 Opinion.

[147] Cf AG Cosmas in Case C–167/97 *R v Seymour-Smith and Perez* [1999] ECR I–623, paras 88–91 Opinion.

[148] Cases C–46 & 48/93 *Brasserie du Pêcheur* and *Factortame III* [1996] ECR I–1029; Cases C–94–95/95 *Bonifaci* [1997] ECR I–3969; Case C–373/95 *Maso* [1997] ECR I–4051.

Procedural Conditions for Exercising the Right to Reparation

In the absence of Community legislation, it is for the internal legal order of each Member State to designate the competent courts and lay down the detailed procedural rules for legal proceedings intended to safeguard the individual's *Francovich* right to reparation, provided that the regime chosen complies with the usual principles of equivalence and effectiveness.[149] For example, the Court affirmed in *Köbler* that, although Member States could incur liability on the basis of an infringement of the Treaty perpetrated by a national court of last instance, and could not avoid such liability simply by reference to the difficulties of designating a court competent to hear disputes relating to such actions for reparation, actually identifying that tribunal remained a matter for domestic law. This reflects the Court's settled principle that the fundamental right of access to judicial process is capable of having only limited direct effect.[150] Similarly, the Court held in *Dounias* that rules governing the admissibility of evidence during the course of *Francovich* actions were to be determined by national law, subject to the requirements of equivalence and effectiveness.[151]

Two issues concerning the scope of the Member State's presumptive procedural autonomy warrant particular mention. First, the Court held in *Brasserie* that, although it was not appropriate to limit the temporal effects of its judgment, any Member State obliged to make good the consequences of a breach of Community law within the framework of its domestic law on liability could apply substantive and procedural conditions which took into account the requirements of the principle of legal certainty (provided those conditions satisfied the principles of equivalence and effectiveness).[152] On that basis, the Court made clear in *Palmisani* that *Francovich* claims must in principle be initiated within the limitation periods provided for under national law.[153] It is also taken for granted that Member States may apply domestic rules limiting the scope of recoverable compensation to within a given period of time.[154] The detailed rules on limitation periods and back-limits on recovery will be discussed further below.

Secondly, the Court in *Brasserie* indicated that Community law would respect domestic rules requiring claimants to mitigate their own losses by showing reasonable diligence to avoid or limit damage. It is therefore open to the Member State to exclude *Francovich* claims where alternative

[149] Cases C–6 and 9/90 *Francovich* [1991] ECR I–5357, paras 42–43; Cases C–46 & 48/93 *Brasserie du Pêcheur* and *Factortame III* [1996] ECR I–1029, para 67.

[150] Case C–224/01 *Köbler* (Judgment of 30 September 2003), paras 44–47. Further: ch 1 (above).

[151] Case C–228/98 *Dounias* [2000] ECR I–577.

[152] Cases C–46 & 48/93 *Brasserie du Pêcheur* and *Factortame III* [1996] ECR I–1029, paras 97–99.

[153] Case C–261/95 *Palmisani* [1997] ECR I–4025.

[154] In accordance with Case C–338/91 *Steenhorst-Neerings* [1993] ECR I–5475.

means of redress exist, but the claimant has failed to use them, or to do so within the applicable time-limits.[155] The Court will exercise a merely supervisory jurisdiction to ensure that domestic mitigation rules comply with the principles of equivalence and effectiveness. In particular, the obligation under national law to exhaust alternative remedies must be qualified with the proviso that such remedies are adequate in nature. Thus, in the *Metallgesellschaft* case, the Court rejected the United Kingdom's argument that an action for reparation based on national legislation which deprived the claimants of a particular tax advantage in breach of Article 43 EC should be dismissed on the grounds that they had failed to mitigate their losses, by applying to the revenue authorities for an inevitably unfavourable decision, which might then be challenged before the domestic courts based on the direct effect and supremacy of the relevant Treaty rules. In the Court's view, the United Kingdom was criticising the claimants for complying with national legislation—but the exercise of rights conferred by Community law would be rendered excessively difficult if actions for compensation were rejected or reduced solely because the claimants had not applied for a tax advantage which national law explicitly denied them.[156]

However, it is unclear whether the 'exhaustion of local remedies' requirement will be transposed into the jurisprudence of the Court itself, and thereby acquire the character of a Community-level restriction on the scope of the right to reparation. Several cases clearly suggest that the Court sees the right to reparation as a remedy of last resort—to be used when the claimant cannot rely on other actions based on directly effective Community provisions (or national law as construed in conformity with non-directly effective Community provisions).[157] But the Court has not yet imposed a formal 'exhaustion of local remedies' requirement as a matter of Community law. For example, *Stockholm Lindöpark* concerned Swedish rules which exempted the supply of certain sports facilities from the obligation to pay VAT, and thus deprived the claimant of the concomitant right to deduct input tax, contrary to the applicable Community directives. The Court observed that, since the claimant was already entitled to pursue the disputed sums by means of an action for the payment of debts, based on directly effective provisions of Community law, a *Francovich* action for compensatory damages seemed unnecessary. The Court nevertheless continued to observe that the principle of Member State liability under *Francovich* was inherent in the system of the Treaty,

[155] Cases C–46 & 48/93 *Brasserie du Pêcheur* and *Factortame III* [1996] ECR I–1029, paras 84–85; Cases C–178–79 & 188–90/94 *Dillenkofer* [1996] ECR I–4845, para 72.
[156] Cases C–397 & 410/98 *Metallgesellschaft* [2001] ECR I–1727.
[157] Eg Case C–334/92 *Wagner Miret* [1993] ECR I–6911; Case C–91/92 *Faccini Dori* [1994] ECR I–3325; Case C–54/96 *Dorsch Consult* [1997] ECR I–4961; Case C–97/96 *Daihatsu Deutschland* [1997] ECR I–6843.

and answered the national court's questions about the existence of a sufficiently serious breach of Community law.[158]

This possibility of double remedies, through the cumulative application of *Francovich* liability and any other actions deriving directly from the relevant Community rights, was criticised by Advocate General Jacobs in *Denkavit*. He believed that *Francovich* could thereby be abused so as to avoid the stricter procedural requirements (such as shorter time-limits) applicable to restitutionary, as compared to compensatory, claims.[159] But the Advocate General's views on this issue have since evolved. In *Fantask*, he observed that the claimant's ability to use *Francovich* as a means of evading the shorter time-limit for restitutionary actions could perhaps be justified by the fact that the Member State had committed not just a breach, but a sufficiently serious breach of its Treaty obligations, warranting a reappraisal of the balance struck between the individual interest in obtaining redress and the collective interest in preserving legal certainty.[160] The caselaw requires further clarification on this issue.[161]

Assessment

With the benefit of hindsight, it is now clear that the primary purpose of the *Francovich* jurisprudence is the furtherance of specific judicial policy objectives relating to the legal accountability of the national authorities. The Court clearly felt that domestic laws offering total or partial immunity from liability in respect of the exercise of public power in general, and legislative prerogatives in particular, were unacceptable within the hierarchical constitutional system established by the Treaty, and strove to establish minimum guarantees of accountability so as to vindicate both the rule of Community law and the individual's rights.

But while *Francovich* affirms the need for the effective judicial protection of the citizen and ensures that this imperative extends to cover the

[158] Case C–150/99 *Stockholm Lindöpark* [2001] ECR I–493. Also, eg Cases C–397 & 410/98 *Metallgesellschaft* [2001] ECR I–1727. Cf AG Léger in Case C–5/94 *Hedley Lomas* [1996] ECR I–2553. Cf AG Jacobs in Case C–90/94 *Haahr Petroleum* [1997] ECR I–4085.

[159] Case C–2/94 *Denkavit* [1996] ECR I–2827. Cf P Oliver, 'State Liability in Damages Following *Factortame III*: A Remedy Seen in Context' in J Beatson & T Tridimas, (eds) *New Directions in European Public Law* (Hart Publishing, 1998).

[160] Case C–188/95 *Fantask* [1997] ECR I–6783. Cf P Eeckhout, 'Liability of Member States in Damages and the Community System of Remedies' in J Beatson & T Tridimas, (eds) *New Directions in European Public Law* (Hart Publishing, 1998). Further: A Anagnostaras, 'State Liability and Alternative Courses of Action: How Independent Can an Autonomous Remedy Be?' (2002) 21 *Yearbook of European Law* 355.

[161] For further discussion, see: AG Tesauro in Cases C–46 & 48/93 *Brasserie du Pêcheur* and *Factortame III* [1996] ECR I–1029, para 34 Opinion; AG Tesauro in Case C–392/93 *Ex p British Telecommunications* [1996] ECR I–1631, para 30 Opinion. Note that the ECJ applies an 'exhaustion of alternative remedies' rule to claims under Arts 235 and 288(2) EC, eg Case 20/88 *Roquette Frères* [1989] ECR 1553.

actions of all public authorities, it neither imposes uniform substantive conditions for the attribution of liability, nor necessarily requires recognition of a new and universal 'Community action for damages.' As the caselaw has developed, so the remedial innovation of *Francovich* has been diluted, almost to the point that it could slot quite happily into the traditional framework of Community control familiar from *Rewe/Comet*: in the absence of legislation, the enforcement of Community rights is governed by Member State law, subject to the requirements of equivalence and effectiveness. By this means, the Court guarantees for the beneficiary of Community rights an 'adequate remedy,' but leaves the nature and form of such relief primarily within the discretion of the Member State. Only where no adequate domestic remedy is offered will the Court step in and impose by default a supplementary 'Community action for damages.'[162]

Thus, despite the Court's express reference in *Brasserie* to the 'fundamental requirement of the Community legal order that Community law be uniformly applied,'[163] the ability of individuals to obtain compensation in respect of a breach of their Treaty rights will still differ from Member State to Member State, sometimes significantly, depending on the substantive, remedial and procedural conditions for liability recognised within each separate jurisdiction.

Imposition of Limitation Periods

The Court's basic approach to limitation periods was first established, during its early period caselaw, in *Rewe/Comet*: pre-existing national time-limits are acceptable under Community law, provided they comply with the principles of equivalence and effectiveness; the latter requirement is satisfied where the relevant limitation periods are 'reasonable'.[164] This model of negative harmonisation still provides the foundation for the current law; though the situations in which Community law interferes with domestic procedural autonomy, particularly on grounds of effectiveness, have been extended.

The General Principle: Reasonable Limitation Periods

Application of the principle of equivalence may produce a longer limitation period within which the citizen can bring proceedings based on

[162] Further: M Dougan, 'The *Francovich* Right to Reparation: Reshaping the Contours of Community Remedial Competence' (2000) 6 *European Public Law* 103. Similarly, eg C Timmermans, 'Community Directives Revisited' (1997) 17 *Yearbook of European Law* 1.
[163] Cases C–46 & 48/93 *Brasserie du Pêcheur* and *Factortame III* [1996] ECR I–1029, para 33.
[164] Case 33/76 *Rewe-Zentralfinanz v Landwirtschaftskammer für das Saarland* [1976] ECR 1989; Case 45/76 *Comet* [1976] ECR 2043.

Community law, where the Member State is found to have discriminated against Treaty when compared to similar domestic claims. This is illustrated by the case of *Palmisani*: Italian legislation specified a one-year time-limit for bringing proceedings for compensation pursuant to the Court's judgment in *Francovich*; but if the appropriate comparator for the Community right to reparation was found to be the ordinary action for non-contractual damages under the Italian Civil Code, the principle of equivalence required the Italian courts to extend that limitation period to five years.[165]

The principle of effectiveness is concerned with the very different question of whether the claimant enjoys a proper opportunity to exercise his/her Community rights before the national courts (regardless of whether that opportunity is assimilated to the regime governing similar domestic actions). However, effectiveness as formulated in *Rewe/Comet* required only that national limitation periods be 'reasonable.' In particular, the Court held that the laying down of reasonable time-limits with regard to actions of a fiscal nature (*in casu*, the recovery of unlawfully levied charges) is an application of the fundamental principle of legal certainty protecting both the taxpayer and the national administration.[166] For these purposes, the Court seemed to consider one month or 30 days an acceptable temporal opportunity within which to exercise one's Community right to the recovery of unlawfully levied charges. Indeed, under this early caselaw, provided time-limits were reasonable in duration, they could not otherwise be alleged to render the exercise of Community rights virtually impossible, or even excessively difficult. For example, the Court in *Bessin and Salson* rejected the argument that a three-year French time-limit for reclaiming unlawfully levied import duties was incompatible with Community law because there was no possibility of exemption on grounds of *force majeure*. That reflected a legislative choice by the Member State which did not undermine the validity of this otherwise reasonable national limitation period.[167]

The same basic approach now applies, under the current caselaw, not only to domestic limitation periods *stricto sensu*, but also to other forms of time-limit regulating the exercise of Community law rights before the national courts. For example, *Steenhorst-Neerings* concerned Dutch rules refusing incapacity benefits to married women which were struck down in 1988 for breach of Directive 79/7 on the right to equal treatment in matters of social security.[168] Mrs Steenhorst-Neerings claimed that her right

[165] Case C–261/95 *Palmisani* [1997] ECR I–4025. Also, eg Case C–34/02 *Pasquini* [2003] ECR I–6515.

[166] Case 33/76 *Rewe-Zentralfinanz v Landwirtschaftskammer für das Saarland* [1976] ECR 1989, para 5; Case 45/76 *Comet* [1976] ECR 2043, paras 17–18.

[167] Case 386/87 *Bessin and Salson* [1989] ECR 3551.

[168] Dir 79/7, OJ 1979 L6/24.

to equal treatment under the Directive had direct effect from 1984 and that she should therefore receive back-payments of the incapacity benefit to that date. However, under Dutch law, social security benefits were payable not earlier than one year before the date on which they were claimed—limiting the claimant's recoverable backdated benefits to 1987. Asked whether this was compatible with Community requirements, the Court referred to the principles of national autonomy, equivalence and effectiveness, and found that the Dutch rule satisfied the requirements of Community law. This was particularly true having regard to the interests of sound administration (so as one could determine whether and to what extent the claimant satisfied the conditions for eligibility); and the interests of financial balance (since under the Dutch system, claims paid out in principle had to be covered by contributions paid in for each year).[169]

Member State's Margin of Discretion However, this basic test of 'reasonableness' presents certain problems. The first concerns precisely what constitutes a 'reasonable' opportunity to assert one's Community rights before the national courts. Consider the position as regards limitation periods *stricto sensu*. One might expect that 'reasonableness' is to be measured not in the abstract, but by reference to the legal and factual environment within which the relevant time-limit is to be applied. After all, the rationale according to which the Court has consistently defended its presumption of deference to national autonomy over time-limits is the need to respect legal certainty (both in the administration of justice, and as regards the balance of public finances). It is thus arguable that the chief determinant of what constitutes a 'reasonable' limitation period should be the degree of disruption to the work of public authorities at stake in any given category of case, and therefore the degree to which the Community should respect attempts by Member States to restrict access to the domestic courts for the enforcement of Community rights. Considerations of legal and financial certainty may well justify time-limits of one month or 30 days with regard to routine administrative and particularly revenue decisions, but it is doubtful whether similar limits could legitimately extend to a claim for damages in respect of a discriminatory dismissal in breach of the Equal Treatment Directive,[170] or an action for compensation against the Member State for infringing Community law in circumstances such as the *Factortame* dispute.[171] Such disputes do not usually affect interests of legal and financial certainty so pressing as to justify wafer-thin windows of time within which the claimant must assert his/her Community rights.

[169] Case C–338/91 *Steenhorst-Neerings* [1993] ECR I–5475.
[170] Dir 76/207, OJ 1976 L39/40 (and despite new Art 6(4) as introduced by Dir 2002/73, OJ 2002 L269/15).
[171] Cases C–46 & 48/93 *Brasserie du Pêcheur* and *Factortame III* [1996] ECR I–1029.

There is support for this interpretation in the *Pflücke* case, which concerned a limitation period of two months, running from the commencement of insolvency proceedings, within which workers were obliged to lodge with the German guarantee institution, established pursuant to the Insolvency Directive, applications for payment of their outstanding wage claims.[172] The claimant's lawyers failed to notify the German guarantee institution on time, thanks to an apparent misinterpretation of the domestic rules, and his application was dismissed. The Court noted that reasonable limitation periods were justified by the principle of legal certainty, especially in cases involving insolvency; but claims for salary were of great importance to the individual, and time-limits should not be so short as to deprive claimants of the benefits intended by Community law. The national court was therefore obliged to determine whether the German limitation period was justified by overriding reasons of legal certainty relating to the proper working of the guarantee institution. In particular, the Court queried whether two months was considerably shorter than the period within which the guarantee institution must assert its subrogated rights before the competent domestic courts, for the purposes of recovering all or part of the salary payouts from the assets of the insolvent employer.[173] This suggests that 'reasonableness' is to be judged, at least in cases involving vulnerable claimants, in accordance with the Member State's *legitimate need* for legal certainty.[174]

However, *Pflücke* is an exceptional case. In most situations, there is little evidence to suggest that the Court is willing to police the Member State's discretion with any great rigour. Indeed, the Court rarely attempts seriously to look behind the claims raised by domestic authorities, and investigate the true correlation between alleged needs of legal certainty and the length of the time-limits they are being used to justify. The standard of Community control might therefore be more accurately expressed in negative than in positive terms: a time-limit must not be so short as to be wholly unreasonable, such as de facto to deprive the claimant of any genuine opportunity to assert his/her rights judicially.

This generally laissez-faire approach is reinforced by the caselaw on back-limits. *Steenhorst-Neerings* raised certain problems, in particular, as regards its relationship with the judgment in *Marshall II*.[175] After all, the two cases are not easy to reconcile. The Court's hostility towards a straightforward fixed ceiling on the value of financial compensation for a discriminatory dismissal from employment sat uneasily with its tolerance of a rule imposing temporal limits on challenging a discriminatory denial

[172] Dir 80/987, OJ 1980 L283/23.
[173] Case C–125/01 *Pflücke* (Judgment of 18 September 2003).
[174] Support for this approach also comes from AG Jacobs in Case C–2/94 *Denkavit* [1996] ECR I–2827, paras 63–70 Opinion.
[175] Case C–271/91 *Marshall II* [1993] ECR I–4367.

of social security benefits. Both provisions would seem to have the same effect in practice. For example, imagine a breach of Community law in January 2000 which causes €1,000 worth of damage to the citizen each year until he/she seeks legal action in 2004. His/her total loss is €4,000. A statutory ceiling on recovery of €2,000 has the same practical effect as a two-year limit on the retroactive recoupment of one's losses. Insofar as *Marshall II* suggests that the latter rule would be set aside, and *Steenhorst-Neerings* that the former rule would be maintained, this seems to be drawing an unduly formalistic distinction.[176]

Certain possibilities for reconciling the two authorities can be dismissed. First, it is difficult to disentangle *Steenhorst-Neerings* and *Marshall II* by reference to their specific legislative frameworks. Article 6 Directive 79/7 on equal treatment in the field of social security is virtually identical to Article 6 Directive 76/207 on equal treatment in the field of employment. Moreover, the objectives of both measures are the same: to secure real equality between men and women throughout the Community. So, one might have expected that similar principles would apply to the valuation and enforcement of the citizen's Community entitlements under each measure.

Secondly, there was a once-plausible argument that the conclusions reached in *Steenhorst-Neerings* were best explained by the Court's sensitivity towards Member State concerns over interference in the politically and financially controversial sector of social security.[177] But even if this was originally a major consideration in the Court's thinking, that thinking has since extended into Community law more generally. The Court held in *FMC* that Community law does not preclude the application of national rules restricting the back-period in respect of which claimants may obtain reimbursement of undue agricultural levies.[178] The judgment in *Brasserie* recognised that similar procedural restrictions could apply to *Francovich* actions based on the free movement of goods and freedom of establishment.[179] Moreover, the Court held in *Levez* that limits on the payment of arrears were also acceptable within the context of claims for equal pay under Article 141 EC.[180]

[176] Similarly, eg B Fitzpatrick and E Szyszczak, 'Remedies and Effective Judicial Protection in Community Law' (1994) 57 MLR 434; J Coppel, 'Time up for *Emmott*?' (1996) 25 ILJ 153; S Prechal, 'EC Requirements for an Effective Remedy' in J Lonbay & A Biondi (eds), *Remedies for Breach of EC Law* (Wiley, 1997).

[177] Eg J A Sohrab, Commentary on *Steenhorst-Neerings* (1994) 31 CML Rev 875; A Ward, 'New Frontiers in Private Enforcement of EC Directives' (1998) 23 EL Rev 65. Cf Case C–394/93 *Alonso-Pérez* [1995] ECR I–4101: the principles enunciated in *Steenhorst-Neerings* apply not only to claims for equal treatment on grounds of sex under Dir 79/7 but also to claims for social security benefits made by migrant Community workers under Reg 1408/71; a German rule limiting claims for the backdated payment of family allowance to six months was therefore compatible with Community law.

[178] Case C–212/94 *FMC* [1996] ECR I–389.

[179] Cases C–46 & 48/93 *Brasserie du Pêcheur* and *Factortame III* [1996] ECR I–1029.

[180] Case C–326/96 *Levez* [1998] ECR I–7835.

The most likely grounds for distinguishing *Steenhorst-Neerings* from *Marshall II* lies in the idea that the latter judgment concerned national rules limiting the value of Community law rights in the abstract and without any consideration of the temporal context of the claimant's losses; whereas the former judgment concerned domestic restrictions limiting the value of Community law rights by reference to the needs of legal and financial certainty on the part of the relevant domestic authorities. After all, statutory ceilings of the sort at issue in *Marshall II* would apply regardless of when the claimant's losses were incurred: it might 10 years ago, or it might be just 10 days ago; in either case, the value of compensation is capped without any inherent concern to safeguard legitimate interests of legal and budgetary certainty.

This approach is supported by *Magorrian*. Under the statutory occupational pension schemes regime for Northern Ireland, persons who worked as full-time mental health officers for 20 years received certain additional benefits on their retirement. The claimants had worked as mental health officers for longer than the 20-year qualifying threshold, but were refused the additional benefits because a significant proportion of this service had been on a part-time basis. As a result of actions brought in 1992, this was held to constitute unlawful discrimination contrary to Article 141 EC. However, another domestic rule provided that, in proceedings concerning access to membership of occupational pension schemes, the right of admission was to have effect from a date no earlier than two years before the claimant instituted proceedings—which meant 1990 in this case. The Court rejected the United Kingdom's argument that this rule was protected by the *Steenhorst-Neerings* caselaw. The procedural rule at issue in *Steenhorst-Neerings* had merely limited the period prior to commencing proceedings in respect of which backdated benefits could be obtained. But the present provision meant that only service completed by the claimants since 1990 could be taken into account for the purposes of calculating the additional benefits that could be obtained even after the date of their claim. In other words, this rule affected not entitlement to benefits due in the past, but entitlement to a status which in turn conferred a right to benefits due in the future. As such, it rendered any action by individuals relying on Community law impossible in practice and could not be justified by the interests of legal certainty.[181] By implication, the crucial factor at work in *Steenhorst-Neerings* was that the national rules limiting the value of payments due under Community law had only retroactive not prospective effect, and as such could be justified by reference to considerations of legal certainty.[182]

[181] Case C–246/96 *Magorrian* [1997] ECR I–7153. Also: Case C–78/98 *Preston* [2000] ECR I–3201. Further, eg C Kilpatrick, 'Turning Remedies Around: A Sectoral Analysis of the Court of Justice' in G de Búrca & J Weiler (eds), *The European Court of Justice* (OUP, 2001).
[182] Cf AG Jacobs in Case C–2/94 *Denkavit* [1996] ECR I–2827, para 69 Opinion.

However, as with limitation periods *stricto sensu*, the Court often seems reluctant to intrude too far into national procedural autonomy and evaluate the validity of alleged domestic needs as regards legal and financial certainty. For example, *Johnson II* concerned an English provision that no claimant was entitled to severe disablement allowance in respect of any period more than 12 months before the date of claim. As a result, Mrs Johnson's benefit was backdated to 1986 instead of 1984. She argued that there was no difficulty for the authorities in determining whether the claimant satisfied the relevant qualifying conditions prior to bringing her claim; and that this was a non-contributory benefit where payments did not have to be financed from receipts within any given period. The imperatives of sound administration and financial balance present in *Steenhorst-Neerings* did not therefore apply. But while the Court was prepared to recognise certain differences between the two cases, it held that the actual rules in both *Steenhorst-Neerings* and *Johnson II* were identical: such retroactive limits on valuation did not constitute an absolute bar to the claimant bringing proceedings, and therefore did not have the effect of rendering impossible the exercise of the claimant's rights under Directive 79/7.[183] It might therefore seem that Member States will be left with a relatively wide margin of discretion to impose limits to the retroactive valuation of Treaty-based rights, with Community interference being activated only in blatant cases where no possible claim to legal certainty can be sustained. This does not make it impossible to reconcile the *Steenhorst-Neerings* caselaw with the judgment in *Marshall II*—but the greater the extent of the Court's uncritical deference to national autonomy, the less persuasive the idea that back-limits are genuinely justified by domestic needs of legal certainty, and the more such rules begin to resemble the effects of abstract yet apparently unacceptable statutory ceilings.

Role of the National Courts The second main problem with the basic test for judging the compatibility of limitation periods with Community law lies in the fact that the Court has offered little direct guidance as to the consequences of finding that a given limitation period is indeed 'unreasonable.' There is clear support for the view that national judges should simply disapply the offending procedural rule altogether, at least in cases where it would otherwise result in dismissal of a claim which should rightly be allowed to proceed. For example, the Court in *Pflücke* held that, if the domestic court were to find the two-month time-limit for lodging applications for the payment of outstanding wages incompatible with the requirements of the principle of effectiveness, it would be obliged to refuse to enforce that restriction against the claimant.[184] But what about

[183] Case C–410/92 *Johnson II* [1994] ECR I–5483.
[184] Case C–125/01 *Pflücke* (Judgment of 18 September 2003).

situations where *some* limitation period would be justified by the needs of legal certainty, even if the *existing* time-limit exceeds legitimate national requirements, and it is unclear that the claim would be allowed to proceed even under a revised procedural regime? Should the domestic judge be required to assess for him/herself what would be a 'reasonable' limitation period and substitute it for the existing procedural rules—thus possibly resulting in the dismissal or curtailment of the claimant's action in any event? Authorities here exist only by analogy. The judgment in *Grundig Italiana* suggests that the national courts are entitled, as a matter of Community law, to assess for themselves what duration of limitation period is reasonable, having regard to considerations of legal certainty, and apply that revised procedural rule (in preference to the existing time-limit) within the context of pending disputes.[185] However, the ruling in *Eribrand* further suggests that Community law cannot positively require the national courts to undertake such an assessment: whether the judges have the power to fix for themselves a more appropriate limitation period is to be determined by domestic law (subject to the requirements of equivalence and effectiveness). In particular, the Member States enjoy a degree of discretion as regards the duration of their limitation periods, and it is not for Community law to dictate which body should be competent to exercise that discretion within the national legal order.[186]

In any case, the requirements of the modern principle of effectiveness are not exhausted simply by applying a test of 'reasonableness' as regards the duration of national time-limits. It is necessary to examine several further qualifications to the presumption of national autonomy, before assessing just how far Community law has harmonised the standards of judicial protection in this field: the situation of claimants who have been misled as to their rights and thereby miss the relevant domestic time-limit; and the position where Member States attempt to revise the limitation periods applicable to Community law rights.

Limitation Periods and Claimants Who Have Been Misled as to Their Rights

The first main qualification to the general 'reasonable limitation periods' rule concerns situations in which one party's conduct effectively deprived the other party of an opportunity to commence its action before the national courts within the applicable time-limits.

Steps Towards Positive Harmonisation in the Emmott Judgment This qualification finds its origins in the Court's middle-period judgment in *Emmott*. The background to the case may be summarised as follows. In *McDermott and Cotter*, the Court held that Ireland had failed correctly to implement

[185] Case C–255/00 *Grundig Italiana* [2002] ECR I–8003.
[186] Case C–467/01 *Eribrand* (Judgment of 19 June 2003).

Directive 79/7 on equal treatment between men and women in matters of social security.[187] As from 23 December 1984, married women were thus entitled to rely on directly effective provisions of the Directive to claim the same benefits as married men in equivalent circumstances.[188] Immediately after this judgment, Mrs Emmott wrote to the Irish Minister for Social Welfare claiming benefits which had been withheld from her in breach of Community law. However, she was told that no decision would be taken in relation to her claim until on-going litigation in the Irish courts over implementation of the Directive had been resolved. Hearing nothing further, Mrs Emmott brought judicial review proceedings, only for the Minister then to plead that her action was inadmissible because it had not been brought within the applicable three-month time-limit. The Irish court sought guidance as to the position under Community law.

The Court of Justice began by asserting the orthodox *Rewe/Comet* principles. But it continued to observe that, whilst the laying down of reasonable time-limits in principle satisfies the condition of effectiveness, account must nevertheless be taken of the particular nature of directives as set out in Article 249(3) EC, whereby the Member States have discretion as to the form in which a directive is implemented, but nevertheless remain obliged to adopt all measures necessary to ensure the effectiveness of its objectives, so that individuals can ascertain the full extent of any rights the directive intends to create in their favour. During any period when a directive has not been correctly implemented into national law, individuals are unable to ascertain the full extent of their Community rights (even where the directive in question has direct effect). Only proper transposition of the directive can bring this state of uncertainty to an end. Therefore, until such time as a directive has been properly transposed, the Member State may not rely on an individual's delay in initiating proceedings in order to protect rights conferred by the directive; national limitation periods for the initiation of proceedings cannot begin to run before that time.[189]

Emmott seemed to have inaugurated a new rule governing the time from which national limitation periods could begin to run in Community cases: regardless of the non-discriminatory and equivalent nature, or even the reasonable duration, of existing domestic limitation periods, the

[187] Case 286/85 *McDermott and Cotter* [1987] ECR 1453; Dir 79/7 on the progressive implementation of the principle of equal treatment for men and women in matters of social security, OJ 1979 L6/24.

[188] Regardless of national rules prohibiting unjust enrichment through double payment to the same families: Case C–377/89 *Cotter and McDermott* [1991] ECR I–1155.

[189] Case C–208/90 *Emmott* [1991] ECR I–4269. Cf related cases in which the ECJ sought to prevent Member States from benefiting from their own unlawful conduct, in particular, from their failure correctly to implement directives on time, eg Case 152/84 *Marshall* [1986] ECR 723; Case C–377/89 *Cotter and McDermott* [1991] ECR I–1155; Cases C–6 & 9/90 *Francovich* [1991] ECR I–5357.

Community would insist on their straightforward postponement in situations where the Member State had failed to comply with its obligation correctly to implement a directive within the prescribed time-limit. Although the actual duration of national time-limits had not been fully approximated, the Court appeared nevertheless to have taken the initiative in increasing substantially the nature of Community control over this category of national procedural rule.

The degree of that Community control could indeed be construed quite broadly. For example, it is perfectly possible to read the concept of a Member State's failure to implement a directive as including any action by a public authority which fails to comply with the substantive terms of that directive—embracing not just a transpositional breach as regards the relevant national legislative framework, but even an operational breach as regards the application of the directive in any given case.[190] If so, *Emmott* might have appeared effectively to abolish the application of limitation periods in certain categories of cases. So long as a Member State was acting in breach of a directive, the individual could rely upon its provisions vertically against emanations of the state, and the limitation periods ordinarily applicable under national law would have to be postponed. Only when the Member State finally complied with the terms of the directive could time-limits begin to run—by which stage there was unlikely to be any dispute about the conduct of the relevant public authorities. Moreover, the reasoning in *Emmott* need not have been confined to situations involving the non- or incorrect transposition of directives. After all, uncertainty as to the existence and/or content of an individual's Community rights could equally arise in relation to both regulations and Treaty articles, particularly where these leave to the Member States a certain discretion to implement (and thus also to contradict) substantive Community policy. The Member State could thereby benefit just as much from the application of limitation periods to bar actions based on directly effective Treaty articles or regulations as those based on directives, and the reasoning in *Emmott* could just as readily extend to all such situations.[191]

Distinguishing the Judgment in Emmott However, during its most recent period in the caselaw, the Court moved quickly to limit the apparently drastic implications of the *Emmott* judgment for Community intervention

[190] Cf Case C–62/00 *Marks & Spencer* [2002] ECR I–6325.

[191] Cf AG van Gerven in Case C–128/93 *Fisscher* [1994] ECR I–4583: Member States which fail to fulfil their Community obligations cannot rely on time-limits against individuals 'who invoke provisions of Community law having direct effect' (para 31 Opinion); there is no mention of this principle being confined to directives.

in the domestic systems of judicial protection.[192] The attack was launched in *Steenhorst-Neerings*. It will be recalled that Dutch rules restricted to one year claims for the back-payment of certain benefits, again withheld in breach of the Social Security Directive 79/7. On its face, such procedural restrictions fell within the rationale of the *Emmott* judgment: the claimant had been unable to ascertain the full extent of her Community rights; this situation was caused by the Member State's failure properly to implement the Directive; therefore the Dutch authority should have been unable to invoke the restrictive national provision.[193] However, the Court drew a sharp distinction between rules involving back-limits and those purporting to limit the time available for the commencement of actions in the first place: whereas *Emmott*-style limitation periods directly prejudiced access to the courts for the enforcement of Community rights as against the defaulting Member State, *Steenhorst-Neerings*-type rules merely limited the retroactive effect of claims. Back-limits were therefore subject, as we have seen, to the ordinary *Rewe/Comet* principles.[194]

The Court's reasoning in *Steenhorst-Neerings* has again been criticised as unduly formalistic in this regard.[195] Imagine a situation where, on an annual basis commencing from 1998, a public authority refuses to grant to the citizen certain social security benefits. The claimant brings an action in 2004 challenging these decisions as contrary to Community law. If there is a time-limit of three years for challenging each individual decision, the claimant can only obtain benefits in respect of the period 2001–04; claims in respect of prior decisions are time-barred. But if instead there is a rule limiting back-payments to three years, the claimant can still recover only his/her benefits for 2001–04. Thus, in respect of challenges to routine administrative decisions, the effect of both types of limitation period can be the same, so why postpone one (under *Emmott*) but not the other (under *Steenhorst-Neerings*)? Similar inconsistencies also arise in respect of one-off unlawful acts which lead to prolonged damage to the individual. The effect of an *Emmott*-style limitation period is to give the claimant either none or all of his/her rights, depending on whether he/she initiates proceedings within the applicable time. But the effect of a *Steenhorst-Neerings*-style provision will be that, even if the claimant has brought proceedings within time, he/she is always deprived of at least some of

[192] The phrase 'hasty retreat' was coined by A Ward, 'Effective Sanctions in EC Law: A Moving Boundary in the Division of Competence' (1995) 1 *European Law Journal* 205.
[193] This was the conclusion reached by AG Darmon in the case.
[194] Case C–338/91 *Steenhorst-Neerings* [1993] ECR I–5475.
[195] Eg AM Collins, 'Community Law as a Source of Rights and Remedies in the Irish Legal Order' (1994) 3 *Irish Journal of European Law* 173; I Higgins, 'Equal Treatment and National Procedural Rules: One Step Forward, Two Steps Back' (1995) 4 *Irish Journal of European Law* 18; M Hoskins, 'Tilting the Balance: Supremacy and National Procedural Rules' (1996) 21 EL Rev 365.

his/her full entitlement to recovery. In such circumstances, the back-limit rule is actually more restrictive for the effective enjoyment of Community rights than the limitation period *stricto sensu*.

Nevertheless, *Steenhorst-Neerings* indicated an important change in the policy of the Court: *Emmott* was not to be taken at its face value. In particular, *Steenhorst-Neerings* clarified the outer scope of *Emmott*, by excluding from its potential reach a whole category of domestic procedural rules which might otherwise have been thought ripe for disapplication: retrospective limits on the recoverable value of Community rights. The next issue on which attention naturally focused was what sort of Community control *Emmott* represented even as regards those procedural rules to which it was still capable of applying: limitation periods *stricto sensu*.

In this regard, current wisdom holds that *Emmott* sought to establish no new general rule as to the nature of Community control over the commencement of national time-limits. Instead, the decision is to be explained by reference to its particular factual context: the Irish authorities deliberately led Mrs Emmott to believe that she need not initiate legal action to obtain the wrongly withheld social security benefits, only to argue later on that she was time-barred from doing so. In the light of such conduct, small wonder the Court felt obliged to act. The pity is that it did so in such sweeping language, when really it would have been sufficient to say that, in the circumstances, the Irish authorities were estopped from relying on the limitation period.

This interpretation was not apparent from the judgment in *Emmott* itself; it has emerged only through subsequent judicial pronouncements.[196] In this regard, *Steenhorst-Neerings* sowed the seeds of *Emmott*'s demise even in respect of limitation periods for the commencement of proceedings: the Court explicitly referred to the conduct of the Irish authorities as part of the essential factual matrix of the *Emmott* decision.[197] In *Johnston II*, the Court went further: the solution adopted in *Emmott* was justified by the particular circumstances of the case; application of the Irish time-limit would have had the result of depriving the claimant of any opportunity whatever to rely on her right to equal treatment under Directive 79/7.[198]

These dicta have since been applied with full force by the Court. For example, *Fantask* concerned charges levied by Denmark contrary to a Community directive and which the claimant companies now sought to recover, even though the five-year limitation period under domestic law had already expired. The Court expressly rejected the claimant's argument that a broad interpretation of *Emmott* should apply and the time-limits be postponed until Denmark had correctly implemented the

[196] Though note the reasoning used by AG Mischo in Case C–208/90 *Emmott* [1991] ECR I–4269.
[197] Case C–338/91 *Steenhorst-Neerings* [1993] ECR I–5475, para 20.
[198] Case C–410/92 *Johnston II* [1994] ECR I–5483, para 26.

directive, referring again to the specific circumstances of the *Emmott* decision rather than to any more general principle of Community control over the commencement of domestic limitation periods.[199] Similarly, *Edis* concerned actions for the recovery of charges levied by the Italian authorities contrary to a directive, initiated outside the three-year period provided for under national rules. The Court held that three years was a reasonable time for the claimant company to assert its Community rights, after the expiry of which the Member State could legitimately resist actions for the recovery of the unlawfully levied charges. *Emmott* did not interfere with this proposition, since there was no evidence that the conduct of the Italian authorities, combined with the operation of the disputed limitation period, had the effect of depriving the claimant of any opportunity whatever of enforcing its rights before the domestic courts.[200]

It is therefore clear that *Emmott* no longer represents an ambitious first step towards the positive harmonisation of national limitation periods. But *Emmott* still embodies an important aspect of the Court's general principles governing the standards of judicial protection applicable to the decentralised enforcement of Community law. In particular, *Emmott* can perhaps best be understood as an element of the fundamental right to seek judicial redress established in *Johnston v Chief Constable of the RUC*.[201] While, for reasons of legal certainty, reasonable limitation periods do not in themselves deprive citizens of their basic right of access to judicial process, the manner in which such limitation periods are applied in any given case may well have that effect, where the defendant itself was responsible for the claimant's failure to comply with the required time-limits.

Indeed, *Emmott* is no longer the only case which illustrates the application of this particular principle under Community law. *Santex* concerned an Italian public authority which issued an invitation to tender for the supply of certain products, including conditions relating to the hopeful undertaking's overall turnover. The claimant objected to this clause on the grounds that it was contrary to the Public Procurement Directive 93/36.[202] In response, the Italian authority informed all tenderers that the

[199] Case C–188/95 *Fantask* [1997] ECR I–6783. Also, eg Case C–62/93 *BP Supergas* [1995] ECR I–1883 (incorrect transposition); Case C–90/94 *Haahr Petroleum* [1997] ECR I–4085 (incorrect transposition); Case C–261/95 *Palmisani* [1997] ECR I–4025 (non-implementation); Cases C–114–5/95 *Texaco and Olieselskabet Danmark* [1997] ECR I–4263 (recovery of charges levied contrary to Treaty). Cf AG Jacobs in Case C–2/94 *Denkavit* [1996] ECR I–2827, paras 73–76 Opinion.

[200] Case C–231/96 *Edis* [1998] ECR I–4951. Also, eg Case C–260/96 *Spac* [1998] ECR I–4997; Cases C–279–281/96 *Ansaldo Energia* [1998] ECR I–5025; Case C–228/96 *Aprile* [1998] ECR I–7141; Case C–88/99 *Roquette Frères* [2000] ECR I–10465; Cases C–216 & 222/99 *Prisco* [2002] ECR I–6761.

[201] Case 222/84 *Johnston v Chief Constable of the RUC* [1986] ECR 1651.

[202] Dir 93/36 coordinating procedures for the award of public supply contracts, OJ 1993 L199/1.

disputed clause would not be treated as an absolute precondition for eligibility, but merely as a criterion for assessing the quality of tenders. But the Italian authority later changed its mind and decided to exclude all tenderers which did not satisfy the terms of the original notice. By the time the claimant sought judicial review, the 60-day limitation period, running from the date of the original notice, had already expired. The Court held that, although this procedural rule was not itself contrary to the principle of effectiveness, it was necessary to examine whether application of the time-limit would infringe Community law in the particular circumstances of the case. The Italian authority created, by its own conduct, a state of uncertainty as to the interpretation to be given to the disputed clause. That state of uncertainty was removed only by adoption of the final decision reverting to the original terms of the notice, by which point application of the 60-day limitation period had already expired—depriving the claimant of any opportunity to plead a breach of Directive 93/36. The changing conduct of the Italian authority, coupled with the operation of the national limitation period, rendered the exercise of the claimant's Community law rights excessively difficult.[203]

Moreover, the Court's new approach to *Emmott* has permitted it to undo the arbitrary distinctions which seemed to have emerged, after *Steenhorst-Neerings*, between the treatment under Community law of limitation periods *stricto sensu* on the one hand, and back-limits to recovery on the other hand. *Levez* concerned a British employer who assured his new employee that her level of remuneration was equivalent to that of her male predecessor. She was in fact being paid significantly less. By the time the true facts emerged, the employee's claim under the Equal Pay Act 1970 was frustrated by a domestic rule whereby payments by way of arrears of remuneration may only be made in respect of a period of two years before the institution of proceedings. Following *Steenhorst-Neerings*, the Court observed that national law could prescribe reasonable temporal restrictions which, in the interests of legal certainty, might entail the total or partial rejection of Treaty-based actions. However, where the employer provides the claimant with inaccurate or deliberately misleading information, such that the claimant cannot ascertain whether and to what extent there is unlawful discrimination, application of such a procedural rule would deprive the employee of the opportunity to enforce her Community rights before the national courts, and thus contravene the principle of effectiveness.[204]

The Court in *Santex* and *Levez* did not expressly refer to the judgment in *Emmott*.[205] Nevertheless, it seems clear that the same policy was at

[203] Case C–327/00 *Santex* [2003] ECR I–1877.
[204] Case C–326/96 *Levez* [1998] ECR I–7835.
[205] Perhaps feeling that, given the trouble *Emmott* had already caused, it was best to isolate that ruling as far as possible.

work in all three cases: defendants who are guilty of some form of unconscionable conduct cannot benefit from the application of (otherwise perfectly valid) national limitation periods.[206]

Uncertainties Surrounding the Revised Emmott *Principle* Of course, the precise content of this principle of Community law remains uncertain in several important respects. One can usefully begin by observing that the Court now justifies its judgment in *Emmott* on the grounds that the conduct of the Irish minister, coupled with the application of the limitation period, had the effect of depriving the claimant of 'any opportunity whatever' to rely on her right to equal treatment under Directive 79/7.[207] Yet it is difficult to say that the conduct of the Irish government in *Emmott*, or indeed that of the Italian authority in *Santex*, made it objectively impossible for those claimants to pursue their rights under Community law: both Mrs Emmott and the disgruntled tenderer could have chosen not to take the official advice offered to them at face value, and initiated legal proceedings in compliance with the applicable limitation periods. This suggests that the Court's reasoning cannot be taken entirely literally. The true basis of *Emmott* and *Santex* lies in the idea that individuals are reasonably entitled to rely upon representations made by public authorities, giving rise (in effect) to a legitimate expectation that the authority will conduct its affairs in a particular manner. Even though the concept of legitimate expectations is usually confined to the sphere of public law, a similar principle might also underlie disputes arising in a private law or horizontal context, as illustrated by the judgment in *Levez*.[208] Situations where one (private) party has created a misrepresentation, upon which another (private) party detrimentally relies by refraining from taking action to enforce their legal rights, are also capable of raising an estoppel against the application of national limitation periods.

So, on the one hand, even if the inaccurate representations made in *Emmott*, *Santex* or *Levez* did not render exercise of the claimant's Treaty rights theoretically impossible, reliance by the claimant upon those representations constituted a reasonable course of conduct in the circumstances,

[206] Cf L Flynn, 'Whatever Happened to *Emmott*? The Perfecting of Community Rules on National Time-Limits' in C Kilpatrick, T Novitz & P Skidmore (eds), *The Future of Remedies in Europe* (Hart Publishing, 2000).

[207] Eg Case C–410/92 *Johnston II* [1994] ECR I–5483, para 26. Consider also: Case C–327/00 *Santex* [2003] ECR I–1877, para 60. AG Ruiz Jarabo Colomer also seemed to consider that mere obstacles to a claimant's action for the recovery of unlawfully levied taxes are insufficient to trigger an *Emmott*-style estoppel: Case C–231/96 *Edis* [1998] ECR I–4951, para 82 Opinion; Cases C–279–81/96 *Ansaldo Energia* [1998] ECR I–5025, para 24 Opinion; Case C–260/96 *Spac* [1998] ECR I–4997, para 43 Opinion.

[208] Case C–326/96 *Levez* [1998] ECR I–783. Cf AG van Gerven in Case C–128/93 *Fisscher* [1994] ECR I–4583, para 31 Opinion.

which justified Community intervention to remove the unconscionable obstacles placed in the claimant's path to judicial process. But, on the other hand, the Court in *Levez* made clear that, where the claimant in fact has another course of action available before the national courts for fully enforcing their Treaty rights, application of the disputed limitation period cannot have the effect of infringing the principle of effectiveness.[209] After all, detrimental reliance cannot in such cases be said to have deprived the claimant of any realistic opportunity to exercise his/her Community law rights.

From this perspective, it is possible to identify in the judgments in *Emmott*, *Santex* and *Levez* the beginnings of a Community doctrine of legitimate expectations or estoppel as regards the effective exercise of one's fundamental right of access to the national courts, vis-à-vis the application of domestic limitation periods and similar procedural restrictions. This incorporates into the principle of effectiveness familiar questions about the scope of protection offered to individuals in such situations—issues on which the Court has already begun to develop guidance under Community law.

In the first place, there are questions about what sort of unconscionable conduct on the part of the defendant will be required to trigger the principle of effectiveness. For example, must the defendant have set out deliberately to dissuade the claimant from exercising his/her Community rights; or is it sufficient that this was the causal (though possibly unintended) effect of the defendant's conduct? In *Levez*, both the Court and the Advocate General considered that the claimant's failure to act on time was attributable to deliberate misrepresentations made by the employer[210]; but the Court also hinted that the same reasoning would have applied in the case of a merely inaccurate though not necessarily deceitful provision of information.[211] The latter approach is supported by *Santex*: there was no proof that the Italian public authority acted in bad faith when it advised tenderers of its revised interpretation of the disputed clause; reversion to the terms of the original notice of invitation to tender appears to have been prompted by subsequent complaints from another tenderer. In any case, both the Advocate General and the Court relied upon the objective effect of the Italian authority's conduct, which had created a misleading impression about its intentions with regard to the disputed clause, without reference to any sort of subjective evidence that the defendant had set out deliberately to mislead the claimant.[212] Other issues relating to the sorts of conduct sufficient to generate an estoppel will no

[209] Case C–326/96 *Levez* [1998] ECR I–783, para 37.
[210] Case C–326/96 *Levez* [1998] ECR I–7835, paras 28 and 32 Judgment; para 93 Opinion.
[211] Case C–326/96 *Levez* [1998] ECR I–7835, para 31.
[212] Case C–327/00 *Santex* [2003] ECR I–1877, paras 58–61 Judgment; paras 103–8 Opinion.

doubt require similar clarification: for example, the degree of precision or clarity required to engender expectations by the claimant that the defendant will pursue a certain course of conduct; and in particular, whether an estoppel can arise implicitly from the defendant's behaviour as well as by his/her express representations.[213]

In the second place, there are also questions about how far it was reasonable of the claimant to rely upon any representation made by the defendant. For example, was it crucial in *Levez* that the claimant was an employee, dependent upon the cooperation of (or at least a lack of obstruction from) her employer as regards information about comparative levels of remuneration within the business? Or would any situation in which one party's conduct gives rise to some form of representation provide the basis for an estoppel in favour of another party, perhaps of equal bargaining power or commercial resources, which has detrimentally relied upon that representation by failing to commence legal action within the relevant national limitation periods?[214]

One issue which has given rise to discussion in the caselaw is whether the estoppel principle can apply in respect of Community rights arising through legislation other than directives. In principle, there is no reason why this should not be the case. After all, unconscionable conduct in relation to otherwise acceptable limitation periods may readily interfere with the claimant's right of access to judicial process for the purposes of enforcing primary Treaty provisions or regulations, just as much as rights arising under directives. Indeed, the estoppel principle was applied in *Levez* in respect of retrospective limits on the exercise of the right to equal pay arising directly under Article 141 EC. However, the Court in *Haahr Petroleum* rejected an argument that the Danish courts must disapply a five-year time-limit for the commencement of actions seeking the recovery of taxes levied contrary to Article 90 EC, on the basis that this claim for reimbursement was not based on the direct effect of a directive which had been incorrectly transposed into national law, but on the direct effect of a primary Treaty provision. On that basis alone, the *Emmott* ruling could not apply.[215]

It is true that the Court in *Emmott* relied on the 'special characteristics' of directives to justify its reasoning—citing, in particular, considerations of legal certainty in ascertaining the citizen's Community rights, which are exacerbated by the process of transposition inherent in the lifecycle of a directive as defined under Article 249 EC.[216] However, the Court has

[213] On these issues, consider also Case C–481/99 *Heininger* [2001] ECR I–9945.
[214] Again, consider Case C–481/99 *Heininger* [2001] ECR I–9945.
[215] Case C–90/94 *Haahr Petroleum* [1997] ECR I–4085, para 53. Also, eg Cases C–114–5/95 *Texaco and Olieselskabet Danmark* [1997] ECR I–4263, para 49; Case C–228/96 *Aprile* [1998] ECR I–7141, para 44.
[216] Cf AG Jacobs in Case C–188/95 *Fantask* [1997] ECR I–6783, paras 65–66 Opinion.

since redefined the nature of the *Emmott* judgment, replacing its original arguments with the alternative notion of conduct-based estoppel—a notion which enjoys no inherently closer relationship to directives than to Treaty articles or regulations. By failing to distinguish *Haahr* from *Emmott* on the grounds that the Danish authorities in the former case had committed no specific form of misconduct comparable to the misrepresentations of the Irish authorities towards the claimant in the latter case, and choosing instead to rely upon inappropriate arguments based on the peculiar but now essentially irrelevant features of directives, there is a risk that the Court may thus impose upon the scope of the *Emmott* estoppel principle an artificial restriction which elevates one form of Community legislation to an unwarranted position of privilege.[217]

Advocate General Jacobs in *Haahr* did suggest some reconciliation between these two approaches. He observed that the prohibition on discriminatory internal taxation contained in Article 90 EC was complete and legally perfect, having direct effect in Community law from 1966 and in Denmark from the time of its accession in 1973. Thus, not only were the Danish authorities innocent of any form of misconduct in relation to the claimants, but in addition, there could be no question of the claimants being placed in a situation of legal uncertainty comparable to that of Mrs Emmott.[218] Nor, one might add, could there be any question of the claimants being dependent upon the cooperation of the national authorities for the purposes of apprising themselves of all the relevant facts, in a manner comparable to that of Mrs Levez. This approach suggests that considerations of legal certainty, as derived from *Emmott* and reiterated by the Court in *Haahr*, might be best treated simply as factors relevant to the assessment of whether, in all the circumstances, the claimant was reasonably entitled to rely on representations made by the defendant. The fact that a dispute involves a Treaty provision establishing a clear and directly effective right might help to excuse conduct which could otherwise have justified application of the estoppel principle. But it should not of itself act as an automatic bar to the potential disapplication of limitation periods in cases characterised by the claimant's reasonable reliance upon the defendant's misrepresentation.

Revision of Limitation Periods Applicable to Community Law Rights

The second main qualification to the general 'reasonable limitation periods' principle concerns situations in which national rules governing limitation periods are revised so as to render the exercise of Community law rights more difficult than before.

[217] Further, eg M Hoskins, 'Tilting the Balance: Supremacy and National Procedural Rules' (1996) 21 EL Rev 365.
[218] Case C–90/94 *Haahr Petroleum* [1997] ECR I–4085, paras 159–167 Opinion.

Targeting the Exercise of Community Law Rights Our starting point for analysis is the Court's ruling in *Gravier* that the 'minerval'—an admission fee levied upon foreign students attending, inter alia, vocational training courses at non-university institutions in Belgium—was contrary to the principle of non-discrimination on grounds of nationality contained in Article 12 EC.[219] That judgment was delivered on 13 February 1985. Belgium then introduced a special procedural rule that fees paid prior to 13 February 1985 could only be recovered by foreign students who had already commenced legal proceedings by that date. The Court in *Bruno Barra* refused to limit the temporal scope of the *Gravier* judgment, finding that the right to recovery of the minerval applied to applications for admission to vocational training courses made not only after 13 February 1985 but also prior to that date. Despite the presumption of national competence to determine the procedural conditions under which individuals could recover the unlawful minerval, the effect of the Belgian rule was to deprive foreign students who had not brought an action for recovery by 13 February 1985 of their right to obtain repayment and thus render exercise of their Treaty right to equal treatment virtually impossible.[220]

Similarly, the Court in *Humblot* held that a French car tax which indirectly discriminated against imported vehicles as compared to domestically produced cars contravened Article 90 EC.[221] That judgment was delivered on 9 May 1985. France subsequently adopted legislation governing recovery of the illegal charge which preserved existing domestic time-limits in respect of claims submitted before 9 May 1985, but adopted more restrictive time-limits in respect of claims submitted after that date. The Court held in *Deville* that, under the principle of effectiveness, Member States could not, subsequent to a judgment of the Court from which it follows that certain legislation is incompatible with the Treaty, adopt a procedural rule which specifically reduces the possibilities of bringing proceedings for recovery of the taxes which were wrongly levied under that legislation.[222]

Although the Court in *Deville* did not explicitly refer to *Bruno Barra*, it was still possible to identify a single rationale linking the two rulings: Member States should not alter their national rules on limitation periods so as specifically to limit the opportunity for individuals to exercise a particular category of Community law right. Both cases concerned Treaty provisions which had already formed the subject-matter of a judgment from the Court of Justice, but there seems no obvious reason why the same principle should not apply to the exercise of Treaty rights whose full

[219] Case 293/83 *Gravier v City of Liège* [1985] ECR 593.
[220] Case 309/85 *Bruno Barra* [1988] ECR 355. Also: Case C–47/93 *Commission v Belgium* [1994] ECR I–1593.
[221] Case 112/84 *Humblot* [1985] ECR 1367.
[222] Case 240/87 *Deville* [1988] ECR 3513.

import is evident from the Court's existing caselaw, or which have already formed the subject-matter of a judgment from the national courts applying the principles of direct effect and supremacy.

The proper scope of the judgments in *Bruno Barra* and *Deville* was clarified in a series of preliminary references from the Italian courts after the Court found in *Ponente Carni* that an annual registration charge for entering companies on the register of companies was incompatible with Community legislation concerning indirect taxes on the raising of capital. That judgment was delivered on 20 April 1993, and no limit was placed upon its temporal effects.[223] Companies which had paid the unlawfully levied charge brought actions for its reimbursement before the Italian courts. However, the *Corte Suprema di Cassazione* held in a judgment dated 23 February 1996 that recovery of the unlawful registration charge should be governed by a special limitation period of three years, provided for under legislation dating from 1972 governing various categories of registration charge imposed by Italian law. It was argued in the *Edis* case that this constituted a departure from the earlier caselaw of the *Corte Suprema di Cassazione*, which would have led one to expect actions for recovery of this particular registration charge to be governed by the general ten-year limitation period laid down in the Civil Code. The Member State had thus specifically curtailed the claimants' opportunity to bring proceedings to secure repayment of the unlawful registration charge. The Court held that, according to *Bruno Barra* and *Deville*, Member States may not adopt provisions making repayment of a tax held to be contrary to Community law by a judgment of the Court, or whose incompatibility with Community law is apparent from such a judgment, subject to conditions relating specifically to that tax which are less favourable than those which would otherwise be applied to repayment of the tax in question. However, the interpretation given by the *Corte Suprema di Cassazione* related to a national provision which had been in force for several years before the judgment in *Ponente Carni*. Moreover, that provision was concerned not only with repayment of the specific registration charge at issue in *Ponente Carni*, but also with the recovery of all other registration charges levied by the Member State.[224]

Notwithstanding the twin factors referred to in *Edis* as a grounds for distinguishing that case from *Bruno Barra* and *Deville*, the Court's restrained approach to the principle of effectiveness may well extend beyond situations in which, after a judgment from the Court, the national judges interpret *existing* domestic procedural rules so as to assign the claimant's action to a less favourable limitation period than it might previously have enjoyed. The *Edis* caselaw could also cover situations in

[223] Cases C–71 & 178/91 *Ponente Carni* [1993] ECR I–1915.
[224] Case C–231/96 *Edis* [1998] ECR I–4951.

which, after a judgment from the Court, a Member State decides to revise the limitation periods applicable to certain categories of action, through the enactment of *new* legislation, so that the exercise of Community law rights becomes more difficult than would otherwise have been the case. As Advocate General Ruiz-Jarabo Colomer observed in *Aprile*, the rulings in *Bruno Barra* and *Deville* were not meant to imply any obligation to crystallise national procedural rules, such that the Member State—including the national legislature—was totally prohibited from revising its limitation periods after a finding from the Court that it had infringed the Treaty.[225]

This is confirmed by a joint reading of the judgments in *Aprile* (which in fact concerned national legislation *predating* delivery of the relevant judgments of the Court) and *Dilexport* (which indeed concerned the adoption of national legislation *after* delivery of the relevant judgments of the Court). The requirements of effective judicial protection will not be infringed, where a Member State revises the limitation periods applicable to a certain category of claim in the light of a relevant ruling from the Court of Justice, provided that: (a) the new procedural rules do not specifically target the exercise of those Community law rights which formed the subject-matter of the Court's previous judgment, but instead apply to entire categories of similar rights under Community/domestic law; (b) the revised limitation periods correspond to the procedural rules which apply to comparable rights under purely domestic law, in accordance with the principle of equivalence; and (c) the new procedural rules remain reasonable in the sense of the *Rewe/Comet* caselaw, in accordance with the principle of effectiveness.[226]

Retroactive Effects of Revised Limitation Periods The Italian legislation at issue in *Aprile* and *Dilexport* reduced the limitation period applicable to the recovery of various categories of charge (including certain taxes found to be incompatible with Community law) from ten (or, in some cases, five) to three years. However, there was considerable confusion about precisely which classes of action were affected by that revision. It was clear (and uncontroversial) that the new three-year limitation period applied to claims for recovery which had not yet been commenced by the date of its enactment, and which also concerned taxes paid after the date of its enactment. It was less clear (and more controversial) whether the new three-year limitation period could apply to other actions for recovery: those which had already been commenced by the date of enactment, concerning taxes already paid before that date; and those which had not yet been commenced by the date of enactment, but also concerning taxes paid before that date. Advocate General Ruiz-Jarabo Colomer firmly objected to the

[225] Case C–228/96 *Aprile* [1998] ECR I–7141, paras 45–49 Opinion.
[226] Case C–228/96 *Aprile* [1998] ECR I–7141; Case C–343/96 *Dilexport* [1999] ECR I–579.

idea that the Italian legislation could apply to the former category. However, he refrained from taking any hard stance under Community law with regard to the latter category—especially since the national legal orders dealt with issues of non-retroactivity in very different ways. He was content with the fact that, in such cases, the Italian judges permitted proceedings to be instituted before the domestic courts within the revised three-year limitation period as from the date of its own entry into force. Thus, claimants who could have expected their actions to be governed by the old time-limit of ten (or five) years were still being given an adequate time within which to exercise their Treaty rights.[227] The Court followed this restrained approach: in those circumstances, the Italian legislation could not be regarded as having retroactive effect.[228]

Aprile and *Dilexport* established the principle that, where a Member State revises the limitation periods applicable to a certain category of claim in the light of a relevant ruling from the Court of Justice, the imperative of effective judicial protection imposes one further condition: that (d) the new time-limits should not be unduly retrospective in scope.[229] Subsequent cases have now begun to explore more fully what amounts to an 'undue' retroactive effect.

For example, the United Kingdom announced its intention in July 1996 to reform the limitation periods applicable to claims for the reimbursement of various categories of unlawfully levied taxes. The time-limit for seeking recovery would be reduced from six to three years with far-reaching retroactive effects—thus applying not only to claims made after the final enactment of the relevant legislation in March 1997, but also to actions brought after the July 1996 announcement, and to those still pending at that date, in all cases even as regards taxes paid before July 1996. Shortly after this announcement, though before adoption of the relevant legislation, it became apparent, in the light of the Court's judgment in *Argos*, that certain aspects of the United Kingdom's VAT regime were incompatible with Community law.[230] *Marks & Spencer* concerned an action for recovery of such wrongly paid VAT, which was lodged between July 1996 and March 1997. The Court held that the principle of effectiveness precluded the fully retroactive application of the three-year time-limit to claims for the reimbursement of relevant VAT payments, on the grounds that the Member State had failed to make provision for any transitional period in favour of claimants who were entitled to seek recovery in accordance with the original six-year limitation period.[231]

[227] Case C–228/96 *Aprile* [1998] ECR I–7141, paras 40–53 Opinion.
[228] Case C–228/96 *Aprile* [1998] ECR I–7141, para 28; Case C–343/96 *Dilexport* [1999] ECR I–579, para 42.
[229] Also: Cases C–216 & 222/99 *Prisco* [2002] ECR I–6761.
[230] Case C–288/94 *Argos Distributors* [1996] ECR I–5311.
[231] Case C–62/00 *Marks & Spencer* [2002] ECR I–6325. Cf Case C–17/01 *Sudholz* (Judgment of 29 April 2004).

Of course, this case involved an action for recovery which had *already* been commenced by the date of enactment of the British legislation, concerning taxes paid *before* that date, which should have been governed by the original time-limit. In such situations, retroactivity is clearly incompatible with the very principle of legal certainty that limitation periods are meant to embody. Nevertheless, the Court's judgment was phrased broadly enough to catch *also* those actions for recovery which had *not yet* been commenced by the date of enactment of the British legislation, but also concerned taxes paid *before* that date, which again should have been governed by the original time-limit. Retroactivity might deprive the individuals involved in those disputes of the opportunity to exercise their Community law rights, contrary to the legitimate expectation of being able to commence their claims within a much longer period of time.[232] *Marks & Spencer* clearly suggested that, in such situations, the Member State's legitimate interest in preserving the balance of public finances had to be weighed against the effective enjoyment of Community law rights through the provision of suitable transitional arrangements.

This idea was further developed in *Grundig Italiana*, which concerned the same Italian legislation considered by the Court in *Aprile* and *Dilexport*, but this time working on the assumption that the revised three-year limitation period could apply to actions *not yet* commenced by the time of its entry into force, relating to sums paid *before* that date, and calculated from the levying of the unlawful charge (rather than from the date of the revised legislation's own entry into force). The Court held that Community law does not present an absolute bar to the retroactive application of a new and more restrictive limitation period, even so far as concerns actions for recovery which have not yet been commenced by the time of its entry into force relating to charges paid before that date. However, this is subject to the condition that the new procedural regime includes transitional arrangements allowing an adequate period, after the enactment of the legislation, for claiming repayment in accordance with the old limitation period. Otherwise, the immediate application of a shorter limitation period would retroactively deprive some individuals of their right to repayment, when they believed that a much longer period of time was still available. In a situation where Italian legislation had retroactively reduced the original time-limit from 10 (or five) to three years, a transitional period of 90 days was clearly insufficient to allow taxpayers who believed their claims would be governed by the old limitation period a reasonable opportunity to assert their right of recovery in cases where, under the new rules, such claims would already be out of time. In those

[232] Cf AG Geelhoed in Case C–62/00 *Marks & Spencer* [2002] ECR I–6325, para 62 Opinion. Further: S Drake, 'Vouchers and VAT: Issues of Direct Effect and National Time-Limits Raised by the *Marks & Spencer* Case' (2003) 28 EL Rev 418.

circumstances, six months represented the minimum transitional period required to ensure that Community law rights could be effectively exercised.[233]

Moreover, *Grundig Italiana* concerned limitation periods which had been revised by the Member State *before* the Court of Justice ruled the relevant tax incompatible with the Treaty—suggesting that the principle of effectiveness places restrictions on the Member State's competence to curtail the time-limits applicable to the decentralised enforcement of Treaty rights with retroactive effect *in all situations*, not just in the light of an adverse ruling from the Court concerning the relevant Community law provisions.

Two principles have therefore emerged from this caselaw, to supplement the general requirement to provide equivalent and reasonable domestic time-limits. First, the Member State cannot reduce limitation periods specifically to target the exercise of Treaty rights which have been the subject of proceedings before the Court of Justice. For these purposes, a specific ruling from the Court is not necessary, where the legal position was already apparent from existing jurisprudence; though it remains unclear whether the same principle could apply where the Member State specifically targets the exercise of Treaty rights which have been the subject of proceedings before the national courts applying the principles of direct effect and supremacy. Secondly and in any case, the Member State cannot reduce the limitation periods applicable to the exercise of Community law rights in a manner which has retroactive effects, without including adequate transitional provisions. For these purposes, it is immaterial whether the revision took place through the reinterpretation of existing legislation or the enactment of new legislation. It is also unnecessary for claimants to demonstrate that the disputed revision took place following a relevant judgment from the Court of Justice.[234]

Other ad hoc *Examples of Effectiveness in Action*

Besides the jurisprudence established through accumulated bodies of caselaw, the principle of effectiveness can justify Community interference with (even reasonable) domestic limitation periods in more ad hoc situations.

For example, *Preston* concerned United Kingdom legislation which provided for a six-month time-limit, running from the end of their employment contract, within which women could challenge a discriminatory refusal of membership of an occupational pension scheme as prohibited

[233] Case C–255/00 *Grundig Italiana* [2002] ECR I–8003.

[234] Similar principles also apply to the revision of national rules on, eg the payment of interest (Cases C–216 & 222/99 *Prisco* [2002] ECR I–6761); and, eg unjust enrichment (Case C–147/01 *Weber's Wine World* (Judgment of 2 October 2003)).

under Article 141 EC. The Court noted that this time-limit was not in itself objectionable. However, the claimants in *Preston* were employed on a continuous series of short-term contracts. Under English law, the six-month time-limit was deemed to run from the end of each individual contract, thus placing severe temporal restrictions on the claimants' ability to seek redress in respect of past exclusion from the relevant benefits. In such circumstances, the Court ruled that the principle of effectiveness requires domestic limitation periods to run from the end of the parties' overall employment relationship.[235] *Preston* did not involve unconscionable conduct by the defendant, consisting in misrepresentations warranting application of an estoppel, of the sort castigated in *Emmott*, *Santex* and *Levez*. Nor did it concern revisions by the Member State to the limitation periods previously governing certain categories of Treaty rights such as those involved in *Bruno Barra* and *Deville*, or in *Marks & Spencer* and *Grundig Italiana*. The requirements of effective judicial protection nevertheless demanded intervention in domestic procedural rules which, in effect, offered employers a convenient loophole through which to evade proper compliance with the obligations imposed by Community social legislation.

Consider also the judgment in *Heininger*. Directive 85/577 obliges traders to give consumers written notice of their right to cancel contracts entered into away from the trader's own business premises. The right to cancel must be exercised by the consumer within seven days of receiving that written notice.[236] German law provided for a one-year limitation period, running from the conclusion of the relevant contract, within which consumers had *in any event* to exercise their right to cancel. The Court held that both the wording and the purpose of Directive 85/577 precluded application of this limitation period where traders had failed to comply with their own obligation to inform consumers of the right to cancel in the first place. Arguments based on legal certainty did not persuade the Court otherwise: if undertakings choose to market their goods or services by entering into agreements away from their business premises, they can satisfy both the interests of consumers and their own need for legal certainty by complying with the duty to supply information to the consumer.[237] On one level, *Heininger* might simply be considered another expression of the evolving Community principles on estoppel: there was no traditional 'representation' and 'detrimental reliance' of the kind found in *Emmott*, *Santex* and *Levez*; but there was still unconscionable conduct of the sort which justified the disapplication of otherwise reasonable national time-limits. On another level, *Heininger* was surely flavoured by its particular legislative and policy context: traders were under a specific

[235] Case C–78/98 *Preston* [2000] ECR I–3201. Cf Case C–435/93 *Dietz* [1996] ECR I–5223.
[236] Dir 85/577 to protect the consumer in respect of contracts negotiated away from business premises, OJ 1985 L372/31.
[237] Case C–481/99 *Heininger* [2001] ECR I–9945.

duty to inform consumers of the very existence of their right to cancel; and consumer policy is a sector characterised by systemic imbalances in the resources and bargaining power of the contracting parties. So, perhaps *Heininger* is best seen as part of the Court's special caselaw on effective judicial protection within the particular context of consumer relations.[238]

Assessment

After the period of confusion generated by *Emmott* and its subsequent fall from judicial grace, it seems that Community intervention in the time-limits applied to the exercise of Treaty rights before the domestic courts is once again characterised by a firm pattern of negative harmonisation: a presumption of national autonomy, into which the Court is prepared to make only limited incursions. Besides the principles of non-discrimination on grounds of nationality, and equivalence between comparable Community and domestic claims, the principle of effectiveness also curtails the Member State's margin of discretion by insisting that limitation periods must be of 'reasonable' duration. The level of judicial control over what amounts to 'reasonableness' in this context seems relatively low. But even reasonable limitation periods might have to be disapplied in a range of other circumstances: for example, where one party has perpetrated such unconscionable conduct against the other that to enforce the applicable time-limits would constitute an affront to the principle of access to judicial process; where the Member State reforms existing limitation periods in an attempt specifically to undermine the exercise of certain Treaty rights in the aftermath of an unfavourable Court judgment; or where in any case the Member State revises its existing time-limits in a manner which produces retroactive effects without furnishing adequate transitional provisions.

Otherwise, however, limitation periods are accepted by the Court to embody a fundamental and legitimate desire for legal certainty, and do not as such contravene the principle of effectiveness, even if their effect is inevitably to restrict access to judicial process for the purposes of obtaining a determination of one's Community rights.[239] And ultimately, the relatively limited nature of contemporary Community competence over domestic time-limits means that the opportunity for individuals to

[238] Further: ch 4 (above).

[239] Eg Case C–90/94 *Haahr Petroleum* [1997] ECR I–4085; Cases C–114–15/95 *Texaco and Olieselskabet Danmark* [1997] ECR I–4263; Case C–188/95 *Fantask* [1997] ECR I–6783; Case C–261/95 *Palmisani* [1997] ECR I–4025; Case C–231/96 *Edis* [1998] ECR I–4951; Case C–260/96 *Spac* [1998] ECR I–4997; Cases C–279–81/96 *Ansaldo Energia* [1998] ECR I–5025; Case C–228/96 *Aprile* [1998] ECR I–7141; Case C–85/97 *SFI v Belgium* [1998] ECR I–7447; Case C–343/96 *Dilexport* [1999] ECR I–579; Case C–78/98 *Preston* [2000] ECR I–3201; Case C–88/99 *Roquette Frères* [2000] ECR I–10465.

enforce their Treaty entitlements before the domestic courts is clearly capable of varying significantly from Member State to Member State.

SECTORAL CREDENTIALS OF THE GENERAL TREND TOWARDS NEGATIVE HARMONISATION IN THE CURRENT CASELAW

It seems clear that the Court of Justice has, for the most part, given up any general ambition it may have harboured during the middle-period caselaw of achieving the positive harmonisation of domestic remedies and procedural rules by judicial means. Instead, the Court's recent caselaw is, for the most part, characterised by a resurgent presumption of national autonomy, subject to the negative limits imposed by Community law, in particular, through the principle of effectiveness. That principle certainly catches blatant lacunae which are treated as incompatible with the Treaty per se: for example, a total failure to provide for the possibility of interim relief against national measures alleged to breach one's Community law rights;[240] or to provide for the possibility of recovering taxes and other charges levied by the Member State in breach of its Treaty obligations.[241] But otherwise, the Court seems prepared to engage in a process of 'objective justification': national remedies and procedural rules which restrict the exercise of Community law rights are compatible with the Treaty provided they perform some legitimate public interest function, and do so in a legitimate manner which does not exceed the domestic margin of discretion recognised by the Court.[242] Within that framework, the most difficult question is to identify exactly how far the Member State's margin of discretion extends—and thus to appreciate the full nature of the balance struck by the Court between competing Community and Member State interests in the decentralised enforcement of Treaty norms.

For these purposes, it is tempting to see the Court's current approach as concentrating on the accretion of specific bodies of legal doctrine concerning particular types of national remedy or procedural rule. In this regard, we have examined how the caselaw on the *Francovich* right to reparation, and that concerning national limitation periods and back-limits to recovery, each produce incomplete and (in particular) merely minimum standards of judicial protection at the Community level. The same would be true if one were to examine in greater detail the caselaw in fields such as the sanctions imposed upon individuals in the general interest under the Case 68/88 *Commission v Greece* (1989) jurisprudence;[243]

[240] Case C–213/89 *Ex p Factortame* [1990] ECR I–2433.
[241] Case 177/78 *Pigs and Bacon Commission v McCarren* [1979] ECR 2161.
[242] Further: ch 1 (above).
[243] Case 68/88 *Commission v Greece* [1989] ECR 2965. Further: ch 1 (above).

and restrictions on the ability of national courts to raise points of Community law of their own motion.[244]

However, it is also useful to examine several more general models by which the Court might define (with greater predictability and consistency) the Member State's margin of discretion within the principle of effectiveness. Each of these models finds some degree of support in the caselaw on national remedies and procedural rules—and each might help shed light on the Court's attitude towards the imperative of uniformity weighed against the reality of differentiation.

Are Member States Bound by the Principle of Proportionality?

The first general model would be for the Member State's margin of discretion to be defined in accordance with the principle of proportionality: national remedies and procedural rules could restrict the exercise of an individual's Community law right only to the extent necessary to achieve their legitimate public interest objectives.

Such a model could have certain advantages. For example, from the perspective of the imperative of effectiveness, it would suggest a more robust approach to the standards of judicial protection expected under Community law than any test based on whether national rules merely render the exercise of Treaty rights virtually impossible or excessively difficult. But from the perspective of the imperative of uniformity (especially as sketched out by an 'integration through law' analysis), an assessment based upon the proportionality of national rules vis-à-vis their ultimate purpose could also help reduce the wide range of possible enforcement options which currently seem available to Member States. Thus, van Gerven has argued that, although the substantive conditions for obtaining a remedy in respect of one's Treaty rights should be determined uniformly as a matter of Community law, we seem obliged to accept—as a regrettable matter of political and legal necessity—that 'executive rules' concerning issues such as the character of relief, recoverable heads of damage, standards of proof, forms of evidence and applicable limitation periods fall within the presumptive competence of each Member States. However, he advocates an approach whereby all such executive rules should be governed by a requirement of 'adequate judicial protection,' closely akin to the proportionality test applied in other fields of Community law, like the free movement of goods and services. Such

[244] In particular: Case C–312/93 *Peterbroeck* [1995] ECR I–4599; Cases C–430–431/93 *Van Schijndel* [1995] ECR I–4705; Case C–126/97 *Eco Swiss v Benetton* [1999] ECR I–3055. Further: ch 1 (above).

a requirement would help minimise the degree of fragmentation produced by the presumption of national competence; and surely do a better job in that regard than the 'virtually impossible or excessively difficult' principle.[245]

To a certain extent, the principles of effective judicial protection do already employ proportionality as a means of assessing the compatibility of national remedies and procedural rules with Community law. For example, proportionality applies to domestic provisions infringing the principle of equal treatment on grounds of nationality enshrined in Article 12 EC by indirectly discriminating against Union citizens within the scope of application of the Treaty;[246] and to any sanctions imposed upon individuals who have infringed national legislation which itself was found to be in prima facie breach of the Treaty but could be justified on public interest grounds.[247] Moreover, the requirement of proportionality applies to penalties adopted by the Member State, under the Case 68/88 *Commission v Greece* (1989) caselaw, in order to provide effective and dissuasive sanctions against individuals who have breached their Community law obligations.[248] Given that there may be little practical difference between the sanctions imposed directly by a public authority in the criminal or administrative sphere, and the sanctions made available to individual right-holders under civil or private law to enforce exactly the same Community law obligations, the proportionality requirement might be seen as a necessary element of the duty incumbent upon national courts to furnish adequate remedies for any breach of the Treaty.[249] Indeed, one might go further: given that proportionality represents a general principle of Community law, binding upon the Member States *whenever* they act within the scope of application of the Treaty, proportionality should provide the universal benchmark for objectively justifying domestic restrictions on the exercise of Community law rights within the framework of the principle of effectiveness.[250]

245 W van Gerven, 'Of Rights, Remedies and Procedures' (2000) 37 CML Rev 501.

246 Eg Case C–398/92 *Mund and Fester* [1994] ECR I–467; Case C–29/95 *Pastoors* [1997] ECR I–285.

247 Eg Case C–193/94 *Skanavi* [1996] ECR I–929; Case C–348/96 *Calfa* [1999] ECR I–11.

248 Case 68/88 *Commission v Greece* [1989] ECR 2965.

249 Consider, eg Case 14/83 *von Colson* [1984] ECR 1891; Case C–382/92 *Commission v United Kingdom* [1994] ECR I–2435. Consider, in particular, the relationship between Arts 6 and 8d Dir 76/207 on the implementation of the principle of equal treatment for men and women as regards access to employment, vocational training and promotion, and working conditions, OJ 1976 L39/40 (as amended by Dir 2002/73, OJ 2002 L269/15).

250 Note also the argument that, given the conceptual and practical difficulties of telling substantive restrictions from procedural restrictions, a general standard of judicial review based upon the principle of proportionality would be more consistent: R Craufurd Smith, 'Remedies for Breaches of EU Law in National Courts: Legal Variation and Selection' in P Craig & G de Búrca (eds), *The Evolution of EU Law* (OUP, 1999).

The Court itself has sometimes relied directly upon the principle of proportionality as a means of assessing the compatibility of national remedial and procedural restrictions with Community law. For example, *Garage Molenheide* concerned Belgian rules permitting the national tax authorities to retain sums paid by way of VAT but which the claimant argued it was entitled to recover in accordance with Community legislation. The Belgian judge referred questions to the Court of Justice concerning the compatibility with the principle of proportionality of national rules, inter alia, limiting the scope of judicial review over decisions by the tax authorities to retain sums paid by way of VAT; denying the possibility of granting interim relief against such decisions; and severely circumscribing the circumstances in which Belgium was obliged to pay interest on the repayment of wrongly retained sums. The Court found that such measures, adopted by the Member State so as to preserve the interests of the national treasury against tax fraud, went further than was necessary to achieve that purpose; and indeed had the effect of undermining the claimant's Community law right to deduct VAT.[251] That conclusion was reached as a function of the general principle of proportionality, not (as one might perhaps have expected) by reference to the ordinary principles of effective judicial protection.

There is surely something attractive about the Court's approach in *Garage Molenheide*: starting from the usual presumption of national autonomy over the enforcement of Community law, the Member State's margin of discretion is then constrained by the familiar test of proportionality—with all the benefits that (usually) implies in terms of making the 'effectiveness' assessment conducted by domestic courts more structured, transparent and predictable.

However, *Garage Molenheide* belongs to the particular context of the VAT directives. The Court has consistently held that exercise of the individual's right to deduct, which is a fundamental aspect of Community policy in this field, may only be limited by what is necessary to ensure the correct levying of VAT and to permit proper supervision by the national authorities. But the relevant caselaw makes clear that, *in addition*, national measures aimed at ensuring the correct levying of VAT and proper supervision by the domestic authorities must not render exercise of the right to deduct practically impossible or excessively difficult.[252] Proportionality and effectiveness remain conceptually distinct, even if they are sometimes practically interchangeable.[253] In any case, leaving aside *Garage*

[251] Cases C–286, 340 & 401/95 and C-47/96 *Garage Molenheide* [1997] ECR I–7281. Cf Cases C–110–147/98 *Gabalfrisa* [2000] ECR I–1577.

[252] Eg Cases 123 & 330/87 *Jeunehomme* [1988] ECR 4517; Case C–96/91 *Commission v Spain* [1992] ECR I–3789.

[253] Note that AG Fennelly in *Garage Molenheide* referred to caselaw such as Case C–312/93 *Peterbroeck* [1995] ECR I–4599 and Case C–213/89 *Ex p Factortame* [1990] ECR I–2433—but treated the requirements of proportionality and effectiveness interchangeably.

Molenheide and the VAT directives, it is difficult to see proportionality as anything more than a prescriptive rather than a descriptive model for defining the Member State's margin of discretion under the broader principle of effectiveness. Consider the caselaw on limitation periods (as examined above) in which the Court has been asked to strike a balance between the Member State's legitimate interest in safeguarding legal certainty and financial balance (on the one hand) and rules governing the duration and calculation of the time-limit available under national law (on the other hand). The Court's overall approach is closer to what English administrative lawyers might describe as '*Wednesbury* unreasonableness,'[254] rather than a fully-fledged investigation into whether the relevant time-limit goes beyond what is necessary to protect the public interest in any given situation.[255]

The same holds true in other areas of caselaw. Thus, *Dilexport* concerned actions for the recovery of an unlawfully levied consumption charge on bananas. That consumption charge was deductible from taxable income under national law. The question arose whether the principle of effectiveness precluded the application of an absolute precondition that claimants for reimbursement must have given prior notice to the national tax authority which had received their tax return for the relevant financial year. Advocate General Ruiz-Jarabo Colomer noted that the legitimate purpose of the notice requirement (that national revenue authorities should be apprised of situations in which deductible charges were refunded to the taxpayer) could have been achieved by means less restrictive of the claimant's Community right to the recovery of the unlawfully levied charge (such as an obligation upon the public body which repaid the charge to notify the competent revenue authorities). However, he considered that it fell outside the Court's jurisdiction to express any opinion on the appropriateness of the Member State's measures, provided they complied with the principles of equivalence and effectiveness. In this regard, the Court itself simply held that the disputed domestic rules did not have the effect of depriving claimants of the benefit of the practical application of Community law.[256]

Some might argue that even the caselaw on limitation periods, and judgments such as *Dilexport*, can be construed as manifestations of the principle of proportionality—bearing in mind that proportionality is a context-sensitive requirement which can still leave a wide margin of

[254] Based on the ruling in *Associated Provincial Picture Houses v Wednesbury Corporation* [1947] 2 All ER 680: the impugned decision must be so unreasonable that no reasonable authority could ever have reached it.

[255] Despite hints that national time-limits should be 'no more than necessary', eg in Case C–255/00 *Grundig Italiana* [2002] ECR I–8003. Note also the Court's occasional comparative analysis with the time-limits adopted by other Member States, eg Case C–126/97 *Eco Swiss v Benetton* [1999] ECR I–3055; Case C–125/01 *Pflücke* (Judgment of 18 September 2003). Consider, in particular, Case C–30/02 *Recheio* (Judgment of 17 June 2004).

[256] Case C–343/96 *Dilexport* [1999] ECR I–579.

discretion to the Member States in areas which are not readily amenable to judicial review.[257] For example, in free movement cases concerning difficult social or complex technical choices, the Court recognises that Member States are entitled to reach their own assessment of what is necessary to protect the public interest. In particular, the fact that different Member States have adopted different rules to achieve the same underlying public interest objectives does not in itself indicate that more stringent national provisions amount to a disproportionate exercise of national competence.[258] The same could be said of the caselaw on national remedies and procedural rules: the 'virtually impossible or excessively difficult' test is in fact the thin end of the proportionality wedge, which represents an appropriate standard of judicial review over Member State choices about how best to organise their own systems of remedies and procedural rules, particularly given the desire for legal certainty in the administration of justice.

In any case—whether one believes that the caselaw largely rejects any genuine proportionality assessment, or instead thinks that the caselaw largely embodies a legitimate form of proportionality assessment—this is clearly not a model for defining the Member State's margin of discretion under the principle of effectiveness that seems capable in practice of bringing about anything more than a loose form of negative harmonisation as regards national remedies and procedural rules for the decentralised enforcement of Community law.

Cross-Fertilisation Between Centralised and Decentralised Standards of Judicial Protection

The second general model suggested by the caselaw would be for the Member State's margin of discretion to be defined in accordance with the standards of judicial protection applied by the Community courts themselves in comparable situations. Chapter 6 will examine how the Court of Justice has often insisted that its own principles of judicial protection must be applied by the national judges, specifically for the purposes of challenges to the legality of Community action initiated before the domestic courts and then referred to the Court via Article 234 EC, rather than brought directly before the Community judicature via an action for

[257] Further, eg G de Búrca, 'The Principle of Proportionality and its Application in EC Law' (1993) 13 *Yearbook of European Law* 105. Also: E Ellis (ed), *The Principle of Proportionality in the Laws of Europe* (Hart Publishing, 1999).

[258] Eg Case C–275/92 *Schindler* [1994] ECR I–1039; Case C–124/97 *Läärä (Cotswold Microsystems)* [1999] ECR I–6067; Case C–67/98 *Zenatti* [1999] ECR I–7289. Consider also, eg Case C–3/95 *Reisebüro Broede* [1996] ECR I–6511; Case C–108/96 *Mac Quen* [2001] I-837; Case C–309/99 *Wouters and Others* [2002] ECR I–1577.

annulment under Article 230 EC. We shall see that the rationale behind such caselaw lies in the need to preserve the coherency of judicial review against the Community institutions, within the context of a two-track procedural system, where national rules on remedies and procedural rules which differ significantly from those applicable before the Community courts themselves could (at the least) encourage claimants to engage in an abuse of judicial process, or (at the worst) risk the uniform application of secondary Community legislation across the Member States.

However, even in situations concerned with challenges to the legality of purely Member State action, where no such need for coherency exists, the Court has sometimes used its own standards of judicial protection as the basis for developing the remedies and procedural rules to be applied by national courts in disputes involving Community law. For example, the substantive conditions under which Member States should incur liability to make reparation under the *Francovich* caselaw, as developed by the Court in *Brasserie*, are drawn from the caselaw concerning the non-contractual liability of the Community institutions under Article 288(2) EC.[259] Similarly, the appropriate standard of judicial review over decisions adopted by the national authorities in cases involving complex scientific or technical data, as clarified by the Court in *Upjohn*, are based directly upon the caselaw concerning judicial review against measures of the Community institutions under Article 230 EC.[260]

The rationale behind this policy was explained by the Court in *Brasserie* in the following terms: the conditions under which the Member State may incur liability for damage caused to individuals by a breach of Community law cannot, in the absence of particular justification, differ from those governing the liability of the Community institutions in like circumstances. In particular, the protection of the rights which individuals derive from Community law cannot vary depending on whether a national authority or a Community authority is responsible for the damage.[261] From another point of view, this caselaw helps prevent accusations of double standards as regards the levels of effective judicial protection required under the Treaty, especially if Member States were made to labour under more onerous conditions than do the Community institutions themselves (accusations which could in turn undermine the credibility and

[259] Cases C–6 & 9/90 *Francovich* [1991] ECR I–5357; Cases C–46 & 48/93 *Brasserie du Pêcheur* and *Factortame III* [1996] ECR I–1029.

[260] Case C–120/97 *Upjohn* [1999] ECR I–223. Consider also, eg AG Cosmas in Case C–83/98P *France v Ladbroke Racing and Commission* [2000] ECR I–3271 (as regards the protection of legitimate expectations in state aids cases); AG Alber in Case C–63/01 *Evans* (Judgment of 4 December 2003) (as regards the recovery of interest in actions for compensation).

[261] Cases C–46 & 48/93 *Brasserie du Pêcheur* and *Factortame III* [1996] ECR I–1029, para 42. Also: Case C–120/97 *Upjohn* [1999] ECR I–223, paras 34–35.

authority of the Court).[262] Moreover, any model for defining the Member State's obligations under the principle of effectiveness based upon the systematic transposition to the national legal systems of the Court's own remedies and procedural rules could mean a more predictable margin of national discretion *and* the potential for greater convergence towards a common body of Community norms. Indeed, pursued systematically by the Court, such a principle of parallelism could even act as a convincing vehicle by which to achieve extensive positive harmonisation of the domestic rules on decentralised enforcement.

However, any such process of convergence is far from complete. After all, in many other situations, the standards of judicial protection applicable in relations between the individual and Member State (or between private parties) are clearly developed without any reference to the standards of judicial protection applicable in relations between individual and Community institutions in corresponding situations. This is true, to take an obvious illustration, of the caselaw on limitation periods (as examined above).[263] But the apparently random nature of the Court's reliance upon the model of parallelism is also evident from the caselaw on the payment of interest. On the one hand, when it comes to actions for compensation based upon Community law against Member States (or other individuals), the Court draws explicitly from its own caselaw concerning actions for *compensation* against the Community institutions under Article 288(2) EC, in reaching the conclusion that claimants must be entitled to recover losses suffered through the effluxion of time.[264] On the other hand, when it comes to *other forms* of financial remedy (such as restitutionary actions) against Member States or private parties which have infringed the Treaty, the Court has held that effective judicial protection does not necessarily require the payment of interest—without drawing attention to the fact that the Community institutions would be obliged to make redress for losses suffered through the effluxion of time in comparable circumstances.[265]

Indeed, the Court has sometimes consciously refrained from developing the principle of effectiveness at the domestic level in parallel with the treatment afforded to Community institutions in apparently comparable

[262] In particular: A Ward, *Judicial Review and the Rights of Private Parties in EC Law* (OUP, 2000); and 'Individual Rights, EC Directives, and the Case for Uniform Remedies' in J Prinssen & A Schrauwen (eds), *Direct Effect: Rethinking a Classic of EC Legal Doctrine* (Europa Law Publishing, 2002). Cf AG Léger in Case C–5/94 *Ex p Hedley Lomas* [1996] ECR I–2553.
[263] Consider also the substantive conditions for granting interim relief against Member State acts under Case C–213/89 *Ex p Factortame* [1990] ECR I–2433. Further: ch 6 (below).
[264] Eg Case C–63/01 *Evans* (Judgment of 4 December 2003). Compare, eg Case 238/78 *Ireks-Arkady* [1979] ECR 2955; Case C–308/87 *Grifoni* [1994] ECR I–341.
[265] Eg Case C–66/95 *ex p Sutton* [1997] ECR I–2163; Cases C–397 & 410/98 *Metallgesellschaft* [2001] ECR I–1727. Contrast, eg Case 21/86 *Samara* [1987] ECR 795; Case T-171/99 *Corus UK* [2001] ECR II–2967 (which itself relied upon the judgment in *Marshall II* to justify obliging the Community institutions to provide interest, as well as to repay the principal sum wrongly demanded from the claimant).

cases. For example, the judgment in *Muñoz* implicitly but firmly rejected Advocate General Geelhoed's suggestion that the rules on standing for private parties to bring actions before the national courts to enforce obligations contained in Community agricultural regulations should simply reflect the conditions governing standing for natural and legal persons to bring actions for annulment under Article 230(4) EC to enforce Treaty norms against the Community institutions themselves (based upon the stringent requirements of 'direct and individual concern').[266]

Some commentators might breathe a sigh of relief that the Court has not chosen to pursue this particular convergence policy very vigorously. The Court's own rules on judicial protection are not always very effective against the Community institutions, and do not necessarily offer an ideal model for safeguarding Treaty rights before the domestic courts (as the *Muñoz* case itself well illustrates). But it should be borne in mind that the process of cross-fertilisation can run in both directions. For example, the ruling in *Bergaderm* has been taken as concrete evidence that the substantive conditions governing Member State liability under the *Francovich* caselaw, coupled with the *Brasserie* principle that the protection of Community law rights cannot vary depending on whether the relevant breach was perpetrated by a national or Community body, can contribute to a more coherent system of judicial review against the Community institutions as regards their own non-contractual liability under Article 288(2) EC.[267] So, the effectiveness of judicial protection against the Member States might help to bolster (rather than necessarily be constrained by) the principles of judicial protection applicable in respect of the Community itself.[268]

In any case, even in those ad hoc situations where the remedies and procedural rules applicable in relations between individual and Member State (or between individuals) are developed by reference to the standards of judicial protection applicable in relations between individual and Community institutions, the Court's caselaw remains a minimum standard only—placing inherent limits on how far this model of parallelism can really be said to foster positive harmonisation, so as to replace pre-existing national rules with uniform Community-level norms. For example, the substantive conditions established in *Brasserie* on the basis of Article 288(2) EC do not (as we have already seen) prevent Member

[266] Case C–253/00 *Muñoz* [2002] ECR I–7289. On 'direct and individual concern', see further: ch 6 (below). Note Case C–34/02 *Pasquini* [2003] ECR I–6515, which concerned the very different question of whether the claimant could rely on a time-limit applicable under Community law, not against a Community institution in a comparable situation, but against the Member State itself in an entirely different context.

[267] Case C–352/98P *Bergaderm* [2000] ECR I–5291. Also, eg Case C–312/00 P *Camar* [2002] ECR I–11355; Case C–472/00 P *Fresh Marine* (Judgment of 10 July 2003).

[268] Further, eg T Tridimas, 'Liability for Breach of Community Law: Growing Up and Mellowing Down?' (2001) 38 CML Rev 301.

States from adopting more generous liability principles in accordance with their own national rules. Nor would the judgment in *Upjohn* seem to require domestic courts to refrain from exercising a more stringent level of judicial review over decisions adopted by public authorities in fields characterised by complex or technical assessments (if national administrative law so permits).

The Court's preference for parallelism between the levels of judicial protection available in centralised and decentralised enforcement, inspired by the desire to avoid accusations of double standards in the treatment of the Community institutions and the Member States, therefore seems unlikely to do more than reinforce the trend towards the incomplete and (in particular) merely minimum harmonisation of national remedies and procedural rules which already characterises the current caselaw—and certainly appears unlikely to achieve the sort of positive harmonisation necessary to satisfy demands for uniformity of the sort championed by an 'integration through law' analysis.

Direct and Indirect Intervention in National Standards of Judicial Protection

The third general model which finds support in the caselaw consists in the idea that the Member State's margin of discretion should be defined not according to the traditional method of *direct* intervention by the Court within the domestic legal orders via the principle of effectiveness, where there is a patent inadequacy in existing standards of judicial protection; but rather by using the *Francovich* action for reparation as a means of *indirectly* overcoming certain limitations upon the effectiveness of national remedies and procedural rules, and thus only where the claimant can demonstrate the existence of a sufficiently serious breach by the Member State of its obligations under Community law.

This trend is perhaps best illustrated by the caselaw on the availability of interest (which has already been touched upon several times above).[269]

[269] The judgments in Cases C–192–218/95 *Comateb* [1997] ECR I–165 and Case C–242/95 *GT-Link* [1997] ECR I–4449 suggested that the Court was following an 'indirect' route to effective judicial protection in situations where traders paid unlawful taxes, passed them on to third parties, but suffered economic losses as a result, ie by insisting that such losses were not an answer to allegations of unjust enrichment within the context of an action for restitution of the unlawful taxes per se (based on strict liability), but should at most provide the basis for a separate *Francovich* action for reparation against the defaulting Member State (based on the existence of a sufficiently serious breach). However, the more recent judgments in Case C–147/01 *Weber's Wine World* (Judgment of 2 October 2003) and Case C–129/00 *Commission v Italy* (Judgment of 9 December 2003) suggest that the Court is now prepared to adopt a more 'direct' route to effective judicial protection in such cases, ie by insisting that losses suffered as a result of passing on must be taken into account in assessing whether the trader has in fact been unjustly enriched within the context of the action for

In situations where the claimant argues that national remedies fall below the standards of effective judicial protection required under Community law, because Member States fail to make provision for the payment of interest, the Court is sometimes prepared to intervene directly in the domestic legal order and correct the problem at its source. Recall, for example, the judgment in *Marshall II*: effective protection for the victim of a discriminatory dismissal from employment requires that domestic rules must provide for full compensation, including the payment of interest. Domestic rules limiting the jurisdiction of national courts to award interest had thus to be set aside.[270] However, other judgments do not follow that pattern. Recall, for example, the ruling in *ex parte Sutton*: effective protection for the victim of a discriminatory refusal to provide social security benefits did not require the national courts to award interest. The claimant's proper course was to bring a *Francovich* action against the Member State, on the basis of the latter's substantive breach of Community law, seeking damages for losses suffered through the effluxion of time.[271]

The claimants in both *Marshall II* and *ex parte Sutton* alleged that existing national remedies intended to safeguard their Community law rights were unsatisfactory. But in the former case, the Court intervened directly to correct the inadequate domestic remedy; whereas in the latter case, the Court left the inadequate national rule intact and advised citizens who sought payment of wrongly withheld social security benefits to bring a supplementary *Francovich* action. This new trend of indirect intervention poses a number of problems. For example, the claimant may be put to the trouble and expense of having to bring two separate actions instead of one to safeguard his/her Treaty rights.[272] More seriously, cases such as *ex parte Sutton* suggest that the Court is sometimes more concerned to ease the financial consequences for the Member State of its own unlawful conduct, than with ensuring the effective judicial protection of individuals attempting to enforce their Community law rights. After all, the result of *ex parte Sutton* is that, instead of interest being available *as of right* in respect of an infringement of Community law which is enforceable per se, interest can only be recouped if that breach of the Treaty can furthermore be considered *sufficiently serious* in the sense of the *Francovich* caselaw.[273]

restitution itself. Note Case C–63/01 *Evans* (Judgment of 4 December 2003): the ECJ approved—but did not necessarily require—that the claimant bring a *Francovich* action to redress various shortcomings in national remedies/procedural rules vis-à-vis the principles of effective judicial protection.

[270] Case C–271/91 *Marshall* II [1993] ECR I–4367.

[271] Case C–66/95 *ex p Sutton* [1997] ECR I–2163.

[272] Cf AG Tesauro in Cases C–192–218/95 *Comateb* [1997] ECR I–165, para 23 Opinion.

[273] Further: M Dougan, 'The Francovich Right to Reparation: Reshaping the Contours of Community Remedial Competence' (2000) 6 *European Public Law* 103.

In any event, judgments such as *ex parte Sutton* reinforce the more fundamental shift in judicial policy towards the Community's remedial competence during the current period caselaw as identified in the academic discourse. The trend of renewed deference towards domestic competence in the decentralised enforcement of Community rights, already evident in the transition from the middle-period caselaw, is actually accelerated by the Court's strategy of employing *Francovich* to address indirectly the shortcomings of pre-existing national remedies. Indeed, Community law now offers different standards of judicial protection to individuals relying on the same body of substantive Community law, not only according to the Member State in which they happen to live or work, but also according to the specific legal and factual circumstances in which the relevant public authority perpetrated its breach of the Treaty—a situation which is hardly in accordance with the 'integration through law' desire to ensure uniform enforcement conditions across the entire Community.

However, the boundaries of this indirect intervention model remain uncertain. For example, *Marshall II* and *ex parte Sutton* suggest that, for the purposes of determining whether interest should be paid directly in respect of financial remedies, it is necessary to draw a fundamental distinction between 'compensation' and 'wrongly withheld benefits.'[274] But recall further the judgment in *Metallgesellschaft*, where the United Kingdom had adopted discriminatory tax rules contrary to Article 43 EC, permitting the subsidiaries of domestic companies more time within which to pay a particular levy than that offered to the subsidiaries of foreign companies. The question arose whether the claimants could recover a sum equal to the interest which would have accrued between the time of the actual payment and the date on which the tax should have been become chargeable. It was not clear whether the claimants' actions under national law were brought on the basis of restitution or compensation. Insofar as the claimants' remedy consisted of a restitutionary action, the Court seems to have treated their situation as comparable to that of the claimant in *ex parte Sutton*. Affirming its early-period caselaw on the recovery of unlawfully levied charges, the Court held that the payment of interest was governed by national law.[275] However, where the breach of Community law arose, not because the Member State had imposed a tax, but because the Member State did so prematurely, interest should indeed be recoverable even in a restitutionary action, because damage suffered through the effluxion of time represented the claimant's only real loss, and its reimbursement was essential for restoring true equality of treatment in accordance with Article 43 EC. Insofar as the claimant's remedy consisted in a *Francovich* action for reparation against the Member State,

[274] A distinction which, even at the best of times, seems thoroughly unconvincing: see above.
[275] Cf Case 26/74 *Roquette Frères* [1976] ECR 677.

the Court was prepared to hint that, on the authority of *Marshall II*, interest should be seen as an essential element of effective protection as regards all forms of compensatory damages. However, in concrete terms, the Court went no further than deciding that, where losses suffered through the effluxion of time again represented the essential value of the claimant's Treaty rights, and their recovery was essential for restoring true equality of treatment in accordance with Article 43 EC, the domestic courts must be able to award interest as a matter of Community law.[276]

It therefore seems clear that interest must be payable on compensatory damages such as those at issue in *Marshall II*; and possibly also within the context of other compensatory damages actions such as those derived from the *Francovich* right to reparation. The latter assumption is reinforced by the judgment in *Evans*. The claimant suffered personal injuries after being struck by an unidentified vehicle, and sought compensation for his losses from the insurance body which the United Kingdom was obliged to establish in accordance with Directive 84/5.[277] Neither the Directive nor English law provided for the payment of interest. The Court held that, since compensation for loss is intended so far as possible to provide restitution for the victim of an accident, that compensation cannot leave out of account factors (such as the effluxion of time) which may in fact reduce its value—though for these purposes, it was for the Member State to choose between simply awarding interest, or instead paying compensation in the form of aggregate sums which take account of the effluxion of time.[278] That conclusion is all the more important because Directive 84/5 expressly requires the Member States to guarantee 'adequate' (rather than 'full') compensation to victims of injury caused by unidentified vehicles—thus implying that the right to interest recognised under *Marshall II* is not limited to situations involving actions for compensation in respect of a discriminatory dismissal from employment in breach of the Equal Treatment Directive.[279]

However, as regards claims for other types of financial remedy, such as the payment of wrongly withheld benefits or for the recovery of unlawfully levied charges, the presumption of national autonomy remains intact as regards the payment of interest. In such cases, the claimant's proper course of redress lies (as in *ex parte Sutton*) with a *Francovich* action to recover damages suffered through the effluxion of time. For these

[276] Cases C–397 & 410/98 *Metallgesellschaft* [2001] ECR I–1727.
[277] Dir 84/5 on insurance against civil liability in respect of the use of motor vehicles, OJ 1984 L8/17.
[278] Case C–63/01 *Evans* (Judgment of 4 December 2003).
[279] Moreover, the ECJ avoided deciding *Evans* on the narrow grounds that Dir 84/5 requires victims of accidents involving unidentified cars to receive the same levels of compensation as victims of accidents involving identified cars—and English law entitled the latter to the payment of interest. The Court preferred a broader approach, based directly upon the general requirements of effective judicial protection.

purposes, it appears fairly certain that the general *Brasserie* presumption of national competence over recoverable heads of loss should, in practice, give way to the principle of effectiveness. After all, there would seem little point in the Court offering individuals the possibility of *Francovich* damages representing losses suffered through the effluxion of time, if Member States were then free to deny that such losses were even recognised under national law. Nevertheless, there is an exception to this model of indirect intervention in the case of non-compensatory remedies, that is, where damage suffered through the effluxion of time in fact represents the principal loss suffered by the claimant, and its recovery is essential to vindicating the very essence of his/her Community law rights (as in *Metallgesellschaft*). In such situations, the principle of effectiveness will indeed intervene directly in national competence, as in *Marshall II* or *Evans*, and insist upon the award of interest.

It is therefore difficult to see the indirect intervention model as anything more than another strand of judicial practice within the overall corpus of remedies jurisprudence, but which is clearly incapable of offering any coherent or comprehensive definition of the Member State's margin of discretion under the principle of effectiveness.

An Assessment of Uniformity and Differentiation in the Court's General Caselaw

Indeed, the fact that the Court's jurisprudence exhibits tendencies towards all three of these general trends—some exerting pressure for greater harmonisation at the Community level, others pulling the system of decentralised enforcement closer towards national autonomy—clearly illustrates the often contradictory tensions operating within this large and diverse body of caselaw. That merely reinforces the impressions already formed through our detailed analysis of how the Court treats specific types of remedy (such as the right to reparation) and procedural rule (such as limitation periods).

This transition from the relative integration of the middle-period caselaw to the relative disintegration of the current-period caselaw attracts the disapproval of those who reason from an 'integration through law' perspective: the Court appears to have sacrificed vital Treaty interests in constructing a uniform system of legal protection, and seems content instead to prescribe incomplete and merely minimum Community rules, within and beyond which the Member States remain free to construct an independent and potentially divergent framework of remedies and procedural rules.

However, when viewed through the alternative paradigm postulated in Chapter 4, a different picture emerges. By refusing to pursue the logic of positive harmonisation suggested by its middle-period caselaw, the Court seems implicitly to have rejected an 'integration through law' analysis of the compelling need to centralise the legal framework of judicial protection available for the domestic enforcement of Community law. By reaffirming in its place a preference for mere negative harmonisation, the stance currently adopted by the Court appears instead to coincide with an understanding of the increasingly limited quality of uniformity suggested by our alternative sectoral model.

This interpretation is reinforced by the Court's newfound enthusiasm for the requirement of equivalence, as evidenced in recent-period judgments such as *Palmisani, Levez, Dilexport, Dounias* and *Preston*.[280] After all, equivalence seeks to promote equality of treatment only as regards the comparable remedies available within one particular Member State, and does nothing to address or reduce the differing levels of judicial protection applied to comparable situations across the Member States as a whole. By injecting fresh impetus into the principle of equivalence as a vehicle for Community intervention into the domestic judicial systems, the Court seems implicitly to recognise and even legitimise the Community's present state of remedial fragmentation.

Furthermore, the current judicial strategy of mere negative harmonisation for national remedies and procedural rules seems well suited to that category of sectors indeed characterised by only incomplete and minimum levels of substantive approximation: for example, environmental, consumer and social policy—and perhaps even the Single Market itself, insofar as the goals of free movement and equalised competitive conditions have become indelibly marked by the trend towards regulatory differentiation carried into the Treaty heartland via those welfare elements inherent in the process of economic integration.[281]

But it would be misleading to conclude that any overlap between the basic conceptual premises of our sectoral model (on the one hand), and the main thrust of current Community practice as regards national remedies and procedures (on the other hand) is the result of some conscious or even coherent act of judicial will. After all, consider the sorts of factors which help to explain the general change in the Court's remedies policy. First, the Member States were clearly concerned over the financial consequences of the Court's decisions: 'effective judicial protection' as embodied in the relatively generous criteria for damages liability set out in

[280] Case C–261/95 *Palmisani* [1997] ECR I–4025; Case C–326/96 *Levez* [1998] ECR I–7835; Case C–343/96 *Dilexport* [1999] ECR I–579; Case C–228/98 *Dounias* [2000] ECR I–577; Case C–78/98 *Preston* [2000] ECR I–3201.

[281] Note that the same analysis could apply to much of the Community's secondary legislation dealing with remedies and procedural rules (eg in the field of consumer protection): domestic standards of judicial protection are harmonised in an incomplete and (in any case) merely minimum fashion; but that does not seem inappropriate to the balance between regulatory uniformity and differentiation achieved at the substantive level.

Francovich, or the relatively interventionist control over limitation periods suggested by *Emmott*, threatened drastically to increase the costs of failing to comply with Community obligations.[282] Secondly, the Court's approach had created a serious double-standard of protection within each national legal system, since intervention to create more effective remedies for Community rights did nothing to affect the situation of comparable domestic rights. Sometimes the Member States were prepared to let Community rules 'spill-over' into national law.[283] But in many other situations nothing was done, and the resulting anomalies were criticised for being both unfair to citizens and damaging to efforts to integrate Community rights more fully into the domestic legal orders.[284] Thirdly, some practitioners expressed worries that the momentum of Community remedial competence embodied in decisions such as *Francovich* and *Emmott* had attained such levels that no national procedure could be considered truly safe from challenge, threatening to impair the administration of justice through excessive legal uncertainty.[285]

Such explanations suggest that Community control over the national systems of judicial protection has ebbed, flowed and ebbed once more according to the Court's changing perception of the imperative of effectiveness and, in particular, the Court's desire to strike some more appropriate balance between competing Community and domestic interests. This perception is reinforced by the fact that the imperative of uniformity in the application of Community norms does not often warrant a mention in the Court's remedies discourse.[286] Even when the Court does employ the language of uniformity, this is not necessarily a reliable guide to the strength of Community intervention in any particular case. For example, the Court held in *Kefalas* that Community law does not preclude the application of national rules prohibiting the abusive exercise of legal rights—but that the 'full effect and uniform application' of Treaty rules governing rises in company capital would be prejudiced if claimants were prevented from exercising their intended rights merely because they had derived some economic benefit from the relevant breach of Community law.[287]

[282] Eg the submissions of Member States such as Germany in Cases C–46 & 48/93 *Brasserie du Pêcheur* and *Factortame* III [1996] ECR I–1029 as regards liability to make reparation under the *Francovich* principle.

[283] Eg *M v Home Office* [1994] 1 AC 377 (in the light of Case C–213/89 *ex p Factortame* [1990] ECR I–2433). Also: *Woolwich Building Society v IRC* [1993] AC 70 (in the light of Case 199/82 *San Giorgio* [1983] ECR 3595).

[284] Eg AG Jacobs in Cases C–430–431/93 *Van Schijndel* [1995] ECR I–4705; AG Léger in Case C–66/95 *ex p Sutton* [1997] ECR I–2163.

[285] Eg M Hoskins, 'Tilting the Balance: Supremacy and National Procedural Rules' (1996) 21 EL Rev 365.

[286] Eg Case C–271/91 *Marshall II* [1993] ECR I–4367 imposed exacting standards of effective judicial protection without reference to the imperative of uniformity.

[287] Case C–367/96 *Alexandros Kefalas* [1998] ECR I–2843. Also: Case C–441/93 *Pafitis* [1996] ECR I–1347; Case C–373/97 *Diamantis* [2000] ECR I–1705. Cf Case C–36/96 *Günaydin* [1997]

This is clearly a situation of negative harmonisation: the presumption of national competence, subject to supervisory scrutiny by the Court. Moreover, Advocate General Tesauro suggested that it would be inappropriate to attempt to formulate genuinely common principles governing the abusive exercise of legal rights, when the Community's own evolution towards legal integration was so far from complete.[288] Notwithstanding the robust language of the Court, perhaps the true nature of Community intervention would have been better expressed by saying that the full effect and uniform application of the relevant Treaty rules would be *unduly* prejudiced by a totally unrestrained application of the relevant domestic provisions.

However, there is some limited evidence to suggest that the tension between centralisation and differentiation in the construction of Treaty norms, and thus in the elaboration of Community remedial competence, is a policy consideration which influences not only *ex post* academic analysis, but also a priori judicial deliberations. In particular, it will be seen in Chapter 6 that the general trend back towards negative harmonisation which has dominated the recent caselaw is supplemented by several persistent situations of positive remedial and procedural approximation, in which uniformity in the application and enforcement of Community law has played an explicit and prominent part in the Court's reasoning. These situations of positive harmonisation are significant because they demonstrate that the Court feels able to pursue uniformity in the domestic standards of judicial protection when it wants to achieve this goal. Against that background, the Court's silence as regards the impact of uniformity in other situations of decentralised enforcement *in itself* speaks of both an underlying judicial consciousness of the potential relevance of this imperative, and an unarticulated rejection of the 'integration through law' notion that uniformity must play some central role in resolving the enforcement deficit debate—and in particular, that some general strategy of positive harmonisation is necessary to protect the Treaty's legitimate interest in regulating national remedies and procedures.

Thus, before attempting to reach any further conclusions about the tension between uniformity and differentiation in the caselaw, it is necessary to examine precisely those fields in which the Court has pursued some form of positive harmonisation—and to query how far this can be accommodated within our own sectoral model for addressing the Community's enforcement deficit.

ECR I–5143; Case C–212/97 *Centros* [1999] ECR I–1459; Case C–110/99 *Emsland-Stärke* [2000] ECR I–11569; Case C–109/01 *Akrich* (Judgment of 23 September 2003). Further, eg W van Gerven, 'Mutual Permeation of Public and Private Law at the National and Supranational Level' (1998) 5 *Maastricht Journal of European and Comparative Law* 7; D Triantafyllou, Commentary on *Kefalas* (1999) 36 CML Rev 157; D Anagnostopoulou, Annotation of *Diamantis* (2001) 38 CML Rev 767.

[288] Case C–367/96 *Alexandros Kefalas* [1998] ECR I–2843, paras 19–23 Opinion.

6

The Court of Justice's Caselaw on National Remedies and Procedural Rules II

ONE WOULD ANTICIPATE that, insofar as the Court of Justice was truly sensitive to some sectoral understanding of the imperative of uniformity, its general acceptance of mere negative approximation for the domestic standards of judicial protection (appropriate to more welfare-orientated fields such as environmental, consumer or employee protection) would be supplemented by the pursuit of more positive harmonisation in respect of those areas of Treaty activity which remain characterised by a relatively centralised framework of substantive norms.

In this regard, it is true that the recent-period caselaw has confounded expectations that the Court would, as a general policy, replace national with Treaty-level standards of judicial protection. However, to speak of a dominant trend towards negative rather than positive harmonisation fails to capture the true complexity of the Court's contemporary remedies jurisprudence. Judgments such as *Emmott* and *Francovich* seem to have confirmed that the judicial assertion of relatively intensive levels of Community remedial competence is perfectly within the Court's grasp, and can successfully be pursued should sufficient will exist to do so.[1] Indeed, the retreat towards mere negative harmonisation characterising the broad sweep of the current caselaw shows up in even more striking relief certain relatively well-defined categories of situation in which the Court has indeed created and consolidated what may justly be termed 'Community' remedies and procedural rules, to be applied by the national courts in favour of their own pre-existing domestic standards. This prompts the question: what type of uniformity is the Court pursuing in these instances of positive harmonisation? And how far does it support or undermine the claim that the Court is willing to pursue remedial harmonisation where this is justified on the basis of a sectoral approach to the requirements of uniformity?

[1] Case C–208/90 *Emmott* [1991] ECR I–4269; Cases C–6 & 9/90 *Francovich* [1991] ECR I–5357.

Three situations warrant consideration: first, caselaw concerning the problem of maintaining a coherent relationship between the principles governing redress against the Community institutions directly before the Community courts and indirectly through the national courts; secondly, the legal framework governing the repayment or recovery through the domestic courts of unlawful state aids; and thirdly, caselaw dealing with the decentralised enforcement of the Community competition rules under Articles 81 and 82 EC.

CENTRALISED AND DECENTRALISED ENFORCEMENT AGAINST COMMUNITY INSTITUTIONS

The first situation in which the Court has continued to pursue positive harmonisation concerns claimants who seek to challenge the legality of Community action via the domestic courts, on the grounds that it breaches a higher-ranking norm of the Treaty legal order.

Centralised Enforcement Before the Community Courts: Article 230 EC

The primary route for seeking judicial review against acts of the Community institutions, as envisaged by the Treaty itself, is the action for annulment under Article 230 EC. Article 230(1) EC states that the Court of Justice shall review the legality of acts adopted jointly by the European Parliament and the Council, of acts of the Council, of the Commission and of the European Central Bank, other than recommendations and opinions, and of acts of the European Parliament intended to produce legal effects vis-à-vis third parties. The Treaty then continues to establish three main categories of claimant, distinguished according to their rights of standing to initiate such claims before the Community courts.

The first category concerns 'fully privileged applicants' under Article 230(2) EC. Member States, the European Parliament, the Council and the Commission have automatic rights of standing as regards any challengeable act, regardless of the nature of their interest in initiating the claim.[2] The second category concerns 'semi-privileged applicants' under Article 230(3) EC: the Court of Auditors and the European Central Bank have standing to initiate actions for annulment only for the purpose of protecting their own prerogatives (for example, to be consulted before the adoption of a given legal act).[3] The final category concerns 'non-privileged applicants' under Article 230(4) EC: any natural and legal person may

[2] Eg Case 45/86 *Commission v Council* [1987] ECR 1493.
[3] Consider, eg Case C–187/93 *Parliament v Council* [1994] ECR I–2857.

institute proceedings against a decision addressed to that person or against a decision which, although in the form of a regulation or a decision addressed to another person, is of direct and individual concern to the applicant.

Article 230(4) EC thus suggested that, for the purposes of determining the standing of non-privileged applicants, where the claimant was not a direct addressee, the basic legal character of the disputed Community act could (in certain cases) be decisive. In particular, the Treaty text implied that such non-privileged applicants could never challenge measures which could be considered true regulations; or measures which could be described as directives in either form or substance.[4] However, the Court of Justice has chosen to interpret Article 230(4) EC in such a manner that the strict legal classification of the disputed Community act should no longer be considered crucial to the claimant's ability to establish standing. True regulations and even directives may—at least in principle—form the subject of an action for annulment brought under Article 230(4) EC.[5] In all cases where the claimant is not an addressee of the disputed Community measure, attention therefore focuses on the cumulative requirements of direct and individual concern.

Direct Concern

The Court held in *Les Verts* that a Community act will be of direct concern to a non-privileged applicant where that act constitutes a complete set of rules which are sufficient in themselves and which require no further implementing provisions, since their implementation is automatic and leaves no room for any discretion.[6] Similarly, the Court in *Dreyfus* stated that, for a non-privileged applicant to be directly concerned by a Community measure, that measure must directly affect the legal situation of the person concerned and its implementation must be purely automatic and result from Community rules alone without the application of other intermediate rules.[7] Where a Community measure simply requires its addressee to adopt a certain course of conduct, without conferring upon that addressee any independent discretion about whether or not to comply, the measure will be of direct concern to a non-privileged applicant.[8] Even Community acts which appear to leave their addressee

[4] Consider, eg Cases 789–90/79 *Calpak* [1980] ECR 1949; Case T–99/94 *Asocarne* [1994] ECR II–871.

[5] As regards regulations, eg Case C–358/89 *Extramet* [1991] ECR I–2501; Case C–309/89 *Codorniu* [1994] ECR I–1853. As regards directives, eg Case C–10/95P *Asocarne* [1995] ECR I–4149; Cases T-172 & 175–77/98 *Salamander* [2000] ECR II–2487.

[6] Case 294/83 *Les Verts* [1986] ECR 1339.

[7] Case C–386/96P *Dreyfus* [1998] ECR I–2309.

[8] Eg Cases 106–7/63 *Toepfer* [1965] ECR 405; Case C–152/88 *Sofrimport* [1990] ECR I–2477.

some discretion as to implementation may still be of direct concern to a non-privileged applicant where such discretion is in fact more theoretical than real.[9]

However, the direct concern requirement poses particular problems as regards the ability of non-privileged applicants to bring actions for the annulment of directives. According to the Court of First Instance in *Salamander*, such measures cannot be of direct concern to individuals either *before* their transposition into national law by the Member State (since directives are incapable of having any independent legal effects against private parties); or even *after* such transposition (since any legal effects for private parties are then produced by the relevant domestic measures and not by the directive itself).[10] The Court of First Instance did seem to leave open the question of whether an 'emanation of the state' under the *Foster v British Gas* caselaw could claim to be directly concerned by a Community directive.[11] After all, in such situations, directives which are sufficiently clear, precise and unconditional are indeed capable of producing independent legal effects after the deadline for transposition has passed and in the absence of domestic implementation. Even as regards truly private parties, it is arguable that the reasoning adopted by the Court of First Instance may need to be further refined: if a directive sets out rules which are so detailed as to leave no real discretion as to their implementation by the Member State, other than the mechanical act of transposition, it is arguable that the measure should nevertheless be of direct concern to individuals whose legal position will or at least should be affected by its provisions upon implementation into national law. Nevertheless, the Court of First Instance, in cases such as *Japan Tobacco*, has indicated that it will continue to adopt a restrictive approach to the circumstances in which non-privileged applicants might be considered directly concerned by a Community directive.[12]

Individual Concern

Individual concern was defined by the Court in *Plaumann*: the disputed Community act must affect the claimant by reason of certain attributes which are peculiar to the claimant, or by reason of circumstances in which the claimant is differentiated from all other persons, and thus distinguishes the applicant individually just as in the case of the actual addressee.[13] The Court has adopted an extremely restrictive approach to the situations in

[9] Eg Case 11/82 *Piraiki-Patraiki* [1985] ECR 207.
[10] Cases T–172 & 175–77/98 *Salamander* [2000] ECR II–2487.
[11] Case C–188/89 *Foster v British Gas* [1990] ECR I–3313.
[12] Case T–223/01 *Japan Tobacco* [2002] ECR II–3259.
[13] Case 25/62 *Plaumann* [1963] ECR 95.

which claimants will be considered to fulfil these *Plaumann* requirements.[14] In particular, it is possible to identify only two generic categories of dispute in which an applicant will be considered individually concerned by a Community measure.[15]

In the first place, the Court recognises standing for members of a closed class of persons whose membership was unalterably fixed at the time the disputed measure was adopted; and moreover, whose interests the Community institutions were obliged to take into account when adopting the relevant act.[16] It seems that both limbs of this formulation are essential. An applicant who is a member of a closed class cannot be considered individually concerned by the relevant Community measure, if the institutions were not under a specific obligation to take that group's interests into account.[17] Conversely, an obligation to take into account the situation of a particular group is insufficient to generate individual concern, where the applicant did not belong to a closed class of persons affected by the disputed act.[18]

In the second place, the Court also recognises standing for applicants who enjoyed a right to participate in the decision-making process which led to the adoption of the disputed Community act. This is true, for example: of those who complain to the Commission about an alleged infringement of the competition rules under Article 81 or 82 EC and are thus entitled to be heard during the subsequent investigation in accordance with Regulation 1/2003;[19] of persons with a right to make representations during the Commission's analysis of a proposed concentration under the secondary legislation on mergers;[20] and of parties entitled under Article 88(2) EC to submit comments to the Commission during an investigation into the grant of state aid.[21] The key point here is that the applicant must have a *right* to participate. The mere fact that a natural or

[14] Further, eg R Greaves, 'Locus Standi Under Article 230 EEC When Seeking Annulment of a Regulation' (1986) 11 EL Rev 119; A Albors Llorens, *Private Parties in European Community Law: Challenging Community Measures* (Clarendon Press, 1996); A Arnull, 'Private Applicants and the Action for Annulment Under Article 230 of the EC Treaty' (1995) 32 CML Rev 7; N Neuwahl, 'Article 230 Paragraph 4 EC: Past, Present and Possible Future' (1996) 21 EL Rev 17; A Arnull, 'Private Applicants and the Action for Annulment Since *Codorniu*' (2001) 38 CML Rev 7.

[15] Consider also specialised bodies of caselaw, eg in the sphere of anti-dumping duties. Further, eg P Craig and G de Búrca, *EU Law: Text, Cases, & Materials* (OUP, 2002) ch 12.

[16] Eg Case 11/82 *Piraiki-Patraiki* [1985] ECR 207; Case C–152/88 *Sofrimport* [1990] ECR I–2477.

[17] Eg Case C–209/94 *Buralux* [1996] ECR I–615.

[18] Eg Case C–451/98 *Antillean Rice* [2001] ECR I–8949; Case C–452/98 *Nederlandse Antillen* [2001] ECR I–8973.

[19] Reg 1/2003 on the implementation of the rules on competition laid down in Articles 81 and 82 of the Treaty, OJ 2003 L1/1. Eg Case 26/76 *Metro I* [1977] ECR 1875.

[20] Eg Case T–96/92 *Grandes Sources* [1995] ECR II–1213; Case T–12/93 *Vittel* [1995] ECR II–1247.

[21] Eg Case C–313/90 *CIRFS* [1993] ECR I–1125.

legal person has become involved in the Community's decision-making procedures prior to the adoption of the disputed act, as a matter of good administration or institutional courtesy, will be insufficient to differentiate that applicant in the *Plaumann* sense.[22]

There are other (more unpredictable) situations in which the Court has recognised that non-privileged applicants are individually concerned within the scope of the *Plaumann* formula, and thus capable of bringing actions for annulment under Article 230(4) EC, even though those applicants do not fall within either of the two generic categories described above: for example, where the disputed act causes special damage to the applicant,[23] or infringes a specific legal right.[24] Overall, however, the caselaw severely restricts the range of applicants able to claim standing within the terms of Article 230(4) EC. Furthermore, the Court will not permit natural or legal persons effectively to circumvent the requirement to prove direct and individual concern, before seeking the annulment of any given Community measure, by using alternative legal actions based upon the Treaty: for example, an action for failure to act under Article 232 EC;[25] or an action for damages against the Community institutions under Article 288(2) EC.[26]

Decentralised Enforcement Before the National Courts: Article 234 EC

Analysed in isolation, the Treaty's system of centralised enforcement against the Community institutions would appear woefully inadequate, thanks to the Court's restrictive interpretation of the requirements of direct and individual concern as regards the standing of non-privileged applicants. However, that centralised system must in fact be considered alongside the additional *decentralised* route to judicial review against Community measures available via the national courts. In particular, Article 234 EC provides that the Court of Justice shall have jurisdiction to give preliminary rulings concerning, inter alia, the validity of acts adopted by the Community institutions. The Treaty itself therefore contemplated that, if the outcome of a dispute pending before the national courts were to depend upon the validity of a given Community measure, the domestic judges could submit an Article 234 EC reference to the Court of Justice.

On that basis, the Court has often pointed out that natural and legal persons unable to bring an action for annulment directly under

[22] Eg Case C–10/95P *Asocarne* [1995] ECR I–4149; Case C–321/95P *Greenpeace* [1998] ECR I–1651.
[23] Eg Case C–358/89 *Extramet* [1991] ECR I–2501.
[24] Eg Case C–309/89 *Codorniu* [1994] ECR I–1853.
[25] Eg Cases 10 & 18/68 *Eridania* [1969] ECR 459.
[26] Eg Case 543/79 *Birke* [1981] ECR 2669.

Article 230(4) EC may nevertheless plead the illegality of Community measures indirectly before the domestic courts. That is true regardless of the character of the disputed act (decision, regulation or directive); and without any need for the claimant to demonstrate direct and individual concern.[27] Indeed, the Court in *Walter Rau* recognised that even individuals who do in fact satisfy the conditions for commencing judicial review against Community measures under Article 230(4) EC remain at liberty instead to initiate legal proceedings before the national courts based upon the alleged unlawfulness of the relevant act.[28]

On the one hand, given the limited scope of access to judicial process under Article 230(4) EC, the possibility of decentralised enforcement seems essential if the Court is to guarantee an adequate standard of legal protection against the Community institutions in the event of an infringement of the individual's Treaty rights. On the other hand, the existence of parallel—and potentially overlapping—avenues to judicial redress in respect of the same allegedly unlawful Community act poses certain problems. In the first place, if the national courts enjoyed unfettered discretion to adjudicate for themselves over the substantive compatibility of any given Community measure with higher Treaty norms, different Member States might reach different conclusions as to the validity of a single legal instrument. Regardless of any potential for regulatory differentiation through devices such as minimum harmonisation and ad hoc derogations, the uniform application of the common core of rights and obligations established for every Member State by the Community legislature would be endangered. In the second place, if the Member States were completely free to determine the procedural conditions under which Community acts could be challenged via the national courts, there would be a genuine risk that claimants might choose to initiate legal action in a domestic jurisdiction with (say) longer limitation periods than the two-month time-limit provided for in respect of actions for annulment before the Community courts under Article 230(5) EC. Differences between the conditions for centralised and decentralised enforcement could therefore encourage abuse of the national judicial processes, so as to circumvent the procedural guarantees specifically offered to the Community institutions by the Treaty itself in order to protect the general interest.[29]

[27] Eg Case C–209/94 *Buralux* [1996] ECR I–615; Case C–321/95P *Greenpeace* [1998] ECR I–1651; Cases T–172 & 175–177/98 *Salamander* [2000] ECR II–2487.

[28] Cases 133–136/85 *Walter Rau* [1987] ECR 2289.

[29] Cf the situation in English law after the reforms to Order 53 of the Rules of the Supreme Court and the Supreme Court Act 1981, eg *O'Reilly v Mackman* [1982] 3 All ER 1124; *Cocks v Thanet DC* [1982] 3 All ER 1135; *Wandsworth LBC v Winder* [1985] 1 AC 461; *Roy v Kensington and Chelsea Family Practitioner Committee* [1992] 1 AC 624; *Boddington v British Transport Police* [1999] 2 AC 143. Cf the impact of the new Civil Procedure Rules, eg *Clark v University of Lincolnshire* [2000] 3 All ER 752.

The Court has responded to these concerns by imposing more centralised—and more stringent—conditions upon the exercise of national jurisdiction as regards challenges to the legality of Community action than those which usually apply to claims based on the alleged incompatibility of purely domestic action with Treaty norms. Three areas merit attention: the power of the national courts to adjudicate on the substance of the action for judicial review; the conditions under which interim relief may be granted to claimants pending final resolution of the dispute; and the rules governing domestic limitation periods for commencing legal proceedings.

Limited Jurisdiction of the National Courts

The Court in *Granaria* held that every regulation brought into force in accordance with the Treaty must be presumed to be valid so long as a competent court has not made a finding that it is invalid. That presumption was derived, on the one hand, from Treaty provisions such as Article 230 EC reserving to the Court of Justice alone the power to review the legality of regulations and, on the other hand, from Article 234 EC empowering the Court of Justice to give rulings as a court of last instance on the validity of regulations where a dispute on that issue has been brought before a national court.[30] However, *Granaria* did not clarify exactly which courts should be considered competent to make a finding that any given Community measure is invalid. Did the idea that the Court of Justice ruled as a 'court of last instance' under Article 234 EC imply that domestic tribunals were able to settle disputes without the need to make a preliminary reference, by finding for themselves that Community acts were unlawful? Or did the notion that the Court 'alone' had jurisdiction to review the legality of Community measures in accordance with Article 230 EC mean that national courts would instead be obliged to refer issues of validity to the central level?

This issue was settled in *Firma Foto-Frost*, which concerned a Commission decision refusing permission for Germany to waive the post-clearance recovery of certain import duties, on the basis of which the German authorities adopted a notice demanding payment from the claimant. The latter brought an action before the national courts for annulment of the German notice, on the grounds that the Commission decision on which it was based was itself incompatible with superior rules of Community law. The questions arose whether the German court was competent to declare the Commission decision invalid. The Court of Justice held that, if national courts consider that the grounds of invalidity put forward by the claimant are unfounded, they may conclude that the

[30] Case 101/78 *Granaria* [1979] ECR 623.

Community measure is completely valid. However, national courts do not have any power to declare Community acts invalid.[31]

According to the Court, the main purpose of the preliminary reference procedure under Article 234 EC is to ensure that Community law is applied uniformly by national courts. That requirement is particularly imperative when the validity of a Community act is at issue. Divergences between courts in different Member States as to the validity of Community acts would jeopardise the very unity of the Community legal order, and detract from the fundamental requirement of legal certainty. That conclusion was reinforced by the need for coherence in the system of judicial protection established by the Treaty. In Articles 230 and 234 EC, the Treaty had established a complete system of legal remedies designed to permit the Court of Justice to review the legality of Community measures. Since Article 230 EC gives the Court exclusive jurisdiction to declare a Community act void, the coherence of the Treaty system requires that, where the validity of a Community act is challenged before a national court, the power to declare that act invalid must also be reserved to the Court of Justice. Moreover, the Court considered itself to be in the best position to decide on the validity of Community acts. Community institutions whose acts are challenged are entitled to participate in proceedings before the Court under Article 234 EC; and the Court may require the Member States and Community institutions which are not participating in the Article 234 EC proceedings to supply all information which it considers necessary for the purposes of the case before it.

If the validity of a Community measure is seriously in doubt, the domestic judge is therefore obliged to make a reference under Article 234 EC.[32] That is true even of tribunals against which there is still a judicial remedy under national law, and which would in other circumstances enjoy discretion about whether or not to make an Article 234 EC reference.[33] The Court of Justice will then rule definitively on the validity issue for itself. By contrast with the usual effects of a preliminary ruling, the Court's judgment will be binding on all national courts across every

[31] Case 314/85 *Firma Foto-Frost* [1987] ECR 4199.

[32] Eg Case C–6/99 *Greenpeace France* [2000] ECR I–1651.

[33] However, problems arise with measures adopted under Title IV, Part Three EC (relating to visas, asylum and immigration policy). Art 68(1) EC provides that courts of last instance must submit references under Art 234 EC; but it does not confer any power on other tribunals to do the same. This suggests that the jurisdictional principles established in *Firma Foto-Frost* must be adapted, in situations where claimants challenge the validity of Title IV measures before the lower national courts, because the latter are not competent to refer the issue under Art 234 EC. This has been criticised on the grounds that it would require certain claimants to pursue legal proceedings through to the highest possible domestic court, before having any genuine opportunity to challenge the validity of Community acts before the ECJ, eg A Ward, 'The Limits of the Uniform Application of Community Law and Effective Judicial Review: A Look Post-Amsterdam' in C Kilpatrick, T Novitz & P Skidmore (eds), *The Future*

Member State. In particular, if the Community measure is declared by the Court to be invalid, it must be considered a nullity throughout the entire Community territory without the need for the courts of each separate Member State to make a reference of their own.[34]

Interim Relief Before the National Courts

It will be recalled that the Court in *Factortame* insisted that the effective protection of Community rights requires the availability, in principle, of interim relief before the national courts against Member State conduct alleged to infringe Treaty norms.[35] However, the Court appeared to leave determination of the substantive conditions under which such relief might be granted in any particular case within the discretion of domestic law, subject to the minimum requirements imposed by the principles of equivalence and effectiveness.[36]

As regards the availability of interim relief before the national courts in respect of Community measures alleged to infringe superior Treaty norms, the Court in *Firma Foto-Frost* admitted that it might prove necessary to qualify the fundamental rule that national courts may not themselves declare Community acts invalid, but did not find it necessary to express any firm opinion on this issue. In its subsequent judgments in *Zuckerfabrik* and *Atlanta*, the Court indeed addressed the competence of the national courts to grant interim relief in cases involving the alleged invalidity of Community acts—and in doing so, travelled much further towards the positive harmonisation of national procedural rules than even the *Factortame* ruling had achieved.[37]

In *Zuckerfabrik*, the German customs authorities sought to enforce a Community regulation imposing a levy on sugar producers. The claimant sought annulment of the payment order before the German courts, claiming that the Community regulation was itself invalid. The national judge asked the Court of Justice for guidance on whether the Treaty precluded the power of national courts provisionally to suspend the operation

of Remedies in Europe (Hart Publishing, 2000). Cf the proposals contained in the Draft Treaty Establishing a Constitution for Europe, OJ 2003 C169/1; discussed by M Dougan, 'The Convention's Draft Constitutional Treaty: Bringing Europe Closer to Its Lawyers?' (2003) 28 EL Rev 763. See now the 2004 Treaty, CIG 87/04.

[34] Eg Case 66/80 *International Chemical Corporation* [1981] ECR 1191.
[35] Case C–213/89 *ex p Factortame* [1990] ECR I–2433.
[36] This interpretation is supported by, eg E Szyszczak, 'Sovereignty: Crisis, Compliance, Confusion, Complacency?' (1990) 15 EL Rev 480; D Oliver, 'Fishing on the Incoming Tide' (1991) 54 MLR 442; CM Collins, 'The Availability of Interim Relief in National Courts to Uphold Community Law Rights' (1992) 1 *Irish Journal of European Law* 60; P Oliver, 'Interim Measures: Some Recent Developments' (1992) 29 CML Rev 7; M Jarvis, *The Application of EC Law by National Courts: The Free Movement of Goods* (Clarendon Press, 1998) pp 368–70.
[37] Cases C–143/88 and C–92/89 *Zuckerfabrik Süderdithmarshen* [1991] ECR I–415; Case C–465/93 *Atlanta* [1995] ECR I–3761.

of a national administrative measure based on an allegedly invalid Community regulation; and if not, under what conditions such interim relief should be adopted. *Atlanta* concerned a Community regulation establishing a common import regime for the market in bananas. The claimant was allotted an initial quota of import licences for the first half of the 1993 marketing year, but challenged that decision before the German courts on the grounds that the Community regulation was itself invalid. The national court decided to grant interim protection pending final judgment, by ordering the German authorities to grant the claimant additional import licences for the second half of 1993 (on the understanding that, if the claimant eventually lost its case, those additional licences could be set off against its 1994 quota).

The Court in *Zuckerfabrik* and *Atlanta* gave three reasons why the national courts should, in principle, have jurisdiction to grant interim relief against domestic measures implementing an allegedly invalid regulation, notwithstanding their lack of jurisdiction definitively to rule on the legality of such Community acts. First, the right to challenge the legality of a Community act indirectly through the national courts would be compromised if individuals were not able, in principle, to obtain interim relief against national implementing measures. Indeed, the effective judicial protection of individual rights must entail jurisdiction to grant interim relief pending the Court's final ruling on (in)validity. Secondly, the Court drew a parallel between the right to challenge Community legislation indirectly through the domestic courts by way of an Article 234 EC preliminary reference, and the ability to launch a challenge directly before the Community courts under Article 230(4) EC. Under a direct action, Articles 242–43 EC give the Community courts power to order interim suspension of the Community measure, and to adopt other (positive) interim measures. The coherence of the system of legal protection requires that national courts should be able to offer similar safeguards to protect the individual claimant. Thirdly, the Court drew a parallel between interim relief against a purely national measure and interim relief against a Community measure or its national implementing act. In both situations, the dispute is based on an alleged incompatibility with a higher rule of Community law. Since interim relief was available against purely domestic measures under *Factortame*, it should also be available against Community acts or their domestic implementing measures.

When it came to dealing with the substantive conditions for granting interim relief in any given case, *Zuckerfabrik* and *Atlanta* sought directly to establish a single Community standard to be applied across the Member States. In the Court's view, the fact that national rules governing the grant of interim relief differed from country to country might have the effect of prejudicing the uniform application of Community law. Therefore, while the grant of interim relief against national acts based on an allegedly invalid Community measure should be governed by domestic procedural law as regards, for example, the making and examination of the application, interim relief must in every Member State be subject, at the very least, to conditions which are uniform so far as the granting of such protection is concerned. For these purposes, the Court referred again to the need to maintain a parallel between centralised and decentralised challenges to Community measures and therefore looked to the approach applied under Articles 242 and 243 EC. On that basis, *Zuckerfabrik* and *Atlanta* together establish the following test.

First, the national court must entertain serious doubts as to the validity of the disputed Community act, taking into account the extent of the discretion enjoyed by the Community institutions within the relevant sector. Secondly, the domestic judge must, if the validity of the Community act is not already in issue before the Court, make a reference under Article 234 EC setting out the reasons for which it considers the Community act to be unlawful. Thirdly, the relief granted must retain its interim character. Thus, if the Court rules that the questions referred do not disclose any factor affecting the validity of the act, the relief must end. Fourthly, there must be urgency, that is, the interim relief must be necessary to avoid serious and irreparable damage being caused to the party seeking it. For these purposes, the damage must be such as to materialise before the Court can rule on the validity of the Community act. As to the nature of the damage, the national court must decide whether the immediate enforcement of the Community act would be likely to result in irreversible damage to the applicant which could not be made good if the Community act were to be declared invalid. In principle, purely financial damage cannot be regarded as irreparable. Fifthly, the national court must take due account of the Community's interests. It must decide whether the Community act in question would be deprived of all effectiveness if not immediately implemented, having regard to the damage interim relief may cause to the legal regime established by the relevant act for the Community as a whole. Thus, it must consider the cumulative effect of a large number of courts adopting interim measures for similar reasons and the special features of the applicant's situation distinguishing him/her from the other operators concerned. Moreover, Community acts should not be set aside without proper guarantees. Thus, if the grant of interim relief represents a financial risk for the Community, the national court must be in a position to require the applicant to provide adequate security.

In its assessment of all those conditions, the national court must respect any decision of the Court of Justice or Court of First Instance on the lawfulness of the Community act or on the application of interim measures at Community level. Thus, if the Court has already upheld the validity of the act in question, or determined the nature of the damage likely to be suffered as a result of the failure to grant relief, or assessed the balance between the Community interest and that of the economic sector concerned, the national court must respect those findings—unless (for example) the alleged grounds of invalidity are different, or the individual applicant shows specific considerations which distinguish him/her from other economic operators concerned. The Court added in *Krüger* that a national court which has provisionally suspended the disputed measure and referred its validity to the Court may still grant leave to appeal against that decision to a higher domestic forum. If the latter reverses the earlier finding, the Article 234 EC reference would serve no further purpose, and the Community measure would again become fully applicable.[38]

These principles must be applied by the Member States in preference to their own pre-existing domestic rules.[39] *Zuckerfabrik* and *Atlanta* therefore represent a strong assertion by the Court of centralised Community remedial competence, explicitly justified by reference to the fundamental imperative of uniformity in the application of Treaty norms.[40]

On its face, the Court's approach in *Zuckerfabrik* and *Atlanta* to the substantive conditions for granting interim relief differs markedly from that adopted in *Factortame*. However, many commentators believe that the principles established in *Zuckerfabrik* and *Atlanta* are also intended to apply to situations where claimants challenge the compatibility of purely national action with Community law. That assessment is based on two strands of the Court's reasoning in *Zuckerfabrik*. In the first place, the Court's assertion that 'the interim legal protection which Community law ensures for individuals before national courts must remain the same, irrespective of whether they contest the compatibility of national legal provisions with Community law or the validity of secondary Community law, in view of the fact that the dispute in both cases is based on Community law itself' could equally apply as regards the substantive conditions for protection in *Factortame*-style situations (even though that statement was made only in the context of establishing the national court's jurisdiction *in principle* to grant interim relief).[41] In the second place, the Court's reasoning that divergent domestic rules governing the grant of interim relief might jeopardise the uniform application of Community law, thereby justifying the prescription of common conditions for relief in their place, could apply as much to the existence of national as of Community

[38] Case C–334/95 *Krüger* [1997] ECR I–4517.
[39] Eg Case C–17/98 *Emesa Sugar* [2000] ECR I–675. Cf AG Léger in Case C–213/01P *Port* [2003] ECR I–2319.
[40] Further, eg P Oliver, 'Interim Measures: Some Recent Developments' (1992) 29 CML Rev 7; H Schermers, Commentary on *Zuckerfabrik* (1992) 29 CML Rev 133; E Sharpston, 'Interim Relief in the National Courts' in J Lonbay & A Biondi (eds), *Remedies for Breach of EC Law* (Wiley, 1997).
[41] Cases C–143/88 and C-92/89 *Zuckerfabrik Süderdithmarshen* [1991] ECR I–415, para 20, Case C–465/93 *Atlanta* [1995] ECR I–3761, para 24.

provisions allegedly in breach of higher Treaty norms.[42] After all, according to an 'integration through law' analysis, both situations involve the same risk that the protection of Community interests will vary as between Member States depending on the rules applied by the latter for the grant of interim protection.[43]

However, the Court itself has never insisted that the substantive conditions for granting interim relief against purely domestic measures must mirror those established in *Zuckerfabrik* and *Atlanta* as regards the validity of Community acts.[44] Moreover, there are good reasons why the Court need not feel obliged to adopt such a position in the future. Advocate General Jacobs argued in *Peters* that there is a quantitative difference, as regards the seriousness of the risk posed to the uniform application of the Treaty, between suspending the application of a Community regulation and merely permitting national divergences between its operational effectiveness in particular cases.[45] For present purposes, we might elaborate on that reasoning by pointing out that, in situations such as *Zuckerfabrik* and *Atlanta*, divergent standards of judicial protection between the Member States directly threaten the common core of rights and obligations imposed by any binding measure adopted by the Community institutions. But in disputes such as *Factortame*, that threat surely cannot be described as generic. If substantive Community norms are indeed uniform, there may well be a sectoral argument for harmonising the conditions for granting interim relief against purely domestic conduct which is alleged to infringe the Treaty. But where substantive Community norms are themselves located within a landscape of regulatory differentiation, there is no need for anything more than the minimum level of judicial protection guaranteed by the ordinary presumption of national competence, subject to the requirements of equivalence and effectiveness.

Furthermore, in the case of interim relief against purely domestic measures, the Court was confronted from the outset with a set of divergent national practices. *Factortame* sought to impose some sort of Community-level order, by insisting that national courts must meet the basic standards of judicial protection required by the principle of effectiveness. But in the

[42] Cases C–143/88 and C–92/89 *Zuckerfabrik Süderdithmarshen* [1991] ECR I–415, paras 25–26.
[43] See further, eg AG Mischo in Cases C–6 & 9/90 *Francovich* [1991] ECR I–5357, para 55 Opinion. This option is supported by, eg AG Toth, Commentary on *ex p Factortame* (1990) 27 CML Rev 573; S Weatherill, 'Beyond "EC Law Rights, National Remedies"' in A Caiger & DA Floudas (eds), *1996 Onwards: Lowering the Barriers Further* (Wiley, 1996); A Ward, *Judicial Review and the Rights of Private Parties in EC Law* (OUP, 2000).
[44] Though note the broad formulation used in Case C–17/98 *Emesa Sugar* [2000] ECR I–675: the *Zuckerfabrik/Atlanta* conditions apply to interim relief before the national courts 'when the dispute concerns a matter of Community law' (para 70). Further: L Flynn, 'Taking Remedies Too Seriously? National Procedural Autonomy in the European Court of Justice' (1996) XXXI *The Irish Jurist* 110.
[45] Case C–290/91 *Johannes Peter* [1993] ECR I–2981, para 24 Opinion.

case of interim relief against Community measures, *Zuckerfabrik* and *Atlanta* started from the opposite pole. Because of the Court's exclusive jurisdiction under *Firma Foto-Frost*, the conditions for judicial protection against Community measures were already uniform (under Articles 242–43 EC). In the interests of the more efficient enforcement of individual rights, the Court sanctioned a limited devolution of jurisdiction (to order interim relief) onto the national courts. In that devolution of power, the Court had a legitimate interest in preserving the pre-existing state of uniformity by harmonising the substantive conditions for granting interim relief against the Community institutions in accordance with its own caselaw.

Time-limits Before the National Courts

Chapter 5 described how the Court's general approach to national limitation periods consists in the presumption of national autonomy, subject to the principle of equivalence, and the ad hoc requirements imposed by the principle of effectiveness. This basic framework applies whether the claimant seeks to challenge the legality of conduct by the Member State, another private party, or indeed the Community institutions themselves. However, in the last category of situation, more specialised conditions may come into operation. In particular, where an individual wishes to query the validity of a Community measure in proceedings before the national courts, ordinary domestic time-limits must be replaced by a mandatory two-month Community limitation period, if the individual could clearly have challenged the measure directly before the Community courts under Article 230(4) EC, but failed to do so within the time-limit provided for under Article 230(5) EC. Claimants might otherwise abuse the Community's dual system of judicial review, so as to evade the procedural guarantees, intended to safeguard legal certainty and efficient public administration, laid down in the Treaty text itself.

For example, *TWD* concerned payments made by a German public authority to a private undertaking which the Commission subsequently declared to be unlawful under Article 88 EC and ordered should be recovered from the recipient. In September 1986, the German authorities informed the recipient of the Commission's decision and of the option of challenging it through proceedings under Article 230(4) EC. No such action was launched. In March 1987, the German authorities sought recovery of the unlawful state aid. The recipient appealed before the national courts on the basis that the Commission decision ordering repayment was itself unlawful. The Court of Justice observed that a Commission decision adopted under Article 88 EC can be challenged by both the Member State to which it is addressed and the recipient of the aid who is to be considered directly and individually concerned.

Expiry of the two-month time-limit imposed by Article 230(5) EC rendered the decision definitive as against the Member State, which could not then raise its validity during enforcement proceedings brought under Article 226 EC for failing to recover the unlawful aid. Such a result was justified by considerations of legal certainty, so as to prevent Community measures from being called into question indefinitely. For the same reason, expiry of the limitation period under Article 230(5) EC rendered the decision definitive as against the recipient, who could not then raise its validity during proceedings before the national court challenging revocation of the aid by the public authorities.[46]

Consider also the judgment in *Wiljo*. The claimant applied for exemption from the obligation to make special contributions to a scrapping fund established under the Community's scheme for improving inland water transport infrastructures. That application was rejected by a Commission decision communicated to both the claimant and the competent national authorities in May 1993. The national authorities therefore sought payment of the special contribution. In April 1995, the claimant brought an action before the domestic courts challenging the demand for payment on the grounds that the Commission decision was itself incompatible with superior Treaty rules. The Court observed that the claimant had failed to challenge the Commission decision under Article 230(4) EC even though, as an addressee, it could clearly have done so. Since the two-month time-limit laid down in Article 230(5) EC had now expired, the principle of legal certainty required that the decision could no longer be challenged either directly before the Community courts or indirectly before the national tribunals.[47]

The effect of judgments such as *TWD* and *Wiljo* is to impose upon certain claimants a time-limit of two months within which to seek annulment of the relevant Community measure, before either the Community or the national courts, regardless of the limitation period which would ordinarily apply under domestic rules in respect of challenges to administrative acts.

But it remains uncertain just how cast-iron the claimant's entitlement to standing under Article 230(4) EC must be, before the Community's own time-limits will apply also before the domestic courts. The Court in *Banks* referred to the idea that, for the principle in *TWD* to apply, the claimant must 'undoubtedly' have been able to bring an action for annulment under Article 230(4) EC.[48]

At one extreme, the Court held in *Wiljo* that the restrictive two-month limitation period should apply vis-à-vis the addressee of a disputed Community act, who was very clearly entitled to launch an action for

[46] Case C–188/92 *TWD* [1994] ECR I–833.
[47] Case C–178/95 *Wiljo* [1997] ECR I–585. Cf also AG Fennelly in Case C–246/95 *Coen v Belgium* [1997] ECR I–403.
[48] Case C–390/98 *Banks* [2001] ECR I–6117, para 111.

annulment under Article 230(4) EC. The judgment in *National Farmers' Union* confirms that the same rigorous approach will apply to Member States as addressees of Community measures when they fail to bring a challenge under Article 230 EC within the two-month time-limit.[49] At the other extreme, it seems that claimants who are not clearly able to satisfy the requirements of direct and individual concern under Article 230(4) EC will not find themselves caught by the restrictive two-month time-limit should they mount a challenge via the national courts. For example, *ex parte Accrington Beef* concerned an action before the English courts challenging the validity of a Community agricultural regulation. The measure was, on its face, a true regulation rather than a disguised decision. It was therefore objectively unclear whether the applicant could have established individual concern under the *Plaumann* caselaw, and it was not appropriate to invoke the Article 230(5) EC limitation period.[50] But *TWD* itself lies between these two extremes. The claimant was not an addressee of the Commission's state aid decision, but as recipient of the disputed monies indisputably enjoyed standing under Article 230(4) EC. In addition, however, the claimant had been specifically informed by the German authorities about the possibility of bringing an action for annulment directly before the Community courts, and the Court was careful to refer to 'the factual and legal circumstances of the case' in reaching its judgment.[51]

Subsequent rulings have sent mixed messages about whether the test to be applied to non-addressees contains merely an objective element (based upon whether the claimant would clearly have enjoyed standing to bring an action for annulment under Article 230(4) EC); or also a subjective requirement (dependent upon whether the claimant actually knew that they would have enjoyed standing under Article 230(4) EC). For example, both the Advocate General and the Court in *Eurotunnel* suggested that the principle in *TWD* requires not only an objectively clear entitlement to standing under Article 230(4) EC, but also subjective knowledge of the right to pursue that route to judicial review.[52] But the Court in *Nachi Europe* applied the principle in *TWD* to time-bar a decentralised challenge to a Community anti-dumping regulation on the basis that, although the applicant was a non-addressee, caselaw had clearly established its right to standing under Article 230(4) EC. There was no evidence that the applicant was also subjectively aware of the right to challenge the regulation directly before the Community courts.[53] Academic opinion seems to favour restricting the potential scope of the principle in *TWD*: given the

[49] Case C–241/01 *National Farmers' Union* [2002] ECR I–9079.
[50] Case C–241/95 *ex p Accrington Beef* [1996] ECR I–6699.
[51] Case C–188/92 *TWD* [1994] ECR I–833, para 25. Cf paras 11–12 Judgment; and AG Jacobs, para 24 Opinion.
[52] Case C–408/95 *Eurotunnel v SeaFrance* [1997] ECR I–6315.
[53] Case C–239/99 *Nachi Europe* [2001] ECR I–1197.

unsatisfactory nature of the caselaw on the direct and individual concern of non-privileged applicants, it could be detrimental to the imperative of effective judicial protection for the Court to deny access to the domestic courts for the purposes of challenging the validity of Community measures in all but the very clearest situations.[54]

In any case, the desire to ensure that challenges to the legality of Treaty acts are governed by a coherent system of judicial protection—and in particular, to ensure that the possibility of initiating action through the domestic courts does not compromise the integrity of the centralised system of judicial review operating under Article 230 EC—has led the Court to make certain modifications to the principles which usually govern the application of domestic limitation periods to Community cases. Indeed, the Court has again created a centralised Community procedural competence, which usurps the pre-existing domestic standards of judicial protection.

Assessment

Relevance of Uniformity

Caselaw such as *Zuckerfabrik* and *Atlanta* on interim relief, and *TWD* and *Wiljo* as regards limitation periods, embodies a highly interventionist approach to national remedies and procedural rules. On its face, this caselaw does not exactly correspond to the sectoral conception of uniformity postulated in Chapter 4. After all, *Zuckerfabrik* and *Atlanta*, and *TWD* and *Wiljo*, could apply as much when challenging a Community measure on social or consumer policy (relatively differentiated sectors), as a Community measure on competition law or state aids (relatively centralised sectors). But nor does this caselaw simply support an 'integration through law' approach to the Community's enforcement deficit. After all, it seems equally clear that *Zuckerfabrik* and *Atlanta*, and *TWD* and *Wiljo*, are not intended to act as a springboard for the wholesale positive harmonisation of the rules on interim relief or time-limits before the national courts.

In fact, this caselaw is the result of factors particular to the context of decentralised challenges to the validity of Community acts: the need to guarantee that differences in the domestic standards of judicial protection do not seriously undermine the uniform application of Community legislation; coupled with the desire to ensure that the possibility of initiating

[54] Further, eg M Hoskins, Commentary on *TWD* (1994) 31 CML Rev 1399; D Wyatt, 'The Relationship Between Actions for Annulment and References on Validity After *TWD Deggendorf*' in J Lonbay & A Biondi (eds), *Remedies for Breach of EC Law* (Wiley, 1997); P Stanley, Commentary on *Eurotunnel* (1998) 35 CML Rev 1205; N Moloney, Commentary on *Nachi Europe* (2002) 39 CML Rev 393.

action through the national courts does not compromise the integrity of the system for judicial review under Article 230 EC itself. Judgments such as *Zuckerfabrik* and *Atlanta*, and *TWD* and *Wiljo*, therefore address justified concerns about the imperative of uniformity—concerns which are legitimate even from the perspective of our sectoral analysis, insofar as they seek to protect the common core of rights and obligations which are intended to bind every Member State.

The drastic implications which these factors may have, as regards national remedial and procedural autonomy, are reinforced when one considers other situations in which claimants have attempted to challenge alleged Community misconduct through the domestic courts. For example, jurisdiction over claims that the Community institutions have failed to act vests in the Community courts under Article 232 EC. But this time, there is no (alternative or concurrent) possibility of pursuing decentralised action: the national courts cannot make references under Article 234 EC in respect of that particular category of wrongdoing. Against that background, the dispute in *Port* concerned Regulation 404/93 on the common organisation of the market in bananas, which introduced a system of import quotas in respect of third–country produce, and discontinued the annual duty-free quota previously enjoyed by German importers. Article 30 of the Regulation provided that, if specific measures were required to assist in the transition from the old to the new regime, the Commission should take any necessary transitional measures—a provision which authorised, and in some cases required, the Commission to adopt rules catering for cases of hardship.[55] The claimant argued that it was likely to go bankrupt as a result of the new regime, and sought interim relief from the German courts in the form of additional import licences, pending the exercise by the Commission of its Article 30 powers.

Advocate General Elmer observed that, in such circumstances, the Court of Justice itself could only find the Commission guilty of a failure to act under Article 232 EC, and should not usurp the Commission's functions by using the power to order interim relief under Articles 242 and 243 EC. And if the Court had no power to award interim relief, nor should the national judges. The latter's jurisdiction, as recognised under *Zuckerfabrik* and *Atlanta*, was based on the need to ensure the efficacy of the Court's judgments, when delivered via Article 234 EC proceedings rather than by direct action under Article 230 EC. This consideration did not apply in cases such as Article 232 EC, where the Court itself was debarred from ordering provisional measures.

However, the Court adopted a different stance. This situation was different from those at issue in *Zuckerfabrik* and *Atlanta*. In particular,

[55] Reg 404/93 on the common organisation of the market in bananas, OJ 1993 L47/1.

interim relief was being sought not to protect the claimant's Community law rights against an allegedly invalid measure, but to protect the position of a claimant whose rights were to be established by a Commission measure which had not yet been adopted. Since the Treaty made no provision for an Article 234 EC reference by which the national judges could ask the Court for a ruling that a Community institution had failed to act, the national courts could have no jurisdiction to order interim measures pending action on the part of the relevant Community institution. Only the Community courts could carry out judicial review of an alleged failure to act. In this regard, if a Member State or an individual trader were to bring an action against the Commission under Article 232 EC, the Court could indeed adopt interim measures under Article 243 EC, since the latter provision is framed in general terms and does not exclude any particular procedures.[56] *Port* thus affirms the view that the national courts' jurisdiction to order interim relief in situations involving alleged misconduct by the Community institutions is founded entirely upon principles developed under the Treaty system: Community law not only provides the basis upon which national courts may offer interim protection (in actions challenging the legality of Community measures), but also actively denies the domestic judges any jurisdiction to adopt provisional measures in certain categories of dispute (in claims based upon a failure to act).[57]

However, even if one admits that the Court has valid policy reasons for adopting a relatively stringent approach to national remedial and procedural competence in cases involving challenges to the validity of Community action, this caselaw does raise difficult constitutional problems, in particular, for Member States now obliged to provide lower standards of judicial protection than would ordinarily be available in purely domestic disputes. For example, some of the conditions set out by the Court in *Zuckerfabrik* and *Atlanta*, for the purposes of granting interim relief in respect of allegedly unlawful Community acts, are hardly novel.[58] But the standards prescribed by Community law are still less favourable towards individuals than the test for granting interim relief under (say) ordinary German law.[59] Moreover, the Court in judgments such as *Brasserie de Pêcheur* and *Upjohn* drew upon its own caselaw concerning judicial protection against the Community institutions so as to inform the development of the principle of effectiveness vis-à-vis the

[56] Case C–68/95 *Port* [1996] ECR I–6065.

[57] Consider also damages claims against the Community institutions, as regards which the Community courts have exclusive jurisdiction under Article 288(2) EC, eg Case 101/78 *Granaria* [1979] ECR 623. This exclusivity again places severe restrictions on the remedial and procedural competence of the national judges, eg Case C–275/00 *First and Franex* [2002] ECR I–10943.

[58] Such as the idea that purely financial damage cannot be considered irreversible.

[59] As noted by A Barav, 'Omnipotent Courts' in D Curtin & T Heukels (eds), *Institutional Dynamics of European Integration* (Martinus Nijhoff, 1994).

Member States, in order to avoid accusations of double standards in comparable situations—but without going further than laying down merely minimum standards which national courts remain free to supplement with better legal safeguards for claimants.[60] By contrast, the Court in judgments such as *Zuckerfabrik* and *Atlanta* invokes its own caselaw concerning judicial protection against the Community institutions so as to establish exhaustive conditions for judicial review before the national courts—prompting concerns that the Court went too far in protecting the Community's interests, at the expense of individuals whose rights may have been infringed.[61]

Limits to Uniformity

In any case, even if the Court's approach to national competence in cases involving challenges to the validity of Community measures goes beyond the requirements of effective judicial protection applicable to disputes involving Member State or private conduct, the process of positive harmonisation is not entirely complete. Indeed, one might query whether the Court has yet achieved a level of remedial and procedural centralisation sufficient to guarantee the uniform application of the common Community core, and to establish a truly coherent relationship between the twin centralised and decentralised tracks to judicial review.

For example, some commentators have argued that the substantive conditions for interim relief set out in *Zuckerfabrik* and *Atlanta* are inadequate for securing the desired level of uniformity. Consider the duty cast upon national courts to take into account the Community's interest when deciding whether or not to suspend application of a disputed Community act. It may be very difficult for the national court to discover (let alone evaluate) the cumulative effects of other interim measures across the Community; or to determine the general Community interest and its relationship to that of the individual claimant.[62] Nevertheless, the judgment in *Krüger* suggests that the Court is content to adopt a laissez-faire approach here. The case concerned a decision by the national authorities to recover export refunds granted to the claimant. The latter argued that the decision was based upon an invalid Community regulation, and sought suspension of its implementation. The Commission argued that, for the purposes of taking into account the Community interest as required by *Zuckerfabrik* and *Atlanta*, the national court should be obliged

[60] Cases C–46 & 48/93 *Brasserie du Pecheur* and *Factortame III* [1996] ECR I–1029; Case C–120/97 *Upjohn* [1999] ECR I–223. Further: ch 5 (above).

[61] Eg E Sharpston, 'Interim Relief in the National Courts' in J Lonbay & A Biondi (eds), *Remedies for Breach of EC Law* (Wiley, 1997).

[62] See: E Sharpston, 'Interim Relief in the National Courts' in J Lonbay & A Biondi (eds), *Remedies for Breach of EC Law* (Wiley, 1997) p 54.

to give the Community institution which adopted the disputed measure an opportunity to express its views. However, the Court rejected this proposal: it was for the national court, in accordance with its own rules of procedure, to decide the most appropriate way of obtaining all relevant information relating to the Community act in question.[63] Such deference to national procedural autonomy does little to soothe concerns that, without a more formal channel of communication, the general Community interest may not be correctly understood or protected by the national courts.

Moreover, even if *Zuckerfabrik* and *Atlanta* do guarantee the availability of interim relief in respect of allegedly invalid Community acts under uniform conditions within each Member State, it has been pointed out that such interim relief remains confined to the territory of the relevant Member State.[64] If the claimant wants to secure the same level of judicial protection for its interests across the rest of the Community, it will have to engage upon the very expensive and highly inconvenient task of securing interim relief across all 25 Member States. In any case, claimants awarded interim relief in one country will be treated differently from claimants who are not granted such protection in other Member States—with all that implies about comparability of regulatory compliance costs between economic undertakings, and equality of treatment between Union citizens in their rights and obligations. 'That would … prejudice the uniform application of Community law, and in extreme cases could totally subvert it.'[65]

There are other weak links in the decentralised system for challenging the validity of Community acts. For example, limitation periods which fall outside the scope of the principle established in *TWD* remain subject to the ordinary caselaw based on *Rewe/Comet*: the basic rule on reasonable time-limits, the punishment of conduct which wrongly prevents the claimant from exercising his/her rights, and restrictions on deliberately targeting the exercise of Community law rights, or revising limitation periods with unduly retroactive effects.[66] Thus, access to judicial review via the national courts, for claimants whose standing under Article 230(4) EC is not sufficiently clear to justify imposing the two-month *TWD* bar, will still vary significantly thanks to the procedural restrictions applicable in different Member States.[67]

[63] Case C–334/95 *Krüger* [1997] ECR I–4517.
[64] By contrast with interim relief ordered under Arts 242/243 EC, which is effective in every Member State.
[65] AG Jacobs in Case C–50/00 *Unión de Pequeños Agricultores* [2002] ECR I–6677, para 44 Opinion.
[66] Case 33/76 *Rewe-Zentralfinanz v Landwirtschaftskammer für das Saarland* [1976] ECR 1989; Case 45/76 *Comet* [1976] ECR 2043. Further: ch 5 (above).
[67] Note that the domestic remedies available against national implementing measures, following a finding by the Court that any given Community act is in fact invalid—such as the recovery of wrongly levied charges—are governed by the ordinary caselaw on effective judicial protection, eg Case C–212/94 *FMC* [1996] ECR I–389.

National Rules on Standing to Seek Judicial Review

This analysis has been reinforced by recent developments in the field of access to justice under Article 230(4) EC. In particular, Advocate General Jacobs in *Unión de Pequeños Agricultores* queried how far preliminary references under Article 234 EC really offer an adequate alternative to direct access to judicial review before the Community courts as regards Community measures of general application. For these purposes, the Advocate General identified a series of problems with Article 234 EC. For example, the decentralised route to judicial review depends heavily upon the discretion of national judges: about whether there are sufficient doubts over the validity of the Community act; and as to the precise terms of any reference sent to the Court of Justice. Moreover, there are procedural drawbacks to using Article 234 EC proceedings as a means of settling validity issues, as compared to actions for annulment heard directly under Article 230 EC: besides the possibility of substantial additional delays and costs, Article 234 EC references do not involve a full exchange of pleadings; while Article 230 EC actions offer greater opportunities for participation by interested parties.[68]

Another problem with the decentralised route to judicial review against the Community institutions—which assumed particular importance in *Unión de Pequeños Agricultores*—is the fact that national rules of standing, determining the range of persons entitled to initiate proceedings against any given type of act, differ widely from Member State to Member State.

The Court has rarely addressed the existence of significant variations between the domestic regimes on standing to seek judicial review, and their potential to distort the system for decentralised enforcement against the Community institutions. On the one hand, the caselaw seems to assume that national law will be more generous than the *Plaumann* formula. After all, it would make little sense for the Court to encourage unsuccessful applicants under Article 230(4) EC to seek redress through their national courts, if those national courts then simply applied standing requirements as (or even more) restrictive than the Court itself.[69] On the other hand, even that proposition remains untested in the caselaw—let alone any more adventurous attempt to establish common criteria regarding standing to challenge the validity of Community acts through the domestic courts. Such differences in the legal framework for decentralised enforcement against the Community institutions—to a greater

[68] Case C–50/00 *Unión de Pequeños Agricultores* [2002] ECR I–6677.

[69] Which thereby implicitly rules out the principle of parallelism suggested by cases like Cases C–46 & 48/93 *Brasserie du Pecheur* and *Factortame III* [1996] ECR I–1029; Case C–120/97 *Upjohn* [1999] ECR I–223. Further: ch 5 (above).

degree than the remaining rules on interim relief or limitation periods—threaten to undermine the uniform application of Community law.

The problem becomes particularly acute because, in several Member States, access to the domestic courts depends upon the national authorities adopting an act, under licence from the disputed Community measure, which is capable of providing a basis for legal proceedings. Such a requirement does not sit easily with 'self-executing' Community acts which are capable of producing autonomous effects within the national legal orders without requiring any particular implementing action by the domestic authorities. This was true of the agricultural regulation at issue in *Unión de Pequeños Agricultores*, which simply terminated an existing Community aid scheme. The requirement of a national implementing measure can also cause problems with 'self-executing' Community acts which prohibit certain types of private conduct. In such cases, the only way for claimants to obtain access to judicial review may be to break the law, then plead the unlawfulness of the relevant Community act before the national courts, as a defence to his/her subsequent prosecution. This was true of the fisheries regulation under dispute in *Jégo-Quéré*, which prohibited the use of a certain type of fishing net in Community waters.[70] In such situations, there is a genuine danger of claimants being squeezed between two illiberal regimes on standing—certainly one which is Community in origin, possibly another which is national in origin—threatening not only legitimate concerns for uniformity of enforcement across the Member States, but also the basic effectiveness of judicial protection within the Community legal order as a whole.

For all these reasons, Advocate General Jacobs in *Unión de Pequeños Agricultores* proposed that the Court should adopt a new test for standing under Article 230(4) EC: an applicant is individually concerned by a Community measure when the measure has, or is liable to have, a substantial adverse effect on his/her interests. The Court of First Instance in *Jégo-Quéré* accepted much of the Advocate General's critical analysis of the current state of affairs, but proposed a different (and in some respects less generous) reform to the test for standing under Article 230(4) EC: a person is to be regarded as individually concerned by a Community measure of general application if the measure in question affects his/her legal position, in a manner which is both definite and immediate, by restricting his/her rights or by imposing obligations on him/her. For these purposes, the Court of First Instance believed that the number and the position of other persons who are likewise affected by the measure, or who may be so, should be irrelevant.[71]

[70] Case T–177/01 *Jégo-Quéré* [2002] ECR II–2365; Case C–263/02P *Jégo-Quéré'* (Judgment of 1 April 2004).

[71] Case T–177/01 *Jégo-Quéré* [2002] ECR II–2365. Further, eg A Ward, 'Judicial Architecture at the Cross-Roads: Private Parties and Challenge to EC Measures Post-*Jégo-Quéré*' (2001) 4 *Cambridge Yearbook of European Legal Studies* 413.

However, the Court of Justice in its judgment in *Unión de Pequeños Agricultores* rejected this mounting pressure to reform the *Plaumann* caselaw. The Court noted that the Community is one based on the rule of law: its institutions are subject to judicial review of the compatibility of their acts with the Treaty and the general principles of Community law; and individuals have a fundamental entitlement to effective judicial protection of the rights they derive from the Community legal order. In this regard, the Court recalled that, by provisions such as Article 230 EC on the one hand, and by Article 234 EC on the other hand, the Treaty had established a complete system of legal remedies and procedures designed to ensure judicial review of the legality of acts of the institutions. Under that system, where natural or legal persons cannot, by reason of the conditions for admissibility laid down in Article 230(4) EC, directly challenge Community measures of general application, they are able to plead the invalidity of such acts before the national courts and ask them to make a preliminary reference to the Court under Article 234 EC. But while the requirement of individual concern must be interpreted in the light of the principle of effective judicial protection by taking account of the various circumstances that may distinguish an applicant individually, the Court was not prepared to adopt an interpretation that would have the effect of setting aside a condition expressly laid down in the Treaty text.[72]

Many commentators seem unpersuaded by the Court's reasons for refusing to revise its own caselaw on individual concern.[73] After all, the restrictive interpretation set out in *Plaumann* and subsequent judgments was adopted by the Court itself, not imposed by the bare Treaty text; and the Court could easily have chosen to adopt an alternative, more liberal interpretation, without calling into question its basic respect for the exact same Treaty text.[74] Moreover, the Court has not always demonstrated so deep an attachment to the strict wording of Article 230 EC: it was prepared to recognise that the European Parliament was capable of bringing actions for annulment, even though the Treaty did not expressly confer any such right to standing;[75] and to concede that non-privileged

[72] Case C–50/00 *Unión de Pequeños Agricultores* [2002] ECR I–6677. And since that judgment, eg Case C–142/00P *Nederlandse Antillen* [2003] ECR I–3483; Case C–167/02P *Rothley* (Judgment of 30 March 2004); Case C–263/02P *Jégo-Quéré* (Judgment of 1 April 2004).

[73] Eg A Albors Llorens, 'The Standing of Private Parties to Challenge Community Measures: Has the European Court Missed the Boat?' [2003] CLJ 72; F Ragolle, 'Access to Justice for Private Applicants in the Community Legal Order: Recent (R)evolutions' (2003) 28 EL Rev 90; P Craig, 'Standing, Rights and the Structure of Legal Argument' (2003) 9 *European Public Law* 493; R Mehdi, 'La recevabilité des recours formés par les personnes physiques et morales à l'encontre d'un acte de portée générale: l'aggiornamento n'aura pas eu lieu …' (2003) 39 *Revue trimestrielle de droit européen* 23.

[74] Cf Case 145/88 *Torfaen BC v B&Q* [1989] ECR 3851; Cases C–267–268/91 *Keck and Mithouard* [1993] ECR I–6097.

[75] Case C–70/88 *Parliament v Council* [1990] ECR I–2041. Consider also, eg Case 294/83 *Les Verts* [1986] ECR 1339: Parliament is susceptible to actions for annulment under Art 230 EC, even though the Treaty did not expressly provide for this possibility.

applicants should be capable in principle of bringing actions for annulment against true regulations and directives, even though Article 230(4) EC seemed to rule out such challenges altogether.[76]

Nevertheless, the Court in *Unión de Pequeños Agricultores* did suggest two other avenues for overcoming the difficulties associated with judicial review against the Community institutions. First—and this seems to have been intended as a long-term solution—the Court stated that, while it is possible to envisage a system of judicial review of the legality of Community measures of general application different from that established by the Treaty, it is for the Member States in accordance with Article 48 TEU to reform the system currently in force. That was the gauntlet picked up by the Convention on the Future of Europe. Article III–270(4) of the draft Treaty establishing a Constitution for Europe, as presented to the European Council in July 2003, provides that any non-privileged applicant may institute proceedings against an act addressed to that person or which is of direct and individual concern to him/her, and against a regulatory act which is of direct concern to him/her and does not entail implementing measures.[77] As regards non-addressees, the requirement of individual concern would therefore be retained save for situations where the disputed act is both self-executing in the sense of the *Unión de Pequeños Agricultores* or *Jégo-Quéré* cases; and non-legislative in nature in accordance with the newly proposed hierarchy of legal instruments. Conversely, the requirement of individual concern would remain intact as regards non-legislative acts which do entail implementing measures; and also as regards legislative acts, regardless of whether or not these are self-executing in nature.[78]

Secondly—and this seems to have been intended as a short-term solution—the Court in *Unión de Pequeños Agricultores* pointed out that it is for the Member States to establish a system of legal remedies and procedures which ensure respect for the right to effective judicial protection. At first sight, this suggests that Member States will be expected to reform their own rules on standing, so as to address the need for effective judicial protection in respect of claimants unable either to demonstrate direct and individual concern under Article 230(4) EC or to identify any specific national implementing measure capable of being challenged before the domestic courts. However, the Court then continued to observe that Article 10 EC requires the domestic courts to interpret and apply national procedural rules in a way that enables natural and legal persons

[76] Eg Case C–358/89 *Extramet* [1991] ECR I–2501; Cases T–172 & 175–177/98 *Salamander* [2000] ECR II–2487.

[77] OJ 2003 C169/1.

[78] Further, eg J Usher, 'Direct and Individual Concern: An Effective Remedy or a Conventional Solution?' (2003) 28 EL Rev 575; J Schwarze, 'The Legal Protection of the Individual Against Regulations in European Union Law' (2004) 10 *European Public Law* 285. See now Art I-365(4) of the 2004 Treaty, CIG 87/04.

to challenge the legality of any decision or other national measure relating to the application to the claimant of a Community act of general application, by pleading the invalidity of such an act. This puzzling dictum—which seems still to wed the Member State's obligation to provide effective judicial protection firmly to the existence of national implementing measures—hardly encourages the idea that the Court in *Unión de Pequeños Agricultores* was seriously concerned to solve the problem of decentralised access to judicial process for claimants seeking to challenge the validity of self-executing Community measures.

It therefore remains for future caselaw to clarify how far the Member States will be required to furnish rights of standing to individuals before the domestic courts even in the absence of specific national implementing measures.[79] In this regard, the Court has so far done little more than indicate its willingness to welcome references from Member States with relatively generous standing rules. For example, the English courts seem prepared to make preliminary references to the Court concerning the validity of Community directives, even where the deadline for transposition has not yet expired and the United Kingdom has not yet adopted the necessary national implementing measures.[80] The Court was asked in *ex parte British American Tobacco* to rule on whether such references should in fact be considered inadmissible, on the grounds that they circumvent the conditions of direct and individual concern contained in Article 230(4) EC. The Court replied that the opportunity for individuals to plead the invalidity of a Community act of general application before the national courts is not conditional upon that act actually having been the subject of implementing measures adopted pursuant to national law. It is sufficient if the national court is called upon to hear a genuine dispute in which the question of the validity of such an act is raised indirectly.[81] But for the Court to *welcome* references from national courts which choose not to make recognition of standing conditional upon the existence of domestic implementing acts is hardly the same as the Court insisting that all national courts are under an *obligation* to admit actions for judicial review against self-executing Community measures in comparable circumstances. Indeed, the Court in *Jégo-Quéré* expressly contemplated the possibility that, despite the impact of the duty of loyal cooperation under Article 10 EC, national procedural rules might still not allow an individual to contest the validity of a disputed Community measure unless

[79] For discussion, see J Temple Lang, 'Actions for Declarations that Community Regulations are Invalid: The Duties of National Courts Under Article 10 EC' (2003) 28 EL Rev 102; X Groussot, 'The EC System of Legal Remedies and Effective Judicial Protection: Does the System Really Need Reform?' (2003) 30 *Legal Issues of Economic Integration* 221.

[80] Consider the position under English law, as illustrated by Case C–74/99 *Ex p Imperial Tobacco* [2000] ECR I–8599.

[81] Case C–491/01 *Ex p British American Tobacco* [2002] ECR I–11453.

he/she has already contravened it.[82] So far as concerns any more advanced form of harmonisation over the domestic rules on standing, whether or not related to self-executing Community measures, the caselaw has therefore progressed no further than the ad hoc collection of judgments, such as *Kraaijeveld* and *Muñoz*, decided under the general principles of direct effect, supremacy and effective judicial protection.[83]

Should future judgments eventually lead to a more intrusive degree of interference with national standing rules, Community law will no doubt be accused of posing yet further constitutional problems for the Member States. In particular, the willingness of the Court to solve the problem of having self-imposed restrictive rules of standing at the Union level, at least in part by obliging the Member States to liberalise their own rules of standing at the domestic level, perhaps underestimates the potentially disruptive effects which such intervention can produce when they spill-over (as often occurs) into situations unconnected with Union law. After all, national rules on standing will often embody fundamental social and cultural choices about the nature and purpose of administrative law—choices which might soon be threatened, albeit indirectly, by demands for effective judicial protection emanating from Luxembourg in the wake of *Unión de Pequeños Agricultores*.[84]

But for the time being, the position as regards rights of standing before the national courts to seek judicial review in respect of allegedly invalid Community measures reinforces the provisional conclusion set out above. The Court has done much to harmonise the remedies and procedural rules applicable to decentralised enforcement against the Community institutions—surely going further in this regard than the general caselaw concerning the effective enforcement of Treaty rights against the Member States and other private parties. But even within this limited field of endeavour, the legitimate task of constructing a truly uniform and coherent legal framework for judicial protection remains unfinished.

RECOVERY OF UNLAWFUL STATE AIDS

The second category of situation in which the Court of Justice has attained centralised standards of national judicial protection, going beyond the general caselaw, concerns the principles applicable to the repayment or recovery of unlawful state aids. This particular body of jurisprudence

[82] Case C–263/02P *Jégo-Quéré* (Judgment of 1 April 2004).

[83] Case C–72/95 *Kraaijeveld* [1996] ECR I–5403; Case C–253/00 *Muñoz* [2002] ECR I–7289. Further: ch 1 (above).

[84] Further, eg M Dougan, 'The Convention's Draft Constitutional Treaty: Bringing Europe Closer to Its Lawyers?' (2003) 28 EL Rev 763.

provides more solid support for establishing some direct nexus between the relative degree of substantive and remedial harmonisation pursued by the Community institutions, such as might appear justified from our sectoral perspective.

Centralised and Decentralised Enforcement of the State Aids Rules

Article 87(1) EC sets out the basic prohibition on state aids that are incompatible with the Common Market. Articles 87(2) and (3) EC then list the mandatory and discretionary grounds upon which state aids shall be, or may be considered, compatible with the Common Market. For the purposes of ensuring that state aids are granted by the Member States in conformity with these rules, the Treaty establishes a special supervision and control procedure centred upon the Commission. In particular, Article 88(1) EC provides that the Commission shall, in cooperation with the Member States, keep under constant review all systems of aid existing in those States. According to Article 88(2) EC, if the Commission finds that aid granted by a Member State is not compatible with the Common Market, or that such aid is being misused, it shall decide that the Member State concerned shall abolish or alter such aid within a specified period.[85] Article 88(3) EC states that the Commission shall be informed, in sufficient time to enable it to submit its comments, of any plans to grant or alter state aid. If the Commission considers that any such plan is not compatible with the Common Market, it shall without delay initiate the procedure provided for under Article 88(2) EC. The relevant Member State shall not put its proposed measures into effect until this procedure has resulted in a final decision.

As the Court observed in *Iannelli & Volpi*, the rules governing the substantive compatibility of state aids with the Common Market are neither absolute nor unconditional; and the Treaty gives the Commission a wide discretion to sanction the grant of state aid in derogation from the general prohibition under Article 87(1) EC. The Treaty thereby intended that any finding that aid might be incompatible with the Common Market should (subject to judicial review by the Community courts) be the outcome of the procedures envisaged by Article 88 EC under the responsibility of the Commission.[86] For that reason, individuals are not entitled to rely upon

[85] Art 88(2) EC also provides for expedited judicial proceedings against defaulting Member States; and for the Council (exceptionally) to decide for itself upon the compatibility of state aids with Art 87 EC. Note Case C–110/02 *Commission v Council* (Opinion of 11 December 2003; Judgment of 29 June 2004).

[86] On judicial control over the Commission in the state aids sector, eg C Nordberg, 'Judicial Remedies for Private Parties Under the State Aid Procedure' (1997) 24 *Legal Issues of Economic Integration* 35; J Winter, 'The Rights of Complainants in State Aid Cases: Judicial Review of Commission Decisions Adopted Under Article 88 EC' (1999) 36 CML Rev 521; L Flynn,

Article 87 EC to challenge the substantive compatibility of state aids with Community law before the national courts.[87]

Procedurally Defective State Aids

According to the Court in *Heineken Brouwerijen*, the notification and standstill obligations contained in the last sentence of Article 88(3) EC safeguard the machinery for supervision and control laid down by Article 88 EC—itself essential for ensuring the proper functioning of the Common Market—by ensuring that state aids cannot become operational before the Commission has had an opportunity to examine the proposed measures and (if necessary) initiate the procedure under Article 88(2) EC.[88] In situations where the Member State grants or alters state aid in breach of the procedural requirements laid down in the last sentence of Article 88(3) EC, the Commission may adopt certain measures against the defaulting national authorities under Regulation 659/1999.[89] For example, Article 11(1) empowers the Commission to issue a 'suspension injunction' requiring the Member State to suspend the unlawful aid, pending the Commission's final decision on its substantive compatibility with the Common Market. Moreover, Article 11(2) permits the Commission to adopt a 'recovery injunction' ordering the Member State provisionally to recoup the unlawful aid, pending the Commission's final decision on its substantive compatibility with the Common Market.[90] However, the Commission cannot refuse to examine the substantive compatibility of state aid with the Common Market in accordance with the procedure under Article 88 EC, or order state aid definitively to be repaid, on the sole grounds that the relevant aid was granted or altered in breach of the notification or standstill requirements contained in Article 88(3) EC.[91]

The Court established in its judgment in *Lorenz* that the procedural requirements of notification and standstill imposed upon the Member States by the last sentence of Article 88(3) EC have direct effect and give

'Remedies in the European Courts' in A Biondi, P Eeckhout & J Flynn (eds), *The Law of State Aid in the European Union* (OUP, 2004).

[87] Case 74/76 *Iannelli & Volpi* [1977] ECR 557. Also, eg Case 78/76 *Steinike und Weinlig* [1977] ECR 595.

[88] Cases 91 & 127/83 *Heineken Brouwerijen* [1984] ECR 3435. For that reason, Member States are not entitled to ignore the procedure under Art 88 EC, even where they believe that the relevant aid fulfils the conditions for exemption under Art 87 EC, eg Case C–332/98 *France v Commission* [2000] ECR I–4833.

[89] Reg 659/99 laying down detailed rules for the application of Article 88 of the EC Treaty, OJ 1999 L83/1. These provisions are based on previous caselaw, eg Case C–301/87 *France v Commission* [1990] ECR I–307.

[90] Provided certain conditions are fulfilled, eg according to an established practice, there must be no doubts about the aid character of the relevant measure; there must be an urgency to act; and there must be a serious risk of substantial and irreparable damage to a competitor.

[91] Eg Case C–142/87 *Belgium v Commission* [1990] ECR I–959.

rise to rights in favour of individuals which national courts are bound to safeguard.[92] In particular, the Court subsequently decided in the *French Salmon* case that national courts must offer to individuals able to rely on the direct effect of the last sentence of Article 88(3) EC the certain prospect that all the necessary inferences will be drawn as regards the validity of measures giving effect to the unlawful aid and the recovery of financial support granted in disregard of the Member State's notification or standstill obligation.[93] The Court clarified in the *SFEI* case that the national court's power cannot be limited to suspending the payment of new state aid. If the national court finds that state aid has already been granted in breach of the last sentence of Article 88(3) EC, it must in principle allow an application for its repayment.[94]

Within the system for supervising state aids established by the Treaty, the Commission and national courts therefore perform separate though complementary roles. The Commission must examine the compatibility of state aid with the Common Market, even where the Member State has failed to observe the procedural obligations imposed by the last sentence of Article 88(3) EC. The national courts do no more than preserve (until the Commission's final decision) the rights of individuals faced with a breach of the notification or standstill requirements contained in the last sentence of Article 88(3) EC. On the one hand, the national courts, in exercising their jurisdiction, do not decide upon the substantive compatibility of the unlawful aid with the Common Market—since that falls within the exclusive competence of the Commission. On the other hand, the initiation by the Commission of the procedure for carrying out a preliminary examination or substantive assessment of state aid cannot release the national courts from their duty to safeguard the individual's rights in the event of an infringement by the Member State of the last sentence of Article 88(3) EC.[95] Indeed, even a final decision adopted by the Commission finding that the relevant aid is in fact compatible with the Common Market cannot have the effect of regularising *ex post facto* the unlawful implementing measures originally adopted in breach of the last sentence of Article 88(3) EC.[96]

Substantively Unlawful State Aids

The Court held in *Deufil* that, where the Commission reaches a final decision that proposed aid is incompatible with the Common Market, and

[92] Case 120/73 *Lorenz* [1973] ECR 1471. Also, eg Case 121/73 *Markmann* [1973] ECR 1495; Case 122/73 *Nordsee* [1973] ECR 1511.
[93] Case C–354/90 *FNCE ('French Salmon')* [1991] ECR I–5505.
[94] Case C–39/94 *SFEI* [1996] ECR I–3547.
[95] Case C–39/94 *SFEI* [1996] ECR I–3547.
[96] Case C–354/90 *FNCE ('French Salmon')* [1991] ECR I–5505.

that aid has already been granted in breach of the last sentence of Article 88(3) EC, the Commission may order the national authorities to recover the unlawful aid.[97] Indeed, it was established in the *Tubemeuse* case that the recovery of unlawful aid is the logical consequence of finding that it is unlawful, since this has the purpose of restoring the *status quo ante*.[98] By repaying the unlawful aid, the recipient forfeits the advantage it enjoyed over its competitors on the Common Market.[99] For that reason, neither the Member State nor the recipient can challenge the legality of a Commission decision ordering recovery on the grounds that it is disproportionate to the objectives of Articles 87 and 88 EC.[100] Only in exceptional circumstances will the Commission exceed the boundaries of its discretion by requiring the national authorities to recover the sums unlawfully granted.[101] In any case, the precise terms of an order for recovery, by which the Commission seeks to remove any distortions of competition and restore the *status quo ante* within the Common Market, will depend upon the exact nature of the unlawful aid: for example, aid granted in the form of a capital injection transferred on a permanent basis will normally have to be recovered in its entirety; whereas aid granted in the form of a temporary loan at a preferential interest rate may not require recovery of the principal sum, but rather of the difference between the interest actually charged at the preferential rate and the interest that would have been charged under normal market conditions.[102]

Where the Member State is ordered to recover unlawful state aid, it is obliged under Article 249 EC to take all measures necessary to ensure implementation of the Commission's decision.[103] The only defence available to the Member State, in the event of enforcement proceedings initiated by the Commission for failing to secure repayment of the unlawful state aid, is that recovery was 'absolutely impossible.'[104] This defence is very restrictively interpreted.[105] In any event, the Member State must

[97] Case 310/85 *Deufil* [1987] ECR 901.
[98] Case C–142/87 *Belgium v Commission* [1990] ECR I–959.
[99] Eg Case C–310/99 *Italy v Commission* [2002] ECR I–2289. On recovery orders in respect of third parties who have dealings with the recipient undertaking, consider, eg Case C–277/00 *Germany v Commission* (Judgment of 29 April 2004).
[100] Case C–142/87 *Belgium v Commission* [1990] ECR I–959.
[101] Eg Case C–310/99 *Italy v Commission* [2002] ECR I–2289.
[102] Eg Case T–16/96 *Cityflyer Express* [1998] ECR II–757; Case T–55/99 *CETM* [2000] ECR II–3207. For a general critique of the current system of recovery orders, see J Lever, 'The EC State Aids Regime: The Need for Reform' in A Biondi, P Eeckhout & J Flynn (eds), *The Law of State Aid in the European Union* (OUP, 2004).
[103] Eg Case C–404/00 *Commission v Spain* [2003] ECR I–6695.
[104] Eg Case 52/84 *Commission v Belgium* [1986] ECR 89.
[105] Eg Case C–6/97 *Italy v Commission* [1999] ECR I–2981; Case C–404/97 *Commission v Portugal* [2000] ECR I–4897; Case C–310/99 *Italy v Commission* [2002] ECR I–2289.

cooperate closely with the Commission in all situations where recovery might well prove absolutely impossible to secure.[106]

The state aids regime thus envisages two situations—actions for the repayment of unlawful aid brought on the basis of the direct effect of the last sentence of Article 88(3) EC, and actions for the recovery of unlawful aid following a final Commission decision establishing that such aid is incompatible with the Common Market—in which enforcement takes effect through the domestic courts. At this point, the principle of national autonomy becomes applicable: in the absence of relevant Community legislation, actions for repayment or recovery must take effect within the procedural framework of the Member State's own legal system.[107] As regards the limits imposed by Community law upon that presumption of national autonomy in the field of wrongly paid state aids, the Court has drawn inspiration from its caselaw on the repayment or recovery of wrongly paid Community subsidies.

Repayment or Recovery of Wrongly Paid Community Subsidies

Deutsche Milchkontor concerned Community agricultural subsidies which had been wrongly paid by the German authorities to the recipient undertakings. Questions arose about the power of the national authorities, under Community and domestic law, to adopt decisions ordering the recovery of those monies. The Court held that, according to the general principles on which the institutional system of the Community is based, it is for the Member States (by virtue of Article 10 EC) to ensure that Community regulations concerning the common agricultural policy are implemented within their territory. Insofar as Community law does not include common rules to this effect, the national authorities must act in accordance with the procedural and substantive rules of their own domestic law. However, this rule must be reconciled with the need to apply Community law uniformly so as to avoid unequal treatment of producers and traders. Against this background, Article 8(1) Regulation 729/70 obliged the national authorities to take the measures necessary to prevent and deal with irregularities, and to recover sums lost as a result of irregularities or negligence.[108] However, that legislation did not lay

[106] Eg Case 94/87 *Commission v Germany* [1989] ECR I–175; Case C–183/91 *Commission v Greece* [1993] ECR I–3131; Case C–261/99 *Commission v France* [2001] ECR I–2537; Case C–378/98 *Commission v Belgium* [2001] ECR I–5107.

[107] Eg Case 120/73 *Lorenz* [1973] ECR 1471 on repayment. Eg Case 94/87 *Commission v Germany* [1989] ECR 175 on recovery.

[108] Reg 729/70 on the financing of the common agricultural policy, OJ Special English Edition 1970 (Series I) 218. Repealed and replaced by Reg 1258/99 on the financing of the common agricultural policy, OJ 1999 L160/103.

down any specific provisions relating to the exercise of such supervision by the national authorities. In those circumstances, the Court held that disputes concerning the recovery of amounts unduly paid under Community law are to be decided by the national courts pursuant to their own domestic rules, subject to the limits imposed by Community law: national rules must be applied in a manner which is not discriminatory compared to the treatment of similar but purely domestic disputes; and national rules cannot have the effect of making it virtually impossible to implement Community law.[109]

The obligation incumbent upon Member States to recover wrongly paid Community monies from their recipients precludes the national authorities from exercising any discretion about whether or not it would be expedient to seek repayment.[110] Otherwise, within the framework of national autonomy (subject to the principles of equivalence and effectiveness),[111] the Court has ruled that Member States may take account of the need for legal certainty by requiring recovery proceedings against the recipients of wrongly paid subsidies to be commenced by the national authorities within domestic limitation periods.[112] Moreover, it is permissible for national courts to apply domestic rules protecting the legitimate expectations of the recipients of wrongly paid Community subsidies, provided in all cases that the recipient itself has acted in good faith.[113] Similarly, national law may preclude an action for repayment where the error which gave rise to the wrongful payment did not arise from incorrect information supplied by the recipient; or where the recipient supplied incorrect information in good faith and the relevant error could easily have been detected by the national authorities.[114] In addition, Member States may be restrained from securing the recovery of wrongly paid Community monies where the recipient demonstrates 'loss of enrichment,' again provided that he/she has acted in good faith.[115] However, the Court insists that the Community's interest in recovering wrongly paid aid must be taken fully into consideration in the application of any national provision which requires the various interests

[109] Cases 205–15/82 *Deutsche Milchkontor* [1983] ECR 2633.

[110] Eg Cases 146 & 192–93/81 *BayWa* [1982] ECR 1503.

[111] Effectiveness now covering either 'virtually impossible' or 'excessively difficult', eg Case C–336/00 *Huber* [2002] ECR I–7699.

[112] Eg Cases 205–15/82 *Deutsche Milchkontor* [1983] ECR 2633; Case C–366/95 *Steff-Houlberg* [1998] ECR I–2661.

[113] Eg Cases 205–15/82 *Deutsche Milchkontor* [1983] ECR 2633; Cases C–80–82/99 *Flemmer* [2001] ECR I–7211; Case C–366/95 *Steff-Houlberg* [1998] ECR I–2661; Case C–336/00 *Huber* [2002] ECR I–7699.

[114] Eg Case 265/78 *Ferwerda* [1980] ECR 617; Case C–366/95 *Steff-Houlberg* [1998] ECR I–2661.

[115] Eg Cases 205–15/82 *Deutsche Milchkontor* [1983] ECR 2633; Case C–298/96 *Oelmühle Hamburg* [1998] ECR I–4767.

involved in a dispute to be weighed against each other before a defective administrative measure is revoked.[116]

National autonomy (subject to the principles of equivalence and effectiveness) also applies to other ancillary rules relating to the repayment of wrongly paid Community monies: for example, domestic law may determine the allocation of the burden of proof, provided the recovery required by Community law is not rendered virtually impossible.[117] In particular, Member States may choose whether or not to charge interest on wrongly paid Community subsidies (even where such interest accrues to their own budget), provided they do not treat such disputes more harshly than actions for the repayment of comparable wrongly paid national monies.[118]

Clearly, the Court's approach to the repayment or recovery of wrongly granted Community subsidies is closely aligned to the current period of general caselaw concerning national remedies and procedural rules for the enforcement by individuals of their subjective Treaty rights.[119]

Repayment or Recovery of Wrongly Paid State Aids

In principle, the *Deutsche Milchkontor* approach applies to actions for the repayment of unlawful state aids brought on the basis of the direct effect of the last sentence of Article 88(3) EC; and to actions for the recovery of unlawful state aid following a final Commission decision establishing that such aid is incompatible with the Common Market.

Thus, the Court has held that, although in the absence of Community provisions relating to the procedure applicable to the recovery of illegal state aids, such recovery must take place in accordance with the relevant provisions of domestic law, those provisions must nevertheless conform to the requirements of equivalence (as regards the treatment of comparable but purely national disputes),[120] and effectiveness (so that the recovery required by Community law is not rendered practically impossible).[121] In any case, the national courts must ensure that the Community's interests in securing the repayment or recovery of unlawful state aids are taken fully into consideration.[122] For example, Member States which are required to recover unlawful aid are free to choose the

[116] Eg Cases 205–15/82 *Deutsche Milchkontor* [1983] ECR 2633; Case C–366/95 *Steff-Houlberg* [1998] ECR I–2661; Case C–298/96 *Oelmühle Hamburg* [1998] ECR I–4767; Case C–336/00 *Huber* [2002] ECR I–7699.
[117] Eg Cases 205–15/82 *Deutsche Milchkontor* [1983] ECR 2633.
[118] Eg Case 54/81 *Fromme* [1982] ECR 1449.
[119] As discussed in ch 5 (above).
[120] Eg Case C–382/99 *Netherlands v Commission* [2002] ECR I–5163.
[121] Eg Case 94/87 *Commission v Germany* [1989] ECR 175.
[122] Eg Case C–404/97 *Commission v Portugal* [2000] ECR I–4897.

means of fulfilling that obligation—not necessarily by means of a simple cash transfer from the recipient undertaking, but perhaps through other more complex measures—provided that such measures are actually suitable to re-establish the normal conditions of competition which were distorted by the grant of the relevant aid (and thus act as the functional equivalent to repayment by way of a simple transfer of funds).[123] Similarly, Community law does not necessarily require that the Member State be treated as a privileged creditor, for the purposes of recovering unlawful state aids from a recipient undertaking which has become insolvent, to the detriment of the financial interests of that undertaking's other unsecured creditors.[124]

This caselaw has now been partially codified by Regulation 659/1999. Article 14(3) provides that, where the Commission orders the recovery of unlawful state aids, either by way of a recovery injunction (in the case of aid granted in breach of the last sentence of Article 88(3) EC) or by a final decision (establishing that the aid is incompatible with the Common Market), such recovery shall be effected without delay and in accordance with the procedures under the national law of the Member State, provided that they allow the immediate and effective execution of the Commission's decision. To this effect, and in the event of a procedure before the national courts, the Member State shall take all necessary steps which are available under its legal system, without prejudice to Community law.

However, the Court has adapted the basic framework provided by *Deutsche Milchkontor* so as to meet certain specific characteristics of the state aids sector.[125] This can be illustrated by the caselaw on limitation periods for the commencement of recovery actions; the protection of the recipient's legitimate expectations; and other aspects of recovery, such as defences based on passing on by the recipient of the unlawful state aids, and the charging of interest on the recoverable monies.

Time-limits for Recovery

The Court in Case C–5/89 *Commission v Germany* (1990) considered the relevance in state aids cases of a one-year time-limit under national law for revoking administrative measures conferring benefits upon individuals, running from the date when the national authorities became aware of

[123] Eg Case C–209/00 *Commission v Germany* [2002] ECR I–11695. The Court also held that, in situations where the Member State chooses a method other than simple cash transfer, the national authorities are required to cooperate closely with the Commission as it supervises the process of recovery.

[124] Consider, eg Case C–142/87 *Belgium v Commission* [1990] ECR I–959.

[125] Further, eg H-J Priess, 'Recovery of Illegal State Aid: An Overview of Recent Developments in the Case Law' (1996) 33 CML Rev 69.

the grounds for revocation. It was held that this domestic procedural rule must be applied in such a way that the recovery required by Community law is not rendered practically impossible.[126] However, the full implications of this ruling were unclear. Was the Court suggesting that national limitation periods (even if they satisfied the familiar *Rewe/Comet* criteria) could never justify a failure to secure the recovery of unlawful state aids? And if so, would that principle apply not just in the context of enforcement proceedings brought against the Member State by the Commission; but also in actions for repayment brought before the national courts by third parties on the basis of the direct effect of the last sentence of Article 88(3) EC, and in recovery actions commenced before the same courts by the national authorities for the purposes of implementing a final Commission decision?

These issues were explored by the Court in *Alcan Deutschland*. The case concerned a final Commission decision finding that state aid which had been provided by a German public authority to Alcan in breach of the procedural obligations imposed by Article 88(3) EC was substantively incompatible with the Common Market. Neither Germany nor Alcan challenged the validity of this decision. Germany was subsequently found to have breached its obligations under Community law for having failed to recover the unlawful aid.[127] When the public authority eventually demanded repayment, Alcan argued that recovery was now time-barred by the same domestic rule at issue in Case C–5/89 *Commission v Germany* (1990), prohibiting the revocation of administrative acts more than one year after the national authorities became aware of the circumstances constituting grounds for revocation.

On an Article 234 EC reference, the Court held that, where the national authorities seek the recovery of state aid found by the Commission to be incompatible with the Common Market and thus to have been granted contrary to Articles 87–88 EC, the recipient cannot rely on the expiry of domestic time-limits (even those of reasonable duration) to resist repayment.

In particular, the Court observed that the regulation of state aids under the Treaty is characterised by a mandatory system of notification to and verification by the Commission, with the operation of which it is presumed that any diligent businessman will be aware. When the grant of state aid is found to be incompatible with Community law, the role of the national authorities is merely to give effect to the Commission's decision. The national authorities thus lack any discretion as regards revocation of a decision granting aid, and are not entitled to reach any finding other than the Commission's order for recovery. Where the national authorities nevertheless allow a national time-bar to expire, that situation cannot be

[126] Case C–5/89 *Commission v Germany* [1990] ECR I–3437.
[127] Case 94/87 *Commission v Germany* [1989] ECR 175.

treated in the same way as the situation where an individual does not know whether the national authorities are going to reach a decision at all. In the latter type of case, the principle of legal certainty requires that such uncertainty be brought to an end after a given period of time has elapsed. But in the case of state aids, since the national authorities have no discretion in the matter, recipients of unlawful aid cease to be in a position of legal uncertainty once the Commission has adopted a decision finding the aid incompatible with the Common Market and requiring its recovery. Such recovery cannot therefore be precluded on the grounds that the national authorities have permitted the expiry of domestic limitation periods. Otherwise, the recovery of unlawful state aids would be rendered practically impossible and the relevant Treaty provisions would be deprived of their effectiveness.[128]

One reading of the judgment in *Alcan Deutschland* is that this was merely an example of the sort of estoppel principle we now see embodied in cases such as *Emmott*.[129] Indeed, the Court highlighted the blatantly uncooperative conduct of the German authorities in their connivance with Alcan: the disputed aid had not been notified to the Commission in accordance with Article 88(3) EC; a second instalment had been paid despite a specific Commission request not to do so; and the relevant domestic time-limits were allowed to expire while the German authorities deliberately refrained from taking action to enforce the Commission's final decision.[130] In the face of such behaviour, the Court was perfectly justified in imposing the punitive sanction of setting aside otherwise acceptable limitation periods.

However, the language of the judgment does not support so narrow an interpretation. The Court clearly envisaged that, in *all* cases where the national authorities must seek the recovery of state aids found by the Commission to be incompatible with the Common Market, the recipient cannot rely upon the expiry of domestic time-limits so as to resist repayment. It remains unclear only whether *Alcan Deutschland* should apply *also* in situations where the Commission has not yet reached a final decision, but the Member State has acted in disregard of its procedural (notification and standstill) obligations, entitling third parties to rely upon the direct effect of the last sentence of Article 88(3) EC before the national courts, so as to seek an order for repayment of the unlawful state aids. On the one hand, we might expect that *Alcan Deutschland* will extend to such situations. After all, the mandatory state aids notification and verification regime has again been ignored, as any diligent businessman should

[128] Case C–24/95 *Alcan Deutschland* [1997] ECR I–1591.
[129] Case C–208/90 *Emmott* [1991] ECR I–4269. Further: ch 5 (above).
[130] Case C–24/95 *Alcan Deutschland* [1997] ECR I–1591, paras 30–33.

presumably be aware. Moreover, the national authorities still lack any appreciable discretion about the implementation of substantive state aid policy, being unable to reach any unilateral judgment about the compatibility of their proposed state aids with the Treaty. On the other hand, perhaps recipients of the unlawful aid this time remain in a certain position of legal uncertainty, until the Commission has adopted a final decision finding the aid contrary to the Common Market. Indeed, that uncertainty might last for many years: Regulation 659/1999 states that the ordinary time-limits applicable to the Commission's conduct of preliminary investigations and adoption of final decisions shall not apply to unlawful aid;[131] the Commission's powers to order the recovery of unlawful aid are instead subject to a ten-year limitation period running from the date on which the aid was awarded to its recipient.[132] Yet, in keeping with the principle that centralised and decentralised enforcement perform separate roles in state aids law, the status of the Commission's substantive investigations should not relieve the national courts of their obligation to safeguard the direct effect of the last sentence of Article 88(3) EC. There are therefore good grounds for arguing that individuals relying upon the last sentence of Article 88(3) EC may safely ignore domestic limitation periods which would otherwise block actions seeking an order for repayment of the unlawful aid.

In any event, *Alcan Deutschland* departs from the template of negative harmonisation provided for by *Deutsche Milchkontor* (and the caselaw based upon *Rewe/Comet*).[133] Despite the Court's insistence that the Community legal order cannot simply ignore national legislation providing for time-limits in actions for repayment,[134] the practical effect of *Alcan Deutschland* is to create a uniform approach to the limitation periods which must be applied by domestic courts in state aid recovery cases, in preference to the pre-existing national procedures of the various Member States, at least in cases where the Commission has adopted a final negative decision. In this regard, *Alcan Deutschland* should also be considered alongside other developments in the state aids field: first, the ten-year limitation period within which the Commission must exercise its power to order the recovery of unlawful aid under Regulation 659/1999;[135] the two-month time-limit within which individuals may challenge Commission aid decisions before the Community courts;[136] and the

[131] Art 13(2) Reg 659/99, OJ 1999 L83/1—unless the Commission has adopted a recovery injunction (and the aid has in fact been recovered) under Art 11(2).
[132] Art 15 Reg 659/99, OJ 1999 L83/1.
[133] Case 33/76 *Rewe-Zentralfinanz v Landwirtschaftskammer für das Saarland* [1976] ECR 1989; Case 45/76 *Comet* [1976] ECR 2043. Further: ch 5 (above).
[134] Case C–24/95 *Alcan Deutschland* [1997] ECR I–1591, para 25.
[135] Art 15 Reg 659/1999, OJ 1999 L83/1.
[136] Art 230(5) EC.

Court's strict approach to the application of time-limits within which individuals may instead challenge such Commission decisions via the domestic courts.[137] Taken together, these developments create a highly centralised procedural regime applicable to the enforcement of Treaty state aids policy, embracing the limitation periods both for challenging Commission recovery decisions and for resisting recovery actions brought by the national authorities. Moreover, the harmonisation of limitation periods which results from *Alcan Deutschland* was expressly justified by reference to the corresponding degree of substantive centralisation achieved under the Treaty, whereby the state aids regime is promulgated and applied by the Community institutions, with only very limited scope for any independent exercise of Member State discretion.[138] To this extent, *Alcan Deutschland* provides clear support for the sort of sectoral model argued for in Chapter 4.

Protection of Legitimate Expectations

The protection of legitimate expectations within the context of the Treaty regime on state aids operates at two separate levels.

First, respect for legitimate expectations constitutes a general principle of Community law binding upon the Community institutions in the exercise of their powers, and thus capable of providing the grounds for judicial review against Community measures at the suit of Member States and private parties.[139] Within this context, the constituent elements of the legitimate expectations claim clearly should be defined by Community law itself. On that basis, the legality of final decisions finding that state-aid programmes are incompatible with the Common Market may be challenged (for example) because the Commission was guilty of undue or unreasonable delay in concluding its investigations.[140] However, the Court refuses to recognise that Commission decisions may be vitiated on grounds of legitimate expectations in this manner, where the relevant state aids were granted by the Member State in breach of its procedural obligations under Article 88(3) EC. The Court relies upon the mandatory

[137] Case C–188/92 *TWD* [1994] ECR I–833; Case C–239/99 *Nachi Europe* [2001] ECR I–1197. See above.
[138] Further, eg A Arnull, A Dashwood, M Ross and D Wyatt, *Wyatt and Dashwood's European Union Law* (Sweet & Maxwell, 2000) ch 24; P Craig and G de Búrca, *EU Law: Text, Cases, & Materials* (OUP, 2002) ch 27.
[139] See, eg Case 112/77 *Toepfer* [1978] ECR 1019; Cases C–31–44/91 *Lageder* [1993] ECR I–1761.
[140] Eg Case 223/85 *RSV* [1987] ECR 4617. Contrast, eg Case T–55/99 *CETM* [2000] ECR II–3207; Case C–334/99 *Germany v Commission* [2003] ECR I–1139; Case T-109/01 *Fleuren Compost* (Judgment of 14 January 2004); Case C–278/00 *Greece v Commission* (Judgment of 29 April 2004). Consider also, eg Case 310/85 *Deufil* [1987] ECR 901; Case T–129/96 *Preussag Stahl* [1998] ECR II–609.

nature of the supervision of state aids by the Commission to assert that recipients cannot, in principle, entertain any legitimate expectation that the aid is lawful *unless* it has been granted in compliance with the procedure under Article 88 EC—taking into account the fact that any diligent operator should normally be able to determine whether that procedure has been followed.[141]

Secondly, respect for legitimate expectations may also constitute a principle of national administrative law—clearly incapable of providing any grounds for questioning the validity of Community measures, but nevertheless relevant to the legal framework for the decentralised enforcement of Treaty norms. In this regard, the Court in Case C–5/89 *Commission v Germany* (1990) relied upon its *Deutsche Milchkontor* caselaw to find that, in theory, the domestic courts are entitled to protect the legitimate expectations held by individuals in accordance with national law within the framework of actions for the repayment or recovery of state aids granted contrary to Community law.[142] Here, one is entitled to assume that the constituent elements of the legitimate expectations claim should be defined by national law—subject (as the Court observed in *Alcan Deutschland*) to the limits imposed by the Treaty: the principles of equivalence and effectiveness, including the obligation to take the Community's interests fully into account.[143] For these purposes, however, the Court has established that the mandatory system of state aids supervision provided for under Article 88 EC means that recipients cannot, in principle, entertain any legitimate expectation that procedurally defective state aid has been lawfully granted by the Member State—not only as a matter of Community law (going to the validity of any final Commission decision), but also under national law (as a grounds for resisting recovery of the relevant aid).[144] Nevertheless, the Court in Case C–5/89 *Commission v Germany* (1990) was prepared to accept that recipients might rely upon 'exceptional circumstances' justifying the assumption that state aids were lawful, and thus providing a legitimate basis under domestic law for refusing their repayment. If such a case arose, the national court would be obliged to assess the material circumstances and (if necessary) refer the matter to the Court under Article 234 EC for guidance.[145] However, it

[141] Eg Case C–169/95 *Spain v Commission* [1997] ECR I–135; Case T–129/96 *Preussag Stahl* [1998] ECR II–609; Case C–334/99 *Germany v Commission* [2003] ECR I–1139; Case C–91/01 *Italy v Commission* (Judgment of 29 April 2004). However, as such judgments demonstrate, the Community courts do sometimes continue to evaluate (and dismiss) arguments that the recipient was exceptionally entitled to hold legitimate expectations, under Community law, that procedurally defective state aid was nevertheless lawfully granted.

[142] Case C–5/89 *Commission v Germany* [1990] ECR I–3437.

[143] Case C–24/95 *Alcan Deutschland* [1997] ECR I–1591.

[144] Case C–5/89 *Commission v Germany* [1990] ECR I–3437; Case C–24/95 *Alcan Deutschland* [1997] ECR I–1591.

[145] Case C–5/89 *Commission v Germany* [1990] ECR I–3437; Case C–310/99 *Italy v Commission* [2002] ECR I–2289.

seems that 'exceptional circumstances' of that nature cannot depend solely upon the conduct of the national authorities, even if (for example) the latter were responsible for the illegality of the aid measure to such a degree that its revocation would amount to a breach of good faith towards the recipient.[146] It would therefore appear that claimants seeking to establish the existence of 'exceptional circumstances' must be able to demonstrate that the Commission itself somehow contributed to their reasonable belief that the procedurally defective aids were nevertheless lawful.

In any case, a Member State whose public authorities have granted aid in breach of the procedural rules contained in Article 88 EC cannot invoke any (even exceptional) legitimate expectations held by recipients as a matter of national law, within the context of litigation before the Community courts, so as to justify its own failure to comply with the obligation to take all necessary steps to implement a Commission final decision ordering recovery. Otherwise, the Treaty rules on state aids could be set at naught, since national authorities could rely upon their own unlawful conduct to deprive Commission decisions of their effectiveness.[147] Moreover, the Court of First Instance has taken the view that undertakings which have received aid in breach of the procedural rules contained in Article 88 EC are likewise debarred from relying upon their own (even exceptional) legitimate expectations arising under domestic law, within the context of litigation before the Community courts, so as to challenge the validity of Commission final decisions ordering recovery of the unlawful aid.[148]

As with domestic limitation periods, the Court therefore pays little more than lip-service to the idea of respecting national autonomy in the protection of legitimate expectations within the particular sphere of the decentralised enforcement of the Treaty state aids rules. Indeed, the Court treats the principle that there can be no legitimate expectations in situations of procedurally defective aid as completely interchangeable, as between its caselaw on the definition of legitimate expectations under Community law, and its caselaw on the limits to national definitions of legitimate expectations under the principle of effectiveness. Only the ill-defined idea of 'exceptional circumstances' remains within the Member State's margin of discretion to define the conditions for recognising

[146] Eg Case C–24/95 *Alcan Deutschland* [1997] ECR I–1591; Case T–109/01 *Fleuren Compost* (Judgment of 14 January 2004).

[147] Eg Case C–5/89 *Commission v Germany* [1990] ECR I–3437; Case C–169/95 *Spain v Commission* [1997] ECR I–135; Case C–310/99 *Italy v Commission* [2002] ECR I–2289; Case C–334/99 *Germany v Commission* [2003] ECR I–1139; Case C–99/02 *Commission v Italy* (Judgment of 1 April 2004).

[148] Eg Case T–459/93 *Siemens* [1995] ECR II–1675. Cf Case T–67/94 *Ladbroke Racing* [1998] ECR II–1: the Commission itself may not limit the Member State's obligation to recover unlawful state aids, by reference to the recipient's (even exceptional) legitimate expectations as recognised under national law.

the recipient's legitimate expectations—and even that is clearly a very narrow concept, subject to potentially unlimited scrutiny by the Community judiciary.[149]

Against that background, Advocate General Cosmas in *France v Ladbroke Racing and Commission* proposed that the Court should carry the caselaw through to its logical conclusion: extend Community competence into the territory currently (but largely theoretically) occupied by domestic law, in particular, so that Community law defines for itself the substantive conditions for the application of any defence based on legitimate expectations, even within the particular context of actions for the repayment or recovery of unlawful state aids before the national courts, to the complete exclusion of the pre-existing domestic jurisdiction otherwise recognised under *Deutsche Milchkontor*. In the Advocate General's view, such an approach would ratify de jure the extensive intrusion into national remedial autonomy which already exists de facto after judgments such as Case C–5/89 *Commission v Germany* (1990) and *Alcan Deutschland*. It would also better reflect the allocation of competences between the Community and domestic authorities as regards the substantive regulation of state aids; promote legal certainty by clarifying exactly when legitimate expectations may constitute a valid grounds for resisting repayment or recovery; and reinforce the legal framework for preserving fair competition within the Single Market by remedying the severe damage to the objective of uniform conditions for intra-Community trade caused by the payment of unlawful state aids.[150]

Other Issues Relating to Repayment or Recovery

Other elements of the state aids caselaw illustrate the same phenomenon of increasingly centralised competence to determine the remedies and procedural rules applicable to repayment or recovery actions.

Consider the position as regards the passing on of unlawful state aid by its recipient. It will be recalled that the Court respects domestic rules permitting individuals to resist actions for the recovery of wrongly paid Community subsidies on the grounds that the monies have been passed on to third parties.[151] This basically mirrors the position as regards actions brought by individuals for the recovery of charges levied by the Member

[149] Consider the fact that the Community courts sometimes evaluate (and dismiss) the recipient undertaking's argument that it was exceptionally entitled to hold legitimate expectations that procedurally defective aid was nevertheless lawful, without necessarily making clear whether that argument is being considered on the basis of the Community or domestic legal order, eg Case T–55/99 *CETM* [2000] ECR II–3207; Case T–109/01 *Fleuren Compost* (Judgment of 14 January 2004).
[150] AG Cosmas in Case C–83/98P *France v Ladbroke Racing and Commission* [2000] ECR I–3271.
[151] Cases 205–15/82 *Deutsche Milchkontor* [1983] ECR 2633.

States (whether on their own initiative or in accordance with Community secondary legislation) which are in fact contrary to Treaty rules, whereby the Member State may deny reimbursement if the tax has in fact been passed on by the payor and the latter would be unjustly enriched.[152]

By contrast, the Court in *Alcan Deutschland* ruled out the ability of recipients to resist the repayment or recovery of unlawful state aids, based on loss of the enrichment through passing on to third parties. In particular, the Court rejected the recipient's argument that state aid disputes where an unlawful gain has ceased to exist would be very rare, so that for Community law to recognise the validity of a national defence based on passing on could not be said to render repayment or recovery practically impossible. According to the Court, it is not unusual from an accounting viewpoint for gains to cease to exist. In fact, that is the rule in state aids cases, which generally involve undertakings in difficulty, and whose balance sheet no longer reveals the added value which results from the unlawful payment. Moreover, just because an unlawful gain no longer appears on the recipient's balance sheet does not mean that the benefit of that payment also ceases to exist. An undertaking which incurs post-payment losses may nevertheless have obtained ongoing benefits in terms of the retention of its place on the relevant market, reputation and commercial goodwill.[153]

In the subsequent case of *Oelmühle*, the Court was asked whether this usurpation by Community law of national remedial competence over defences based on passing on should apply beyond the state aids sector, so as also to govern the recovery of wrongly paid Community subsidies within the context of the common organisation of an agricultural market—thus effectively overruling *Deutsche Milchkontor*.[154] However, the Court refused to extend *Alcan Deutschland* in this manner. As regards the recovery of illegal state aid, the Court reiterated that some defence of passing on would almost always be available to undertakings which received the aid to bail themselves out of difficult financial circumstances. Moreover, that defence would grant recipients an unjustified competitive advantage over rival undertakings operating on the relevant Community market for goods/services. But no such significant distortion of competition could arise on an agricultural market where Community law

[152] Eg Case 68/79 *Hans Just* [1980] ECR 501; Case 61/79 *Denkavit Italiana* [1980] ECR 1205; Cases 142–43/80 *Essevi and Salengo* [1981] ECR 1413; Case 199/82 *San Giorgio* [1983] ECR 3595; Cases 331, 376 & 378/85 *Bianco* [1988] ECR 1099; Case 104/86 *Commission v Italy* [1988] ECR 1799; Cases C–192–218/95 *Comateb* [1997] ECR I–165; Cases C–441–42/98 *Mikhailidis* [2000] ECR I–7145; Cases C–397 & 410/98 *Metallgesellschaft* [2001] ECR I–1727; Case C–147/01 *Weber's Wine World* (Judgment of 2 October 2003); Case C–129/00 *Commission v Italy* (Judgment of 9 December 2003).

[153] Case C–24/95 *Alcan Deutschland* [1997] ECR I–1591.

[154] Case C–298/96 *Oelmühle Hamburg* [1998] ECR I–4767.

recognises a defence under national law, based on passing on to third parties, favouring the recipients of wrongly paid Community subsidies.[155] After all, the unlawful payment of Community aid means merely that the undertaking in question failed to meet the applicable preconditions—but this cannot distort competitive conditions in a market which is already subject to extensive Community intervention with a view precisely to interfering in ordinary economic forces for the public good.[156]

Consider also the situation as regards the charging of interest. It will be recalled that questions concerning interest on the recovery of wrongly paid Community monies (including not only whether interest is charged at all, but also the timing and calculation of any interest payable by the recipient) are governed by the usual presumption of national autonomy.[157] However, the Court in Case C–169/95 *Spain v Commission* (1997) held that, for the purposes of restoring the *status quo ante* within the context of unlawful state aids, the Commission was entitled to order not only the recovery of the principal sum, but also the charging of interest in respect of the period between payment of the aid and its actual repayment.[158] The Court of First Instance clarified in *Siemens* that, for the purposes of eliminating the financial and competitive advantages which the relevant undertaking enjoyed during the period between payment and repayment, the Commission (rather than the national authorities) may determine the date from and rate at which interest must be paid.[159] Such judgments have now been codified in Regulation 659/1999. Article 14(2) provides that aid recovered pursuant to a final decision of the Commission shall include interest at an appropriate rate fixed by the Commission, calculated from the date on which the unlawful aid was at the recipient's disposal until the date of its recovery.

This expansion of the Community's usual remedial competence in the field of interest is not unlimited. For example, the Court held in Case C–480/98 *Spain v Commission* (2000) that, although the absence of any claim to interest on unlawfully granted state aids at the time of their recovery would amount to maintaining incidental financial advantages consisting of the grant of an interest-free loan for the recipient undertaking, Community law does not preclude the application of domestic rules whereby the prior debts of insolvent undertakings cease to produce

[155] Case C–298/96 *Oelmühle Hamburg* [1998] ECR I–4767, paras 36–37; and paras 46–51 Opinion.

[156] Eg AG Cosmas in Case C–83/98P *France v Ladbroke Racing and Commission* [2000] ECR I–3271, paras 57–58 Opinion.

[157] Eg Case 54/81 *Fromme* [1982] ECR 1449. Cf AG Fennelly in Cases C–397 & 410/98 *Metallgesellschaft* [2001] ECR I–1727.

[158] Case C–169/95 *Spain v Commission* [1997] ECR I–135.

[159] Case T-459/93 *Siemens* [1995] ECR II–1675. Upheld by the ECJ on other grounds in Case C–278/95P *Siemens* [1997] ECR I–2507.

interest as from the declaration of insolvency, which are intended to protect the common interest of all creditors by not burdening the undertaking's assets with new debts likely to worsen the situation, provided that such rules apply to all creditors without discrimination.[160] Nevertheless, the usual presumption of remedial competence has clearly been reversed: under the Court's general caselaw, Member States determine the payment of interest, subject to the ad hoc requirements of the principle of effectiveness; whereas in the state aids caselaw, Community law systematically requires the charging of interest, unless the Member States can demonstrate some legitimate grounds for refusing to do so.

Assessment

The above caselaw suggests that state aids has been identified by the Court as a distinct sector ripe for a distinct solution to the problems posed by Community reliance upon national remedies and procedures for the decentralised enforcement of Treaty norms. Moreover, these judgments also suggest that the Court's motivation lies in the need to reinforce at a procedural level the highly centralised substantive framework which regulates the grant of state aid; as well as to maintain undistorted competition between economic operators within the Common Market, such as might be undermined at a remedial level by disparate Member State defences purporting to block the recovery of illegal aid. Such reasoning reflects both an economic and a sectoral understanding of the imperative of uniformity.

However, the process of harmonising the conditions for decentralised enforcement in state aids disputes is not complete, in particular, as regards the treatment of actions other than those aimed at ordering the repayment or recovery of unlawful state aids. First, it seems clear that domestic courts must be able, at the request of a third party relying upon the direct effect of the last sentence of Article 88(3) EC, to order interim relief against the national authorities so as to restrain the payment (or further payment) of unlawful state aids.[161] That follows from the general principle established in *Factortame*.[162] Moreover, Article 14(3) Regulation 659/1999 expressly states that, in the event of a procedure before the national courts, Member States must take all necessary steps available within their respective legal systems—including provisional measures—to ensure the immediate and effective execution of a final Commission decision ordering recovery. But the Court has not (yet) taken any steps

[160] Case C–480/98 *Spain v Commission* [2000] ECR I–8717.
[161] Eg Case C–39/94 *SFEI* [1996] ECR I–3547; Case C–143/99 *Adria-Wien Pipeline* [2001] ECR I–8365.
[162] Case C–213/89 *Ex p Factortame* [1990] ECR I–2433.

towards harmonising the substantive conditions governing the grant of interim relief in practice (over and above the minimum requirements implicit in the ordinary principles of equivalence and effectiveness). The ability of third parties to obtain provisional measures against national authorities proposing to grant state aid in breach of the procedural requirements imposed by Article 88(3) EC, or of the national authorities themselves to obtain interim relief against recipients of unlawful state aid pending the full hearing of an action for recovery, will therefore continue to differ from Member State to Member State.[163]

Secondly, the Court established in *Van Calster* that, insofar as any given system of national subsidies constitutes state aid within the scope of Articles 87 and 88 EC, the procedural requirements imposed by Article 88(3) EC embrace not only the proposed payments per se, but also the method of financing those payments, inasmuch as that method forms an integral part of the planned regime. Therefore, the consequences of the Member State's failure to comply with its obligations under Article 88(3) EC affect the legality of not only the state aid, but also its method of financing. In particular, national courts must in principle order reimbursement of any charges levied specifically for the purpose of financing the unlawful subsidies.[164] For these purposes, the Court referred to its judgment in *Comateb*—one of the key decisions dealing with the Member State's general obligation to repay charges levied contrary to Community law, in accordance with the ordinary framework of national autonomy, equivalence and effectiveness.[165] While that caselaw undoubtedly imposes severe restrictions on the scope of the Member State's remedial and procedural discretion to limit exercise of the claimant's Community right to reimbursement,[166] it remains to be seen whether the Court, in its caselaw after *Van Calster*, will further adapt that jurisprudence to the special characteristics of the state aids sector (for example) by harmonising the rules on limitation periods to a further degree than the ordinary *Rewe/Comet* caselaw.[167]

Thirdly, it seems clear that third parties are entitled to seek compensation from the defaulting Member State in respect of any damage caused by the competitive advantages enjoyed by a recipient undertaking thanks to the unlawful payment of state aids in contravention of the directly effective procedural obligations contained in Article 88(3) EC.[168]

[163] See above (particularly the contrast with Cases C–143/88 and C–92/89 *Zuckerfabrik Süderdithmarshen* [1991] ECR I–415 and Case C–465/93 *Atlanta* [1995] ECR I–3761).
[164] Cases C–261–62/01 *Van Calster* (Judgment of 21 October 2003).
[165] Cases C–192–218/95 *Comateb* [1997] ECR I–165.
[166] See further below.
[167] Case 33/76 *Rewe-Zentralfinanz v Landwirtschaftskammer für das Saarland* [1976] ECR 1989; Case 45/76 *Comet* [1976] ECR 2043. Further: ch 5 (above).
[168] Eg Case C–390/98 *Banks* [2001] ECR I–6117, para 80.

However, the Court has not (yet) indicated that the substantive and procedural conditions for obtaining compensation in such circumstances will differ from the general framework established under the *Francovich* caselaw.[169] Issues may well arise, within the context of the Community conditions for liability elaborated after *Brasserie de Pêcheur*, about the circumstances in which the Member State's failure to notify proposed state aid to the Commission may constitute a 'sufficiently serious breach' of its Treaty obligations.[170] But in any event, the requirement of a direct causal link between the Member State's breach of Article 88(3) EC and the damage suffered by the claimant will be governed in the first instance by domestic rules; Member States may choose to make the availability of reparation subject to less stringent conditions than those contained in the Court's own 'sufficiently serious breach' caselaw; and rules governing the valuation of compensation payable by the Member State, or the time-limits within which claimants may initiate actions for reparation, will be determined by the ordinary principles of national autonomy, equivalence and effectiveness.[171]

Finally, the Court has adopted a strikingly laissez-faire approach to the types of action available to third parties under Community law against the recipients of unlawful state aids (as opposed to the defaulting national authorities which acted in breach of their Treaty obligations). In particular, the Court held in *SFEI* that the machinery for reviewing state aids established by Article 88 EC does not impose any specific obligations upon the recipient: the procedural requirements contained in Article 88(3) EC are directed towards the Member States; as are final Commission decisions establishing that state aids are incompatible with the Common Market and ordering their recovery. In those circumstances, the Court found that Community law does not provide a sufficient basis for the recipient to incur liability for having failed to verify (as any diligent businessman presumably should) that state aids were in fact duly notified to the Commission. The principle of equivalence might require that, where national rules recognise the potential liability of an economic operator for having accepted unlawful assistance of such a nature as might damage other economic operators, recipients of state aids accepted in breach of Article 88(3) EC should incur liability in comparable circumstances.[172]

[169] Cases C–6 & 9/90 *Francovich* [1991] ECR I–5357. Cf Commission, *Notice on Cooperation Between National Courts and the Commission in the State Aid Field*, OJ 1995 C312/8 assumes that the *Francovich* caselaw provides the relevant legal framework for damages actions against defaulting Member States for the purposes of state aids law. Similarly, eg J Flynn, 'The Role of National Courts' in A Biondi, P Eeckhout & J Flynn (eds), *The Law of State Aid in the European Union* (OUP, 2004).
[170] Cases C–46 & 48/93 *Brasserie du Pêcheur* and *Factortame III* [1996] ECR I–1029. Further: M Struys and H Abbott, 'The Role of National Courts in State Aid Litigation' (2003) 28 EL Rev 172.
[171] Further: ch 5 (above).
[172] Case C–39/94 *SFEI* [1996] ECR I–3547, paras 72–76.

But otherwise, Community law does not seek to overcome the clear disparities which exist between the domestic legal orders when it comes to the direct liability of recipients.[173]

Thus, as with the caselaw on decentralised enforcement against acts of the Community institutions, the Court's approach to national remedies and procedural rules in the sphere of unlawful state aids supports the idea of a selective approach to the imperative of uniformity—and indeed goes further than the jurisprudence on judicial review of Community measures by suggesting that the Court is sensitive to a sectoral understanding of the imperative of uniformity within the state aids field, whereby the degree of harmonisation pursued as regards the domestic standards of judicial protection is linked directly to the level of centralisation which characterises substantive Community policy. But although the Court's specific caselaw on state aids reaches beyond the general caselaw on effective judicial protection, it does not necessarily go far enough towards guaranteeing the uniform application of the relevant Treaty rules—and thus fails to avoid certain artificial distortions of competition within the Internal Market, arising purely from the existence of discrepancies between national remedies and procedural rules.

DECENTRALISED ENFORCEMENT OF COMPETITION POLICY

Centralised enforcement does not play quite so prominent a role in Articles 81 and 82 EC as it does under Articles 87 and 88 EC. We saw that the substantive state aid rules contained in Article 87 EC do not have direct effect.[174] Only the procedural requirements contained in the last sentence of Article 88(3) EC (as well as block exemptions and binding Commission decisions) can be enforced before the national courts.[175] By contrast, before 1 May 2004, Articles 81(1) and (2) EC, block exemptions for various categories of agreement and practice, and Article 82 EC in its entirety, all enjoyed direct effect.[176] Only individual exemptions under Article 81(3) EC could not be granted by the national authorities or domestic judges.[177] Since the entry into force of Regulation 1/2003, on

[173] Further: AEA Comité de Concertation, *Report on the Application of EC State Aid Law by the Member State Courts* (4 June 1999), available at http: <www.europa.eu.int/comm/competition/ state_aid/legislation/app_by_member_states>. In particular, the *SFEI* approach makes it unlikely that third parties could bring an action for damages against state aid recipients relying upon the judgment in Case C–453/99 *Courage v Crehan* [2001] ECR I–6297 (see further below). Consider, eg M Ross, 'Decentralisation, Effectiveness and Modernisation: Contradictions in Terms?' in A Biondi, P Eeckhout & J Flynn (eds), *The Law of State Aid in the European Union* (OUP, 2004).

[174] Eg Case 78/76 *Steinike und Weinlig* [1977] ECR 595.

[175] Eg Case C–354/90 *'French Salmon'* [1991] ECR I–5505.

[176] Eg Case 127/73 *BRT v SABAM* [1974] ECR 51.

[177] Art 9(1) Reg 17/62 implementing Articles 85 and 86 of the Treaty, OJ Special English Edition 1959–62 (Series I) 87.

1 May 2004, the abolition of both the notification system for potentially anti-competitive agreements and practices, and the Commission's monopoly over the grant of individual exemptions, means that all the competition rules contained in Articles 81 and 82 EC can now be applied by the national courts.[178] The contrast with the state aids regime has therefore become even more marked.[179]

Nevertheless, competition policy shares with state aids certain common features: a crucial role in the functioning of an Internal Market based upon fair and equal conditions of competition; and therefore the pursuit of a high degree of substantive uniformity, with little scope for the Member States independently to construct differentiated regulatory regimes. For this reason, it was argued in Chapter 4 that the Community has a genuine interest in approximating the remedies and procedural rules applicable to the decentralised enforcement of its substantive competition policy. But it was also noted that the Community legislature has so far made little serious effort towards achieving the harmonisation of domestic standards of judicial protection. It is now time to examine the situation in greater detail, having specific regard to the Court's developing caselaw. Two main issues warrant attention: the special procedural obligations imposed upon national courts by virtue of their duty to cooperate in good faith with the Commission; and the broader question of harmonising, by judicial means, the remedies available in decentralised competition disputes (which should be considered both before and after the important judgment in *Courage v Crehan*).[180]

Cooperation Between the Commission and the National Courts

The centralised and decentralised authorities responsible for enforcing Community competition law might both exercise jurisdiction over exactly the same agreement or practice. But each set of institutions also has a particular role to play (and expertise to offer) within the overall network of competition policy actors. There is therefore a need for the Community legal order to promote a coherent relationship between these twin enforcement channels. For present purposes, that relationship focuses

[178] Reg 1/2003, OJ 2003 L1/1. Further: ch 3 (above).
[179] Notwithstanding the increased scope for decentralisation in the state aids sphere brought about by the greater use of block exemptions. Further, eg M Ross, 'State Aids and National Courts: Definitions and Other Problems—A Case of Premature Emancipation?' (2000) 37 CML Rev 401; A Sinnaeve, 'Block Exemptions for State Aid: More Scope for State Aid Control by Member States and Competitors' (2001) 38 CML Rev 1479; M Ross, 'Decentralisation, Effectiveness and Modernisation: Contradictions in Terms?' in A Biondi, P Eeckhout & J Flynn (eds), *The Law of State Aid in the European Union* (OUP, 2004).
[180] Case C–453/99 *Courage v Crehan* [2001] ECR I–6297.

upon the obligations of mutual cooperation binding the Commission and the national courts, and the impact such obligations might have upon domestic procedural rules.[181]

Concurrent Jurisdiction and Parallel Proceedings

The main principles dealing with the consequences of concurrent jurisdiction between the Commission and the national courts, before the entry into force of Regulation 1/2003, were established by the Court in *Delimitis* and *Masterfoods*,[182] and elaborated by the Commission in its 1993 Cooperation Notice.[183] The basic problem was to avoid situations in which judgments adopted by the domestic judges might conflict with decisions adopted or contemplated by the Commission in respect of the same agreement or practice, taking account (in particular) of the Commission's old monopoly over the grant of individual exemptions under Article 81(3) EC, with a view to preserving adequate conditions of legal certainty for the economic undertakings involved. The basic solution—much of it still relevant now—was that, before deciding whether there has been a breach of Article 81 or 82 EC, the national court must ascertain whether the relevant agreement or practice has already been the subject of a decision by the Commission.

If a formal decision exists, it is binding on the national court by virtue of the principle of supremacy. Indeed, the Commission cannot be bound by decisions of the national courts concerning the application of Article 81 or 82 EC, and is entitled to adopt its own decisions at any time, even where this would conflict with a judgment already delivered by a domestic judge with regard to the same agreement or practice.[184] It has been argued that the latter principle could result in quite significant incursions into national procedural autonomy: for example, if a national court of first instance found an agreement to be compatible with Article 81 EC, but the Commission subsequently adopted a decision establishing an infringement of the Treaty's competition rules, the higher domestic courts could be obliged by the principle of effectiveness to entertain an appeal, even if the time-limit for initiating further action had already expired.[185] However, the judgment in *Kühne & Heitz* suggests that the Court of Justice

[181] See generally, on competition law enforcement, eg R Whish, *Competition Law* (Butterworths, 2003) chs 7 and 8; D Goyder, *EC Competition Law* (OUP, 2003) chs 20 and 21.
[182] Case C–234/89 *Delimitis* [1991] ECR I–935; Case C–344/98 *Masterfoods* [2000] ECR I–11369.
[183] Commission, *Notice on Cooperation Between National Courts and the Commission in Applying Articles 81 and 82 of the EEC Treaty*, OJ 1993 C39/6.
[184] In particular: Case C–344/98 *Masterfoods* [2000] ECR I–11369.
[185] Eg S Preece, Annotation of *Masterfoods* [2001] ECLR 281. Cf L Kjølbye, Annotation of *Masterfoods* (2002) 39 CML Rev 175.

will not lightly set aside the principle of legal certainty, by requiring Member States to reopen decisions which have acquired definitive effect under the national legal systems, for the sake of securing the supremacy of Community law.[186] In any case, if a formal Commission decision concerning Article 81 or 82 EC is being challenged before the Community courts by way of an Article 230 EC action for annulment, and its validity is crucial to the outcome of a dispute pending before the national court, the latter is obliged either to stay proceedings pending final determination of the action for annulment, or to make a reference to the Court of Justice under Article 234 EC.

By contrast, if there is no formal Commission ruling in respect of the same agreement or practice, the national court is to be guided in its interpretation and application of the Treaty rules by the caselaw of the Community courts, and any relevant Commission decisions. However, if the Commission has already opened procedures in respect of the disputed agreement or practice, the national court is free to suspend its proceedings and await the outcome of the Commission investigation. Suspension is to be envisaged where there is a risk of conflicting positions being taken by the domestic judge and the Commission on the application of Article 81 or 82 EC.[187] Moreover, it used to be the case that, where one party claimed the benefit of an individual exemption under Article 81(3) EC, the national court was obliged to consider the possibility of such an exemption being granted, taking into account the notification requirements set out in Regulation 17/62.[188] If there was no possibility of an individual exemption being granted, the national court could continue to rule definitively on the dispute. But if the national court considered individual exemption possible, it might decide to suspend its proceedings and await a final Commission decision on the matter. In any event, the national court could, if necessary, make a preliminary reference to the Court of Justice under Article 234 EC.

As from 1 May 2004, Regulation 1/2003 adapts those principles to the modernised framework on competition enforcement, in particular, having regard to the newfound direct effect of Article 81(3) EC. There is no provision, equivalent to that applicable to national competition authorities, whereby initiation of a formal procedure by the Commission automatically divests the national courts of their own competence to apply Articles 81 and 82 EC.[189] Instead, Article 16 provides that any final

[186] Case C–453/00 *Kühne & Heitz* (Judgment of 13 January 2004). Cf Case C–207/03 *Novartis* (Opinion of 7 September 2004; Judgment pending).

[187] In this regard, national courts are not bound by any informal Commission opinion (such as a comfort letter) on the relevant agreement/practice, though they may take such opinions into account when assessing the application of Articles 81 and 82 EC, eg Case 99/79 *Lancôme v Etos* [1980] ECR 2511.

[188] Reg 17/62, OJ Special English Edition 1959–62 (Series I) 87.

[189] Cf Art 11(6) Reg 1/2003, OJ 2003 L1/1.

Commission decisions are binding upon the domestic judges; while national courts must avoid reaching judgments which would conflict with decisions being contemplated by the Commission in respect of the same agreement or practice (and may thus have to assess whether it is necessary to stay proceedings).[190]

Provision of Information and Protection of Professional Secrecy

The judgment in *Delimitis*,[191] again as elaborated by the Commission in its 1993 Cooperation Notice,[192] dealt with the national court's right to seek information from the Commission concerning the application of Articles 81 and 82 EC. Thus, the domestic judges were entitled to ask (for example) whether a case was currently pending before the Commission, whether an official investigation had been conducted, and whether any formal decision or informal opinion had been adopted. Similarly, the national courts were entitled to seek more abstract economic and legal guidance from the Commission on the interpretation and application of Articles 81 and 82 EC as regards (for example) when an agreement or practice has an effect on intra-Community trade, current institutional practice on the granting of individual exemptions, and statistical data available in respect of particular markets. These principles are now reflected in Regulation 1/2003. Article 15(1) states that, in proceedings for the application of Article 81 or 82 EC, domestic judges may ask the Commission for information in its possession, or for its opinion on questions concerning the application of the Community competition rules. In all cases involving requests for information from the national courts, the Commission is obliged to comply with the duty of loyal cooperation under Article 10 EC.[193]

However, issues have arisen about the Commission's obligation to cooperate with the national courts in the provision of confidential information. Article 287 EC provides that members and servants of the Community institutions are required not to disclose information covered by the obligation of professional secrecy, in particular, information about undertakings and their business relations. For these purposes, Article 20(2) Regulation 17/62 provided that the Commission and national competition authorities should not disclose information acquired as a result of the application of the Regulation (for example, through notifications and investigations) and of the kind covered by the obligation of professional

[190] See also Commission, *Notice on the Cooperation Between the Commission and the Courts of the EU Member States in the Application of Articles 81 and 82 EC*, OJ 2004 C101/54.
[191] Case C–234/89 *Delimitis* [1991] ECR I–935.
[192] Commission, *Notice on Cooperation Between National Courts and the Commission in Applying Articles 81 and 82 of the EEC Treaty*, OJ 1993 C39/6.
[193] Eg Case C–2/88 *Zwartveld I* [1990] ECR I–3365.

secrecy. At first sight, this seemed to limit the Commission's obligation under Article 10 EC to accede to requests from national courts for information.[194] However, it was established by the Court of First Instance in *Postbank* that the duty of loyal cooperation requires the Commission to provide domestic judges with whatever information they ask for, in principle, even if that information is covered by the obligation of professional secrecy.[195] Accordingly, Article 28(2) Regulation 1/2003 now states that, without prejudice to the exchange and use of information foreseen (inter alia) in Article 15, neither Commission nor Member State officials shall disclose information acquired or exchanged pursuant to the Regulation and of the kind covered by the obligation of professional secrecy.

Nevertheless, the Court of First Instance in *Postbank* did acknowledge that, in discharging its duty of cooperation towards the national courts, the Commission may not in any circumstances undermine the guarantees as regards professional secrecy offered to individuals by Article 287 EC. For these purposes, the Commission is obliged to take certain precautions: for example, by giving undertakings an opportunity to state their views on the existence of confidential information and the potential damage which might result from its disclosure; and also by informing the national courts of documents which contain confidential information or business secrets. But otherwise, it is the responsibility of the domestic judge to guarantee, on the basis of national procedural law, protection of the undertaking's rights as regards the production of documents containing information obtained in the course of procedures before the Commission.[196] The proper implications of this aspect of the judgment are unclear. On the one hand, the Court of First Instance clearly assumed that the national courts must indeed guarantee the protection of confidential information (especially business secrets) pursuant to the principles of effective judicial protection.[197] This seems to imply that national courts are obliged, under Community law, to comply with certain procedural standards—even if they are harmonised only to a minimum level, in accordance with the general thrust of the Court of Justice's current caselaw. On the other hand, the Court of First Instance also recognised that a refusal by the Commission to disclose the documents requested by a national court could be justified in exceptional cases. In particular, there may be situations where, even if the Commission takes

[194] Consider: Commission, *Notice on Cooperation Between National Courts and the Commission in Applying Articles 81 and 82 of the EEC Treaty*, OJ 1993 C39/6, paras 41–42. Also: Case C–234/89 *Delimitis* [1991] ECR I–935, para 53.

[195] Case T-353/94 *Postbank* [1996] ECR II–921. Further: CS Kerse, Commentary on *Postbank* (1997) 34 CML Rev 1481. On the situation of the national competition authorities, consider, eg Case C–67/91 *Asociación Española de Banca Privada* [1992] ECR I–4785; Case T-112/98 *Mannesmannröhren-Werke* [2001] ECR II–729.

[196] Case T–353/94 *Postbank* [1996] ECR II–921, paras 72 and 90.

[197] Case T–353/94 *Postbank* [1996] ECR II–921, para 69.

the precautions outlined above, a refusal to disclose remains the only way of ensuring the protection of the rights of third parties under Article 287 EC 'which in principle is a matter for the national courts.'[198] The Commission has interpreted this to mean that, where national procedural rules in fact fail to make adequate provision for the protection of confidential information, the Commission will not be obliged under Article 10 EC to supply documents requested by the domestic judges.[199] This implies that there is, in the final analysis, no binding obligation under Community law for Member States to guarantee any particular level of judicial protection as regards professional secrecy.[200]

Written and Oral Observations Before the National Courts

In any event, Regulation 1/2003 provides for additional forms of cooperation between the domestic courts and other members of the enforcement network which might have an impact upon national procedural autonomy in competition cases. In particular, Article 15(3) states that a national competition authority may submit written and (with the permission of the domestic judge) oral observations to its own national courts on issues relating to the application of Articles 81 and 82 EC. Where the coherent application of Community competition rules so requires, the Commission itself may also submit written and (again with the permission of the competent tribunal) oral observations during the course of domestic judicial proceedings. Some commentators foresee difficult issues arising from this provision in certain Member States, particularly where the national competition authority or the Commission makes written observations on its own initiative, whilst being involved in a separate investigation of the same agreement or practice now being adjudicated upon before the national court.[201] In any case, Article 15(4) makes clear that the Regulation is without prejudice to wider powers to make observations before domestic courts conferred upon the Member State's competition authorities by national law.

Domestic Judicial Control Over Commission Investigations

Like Regulation 17/62 before, Regulation 1/2003 empowers the Commission to conduct investigations into allegedly anti-competitive

[198] Case T-353/94 *Postbank* [1996] ECR II–921, para 93. Cf Case C–2/88 *Zwartveld II* [1990] ECR I–4405.

[199] Commission, *Notice on the Cooperation Between the Commission and the Courts of the EU Member States in the Application of Articles 81 and 82 EC*, OJ 2004 C101/54, paras 23–25.

[200] Cf Cases C–174 & 189/98P *van der Wal* [2000] ECR I–1 on national procedural autonomy as regards the disclosure of documents supplied to the national courts by the Commission in competition cases.

[201] Eg H Gilliams, 'Modernisation: From Policy to Practice' (2003) 28 EL Rev 451.

agreements and practices. Such investigations will usually involve requests for information from undertakings and associations of undertakings,[202] and may also involve voluntary interviews with natural and legal persons,[203] subject to respect for fundamental rights (such as the right to protection against self-incrimination).[204]

Under Article 20 Regulation 1/2003, the Commission is empowered to undertake all necessary inspections into undertakings and associations of undertakings. This includes the power to enter any premises or means of transport of the relevant undertaking; to examine and copy its books and other records; to seal any premises, books or records of the undertaking as required; and to ask for oral explanations on-the-spot from the undertaking's staff and representatives—again subject to respect for fundamental rights (such as the privileged nature of correspondence between an independent lawyer and his/her clients).[205] In all cases, the Commission must give prior notification of an inspection to the competition authority of the relevant Member State. In situations where the undertaking is to be obliged by formal decision to undergo an inspection, the Commission must consult the competent national competition authority before adopting that decision. The Commission may request assistance from the national authorities for the purposes of conducting the inspection. However, in cases where an undertaking opposes an inspection, the Member State is obliged to afford the Commission all necessary assistance, including (in appropriate cases) that of the police or an equivalent enforcement body. The Commission may also request the Member State's assistance on a precautionary basis, where the undertaking is likely to oppose an inspection, or might attempt to conceal or dispose of evidence.[206] If such assistance requires judicial authorisation under national law, that authorisation must be applied for. Article 21 Regulation 1/2003 has now extended the Commission's powers to conduct inspections so as to cover 'other premises' (including the private homes of the undertaking's managers and staff), if the Commission reasonably suspects that books or other records related to the business and to the subject-matter of the inspection are being kept there, and these may be relevant to prove a serious violation of Article 81 or 82 EC. The Commission must consult the competition authority of the relevant Member State before adopting a formal decision to undertake any such inspection; and must also obtain prior authorisation from the national courts before executing its investigation.

[202] Art 18 Reg 1/2003, OJ 2003 L1/1.
[203] Art 19 Reg 1/2003, OJ 2003 L1/1.
[204] Eg Case 374/87 *Orkem* [1989] ECR 3283.
[205] Eg Case 155/79 *AM & S Europe* [1982] ECR 1575.
[206] Cf Cases 46 & 227/88 *Hoechst* [1989] ECR 2859; Case C–94/00 *Roquette Frères* [2002] ECR I–9011.

Disputes have arisen about the nature and extent of the domestic courts' jurisdiction in cases where the Commission and the national authorities seek judicial authorisation to carry out coercive competition inspections. The basic principles are now referred to in Articles 20(8) and 21(3) Regulation 1/2003, though the detailed legal framework was already established by the Court of Justice in its judgments in *Hoechst* and *Roquette Frères*.[207] Where the Commission intends, with the assistance of the national authorities, to carry out an investigation otherwise than with the cooperation of the undertakings concerned, it is required to respect the relevant procedural guarantees laid down by national law. However, for their part, the Member States are required to ensure that the Commission's action is effective, while at the same time respecting various general principles of Community law. In particular, in accordance with the general principle affording protection against arbitrary or disproportionate intervention by public authorities in the sphere of the private activities of any natural or legal person, the competent national courts are required—as a matter of Community law—to verify that the coercive measures requested by the Commission are not arbitrary or disproportionate to the subject-matter of the investigation. But otherwise, Community law precludes any further review by the national court of the justification for the Commission's proposed coercive measures. In particular, the domestic judge may not substitute his/her own assessment of the need for an investigation for that of the Commission, the lawfulness of whose assessments of fact and law is subject only to review by the Community judicature.[208]

On the one hand, Article 10 EC requires the Commission to ensure that the national court has at its disposal all the information necessary to carry out the judicial review required by Community law, for example: a description of the essential features of the suspected infringement and the undertaking's alleged involvement; detailed explanations showing that the Commission possesses solid factual information and evidence providing grounds for suspecting such infringement by the undertaking; some indication of the evidence sought; and explanations enabling the national court to satisfy itself that, if authorisation for the coercive measures were not granted on precautionary grounds, it would be impossible or very difficult to establish the facts amounting to the infringement. On the other hand, where the national court considers that the information provided by the Commission is inadequate, it is obliged under Article 10 EC to ask for any necessary clarification. Only after receiving such clarification, or

[207] Cases 46 & 227/88 *Hoechst* [1989] ECR 2859; Case C–94/00 *Roquette Frères* [2002] ECR I–9011.

[208] For a summary of the relevant (procedural and substantive) safeguards contained in Community law and enforced by the Community courts: Case C–94/00 *Roquette Frères* [2002] ECR I–9011, paras 43–50.

where the Commission fails to take any practical steps in response to its request, may the national court refuse to grant authorisation on the grounds that the coercive measures envisaged are arbitrary or disproportionate. In any event, the national court does not have any right to demand access to the information and evidence contained in the Commission's file. According to the Court in *Roquette Frères*, it is of crucial importance to an effective system of competition law enforcement that the Commission should be able to guarantee the anonymity of certain of its sources. Were the Commission to be obliged to disclose its file to the national judicial authorities, domestic procedural rules might well increase the risk of informants' identities being revealed to third parties.[209]

Thus, as with the principles governing the disclosure of confidential information by the Commission at the request of a national court adjudicating upon a competition dispute by virtue of the direct effect of Articles 81 and 82 EC, so too with the legal framework governing the disclosure of the Commission's evidence at the request of a domestic judge considering an application for assistance to conduct coercive investigations under Regulation 1/2003: in neither situation is there a serious attempt by the Community courts to harmonise the applicable domestic procedural rules, for the sake of facilitating smooth cooperation between the Community and national authorities when called upon to assist in the enforcement of the Treaty's competition regime through the coordinated exercise of their respective powers. Indeed, while the Court of First Instance in *Postbank* at least left open the question whether the principles of effective judicial protection might impose certain minimum obligations upon the national courts to respect professional secrecy as referred to in Article 287 EC, the Court of Justice in *Roquette Frères* seemed to assume that domestic rules for protecting the identity of informants in competition investigations would simply be left to differ from Member State to Member State—and thus to hamper access to the Commission's file by national courts called upon to assess the arbitrary or disproportionate nature of the Commission's request for coercive measures.

Harmonisation of Remedies and Procedural Rules in Competition Cases: Pre-*Courage v Crehan*

Besides the alterations to domestic procedural rules necessitated by the special obligations of mutual cooperation imposed upon the Commission and the national courts under Article 10 EC, the Court of Justice has tended to apply the ordinary presumption of national autonomy in cases

[209] Case C–94/00 *Roquette Frères* [2002] ECR I–9011, paras 64–66.

involving the decentralised enforcement of Articles 81 and 82 EC—subject to ad hoc negative harmonisation through the principles of equivalence and effectiveness.[210]

For example, the consequences which flow from the sanction of nullity under Article 81(2) EC, where certain provisions of an agreement are found to contravene Article 81(1) EC and fail to secure exemption under Article 81(3) EC, as regards the remainder of the parties' contractual relations, are to be determined in accordance with national law.[211] That is perhaps not surprising, given that the Community's interests are fulfilled when domestic courts enforce the nullity of those specific contractual provisions which infringe Article 81 EC. Questions about the legal status of the rest of the agreement therefore fall outside the scope of application of the Treaty.[212]

Other examples are more pertinent for present purposes. Take, for instance, allocation of the burden of proof as regards the conditions for the application of Articles 81 and 82 EC, where the Court in *GT-Link* applied the ordinary presumption of national procedural autonomy, subject to the principles of equivalence and effectiveness, covering (say) restrictions on the admissibility of evidence which might render the exercise of Community law rights virtually impossible or excessively difficult in practice.[213] That particular example has since been the subject of intervention of the Community legislature. Regulation 1/2003 now provides that, in any proceedings for the application of Articles 81 and 82 EC, the burden of proving an infringement of Article 81(1) or Article 82 EC shall rest on the party alleging the infringement; whereas the undertaking claiming the benefit of Article 81(3) EC shall bear the burden of proving that the conditions for exemption are fulfilled.[214] However, the caselaw provides other illustrations of how the Court's general approach towards effective judicial protection—as embodied in the current caselaw and discussed in Chapter 5—applies to further aspects of the decentralised enforcement of Community competition law. This is true of procedural rules such as limitation periods for the initiation of actions based on Articles 81 and 82 EC;[215] and the legal framework governing the general admissibility of evidence.[216] It also seems true of the remedies available for breach of the Treaty's competition rules: for example, interim relief

[210] For its part, the Commission (at least according to its 1993 and 2004 Cooperation Notices) does not seem to expect much more from the ECJ and the national courts than application of the general remedies caselaw as outlined below.
[211] Eg Case 319/82 *Société de vente de ciments* [1983] ECR 4173; Case 10/86 *VAG France* [1986] ECR 4071.
[212] Eg Case 56/65 *Société Technique Minière v Maschinenbau Ulm* [1966] ECR 235.
[213] Case C–242/95 *GT-Link* [1997] ECR I–4449.
[214] Art 2 Reg 1/2003, OJ 2003 L1/1.
[215] Eg Case C–126/97 *Eco Swiss v Benetton* [1999] ECR I–3055.
[216] Eg Case C–340/99 *TNT Traco v Poste Italiane* [2001] ECR I–4109.

in respect of an alleged infringement of Article 81 or 82 EC;[217] and restitutionary actions for the recovery of unlawfully levied charges (at least where the case involves public or semi-public authorities which can be directly assimilated to the Member State itself;[218] but probably also where the dispute involves a private undertaking which has obtained monies from third parties through the abuse of its dominant market position).[219]

Two judgments warrant special attention. The first is *Otto v Postbank*, which concerned an application by the claimant for the provisional examination of witnesses with a view to establishing certain facts, prior to a possible civil action based upon Articles 81 and 82 EC. Those witnesses included members of the managerial staff from the defendant undertaking. Under Dutch law, a party called as a witness in his/her own case could in principle be obliged to give evidence (save where this would expose that party to criminal prosecution). The basic thrust of the defendant's argument was that the principles of effective judicial protection applicable to the decentralised enforcement of Articles 81 and 82 EC should be developed in tandem with the standards required of the Commission itself within the context of centralised enforcement procedures. In particular, it was claimed that the privilege against self-incrimination, as recognised by the Court of Justice in *Orkem* in relation to Commission investigations under Regulation 17/62, should extend also to civil proceedings before the domestic courts (thus precluding the application of the relevant Dutch legislation).[220] If it had succeeded, this approach could have paved the way for a significant harmonisation of the remedies applicable in decentralised competition law disputes—based upon the general model favoured by certain academics whereby the Member State's margin of procedural discretion should be defined by analogy with any comparable standards of judicial protection governing direct actions before the Community courts.[221]

However, Advocate General Gulmann rejected this argument: without demurring from the possibility that the *Orkem* principle could apply in contexts other than Commission investigations under Regulation 17/62, it would not be appropriate for Community law to prescribe the application of any such principle within the framework for the decentralised enforcement of Articles 81 and 82 EC before the national courts. In particular, the uniform application of Community competition law did not demand that the presumption of domestic procedural autonomy be displaced in favour of judicially-led harmonisation based upon the

[217] Eg Case C–234/89 *Delimitis* [1991] ECR I–935; Case C–344/98 *Masterfoods* [2000] ECR I–11369.
[218] Eg Case C–242/95 *GT-Link* [1997] ECR I–4449.
[219] See further below.
[220] Case 374/87 *Orkem* [1989] ECR 3283.
[221] Further: ch 5 (above).

standards applicable to the Commission's own investigations. After all, every Member State is a signatory to the European Convention on Human Rights, and thus bound to respect the guarantee of a fair hearing before an independent and impartial tribunal contained therein.[222] In any case, true uniformity in the conditions for the decentralised enforcement of Articles 81 and 82 EC was not necessarily a viable goal. There would be difficult choices to make about which procedural principles the Member States should be obliged to respect, especially where there was no existing Community paradigm appropriate for straightforward transposition. Moreover, the Community could hardly insist that those Member States with better standards of judicial protection than that embodied in cases like *Orkem* should conform to a lower common denominator.[223]

The Court of Justice was also unreceptive to the defendant's argument. In principle, the decentralised enforcement of Articles 81 and 82 EC is governed by national procedural rules, provided that the Member State respects the fundamental principles of Community law. In that regard, the guarantees necessary to secure the rights of the defence in the course of an administrative procedure before the Commission differ from the guarantees required to safeguard the rights of the defence in the context of civil proceedings before a national court. The latter did not involve any possibility that the defendant would be compelled to admit to conduct exposing him/her to administrative or criminal penalties imposed by a public authority, so Community law did not—in such circumstances—require the domestic judges to observe the *Orkem* principle of protection against self-incrimination.[224] By focusing on the duty to respect fundamental rights within the scope of application of the Treaty, rather than on the imperative of either effectiveness or uniformity, the Court therefore went further than Advocate General Gulmann, by leaving open the possibility that the national courts could—in appropriate cases—be required to adapt their procedural rules to meet the minimum requirements imposed directly under Community law (rather than those expected indirectly through adherence to the European Convention on Human Rights).[225]

222 Art 6(1) ECHR. Further: ch 1 (above).

223 This last consideration seems rather unpersuasive, given that lowering the procedural safeguards previously available in certain Member States was precisely the outcome of judicial harmonisation in situations such as Cases C–143/88 and C–92/89 *Zuckerfabrik Süderdithmarshen* [1991] ECR I–415; Case C–188/92 *TWD* [1994] ECR I–833; Case C–24/95 *Alcan Deutschland* [1997] ECR I–1591.

224 Case C–60/92 *Otto v Postbank* [1993] ECR I–5683. In particular, the Commission and any competent national authority would be prevented from using information obtained during the course of domestic civil proceedings, for the purposes of establishing an infringement of Community competition rules, in proceedings which could lead directly or indirectly to the imposition of administrative or criminal penalties.

225 Eg where national competition authorities are pursuing administrative or criminal penalties through the courts, in respect of an alleged infringement of Art 81 or 82 EC, and the defendant undertaking would otherwise be denied the right to protection against self-incrimination.

However, even that implicit obligation to meet certain minimum standards of judicial protection relating to the observance of fundamental rights fell far short of any attempt to prescribe, in a genuinely harmonised manner, the conditions for relying upon the privilege against self-incrimination in civil (or any other type of domestic) proceedings. Indeed, the Court expressly rejected the idea that national procedural autonomy in fields such as protection of the rights of the defence should be replaced by a policy of systematic harmonisation on the basis of the rules applicable to Community proceedings.[226] While the Court did not engage in any explicit discussion of the defendant's broader submission that deference to national autonomy as regards procedural rules relating to self-incrimination would endanger the uniform application of Community competition law, it is implicit in the judgment that such rules may legitimately differ, not only from those governing the conduct of the Commission under Regulation 17/62, but also from those applicable in civil proceedings in other Member States. In any case, the Court's approach—based upon respect for fundamental rights rather than the uniform application of Community competition law—should apply as regards the enforcement not only of Articles 81 and 82 EC, but of any corpus of Community law, regardless of how far its substantive content might (from a sectoral perspective) be considered relatively differentiated.

The second judgment is *Eco Swiss v Benetton*, which concerned a private arbitration award relating to a licensing agreement. Neither the parties nor the arbitration tribunal had considered the application of Community competition law, but Benetton subsequently brought an action for annulment of the award on the grounds that the contract was in fact contrary to Article 81 EC. Dutch law permitted the courts to annul arbitration awards only on narrow grounds, including inconsistency with public policy; but national jurisprudence did not treat a mere infringement of domestic competition rules as falling within the scope of that concept. The Court of Justice recognised that it was in the interests of having efficient arbitration proceedings to limit the scope of judicial intervention. However, the Court continued to observe that Article 81 EC constitutes a fundamental provision which is essential for accomplishing the tasks entrusted to the Community, in particular, as regards the functioning of the Internal Market. The importance of that provision led the Treaty framers to provide expressly, in Article 81(2) EC, that prohibited agreements are to be automatically void. The Court then offered two reasons why the possibility of judicial intervention was necessary in this case.

First, where domestic law permits the courts to annul an arbitration award on the basis of failure to observe national rules of public policy, annulment must also be possible if the award is in fact contrary to

[226] Case C–60/92 *Otto v Postbank* [1993] ECR I–5683, para 14.

Article 81 EC. In effect, the Court treated Article 81 EC as a rule of Community public policy, triggering the application of the principle of equivalence, so as to ensure that enforcement of the Treaty was treated in the same manner as enforcement of comparable domestic norms. Secondly, private arbitration tribunals do not constitute courts or tribunals within the meaning of Article 234 EC. Yet it is manifestly in the interests of the Community legal order that every Treaty provision should be given a uniform interpretation, irrespective of the circumstances in which it is to be applied. Community law therefore required that questions concerning the interpretation of Article 81 EC should be open to examination by national courts when asked to rule on the validity of an arbitration award, so that it remained possible for such questions to be referred (if necessary) to the Court itself.[227]

By treating the prohibition on anti-competitive agreements and practices under Article 81 EC as a principle of Community public policy, essential for the functioning of the Internal Market, the judgment in *Eco Swiss v Benetton* hinted at a 'special status' for the Treaty competition rules which could lay the foundations for greater control over the legal framework available for their decentralised enforcement. However, the judgment did not in itself mark any radical departure from ordinary judicial practice under the general remedies caselaw. After all, the Court refused to establish any uniform requirement (for example) that the imperative of full implementation for Article 81 EC should always supersede procedural restrictions on raising new legal arguments on appeal (against arbitration awards or any other type of decision). The principle of equivalence merely requires that, where the Member State already recognises an exception for domestic public policy rules, Treaty competition principles must benefit from the same privilege. Similarly, the principle of effectiveness merely requires that national procedural rules may limit, just never exclude entirely, the possibility of communication between the domestic and Community judiciaries via the Article 234 EC preliminary reference procedure.[228]

Harmonisation of Remedies and Procedural Rules in Competition Cases: Post-*Courage v Crehan*

Despite the tone of the judgment in *Eco Swiss*, there was little indication that the Court was prepared to construct a more comprehensive

[227] Case C–126/97 *Eco Swiss v Benetton* [1999] ECR I–3055. Further, eg M Furse and L D'Arcy, Commentary on *Eco Swiss v Benetton* [1999] ECLR 392; AP Komninos, Commentary on *Eco Swiss v Benetton* (2000) 37 CML Rev 459; C Baudenbacher and I Higgins, 'Decentralisation of EC Competition Law Enforcement and Arbitration' (2002) 8 *Columbia Journal of European Law* 1.
[228] Cf Case C–312/93 *Peterbroeck* [1995] ECR I–4599; Cases C–430–31/93 *Van Schijndel* [1995] ECR I–4705. Further: ch 1 (above).

framework of Community-prescribed procedural law within the particular context of domestic competition law enforcement. However, the dispute in *Courage v Crehan* provided the Court with an opportunity to reconsider its caselaw, taking into account the changing legal environment provided by the Commission's proposals for greater decentralisation in the application of Articles 81 and 82 EC.[229]

Background Debate on Private Liability in Damages

Where a Member State commits an infringement of the Treaty's competition rules—in particular, by creating a situation in which a public undertaking cannot avoid infringing Article 82 EC (read together with Article 86 EC)—the Court held in *GT-Link* that third parties who have sustained damage may obtain compensation for their losses in accordance with the *Francovich* caselaw.[230] However, for many years there has been extensive academic debate about the possibility of imposing liability to make reparation, as a matter of Community law, upon private undertakings which commit an infringement of Article 81 or 82 EC. Three viewpoints are relevant for present purposes.

First, the Commission in its 1993 Cooperation Notice seemed to assume that national courts should be required to award damages against undertakings for having breached the Community's competition rules, only where such remedies were available in respect of comparable infringements of purely domestic norms, in straightforward application of the principle of equivalence.[231]

Secondly, other commentators believe that the principle of effectiveness could in fact justify more extensive intrusions into the realm of national procedural autonomy, specifically as regards Articles 81 and 82 EC, which impose directly effective obligations upon private undertakings.[232] In particular, the effective and uniform application of Articles 81 and 82 EC demand that Community law should prescribe for itself the conditions under which defaulting undertakings incur liability to make reparation.[233] It is argued that damages liability constitutes an essential element of a functioning competition regime: it provides an incentive for third parties to engage in the process of decentralised enforcement; and helps restore conditions of competition to an undistorted state.[234] It is

[229] Case C–453/99 *Courage v Crehan* [2001] ECR I–6297.
[230] Case C–242/95 *GT-Link* [1997] ECR I–4449, para 60. Further: ch 5 (above).
[231] Commission, *Notice on Cooperation Between National Courts and the Commission in Applying Articles 81 and 82 of the EEC Treaty*, OJ 1993 C39/6, para 11.
[232] Eg M Hoskins, 'Garden Cottage Revisited: The Availability of Damages in the National Courts for Breaches of the EEC Competition Rules' [1992] ECLR 257.
[233] Eg L Hiljemark, 'Enforcement of EC Competition Law in National Courts: The Perspective of Judicial Protection' (1997) 17 *Yearbook of European Law* 83.
[234] Eg A Winterstein, 'A Community Right in Damages for Breach of EC Competition Rules?' [1995] ECLR 49.

further argued that Community law should actively promote third-party actions as a means of deterring undertakings from engaging in anti-competitive conduct in the first place, for example, by empowering the national courts to award punitive (double or triple) damages. After all, the provision of an effective remedy within the context of decentralised enforcement may provide ad hoc relief to individuals, but without some more punitive form of sanction, it will not fulfil the same public interest function of *deterring* anti-competitive conduct currently performed by the imposition of hefty fines by the Commission.[235]

Thirdly, yet another body of academic opinion locates the particular issue of private liability under Articles 81 and 82 EC within the broader context of private liability to make reparation for breach of *any* Community law obligation. The most famous exponent of this viewpoint is Advocate General van Gerven in *Banks v British Coal Corporation*. He argued that, according to Article 288 EC, the conditions underpinning the non-contractual liability of the Community institutions and (since *Brasserie*) underpinning also the non-contractual liability of the national authorities, represent general principles derived from the common legal traditions of the Member States.[236] As such, they could readily extend across every kind of non-contractual liability. Of course, this is not to say that the *Francovich* caselaw should simply extend to catch the actions of private parties as well as those of Member States. After all, that would permit individuals to benefit from culpability requirements (such as the 'manifest and grave disregard' test) developed specifically to evaluate the conduct of public authorities exercising broad discretionary powers. Rather, the idea would be for Community law to tailor the general liability conditions developed under the *Francovich* caselaw to the different circumstances—public and private law situations, vertical and horizontal disputes—in which Treaty obligations might be infringed and a Community remedy in damages required. For example, in *Banks* itself, Advocate General van Gerven submitted that, for the purposes of applying the general principles of non-contractual liability underlying Article 288 EC to infringements of Community competition law, liability to make reparation should be engaged, within the over-arching framework of the *Francovich* caselaw, on the basis of a breach of the Treaty per se.[237]

[235] On this issue, see further: C Jones, *Private Enforcement of Antitrust Law in the EC, UK and USA* (OUP, 1999) esp ch 19.

[236] Eg Cases C–46 & 48/93 *Brasserie du Pêcheur* and *Factortame III* [1996] ECR I–1029, paras 29 and 41.

[237] Case C–128/92 *Banks v British Coal Corporation* [1994] ECR I–1209. Similarly, eg R Caranta, 'Governmental Liability after *Francovich*' [1993] CLJ 272; C Lewis and S Moore, 'Duties, Directives and Damages in European Community Law' [1993] PL 151; W van Gerven, 'Non-contractual Liability of Member States, Community Institutions and Individuals for Breaches of Community Law with a View to a Common Law for Europe' (1994) 1 *Maastricht Journal of European and Comparative Law* 6; D Edward and W Robinson, 'Is There a Place for

These three viewpoints reflect the various models which have structured our debate about the Community's enforcement deficit: at one extreme (represented by the Commission's 1993 Cooperation Notice), the idea that Community law should adopt a laissez-faire approach to national procedural autonomy which does not place any particular emphasis on the imperative of uniformity; at the other extreme (embodied in Advocate General van Gerven's Opinion in *Banks*), the proposal for a general Community system of private liability in damages which seems infused with the spirit of an 'integration through law' concern for remedial harmonisation so as to promote the effective and uniform enforcement of Treaty norms before the domestic courts; and resting between the two extremes (articulated primarily by competition specialists), a sectoral approach to damages liability which stresses the particular need for uniformity as regards Articles 81 and 82 EC—but without necessarily extending that concern to other areas of regulatory activity falling within the scope of the Treaty.

The Judgment in Courage v Crehan

Courage v Crehan presented the Court with an opportunity to express its preference between these models. The English courts treat agreements which breach Article 81(1) EC not merely as void under Article 81(2) EC, but also as illegal for the purposes of national law. Furthermore, English law prohibits the parties to any illegal contract from seeking damages *inter se*, based on the principle *in pari delicto potior est conditio defendentis*.[238] As a result, the publican Crehan was prevented from obtaining compensation in respect of losses suffered under a beer tie agreement with the brewery Courage which allegedly infringed Article 81 EC. The Court of Appeal sought guidance under Article 234 EC as to whether this situation was compatible with the principles of effective judicial protection, and whether Community law might even prescribe more detailed rules to govern private liability in damages under Articles 81 and 82 EC.[239]

The Court of Justice began by clarifying that *any* individual can rely on a breach of Article 81 EC before the national courts, even where he/she is a party to the relevant anti-competitive contract. In particular, Article 81 EC constitutes a fundamental provision essential for the accomplishment of the Community's tasks relating to the functioning of the Internal Market. The importance of that provision led the Treaty framers

Private Law Principles in Community Law?' in T Heukels & A McDonnell (eds), *The Action for Damages in Community Law* (Kluwer Law, 1997); C Jones, *Private Enforcement of Antitrust Law in the EC, UK and USA* (OUP, 1999) esp ch 6.

238 *Gibbs Mew v Gemmell* [1998] EuLR 588.
239 *Courage v Crehan* [1999] ECC 455.

to provide expressly that all agreements prohibited by Article 81(1) EC are to be automatically void under Article 81(2) EC. That principle of automatic nullity can be relied on by anyone: an agreement which is rendered null under the Treaty has no effect as between the contracting parties, and cannot be set up against third parties.

The Court then turned to the question of seeking compensation for loss caused by an anti-competitive contract (or other conduct). It recalled how national judges must ensure that Community rules take full effect, and must protect the rights which those rules confer upon individuals. The full effectiveness of Article 81 EC would be put at risk if it were not open to any individual to claim damages for loss caused by an anti-competitive contract (or other conduct). Indeed, the existence of such a right strengthens the working of the Community competition rules and discourages agreements or practices—frequently covert—which are liable to restrict or distort competition. From that viewpoint, actions for damages before the national courts can make a significant contribution to the maintenance of effective competition in the Community. From those considerations, the Court held that there should not be any absolute bar to such an action being brought by a party to an anti-competitive contract.

However, the Court continued to observe that, in the absence of harmonised Community rules, it is for the domestic legal system of each Member State to lay down the detailed procedural rules governing actions for safeguarding rights which individuals derive directly from Community law, subject to respect for the principles of equivalence and effectiveness. In that regard, the Court recalled that Community law does not, in principle, prevent national courts from ensuring that the protection of Treaty rights does not entail the unjust enrichment of their beneficiaries. Similarly, Community law does not, in principle, preclude national law from applying the rule that litigants should not profit from their own unlawful conduct—which could justify preventing a party found to bear significant responsibility for an anti-competitive agreement from obtaining damages from the other contracting party.

For the purposes of making these assessments, the competent national court should take into account the economic and legal context of the dispute, and the respective bargaining power and conduct of the two parties to the contract. In particular, the national court should ascertain whether the party who claims to have suffered loss through concluding an anti-competitive contract found him/herself in a markedly weaker position than the other party, such as seriously to compromise or even eliminate his/her freedom to negotiate the terms of the contract and his/her capacity to avoid the loss or reduce its extent (for example) by availing him/herself in good time of all the legal remedies available. It should also be borne in mind that a contract might prove to be contrary to Article 81 EC for the sole reason that it is part of a network of similar contracts which have a cumulative effect upon competition. In such a case, a party contracting with the person controlling the network cannot bear significant responsibility for the breach of Article 81 EC, particularly where in practice the terms of the contract were imposed upon him / her by the party controlling the network.

The Court therefore concluded that Article 81 EC precludes a rule of national law under which a party to an anti-competitive contract is barred from claiming damages for loss caused by performance of that contract on the sole ground that the claimant is party to the agreement. However, Community law does not preclude a rule of national law barring a party to an anti-competitive contract from relying on his / her own unlawful actions to obtain damages where it is established that that party bears significant responsibility for the distortion of competition.[240]

Implications of Courage v Crehan

The judgment in *Courage v Crehan* is riddled with ambiguity, and has given rise to extensive academic comment.

Is there a Community Right to Damages? What at least seems clear is that *Courage v Crehan* does not mark any adaptation of the *Francovich* caselaw to the conduct of private parties—along the lines suggested by Advocate General van Gerven in *Banks v British Coal Corporation*—so as to establish some sort of 'unified approach' to non-contractual liability for breaching the Treaty. Indeed, there was no attempt by the Court to integrate the liability of private parties into the same conceptual or legal framework as that governing the conduct of the Community institutions and the Member States, based upon the 'inherency' of a right to reparation within the Treaty system, defined in accordance with the general principles common to the national legal orders and Article 288(2) EC. In particular, the Court did not direct the national judges formally to apply the substantive conditions for incurring *Francovich* liability, as established in cases such as *Brasserie de Pêcheur* and *Dillenkofer*, albeit tailored more appropriately to the context of a horizontal dispute concerning private law obligations.[241] Thus, there was no question of asking whether Article 81 EC is intended to confer rights on individuals (though it clearly satisfies that criterion); whether Courage's breach was sufficiently serious to justify imposing liability (regardless of the precise factors relevant to that assessment); and whether there was a direct causal link to the damage suffered by Crehan (even if that would in any case be left primarily to the determination of national law).[242]

[240] Case C–453/99 *Courage v Crehan* [2001] ECR I–6297.

[241] Cases C–46 & 48/93 *Brasserie du Pêcheur* and *Factortame III* [1996] ECR I–1029; Cases C–178–79 & 188–90/94 *Dillenkofer* [1996] ECR I–4845.

[242] Cf Commission, *Notice on the Cooperation Between the Commission and the Courts of the EU Member States in the Application of Articles 81 and 82 EC*, OJ 2004 C101/54, para 10(b), which

But beyond this, the question arises: should *Courage v Crehan* nevertheless be seen as authority for the existence of some sort of 'Community right to damages' against private parties—either for breach of the Treaty in general, or for infringement of the competition provisions in particular?

One view would be to focus as much on the factual and legal context of the dispute in *Courage v Crehan* as on the actual text of the judgment. There was no question that English law did, in principle, provide for a remedy in damages in respect of a breach of Article 81 EC. The only issue was whether that remedy could be withheld in the circumstances of this particular dispute, on the basis of the principle *in pari delicto potior est conditio defendentis*. That is also how the Court answered the question: the Member State cannot impose an *absolute bar* on one party to the unlawful contract seeking compensation from the other party, and any such restriction would have to be set aside as incompatible with the principles of effective judicial protection.

This might suggest that *Courage v Crehan* is no more than an ordinary application of the Court's general caselaw. All breaches of Community law must lead to judicial protection for the right-holder through the provision of some form of effective remedy; whereas English law barred the provision of the usual remedy in damages to this particular claimant, on the (potentially legitimate) grounds of *in pari delicto potior est conditio defendentis*. The principle of effectiveness was called upon to perform its usual task of determining the relationship between the Community law imperative and the presumptive national competence. But there was no need for the Court to create some 'Community remedy in damages.' It was sufficient to order the disapplication of an obstructive national rule which (by punishing non-culpable as well as entirely complicit undertakings) in fact went beyond what was necessary to achieve its own policy objectives.[243]

This relatively modest interpretation is supported by the Opinion of Advocate General Mischo in *Courage v Crehan* itself. It is also implicit in the judgment of the Court of First Instance in the *Atlantic Container Line* case, where *Courage v Crehan* was cited as authority for the proposition that, besides the basic sanction of automatic nullity, the consequences in civil law attaching to an infringement of Article 81 EC (such as an obligation to make good the damage caused to a third party or to enter into a contract) are to be determined under national law, subject to this not undermining the effectiveness of the Treaty.[244] It is perhaps telling

envisages using the *Francovich* caselaw against Member States, and *Courage v Crehan* against private parties. Contrast with, eg A Alvizou, 'Individual Tort Liability for Infringements of Community Law' (2002) 29 *Legal Issues of Economic Integration* 177; W van Gerven, 'Harmonization of Private Law: Do We Need It?' (2004) 41 CML Rev 505.

[243] Further, eg A Albors Llorens, 'The Ruling in *Courage v Crehan*: Judicial Activism or Consistent Approach?' [2002] CLJ 38.

[244] Case T–395/94 *Atlantic Container Line* [2002] ECR II–875, para 414.

(though hardly decisive) that the Court of Justice itself has also referred to *Courage v Crehan* in subsequent cases primarily as authority for the basic legal framework of national autonomy, equivalence and effectiveness.[245] If this interpretation is correct, then clearly the approach in *Courage v Crehan* is a very modest achievement in the field of harmonising national remedies, which should apply not just in some sectoral sense to the domestic enforcement of competition law, but also to any other field of Community law in which the Member State attempts to restrict access to the ordinary range of national remedies available to beneficiaries of Treaty rights.

However, another view would be to admit that, despite the particular factual and legal context of the dispute in *Courage v Crehan*, the judgment was nevertheless intended to establish the existence, in principle, of a Community-based remedy in damages in respect of private conduct which infringes the prohibition contained in Article 81 EC. After all, and by contrast with Advocate General Mischo, the Court went out of its way to stress the fundamental importance of Article 81 EC for the proper functioning of the Single Market, and the fact that the effective enforcement of Community competition law would be endangered without the availability of an action for compensation for losses suffered through an anti-competitive agreement. To that extent, *Courage* would appear to reinforce the Court's previous suggestion in *Eco Swiss* that the 'special status' of the Treaty's competition regime justifies a certain level of 'special treatment' as regards the problems posed by decentralised enforcement.[246] Moreover, whether consciously or not, such an interpretation helps to build a more uniform system of remedies before the national courts, particularly in the light of the Commission's modernisation programme—and its potential threat to the coherent cross-border application of Community competition law.[247]

How Uniform is the Community Right to Damages? But even if we were to accept (on the basis of those dicta) that the Court was consciously setting out to oblige the Member States, as a matter of Community law, to provide claimants under Article 81 EC with an action for compensation, three issues arise in determining the exact scope of that obligation and its significance for any sectoral understanding of the imperative of uniformity.

Damages, Restitution and Injunctions First, the idea that the Court created a Treaty-based right to damages would seem to make the ruling

[245] Eg Case C–276/01 *Steffensen* [2003] ECR I–3735; Case C–13/01 *Safalero* (Judgment of 11 September 2003). Also, eg AG Mischo in Case C–448/01 *EVN* (Opinion of 27 February 2003; Judgment of 4 December 2003).

[246] Case C–126/97 *Eco Swiss v Benetton* [1999] ECR I–3055.

[247] Further, eg A Komninos, 'New Prospects for Private Enforcement of EC Competition Law: *Courage v Crehan* and the Community Right to Damages' (2002) 39 CML Rev 447.

in *Courage v Crehan* more intrusive as regards national procedural autonomy than judicial practice in other circumstances. For example, the Court held in *Marshall II* that Member States are free to choose the most appropriate remedy in respect of discriminatory dismissals from employment in breach of the Equal Treatment Directive—which might consist in simple reinstatement back to one's post, rather than an action for compensatory damages.[248] Indeed, it was argued in Chapter 5 that the same philosophy may well underpin the *Francovich* caselaw, as construed in judgments such as *Maso* and *Bonifaci*, so far as concerns the public law liabilities of the Member States under Community law—creating a right to reparation, rather than a right specifically to damages, and leaving national rules a certain margin of discretion to determine the precise character such reparation might properly take.[249]

However, the fact that the Court may have gone further in *Courage v Crehan*, by indeed creating an autonomous action for compensation, does not necessarily mean that Community law will always insist upon claimants being able to pursue a remedy in damages in respect of every breach of Article 81 EC. After all, the *in pari delicto* principle meant that English law would have denied the parties to an agreement deemed illegal for contravening Article 81 EC not only the possibility of seeking compensation *inter se*, but also the availability of other remedies such as the restitution of sums paid under the void contract.[250] Of course, the preliminary reference in *Courage v Crehan* was phrased in terms of a remedy in damages. But if the Court of Appeal had instead asked the Court of Justice whether national law could absolutely prohibit the parties to an anti-competitive agreement from seeking a remedy in restitution *inter se*, it seems unlikely that the Court would have stressed the importance of damages liability for the effective enforcement of Article 81 EC. Instead, one would have expected the Court to carry to its logical conclusion the judgment in *GT-Link*, whereby the principle of effectiveness requires the availability in principle of actions for the repayment of sums paid but not due, not just as regards Member States and public undertakings, but also where the defendant is a purely private party.[251] Exactly the same approach should apply to other types of remedy deemed to form an essential component of the general Community law guarantee of effective judicial protection. For example, the ruling in *Courage v Crehan* could stand

[248] Case C–271/91 *Marshall II* [1993] ECR I–4367; Dir 76/207 on the implementation of the principle of equal treatment for men and women as regards access to employment, vocational training and promotion, and working conditions, OJ 1976 L39/40.
[249] Case C–373/95 *Maso* [1997] ECR I–4051; Cases C–94–95/95 *Bonifaci* [1997] ECR I–3969.
[250] In particular: *Gibbs Mew v Gemmell* [1998] EuLR 588.
[251] Case C–242/95 *GT-Link* [1997] ECR I–4449. Consider, eg AG Jacobs in Cases C–261 & 262/01 *Van Calster* (Opinion of 10 April 2003; Judgment of 21 October 2003). Further, eg A Jones, 'Recovery of Benefits Conferred Under Contractual Obligations Prohibited by Article 81 or 82 of the Treaty of Rome' (1996) 112 LQR 606.

as authority for the idea that national law should provide not only a remedy in damages, but also (in appropriate circumstances) for injunctive relief, in respect of anti-competitive conduct which breaches Article 81 EC.[252]

All of this merely reflects the elementary idea that the most appropriate remedy to secure effective judicial protection in any given situation will not necessarily be financial compensation. Other types of relief (including restitutionary actions, injunctions, and specific relief) might well be preferable depending on the circumstances of the relevant dispute. One would expect Community law to furnish claimants with one or more from among that range of remedies, as the situation demands; or at least to respect the competence of Member States to restrict the availability of damages, where a functionally equivalent form of relief was offered under national law, and the claimant failed to take advantage of it, or to do so within the applicable time-limits.[253]

Negative, Not Positive, Harmonisation Secondly, insofar as a Community action for damages has indeed been established in principle, that remedy is clearly being developed on the basis of the ordinary negative harmonisation model, not through systematic positive harmonisation by the Court.

Consider, for example, the Court's guidance as to the precise circumstances in which private parties will incur liability in damages for a breach of Article 81 EC. It is clear from *Courage v Crehan* that Member States may restrict the availability of relief (for example) where the parties negotiated an anti-competitive contract from an equal bargaining position and there is a genuine risk that the claimant might benefit from his/her own wrongdoing; whereas the Member State cannot rule out judicial protection (for example) where the claimant occupied a position of relative weakness in concluding the relevant agreement, and therefore cannot be held responsible to any significant degree for its anti-competitive terms or effects.[254] On its face, this might look like the setting of Community rules on the thresholds of culpability required to incur liability—similar to (even if not directly based upon) the idea of a 'sufficiently serious breach' under the *Francovich* caselaw, albeit suited to the private law context of the dispute, and focusing as much on the contribution of the claimant as on the behaviour of the defendant.

However, it seems more accurate to say that the Court's reasoning is based firmly upon the presumption of national autonomy, subject to ad hoc surveillance through the principles of equivalence and effectiveness: the Member State is applying its own national rules prohibiting unjust

[252] Consider, eg AG Jacobs in Cases C–264, 306, 354, & 355/01 *AOK Bundesverband* (Opinion of 22 May 2003; Judgment of 16 March 2004).

[253] Further, eg O Odudu and J Edelman, 'Compensatory Damages for Breach of Article 81' (2002) 27 EL Rev 327.

[254] For critical comments about the Court's approach here, see G Monti, 'Anticompetitive Agreements: The Innocent Party's Right to Damages' (2002) 27 EL Rev 282.

enrichment or profiting from one's own wrong; Community law is relevant only for the purpose of scrutinising whether those national rules are being applying in an unreasonable manner. In fact, the Court made no attempt to prescribe, as a matter of Community law, the substantive conditions which national courts must apply to determine private liability in damages under Article 81 EC. To that extent, the legal framework for private liability as regards the Treaty's competition rules (as developed under *Courage v Crehan*) is capable of differing from Member State to Member State to an even more considerable degree than the legal framework for Member State liability (as developed under *Francovich*) which was transposed into the context of Community competition law by the Court in *GT-Link*.[255]

Similar analysis applies to other important aspects of our 'Community right to compensation' against private parties who have breached Article 81 EC: for example, the rules on calculating recoverable damages (in particular, whether there should be a system of double or triple damages); and the procedural conditions for bringing an action before the domestic courts (such as the applicable rules on admissibility of evidence, and limitation periods for commencing proceedings). Of course, the Court was not asked to deal with these issues directly in *Courage v Crehan*, but the explicit reference to national autonomy (subject to the principles of equivalence and effectiveness) clearly indicates that only minimum Community requirements will be imposed, in accordance with the general caselaw discussed in Chapter 5.

On the one hand, it might therefore seem fair to say that the system of private liability in damages for breaching Article 81 EC, as established by the Court in *Courage v Crehan*, lies closer to the model provided by the *Factortame* judgment on interim relief against national measures which are allegedly in breach of the Treaty (whereby a remedy must be available in principle, but its substantive and procedural conditions are presumptively for domestic law),[256] than to the model adopted in cases like *Francovich* on the right to reparation against Member States for having breached their public law obligations under the Treaty (whereby a remedy must be available in principle, and its basic substantive conditions are determined under Community law, even if the procedural conditions are presumptively left to national law).[257]

On the other hand, it is perhaps instructive to consider experience with the Court's caselaw on the reimbursement by Member States of unlawful taxes. It was established in *Pigs and Bacon Commission v McCarren* that Community law confers directly upon individuals the right to recover

[255] Case C–242/95 *GT-Link* [1997] ECR I–4449.
[256] Case C–213/89 *Ex p Factortame* [1990] ECR I–2433.
[257] Cases C–6 & 9/90 *Francovich* [1991] ECR I–5357.

charges levied by the national authorities in breach of the Treaty.[258] However, the Court has consistently held that the conditions under which that Community right to recovery must be exercised are a matter for national law, subject to the principles of equivalence and effectiveness. As regards issues such as the payment of interest and the imposition of limitation periods, that approach remains true in both letter and spirit.[259] In other respects, however, it is perhaps true to say that the Court now pays little more than lip-service to the idea of domestic competence. Community intervention through the principle of effectiveness has reached such an extent as to amount de facto to positive harmonisation of the circumstances in which Member States may legitimately resist claims for reimbursement.[260] For example, the Court in judgments such as *FMC* and *Fantask* made clear that liability to repay is imposed upon the defaulting Member State on the basis of illegality per se; national rules cannot require proof of the existence of fault or unreasonableness on the part of the relevant public authorities.[261] In fact, the only defence available to the Member State faced within an action for recovery is to argue that the quantum due for reimbursement should be reduced to the extent that the claimant would otherwise be unjustly enriched, having already passed on a proportion of the charge to his/her customers.[262] Moreover, successful reliance upon this defence is subject to strict conditions concerning the allocation of the burden of proof—in effect, requiring the national authorities to demonstrate on a case-by-case basis the existence of both passing on and unjust enrichment, and limiting the claimant's possible obligations to cooperation as regards access to relevant documentation (such as the undertaking's balance sheets).[263]

Against that background, one might speculate that the Court's negative harmonisation approach to domestic rules on unjust enrichment in *Courage v Crehan* will not necessarily mark the end of the story for

[258] Case 177/78 *Pigs and Bacon Commission v McCarren* [1979] ECR 2161.

[259] As regards interest, eg Case 26/74 *Roquette Frères* [1976] ECR 677; Cases C–279–81/96 *Ansaldo Energia* [1998] ECR I–5025; Cases C–397 & 410/98 *Metallgesellschaft* [2001] ECR I–1727. As regards limitation periods, eg Case C–231/96 *Edis* [1998] ECR I–4951; Case C–228/96 *Aprile* [1998] ECR I–7141; Case C–88/99 *Roquette Frères* [2000] ECR I–10465; Cases C–216 & 222/99 *Prisco* [2002] ECR I–6761.

[260] Further: M Dougan, 'Cutting Your Losses in the Enforcement Deficit: A Community Right to the Recovery of Unlawfully Levied Charges?' (1998) 1 *Cambridge Yearbook of European Legal Studies* 233. Also, eg LJ Smith, 'A European Concept of Condictio Indebiti' (1982) 19 CML Rev 269; K Magliveras, 'Unjust Enrichment and Restitution in Community Law' (1997) 6 *Irish Journal of European Law* 190; A Biondi and L Johnson, 'The Right to Recovery of Charges Levied in Breach of Community Law: No Small Matter' (1998) 4 *European Public Law* 313.

[261] Case C–212/94 *FMC* [1996] ECR I–389; Case C–188/95 *Fantask* [1997] ECR I–6783.

[262] In particular: Case 68/79 *Hans Just* [1980] ECR 501. Also, eg Case 61/79 *Denkavit* [1980] ECR 1205; Case 130/79 *Express Dairy Foods* [1980] ECR 1887; Case 811/79 *Ariete* [1980] ECR 2545; Case 826/79 *MIRECO* [1980] ECR 2559; Cases 142–43/80 *Essevi and Salengo* [1981] ECR 1413.

[263] Eg Case 199/82 *San Giorgio* [1983] ECR 3595; Case 104/86 *Commission v Italy* [1988] ECR 1799; Cases 331, 376 & 378/85 *Bianco* [1988] ECR 1099; Cases C–192–218/95 *Comateb* [1997] ECR I–165; Cases C–441 & 442/98 *Mikhailidis* [2000] ECR I–7145; Case C–343/96 *Dilexport* [1999] ECR I–579; Case C–147/01 *Weber's Wine World* (Judgment of 2 October 2003); Case C–129/00 *Commission v Italy* (Judgment of 9 December 2003).

Community intervention in national procedural autonomy.[264] That would be particularly true, insofar as Community law will provide not only an action for damages, but also (as suggested above) an action for restitution of sums paid but not due—the latter being particularly apt for transposition of the detailed caselaw concerning allocation of the burden of proof as regards unjust enrichment and passing on by the payor. But in the meantime, having regard to the overall legal framework for exercising the Community right to damages against private parties who have breached Article 81 EC, there are good grounds for querying whether this action is really uniform enough to meet the genuine needs of Community competition law. Indeed, some commentators have already called for intervention by the Community legislature, so as to establish harmonised conditions for private liability in damages under the ruling in *Courage v Crehan*, and thereby prevent distortions in the conditions of competition and possible forum-shopping by undertakings across the Member States.[265]

Beyond Article 81 EC to Other Treaty Activities? Thirdly, it remains to be seen whether the Community action for damages against private parties, as established in *Courage v Crehan*, will extend beyond Article 81 EC to cover individual liability as regards breach of other Treaty norms. One would certainly expect the Court's reasoning to benefit also the victims of abusive market conduct as perpetrated by dominant undertakings under Article 82 EC—as regards which it seems even less likely that national rules purporting to withhold a remedy on grounds of unjust enrichment and profiting from one's own wrong could survive scrutiny under the principle of effectiveness.

Nevertheless, it seems unlikely that *Courage v Crehan* will be limited in its potential scope of application to Community competition law. After all, the Court's reasoning was based primarily upon the imperative of effectiveness in the enforcement of Treaty rules, rather than their simple uniformity across the Member States. As such, the Community action for damages against private parties could, in principle, apply to other policies essential for the functioning of the Internal Market, such as the provisions on free movement of persons, which are now recognised as having horizontal direct effect.[266] Furthermore, Articles 2 and 3 EC entrust the Community with many other tasks than achieving market integration across the Member States, tasks which many commentators

[264] A view shared by, eg A Komninos, 'New Prospects for Private Enforcement of EC Competition Law: *Courage v Crehan* and the Community Right to Damages' (2002) 39 CML Rev 447; C Kremer, 'Liability for Breach of European Community Law: An Analysis of the New Remedy in the Light of English and German Law' (2003) 22 *Yearbook of European Law* 203.
[265] Eg A Jones and D Beard, 'Co-Contractors, Damages and Article 81: The ECJ Finally Speaks' [2002] ECLR 247; E Ballon, Annotation of *Courage v Crehan* (2002) 8 *Columbia Journal of European Law* 499.
[266] In particular: Case 36/74 *Walrave and Koch* [1974] ECR 1405; Case C–415/93 *Bosman* [1995] ECR I–4921; Case C–281/98 *Angonese* [2000] I-4139; Case C–411/98 *Ferlini* [2000] ECR I–8081.

believe are equally fundamental in defining the character of European integration: for example, the strengthening of consumer protection, and achieving a high level of social protection.[267] In these cases too, the existence of a basic Community right to compensation before the national courts could make a significant contribution to the effective functioning of the applicable Treaty rules and secondary legislation.[268]

This is not to say that the same sorts of national rule will require scrutiny through the principle of effectiveness in disputes about competition law as in cases concerning consumer or employment rights, or that the same sorts of result will be required to ensure that exercise of the relevant individual rights is not rendered virtually impossible or excessively difficult.[269] But it is to observe that, by establishing no more than a minimalist principle of private liability in damages, without further steps towards harmonising the necessary substantive and procedural conditions, the Court in *Courage v Crehan* has created a Community remedy which lacks any necessary connection to the enforcement of the Treaty's competition rules, and which is capable of applying to any sector of Community regulatory activity imposing enforceable rights and obligations between individuals, regardless of the degree of substantive uniformity pursued thereunder.[270]

Assessment

There are certain respects in which the peculiar characteristics of the competition law sector have necessitated a special approach to the question of national procedural autonomy.

That is true, in particular, of the obligations of cooperation between members of the modernised enforcement network which the Court has derived from Article 10 EC, and which have specific implications for the conduct of domestic judicial proceedings in cases which might affect the exercise by the Commission of its own investigatory powers. Yet even here, the caselaw suggests a certain reticence on the part of the Community courts to interfere extensively with national

[267] Further: ch 2 (above).

[268] Also: A Komninos, 'New Prospects for Private Enforcement of EC Competition Law: *Courage v Crehan* and the Community Right to Damages' (2002) 39 CML Rev 447.

[269] Eg consider the very different legal framework provided by Dir 76/207 on the implementation of the principle of equal treatment for men and women as regards access to employment, vocational training and promotion, and working conditions, OJ 1976 L39/40 (as construed by the Court, eg in Case C–177/88 *Dekker* [1990] ECR I–3941; Case C–180/95 *Draehmpaehl* [1997] ECR I–2195).

[270] However, the Court's denial that the Treaty rules on state aids impose any obligations directly upon recipient undertakings (consider, in particular, Case C–39/94 *SFEI* [1996] ECR I–3547) makes it unlikely that *Courage v Crehan* will apply in horizontal disputes concerning Arts 87–88 EC. Further, eg M Ross, 'Decentralisation, Effectiveness and Modernisation: Contradictions in Terms?' in A Biondi, P Eeckhout & J Flynn (eds), *The Law of State Aid in the European Union* (OUP, 2004).

procedural autonomy, through the principle of effectiveness, even where this would could significantly facilitate effective coordination between the competent centralised and decentralised authorities: consider, for example, *Postbank* on the obligations of domestic judges to respect professional secrecy; and *Roquette Frères* on the rules governing protection of the identity of informants in competition investigations. But we have seen that this reticence simply reflects a more general trend in the caselaw concerning the enforcement of Articles 81 and 82 EC, as epitomised in judgments such as *Otto v Postbank* and *Eco Swiss v Benetton*: the Court has chosen not to pursue any more far-reaching degree of remedial or procedural harmonisation than the general model embodied in its current caselaw, whatever its failings in terms of achieving fair and equal conditions of competition within the Single Market.

Recent developments centred around the judgment in *Courage v Crehan* have clearly advanced the *effective* enforcement of Community competition law, especially when located within the broader context of the Commission's modernisation programme. Indeed, the guarantee that every Member State will provide for the possibility of damages liability (in appropriate cases) for infringements of Articles 81 and 82 EC amounts to a significant contribution to the practical success of the reforms initiated by the 1999 White Paper and culminating in Regulation 1/2003. However, it seems more difficult to argue that *Courage v Crehan* so clearly advances the cause of securing the *uniform* enforcement of Community competition law. Indeed, whether one supports the traditional 'integration through law' or an alternative 'sectoral' interpretation of the Community's enforcement deficit, the Court's approach does not mark any radical departure from its previous caselaw—establishing certain minimum standards of judicial protection it is true, and perhaps even tailored in some way to the specific needs of competition policy, but still falling far short of creating a centralised framework of private liability in a sector of Community activity where it is possible to construct a plausible case for uniformity in the conditions for decentralised enforcement.

All of this suggests that the Court approaches the Community's enforcement deficit without any clear or confident conception of the appropriate role to be performed by the imperative of uniformity, and demonstrates that the Court's continued attempts to regulate national remedies and procedural rules remain difficult to explain by reference to the sort of sectoral model developed in Chapter 4 alone.[271]

[271] This interpretation is further supported by reference to Cases C–58, 75, 112, 119, 123, 135, 140–41, 154 & 157/95 *Gallotti* [1996] ECR I–4345: Dir 91/156 on waste, OJ 1991 L78/32 was adopted under Art 175 EC on environmental policy, and thus demanded only minimum standards of Community intervention in the Member State's remedial competence; but the ECJ also hinted that the same approach would have applied even if the measure had been adopted under Art 95 EC with a view to equalising conditions of economic competition within the Internal Market.

7

Conclusion

The findings of this study may be summarised as follows.

Traditional understandings of the Community's enforcement deficit focus on the idea of 'integration through law': the purpose of the Treaty is to advance the economic, social and/or political convergence of the European states; a vital component in achieving this objective is the construction of a legal order committed to the twin ideals of uniformity and effectiveness in the formulation and application of Community norms. Against this background, national remedies and procedural rules are portrayed as presenting a serious problem, through their tendency to offer inadequate and, in any case, fragmented standards of enforcement in respect of Treaty norms. The solution is to manufacture—by either legislative or, if necessary, judicial means—a harmonised system of legal protection within Europe.

Although many commentators have criticised this analysis in light of the practical, political and cultural problems posed by Community intervention in the domestic systems of justice, few have actually challenged the internal assumptions of integration and uniformity upon which it is based. Yet the recent history of European union suggests that the time is ripe for these assumptions to be reconsidered and updated. Differentiation has attained the status of a central regulatory principle within the Community legal order, supported by important socio-political forces operating within the fabric of the European project. This development prompts a process of doctrinal reconsideration, seeking to update certain assumptions about the Treaty system which are too closely wedded to an untenable ideal of integration.

Such a process of doctrinal reconsideration extends to traditional analysis of the Community's enforcement deficit. The Treaty project is now as much about managing diversity as it is about promoting integration. Community law has a valid role in accommodating both these aims. Accordingly, the idea of some overarching principle of regulatory uniformity must be refined, and with it the assumptions *both* that national remedies and procedures necessarily frustrate substantive Community objectives *and* that their harmonisation would necessarily represent the most appropriate solution. What is suggested instead is a 'sectoral approach' to the enforcement deficit. The demand for uniformity at both a substantive and a remedial level is purely relative, changing according to the field of Community activity in question. In some sectors (such as state aids and competition law), uniformity remains a valid goal of Treaty policy, and the harmonisation of domestic remedies and procedural rules might well seem justified. In other sectors (such as environmental, consumer and employee protection), the Treaty does not appear to harbour ambitions of achieving any genuine degree of regulatory uniformity, and the principles of subsidiarity and proportionality suggest that we should adopt a correspondingly more restrained interpretation of the need for remedial approximation.

While acknowledging the limitations of this 'sectoral approach' insofar as it might purport to represent some practical legislative blueprint, one can still emphasise its strengths as a critical conceptual tool by which to analyse the Court of Justice's volatile caselaw on national remedies and procedural rules. In this regard, three main observations seem pertinent.

First, the most recent phase in the Court's jurisprudence—as illustrated in fields such as the *Francovich* right to reparation, and the imposition of domestic limitation periods—rejects implicitly the pressure for greater remedial harmonisation exerted by a traditional 'integration through law' analysis, and flirts instead with the challenges of doctrinal reconsideration stimulated by the rise of regulatory differentiation within the Community legal order. In particular, the general remedies caselaw reflects a more limited sympathy with the imperative of uniformity, both as regards its role within the contemporary Treaty order in general, and as a legitimate policy aspiration for the Community's developing procedural competence in particular, such as forms the basic conceptual premises of our alternative 'sectoral model'.

Secondly, the general trend of mere negative approximation which has dominated the recent caselaw provides an adequate standard for Community intervention in the national systems of judicial protection, on grounds of securing the uniform application of Treaty norms, in respect of sectors such as environmental, consumer and social policy. It is arguable that this general trend is also appropriate for related aspects of the Internal Market. The ideal of free movement across a regulatory level playing-field has been compromised by the Treaty's commitment to pursuing higher standards of social protection within the process of economic integration itself, and thus by the Treaty's need to furnish a legal infrastructure capable of accommodating differences in the capacity and willingness of the various Member States to agree a common welfare agenda. Against such a background, some degree of diversity in the mechanisms available for decentralised enforcement cannot be described as inherently incompatible with the contemporary process of Community market-building.

Thirdly, it is nevertheless possible to identity certain sectors of Community policy, intimately related to the functioning of the Single

Market, which remain relatively untouched by the process of regulatory differentiation, and may thus claim a legitimate interest in attaining some more advanced state of remedial harmonisation so as to safeguard the goal of uniformity still being pursued at a substantive level.[1] In this regard, the caselaw on state aids demonstrates that the Court of Justice is sometimes prepared to recognise and address this problem head-on. However, the caselaw on the domestic enforcement of Treaty competition policy suggests that the Court's approach is not entirely consistent, creating a genuine enforcement deficit through undesirable inequalities in the standards of judicial protection available to economic undertakings operating on the Community market which remains to be resolved by future judicial or legislative intervention.

It seems generally agreed that the Court's caselaw on national remedies and procedural rules reveals an underlying sense of uncertainty about the optimal allocation of competence in the decentralised enforcement of Treaty norms as between the Community and its Member States. It would be tempting to conclude, on the basis of this study, that there are good grounds, in particular, for suspecting that the Court approaches the enforcement deficit without any clear understanding of the appropriate role to be performed by the imperative of uniformity.

However, it is one thing to apply a framework of analysis which assesses the sectoral credentials of the current law in an objective manner—finding that the caselaw in some respects fulfils, and in other respects frustrates, the Community's legitimate interest in harmonising the domestic standards of judicial protection. But it might seem premature to draw from that assessment any necessary conclusions about the subjective policy preferences of the Court of Justice itself. In particular, the apparently haphazard judicial approach to the division between Community and Member State competences evidenced in the caselaw may well be the result, not of any fundamental conceptual diffidence as regards the nature and scope of the imperative of uniformity *per se*, but rather of an underlying sense of institutional insecurity on the part of the Court as regards its relations with other key players in the Treaty's legal order. Indeed, future research might build upon the findings of the present study by seeking explanations for the evolving caselaw in the complex institutional position of the Court of Justice.[2]

[1] Leaving aside the caselaw on decentralised enforcement against the Community institutions as discussed in ch 6 (above).

[2] From a massive literature on the ECJ's institutional position, a representative survey would include: Lord Slynn, 'The Court of Justice of the European Communities' (1984) 33 ICLQ 409; H Rasmussen, *On Law and Policy in the European Court of Justice* (Martinus Nijhoff, 1986); M Cappelletti, 'Is the European Court of Justice "Running Wild"?' (1987) 12 EL Rev 3; G Mancini, 'The Making of a Constitution for Europe' (1989) 26 CML Rev 595; K Lenaerts, 'Some Thoughts About the Interaction Between Judges and Politicians in the European

This position embraces the very real practical limitations of the Court as a lawmaking body. Legal development through the process of litigation suffers from several well-known flaws, for example: the ad hoc and uncontrolled manner by which issues are presented to the courts for resolution; and the inevitable influence of the particular factual circumstances of each dispute upon the more abstract legal principles enunciated by the judges. Such flaws are exacerbated within the context of litigation before the Court of Justice: for example, whether sitting in chambers or plenary session, the body is bound to speak with a single voice, and thus to find some acceptable consensus between the differing opinions which must inevitably emerge between the judges, perhaps to the detriment of clear and/or confident lawmaking.[3] For such reasons, many commentators have queried whether any process of remedial harmonisation would not better be entrusted to the systematic consideration of the Treaty's political institutions.[4]

These concerns help to highlight related difficulties over the Court's constitutional relationship with the Treaty legislature. As regards the period from the 1970s until the late 1980s/early 1990s, many commentators believe that the Court enjoyed a valid mandate to take the lead in developing the legal framework of European integration, to overcome the vacuum at the heart of the Treaty system caused by the stagnant political energy of institutions such as Council, Commission and

Community' (1992) 12 *Yearbook of European Law* 1; J Weiler, 'Journey to an Unknown Destination: A Retrospective and Prospective of the European Court of Justice in the Arena of Political Integration' (1993) 31 JCMS 417; T Hartley, 'The European Court, Judicial Objectivity and the Constitution of the European Union' (1996) 112 LQR 95; A Arnull, 'The European Court and Judicial Objectivity: A Reply to Professor Hartley' (1996) 112 LQR 411; P Kapteyn, 'The Court of Justice After Amsterdam: Taking Stock' in T Heukels, N Blokker & M Brus (eds), *The European Union After Amsterdam: A Legal Analysis* (Kluwer Law International, 1998); A-M Slaughter, A Stone Sweet & J Weiler (eds), *The European Court and National Courts: Doctrine and Jurisprudence* (Hart Publishing, 1998); A Albors Llorens, 'The European Court of Justice, More Than a Teleological Court' (1999) 2 *Cambridge Yearbook of European Legal Studies* 373; T Hartley, *Constitutional Problems of the European Union* (Hart Publishing, 1999) ch 3; M Shapiro, 'The European Court of Justice' in P Craig & G de Búrca (eds), *The Evolution of EU Law* (OUP, 1999).

[3] Eg F Snyder, 'The Effectiveness of European Community Law: Institutions, Processes, Tools and Techniques' (1993) 56 MLR 19; Editorial, 'Safeguarding the Union's Legal Order?' (1994) 31 CML Rev 687; G Mancini, 'Crosscurrents and the Tide at the European Court of Justice' (1995) 4 *Irish Journal of European Law* 120; T Tridimas, 'The Court of Justice and Judicial Activism' (1996) 21 EL Rev 199.

[4] Eg C Himsworth, 'Things Fall Apart: The Harmonisation of Community Judicial Procedural Protection Revisited' (1997) 22 EL Rev 291; L Neville Brown, 'National Protection of Community Rights: Reconciling Autonomy and Effectiveness' in J Lonbay & A Biondi (eds), *Remedies for Breach of EC Law* (Wiley, 1997); J Steiner, 'The Limits of State Liability for Breach of European Community Law' (1998) 4 *European Public Law* 69; R Craufurd Smith, 'Remedies for Breaches of EU Law in National Courts: Legal Variation and Selection' in P Craig & G de Búrca (eds), *The Evolution of EU Law* (OUP, 1999).

Parliament.[5] This was true across a range of policy fields: from the principles of direct effect and supremacy; to the free movement of goods, persons and services within the Common Market; and indeed the standards of judicial protection offered by the Member States. However, since at least the early 1990s, the Community legislature has proven itself willing and able to reassert its pre-eminent (and more democratically defensible) role in shaping Treaty policy—in particular, by adopting legislation to address the threat to substantive Community norms allegedly posed by inadequate and/or fragmented domestic remedies and procedural rules.[6] One might wonder whether the legislature's increasing willingness to resolve the enforcement deficit for itself has undermined the legitimacy of the Court's caselaw, or at least of any more ambitious judicial attempts at remedial harmonisation. After all, several Advocates General and the Court itself have recently suggested that, whilst uniformity may remain a valid and indeed essential component of Treaty regulation, responsibility for drawing up any more advanced plans for Community intervention in national remedial and procedural law lies with the Commission, Council and Parliament.[7]

However, such influences cannot be considered decisive. The Court clearly felt sufficiently secure of its own lawmaking mandate to deliver relatively intrusive judgments such as *Alcan* or *Köbler*, even after the political institutions had found their legislative teeth and the great era of judicially-led European integration passed into history.[8] Moreover, the Community legislature's efforts in the sphere of the enforcement deficit remain relatively limited, leaving significant regulatory gaps within

[5] Eg K Lenaerts, 'Some Thoughts About the Interaction Between Judges and Politicians in the European Community' (1992) 12 *Yearbook of European Law* 1; A Arnull, 'Judging the New Europe' (1994) 19 EL Rev 3; N Fennelly, 'Where Power Now Lies: Institutional Reform' (1998) 7 *Irish Journal of European Law* 10. Cf H Rasmussen, *On Law and Policy in the European Court of Justice* (Martinus Nijhoff, 1986).

[6] Eg Dir 84/450 concerning misleading and comparative advertising, OJ 1984 L250/17; Dir 89/665 on public supply, works and service contracts, OJ 1989 L395/33; Dir 92/13 coordinating the laws, regulations and administrative provisions relating to the application of Community rules on the procurement procedures of entities operating in the water, energy, transport and telecommunications sectors, OJ 1992 L76/14; Reg 2988/95 on the protection of the European Communities' financial interests, OJ 1995 L312/1; Dir 97/80 on the burden of proof in cases of discrimination based on sex, OJ 1998 L14/6; Dir 98/27 on injunctions for the protection of consumers' interests, OJ 1998 L166/51; Dir 99/44 on certain aspects of the sale of consumer goods and associated guarantees, OJ 1999 L171/12. Not to say the Community's competence to harmonise civil procedure rules under Art 65 EC: see chs 1 and 2 (above).

[7] Eg Case C–290/91 *Johannes Peter* [1993] ECR I–2981; Case C–132/95 *Jensen and Korn* [1998] ECR I–2975; Case C–298/96 *Oelmühle Hamburg* [1998] ECR I–4767; Case C–231/96 *Edis* [1998] ECR I–4951; Case C–260/96 *Spac* [1998] ECR I–4997; Cases C–279–81/96 *Ansaldo Energia* [1998] ECR I–5025; Case C–228/96 *Aprile* [1998] ECR I–7141; Case C–343/96 *Dilexport* [1999] ECR I–579.

[8] Case C–24/95 *Alcan* [1997] ECR I–1591; Case C–224/01 *Köbler* (Judgment of 30 September 2003).

which judicial creativity might still enjoy some credible freedom of manoeuvre.[9] For example, Advocate General Cosmas in the *France v Ladbroke Racing and Commission* was adamant that, in the continuing absence of legislative intervention, the Court was justified in pursuing for itself the Community-level harmonisation of remedies and procedural rules required to ensure the fair and equal application of Articles 87 and 88 EC as regards the recovery of unlawful state aids before the national courts.[10] Similarly, the Commission's failure to endorse proposals for harmonising the domestic standards of judicial protection within the context of its programme for greater decentralised enforcement of Articles 81 and 82 EC might be interpreted as an invitation to legitimate judicial action.[11] Yet, whereas in the situation of state aids, the Court has indeed embarked upon an ambitious campaign of remedial harmonisation, in the context of competition policy, it has pursued the minimalist strategy evidenced by *Otto v Postbank* and *Eco Swiss v Benetton*.[12] The judgment in *Courage v Crehan* has been widely interpreted as marking the beginning of a new and more integrationist approach to the domestic enforcement of Articles 81 and 82 EC—though we have argued that, for the time being, such an interpretation must rely upon a certain degree of wishful thinking.[13]

Thus, the relationship between judiciary and legislature is clearly relevant, but cannot in itself offer an entirely convincing explanation for the Court's current approach to the imperative of uniformity—particularly when viewed from a sectoral perspective. Other factors might therefore warrant investigation, such as the Court's delicate process of dialogue with the national courts—essential but often temperamental partners in the tasks of elaborating a European judicial order, and of enforcing Community rules in practice;[14] and the impact upon judicial confidence

[9] Cf the ECJ's observations on the scope of its own judicial function in Cases C–46 & 48/93 *Brasserie du Pêcheur* and *Factortame III* [1996] ECR I–1029, paras 24–27.

[10] AG Cosmas in Case C–83/98P *France v Ladbroke Racing and Commission* [2000] ECR I–3271, paras 86f Opinion.

[11] Further: chs 4 and 6 (above).

[12] Case C–60/92 *Otto v Postbank* [1993] ECR I–5683; Case C–126/97 *Eco Swiss v Benetton* [1999] ECR I–3055.

[13] Case C–453/99 *Courage v Crehan* [2001] ECR I–6297.

[14] Eg J Weiler, 'Journey to an Unknown Destination: A Retrospective and Prospective of the European Court of Justice in the Arena of Political Integration' (1993) 31 JCMS 417; I Maher, 'National Courts as European Community Courts' (1994) 14 LS 226; D Chalmers, 'Judicial Preferences and the Community Legal Order' (1997) 60 MLR 164; K Alter, 'Explaining National Court Acceptance of European Court Jurisprudence: A Critical Evaluation of Theories of Legal Integration' in A-M Slaughter, A Stone Sweet & J Weiler (eds), *The European Court and National Courts: Doctrine and Jurisprudence* (Hart Publishing, 1998); A Biondi, 'The European Court of Justice and Certain National Procedural Limitations: Not Such a Tough Relationship' (1999) 36 CML Rev 1271.

of the sometimes hostile reactions of the Member States—the 'masters of the Treaty' on whose tacit acceptance the Court's authority might ultimately appear to rest.[15]

In short: the twin goals of both understanding the Court's underlying attitude towards the imperative of uniformity as a matter of theory, and ascertaining the true possibilities for adopting a genuinely 'sectoral approach' to resolution of the Community's enforcement deficit as a matter of practice, are inextricably intertwined with wider and as-yet-unresolved considerations relating to the Court's self-perception and sense of purpose. Indeed, one might ultimately feel pressed towards the conclusion that remedial harmonisation (whether based on the traditional 'integration through law' or an alternative 'sectoral' model) is a task to which the Court is inherently unsuited.

[15] Eg B Fitzpatrick and E Szyszczak, 'Remedies and Effective Judicial Protection in Community Law' (1994) 57 MLR 434; G Mancini, 'Crosscurrents and the Tide at the European Court of Justice' (1995) 4 *Irish Journal of European Law* 120; S Weatherill, 'Beyond "EC Law Rights, National Remedies"' in A Caiger & D A Floudas (eds), *1996 Onwards: Lowering the Barriers Further* (Wiley, 1996).

Select Bibliography

This bibliography seeks to provide only a representative sample of the relevant academic literature. The footnotes to individual chapters contain extensive further references.

ALBORS LLORENS A, *Private Parties in European Community Law: Challenging Community Measures* (Clarendon Press, 1996)

—— 'The Standing of Private Parties to Challenge Community Measures: Has the European Court Missed the Boat?' (2003) *Cambridge Law Journal* 72

ANAGNOSTARAS G, 'The Allocation of Responsibility in State Liability Actions for Breach of Community Law: A Modern Gordian Knot?' (2001) 26 *European Law Review* 139

—— 'State Liability and Alternative Courses of Action: How Independent Can an Autonomous Remedy Be?' (2002) 21 *Yearbook of European Law* 355

ARMSTRONG K, 'Legal Integration: Theorising the Legal Dimension of European Integration' (1998) 36 *Journal of Common Market Studies* 155

ARNULL A, 'Private Applicants and the Action for Annulment Under Article 230 of the EC Treaty' (1995) 32 *Common Market Law Review* 7

—— 'Private Applicants and the Action for Annulment Since *Codorniu*' (2001) 38 *Common Market Law Review* 7

BAKER E, 'Criminal Jurisdiction, the Public Dimension to "Effective Protection" and the Construction of Community-Citizen Relations' (2001) 4 *Cambridge Yearbook of European Legal Studies* 25

BARAV A, 'Enforcement of Community Rights in the National Courts: The Case for Jurisdiction to Grant an Interim Relief' (1989) 26 *Common Market Law Review* 369

BARNARD C, *EC Employment Law* (OUP, 2000)

—— 'Social Dumping and the Race to the Bottom: Some Lessons for the European Union from Delaware?' (2000) 25 *European Law Review* 57

BARNARD C & SCOTT J (eds), *The Legal Foundations of the Single Market: Unpacking the Premises* (Hart Publishing, 2002)

BEATSON J & Tridimas T (eds), *New Directions in European Public Law* (Hart Publishing, 1998)

BEAUMONT P, LYONS C & WALKER N (eds), *Convergence and Divergence in European Public Law* (Hart Publishing, 2002)

BERNARD N, 'The Future of European Economic Law in the Light of the Principle of Subsidiarity' (1996) 33 *Common Market Law Review* 633

—— *Multilevel Governance in the European Union* (Kluwer Law International, 2002)

BIONDI A, 'The European Court of Justice and Certain National Procedural Limitations: Not Such a Tough Relationship' (1999) 36 *Common Market Law Review* 1271

—— EECKHOUT P & FLYNN J (eds), *The Law of State Aid in the European Union* (OUP, 2004)

BOVIS C, *The Liberalisation of Public Procurement and its Effects on the Common Market* (Ashgate, 1998)

BREALEY M and HOSKINS M, *Remedies in EC Law: Law and Practice in the English and EC Courts* (Sweet & Maxwell, 1998)

BRIDGE J, 'Procedural Aspects of the Enforcement of European Community Law through the Legal Systems of the Member States' (1984) 9 *European Law Review* 28

BRONCKERS M, 'Private Enforcement of 1992: Do Trade and Industry Stand a Chance Against the Member States?' (1989) 26 *Common Market Law Review* 513

DE BÚRCA G, 'Giving Effect to European Community Directives' (1992) 55 *Modern Law Review* 215

—— 'The Principle of Proportionality and its Application in EC law' (1993) 13 *Yearbook of European Law* 105

DE BÚRCA G & SCOTT J (eds), *Constitutional Change in the EU: From Uniformity to Flexibility?* (Hart Publishing, 2000)

CAPORASO J, 'The European Union and Forms of State: Westphalian, Regulatory or Post-Modern?' (1996) 34 *Journal of Common Market Studies* 29

CARANTA R, 'Judicial Protection Against Member States: A New *Jus Commune* Takes Shape' (1995) 32 *Common Market Law Review* 703

—— 'Learning from our Neighbours: Public Law Remedies, Homogenisation from Bottom Up' (1997) 4 *Maastricht Journal of European and Comparative Law* 220

CHALMERS D, 'Judicial Preferences and the Community Legal Order' (1997) 60 *Modern Law Review* 164

CHITI M P, 'Towards a Unified Judicial Protection in Europe(?)' (1997) 9 *European Review of Public Law* 553

CHRYSSOCHOOU D, 'New Challenges to the Study of European Integration: Implications for Theory-Building' (1997) 35 *Journal of Common Market Studies* 521

CRAIG P, '*Francovich*, Remedies and the Scope of Damages Liability' (1993) 109 *Law Quarterly Review* 595

—— 'Once More Unto the Breach: The Community, the State and Damages Liability' (1997) 113 *Law Quarterly Review* 67

—— 'Standing, Rights and the Structure of Legal Argument' (2003) 9 *European Public Law* 493

CRAIG P & DE BÚRCA G (eds), *The Evolution of EU Law* (OUP, 1999)

CREMONA M, 'A Policy of Bits and Pieces? The Common Commercial Policy After Nice' (2001) 4 *Cambridge Yearbook of European Legal Studies* 61

CROSS E D, 'Pre-emption of Member State Law in the European Economic Community: A Framework for Analysis' (1992) 29 *Common Market Law Review* 447

CURTIN D, 'Directives: The Effectiveness of Judicial Protection of Individual Rights' (1990) 27 *Common Market Law Review* 709

—— 'The Constitutional Structure of the Union: A Europe of Bits and Pieces' (1993) 30 *Common Market Law Review* 17

CURTIN D & HEUKELS T (eds), *Institutional Dynamics of European Integration* (Martinus Nijhoff, 1994)

DASHWOOD A, 'The Limits of European Community Powers' (1996) 21 *European Law Review* 113

—— 'States in the European Union' (1998) 23 *European Law Review* 201

DASHWOOD A & O'LEARY S (eds), *The Principle of Equal Treatment in EC Law* (Sweet & Maxwell, 1997)

DEAKIN S, 'Two Types of Regulatory Competition: Competitive Federalism Versus Reflexive Harmonisation. A Law and Economics Perspective on *Centros*' (1999) 2 *Cambridge Yearbook of European Legal Studies* 231

DEARDS E, '*Brasserie du Pêcheur*: Snatching Defeat from the Jaws of Victory?' (1997) 22 *European Law Review* 620

—— 'Curiouser and Curiouser? The Development of Member State Liability in the Court of Justice' (1997) 3 *European Public Law* 117

DEHOUSSE R (ed), *Europe After Maastricht: An Ever Closer Union?* (Law Books in Europe, 1994)

DELCOURT C, 'The *Acquis Communautaire*: Has the Concept Had Its Day?' (2001) 38 *Common Market Law Review* 829

DELMAS-MARTY M, 'The European Union and Penal Law' (1998) 4 *European Law Journal* 87

DOUGAN M, 'Cutting Your Losses in the Enforcement Deficit: A Community Right to the Recovery of Unlawfully Levied Charges?' (1998) 1 *Cambridge Yearbook of European Legal Studies* 233

—— 'The Equal Treatment Directive: Retaliation, Remedies and Direct Effect' (1999) 24 *European Law Review* 664

—— 'The *Francovich* Right to Reparation: Reshaping the Contours of Community Remedial Competence' (2000) 6 *European Public Law* 103

—— 'Minimum Harmonisation and the Internal Market' (2000) 37 *Common Market Law Review* 853

—— 'Vive la différence? Exploring the Legal Framework for Reflexive Harmonisation within the Single European Market' in R Miller & P Zumbansen (eds), *Annual of German and European Law (Volume 1: 2003)* (Berghahn Books, 2004)

—— 'What is the Point of *Francovich*?' in T Tridimas & P Nebbia (eds), *European Union Law for the Twenty-First Century: Rethinking the New Legal Order* (Hart Publishing, 2004)

EDWARDS G and PHILIPPART E, *Flexibility and the Treaty of Amsterdam: Europe's New Byzantium?*, Centre for European Legal Studies Occasional Paper Number 3 (CUP, 1997)

EHLERMANN C-D, 'How Flexible is Community Law? An Unusual Approach to the Concept of Two Speeds' (1984) 82 *Michigan Law Review* 1274

—— 'Differentiation, Flexibility, Closer Cooperation: The New Provisions of the Amsterdam Treaty' (1998) 4 *European Law Journal* 246

—— 'The Modernisation of EC Antitrust Policy: A Legal and Cultural Revolution' (2000) 37 *Common Market Law Review* 537

EMILIOU N, 'State Liability Under Community Law: Shedding More Light on the *Francovich* Principle?' (1996) 21 *European Law Review* 399

DE ENTERRÍA E G, 'The Extension of the Jurisdiction of National Administrative Courts by Community Law: the Judgment of the Court of Justice in *Borelli* and Article 5 of the EC Treaty' (1993) 13 *Yearbook of European Law* 19

ESTEBAN M L F, 'National Judges and Community Law: The Paradox of the Two Paradigms of Law' (1997) 4 *Maastricht Journal of European and Comparative Law* 143

ESTY D & GERADIN D (eds), *Regulatory Competition and Economic Integration: Comparative Perspectives* (OUP, 2001)

FÉDÉRATION International pour le Droit Européen, *The Availability and Appropriateness of National Remedies in the Event of a Breach of Community Law (a) by National Authorities and (b) by Private Bodies*, Volume I, Reports of the Ninth Congress (FIDE and Sweet & Maxwell, 1980)

FERNÁNDEZ MARTÍN J M, *The EC Public Procurement Rules: A Critical Analysis* (Clarendon Press, 1996)

FITZPATRICK B and SZYSZCZAK E, 'Remedies and Effective Judicial Protection in Community Law' (1994) 57 *Modern Law Review* 434

FLYNN L, 'Taking Remedies Too Seriously? National Procedural Autonomy in the European Court of Justice' (1996) 31 *The Irish Jurist* 110

GAJA G, 'How Flexible is Flexibility Under the Amsterdam Treaty?' (1998) 35 *Common Market Law Review* 855

GERADIN D, 'Trade and Environmental Protection: Community Harmonisation and National Environmental Standards' (1993) 13 *Yearbook of European Law* 151

VAN GERVEN W, 'Non-contractual Liability of Member States, Community Institutions and Individuals for Breaches of Community Law with a View to a Common Law for Europe' (1994) 1 *Maastricht Journal of European and Comparative Law* 6

——'Bridging the Gap Between Community and National Laws: Towards a Principle of Homogeneity in the Field of Legal Remedies' (1995) 32 *Common Market Law Review* 679

——'Bridging the Unbridgeable: Community and National Tort Laws after *Francovich* and *Brasserie*' (1996) 45 *International and Comparative Law Quarterly* 507

——'Of Rights, Remedies and Procedures' (2000) 37 *Common Market Law Review* 501

——'Substantive Remedies for the Private Enforcement of EC Antitrust Rules Before National Courts' in C-D Ehlermann & I Atanasiu (eds), *European Competition Law Annual 2001* (Hart Publishing, 2003)

——'Harmonization of Private Law: Do We Need It?' (2004) 41 *Common Market Law Review* 505

GILLIAMS H, 'Modernisation: From Policy to Practice' (2003) 28 *European Law Review* 451

GIRERD P, 'Les principes d'équivalence et d'effectivité: encadrement ou désencadrement de l'autonomie procédurale des Etats membres?' (2002) 38 *Revue trimestrielle de droit européen* 75

GREAVES R, 'Locus Standi Under Article 173 EEC When Seeking Annulment of a Regulation' (1986) 11 *European Law Review* 119

HARDING C, 'Member State Enforcement of European Community Measures: The Chimera of "Effective" Enforcement' (1997) 4 *Maastricht Journal of European and Comparative Law* 5

——'Exploring the Intersection of European Law and National Criminal Law' (2000) 25 *European Law Review* 374

HARDING C & SWART B (eds), *Enforcing European Community Rules: Criminal Proceedings, Administrative Procedures and Harmonization* (Dartmouth, 1996)

HARLOW C, 'Towards a Theory of Access for the European Court of Justice' (1992) 12 *Yearbook of European Law* 213

——'*Francovich* and the Problem of the Disobedient State' (1996) 2 *European Law Journal* 199

HARMSEN R, 'A European Union of Variable Geometry: Problems and Perspectives' (1994) 45 *Northern Ireland Law Quarterly* 109

HEUKELS T & MCDONNELL A (eds), *The Action for Damages in Community Law* (Kluwer Law International, 1997)

HILJEMARK L, 'Enforcement of EC Competition Law in National Courts: The Perspective of Judicial Protection' (1997) 17 *Yearbook of European Law* 83

HIMSWORTH C, 'Things Fall Apart: The Harmonisation of Community Judicial Procedural Protection Revisited' (1997) 22 *European Law Review* 291

HOSKINS M, 'Tilting the Balance: Supremacy and National Procedural Rules' (1996) 21 *European Law Review* 365

HOWELLS G and Wilhelmsson T, *EC Consumer Law* (Dartmouth, 1997)

JACHTENFUCHS M, 'Theoretical Perspectives on European Governance' (1995) 1 *European Law Journal* 115

——'The Governance Approach to European Integration' (2001) 39 *Journal of Common Market Studies* 245

JANS J, *European Environmental Law* (Europa Law Publishing, 2000)

JONES C, *Private Enforcement of Antitrust Law in the EC, UK and USA* (OUP, 1999)

KAKOURIS C N, 'Do the Member States Possess Judicial Procedural "Autonomy"?' (1997) 34 *Common Market Law Review* 1389

KARPENSCHIF M, 'La récupération des aides nationales versées en violation du droit communautaire à l'aune du règlement no. 659/1999: du mythe à la réalité?' (2001) 37 *Revue trimestrielle de droit européen* 551

KILPATRICK C, 'Turning Remedies Around: A Sectoral Analysis of the Court of Justice' in G de Búrca & J Weiler (eds), *The European Court of Justice* (OUP, 2001)

KILPATRICK C NOVITZ T & SKIDMORE P (eds), *The Future of Remedies in Europe* (Hart Publishing, 2000)

KLIMISCH A and KRUEGER B, 'Decentralised Application of EC Competition Law: Current Practice and Future Prospects' (1999) 24 *European Law Review* 463

KOMNINOS A, 'New Prospects for Private Enforcement of EC Competition Law: *Courage v Crehan* and the Community Rights to Damages' (2002) 39 *Common Market Law Review* 447

KON S and MAXWELL A, 'Enforcement in National Courts of the EC and New UK Competition Rules: Obstacles to Effective Enforcement' [1998] *European Competition Law Review* 443

KORTENBERG H, 'Closer Cooperation in the Treaty of Amsterdam' (1998) 35 *Common Market Law Review* 833

KOUTRAKOS P, 'The Elusive Quest for Uniformity in EC External Relations' (2001) 4 *Cambridge Yearbook of European Legal Studies* 243

KRÄMER L, *EC Treaty and Environmental Law* (Sweet & Maxwell, 2000)

KREMER C, 'Liability for Breach of European Community Law: An Analysis of the New Remedy in the Light of English and German Law' (2003) 22 *Yearbook of European Law* 203

LEWIS C and MOORE S, 'Duties, Directives and Damages in European Community Law' [1993] *Public Law* 151

LONBAY J & BIONDI A (eds), *Remedies for Breach of EC Law* (Wiley, 1997)

MACCRORY R and TURNER S, 'Participatory Rights, Transboundary Environmental Governance and EC Law' (2002) 39 *Common Market Law Review* 489

MAHER I, 'National Courts as European Community Courts' (1994) 14 *Legal Studies* 226

—— 'Community Law in the National Legal Order: A Systems Analysis' (1998) 36 *Journal of Common Market Studies* 237

MALMBERG J (ed), *Effective Enforcement of EC Labour Law* (Kluwer Law International, 2003)

MANCINI G, 'The Making of a Constitution for Europe' (1989) 26 *Common Market Law Review* 595

MEHDI R, 'La recevabilité des recours formés par les personnes physiques et morales à l'encontre d'un acte de portée générale: l'aggiornamento n'aura pas eu lieu...' (2003) 39 *Revue trimestrielle de droit européen* 23

MONAR J, 'Justice and Home Affairs in the Treaty of Amsterdam: Reform at the Price of Fragmentation' (1998) 23 *European Law Review* 320

NORDBERG C, 'Judicial Remedies for Private Parties Under the State Aid Procedure' (1997) 24 *Legal Issues of Economic Integration* 35

ODUDU O and EDELMAN J, 'Compensatory Damages for Breach of Article 81' (2002) 27 *European Law Review* 327

OGUS A, 'Competition Between National Legal Systems: A Contribution of Economic Analysis to Comparative Law' (1999) 48 *International and Comparative Law Quarterly* 405

O'KEEFFE D & TWOMEY P (eds), *Legal Issues of the Maastricht Treaty* (Wiley, 1994)

—— (eds), *Legal Issues of the Amsterdam Treaty* (Hart Publishing, 1999)

OLIVER P, 'Interim Measures: Some Recent Developments' (1992) 29 *Common Market Law Review* 7

PELKMANS J and SUN J-M, 'Regulatory Competition in th Single Market' (1995) 33 *Journal of Common Market Studies* 67

PETERSEN N, 'National Strategies in the Integration Dilemma: An Adaptation Approach' (1998) 36 *Journal of Common Market Studies* 33

PLAZA MARTIN C, 'Furthering the Effectiveness of EC Directives and the Judicial Protection of Individual Rights Thereunder' (1994) 43 *International and Comparative Law Quarterly* 26

PRECHAL S, 'Remedies after *Marshall*' (1990) 27 *Common Market Law Review* 451

—— *Directives in European Community Law: A Study of Directives and Their Enforcement in National Courts* (Clarendon Press, 1995)

—— 'Community Law in National Courts: The Lessons From *Van Schijndel*' (1998) 35 *Common Market Law Review* 681

PRECHAL S and HANCHER L, 'Individual Environmental Rights: Conceptual Pollution in EU Environmental Law?' (2001) 2 *Yearbook of European Environmental Law* 89

PRIESS H-J, 'Recovery of Illegal State Aid: An Overview of Recent Developments in the Case Law' (1996) 33 *Common Market Law Review* 69

PRINSSEN J & SCHRAUWEN A (eds), *Direct Effect: Rethinking a Classic of EC Legal Doctrine* (Europa Law Publishing, 2002)

REICH N, 'Competition Between Legal Orders: A New Paradigm of EC Law?' (1992) 29 *Common Market Law Review* 861

RODGER B, 'The Commission White Paper on Modernisation of the Rules Implementing Articles 81 and 82 of the EC Treaty' (1999) 24 *European Law Review* 653

ROSS M, 'Refining Effective Enjoyment' (1990) 15 *European Law Review* 476

——'Beyond *Francovich*' (1993) 56 *Modern Law Review* 55

——'State Aids and National Courts: Definitions and Other Problems—A Case of Premature Emancipation?' (2000) 37 *Common Market Law Review* 401

ROTT P, 'Minimum Harmonisation for the Completion of the Internal Market: the Example of Consumer Sales Law' (2003) 40 *Common Market Law Review* 1107

RUFFERT M, 'Rights and Remedies in European Community Law: A Comparative View' (1997) 34 *Common Market Law Review* 307

SCHERMERS H and WAELBROECK D, *Judicial Protection in the European Union* (Kluwer Law International, 2002)

SCHILLING T, 'The Autonomy of the Community Legal Order: An Analysis of Possible Foundations' (1996) 37 *Harvard International Law Journal* 389

SCOTT J, *EC Environmental Law* (Longman, 1998)

SEVENSTER H, 'Criminal Law and EC Law' (1992) 29 *Common Market Law Review* 29

SHAW J, 'European Union Legal Studies in Crisis? Towards a New Dynamic' (1996) 16 *Oxford Journal of Legal Studies* 231

——'The Treaty of Amsterdam: Challenges of Flexibility and Legitimacy' (1998) 4 *European Law Journal* 63

SHAW J & MORE G (eds), *New Legal Dynamics of European Union* (Clarendon Press, 1995)

SINNAEVE A and SLOT P J, 'The New Regulation on State Aid Procedures' (1999) 36 *Common Market Law Review* 1153

SLAUGHTER A-M, STONE SWEET A & WEILER J (eds), *The European Court and National Courts: Doctrine and Jurisprudence* (Hart Publishing, 1998)

SLOT P J, 'Harmonisation' (1996) 21 *European Law Review* 378

SMITH F and WOODS L, 'Causation in *Francovich*: The Neglected Problem' (1997) 46 *International and Comparative Law Quarterly* 925

SMITS J, 'A European Private Law as a Mixed Legal System: Towards a Ius Commune through the Free Movement of Legal Rules' (1998) 5 *Maastricht Journal of European and Comparative Law* 328

SNYDER F, 'The Effectiveness of European Community Law: Institutions, Processes, Tools and Techniques' (1993) 56 *Modern Law Review* 19

SOARES A G, 'Pre-emption, Conflicts of Powers and Subsidiarity' (1998) 23 *European Law Review* 132

SOMSEN H, 'The Private Enforcement of Member State Compliance with EC Environmental Law: An Unfulfilled Promise?' (2000) 1 *Yearbook of European Environmental Law* 311

STEIN E, 'Lawyers, Judges, and the Making of a Transnational Constitution' (1981) 75 *American Journal of International Law* 1

STEINER J, 'From Direct Effects to *Francovich*: Shifting Means of Enforcement of Community Law' (1993) 18 *European Law Review* 3

——*Enforcing EC Law* (Blackstone Press, 1995)

——'The Limits of State Liability for Breach of European Community Law' (1998) 4 *European Public Law* 69

STORME M (ed), *Approximation of Judiciary Law in the European Union* (Martinus Nijhoff, 1994)

STRUYS M and ABBOTT H, 'The Role of National Courts in State Aid Litigation' (2003) 28 *European Law Review* 172

STUBB A, 'A Categorization of Differentiated Integration' (1996) 34 *Journal of Common Market Studies* 283
STUYCK J, 'European Consumer Law After the Treaty of Amsterdam: Consumer Policy In or Beyond the Internal Market?' (2000) 37 *Common Market Law Review* 367
SZYSZCZAK E, 'European Community Law: New Remedies, New Directions?' (1992) 55 *Modern Law Review* 690
——'Making Europe More Relevant to Its Citizens: Effective Judicial Process' (1996) 21 *European Law Review* 351
TASH A P, 'Remedies for European Community Law Claims in Member State Courts: Toward a European Standard' (1993) 31 *Columbia Journal of Transnational Law* 377
TEMPLE LANG J, 'Community Constitutional Law: Article 5 EEC Treaty' (1990) 27 *Common Market Law Review* 645
——'The Duties of National Courts under Community Constitutional Law' (1997) 22 *European Law Review* 3
TESAURO G, 'The Effectiveness of Judicial Protection and Cooperation between the Court of Justice and the National Courts' (1993) 13 *Yearbook of European Law* 1
TEUBNER G, *Law as an Autopoietic System* (Blackwell, 1993)
——'Legal Irritants: Good Faith in British Law or How Unifying Law Ends Up in New Divergences' (1998) 61 *Modern Law Review* 11
TODINO M, 'Modernisation From the Perspective of National Competition Authorities: Impact of the Reform on Decentralised Application of EC Competition Law' [2000] *European Competition Law Review* 348
TRIDIMAS T, *The General Principles of EC Law* (OUP, 1999)
——'Liability for Breach of Community Law: Growing Up and Mellowing Down?' (2001) 38 *Common Market Law Review* 301
TUYTSCHAEVER F, *Differentiation in European Union Law* (Hart Publishing, 1999)
USHER J, 'Direct and Individual Concern: An Effective Remedy or a Conventional Solution?' (2003) 28 *European Law Review* 575
VAN DEN BERGH R, 'Subsidiarity as an Economic Demarcation Principle and the Emergence of European Private Law' (1998) 5 *Maastricht Journal of European and Comparative Law* 129
VAN DEN BERGH R and SCHÄFER H-B, 'State Liability for Infringement of the EC Treaty: Economic Arguments in Support of a Rule of "Obvious Negligence"' (1998) 23 *European Law Review* 552
VENIT J, 'Brave New World: The Modernisation and Decentralisation of Enforcement Under Articles 81 and 82 of the EC Treaty' (2003) 40 *Common Market Law Review* 545
VERVAELE J (ed), *Compliance and Enforcement of European Community Law* (Kluwer Law International, 1999)
VIGNES D, 'The Harmonisation of National Legislation and the EEC' (1990) 15 *European Law Review* 358
VON BOGANDY A and BAST J, 'The European Union's Vertical Order of Competences: The Current Law and Proposals For Its Reform' (2002) 39 *Common Market Law Review* 227
WALKER N, 'Sovereignty and Differentiated Integration in the European Union' (1998) 4 *European Law Journal* 355

WARD A, 'Effective Sanctions in EC Law: A Moving Boundary in the Division of Competence' (1995) 1 *European Law Journal* 205
——'New Frontiers in Private Enforcement of EC Directives' (1998) 23 *European Law Review* 65
——*Judicial Review and the Rights of Private Parties in EC Law* (OUP, 2000)
——'Judicial Review of Environmental Misconduct in the European Community: Problems, Prospects and Strategies' (2000) 1 *Yearbook of European Environmental Law* 137
WEATHERILL S, 'Beyond "EC Law Rights, National Remedies"' in A Caiger & D A Floudas (eds), *1996 Onwards: Lowering the Barriers Further* (Wiley, 1996)
——*EC Consumer Law and Policy* (Longman, 1997)
——'On the Depth and Breadth of European Integration' (1997) 17 *Oxford Journal of Legal Studies* 537
——'Flexibility or Fragmentation: Trends in European Integration' in J Usher (ed), *The State of the European Union: Structure, Enlargement and Economic Union* (Longman, 2000)
WEILER J, 'The Community System: the Dual Character of Supranationalism' (1981) 1 *Yearbook of European Law* 267
——'The Reformation of European Constitutionalism' (1997) 35 *Journal of Common Market Studies* 97
WERLAUFF E, *Common European Procedural Law: European Law Requirements Imposed on National Administration of Justice* (DJØF Publishing, 1999)
WESSELS W, 'An Ever Closer Fusion? A Dynamic Macropolitical View on Integration Processes' (1997) 35 *Journal of Common Market Studies* 267
——'Flexibility, Differentiation and Closer Cooperation: the Amsterdam Provisions in the Light of the Tindemans Report' in M Westlake (ed), *The European Union Beyond Amsterdam: New Concepts of European Integration* (Routledge, 1998)
WHISH R, 'The Enforcement of EC Competition Law in the Domestic Courts of Member States' [1994] *European Competition Law Review* 60
——*Competition Law* (Butterworths, 2003)
WINTERSTEIN A, 'A Community Right in Damages for Breach of EC Competition Rules?' [1995] *European Competition Law Review* 49
DE WITTE B, HANF D & VOS E (eds), *The Many Faces of Differentiation in EU Law* (Intersentia, 2001)
DE ZWAAN JW, 'Opting In and Opting Out of Rules Concerning the Free Movement of Persons: Problems and Practical Arrangements' (1998) 1 *Cambridge Yearbook of European Legal Studies* 107

Index